Shake Hands with the Devil

Lt. General Roméo Dallaire served as force commander of the UN Assistance Mission for Rwanda from July 1993 to September 1994. *Shake Hands with the Devil*, his eyewitness account of the Rwandan genocide, won the Shaughnessy Cohen Award and the Governor General Award.

'All international peacekeeping missions face problems. What Dallaire confronted was the perfect storm... He describes with anguish and anger how his prescient warnings were ignored and how he was forced to cope with the unfolding catastrophe assisted only by a small staff and several hundred courageous but ill-equipped troops... Throughout this harrowing narrative, Dallaire strives desperately to arrange cease-fires, clear the way for humanitarian assistance and protect terrified civilians. He pushes himself to the edge of sanity...and miraculously retains his moral bearings while so many others are abandoning theirs... Read Roméo Dallaire's profoundly sad and moving book.' Madeleine Albright, *Washington Post*

'Roméo Dallaire is not your average General. Nor is his memoir an ordinary account of the role of the UN in Rwanda... Tens of thousands of people survived because of his extraordinary actions; they walk today on the dirt-red roads hand in hand with his soul.' Clea Koff, *Financial Times*

'It has become customary to think of the genocide in Rwanda as a sudden catastrophe, triggered by the plane crash in which its president was killed. But as Dallaire makes clear, the build-up to the massacre was absolutely clear long before the plane came down on 6 April 1994. For months, he had been warning the UN and the West of the imminent bloodshed, while calling loudly for more soldiers and equipment. That these failed to be sent, that the UN blocked all attempts to mount an effective force, that individual representatives and advisers chose to look after their own needs rather than confront the realities in the field, are the themes of Dallaire's angry, accusatory and extremely moving book.' Caroline Moorhead, *Spectator*

'An important historical record of the UN's failure in Rwanda and an impassioned plea against the moral cowardice that allowed the genocide to happen.' *Independent*

'*Shake Hands with the Devil* is an uncommonly courageous work, wrung from the depths of despair and wrought in plain, forthright prose... A humanitarian needs a saint's compassion, a scholar's knowledge, and a soldier's strength. Bravely and passionately, Roméo Dallaire has shown us where to start.' *Literary Review of Canada*

SHAKE HANDS WITH THE DEVIL

THE FAILURE OF HUMANITY IN RWANDA

LIEUTENANT-GENERAL ROMÉO DALLAIRE

WITH MAJOR BRENT BEARDSLEY

arrow books

First published in the United Kingdom in 2004 by Arrow Books

11

Copyright © Romeo A. Dallaire, LGen (ret) Inc., 2003

Romeo A. Dallaire has asserted his right under the Copyright, Designs
and Patents Act, 1988 to be identified as the author of this work

First published in Canada by Random House Canada 2003

First published in Great Britain in 2004 by
Arrow Books
Random House, 20 Vauxhall Bridge Road,
London SW1V 2SA

www.rbooks.co.uk

Addresses for companies within The Random House Group Limited can
be found at: www.randomhouse.co.uk/office.htm

A CIP catalogue record for this book
is available from the British Library

ISBN 9780099478935

The Random House Group Limited supports The Forest Stewardship
Council (FSC), the leading international forest certification organisation.
All our titles that are printed on Greenpeace approved FSC certified paper
carry the FSC logo. Our paper procurement policy can be found at:
www.rbooks.co.uk/environment

Part of the proceeds of the sale of Shake Hands with the Devil will go
to support the work of the LGen Romeo A. Dallaire Foundation
for children

Printed in the UK by CPI Bookmarque, Croydon, CR0 4TD

To my family and the families of all those who served
with me in Rwanda, with deepest gratitude

To the Rwandans, abandoned to their fate, who were slaughtered
in the hundreds of thousands

To the fifteen UN soldiers under my command who died bravely in
the service of peace and humanity

Lt. Lotin	Belgium	Killed in Action	7 April 94
1ˢᵗ·Sgt. Leroy	Belgium	Killed in Action	7 April 94
Cpl. Bassine	Belgium	Killed in Action	7 April 94
Cpl. Lhoir	Belgium	Killed in Action	7 April 94
Cpl. Meaux	Belgium	Killed in Action	7 April 94
Cpl. Plescia	Belgium	Killed in Action	7 April 94
Cpl. Dupont	Belgium	Killed in Action	7 April 94
Cpl. Uyttebroeck	Belgium	Killed in Action	7 April 94
Pte. Debatty	Belgium	Killed in Action	7 April 94
Pte. Renwa	Belgium	Killed in Action	7 April 94
L/Cpl. Ahedor	Ghana	Killed in Action	17 April 94
Pte. Mensah-Baidoo	Ghana	Killed in Action	9 May 94
Capt. Mbaye	Senegal	Killed in Action	31 May 94
Major Sosa	Uruguay	Killed in Action	17 June 94
Capt. Ankah	Ghana	Killed in Action	8 July 94

To Sian Cansfield, researcher, journalist and dear friend, who died
on June 1, 2002, while working so hard to tell this story

CONTENTS

PREFACE

This book is long overdue, and I sincerely regret that I did not write it earlier. When I returned from Rwanda in September 1994, friends, colleagues and family members encouraged me to write about the mission while it was still fresh in my mind. Books were beginning to hit the shelves, claiming to tell the whole story of what happened in Rwanda. They did not. While well-researched and fairly accurate, none of them seemed to get the story right. I was able to assist many of the authors, but there always seemed to be something lacking in the final product. The sounds, smells, depredations, the scenes of inhuman acts were largely absent. Yet I could not step into the void and write the missing account; for years I was too sick, disgusted, horrified and fearful, and I made excuses for not taking up the task.

Camouflage was the order of the day and I became an expert. Week upon week, I accepted every invitation to speak on the subject; procrastination didn't help me escape but pulled me deeper into the maze of feelings and memories of the genocide. Then the formal processes began. The Belgian army decided to court-martial Colonel Luc Marchal, one of my closest colleagues in Rwanda. His country was looking for someone to blame for the loss of ten Belgian soldiers, killed on duty within the first hours of the war. Luc's superiors were willing to sacrifice one of their own, a courageous soldier, in order to get to me. The Belgian government had decided I was either the real culprit or at least an accomplice in the deaths of its peacekeepers. A report from the Belgian senate reinforced the idea that I never should have permitted its soldiers to be put in a position where they had to defend themselves—despite our moral responsibility to the Rwandans and the mission. For a time, I became the convenient scapegoat for all that had gone wrong in Rwanda.

I used work as an anodyne for the blame that was coming my way and to assuage my own guilt about the failures of the mission. Whether I was restructuring the army, commanding 1 Canadian Division or Land Force Quebec Area, developing the quality of life program for the Canadian Forces or working to reform the officer corps, I accepted all tasks and worked hard and foolishly. So hard and so foolishly that in September 1998, four years after I had gotten home, my mind and my body decided to give up. The final straw was my trip back to Africa earlier that year to testify at the International Criminal Tribunal for Rwanda. The memories, the smells and the sense of evil returned with a vengeance. Within a year and a half, I was given a medical discharge from the army. I was suffering, like so many of the soldiers who had served with me in Rwanda, from an injury called post-traumatic stress disorder. With retirement came the time and the opportunity to think, speak and possibly even write. I warmed to the idea of a book, but I still procrastinated.

Since my return from Rwanda in 1994, I had kept in close touch with Major Brent Beardsley, who had served as the first member of my mission and had been with me from the summer of 1993 until he was medically evacuated from Kigali on the last day of April 1994. Brent used every opportunity to press me to write the book. He finally persuaded me that if I did not put my story on paper, our children and our grandchildren would never really know about our role in and our passage through the Rwandan catastrophe. How would they know what we did and, especially, why we did it? Who were the others involved and what did they do or not do? He said we also had an obligation to future soldiers in similar situations, who might find even a tidbit from our experience valuable to the accomplishment of their missions. Brent collaborated at every stage in the writing of this book. I thank him for his prompting and his support. I am also grateful to his wife, Margaret, and his children, Jessica, Joshua and Jackson, for loaning him to me through the initial research and drafting, through the reviews and most recently for his work to help me finish the manuscript. Brent was the catalyst, the disciplinarian and the most prolific scribe; he committed day after day to the work in order that I could complete this project. Even in periods of enormous suffering from the debilitating effects of overwork, lack of sleep and his own affliction with post-traumatic stress disorder, Brent always went well beyond the effort required of him. He has become my soulmate for all things Rwandan; he provides the sober second thought and voice to my efforts surrounding the Rwandan debacle. His willingness to be a witness for the prosecution at the never-ending International Criminal Tribunal for Rwanda, and his support for my own involvement have cemented our lives together in the best tradition of ex-warriors returning from the front. He has saved me from myself, and I owe my life, as well as the guts of this book, in part to him.

I am especially grateful to Random House Canada for taking a chance on a non-author and a sick veteran. I am grateful for their understanding, their encouragement and their support. A very special thanks goes to my editor and friend, Anne Collins. Without her advice, encouragement and discipline, this project might not have been completed. She kept telling me that this book must be written and that it would be written. For many months I did not put in the effort required, but she held firm, showed genuine concern for me and proved to be the most patient person of us all. She is a lady who takes risks, and I admire her courage and determination. I also wish to thank my agent, Bruce Westwood, for his belief that somewhere in me, we would find the man who could write this story. He kept a friendly eye on me and encouraged me every step of the way. He has become a close colleague, and I respect his skills and experience in the complex world of publishing.

I assembled an ad hoc staff for this project, who worked together magnificently in mutual respect and co-operation. Major James McKay, a long-time researcher for my efforts with the tribunal and on matters of conflict resolution, was my "futures" person. I thank him for his support. Lieutenant Commander Françine Allard, a dogged researcher and "keeper of the documents," worked for me while I was still serving in the Canadian Forces. Fluent and articulate in six languages, she was committed to this book and a cherished member of the team. A special thanks must also go to Major (Retired) Phil Lancaster, who replaced Brent in Rwanda as my military assistant during my final months in the mission area. He helped me draft the chapters on the war and the genocide. A soldier, doctor of philosophy, and a compassionate humanitarian, Phil has worked with war-affected children in the Great Lakes region of Africa almost full-time since his retirement. He has never really returned from Rwanda, and I admire him and the work he does.

Dr. Serge Bernier, the Director of History and Heritage at the Canadian National Defence Headquarters and a classmate of mine from cadet days, provided very personal encouragement and constant contact throughout the project. He reviewed the French version and also provided resources and support for the official history of the mission as debriefed by me to Dr. Jacques Castonguay. He remains a voice of stability in my life.

In addition, there were many extended family members, friends, colleagues and even strangers who encouraged me throughout the writing of this book. I needed that often very timely encouragement and I will be eternally grateful.

In Rwanda today there are millions of people who still ask why the United Nations Assistance Mission for Rwanda (UNAMIR), the United Nations (UN) and the international community allowed this disaster to happen. I do not have all the answers or even most of them. What I do have to offer the survivors and Rwanda's future generations is my story as best as I can remember it. I kept daily notes of my activities, meetings, comments and musings, but there were many days, particularly in the early stages of the genocide, when I did not have the time, the will or the heart to record the details. This account is my best recollection of events as I saw them. I have checked my memory against the written record as it survives, in code cables, UN documents and my papers, which were released to me by the Canadian Forces. If there are any errors in the spelling of the names of places or persons, or misremembered dates, I offer my apologies to the reader. I remain fully responsible and accountable for every decision and action I took as the sometime Head of Mission and full-time Force Commander of UNAMIR.

My wife, Elizabeth, has given more than I can ever repay. Beth, thank you for the days, weeks, months and years when I was absent and you held the home front and the family together, whether I was off serving around the world, at home in my workaholic bubble, or just out in the back forty on exercise, waking you and everyone else in the married quarters with the sound of our guns. Thank you for your support during this last duty, which has been one of the hardest and most complex efforts of my life. I thank my children, Willem, Catherine and Guy, who grew up without a full-time dad but who have always been the pride of my life, the true test of my mettle, and who continue to make their own place in the world. Be yourselves and thank your mother. One of the reasons I wrote this book was for you, my very close family, so that in these pages you may find some solace for the toll my experience in Rwanda has exacted, and continues to exact, from you—far beyond the call of duty or "for better or for worse." I am not the man who left for Africa ten years ago, but you all stayed devoted to this old soldier, even when you were abandoned by the military and the military community in the darkest hours of the genocide. You saw first-hand what happens to the spouses and families of peacekeepers. I remain forever thankful that you so clearly opened my eyes to the plight of the families of a new generation of veterans. You are the ones who really started the Canadian Forces Quality of Life Initiative.

I have dedicated this book to four different groups of people. First and foremost, I have dedicated it to the 800,000 Rwandans who died and the millions of others who were injured, displaced or made refugees in the genocide. I pray that this book will add to the growing wealth of information that will expose and help eradicate genocide in the twenty-first century. May this book help inspire people around the globe to rise above national interest and self-interest to recognize humanity for what it really is: a panoply of human beings who, in their essence, are the same.

This book is also dedicated to the fourteen soldiers who died under my command in the service of peace in Rwanda. The hardest demand on a commander is to send men on tasks that may take their lives, and then the next day to send others to face possibly similar fates. Losing a soldier is also the hardest memory to live with. Such decisions and actions are the ultimate responsibility of command. To the families of those courageous, gallant and devoted soldiers I offer this book to explain. When the rest of the world failed to even offer hope, your loved ones served with honour, dignity and loyalty, and paid for their service with their lives.

This book is also dedicated to Sian Cansfield. Sian was this book's shadow author, but she did not live to see it finished. For almost two years, she immersed herself in everything Rwandan. Her uncanny memory was a researcher's gift. I enjoyed her sparkle, her enthusiasm, her love of Rwanda and its people, whom she came to know in the field a few years after the war. Her journalistic aggressiveness to get at the truth combined with her energy and her zeal to evoke the heart of the story earned her the title of "regimental sergeant major" of our team. We worked well together and enjoyed many laughs and too many tears as I recounted hundreds of incidents and experiences, tragic, revolting, sickening and painful. In the last stages of the drafting of the book, I noticed she was tiring as the content and the workload ate away at her sense of humour and objectivity. I sent her on leave for a long weekend to rest, sleep, eat and recharge her batteries, as I have done so often with officers or soldiers who showed the same symptoms. The morning after she left for the weekend, a phone call broke the news to me that she had committed suicide. Sian's death hit me with a pain I had not felt since Rwanda. It seemed to me that the UNAMIR mission was still killing innocent people. The following week, I joined her family in attending her funeral and mourned her passing. The sense of finality and the shock that came from her death brought to life the spirits that have been haunting me since 1994. I wanted to cancel the project and let my tale die with me. Encouraged by her family and my own, especially Beth, by the rest of the team and many friends, I came to realize that the best tribute I could pay to Sian was to finish the book and tell the story of how the world abandoned millions of Rwandans and its small peacekeeping force. Sian, so much of this book is dedicated to you; your spirit lives with me as if you were another veteran of Rwanda. May you now find the peace in death that so eluded you in life.

The fourth group to whom this book is dedicated comprises the families of those who serve the nation at home and in far-off lands. There is nothing normal about being the spouse or child of a soldier, sailor or airperson in the Canadian Forces. There are very good and exciting times and there are also hard and demanding times. In the past, this way of life was very rich and worthwhile. But since the end of the Cold War, the nature, tempo and complexity of the missions on which our government has sent members of the Canadian Forces have caused a significant toll in marriage casualties. The demands of single parenthood, loneliness and fatigue, and the visual and audio impact of twenty-four-hour news reporting from the zones of conflict where loved ones have been sent create stress levels in the families of our peacekeepers that simply go off the chart. Our families live the missions with us, and they suffer similar traumas, before, during and after. Our families are inextricably linked to our missions, and they must be supported accordingly. Until the last few years, the quality of life of our members and their families was woefully inadequate. It took nearly nine years of hurt all round before the government began to accept its responsibilities in this regard. Witnessing the deep emotion and genuine empathy of Canadians for our soldiers who were wounded or killed in Afghanistan, I am optimistic that the nation as a whole will finally and fully accept its responsibility for these young and loyal veterans and their families. I pray that this book will assist Canadians in understanding the duty they and the nation owe to the soldiers who serve us, and to their families.

The following is my story of what happened in Rwanda in 1994. It's a story of betrayal, failure, naïveté, indifference, hatred, genocide, war, inhumanity and evil. Although strong relationships were built and moral, ethical and courageous behaviour was often displayed, they were overshadowed by one of the fastest, most efficient, most evident genocides in recent history. In just one hundred days over 800,000 innocent Rwandan men, women and children were brutally murdered while the developed world, impassive and apparently unperturbed, sat back and watched the unfolding apocalypse or simply changed channels. Almost fifty years to the day that my father and father-in-law helped to liberate

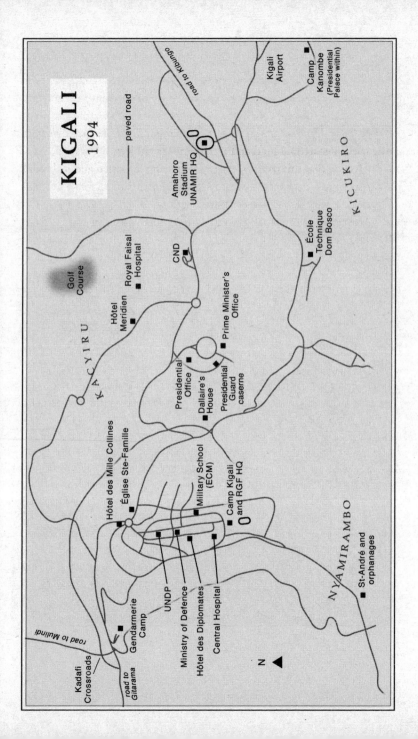

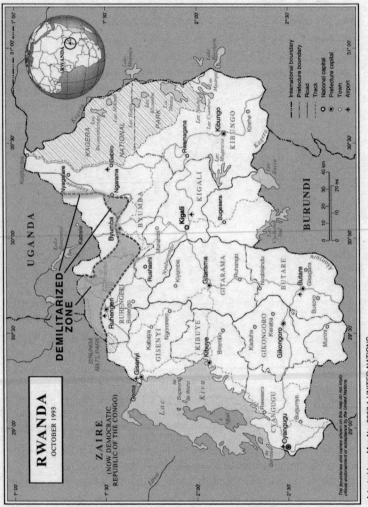

RWANDA
OCTOBER 1993

ZAIRE
(NOW DEMOCRATIC
REPUBLIC OF THE CONGO)

UGANDA

BURUNDI

DEMILITARIZED
ZONE

Adapted from Map No. 3807.1 UNITED NATIONS
September 1993

*The boundaries and names shown on this map do not imply
official endorsement or acceptance by the United Nations.*

International boundary
Prefecture boundary
Road
Track
National capital
Prefecture capital
Town
Airport

RWANDA
JULY 1994

ZAIRE
(NOW DEMOCRATIC
REPUBLIC OF
THE CONGO)

UGANDA

UNITED
REPUBLIC OF
TANZANIA

BURUNDI

RGF CONTROLLED AREA

RPF CONTROLLED AREA

FRENCH HUMANITARIAN PROTECTION ZONE

Adapted from Map No. 3717 Rev. 7 UNITED NATIONS
December 1997 (Colour)

Introduction

It was an absolutely magnificent day in May 1994. The blue sky was cloudless, and there was a whiff of breeze stirring the trees. It was hard to believe that in the past weeks an unimaginable evil had turned Rwanda's gentle green valleys and mist-capped hills into a stinking nightmare of rotting corpses. A nightmare we all had to negotiate every day. A nightmare that, as commander of the UN peacekeeping force in Rwanda, I could not help but feel deeply responsible for.

In relative terms, that day had been a good one. Under the protection of a limited and fragile ceasefire, my troops had successfully escorted about two hundred civilians—a few of the thousands who had sought refuge with us in Kigali, the capital of Rwanda—through many government- and militia-manned checkpoints to reach safety behind the Rwandese Patriotic Front (RPF) lines. We were seven weeks into the genocide, and the RPF, the disciplined rebel army (composed largely of the sons of Rwandan refugees who had lived over the border in camps in Uganda since being forced out of their homeland at independence), was making a curved sweep toward Kigali from the north, adding civil war to the chaos and butchery in the country.

Having delivered our precious cargo of innocent souls, we were headed back to Kigali in a white UN Land Cruiser with my force commander pennant on the front hood and the blue UN flag on a staff attached to the right rear. My Ghanaian sharpshooter, armed with a new Canadian C-7 rifle, rode behind me, and my new Senegalese aide-de-camp, Captain Ndiaye, sat to my right. We were driving a particularly dangerous stretch of road, open to sniper fire. Most of the people in the surrounding villages had been slaughtered, the few survivors escaping with little more than the clothes on their backs. In a few short weeks, it had become a lonely and forlorn place.

Suddenly up ahead we saw a child wandering across the road. I stopped the vehicle close to the little boy, worried about scaring him off, but he was quite unfazed. He was about three years old, dressed in a filthy, torn T-shirt, the ragged remnants of underwear, little more than a loincloth, drooping from under his distended belly. He was caked in dirt, his hair white and matted with dust, and he was enveloped in a cloud of flies, which were greedily attacking the open sores that covered him. He stared at us silently, sucking on what I realized was a high-protein biscuit. Where had the boy found food in this wasteland?

I got out of the vehicle and walked toward him. Maybe it was the condition I was in, but to me this child had the face of an angel and eyes of pure innocence. I had seen so many children hacked to pieces that this small, whole, bewildered boy was a vision of hope. Surely he could not have survived all on his own? I motioned for my aide-de-camp to honk the horn, hoping to summon up his parents, but the sound echoed over the empty landscape, startling a few birds and little else. The boy remained transfixed. He did not speak or cry, just stood sucking on his biscuit and staring up at us with his huge, solemn eyes. Still hoping that he wasn't all alone, I sent my aide-de-camp and the sharpshooter to look for signs of life.

We were in a ravine lush with banana trees and bamboo shoots, which created a dense canopy of foliage. A long straggle of deserted huts stood on either side of the road. As I stood alone with the boy, I felt an anxious knot in my stomach: this would be a perfect place to stage an ambush. My colleagues returned, having found no one. Then a rustling in the undergrowth made us jump. I grabbed the boy and held him firmly to my side as we instinctively took up defensive positions around the vehicle and in the ditch. The bushes parted to reveal a well-armed RPF soldier about fifteen years old. He recognized my uniform and gave me a smart salute and introduced himself. He was part of an advance observation post in the nearby hills. I asked him who the boy was and whether there was anyone left alive in the village who could take care of him. The soldier answered that the boy had no name and no family but that he and his buddies were looking after him. That explained the biscuit but did nothing to allay my concerns over the security and health of the boy. I protested that the child needed proper care and that I could give it to him: we were protecting and supporting orphanages in Kigali where he would be much better off. The soldier quietly insisted that the boy stay where he was, among his own people.

I continued to argue, but this child soldier was in no mood to discuss the situation and with haughty finality stated that his unit would care and provide for the child. I could feel my face flush with anger and frustration, but then noticed that the boy himself had slipped away while we had been arguing over him, and God only knew where he had gone. My aide-de-camp spotted him at the entrance to a hut a short distance away, clambering over a log that had fallen across the doorway. I ran after him, closely followed by my aide-de-camp and the RPF child soldier. By the time I had caught up to the boy, he had disappeared inside. The log in the doorway turned out to be the body of a man, obviously dead for some weeks, his flesh rotten with maggots and beginning to fall away from the bones.

As I stumbled over the body and into the hut, a swarm of flies invaded my nose and mouth. It was so dark inside that at first I smelled rather than saw the horror that lay before me. The hut was a two-room affair, one room serving as a kitchen and living room and the other as a communal bedroom; two rough windows had been cut into the mud-and-stick wall. Very little light penetrated the gloom, but as my eyes became accustomed to the dark, I saw strewn around the living room in a rough circle the decayed bodies of a man, a woman and two children, stark white bone poking through the desiccated, leather-like covering that had once been skin. The little boy was crouched beside what was left of his mother, still sucking on his biscuit. I made my way over to him as slowly and quietly as I could and, lifting him into my arms, carried him out of the hut.

The warmth of his tiny body snuggled against mine filled me with a peace and serenity that elevated me above the chaos. This child was alive yet terribly hungry, beautiful but covered in dirt, bewildered but not fearful. I made up my mind: this boy would be the fourth child in the Dallaire family. I couldn't save Rwanda, but I could save this child.

Before I had held this boy, I had agreed with the aid workers and representatives of both the warring armies that I would not permit any exporting of Rwandan orphans to foreign places. When confronted by such requests from humanitarian organizations, I would argue that the money to move a hundred kids by plane to France or Belgium could help build, staff and sustain Rwandan orphanages that could house three thousand children. This one boy eradicated all my arguments. I could see myself arriving at the terminal in Montreal like a latter-day St. Christopher with the boy cradled in my arms, and my wife, Beth, there ready to embrace him.

That dream was abruptly destroyed when the young soldier, fast as a wolf, yanked the child from my arms and carried him directly into the bush. Not knowing how many members of his unit might already have their gunsights on us, we reluctantly climbed back into the Land Cruiser. As I slowly drove away, I had much on my mind.

By withdrawing, I had undoubtedly done the wise thing: I had avoided risking the lives of my two soldiers in what would have been a fruitless struggle over one small boy. But in that moment, it seemed to me that I had backed away from a fight for what was right, that this failure stood for all our failures in Rwanda.

Whatever happened to that beautiful child? Did he make it to an orphanage deep behind the RPF lines? Did he survive the following battles? Is he dead or is he now a child soldier himself, caught in the seemingly endless conflict that plagues his homeland?

That moment, when the boy, in the arms of a soldier young enough to be his brother, was swallowed whole by the forest, haunts me. It's a memory that never lets me forget how ineffective and irresponsible we were when we promised the Rwandans that we would establish an atmosphere of security that would allow them to achieve a lasting peace. It has been almost nine years since I left Rwanda, but as I write this, the sounds, smells and colours come flooding back in digital clarity. It's as if someone has sliced into my brain and grafted this horror called Rwanda frame by blood-soaked frame directly on my cortex. I could not forget even if I wanted to. For many of these years, I have yearned to return to Rwanda and disappear into the blue-green hills with my ghosts. A simple pilgrim seeking forgiveness and pardon. But as I slowly begin to piece my life back together, I know the time has come for me to make a more difficult pilgrimage: to travel back through all those terrible memories and retrieve my soul.

I did try to write this story soon after I came back from Rwanda in September 1994, hoping to find some respite for myself in sorting out how my own role as Force Commander of UNAMIR interconnected with the international apathy, the complex political manoeuvres, the deep well of hatred and barbarity that resulted in a genocide in which over 800,000 people lost their lives. Instead, I plunged into a disastrous mental health spiral that led me to suicide attempts, a medical release from the Armed Forces, the diagnosis of post-traumatic stress disorder, and dozens upon dozens of therapy sessions and extensive medication, which still have a place in my daily life.

It took me seven years to finally have the desire, the willpower and the stamina to begin to describe in detail the events of that year in Rwanda. To recount, from my insider's point of view, how a country moved from the promise of a certain peace to intrigue, the fomenting of racial hatred, assassinations, civil war and genocide. And how the international community, through an inept UN mandate and what can only be described as indifference, self-interest and racism, aided and abetted these crimes against humanity—how we all helped create the mess that has murdered and displaced millions and destabilized the whole central African region.

A growing library of books and articles is exploring the tragic events in Rwanda from many angles: eyewitness accounts, media analyses, assaults on the actions of the American administration at the time, condemnations of the UN's apparent ineptitude. But even in the international and national inquiries launched in the wake of the genocide, the blame somehow slides away from the individual member nations of the UN, and in particular those influential countries with permanent representatives on the Security Council, such as the United States, France and the United Kingdom, who sat back and watched it all happen, who pulled their troops or didn't offer any troops in the first place. A few Belgian officers were brought to court to pay for the sins of Rwanda. When my sector commander in Kigali, Colonel Luc Marchal, was courtmartialled in Brussels, the charges against him were clearly designed to deflect any responsibility away from the Belgian government for the deaths of the ten Belgian peacekeepers under my command. The judge eventually threw out all the charges, accepting the fact that Marchal had performed his duties magnificently in a near-impossible situation. But the spotlight never turned to the reasons why he and the rest of the UNAMIR force were in such a dangerous situation in the first place.

It is time that I tell the story from where I stood—literally in the middle of the slaughter for weeks on end. A public account of my actions, my decisions and my failings during that most terrible year may be a crucial missing link for those attempting to understand the tragedy both intellectually and in their hearts. I know that I will never end my mourning for all those Rwandans who placed their faith in us, who thought the UN peacekeeping force was there to stop extremism, to stop the killings and help them through the perilous journey to a lasting peace. That mission, UNAMIR, failed. I know intimately the cost in human lives of the inflexible UN Security Council mandate, the penny-pinching financial management of the mission, the UN red tape, the political manipulations and my own personal limitations. What I have come to realize as the root of it all, however, is the fundamental indifference of the world community to the plight of seven to eight million black Africans in a tiny country that had no strategic or resource value to any world power. An overpopulated little country that turned in on itself and destroyed its own people, as the world watched and yet could not manage to find the political will to intervene. Engraved still in my brain is the judgment of a small group of bureaucrats who came to "assess" the situation in the first weeks of the genocide: "We will recommend to our government not to intervene as the risks are high and all that is here are humans."

My story is not a strictly military account nor a clinical, academic study of the breakdown of Rwanda. It is not a simplistic indictment of the many failures of the UN as a force for peace in the world. It is not a story of heroes and villains, although such a work could easily be written. This book is a *cri de coeur* for the slaughtered thousands, a tribute to the souls hacked apart by machetes because of their supposed difference from those who sought to hang on to power. It is the story of a commander who, faced with a challenge that didn't fit the classic Cold War-era peacekeeper's rule book, failed to find an effective solution and witnessed, as if in punishment, the loss of some of his own troops, the attempted annihilation of an ethnicity, the butchery of children barely out of the womb, the stacking of severed limbs like cordwood, the mounds of decomposing bodies being eaten by the sun.

This book is nothing more nor less than the account of a few humans who were entrusted with the role of helping others taste the fruits of peace. Instead, we watched as the devil took control of paradise on earth and fed on the blood of the people we were supposed to protect.

1

MY FATHER TOLD ME THREE THINGS

My first love has always been the army. It has been my mistress, my muse and my family. Even as a child, I never had any doubt about where I wanted to go or what I wanted to do. My first toy, brought with me from war-ravaged Holland when my mother and I came over to join my father in Quebec after the Second World War, was a very crude replica of a Canadian Army Jeep. As a boy, I would create battlefields on the large living-room rug, happy when my parents left me home alone to hold the fort while they ran errands. At the cottage in the summer, I would build massive sand fortresses and defensive works. Totally absorbed by the manoeuvres of my large Dinky Toys inventory and hundreds of plastic soldiers, I would dream of the battlefields of old, where the guns dominated the flow of combat. I was always an artillery-man, peppering the impressive and gallant oncoming cavalry and massed infantry with large gobs of sand.

I wasn't playing war, I was living it, alone in a time far gone yet very alive for me. When not conducting my campaigns on the carpet or in the sand, I would pore over military history books and dream I was a captain dressed in a dashing red and blue serge uniform, commanding a battery of guns and light artillery in the Napoleonic Wars. Those scenes were so real to me, I could smell the gunpowder and hear the screams of the horses. The thrill and excitement of battle would course through me, and I would be lifted out of the depressing grey of east-end Montreal where I grew up.

I was born into a military family, the eldest of three children and the only boy, so perhaps it's not surprising that soldiering became not only my profession but my passion. My father was a non-commissioned officer (NCO) in the Canadian Army, my mother a war bride from Holland. They had met when my father was stationed in Eindhoven behind the winter static line of 1945. My mother had been a student nurse, and she and her friends had walked by the temporary bivouacs in the town square on their way to the hospital. They saw the truly awful conditions that the Canadians were living in, under canvas in the freezing winter rain, with no heat or running water. Local families, including my mother's, were asked to billet the Canadian troops in their homes. Staff-Sergeant Roméo Louis Dallaire was hard to ignore, a huge man with piercing blue eyes. My mother was still single at twenty-six. One thing led to another, and before you knew it, I was born in June of 1946.

My father was forty-four at that time, a strong, impressive-looking man who always appeared younger than his years. He had led a difficult, rather lonely life. He'd been born in the asbestos-mining town of Thetford Mines, in Quebec's Eastern Townships, in 1902. His parents had died young and he had been sent out west to live with a cold and miserly spinster aunt who had a large but unprofitable farm near North Battleford, Saskatchewan. Life with his aunt was full of hard manual labour. In order to have a decent supper once in a while, my father would catch a chicken, wring its neck and throw it on the manure pile. Then he'd tell his aunt the chicken must have died of cold. So as not to waste it, she would cook it for their dinner. Life with her was so unbearable that as soon as he attained the age of majority he left the farm and slowly worked his way back to Quebec.

He drifted through his twenties, picking up whatever work he could find, a robust man with the hard scars of physical labour on him. In 1928, he finally fell into soldiering at the age of twenty-six, when he joined the Royal 22ième Régiment as a private. At the time, the Royal 22ième, commonly called "the Vandoos," was the only francophone unit in the Canadian Army.

In the Vandoos, my father found a family at last, and he relished the companionship and the deep bonds of trust that develop between soldiers. In 1931 he was posted to the Army Service Corps, a logistics branch that handled transportation, equipment, maintenance, payroll and the things that kept an army functioning. Back then the Service Corps was still horse-drawn, and Dad was in his element, having acquired a knack with horses while caring for his aunt's plough team.

When the Second World War began, he was posted overseas, first to northern Scotland, where he trained General Charles de Gaulle's Free French paratroopers. But the cold and damp rendered even that plum job depressing. He was finally posted to the 85th Bridge Company, Second Canadian Corps, and after endless dry manoeuvres in the south of England, his unit landed in Normandy a month after D-Day 1944. During the winter of 1944 to 1945, the Canadian Army held a line of more than 322 kilometres, extending from near the German frontier, south of Nijmegen, along the Maas River and through the Dutch islands to Dunkirk on the channel coast. During that long, bitter winter, he saw many of his friends blown to bits or mangled into screaming messes of bloodied flesh in the desperate battle to shove the Germans back across the Rhine.

Dad by then was a staff-sergeant in charge of a workshop that kept 250 vehicles and bridge-building equipment on the road. Already in his forties, he was the old man, the dean of the shop, and his skill in maintaining and repairing just about any war-fighting machine had earned him an enviable reputation. He was an excellent scrounger, an essential skill for senior NCOs in the nuts-and-bolts Canadian Army, which always seemed to have so much less than other forces. Canadian soldiers became notorious for making deals, bartering anything to help the unit. Thirty years later, along the border between East and West Germany, I saw the same skills being exercised by my own NCOs, usually upon unsuspecting Americans. Whole engines were exchanged for a forty-ounce bottle of Canadian Club whisky. On one occasion, a guarantee of hot meals from my unit's mobile field kitchen gave me access to eight air-defence missile systems for a week. This trade has its own rough law: anyone caught scrounging for personal gain is ostracized. As far as Dad was concerned, doing deals for yourself was like stealing from your buddies, the worst crime one could commit in the army.

After the war, my father stayed on in Holland for nearly a year, working on a post-war program that oversaw the gifting of Canadian vehicles to the Dutch and Belgian governments. His work gave him the opportunity to visit Eindhoven and the lovely young Dutch woman soon to become my mother.

When he returned to Canada, demobilization was in full swing and Dad was immediately stripped of his pre-war rank of sergeant and given a corporal's two bars. My mother was outraged by his treatment; she went all the way to Ottawa to fight tooth and nail with the Adjutant-General for the Canadian Army. Soon after, my father's rank was restored. Even so, he brushed aside chances at retraining or promotion, and spent ten years on the road throughout Quebec doing equipment inspections. After he retired in 1957, he took a civilian job, working for ten more years under punishing conditions at the army's heavy equipment workshop in east-end Montreal.

Parts of the war still haunted him, though he rarely spoke of his experiences to me or anyone outside his tight circle of fellow veterans. The father I knew was tough and taciturn, given to long bouts of brooding introspection. The family learned to avoid him when these black moods descended.

My mother, Catherine Vermeassen, was very Dutch, devout and house proud. She had left a large family behind to travel with a six-month-old baby across the ocean to join a man fifteen years her senior whose primary emotional bond was with the army. She had arrived with me at Pier 21 in Halifax and joined thousands of other war brides on one of the Red Cross trains that delivered wives and children to sometimes extremely reluctant husbands and fathers. There was a fair amount of hostility directed toward the war brides and their offspring. Though my mother became a force to be reckoned with, she never quite adjusted to the parochial world of east-end Montreal and was a little lost in a culture that viewed her as an outsider, different, with odd foreign ideas.

She wasn't the kind of woman who wasted words or emotion, but the war had left some very deep scars. Sometimes, perhaps out of sheer loneliness, she would confide in me, and stories would bubble out of her. I would be swept away with her to the dark, dangerous streets of wartime Holland. She would tell me about the friends she had lost—especially vivid to her was a young Jewish man who had been rounded up in the middle of the night by the Gestapo and disappeared into the nightmare of the Holocaust. With every retelling, I would hear the sharp rap on the door, see the ominous gleam of boots in the moonlight, the white, staring face of the young man, his dark eyes wide with terror.

She would tell me of the noise and fear—and hope—brought by the Allied bombers as they pounded cities and farmland in front of the Canadian Army's advance to the Rhine. She would describe the sound of the transport aircraft and the sight of thousands of paratroopers filling the sky as far as the eye could see during the Allied push to Nijmegen and Arnhem. I felt her mute horror as she told me of how she and her family had watched flames engulf the centuries-old towers and graceful cathedrals that had been the landmarks of her childhood. She showed me the devastating costs of war, but even as she did so, she always cast the Canadian soldiers as the heroes in her tales, larger-than-life saviours who brought light, hope and joie de vivre into a wartorn land. She instilled in me a thrill of pride in Canada, a nation unthreatened by war, which had sacrificed its youth to save the world from the dark power of the Nazis. These stories had a profound impact on me. Unlike many of my generation, who became passionate peace activists determined to put an end to war, I took the opposite lesson. I saw in my parents a courage that had led them to look beyond their own self-interest, to offer their own lives to defeat an evil that had threatened the peace and security of much of the world. It was a model of self-sacrifice that I tried to follow, playing with my soldiers on the rug.

Our first family home was a tarpaper temporary barracks, or H-hut, which we shared with two other families. Dad and some friends from the Service Corps managed to scrounge building materials to divide up the space for more privacy, but the toilets and bathing facilities remained communal. We lived there until 1951, when my father was finally able to afford our own home.

Military pay was low. Dad sometimes earned extra dollars fixing his neighbours' cars to support his growing brood; he was fifty when my youngest sister, Yolande, was born. We lived in basic wartime housing, cheek by jowl with oil refineries and chemical plants that spewed their poison in thick, dense clouds over the neighbourhood. At the time, east-end Montreal was one of the largest centres of the petrochemical industry in North America. There were days when the air was so foul we couldn't play outside—it would burn our throats and send us back indoors, choking. The houses were cheaply and shoddily built; there were no basements and no central heating, just an oil stove, the huge fuel drum that fed it hunkered outside the window. In the winters, ice would form small mounds along the sills and freeze the towels we put there to stop the drafts. The winter wind whistled under the doors and around the window frames, sending sharp fingers of cold into the cozy nests of our beds.

It was a tough, gritty, blue-collar district and you had to be scrappy to survive. Our neighbourhood was divided into two parishes, one French and Catholic, the other English or allophone (immigrants who had chosen English as their second language) and Protestant, each with its own separate schools, churches and institutions. People tended to stick with their own. But even though we lived in the French parish and were devoutly Catholic, my mother, who spoke English well, found herself more comfortable with the allophones—many of them new Canadians like herself. She was nostalgic for the scouting movement of her childhood in Holland and got involved with Scouts Canada, which operated out of the English Protestant school. She dragged me along with her to the first meeting, sternly telling me that the only reason I was being allowed to go was so that I could improve my English. I loved Cubs and made some great friends there, but at that time, it was an Anglican as well as an anglophone outfit. I used to joke that if I went to Cubs on Tuesday night, I was off to confession on Wednesday at the crack of dawn.

Being a Cub had social as well as religious consequences. The francophone kids and the anglophone kids formed separate neighbourhood gangs and were bitter foes; the fact that I had friends on both sides marked me as suspect, possibly a traitor. This did not make life easy for me. I remember my sister Juliette, only five or six, being caught in a crossfire of rock-throwing between French and English gangs in our back alley. My francophone friends and I rescued her. She was cut and bleeding from the back of her head, and we lifted her to safety over a fence. We then launched a counterattack that sent the anglos scurrying into a tarpaper shed, which we proceeded to set on fire. Our siege abruptly ended when a seemingly enormous mother intervened. Days later, I was still harassing those anglos for hurting my little sister. Eventually we struck a ceasefire, and in the next encounter, I found myself in the anglo ranks. So it went, back and forth.

I attended the local boys-only Catholic school, which was run by the Brothers of Saint Gabriel. The brothers often dropped by our house, usually in time for supper, to visit with my parents. My father was a member of the Knights of Columbus and was also a well-known and respected grassroots Liberal Party organizer; my mother was heavily involved in the women's Liberal organization and in charity work. A visit from the brothers was not always a comfortable occasion for me, however, as they often complained about my lacklustre performance in the classroom.

My saving grace was that I was a soloist in the choir. Brother Léonidas, the choirmaster, though quite stern, was a gifted musician, and he was thrilled that I could sing the few English songs in our repertoire. He was constantly hauling us off to choir competitions where we generally did quite well.

I also secured the coveted position of altar boy, a nice sideline that netted me twenty-five cents a week, plus an additional dime or more for weddings and funerals. I soon learned that funerals were often far more elaborate, and therefore more profitable, than weddings and that the music tended to be better, too.

But it was my dancing that raised my profile among the girls segregated in the convent school across the street, though I had to be careful that the brothers never caught me holding hands with one. Punishment for that sort of fraternization was immediate: transcription of pages out of the dictionary, down on my knees in the corner of the classroom. The brothers and nuns would station themselves at strategic windows to keep a watchful eye out for any hanky-panky on the way to or from school. The only time the two sexes were allowed to mix was during folk-dancing-club practices, which were organized by the parish and later by the schools—under heavy supervision. We learned all the traditional French-Canadian folk dances, but also the dances of other nations. I remember especially loving the Jewish dances, because in order to be authentic, we performed them barefoot, imagining that the hard, cold gymnasium floor was actually soft, warm desert sand. The thrill of seeing a girl's naked feet and ankles was almost unbearable.

In high school I carried on as an indifferent scholar, more interested in sports than studying, until the day an old friend of my father's stopped in at the house for a visit. He was a major who had served with my dad in the war. They talked army all night, and I eavesdropped. The dream of soldiering was still with me; I had joined the cadets and spent all of my summers under canvas at Farnham, an old First World War military camp south of Montreal. There I learned tactical manoeuvres and how to use a machine gun from Korean and Second World War vets. I idolized those teachers.

Pausing between reminiscences, my father said to his friend, "You know, my son is thinking of going to military college."

The major smiled and turned to me. "That's fine, son. How are your marks?"

I told him.

"Well, you know, young man, you're not even going to get close to the military college with marks like that. You have to be in the eighties—and solidly in the eighties—to even be considered." Lending weight to his remark was the fact that for my father's generation, military college was only for the sons of senior officers; an NCO's child would never have been admitted.

After the major left, my father didn't say much, undoubtedly sparing my feelings. But I had sensed a different message in the way the old major had spoken to me, the way his eyes had held mine: I was sure that he actually thought I could do it and was challenging me to succeed. With the help of my friend, Michel Chevrette, whose work ethic to that point had totally eclipsed mine, I learned how to knuckle down. Surprising my family and myself, my average rose from 72 per cent in grade nine to 91 per cent in grades ten, eleven and twelve. I'd close the door to my room and put the radio on, creating my own bubble to study in. On the weekends, Michel and I would sometimes study for twelve hours straight. When I was in grade eleven, my parents actually marched me downstairs one Sunday afternoon and told me that I was not living with the family anymore, that they were tired of seeing me only at mealtimes. They were right; I'd eat quickly, do the dishes and then disappear back into my room. But I had broken the code; I had found the determination to stick to that desk and work, and I wasn't about to give up now.

Just before graduation, the brothers sent us on a silent retreat so we could meditate and seek divine guidance on our future direction in life. For most of us, going on a retreat meant stocking up on *Playboy* magazines and chocolate bars, but while we were there, the odd bit of wisdom stuck. We went to confession and I ended up with a fat, old priest who was a retired army padre. He was a bit of a mess, his black soutane stained with ketchup, his ill-shaven face pale and his eyes bloodshot. And there was me, with my bony knees pressed into the cold, stone floor, and no clue what to say. After a long uncomfortable silence, he looked at me through his grubby glasses and asked me what I planned to do with my life. I told him that I'd applied to military college and wanted a career in the army like my dad. He settled back in his chair, his voice taking on a wistful note. "Ahh, soldiers," he said. "You know, soldiers are very unusual people. On the outside, they are the hardest, most demanding, severe people, but underneath that, they are the most human, the most feeling, the most emotionally attached people who exist." Those words perfectly expressed the depth of feeling I saw between my father and his army buddies, and the feeling that had passed between me and the old major, and they would come to describe the deep regard that always existed between my troops and I. I wanted more of that feeling.

I came of age in the Quebec of the Quiet Revolution and, like my parents, was an ardent believer in the vision of Jean Lesage, the premier of Quebec in the early sixties. With the defeat of Maurice Duplessis, who had run the province as his personal fiefdom for close to twenty years,

Quebec burst from the dark, church-bound isolation of the forties and fifties with a boldness and energy that seemed perfectly in tune with the times. In school I was part of a massive movement spearheaded by our teachers, called "Le Bon Parler français," which emphasized respect, even reverence, for French and was an assault on the anglicisms that were creeping into the language. My generation became both confident and passionate about seeking equal recognition for the rights of the French-Canadian minority within Canada. In the words of Jean Lesage, "In Canada, 'French' and 'English' are our first names. Our surname is 'Canadian.' We must be true to our heritage, but we must also be true to our first name as it is our individuality, our soul, and we must not have any inferiority or superiority complex."

But I was about to enter a military culture that lagged far behind the rest of the country in recognizing the rights and differences of French-speaking Canadians. In the fifties, the Canadian Forces had opened up recruitment to meet the demands of the Korean War and the newly formed North Atlantic Treaty Organization (NATO). The numbers enlisting from Quebec were embarrassingly low; potential recruits from that province were repelled by an armed forces that was English-dominated and highly intolerant of French Canadians. In 1952, a courageous member of the Opposition from Trois-Rivières, Léon Balcer, stood up in the House of Commons and challenged Prime Minister Louis St. Laurent, a fellow francophone, about the reasons for the low recruitment figures and especially for the lack of French-speaking officers in all the branches of the service. He sparked a political fracas that had a huge impact in Quebec. After all kinds of studies and commissions, the Collège militaire royal de Saint-Jean (CMR) was set up in 1952. Visionaries such as Major General J.E.P. Bernatchez and General Jean Victor Allard, the only francophones who had reached the rank of general at the time, pushed and prodded behind the scenes to eradicate inequalities and to educate and nurture French-speaking officers. I became one of the many beneficiaries of this monumental effort to eliminate the redneck policies that had ruled the Canadian Armed Forces in the past.

•••

The night before I left for military college, my father and I took a walk around the block. I was eighteen and about to leave home for good, and he seemed to believe that I was ready for the most profound advice he could offer. Though he was enormously proud that the son of an NCO had been accepted at military college, he recommended that if I wanted to make the army my career I should change my name from Dallaire to Dallairds. Artillery was my passion, and in his experience, no French Canadian had gone anywhere in the artillery. He gave me this advice with no hint of bitterness, as if changing my name was simple pragmatism. If I did decide to make a career in the army, he said, I would never be rich, but I would live one of the most satisfying lives there was to be had. Then he warned me that that satisfaction would come at great cost to me and any family I might have. I should never expect to be thanked; a soldier, if he was going to be content, had to understand that no civilian, no government, sometimes not even the army itself, would recognize the true nature of the sacrifices he made. I decided not to change my name, but I have tried to understand and live by the rest of his hard-won wisdom.

At military college, a whole new world opened up to me. It had been founded on the site of old Fort St-Jean, where in 1775 Major Charles Preston and his band of French-Canadian militia, Indians, and a few British regulars resisted the American general, Richard Montgomery. They wiped out enough of Montgomery's men and delayed him so long that he was ultimately defeated in a blinding snowstorm on New Year's Eve at the gates of Quebec. The fort had been continuously occupied by soldiers since it was built in 1666. The site was alive with the ghosts of battles past, and it thrilled me to walk the halls.

On the weekends, my classmates and I would go into Montreal, where I experienced a totally different city from the narrow east-end parish in which I'd grown up. Montreal in the sixties was vibrating with theatre, bistros and music, the *gitane* atmosphere created by a wave of young French-Canadian artists and intellectuals fiercely proud of their distinct heritage and culture. We would go dancing at the many disco-bars, wearing wigs over our military haircuts to get by the bouncers, who often mistook us for vice cops or members of the RCMP. Of course, we would run into Quebec nationalists, who would engage us in heated debate about joining that bastion of *anglophonie*, the Canadian Armed Forces, and we'd meet peaceniks, who were against anything military because of what was going on in Vietnam and the nuclear buildup of the Cold War. Sometimes we were hounded out of the more bohemian clubs and bistros, and at other times the opposition would make a particularly cogent argument and we would almost be persuaded to change our minds. Of course, there were times when we chose to compromise, heavily influenced by drink, beautiful young women and the pungent aroma of certain illicit substances floating in the air. Every possible moment of leave was used to escape the regimented, all-male campus, to plunge into the rich youth culture so alive in the streets of Montreal at the time.

My three years at CMR were happy ones, even though I lagged behind academically. To be truthful, I graduated at the absolute bottom of my class. I had arrived as a virgin in every sense of the word and was determined to remedy that lack of experience in the shortest possible time. I lost (or found) myself in varsity sports, political debates, sex, booze and rock 'n' roll, my work ethic shot to hell.

My classmates and I were a mixed bag. Some of us were serious about a military career, but many were not. And there were even some closet hippies among us who struggled to keep their hair long and cut class to spend time in smoke-filled coffee houses, listening to Gilles Vigneault or Tex Lecor, the francophone equivalents of Bob Dylan and Leonard Cohen. These guys were as much a part of the gang that I ran around with as the more macho science-and-engineering types like myself. It was stimulating to rub up against people who came from totally different milieux, people who loved art and literature and who held antithetical political views to mine.

The student population at CMR was 70 per cent francophone and 30 per cent anglophone, but I moved as easily between the groups as I had in my old neighbourhood. Familiar with the insecurities that plagued the two solitudes, particularly when anglophones were forced into a largely francophone environment and suddenly found themselves a minority, I would defend each group to the other. I never fully belonged to either gang. I wasn't sitting on the fence, but I was always a little apart. There were often times when I'd lose arguments and be furious with myself because I hadn't been able to make the words come out right in either French or English. But by not limiting myself to one side or the other I was often able to pick up nuances missed by my more hardline classmates.

Over a hundred of us, out of an original class of 183, graduated and made our way to the Royal Military College (RMC) in Kingston, Ontario, for two more years of education. There we encountered a very different and not always sympathetic environment. In Kingston you touched the heart of Upper Canada, still very much tied to its British colonial past. Though our education was supposed to be bilingual, there was a deep divide between anglophones and francophones. The Quebeckers formed a tight clique and socialized amongst ourselves, often escaping the strict Protestant Orange of Kingston and the continual ragging of our English comrades for the familiar vibrancy of a weekend in Montreal.

Still, we were probably among the most confident French Canadians that the extremely conservative institution had ever encountered. We did not back down and become assimilated. Seized by the spirit of the times, we fought the sometimes petty battles required to achieve equity.

In the summer of 1967, when some of my friends had chosen to do their summer training in Montreal so they could soak up the life of the city and the excitement of Expo, I found myself in Shilo, Manitoba, smack in the middle of the Prairies. Shilo was where I first confirmed my vocation as a combat arms officer and a gunner. During my first time there, in the summer of 1965, they had us sit on the side of a hill to watch a live firing exercise. It was a splendid setting, with the white sand dunes of the Carberry Desert (the only one in Canada) glistening under a clear blue sky. A young officer, who had graduated from RMC only the previous year, explained his duties to us. He was responsible for the live firing of heavy artillery guns and had about ninety people reporting directly to him in the field. He was just glowing, imbued with the deep inner excitement and concentration that comes with command. He had his gunners demonstrate a fast-action deployment. We watched the guns come in from behind a hill to our left to take aim at the simulated Warsaw Pact target, about three kilometres away. The young officer stood on a truck in the middle of it all, like a conductor on his podium, and ordered the immediate disposition of the guns, the ammunition vehicles, the survey teams and the heavy, mounted machine guns for self-defence. When all was in place, he bellowed, "Fire!" There was a colossal bang as the gun spat out a projectile that exploded in a huge plume of dust just to the right of the target. He immediately yelled, "Left 200. Fire!" and the gunners went about their tasks fluidly and efficiently, barely making a sound, firing to his command again and again. I became consumed by the noise and the awesome destruction, intoxicated by the smell of burnt cordite. Seeing all that raw power under the command of one young officer, I decided then and there that this was the branch of the army I would join.

So when my friends went home to Montreal for the summers, I went back to Shilo, even though any failure there would have resulted in me being dismissed from the military college. Each summer, I survived the milieu only because of the help my classmates gave me with the finer elements of the artillery fire discipline jargon. The summer of 1967 was particularly difficult as I was the only French Canadian in a class of forty. To make matters worse, our course officer, a rotund artillery pilot who disliked the "smart-ass" RMC gang, decided to make my life miserable. He paraded me in front of the chief instructor, where he upbraided me for being "flippant," among other failings. I acknowledged his criticism, saluted and returned to my quarters, certain that I was destined to flunk. I had no idea what he meant. Only at the insistence of my roommate did I decide not to cave in to the pressure. I even finally asked my instructor the meaning of *flippant*. "Cocky," he said. Bewildered, I carried on.

Then, on the evening of July 24, things got a whole lot worse. I arrived at the mess a little late and found a place not far from the door in the TV room. The supper-hour news came on. The top story of the day was Charles de Gaulle, the president of France, saluting massive crowds from the balcony of the Montreal city hall with "Vive le Québec. Vive le Québec libre!" The crowd on TV roared with obvious delight while the mess went dead silent—except for muffled scraping as people shifted in their seats to stare at the only Quebecker in the room. It seemed to me that the clip was repeated twenty times during that newscast, and each time I could feel more daggers coming at me. When the newscast was over, the room emptied slowly. Nobody came up to me, nobody talked to me. I was part of the evil empire that was threatening to tear the country apart. The silence lasted for about two days. I was shunned not for who I was but for who I was assumed to be, and that experience remains burnt into my memory.

When I returned to RMC that fall, my future was in serious doubt. My poor mark from summer training and my even poorer academic performance at the college made failure seem inevitable. But at the last minute I locked into my old habit of creating a bubble of concentration and slowly and steadily pulled myself out of the hole.

In the fall of 1968, with the election of Pierre Trudeau and the publishing of the preliminary report of the Royal Commission on Bilingualism and Biculturalism, the language issue became more and more significant at RMC. In November, four of my francophone classmates convened a bilingualism committee and drafted a memorandum outlining the problems that francophones encountered at the college. They presented it to the commandant, which caused a minor explosion. The committee members were paraded in front of the commandant and asked to explain themselves—a frightening experience for the young officer cadets, who were being accused of harbouring nationalistic tendencies. But their quiet logic and commitment to their principles won the day, and they succeeded in forcing some small changes. Those of us who stayed in the Canadian Forces resolved to continue to monitor and defend French rights within the army. We were one of the first classes of French Canadians at RMC who were comfortable with our cultural identity; even so, only 58 of the 130 French-speaking cadets who had begun military college with me actually graduated in the spring of 1969.

I was posted to one of the brand new French-Canadian artillery units, the 5ième Régiment d'artillerie légère du Canada in Valcartier. It had been stood up in the winter of 1968 by General Allard and Prime Minister Trudeau, and had caused considerable acrimony as older English-speaking regiments were disbanded to make way for the francophone units. We were starting from scratch, actually building the regiment, which was housed in borrowed offices with little equipment or clerical help. Out of the four thousand gunners in the Canadian Forces at the time, fewer than a hundred spoke French. We ended up with a lot of English-Canadian soldiers with French surnames but zero French language skills, and French Canadians who had worked outside of Quebec and had operated in English for so long that they had forgotten their French almost entirely. It was often frustrating, because I was forced to spend so much time translating all kinds of English paperwork into French. But there in Valcartier I had a taste of actually participating in regimental history.

By 1969 the mood in Quebec had begun to darken, fuelled by strikes and student protests, some of them pretty violent. A sudden wave of anger ripped through the province, setting hearts and minds on fire. Extremist separatist factions recast the complex struggle for cultural and linguistic identity into a fight against the anglo bosses. It seemed like the province was hovering on the brink of insurrection as Quebeckers—everyone from taxi drivers to medical workers—took to the streets in a series of crippling strikes and mass demonstrations.

Then there were the terrorists. The Front de libération du Québec (FLQ) had been active in the province since 1963, calling for the violent overthrow of the capitalist system and the establishment of an independent French socialist nation. The FLQ announced itself by conducting a serious bombing campaign, which targeted three Montreal-area armouries and included a thwarted attack on former Prime Minister John Diefenbaker's train. Another attack resulted in the maiming of a soldier, working as a bomb expert. The scale and violence of the assaults increased throughout 1969 and into 1970.

In Valcartier we were quietly training to withstand armed revolt. We all knew there was a strong possibility that we would be called in to help the civilian authorities quell riots, but just how serious the situation would get, nobody could guess. During my first year with the 5ième Régiment, we conducted exercises in crowd control and VIP and vital point protection. We were called out several times to restore order in prisons when guards walked out on strike, and we helped disperse crowds at some of the bigger demonstrations, including the Murray Hill bus drivers' strike where shots were fired. When three thousand

members of the Montreal police force walked off the job in October
1969, we were called in to keep the peace. The strike lasted five days.
Later that month we were put on alert when forty thousand demonstrators marched on the National Assembly in Quebec City. We spent
many nights and weekends camped out in our gun sheds standing
guard over our weapons. A current of nervous excitement ran through
the troops; we felt we would be tested sooner or later.

On October 5, 1970, the British trade commissioner to Quebec,
James Cross, was kidnapped from his home in Westmount. The FLQ
demanded that their manifesto be read in French and English live on
the CBC, and the government acquiesced in order to save Cross's life.
The manifesto talked of "total independence of all Québécois" and the
release of "political prisoners." General Allard, the former Chief of
Defence Staff, and his family were stalked by an FLQ cell, and there were
rumours of a plot to assassinate Trudeau. It was hard to believe this was
happening in Canada. No one could tell if the FLQ were just a bunch of
hotheads causing trouble or if they represented something more sinis-
ter. Then, on October 10, Pierre Laporte was kidnapped. It was as if the
other shoe had dropped.

It was Thanksgiving and bitterly cold in Montreal. I was at home with
my family for the long weekend. On Monday, my father said we'd probably be called out. At that point, I still couldn't believe the situation was
so serious. I drove back to Quebec City that evening, arriving at my little
basement apartment at about eleven-thirty. I had just settled in when the
phone rang. We were being called out. I struggled into my combat gear
and rushed upstairs to tell my landlord and his wife that I'd be away for a
while and to hold my mail. I can only imagine what ran through the
minds of that respectable, middle-aged couple when they woke in the
middle of the night to find me on their doorstep, fully suited and wearing
my helmet. The woman screamed and almost fainted, sure that civil war
had broken out in Quebec. I hastened to reassure them.

At Valcartier, we trained hard for three days and then got the order
to move; the government had invoked the War Measures Act, suspend-
ing civil law for the duration of the crisis. Our rules of engagement
included the use of live ammunition to prevent acts of insurrection,

which meant that opening fire and shooting to kill were real possibilities. This situation presented me, at the age of twenty-four, with one of the most difficult ethical and moral dilemmas of my military career. Members of my own extended family, as well as friends from my old neighbourhood, were supporting the separatist movement. At any time I might see faces I knew in the hostile crowds that I was ordered to control. How would I react? Could I open fire on members of my own family?

As a young lieutenant, I had forty-one soldiers under my command. If I gave the order to shoot, I could not let my men sense the slightest shiver of doubt in my belief in the rightness of that order. Any uncertainty on my part would communicate itself to my men; any hesitation on their part could result in chaos and innocent casualties. In a nanosecond I had to be able to set aside deep personal loyalties and put the mission first. I spent many hours wrestling this issue before I could put aside my loyalty to my roots and wholeheartedly embrace my loyalty to my nation. I had to connect to a deeper commitment, past friendship, kinship or ethnicity, to absolutely believe in the rightness and justness of my path.

On October 17, the whole of the Canadian Army was deployed. Troops moved into the Ottawa-Hull area from out west; units from Petawawa moved into Montreal; the Airborne Regiment flew from Edmonton and was held in reserve at the military college in Saint-Jean. The bulk of our brigade was deployed to Quebec City. My regiment was posted to protect the National Assembly and other government buildings, as well as provincial politicians. There were huge convoys of troops entering Montreal, dozens upon dozens of Hercules transports thundering into Ottawa. We travelled from Valcartier in long columns, taking several routes into the heart of the city. I remember driving at the head of my column while people either honked their car horns and waved, or watched us pass in shocked disbelief that this was happening in Canada.

Later that day, the Quebec cabinet minister Pierre Laporte was found murdered, his body stuffed into the trunk of a car that had been abandoned in Montreal—the FLQ had answered our massive show of force unequivocally and violently.

Once deployed, we established our routine. For three months we worked constantly, six hours on post, six hours off, with a day off every three weeks. We "hot-bedded" it, that is, we hauled out our sleeping bags to crash in the cots just vacated by the soldiers who relieved us. My troop rotated between standing guard outside the National Assembly and the main courthouse near the Château Frontenac in the heart of the old town. Through the bone-chilling cold of a Quebec fall and winter, we did six-hour shifts with only one twenty-minute break inside to warm up. We used to joke that if anyone wanted to start shooting, we wouldn't be able to handle the extra work. We took a fair amount of flak from separatist supporters who jeered and hassled us. A number of English-speaking troops in the regiment had families who lived off base and had no real protection from the mischief-makers who tracked them down and subjected them to harassment. The troops were allowed very little leave time, and they worried about their families. Their anxiety often boiled over in nasty scenes between them and the young French Canadians who served alongside them. The francophone soldiers were getting hostility from both sides. Some of them came from pro-separatist families who viewed them as traitors; at the same time, they were being branded by some of their comrades as untrustworthy "frogs."

I would do my rounds with a crusty old sergeant, Roy Chiasson, a veteran from the Korean War. Because there was no action whatsoever, the troops needed constant reminders of the nature of the operation. They also needed a sounding board to talk over their difficulties. The sergeant and I spent countless hours out in the cold reinforcing and encouraging them. I have often been criticized for being an "emotional" leader, for not being macho enough, but even during this early stage in my career, I believed that the magic of command lies in openness, in being both sympathetic to the troops and at the same time being apart, in always projecting supreme confidence in my own ability and in theirs to accomplish whatever task is set for us.

Luckily, the October Crisis did not escalate to the point where lethal force was necessary, although there were some close calls that seemed pretty ugly at the time. One bitter evening late in November, my soldiers were guarding the Quebec Ministry of Justice and central courthouse. I was inside with a small reserve force of five or six men. Everything was quiet, so quiet that the Quebec City cops who shared the building with us complained that since we'd arrived they were bored. All of a sudden a car came screeching down the street and stopped dead in front of one of my soldiers. The driver got out of the car, cursing a blue streak, and without any provocation, started beating up the soldier so severely that he ended up in hospital. I had guards posted around the building so that everybody was covered off and no one was isolated, but none of them could move from their positions to help their buddy because of the possibility that this was a trap or decoy. They radioed for backup and we raced out to assist. But the police, who were monitoring our radio frequency and were desperate for a little action, heard the call, too. In seconds, a half-dozen cop cars with sirens blaring and roof lights blazing came barrelling down the narrow street. Brawny cops leapt out, hauled the guy off and proceeded to make him regret whatever impulse had caused him to attack soldiers. As one officer said afterwards, "Nobody is going to hurt our soldiers and get away with it." The police were protecting the soldiers who were there to protect law and order!

I was proud of my men. They had endured incredible provocation and responded exactly as trained. It pleased me that Sergeant Chiasson and I had been able to build that level of skill and discipline in the troop, that they had used their heads and followed orders. It was my first taste of true command.

On December 3, 1970, an army intelligence unit uncovered the approximate location of the FLQ cell that was holding James Cross prisoner. Almost an entire battalion of the Royal 22ième formed a tight circle around a block of nondescript row houses in north Montreal, and as the nation waited, the final tense negotiations to resolve the crisis began. Hours later, a thin, pale James Cross was hustled out of the house along with his kidnappers, who were placed on board a Yukon transport aircraft and flown to Cuba. The crisis was over. By January, I was back in Valcartier and the routine of peacetime soldiering.

2

"RWANDA, THAT'S IN AFRICA, ISN'T IT?"

In every regiment of the Canadian Forces, there is an informal council of elders—senior or retired officers who remain intimately connected to the life of the regiment. These elders determine a regiment's individual culture and character. One of their key responsibilities is to select the so-called streamers, the young men or women who the elders believe have the right stuff to become future generals. There is never any official announcement or acknowledgement of this process, but once you are chosen, it's as if an invisible hand is reaching out to guide you, nurturing your career through a carefully selected series of command and staff positions that test and prepare you for higher command. Becoming a streamer doesn't mean success is assured; on the contrary, if you blow any of the commands you are offered, your career is over, or at least stalled.

My first shot at becoming a streamer came in the spring of 1971. I had been on exercise with the regiment for about three weeks, and on the last day, two CF5 fighter planes that had been dogfighting north of Bagotville, Quebec, crashed in mid-air. The pilots were lost in the dense bush. The air base at Bagotville tried to mount a rescue, but one of its helicopters crashed while attempting to land, which resulted in more casualties. My regiment was the designated rapid reaction force and was called out to support the search.

The previous evening, we had celebrated the end of the exercise with a smoker, a huge party with plenty of food and beer bought with the profits from the canteen; there wasn't a man in the battery that was not severely hungover. As usual I had totally immersed myself in the festivities and was nursing a wicked headache when the battery commander, Major Bob Beaudry, called me over. A dignified gentleman of few words, he got right to the point. "You've been chosen to lead the advance party," he said. "There are helicopters waiting for you and your troops back at Valcartier. They'll fly you up north where you'll link up with the air force and commence the search. The rest of the regiment will join you in about two days."

I couldn't believe my ears. Hungover or not, I was being offered a chance at an independent command. Even though it was a grim assignment, it offered a fantastic opportunity for us to test our mettle.

Forty of us jammed into a couple of helicopters and flew up to a remote logging camp close to the last known position of the aircraft. I quickly established a base camp, and we started the gruelling work of searching the dense, trackless bush of northern Quebec. By the third day, our muscles ached so badly from the effort of stepping over dead trees and rotting stumps that we could no longer lift our legs and had to drop and roll over the logs and low-lying scrub.

By then the rest of the regiment had joined us, but we had set such a blistering pace that we were way out in front. Finally, on our fifth day, one of my party let out a yell. He had stumbled across the helmet of one of the missing pilots. We searched the area until it got dark, without success. The next morning, a low-flying search and rescue team from Bagotville found the pilot's body, sitting upright beside a tree, his parachute caught in the branches. Any rush of satisfaction we might have felt at achieving our aim was quickly chastened by the thought of that shattered young body. I can still remember the hush that fell over us when we got the news. We didn't know him, but he was a soldier who had died serving his country, and there wasn't a man among us who didn't utter a prayer for him and his family.

Another group eventually located the other pilot's body, and we were flown out ahead of the rest of the regiment to Bagotville, where we stayed overnight. My troops were billeted, and I was given a room in the officer's mess. I stowed my gear and made my way to the bar, still dressed in the army combat greens that I had been wearing for close to a month—I didn't smell too fresh. There was a bunch of pilots at the bar, mourning the loss of their colleagues. These men knew who I was and that my troops had spent the last five days combing the bush looking for them. Instead of offering to buy me a beer, they scattered, leaving me alone at the bar. Not one of them came up and said a word to me. I worked myself into a righteous rage over this silent treatment, and after I had drunk about half of my beer, I slammed my glass down so hard on the bar that the beer spilled all over the place and stormed out of the room. Not until I had calmed down did my father's words come back to me: if you want to be content in the military, never expect anyone to say thank you. Even your own brother officers may not be able to reach over the line of stupid inter-force rivalries to shake your hand.

What is a peacetime career in the army? How do you grow as a leader when there is no armed conflict to test you? You train and train, and then you train others. I received a number of good training assignments, due in part, I believe, to the fact that I was still single and available, unlike many of my peers who were already married and raising young families. For some of us, the army had to be a higher calling. The old attitude was that if the army wanted you to have a family, they would've issued you one. I was more than willing to dedicate myself and soon learned another hard military lesson. Even in training, mistakes can cost lives.

I had a two-year posting to militia units in the Quebec area, and in the summer of 1971, we were running a very large program called Katimavik, which offered basic reserve-force training to young people. Soldiers with families were given priority for leave, and many of the more senior officers were away at the same time. I had to work flat out to get the program off the ground—it was a last-minute initiative imposed by the federal minister responsible for youth employment. I had to put together, almost overnight, a training and support plan for close to six hundred young people. Blinded by my own can-do attitude, I didn't realize I was actually in way over my head.

One of my old classmates, who was now a reservist, had been hired to take care of about sixty of these potential recruits. He told me he couldn't find a suitable training site near the garrison and so had made an arrangement with a farmer in the Charlevoix area, a fair distance away. Once he had assured me that he'd ironed out the logistics problems, I gave him the go-ahead.

My buddy took off with three heavy army trucks, with eighteen candidates sitting on metal benches in the back of each one—close to the load limit. Unfortunately, the drivers of the trucks were inexperienced and the old highway along the St. Lawrence River was hilly and dangerous in spots, with S bends that swooped down close to the water. One of the drivers missed a curve and his truck spun out of control, tossing most of the young men out along the embankment close to the river's edge. Six were killed.

Six young lives lost because of one stupid decision. I was devastated. There was a huge investigation and blame was apportioned—I received a reproof. But I couldn't escape the thought that I hadn't done enough, that I should have asked more questions, that I should have known better. The rawness of the grief of those six families remains seared in my memory, a constant reminder of the particular trust of command.

I had met Elizabeth Roberge at a regimental wedding in the fall of 1969, and we had begun dating. Beth taught kindergarten at one of the Valcartier base schools. She and her colleagues would come for lunch at the mess, and I was smitten by her liveliness and charm. She was the daughter of Lieutenant Colonel Guy Roberge, who had served with my father in the Vandoos in the late twenties and early thirties, and he had also commanded the prestigious old French-Canadian reserve regiment les Voltigeurs de Québec. I was a young subaltern, "living in" (staying in the officer's mess) and sending a portion of my small salary home to my parents. Beth's family was two generations army, and they understood that a good meal was a welcome treat to a young, near-impoverished officer.

From the moment I stepped in the door of the Roberges' lovely house, with its wonderful warm smell of spices, its clean, starched linen, and family treasures, I felt at home. Beth's mother was a gracious lady, extremely cultured and a superb *cuisinière*. But her father was especially dear to me; he became both a mentor and a second father. The Roberges had four daughters and no sons, which I suspect was a bit of a disappointment to Colonel Roberge, as he had rare occasion in the family to talk army. He seemed lonely for the companionship of another soldier.

Sunday dinner at the Roberges' was a formal family occasion and everybody had their assigned seat at the beautiful old hardwood table. As soon as I sat down to my first dinner, Colonel Roberge rearranged the seating order so that I was in the place of privilege at his right-hand side. I kept that seat every Sunday for all the years I was posted in Quebec City.

My father-in-law had an impressive career, from commanding a regiment to serving in the Italian campaign as the liaison officer between the Free French and the 1st Canadian Corps. He had watched top-ranked generals as they plotted the battles of the campaign, and his stories held me spellbound. On his return to Canada in 1943, he had nurtured and trained two mobilized reserve infantry regiments for service overseas. His many insights into leadership helped shape my own thoughts and practices. We became very close over the years, and he gave me much wise counsel. I remember that just before I was promoted to brigadier-general, my father-in-law lay dying in the old veterans' hospital, which is now the Laval University Medical Centre. When I went to see him the last time, his breathing was very shallow, his eyes closed, and it was obvious he was slipping away. I leaned over and whispered that I had been promoted general. His eyelids flickered for a moment and I could swear that a shadow of a smile played about his mouth. He was as proud of me as he would have been of a son. He died two days later in his sleep.

Elizabeth had been teaching on the Canadian base in Lahr, Germany, since 1970. She loved the life there and invited me over for a vacation. We had a wonderful time together skiing the Swiss Alps and running around in her new Peugeot 504. But I did have an ulterior motive for making the visit. Back home the word was that there was no way that I, as one of the few French-Canadian officers in the regiment, was going to get posted to either the Airborne, or 4 Brigade in Germany. I intended to lobby the commanding officer of the artillery regiment for a posting. I spent some time in the garrison, mingling with the troops and officers at the mess and having a great time. I guess I must have made an impression, because Lieutenant Colonel Harry Steen, the commanding officer at the time, says he still remembers the mad French Canadian who injected so much fun into the place. He became an enthusiastic supporter of my efforts to get posted to Germany.

It was 1973 and we were still in the middle of the Cold War; Germany was definitely an operational theatre with all the attendant realities. After I arrived, we were continually on long, live-fire exercises and huge NATO manoeuvres that lasted weeks. However, the life in the field as well as in garrison was outstanding. It had to be, since there were no phones and no TV, just a nascent radio station run by the CBC and Radio-Canada. The folks on the French broadcast were left-wing peaceniks who were just a whisper away from being outright Quebec nationalists, but they were such good company I couldn't resist hanging out with them. I remember when René Lévesque's pro-sovereignty government was elected in 1976. We had a great party inside the radio station, with me continually looking over my shoulder to make sure none of the troops saw me. It was in Lahr that I first met Maurice Baril, a fellow officer who would be crucial to my posting in Rwanda. He was from the legendary Vandoos, some years my senior, a major and second-in-command of his battalion.

I married Beth, after a seven-year courtship, on June 26, 1976. It was a small wedding, since most of the Valcartier regiment was in Montreal to provide security for the Olympic Games. After we got back from a six-week honeymoon in Germany, I was caught up in a whirl of activity, attending courses as well as being called out on a NATO exercise. Beth returned to her teaching job at Valcartier. I was supposed to be posted to Army Headquarters in Montreal. At the last minute, however, I was sent to Gagetown, New Brunswick, as head of a national program called Francotrain, which was set up to translate all the forces' manuals, documents, and pedagogical tools used from English into French. It was a stressful time for Beth. Amidst all this upheaval and uncertainty, she had a miscarriage the night I flew out to Germany on exercise. Alone, she soldiered on as so many military wives do.

Located in the little town of Oromocto on the St. John River, the Gagetown base is a pretty place but was a bit of a letdown after Germany. While at Gagetown, I was promoted major. Since I was young, only thirty-two, many of the older guys complained that I was being fast-tracked because I was a francophone. This was the first time I had encountered the bitter jealousy that can sour regimental life. Being separated out from your brother officers can be a lonely and vulnerable position.

Eighteen months into the posting, my eldest son, Willem, was born, and for a while at least, all the back-biting took a back seat to my family. My father was over the moon. For someone who had grown up without any family to speak of, seeing that third generation was important to him. I never saw him so full of love and pride as he was when he first held Willem in his arms. He died suddenly a few months after Willem was born, having suffered a stroke.

I was posted back to Valcartier in 1978 to assume command of a battery— 120 gunners. I was in my element. I noticed that my battery, and for that matter the entire regiment, was not working to potential during exercises because many of the signallers were unilingual French Canadians, and the fire discipline orders were always given in a special jargon that required mastery of military English. French-speaking gunners simply couldn't cope. I pushed for some reforms, chiefly the ability to give the orders in French. Almost eleven years after the Offical Languages Act had passed, we were still fighting these stupid language restrictions, and as a result, we were not reaching our potential as an operational artillery regiment.

Luckily, the commanding officer was a reasonable, open-minded man named Tim Sparling, who gave me the go-ahead to try out French commands in the field. I ran a conversion course, translating all the technical stuff into French; it worked like a charm, and our effectiveness increased dramatically. The signallers were ecstatic because they finally understood what they were saying. Over the years there had been much muttering about me being a French-Canadian nationalist, but nobody could argue with the result. When the troops were able to fight in their own language, there was a positive surge in morale and effectiveness.

I was soon given the opportunity to attend the U.S. Marine Corps Command and Staff College in Virginia. It was a great year, although it took my family and me a while to adjust to the culture. Our sponsors were Major Bob List and his wife, Marty. List was an A-6 Intruder fighter bomber pilot who flew off aircraft carriers during his two long tours in Vietnam. He and his wife got a bit of a surprise when their young daughter, listening to Willem speak French, cried out, "He doesn't speak English!" To which I responded, immediately and without thinking, "He doesn't speak American either." Things went uphill from there.

At the staff college in Virginia, I saw first-hand the terrible price exacted by Vietnam. There wasn't one of my instructors and fellow officers whose body had not been horribly scarred in battle. The mental toll was equally apparent, revealing itself in bitter invectives against the U.S. generals and higher command who had either screwed up in the field or stayed comfortably at home. I wondered whether I wouldn't have been equally suspicious of politicians, grand strategists and pencil pushers from NDHQ if I had lost 63 per cent of my classmates in combat.

I put my nose to the grindstone and managed to reasonably distinguish myself academically, producing a research paper on circumpolar threats and the nature of Arctic warfare, which was later used by National Defence Headquarters when it was seriously considering setting up a permanent garrison of army, navy and air force personnel along the Northwest Passage.

Immediately upon returning to Canada I was appointed executive assistant to the deputy commander of the army, Major General Doug Baker, a privileged position. He was known to everybody as "Two Gun" Baker because of his straight-shooting style of command. As the army's senior serving gunner, he was the godfather of the artillery. The war in the Falklands was on, and we seemed to be constantly zipping around the country or back and forth to Britain and the United States, with the general munching on chocolate bars, immersed in one of the several horse operas he always carried with him, while I dutifully read Clausewitz's *On War*.

General Baker was a hard taskmaster with a demanding work ethic and extremely high standards. He never counted his hours and I learned not to count mine. Paperwork was limited during regular working hours, as that time was reserved for decision-making and for his troops.

In the summer of 1982, I was promoted to lieutenant colonel and our daughter Catherine joined the growing ranks of the Dallaire family. I spent less than a year as the deputy chief of staff of a militia area headquarters in Montreal. In March 1983, I returned to Valcartier as the commanding officer of the 5ième Régiment d'artillerie légère du Canada, with a troop strength of over six hundred. It was a very different outfit from the struggling young regiment I had joined as a young lieutenant. For the fifteenth anniversary of the regiment, we were to receive the Freedom of the City of Quebec. Gunners had been a part of the old garrison town's history since 1608 and, during our day of celebration, we marched through the streets of the old walled city with our guns to receive the honour from the mayor, Jean Pelletier.

But there was a feeling in many quarters that because the 5ième was one of the specially created French units, it had never been really tested. In April 1985, there was going to be a big army exercise in Alberta called RV85, and I was determined that during this two-month exercise, my gunners were going to outshoot and outmanoeuvre the rest of the Canadian artillery.

Nine months before the exercise, I brought in a couple of my operations staff officers, Captain André Richard and Captain Michel Bonnet, to devise a training plan guaranteed to produce the best artillery regiment in the army. During the first week of September, I assembled the whole regiment into the big theatre on the base, sat them down and said, "I think it is high time that we show the rest of the artillery that we are not second-class citizens." A hush fell over the room. Although soldiers had muttered these kinds of sentiments to themselves, no senior officer had ever had the temerity to get up and publicly acknowledge that this is how we were viewed. At the very end of the speech, I said, "I need every single one of you there, body and soul, for that exercise, and I don't want to see any of you having to pull out because your wives are expecting." There was much laughter, but those words came back to haunt me.

For the next six months we worked hard. I scrounged ammunition, equipment, more training time in the field, more winter exercises with the guns. I kept pushing the troops to go beyond their own expectations to reach what I believed was their potential. My soldiers were magnificent, focused, diligent and totally committed.

When we arrived in Suffield, Alberta, the largest training area in the country, we were technically and tactically ready. As the exercise went into its second month, the army and divisional commanders confirmed that my regiment was not only the best artillery regiment in the corps, but one of the best combat units in the division.

Two days before the end of the exercise, I got a phone call. Beth was pregnant with Guy at the time and was having complications. The doctor had moved her into the hospital because he was concerned she might lose the baby. I knew I had to be with Beth. I went on the radio net to tell everyone in the regiment that I had to leave. My voice was breaking, and I was keenly aware that I was doing something I had asked them not to do. Later, back in Valcartier, I lost track of the number of gunners who came up to me and thanked me for not keeping a stiff upper lip, for being human, for sharing my life and my struggle with them.

Guy was born a few days later, and both he and Beth came through in fine shape. I bought a beer for every member of the regiment.

In 1986 I was in Ottawa at National Defence Headquarters as a section head, learning the ropes of project management and procurement. Promoted to full colonel, I was appointed the director of the army equipment and research program, a job I relished, since one of the overwhelming problems facing the Canadian military was the lack of expenditure and rational plan for the acquisition of the systems we needed to remain operational. It was a perfect job, with a tolerant boss, Major General Richard Evraire, who gave us guidance, a team of near-workaholics, and the advice of a small inner cabinet to help us keep within the tolerances of the friction war we were fighting with the air force and navy, and with the federal bureaucrats.

In response to increasing pressure from the United States, which under Ronald Reagan was spending trillions to win the Cold War, Brian Mulroney's Conservative government announced that it was committed to increase defence spending. The government asked for a white paper that would plot a fifteen-year strategy to bring the Canadian military up to scratch. At National Defence Headquarters, we were jubilant. Finally we could start to think about real defence budgets, maybe in the $18-billion range for the army alone, and about increasing the forces from about 72,000 to 90,000 regular members, and doubling the reserves from 45,000 to 90,000. Instead of being a shop-window force with no sustainability, we had a chance to become a truly credible defence force able to live up to our NATO commitments.

We worked constantly on the white paper. We believed that if we could come up with the right arguments and the right fiscal package, we might actually persuade the government and the country of the wisdom of supporting a larger, better-equipped and better-financed military. I worked with my small inner core of about sixty dedicated staff of captains, majors, and lieutenant colonels and my sterling deputy, Howie Marsh. We worked nights, weekends and statutory holidays (some of us had cots in our office) for eight months.

Then on March 17, 1987, word came down from the Department of National Defence that cabinet had decided that our plan was not affordable. Some of us cried in shocked anger and disbelief. Still, the young and ambitious minister of national defence, Perrin Beatty, decided that we should continue work on the policy document, and table it in the House of Commons, even though he knew it would never be implemented. We expected an outcry from the senior generals and admirals who had persuaded us that this battle for a new policy base and funding line was the closest we would get to the high stakes of war, but none of them uttered a peep of protest.

I had never seen morale drop so fast and so violently in a group of experienced officers as it did on that day in March 1987.

I sat in the gallery of the House of Commons on June 5 when Beatty tabled a toothless and even hypocritical document. Over the next two years, the Conservatives hacked and slashed what was left of our acquisition programs. I finally left Ottawa in disgust in the summer of 1989. I wouldn't say I was disillusioned, but I had suffered a loss of innocence.

My family and I moved back to the Montreal area. I was promoted brigadier general to take up the position of commandant at the Collège militaire royal. I adored the job. It was not only a magnificent challenge, but it brought me back to the place I had started from and gave me a chance to reappraise myself. The routine helped heal some of the wounds of Ottawa, and my wife and I also revelled in the social life with its extraordinary mixture of academics, officers, and cadets, integrated in one institution and pursuing the same objective: the development of future officers. The principal, Roch Carrier, was an acclaimed writer who hid his strong will and determination behind a calm and serene manner. Our two years together were an absolute joy.

My interest was to try to improve leadership training. When I arrived, little formal military leadership material and experience were being passed on to the future officers. The task was immense, since the Canadian Forces at the time had little to no formal material to provide. My generation had been on the receiving end of experience passed down from our elders, who got theirs from Second World War and Korean War veterans. As the guys with the combat medals retired, with very little of their experience put to paper, leadership training became more and more difficult for those who had not been in battle. It was simpler for most to teach physical fitness or *conciergerie*. The principles of military leadership remain difficult to teach.

Before my work at the college was complete, I was selected to attend the Higher Command and Staff course in Camberley, England. The Gulf War had just started, so we dubbed the course "How to Do Schwarzkopf's Job."

When I returned to Canada, I was appointed commander of the 5ième Group Brigade Mechanisé du Canada at Valcartier. I was taking charge of about 5,200 military personnel, 1,200 civilian support staff and related historic garrison duties in Quebec City, the oldest capital in North America. I was the first officer who had started his career with the 5ième to command it; Valcartier was a superb operational posting at the height of the Gulf War and the beginning of a new era of peacekeeping and conflict resolution for the Canadian military.

I worked constantly. We lived in the brigade commander's historic official residence on the Plains of Abraham; my kids attended Catholic private schools, run by religious orders in the old city; I was driven the twenty-six kilometres to the base in an impeccable black staff car; my wife was a pillar of the community and worked hard to support the families of soldiers away on missions. I was excited by the wealth of possibilities that lay before me, but I was also completely and utterly alone.

I never seemed to have an extra moment to spend with my children, and only now do I realize how much they suffered as they watched me work at my desk or at the dining-room table during the rare hours when I was at home.

Commanding such a large contingent of soldiers in a bastion of Quebec that had nationalist sympathies was a delicate balancing act. That was never clearer to me and my headquarters staff than during an exercise aimed at training a 1,600-person contingent for a high-risk peacekeeping mission in the former Yugoslavia. We were training the troops in escort tasks and convoy protection, and to provide a little more realism, we had planned manoeuvres in local communities on a specific day, alerting the police and the town councils as to what we were doing. It turned out that on that very day Prime Minister Mulroney was in town with other premiers to negotiate the Meech Lake Accord, which was designed to reconcile Quebec to staying in Canada under special status. Someone told the media that the prime minister was trying to intimidate the separatists by ordering up a huge display of military force.

I was ordered to stop the exercise and move the blue berets back to barracks with our tails between our legs. Caught by journalists later that day, I apparently created a small storm in Ottawa by accusing the media of fostering Quebec paranoia and of jumping to conclusions without making the effort to find out what was really going on. Someone in Ottawa must have stood up for me, because I never heard about it again.

From 1991 to 1993, the brigade sent more than four thousand troops on peacekeeping missions in places all over the world, from Cambodia to the Balkans to Kuwait. At one point I called the commander of the army to suggest that my whole brigade headquarters be moved overseas, since it felt like I was the only one left at home. He thanked me for the moment of levity, but told me I should prepare for even more UN taskings. I couldn't figure out where I would get the troops.

We were sending our soldiers, who were ready for classic chapter-six peacekeeping missions, into a world that seemed increasingly less amenable to such interventions. Chapter six of the UN Charter deals with threats to international peace and security. In the fifties, Lester

Pearson, Canada's minister of foreign affairs at the time, had come up with a concept of peacekeeping that had been implemented in conflict areas throughout the Cold War (and had won Pearson a Nobel Peace Prize). In these operations, lightly-armed, multinational, blue-helmeted, impartial and neutral peacekeepers were deployed and inter-posed between two former warring factions, with their consent, either to maintain the status quo, as in Sinai from 1956 to 1967, or to assist the parties in implementing a peace accord, as was at that time the case in Cambodia. The key principles of these operations are impartiality, neutrality and consent. Classic peacekeeping had worked well during the Cold War, where the two camps had used peacekeeping to diffuse conflicts that could draw in the major superpowers and lead to nuclear Armageddon. This was the type of peacekeeping that I had been trained in and the principles with which I was most familiar.

But we were increasingly less certain of the effectiveness of the clas-sic approach. Not only were we stretched in finding enough personnel, but on top of everything else, we started to receive casualties—some even killed in action. On June 18, 1993, one of the soldiers from the brigade, Corporal Daniel Gunther, died on active duty in Bosnia. The report I was given at the time suggested that a mortar bomb had exploded near his armoured personnel carrier and that he had been killed by flying shrapnel. Beth and I attended his funeral, which I found simple to the point of disrespect. Corporal Gunther was buried with a minimum of peacetime honours, and he and his family were treated as if he had been killed in a road accident. I remember his devastated father coming up to me after the service and asking me what, if any-thing, his son had died for? I had no answer to offer him and the rest of the shocked and grieving family.

According to the often gut-wrenching testimony of my young troops, the situations they found themselves in in the field were far more dangerous and complex than we were being led to expect. For instance, I found out much later that Gunther had actually been hit in the chest by an anti-tank rocket that had been fired from a shoulder-held grenade launcher. He had been deliberately targeted, and murdered. And yet the kind of training I was supposed to offer these troops before they went into the theatre was based on a hopelessly outdated model of lightly-armed blue berets monitoring a stable ceasefire. Lessons learned were slowly beginning to emerge, but not fast enough or with the force needed to stimulate any real changes. I was deeply concerned about the impact the combined effects of extreme stress and brutal violence encountered in the field were having on my troops. I harassed army headquarters to send some clinical psychology experts out to try to come up with solutions. The response that came back? Because of troop limitations, there were barely enough bayonets to do the job, let alone resources for such a low-priority effort. A commander should know how to do what needed to be done.

On June 27, 1993, I attended a change-of-command parade for one of my units, the 430th Tactical Helicopter Squadron. It was a lovely, cloudless day with just enough of a breeze that the soldiers were not too uncomfortable in their dress greens. I had made my speech of thanks to the departing commander and of welcome to the incoming one and was coming off the dais when an aide rushed up to me and said that Major-General Armand Roy, the Military Area Commander for Quebec and my boss at that time, was on the phone in my staff car and needed to speak with me immediately. I hurried to the car and picked up the phone. General Roy asked me if there was any reason why I couldn't be deployed overseas in a peacekeeping mission. I said none whatsoever. He said that UN Headquarters was contemplating a mission to Rwanda. I could feel my heart pounding with excitement. I managed to stammer out, "Rwanda, that's somewhere in Africa, isn't it?" He laughed and told me he would call the following day with more details. I almost floated back to the ceremony, I was that exhilarated. I leaned over to Beth and whispered, "I think I'm going to Africa!"

3

"CHECK OUT RWANDA AND YOU'RE IN CHARGE"

I confess that when General Roy called, I didn't know where Rwanda was or exactly what kind of trouble the country was in. The next day, he told me more about the tiny, heavily populated African nation. Rwanda was in the midst of negotiating a peace agreement to end a vicious two-and-a-half-year civil war between a rebel force, the Rwandese Patriotic Front (RPF), and the government. The rebel movement had grown out of a refugee population of Rwandans who had fled north to Uganda in the early sixties, after independence had changed the political balance in their homeland. In the early nineties, the rebel army had twice pushed into the northern region of Rwanda and was now hunkered down behind a demilitarized zone monitored by a group of neutral military observers under the auspices of the Organization of African Unity (OAU). While the parties negotiated the terms of a peace agreement in Arusha, Tanzania, the UN had been asked by the president of Uganda, Yoweri Museveni, to send in a small force to monitor the border to ensure that weapons and soldiers were not crossing from Uganda into Rwanda to reinforce the RPF.

This was to be my mission, dubbed the United Nations Observer Mission in Uganda and Rwanda (UNOMUR). General Roy described it as a classic peacekeeping operation, a confidence-building exercise designed to encourage the belligerents to get down to the serious business of peace. It was extremely modest in scope and size: I would have under my command a total of eighty-one unarmed military observers, who would operate on the Ugandan side of the border.

Why pick me to lead this tiny mission in a place I'd barely heard of?

I was about to begin an unprecedented third year as commander of the 5ième Brigade Group; in four days we were going to celebrate the twenty-fifth anniversary of its founding with more than a thousand troops on parade. The 5th still faced plenty of challenges, many of them in the area of peacekeeping. We were still too ad hoc in our preparation of troops for deployment on ever more challenging missions. Much of our training was still focused on classic war-fighting, even though the conflicts we were sending troops into usually were not unfolding like classic wars. As far as I was concerned, it wasn't yet time for me to leave, but I was being asked—ordered—to deploy. Whether it was a big force, a small force or just me alone, I was going over. Knowing that Major General Maurice Baril was heading up the military component of the UN Department of Peace-keeping Operations (DPKO), I surmised that there must be more to this mission than met the eye. In the end I decided that this was my chance to learn first-hand what would work in the changing nature of conflict in the post–Cold War world.

However, I was stunned to find out that Canada was only willing to supply me, and not a single soldier more, to the mission. I protested to the defence department, which remained adamant about the decision until I noticed a tiny loophole in the arrangement. I was being hired by the UN under a civilian contract—in essence being seconded by the government of Canada to UN service—and so the defence department was still on the hook to supply the one Canadian officer it had approved for UNOMUR. The director of Canadian peacekeeping operations at National Defence Headquarters gave me a list of ten names from which to choose the officer who would become my military assistant. Since the mission was so tiny, picking the right MA was crucial: he would take care of a large portion of the paperwork and the administrative burden so that I could concentrate on operations, training and political matters.

I didn't recognize any of the names on the list of ten, and truth be told I was miffed that none of the officers from my brigade was on it. The people of Rwanda spoke French as well as Kinyarwanda; the RPF spoke English. I wanted my MA to be bilingual, but none of the officers on the list met that requirement—short notice and a lack of volunteers was the department's lame excuse. I finally stopped at one name: Major Brent Beardsley of the Royal Canadian Regiment, the senior infantry regiment in the army. At thirty-nine, he was older than most of the others on the list and he was currently involved in drafting the Canadian Forces peacekeeping manual. On paper he seemed to have the background to balance off my limited experience with UN headquarters and with peacekeeping. Luckily, his boss was my old colleague, Howie Marsh, and I knew he'd give me the straight goods. When I phoned, he told me that Brent was a solid soldier with a tremendous work ethic, but more important, he was *perspicace*—he had that magic combination of insight and foresight.

On July 1, 1993, I handed over my command to my successor, Brigadier General Alain Forand, in front of a surprised audience at the anniversary celebrations of the 5ième. Since my family would have to move from the commander's official residence, Beth launched a search for a new place, hoping to find one in the same area so that the children wouldn't have to switch schools. With my future uncertain, we didn't want to buy a home, so we decided to move into military married quarters next to the old Garrison Club.

As for me, I was already in the Rwandan mission body and soul. I set aside as my temporary headquarters the Artillery Room in the Garrison Club, which had been built in the 1820s by British engineers as their headquaters for the massive defensive works of the old capital. The windows look out toward the lush green of the Plains of Abraham, where generations of French, English and Canadian military leaders plotted campaigns, and beyond the plains to the St. Lawrence River. This room, with its heavy, old oak furniture and yellowing nineteenth-century prints depicting training and fighting scenes in the garrison, always sent a thrill through me. I could almost feel the presence of the military and political leaders who came before me, pacing in front of the fireplace as they pondered strategies and worked through knotty tactical problems.

My mission was hardly on the level of their campaigns, but still I was carried away by the romance of it, by the idea of adventure that Africa represented to me. Growing up Catholic in Quebec in the fifties, I had been captivated by missionary tales from "the dark continent." As a result, my notions of Africa were outdated and Eurocentric. I combed the library for anything I could find on Rwanda and the Great Lakes region of central Africa. There wasn't much. But serious work was afoot, and time was of the essence.

I had spoken to Major Beardsley only once on the phone and had asked him to bring to Quebec City the most up-to-date technical peace-keeping data, after-actions reports and doctrine, along with the results of the DPKO's two brief reconnaissance missions to Rwanda, and any general information he could obtain on the country. I hoped we would receive a very detailed intelligence briefing later on at National Defence Headquarters in Ottawa. As soon as I laid eyes on Brent, I knew I had chosen well. He is the quintessential quiet Canadian, thoughtful, modest to a fault, but with a sparkle in his calm hazel eyes that signals the presence of plenty of fire, determination and humour. With a few faxes from New York on the mission's concept of operations, which had been presented to the UN Security Council only a few days earlier, we set to work. By the end of our first afternoon together, we had become a team of two. Brent had an appetite for work and an ability to anticipate upcoming objectives that was awe-inspiring. But I think the quality that impressed me most about him was his unassuming confidence.

For the next three weeks, Brent produced staff work and gathered material for us in Ottawa. I travelled to New York and Ottawa a couple of times, but I received very limited briefings in both places. I worked with the DPKO desk officer, Major Miguel Martin, an Argentinian who was also the desk officer for missions in Angola, Mozambique, Central America, Liberia and any number of other places, and Isel Rivero, an ex–Cuban freedom fighter who served as the political desk officer for central Africa. The four of us were the entire staff effort devoted to UNOMUR by the UN, and Martin and Rivero were only with us part-time. It was clear that this small mission would not sway anyone, either at the UN or at National Defence Headquarters in Ottawa, away from the many other missions, crises, problems and budget cuts that were overwhelming them on a daily basis.

We tried to cram in as much knowledge about the Great Lakes region of central Africa as we could. Tiny, landlocked Rwanda was tucked between Zaire on the west and Tanzania on the east, with Uganda to the north and Burundi to the south. Rwanda had never been considered important enough by scholars in the West to warrant extensive study. Brent and I managed to piece together a rough history from newspaper accounts and a few scholarly articles, which reduced a highly complex social and political situation to a simple inter-tribal conflict. With a confidence born of ignorance, we soldiered on.

We traced the roots of the current hostilities back to the early twentieth century and Belgian colonial rule. When the Belgians chased the Germans out of the territory in 1916, they discovered that two groups of people shared the land. The Tutsis, who were tall and quite light-skinned, herded cattle; the shorter, darker Hutus farmed vegetable plots. The Belgians viewed the minority Tutsis as closer in kind to Europeans and elevated them to positions of power over the majority Hutu, which exacerbated the feudal state of peasant Hutus and overlord Tutsis. Enlisting the Tutsis allowed the Belgians to develop and exploit a vast network of coffee and tea plantations without the inconvenience of war or the expense of deploying a large colonial service.

Rwanda achieved independence in 1962, after a popular uprising slaughtered or drove out the Tutsi elite, and installed a Hutu-dominated government led by the charismatic Gregoire Kayibanda. Over the next decade, a series of violent pogroms further targeted the Tutsi population of Rwanda and many more fled to the neighbouring states of Uganda, Burundi and Zaire, where they led a precarious existence as stateless refugees.

In 1973, Major General Juvénal Habyarimana, a Hutu, toppled Kayibanda in a *coup d'état* and began a twenty-year dictatorship. It led to a degree of stability in Rwanda that was envied in the volatile Great Lakes region. But the expulsion and persecution of the country's Tutsis sowed permanent seeds of discord. Slowly, the Tutsi diaspora became a force to be reckoned with. Fuelled by the continued oppression in Rwanda and harsh treatment at the hands of their reluctant host countries, the diaspora finally coalesced into the Rwandese Patriotic Front. A small but highly effective military and political movement, the RPF proved capable of engaging and defeating the French-backed Rwandese Government Forces (RGF). By 1991, the Rwandan government was caught between an increasingly formidable rebel army and international pressure for democratic reform. President Habyarimana began the on-again, off-again negotiations that formed the basis for the peace talks then taking place in Arusha, Tanzania.

A few short weeks of snatching at whatever material that came our way was not about to make Africanists of either one of us.

Downtown Manhattan in mid-July was hot, and the streets were lit-tered with tourists. It was not the best time of the year to be in New York, but the shimmering glass tower of the United Nations headquarters beckoned, and sometimes I had to pinch myself to realize I wasn't dreaming.

Like many first-timers at the UN, I was impressed by the grandeur of the chambers of the General Assembly and the Security Council. But I soon learned that the real work went on in a rabbit warren of offices that lay just out of sight of the general public. The drabbest and most cramped offices seemed to belong to the DPKO. Staff were working in dreadful conditions: desks squeezed together, phones jangling constantly, outdated computers crashing (in some cases, employees were still using typewriters), people often short of the most basic office supplies. Not to put too fine a point on it, the DPKO was essentially a thirty-sixth-floor sweatshop. Its sorely under-equipped state was possibly part of the image game that the UN plays in order to avoid the wrath of irresponsible media and the international political vultures who use any excuse to accuse it of "wasting" money. But I soon noticed that other UN agencies, such as the United Nations Childrens Fund (UNICEF) and the United Nations High Commissioner for Refugees (UNHCR), were not only bet-ter quartered but enjoyed a better quality of life all around.

Maurice Baril was a member of a triumvirate that led the DPKO. The other members were Kofi Annan, the under-secretary-general of peacekeeping, and Iqbal Riza, who was Annan's number two and essen-tially the chief of staff for the department. The appointment of Baril in June 1992 had been celebrated as a coup for Canada. But the task he had set himself—building the office into an effective military-strategic, as well as operational, headquarters—was a huge challenge. Critics charged that the DPKO was staffed by a bunch of incompetent boobs who kept bankers' hours and disappeared when situations in the field came to a head. Canada's Major General Lewis MacKenzie, who had led the UN peacekeeping contingent in Sarajevo, had heaped scorn on the DPKO for its generally negative attitude toward those in the field, its lack of response to immediate needs, and the way its staff and leadership seemed to be consistently unavailable when urgent decisions had to be made. His criticisms had made headlines in Canada and most of the capitals in the world and had sunk morale in the DPKO.

Maurice set up an operations room that was now staffed around the clock by talented and dedicated young officers. He'd begged and borrowed most of them directly from the permanent missions and managed to get their home nations to cover their costs as well. He would pose his request simply: "Don't you think it would be an irresistible training opportunity to have one or two of your better qualified officers loaned to me during my buildup of DPKO headquarters?" Many nations responded immediately and positively out of a kind of enlightened self-interest. He also began "borrowing" officers from the field missions in order to bring their expertise back to New York, where he gave them responsibility for sorting out problems that missions were facing on the ground.

Among his enormously diverse staff, he had created an atmosphere of good humour, hard work and co-operation that was quite remarkable under the circumstances. The number of UN missions had nearly tripled in just a few years to seventeen. They now involved more than 80,000 personnel from over 60 contributing nations, with unimaginable logistics, training, ethical and equipment problems, and were all being commanded from an ad hoc, under-staffed and under-funded headquarters in New York. I remember waiting in Maurice's office one time while he was on the phone trying to link up some ancient M-48 tanks from one army with a battalion from another army that was sitting on the border of Croatia, in need not only of tanks but tank training and maintenance. On a second phone, he was keeping U.S. officials in Germany on the line to provide ammunition and spare parts for the tanks, and he still needed to figure out where the mechanic instructors would come from.

Maurice's overextended desk officers particularly admired the way he stickhandled around the clumsy bureaucratic UN procedures and protected his staff so they could actually do their work. What won him particular glory from them was that he did not seem intimidated by the all-powerful Americans; he could negotiate with them and wasn't afraid to go one-on-one in the corner if the interests of the DPKO were at stake. Maurice was definitely in his element, using his shy, self-deprecating humour to win over the crustiest UN time-servers. I had been warned by friends back home that working for the UN could be a nightmare, but seeing the genuine esteem that Maurice had won within the institution in just one year made me think that I would be able to handle it.

I was also tremendously impressed by Annan and Riza. Annan was gentle, soft-spoken and decent to the core. I found him to be genuinely, even religiously, dedicated to the founding principles of the UN and tireless in his efforts to save the organization from itself in these exceptionally troubled times, where conflict and humanitarian catastrophes, often linked, were breaking out around the world. We were not facing a new world order, as George Bush had declared two years earlier, but world disorder, with the destruction of human life in "peacetime" at an all-time high.

Riza wasn't as personable as his boss, but he read his interlocutors rapidly and could set the tone of any encounter. Tall, thin and intense, he did not suffer fools and at times did not hesitate to make you aware of that fact. His occasional intellectual arrogance was offset by his sound common sense and political sophistication.

The relationship between these two men lay at the core of the DPKO as I knew it, Annan very human and concerned, and Riza the cool, calculating master of ceremonies. Articulate, businesslike and direct, Riza made the place dance to their tune. Along with Baril, these two éminences grises seemed determined to force change on their watch and eradicate the stain of recent failures in Somalia and the Balkans.

There was talk of mounting a larger peacekeeping mission inside Rwanda itself but only in passing. Some people in the DPKO thought that a small and quick success story in Rwanda might inspire member nations to place increased confidence in the UN's peacekeeping efforts and be more generous with military and financial resources. The trouble was, as I was bluntly told on a few occasions, no one but the French and possibly the Belgians had any interest in that part of the world. Where would the political will and resources come from? This, at least, was the party line from Hedi Annabi, the head of the Africa Section in the political division of the DPKO. Still, as far as I knew and as far as Brent could find out, the parties in Arusha were close to putting the final touches on the peace agreement. Once that was in place, either the OAU or the UN would be called upon to help implement it. Maurice doubted that the OAU had the expertise or the resources or even the desire to mount a full-fledged peacekeeping operation in Rwanda, and he was certain the DPKO would be asked to pick up the slack. But at that point, the only people motivated to spend any time on preliminary activity for such a mission to Rwanda were my very small team.

From my conversations with Maurice, I was gradually working out the elaborate power relationships that he had to deal with. The DPKO was definitely further down the UN totem pole than the Department of Political Affairs (DPA), under Dr. James Jonah from Sierra Leone. The DPA was a very political place, indeed, where many officers flaunted their connections, particularly with the secretary-general, Boutros Boutros-Ghali. Maurice told me that one of the most difficult problems he and his colleagues faced was the DPA's constant interference and manoeuvring without consulting the DPKO political staff who were in direct contact with the mission in the field.

Maurice and I had become close during our battles with the Ottawa mandarins in the late eighties, and I thought I knew him well. However, New York had changed him in an almost indefinable way. His earthy good humour was still there, but he had begun to take on the coloration of his surroundings. He was becoming more cautious and more politically sensitive. For instance, he and his staff always dressed in civilian clothes. He told me that he had instituted this policy because uniforms made the civilian staff at the UN uncomfortable and created unnecessary friction. The new, more astute Maurice understood that to woo allies he had to become more flexible than his military background generally allowed. He tried to pass this knowledge on to me, and Brent and I also donned civilian clothes, albeit with great reluctance.

Maurice had become masterful at marrying political, diplomatic, humanitarian and military imperatives in an organization full of internecine friction. Had he become more cunning or had he just matured at the grand strategic level? He certainly had become very skilled and attentive to the political dimensions of the use of military force. With so many factors at play when he had to make decisions, how was his fighting edge affected? All I can say is that while he was still a close friend, he had acquired a polished side that field soldiers do not readily understand.

The Security Council of the UN had approved UNOMUR in June, but we couldn't do anything until the Ugandan government signed the status of mission agreement, or SOMA, which would allow our troops to operate within the country. Mozambique had stalled the signing of the SOMA for the peacekeeping mission currently operating there and, when the UN had sent peacekeepers without the signature, they were hit with a crippling series of taxes on soldiers and equipment as soon as the mission arrived on the ground. At the Security Council, the British were refusing to let my mission deploy before the UN had the signed SOMA in hand. Brent became quite adept at collecting corridor intelligence. Some people speculated that the Ugandans weren't signing because they were in a mad scramble to find alternate routes to supply the RPF, while others cynically thought it was a ploy to try and extract cash from the UN.

We had produced the bulk of the necessary paperwork for the mission, including operational documents that still had to be confirmed on the ground; we had pushed all the possible buttons. We hadn't been able to persuade the desk officers from the relevant departments to have a final coordination session on our mission; such a meeting was nearly impossible to organize because the culture of the UN was one of jealously guarded stovepipe fiefdoms where information was power (not the best way to run a complex, multi-national, multidisciplined and international organization that was always in the poorhouse).

Cooling our heels while waiting for the SOMA to be signed was wasting precious time. I had left my family high and dry to serve what I thought was a greater good. At very short notice, they had been forced to vacate the beautiful and spacious garrison commander's home and move into married quarters in a historic building that had been built in 1804 and was not in the best of shape. Brent's wife, Marge, was pregnant with their third child and was going through some difficult days. Finally, I requested leave, which was immediately approved by Maurice.

On the way back home, I stopped in Ottawa for an administrative and intelligence update: the update was, there was no intelligence. Canada's defence department was unconvinced that the Great Lakes region of central Africa was a priority.

In Quebec City I found it hard to gear down and act as if the long separation facing me and my family was just another posting. On the surface we were the perfect military family: three happy kids and a loving wife and mother who, after twelve years of teaching, had chosen to pack up her chalk and her workbooks and devote her time to raising our children and making a home for us all. Underneath there was trouble. Willem, my eldest, was fourteen and having difficulty at school; he was constantly being baited by his pro-sovereignist teachers about his staunchly federalist father. I could see that he was angry, isolated and confused, but I didn't have the time or the patience to connect with him. I had had all kinds of time for the young officers I had guided, mentored and nurtured over the years, but I was unable to offer the same love and support to my own son. Instead, I dealt with the surface details of trying to get my family settled in our new home.

I should have seen that Beth, too, was struggling. She had gone from leading a high-profile, very involved life as the wife of the garrison commander to being brutally shoved aside as the military community hurried to embrace my replacement. What comfort could I offer her when it was my desire and duty to go to Africa that had put her in this position?

On the weekend of August 8, I received an urgent call from Brent. The Rwandans had just signed the Arusha Peace Agreement—which called for, among other things, a speedy deployment of an international peacekeeping force to guarantee the shaky ceasefire on which the peace accords rested. All hell was breaking loose at DPKO as they rushed to cobble together a response, and I was needed back in New York. I threw some clothes into a bag and was off.

• • •

Back at the UN, we immediately immersed ourselves in the text of the Arusha accords, provided to us by a Fijian colonel named Isoa Tikoka, who had been the UN military observer throughout the last months of negotiations at Arusha. The existence of Tikoka was a surprise: no one had thought to tell us that there was a UN military man on the ground in Africa whom we might have tapped for information during my weeks in New York. Tiko, as we soon came to call him, was a veteran peace-keeper, a literal giant of a man, good-hearted and full of life. He had been pulled from the Somalia mission to observe the Arusha peace talks. In Somalia he had had several vehicles shot out from under him, had been frequently robbed at gunpoint and had lost all of his personal kit. In the months ahead, he would become a most valued adviser to me.

The peace agreement was a complex document that was the result of painstaking refereeing by Tanzania's president, Ali Hassan Mwinyi, at Arusha during nearly two years of fractious negotiations. What was not evident to us sitting in New York was that the accords papered over, rather than resolved, the major problems of how to share power between the formerly warring parties and how to resettle refugees in Rwanda, some of whom had left the country forty years earlier and now had children and grandchildren with a claim on Rwandan citizenship. We also did not appreciate the state of human rights in the country after so much fighting. (Such information was available in New York, but because of the lack of sharing between the departments in the UN, the UN agencies and the non-governmental organizations [NGOs], no one filled us in until we actually hit the ground in October 1993.)

Basically the accords set a brisk, twenty-two-month timetable in which the various political parties, including the RPF and the former rul-ing party, the Mouvement républicain national pour la démocratie et le développement (MRND), would first form a broad-based transitional gov-ernment (BBTG). Then the country would proceed through several stages to free, democratic, multi-ethnic elections. Along the way, the BBTG would somehow reintegrate the refugees and the RPF, demobilize both armies and create a new national force, redraft the constitution, revitalize the civil police and rebuild the shattered economy, drawing on the world financial and aid communities, which would be needed to throw money at all the country's complicated problems. All of this depended on a neutral international force deploying immediately to assist in the implementation of the stages of the accords. The deadline that Arusha set for the presence of such a force was September 10, a mere five weeks away.

The DPKO decided to launch a third reconnaissance of Rwanda. Usually each department sent its own team on its own schedule. This time we were trying to achieve a faster turnaround, and representatives from all concerned departments would go at the same time.

Brent and I set to work immediately to produce a plan of attack that focused on military concerns but also took into account the humanitarian side of the mission. The political side remained the purview of the DPA. We worked without an office or support staff or even proper military maps of the area—we were two guys pulling all-nighters on borrowed laptops. We planned our reconnaissance using a tourist map of Rwanda.

On August 10, Brent and I were called into a hastily scheduled meeting with other reconnaissance mission team members to discuss plans and requirements. Nobody had anything useful to bring to the table and most appeared to be totally out of the loop. Even Macaire Pédanou, a slightly-built African with a pensive manner who had been the UN political observer in Arusha and had been appointed head of the reconnaissance mission, had little to offer in the way of a plan of action. Though Maurice and others talked about Rwanda being a chance to redeem the reputation of UN peacekeeping, it was clear to me that the mission was still considered a sideshow to the main event, which was always going on somewhere else far more important, such as Bosnia or Haiti or Somalia or Mozambique, just about anywhere other than the tiny central African country that most people would be hard-pressed to locate on a map.

A few days before we were to leave for Rwanda, Maurice called me into his office to brief him. His workspace was functional and rather depressing, without any creature comforts whatsoever. He spent so much of his time in the field or at innumerable meetings all over the UN that he wasn't in his office much; it lacked the personal trinkets that usually accumulate in a commander's office. The sixties wood panelling was in need of a serious upgrade and the furniture should have been out on the garbage heap.

I was feeling very confident about our plan for the reconnaissance or, in UN-speak, the "technical mission." Maurice listened to me carefully but told me not to come back to him with a request for a brigade-sized mission. His words were roughly, "This thing has to be small and inexpensive, otherwise it will never get approved by the Security Council." I was taken aback. He was asking me to "situate the estimate," as we say in the military, to design the mission to fit available resources rather than to respond to the actual demands of the situation we were being sent to assess.

I struggled with this new information as Brent tackled the UN bureaucracy to get funds released for our technical mission. I rationalized that as a soldier coming from a chronically undermanned and under-equipped army, I was used to making do—that was part of a soldier's job description. But I was in a serious quandary. From what I had determined, the Arusha accords would require a UN mission to meet their milestones. Yet if my technical mission report asked for more than what nations were willing to pay or contribute, there would be no mission. I had a major ethical dilemma on my hands before we had even left New York.

Then we received word that an eye condition had sidelined Pédanou. He would not be joining us in Rwanda because he had to have emergency surgery. Not until the plane tickets were in my hand did Maurice tell me that no one from the DPA would be able to replace Pédanou as mission head. By default I was to be in charge. I was still naive enough to be pleased.

4

ENEMIES HOLDING HANDS

We landed in the Rwandan capital, Kigali, on August 19, 1993. From the first moment I glimpsed its soft, mist-covered mountains, I loved Rwanda. Though it is almost on the equator, its elevation makes it a temperate place, full of fragrant breezes and unbelievable greenness. With its tiny terraced fields against the perpetual backdrop of rolling hills, Rwanda seemed to me then a kind of garden of Eden. Not that there was much time to appreciate its beauties: from the moment the plane touched down, I was caught up in a flurry of diplomatic activity. From the runway, I stepped into my first press conference, which was well-attended by the local and international media.

The atmosphere was friendly and positive. The official airport welcoming party was led by Anastase Gasana, the coalition government's foreign minister; Jean-Damascène Bizimana, the Rwandan ambassador to the UN; and the Rwandan ambassador to Uganda. Gasana had been one of the strong peace supporters within the Rwandan government at Arusha, and he had been appointed official liaison with the technical mission. He was an affable, unpretentious chap, a politician from the Mouvement démocratique républicain (MDR), a party that was in opposition to the Habyarimana regime. He believed that the Arusha Peace Agreement marked the beginning of democracy for his country. He wasn't afraid that Rwanda would fall back into war, but he recognized the dangerous political uncertainty that the transition to a multi-party, power-sharing, democratic system represented for the country. He was unwavering in his insistence that the UN had to form a neutral peace-keeping force and get it on the ground as soon as possible.

I was buoyed by Gasana's optimism; it was hard to keep my neutral face and not respond. Bizimana was a different story. He watched and listened intently and said nothing, his sombre silence more than a little disturbing, as he was Rwanda's man in New York and an important interlocutor on our behalf in front of the media that day. At the time, I didn't know he was from the hardline side of the house.

I stuck closely to my script, emphasizing that my team was embarking on a fact-finding mission, and stressing that our presence was no guarantee that the UN would commit to the full-fledged peace-keeping operation mandated by the Arusha accords. The question of September 10, the day that the BBTG was supposed to be in place, was on many of the journalists' lips. I remember raising my finger to make the point that our presence was only phase one, that a series of deci-sions had yet to be made by the UN and the troop-contributing nations before anybody would be sent to Rwanda. There would definitely be no UN mission on the ground by September 10. However, I promised, if a mission was approved, we would break every possible record, not to say a few rules, to get there as quickly as possible. My news took a lot of the enthusiasm out of the reception.

I was surprised that a formal visit to President Habyarimana wasn't on the immediate agenda, since I thought he might have wanted to make his own appraisal of the person leading the team of UN staff that would sway the decision to send a mission or not. When I mentioned this to Gasana, he assured me that the president did want to see me. He left it at that and so did I for the moment.

In twelve days, my small eighteen-member team and I had to assess the political, humanitarian, administrative and military aspects of a poten-tial UN peacekeeping mission. Because I was now head of the mission, I had to split my time to cover political and humanitarian aspects as well as the military and meet the leading politicians of the seven parties who would be involved in forming the transitional government. I also had to meet members of the diplomatic community of Kigali, and the United Nations Development Programme (UNDP) resident representative, Amadou Ly of Senegal, who was the senior UN presence in the country.

As a result, I had to delegate several military reconnaissance tasks to

Brent, Tiko, Miguel Martin and Brigadier Paddy Blagdon, a retired U.K. army officer and UN de-mining expert, while I took on only the work with the highest military authorities on all sides. As well, I would have to touch base with the humanitarian and aid organizations that would be key to helping the refugee, internally displaced and famine-ridden populations inside and around the country and reintegrating demobilized soldiers later on. A drought had hit southern Rwanda hard, and no let-up seemed to be in sight.

Staff from the Field Operations Division (the UN's field administrative and logistics agency) would examine communications, infrastructure, personnel, local logistics and transportation, and every other aspect of administrative support that the mission would need in this remote, landlocked country.

Even for the technical mission, we needed vehicles, local staff, telephones and all sorts of equipment. We set up a temporary headquarters in a meeting room in the Hôtel des Mille Collines, but we were plagued with logistical problems, and I fumed about the amount of time we were wasting just getting ourselves set up. We had some tourist maps on the wall, some computers on the desks and a conference table with a few chairs. At the end of this brief trip I would have to submit my recommendations and draft concept of operations to the UN for approval, and already administrative problems and shortages were consuming our limited time and attention.

Luckily we were blessed with Amadou Ly, who had been in Rwanda for three years and knew the lay of the land. Unlike many others in the UN, he was neither cynical nor jaded, even though he had witnessed his share of bungling and incompetence. His mild demeanour masked a ferocious appetite for work, which inspired his small but dedicated staff to achieve minor miracles with their scant resources. He managed to supply us with everything from paper and pencils to access to overseas lines, and vehicles with drivers, even though it wasn't his job to do so and his office didn't have the budget to provide this service to us. On that trip, Ly was one of the few people in Rwanda to alert us to the ominous rumblings of the extremist elements and to the presence of militias, which had inserted themselves into the youth wings of the various political parties, even the moderate ones. He warned me that time was of the essence: the UN needed to get a peacekeeping mission on the ground as soon as possible to prevent such forces from increasing their grip.

My first official meeting was with the prime minister of the interim government, Agathe Uwilingiyimana, known far and wide simply as Madame Agathe, and Faustin Twagiramungu, the prime minister designate, who had been chosen in Arusha to lead the BBTG. We met in Madame Agathe's large, airy office. She was a motherly woman, but there was steel in her too. She supported a UN peacekeeping force. Rwanda's future hung in the balance, she said, and we could not miss this historic opportunity for democracy because of a few hard-liners who did not want to share power.

Twagiramungu had studied in Quebec from 1968 to about 1976, living through the War Measures Act and René Lévesque's separatist Parti Québécois taking power democratically. He had participated in the great rally for a McGill University français. He felt that that experience had assisted him greatly in his political life. He was not as inspiring as Madame Agathe, and less prone to be front and centre, but he was very keen on the establishment of the BBTG. Before entering politics, he had been the general manager of a state-run company that had a monopoly on all of Rwanda's international freight movements. Twagiramungu had at one time been accused of pocketing bribes and was briefly incarcerated, an episode he attributed to political persecution. Perhaps that accounted for his cool, chip-on-the-shoulder attitude. Although he seconded Madame Agathe's support of the UN, he did so without her passion.

I found the circuitous talk of the Rwandan politicians whom I met a little trying at times, but I soon realized that if I stopped asking questions and listened, I was often rewarded with amazing insights into the history and culture of the country and what ailed it. For example, individuals from both sides of the ethnic divide betrayed a fear of the future, all the while expressing their desire for the peace accords to be implemented. Their lingering sense of injustice over their treatment in the past, the chaotic uncertainty and their mistrust of authorities, could be potential impediments to grasping the incredible opportunity that the peace process held out. Overall they were a people suffering from psychological depression because of legitimate or imagined past grievances. They had a pessimistic, though perhaps realistic, view of the future.

I was surprised at how many of the people I met had either studied in Canada or had had Canadian teachers in Rwanda. People also had very close ties with the Belgians, the old colonial power, and with the French academic and military milieu. The scanty information I'd collected before arriving in Kigali did not quite describe the decades-long relationship between francophone Rwandans, mostly of Hutu extraction, and Quebec, especially its two largest French universities, Laval and the Université de Montréal. The head of the moderate Parti libéral, Landoald Ndasingwa, was married to a Québécoise, Hélène Pinsky. They made an odd but charismatic couple, Lando with his gentle charm and easy laugh, and Hélène, who called to mind a turbocharged Bella Abzug. He was the minister of social affairs in the interim government, and he expected to be a minister in the BBTG. Hélène ran the family business, which was Chez Lando, a hotel, bar and restaurant, popular with European expatriates and Rwandans alike.

With Hélène it was easy to see how well French-Canadian culture—the language, music, literature and appetite for intense social and political discussion—translated to Rwanda. As the mission continued, I became more and more at ease in this francophone nation. Perhaps I was a willing victim of Rwanda's charms, but the struggles of this little African country began to stir a passionately sympathetic response in me. My eyes were being opened to realities far from my usual military sphere, and I was attempting to absorb every nuance of the culture, every distortion of the double-talk of its political leaders.

While Boutros Boutros-Ghali had not assigned a new political head of the mission after Pédanou dropped out, the DPKO had sent along Rivero as well as Martin to accompany me on all my diplomatic and political meetings. And the DPA had sent a junior political officer to assist me. She was an assistant to Under-Secretary-General James Jonah and was soignée and haughty, a fixer and arranger who thrived in the diplomatic social milieu, filling my diary with a constant stream of meetings and attempts at cocktail parties. We saw the Germans, the Belgians, the Americans, the Chinese, the Russians, the papal nuncio, the Burundian ambassador and, of course, the French—twice, at their insistence. None of them offered me any in-depth political analysis. All of them seemed to be singing from the same song sheet: the UN had to get on the ground as soon as possible. None of them put any troops on the table, however, and most permitted themselves to quibble about the potential size and cost of such a mission.

Our junior political officer, who happened to be French, booked me the two appointments with the French ambassador, one at the beginning of the trip and one on the day before I left. The French had a relationship with the Habyarimana regime that stretched back to the mid-seventies. Over the years, the French government had made a significant investment in French-speaking Rwanda, supplying it with arms and military expertise, support that had escalated to outright intervention against the RPF insurgent force in October 1990 and again in February 1993. But the RPF proved to be a stubborn and persistent foe, and the French finally joined the United States in a diplomatic effort that led to a series of ceasefires and, eventually, the Arusha accords. The French still had a half a para-battalion in Kigali, supposedly to protect the European expatriate community, and they also provided military advisers, both in and out of uniform, to the major units of the RGF. France was the only member on the UN Security Council that had demonstrated a clear interest in Rwanda. Keeping the French ambassador informed was important—the possibility of a UN deployment hung in the balance.

To my delight, during our first meeting at his residence, Ambassador Jean-Phillippe Marlaud was open and friendly, showing none of the usual arrogance that I had encountered with French officials on other occasions. He had only been in Rwanda since March 1993, and he seemed determined to further the objectives of the Arusha accords. He listened to me carefully, expressed genuine enthusiasm for my nascent ideas and even looked over my reconnaissance plan. He was the only person in Rwanda other than Ly to demonstrate more than a superficial interest in my work and its details. He believed that it was imperative to find some means of reassuring the Rwandan people on September 10. Even a simple gesture might allay their fears.

As I survived the rounds of political meetings, Brent and Tiko were busy assessing the military situation. The huge Fijian, who had served in Kashmir, Sinai, Lebanon and Somalia, among other places, had a seemingly inexhaustible stock of war stories and equally inexhaustible good humour. A few days into the trip, we travelled together to meet with the senior leadership of the RPF north of the demilitarized zone in Mulindi, sixty kilometres north of Kigali. As we drove through the blue-green countryside, my thoughts turned to Major Paul Kagame, the military leader of the RPF. I was curious to meet the man who had turned a ragtag group of guerrilla fighters into a force capable of holding its own against French soldiers in the field, not once but twice.

We passed a constant stream of pedestrians, women in brightly coloured dresses, swaying gracefully under the large parcels balanced on their heads, often with small children tucked into shawls slung across their backs. Men pedalled handmade bicycles, fashioned from scrap wood and draped with all manner of vegetables. Gaggles of smiling boys in baggy cotton shorts drove cattle. The route was dotted with neat villages of terracotta, mud-brick cottages, the beauty of the landscape masking what I knew was desperate poverty.

And then, in the middle of this rural idyll, we came across a hellish reminder of the long civil war.

We smelled the camp before we saw it, a toxic mixture of feces, urine, vomit and death. A forest of blue plastic tarps covered an entire hillside where 60,000 displaced persons from the demilitarized zone and the RPF sector were tightly packed into a few square kilometres. When we stopped and got out of our vehicles, we were swarmed by a thick cloud of flies, which stuck to our eyes and mouths and crawled into our ears and noses. It was hard not to gag with the smell, but breathing through the mouth was difficult with the flies. A young Belgian Red Cross worker spotted us and interrupted her rounds to guide us through the camp. The refugees huddled around small open fires, a silent, ghost-like throng that followed us listlessly with their eyes as we picked our way gingerly through the filth of the camp. I was deeply impressed by the young Belgian woman's calm compassion as she gently administered what aid she could to these desperate souls. It was obvious that she could see through the dirt and despair to their humanity.

The scene was deeply disturbing, and it was the first time I had witnessed such suffering unmediated by the artifice of TV news. Most shocking of all was the sight of an old woman lying alone, quietly waiting to die. She couldn't have weighed more than a dozen kilos. Pain and despair etched every line of her face as she lay amid the ruins of her shelter, which had already been stripped of its tarp and picked clean of its possessions. In the grim reality of the camp, she had been given up for dead and her meagre belongings redistributed among her healthier neighbours. The aid worker whispered that the old woman likely would not last the night. Tears stung my eyes at the thought of her dying alone with no one to love or comfort her.

As I stood struggling to regain my composure, I was surrounded by a group of the camp children, who were either laughing outright or smiling shyly at this strange white man in their midst. They had been playing soccer with a ball made out of dried twigs and vines, and they tugged at my pants, eager to have me join their game. I was awed by their resilience. It was too late for the old woman, but these children had a right to a future. I am not being melodramatic when I say that this was the moment when I personally dedicated myself to bringing a UN peacekeeping mission to Rwanda. Until that point, the exercise had been an interesting challenge and a potential route to a field command. As I climbed back into my vehicle, I knew that my primary mission now was to do my best to ensure Rwanda's peace for the sake of these children, and ease this suffering.

We soon passed the RGF checkpoint, eased our way through a marked minefield that delineated the front lines, and entered the demilitarized zone, which was an eerie place, dotted with villages that had been deserted by the displaced persons we had seen in the camp. They had been driven out by fighting in 1990, and their fields and farms were beginning to be reclaimed by the luxuriant native plants and wildflowers. The air was filled with the raucous yet lonely cries of flycatchers and warblers. I would have loved to have gotten out of the vehicle and gone exploring, but we had been warned that this area was heavily mined. So we stuck to the road until we crossed the zone to RPF territory.

The RPF greeted us with an honour guard of about thirty Intore, or warrior dancers. Each of them wore a short underskirt of scarlet cotton draped with a piece of leopard-patterned cloth, and huge flowing head-dresses made to resemble lions' manes. Their bare chests were orna-mented with beads, around their ankles were clusters of tiny bells, and in their hands, they carried ceremonial shields and spears. Tossing their heads and twisting their bodies, they leapt effortlessly into the air like a flock of giant birds, their sweat-streaked torsos gleaming in the sun-light. They danced, drummed and sang for about twenty minutes and ended with a flourish, presenting their weapons to us. Their display wove the discipline and precision of a well-trained modern army with an ancient warrior tradition, setting the tone for what was to follow.

The RPF was using the large complex of buildings belonging to a deserted tea plantation as its headquarters. We drove up a hill lush with unharvested tea and halted in front of a graceful old house with a huge veranda overlooking a formal garden slowly going to ruin. The air was laden with the fragrance of flowers. Inside, we were given a warm welcome by the RPF political and military leadership, including its chairman, Alexis Kanyarengwe, who was plump and bright-eyed and wore a diffi-cult smile; its senior political officer, Pasteur Bizimungu, who was both impatient and eloquent; and Paul Kagame, who seemed more like a stern college professor than a rebel army commander. They led us to a large living room that had been stripped of its domestic furnishings and now functioned as a meeting place.

The trio of Kanyarengwe, Bizimungu and Kagame presented an interesting study in contrasts, and each was very effective in his own way. Kanyarengwe, the RPF's titular head, was a Hutu and seemed a little uneasy with his leadership role, constantly checking for the reac-tions of the others after making a remark. Still, he proved to be solid, serious and well-organized. Bizimungu was the RPF's public political face. He had been a senior civil servant during Habyarimana's regime and as such had been jailed and tortured when he sought to expose its worst excesses. He, too, was a Hutu, passionate, argumentative and inflexible, devoid of real charisma. Then there was Kagame, easily the most interesting of the three, although he was the most self-contained. Almost stereotypically Tutsi, he was incredibly thin and well over six feet tall; he towered over the gathering with a studious air that didn't quite disguise his hawk-like intensity. Behind his spectacles, his glistening charcoal eyes were penetrating, projecting his mastery of the situation.

Most of the group, senior officers included, behaved with quiet confidence and dignity. When we took breaks, they were never idle but talked over points among themselves. The atmosphere was Spartan: there were no flags, pictures or decorations of any kind and no indulgences like alcohol or cigars. We sat at a long table in the centre of the room; three rows of benches were filled with staff officers and civilian leaders observing the meeting.

The RPF was unanimous in its support for Arusha. The chairman stressed that we had to act rapidly to avoid the "gangrene," or wasting away, of the agreement. He also conveyed his concern over the growth and activities of paramilitary groups within Rwanda. He said that if the UN was to form the neutral peacekeeping force mandated by Arusha, the UN had to guarantee the security of the RPF leaders when they came to Kigali to join the transitional government. He also insisted that the UN should pressure France to remove its soldiers from the country as soon as possible. He politely did not mention that the RPF, proudly African, actually preferred the notion of a peacekeeping force run by the OAU to one from the UN.

The RPF portrayed itself as a group of Rwandan refugees who only wanted to go home and live in peace. They claimed that their desire was to build a multi-ethnic, democratic society in Rwanda. While I didn't doubt their sincerity, I was aware that having been successful in the civil war they had nothing to fear and everything to gain from the successful implementation of the peace accords. We hit only one awkward snag: the chairman expressed his concern that, since the signing of the Arusha agreement in early August, the displaced population of the demilitarized zone—which numbered 600,000—had started to wander back into the area. The RPF was worried that its security could be compromised as a result. Having just witnessed the hell of the displaced persons camp, I ventured that these poor people were desperate to return to their homes and small farms and that it should be one of the first orders of business to de-mine the area to prepare it for resettlement. Bizimungu did not agree. According to the provisions of the Arusha agreement, the neutral international force had to keep the area clear and closed. At the time, I put his concern down to the paranoia of an insurgent rebel force. Later on, the thought crossed my mind that the reason the RPF raised the issue had less to do with security and more to do with the resettlement ambitions of Tutsi refugees then in Uganda.

Our inspection of the RPF army was conducted in closely guarded convoys over terrible tracks. This struck me as a deliberate attempt to waste our time and prevent us from taking a really good look at the RPF headquarters and units. However, without helicopters, which could fly over the heavily forested and mountainous terrain, we were going to be very limited in our observations of the force. The officers were good at giving the impression of full co-operation, but they offered very little information about their force structures and true capabilities. The soldiers we did see were clearly well-led, well-trained and motivated. They wore an idiosyncratic combination of East German summer uniforms and rubber boots, but were always clean and neat. The rank and file tended to be young, sometimes even boys; the officers, too, were young but clearly knew how to work their troops. When not training, soldiers had lectures to attend and equipment to clean and maintain. This was a combat-proven and battle-ready army.

The RPF's only limitation was in logistical support. They had very few vehicles, and while their troops appeared to be fit, well-fed and reasonably well-equipped, they were a light infantry army that had to fight and resupply by foot or bicycle. Yet they had won all recent contests because of their superior leadership, training, experience, frugality, mobility, discipline and morale. If Kagame was responsible for nurturing this force, he was a truly impressive leader and perhaps deserved the sobriquet that the media had given him: the Napoleon of Africa.

The RGF was a pronounced contrast. The army's chief of staff, Major General Déogratias Nsabimana, was a big man with facial expressions that betrayed a deceptive nature. He was not an impressive soldier and had proven less than effective in the last campaign against the RPF in the spring of 1993. He hung on to his position after hostilities ended because of his closeness to President Habyarimana. Despite the presence of an interim government, the army and large parts of the Gendarmerie (the Rwandan police) were still controlled by the regime due to the fact that well-placed hard-liners from the president's party, the MRND, had hung on to power in the ministry of defence.

Among the senior officers of the RGF was a cadre of a few colonels who appeared to be committed to Arusha and who eagerly anticipated the end of a conflict they had lost on the battlefield. But there were many others within the officer corps, particularly from northern Rwanda, who seemed less committed to Arusha and made no secret of their hatred of the RPF. It was clear that there was a group to work with and a group to watch.

I visited the RGF side of the demilitarized zone and the southern part of the country in a light Gazelle gunship helicopter and also flew north to see the training camps of the elite units of the RGF in Ruhengeri, close to Habyarimana's birthplace. As we approached Ruhengeri, the Virunga Mountains rose up in front of us like blue giants from the sea of verdant hills. This breathtaking vista (made famous by the film *Gorillas in the Mist*) was the heartland of the former regime.

The elite units in the area were based in a commando camp; a Gendarmerie rapid reaction force and elite military units were based at the Gendarmerie school in Ruhengeri. All were being trained by French and Belgian military advisers.

On the other hand, the front-line units of the army were composed of poorly trained recruits who lacked weapons, food, medical supplies and, above all, leadership and morale. Atrocious living conditions meant desertion rates were high and units had to be frequently rotated due to the high incidence of malaria. There was a double standard in this army: high for the elite units and low for the rest of the army.

The RGF unit that caused me the most concern was the Presidential

Guard, which Brent and Tiko had observed closely at its camp in Kigali near the Meridien hotel. It was made up of highly trained officers, NCOs and soldiers, and was the best equipped and staffed of the elite units as well as the most aggressive. They were Habyarimana's praetorian guard, and they acted with arrogant self-assurance. I did not appreciate their standard of discipline. While they were respectful and obedient to their own officers, they treated all others in the RGF, and even myself, with contempt. It was clear they would have to be handled carefully. Reintegrating them into society when they were released from military service or rolling them into the new army planned for Rwanda would be difficult, to say the least. They would be a first priority during the demobilization phase, and I was sure that controlling them would require the personal intervention of the president.

While the RGF's conscripted troops lived for their two beers a day and well-nigh mutinied when that ration was cut in half, the young officers who commanded them were generally hard-hitting and dynamic. The gulf between officers and enlisted men was explained to me by a senior local commander in the Ruhengeri garrison, who said that the only way for officers to advance was "to make a name for themselves." He didn't elaborate, but I understood him to mean "in the field." This was not a comforting thing for a potential UN peacekeeper to hear, as it meant that the more ambitious young officers with nothing to lose and all to gain might be willing to risk the lives of the men under their command to advance their own careers.

Something else that disturbed and angered me was the RGF's use of children on the front line. I had gotten somewhat used to seeing children doing heavy physical labour in Rwanda, but as I toured the government forces I realized that the soldiers were using children as servants to wash clothes, cook, and clean, and the men demonstrated a disturbing fondness for them while off duty. I was told on more than one occasion that these children were undoubtedly better off with the army—at least they were being fed. But the intimate connection between children and combat troops seemed downright wrong. I never saw children that young with the RPF, though a large number of its soldiers were definitely below eighteen years of age.

The more candid RGF officers told us about the low pay, poor (if any) training, limited reinforcements, troubling desertion rates and lack of confidence among the men, who had been thrown into battle against the proficient RPF and had suffered a heavy toll of casualties, particularly during the last RPF assault in February 1993. An army in this state of disorder could become a very dangerous entity; rallied by a charismatic leader, it could degenerate into a ruthless rabble. I decided that in any mission, the bulk of the UN forces should be deployed south of the demilitarized zone, in the RGF sector.

The Gendarmerie, a paramilitary force built on the French model, was the third structured force in Rwanda and was about six-thousand strong. Its chief of staff, Colonel Augustin Ndindiliyimana, reported to the minister of defence for operational taskings, support and logistics, and to the minister of the interior for day-to-day police work around the country. Bizimana, the defence minister, had a strong hold over the Gendarmerie during periods of war, when it could be mobilized for the front to augment the army. Before the last war, the Gendarmerie had had fewer than two thousand members, but young recruits had tripled its size. In the process, it lost cohesiveness, discipline, training, experience and credibility. Of all the officials with whom we had to work during the mission, Ndindiliyimana was by far the most helpful, candid and open.

Tiko and Major Eddy Delporte, a Belgian military police officer who was attached to us from the UN mission in Western Sahara, conducted the analysis of the Gendarmerie. Their survey revealed an erratically led and undisciplined body of men who ranged from true professional police officers to out-and-out criminals in uniform. Although scattered around the country, the bulk of its force was in Kigali and Ruhengeri. By and large, its members seemed more educated than their colleagues in the army and had a sense of pride. Delporte confirmed that France and Belgium had advisers with the RGF and the Gendarmerie, from their headquarters to their training institutions to their units in the field, an advisory network far more extensive than their ambassadors or military attachés had let on. Delporte tried to get more information from the

Belgians but ran up against a brick wall, which we were never able to penetrate. What was their actual mission in Rwanda?

Our staff also made contact with the French para-battalion in Kigali, but the visit yielded little except some map references of RGF sites around the city. The battalion, too, was close-mouthed about its strength and true mission in Rwanda. We rarely saw French soldiers, except at the airport or at night when they operated patrols and road-blocks in and around the capital. On the whole the situation in the city was quiet and restrained, an atmosphere to which the battalion proba-bly contributed. Nights in Kigali and in central Africa are usually extremely dark. The city usually shuts down at last light. I found African nights a startling contrast between peace and quiet, darkness and danger.

Despite the warning signs I could read in the RGF, as we drew our tech-nical mission to a close, I was certain that Rwanda was a place that could benefit from a classic chapter-six peacekeeping mission, if we could invest it with a sense of urgency. The operation would referee the ex-belligerents to ensure that the peace agreement was being imple-mented and that everybody was playing by the rules. The force would be a combination of armed troops and unarmed observers, deployed with care to all the possible areas of mischief and with strict rules of engagement: we would use our weapons only in self-defence. The alter-native to a chapter-six operation was to try to contain the conflict diplomatically (which was a non-starter in the case of Rwanda) or to go to a chapter-seven, or peace-enforcement mission, where the UN would sanction a coalition of nations to invade the country with offensive mil-itary force and impose peace on the parties. No nation would be prepared to contribute to a chapter-seven mission to a country where there were no strategic national or international interests and no major threat to inter-national peace and security. Chapter seven had only been used in Korea at the start of the Cold War and, more recently, in the Gulf War and Somalia. Chapter seven scared the war-allergic liberals who dominated the govern-ments of the major powers; it reeked of colonialism and violated national sovereignty; it would ultimately cost vast amounts of resources and blood.

If I had even suggested a chapter seven in the case of Rwanda, I would have been on a one-way flight back to Ottawa. Chapter six was the only real option we had.

However, I also knew that given the ethnic nature of the conflict, the presence of some who opposed the agreement, and the potential for banditry or ethnic killings by demobilized soldiers, I needed to be able to confront such challenges with military force. Therefore, in the rules of engagement (ROE) that I proposed for this mission (largely cribbed from the Cambodian rules), we inserted paragraph seventeen, which authorized us to use force up to and including the use of deadly force to prevent "crimes against humanity." We were breaking new ground, though we didn't really understand it at the time. We were moving toward what would later be called "Chapter six and a half," a whole new approach to conflict resolution.

In those twelve days in August in Rwanda, I found plenty of reasons for optimism. Among the most productive and informative meetings I held were two joint sessions between the RPF and the RGF, convened in Kinihira, in the heart of the demilitarized zone, the site where a number of the articles of the Arusha Peace Agreement had been signed over the previous months. The RPF sent Pasteur Bizimungu as its chief spokesman. His counterpart from the RGF was Colonel Théoneste Bagosora, the chef de cabinet of the minister of defence. Bagosora was a bespectacled and pudgy man who seemed slightly bemused by the proceedings. He said he supported Arusha, but more often than not, he was confrontational, especially with the RPF delegation.

Language was a real issue. The RPF delegation, composed mostly of Rwandan refugees who had grown up in English-speaking Uganda, was mostly anglophone, and the Rwandan government representatives were exclusively francophone. I summoned up a lifetime of experience in mediating between the two language groups and expended much energy acting as official translator. I wonder if I might have picked up more of the undercurrents that must have been playing around the negotiating table if I hadn't been put in that position. Then again, as translator I had to be attentive to every word.

We met in the house of the manager of an expansive tea plantation. From the veranda, which commanded a spectacular view of the
surrounding terraced hills and terra cotta cottages, I watched with
fascination and disbelief as members of the opposing delegations
strolled hand in hand, in informal discussion. Veterans of the Cyprus
mission had regaled me with stories of the histrionics employed by
the Greek and Turk Cypriots during their negotiations; at one point
they insisted on meeting rooms with separate entrances so they
wouldn't have to share the same doorway. At the negotiating table,
these men were cold and aggressive, but at breaks and lunch, they
were nothing less than fraternal.

Not all delegates partook in these goodwill gestures. Notable exceptions
were Bagosora and the chiefs of staff of the RGF and the Gendarmerie.

During the formal sessions, I had both parties explain to me aspects
of the peace accords that I did not understand or that required clarification. This strategy enabled me to make sure that everyone understood the
meaning of each article in the accords. We ranged from discussing obscure
points of order to debating the composition of the RPF light battalion of
six hundred soldiers that would be stationed in Kigali to protect their dignitaries during the establishment of the BBTG. That portion of the meeting took a very long time, as every detail was hammered out, from the size
of weapons to ammunition loads. The question of air-defence systems was
raised by Bagosora. Only heavy machine guns with special mounts for air-
defence fire were permitted. No missiles were authorized. The RPF had
declared itself to be in possession of a number of Eastern Bloc short-range
missiles, while the RGF claimed no missile capability at all, although I knew
they had a number of anti-aircraft guns at Kigali airport and an unreported
number of SA-7 missiles. The fact that we had to find a site in the heart of
Kigali for an RPF battalion and that both sides had to agree to it, never
raised an eyebrow. The RGF claimed that they placed their confidence in
the neutral peacekeepers to control the situation.

The biggest problem that I could see was how to handle the demobilization of the armies and the Gendarmerie, and the creation of a new
national force. It would not be enough to disarm them and then just let

them go. We had to ensure that each soldier was provided with the pensions promised in Arusha and with retraining so they could find other employment. Demobilization was supposed to begin as soon as the BBTG was put in place on September 10, which was only thirteen days away. It was unlikely we would even have the technical report finished by then.

I raised the question of where to find the resources to pay for a safe demobilization and reintegration again and again in the meetings I had with the various diplomatic missions, but got no takers. What frustrated me beyond belief was the inability of anybody at the UN to supply me with information on how other missions had dealt with the problem. I was being forced to reinvent the wheel in a crucial arena under such a tight deadline. Amadou Ly, with his usual optimism, suggested that I try to get the International Monetary Fund (IMF) and the World Bank on board, and then use their backing to leverage a roundtable of potential donor governments. Failing that, the only other option was to somehow link up demobilization with the overall aid plan proposed by the humanitarian groups who would operate under the umbrella of the UN for the life of the mission.

To that end, we devoted time during the last days of our technical mission to bringing ourselves up to speed with the major humanitarian organizations in Rwanda. This was a feat in itself, since each of these organizations tended to march to the beat of its own drummer and resisted integration into any outside body's overall plan. Rwanda was one of the most densely populated nations in sub-Saharan Africa. While Arusha had guaranteed the right of return of refugees, none of the terms of their resettlement, such as land ownership and compensation for expropriated property, had been addressed, even by the UNHCR.

As each day passed, bringing with it another debriefing of my team of experts, it became more and more evident that this mission was going to need a lot more money than the initial estimate of $50 million (U.S.). At these daily meetings I insisted that we were not going to leave Kigali until the first draft of the entire report was done. I set such a pace partly to ensure that we covered all the bases while we were in Rwanda and obtained as much information as possible.

But I also knew that all my experts would be returning to their regular jobs; I didn't want to have to chase slippery bureaucrats around the UN for their portions of the report—they knew the building better than I did and therefore knew where to hide. So I held them all to my deadline despite the innovative reasons they offered for pulling out early or for delaying the writing of the report, reasons such as "I'm too tired" or "Can't we go see the gorillas?" or—my absolute favourite—"I need time to reflect."

Our meeting room at the Mille Collines had a large rectangle of tables in the centre and workstations around three of the walls. Brent and a few others had finally acquired a very large military map, and it hung on the fourth wall. The demilitarized zone, new minefields, military camps and some of the displaced persons camps were plotted on the map as more information came in every day.

On August 28, four days before we were due to leave the country, Brent, Miguel Martin, Paddy Blagdon, Tiko and Marcel Savard, an ex–Canadian Forces logistics officer who was the leader of the Field Operations Division team, helped me put to paper my concept of operations for a chapter-six mission in Rwanda. I wanted to present three options. Brent and Miguel had finished a clear estimate of the situation—what we'd need to get the job done if we were operating in an ideal world and could get all the troops and resources we asked for. The two earlier technical missions, the first headed by Colonel Cameron Ross from Canada, and the second under Maurice Baril's direction, had estimated the necessary force initially at 8,000 and then at 5,500 personnel. Our "ideal" recommendation was at the 5,500 level: three battalions (each numbering 800) in the demilitarized zone and two to secure Kigali, with rapid reaction force capability; 350 unarmed military observers to roam the country as the mission's eyes and ears; full logistical support, helicopters, armoured personnel carriers, vehicles, hospital, the works. I knew from my talks with Maurice that this recommendation would never leave the DPKO.

We called our next estimate the "reasonable viable option." It called for a significantly smaller force of about 2,500 personnel and required the mission to take more risks as a result, but it was more likely to be approved and eventually deployed. It was the one we spent the most time refining. Talking it over with Maurice on the UNDP's secure line, he suggested that we work out how to deploy the troops in stages so that we would cause the least burden to the UN and the troop-contributing nations.

The final option was designed to address the concerns of the United States, France and Russia, whose ambassadors had all insisted that the mission needed a force of only five hundred to one thousand personnel. We did not really see how this could work, and concentrated on laying out in the draft all the risks such a course would entail.

We anticipated that, with the support of Maurice, the "reasonable viable option" would be approved. Even before we left Rwanda, Brent and the others began working on how we could accelerate the approval of the mandate and be ready for rapid deployment.

At my meeting with the French ambassador the day before I left, I took the opportunity to run some of my findings past him. The ambassador thought my report reasonable, but as soon as I started to talk actual figures, the French military attaché leapt into the fray. He said he couldn't understand why I needed so many troops. France had a battalion of only 325 personnel stationed in the country and the situation seemed to be well in hand. There was an awkward moment as the ambassador reiterated his support for my plan and the attaché sat back in his chair silently fuming. The attaché's position made no sense to me, and I concluded that he was being deliberately obstructive. The incident alerted me to an outright split between the policy being followed by France's foreign affairs department and its ministry of defence. Another thing to ponder.

I was alarmed that I still hadn't had a meeting with President Habyarimana. He and his regime had signed the accords under some duress. Habyarimana finally sent word that he would see me at the palace on the last day I was to be in Rwanda. The junior political officer from the DPA and Ly were to accompany me; we dressed for a formal meeting.

The presidential palace was a modern condominium complex, understated but elegant, with what looked to be expensive art on the walls. We were ushered out to a patio area where we found the president, dressed in a short-sleeved, open-necked shirt, seated under a

Cinzano umbrella. With him was his chef de cabinet, Enoch Ruhigira; Nsabimana, the RGF's chief of staff; Ndindiliyimana from the Gendarmerie; another RGF colonel; and Bagosora, whom I'd met during the two days of talks between the RGF and the RPF. Surprisingly neither the prime minister, the prime minister designate, the minister of defence nor the minister of justice were present.

Habyarimana must have been a very handsome man when he was younger, and his stature and appearance were still impressive. He welcomed us warmly, and I gave him a short briefing on my findings and recommendations. He listened intently and seemed to find no fault with my report. He pressed me to get a UN force on the ground as soon as possible—no move to install the BBTG could happen without peacekeepers in Kigali. We talked for about forty-five minutes while the others remained quiet. Habyarimana smiled easily and spoke sincerely of the problems of the displaced persons and the drought. He indicated that the country had now embarked on a very complex road to peace and that the international community needed to respond favourably to my report urging the earliest deployment of a UN peacekeeping mission to Rwanda. It still worried me that he had not publicly embraced the mission, but I had no reason not to take him at face value.

As we prepared to leave Rwanda, nothing I had seen or heard swayed me from my initial assessment that a mission was both possible and essential. Brent and the rest of the reconnaissance team were flying back to New York. I was continuing on to Tanzania to meet with President Ali Hassan Mwinyi, the facilitator of the Arusha Peace Agreement, and then to Ethiopia to see Salim Ahmed Salim, secretary-general of the OAU. Both of these men had been key to the Arusha accords, and I was hoping that they could confirm my impressions and give me a sense of the bigger picture. We also had to iron out whether the OAU wanted to continue to play a role in the implementation of the accords, as the RPF certainly wished.

To my surprise, Pédanou, who had recovered nicely from his emergency surgery, joined me in Dar es Salaam. He immediately assumed his position as Head of Mission, treating me as his number two. I tried to shrug this off, reasoning that he already knew Mwinyi well from the Arusha process. It made sense for him to take the lead, but it rankled.

We met with the Tanzanian president at the old governor's palace, which was opulent. I was a little awed by the surroundings and expected an arrogant, high-handed African despot. I couldn't have been more mistaken. Mwinyi was every inch the elder statesman, dignified and courteous, yet with a warmth and charm that immediately put you at ease. He listened attentively to my briefing and judged it to be a reasonable assessment of the situation. He was the first person to tell me that the September 10 milestone had been picked with great care as it marked the beginning of the school year and of the planting season. It was vital to take advantage of the sense that change was in the air, that this movement toward a new unified, democratic Rwanda was natural and inevitable. I was beginning to feel almost ebullient, taking Mwinyi's official blessing of my proposed operational plan as a very good sign.

The following day, we flew on to Addis Ababa and the United Nations Economic Commission for Africa, a palatial building with more black Mercedes in its parking lot than I had ever seen in my life. The UN staff waltzed around in expensive tailored suits and couture dresses as if they were in downtown Geneva rather than smack in the middle of the Third World; it seemed to me that they were inured to the poverty around them. If you had the temerity to raise the issue with them, they would look at you with a world-weary cynicism so cold it could freeze your heart.

At our meeting with Salim, Pédanou presented himself as the reconnaissance expert. In Dar es Salaam I had been patient, but the time had come to shut him down. I waited for him to take a breath, and in that brief pause I just started talking and didn't stop until I had thoroughly briefed the OAU secretary-general on my proposed operational plan. Salim listened attentively to my briefing and then stated quite baldly that though he was most concerned about Rwanda, the OAU didn't have the resources, cash or equipment to sustain beyond the end of October the fifty-five unarmed OAU military observers and the light Tunisian infantry company who were currently monitoring the ceasefire in the demilitarized zone. He was scrambling to put together a three-hundred-member force for Rwanda, but he couldn't do that without UN assistance. He was eager to hand the whole works over to us as soon as possible.

I remember that I settled back in my seat with some satisfaction as our plane left Africa. I felt that I had worked very hard and had come up with a mission plan that could work. I had taken into account all the major political, military and humanitarian concerns and had gotten positive feedback from all the major players of the Arusha process. Real peace and contentment washed over me. I truly did not realize that the devil was already afoot.

I did not understand that I had just met men in Rwanda who would become génocidaires. While I thought I was the one who had been doing the assessing, I was the one who had been carefully measured. I still thought that for the most part people said what they meant; I had no reason to think otherwise. But the hard-liners I had met on my reconnaissance of Rwanda had attended the same schools that we do in the West; they read the same books; they watched the same news; and they had already concluded that the developing world, as represented by the OAU, would not have the resources or the means to deploy in force to Rwanda. They had judged that the West was too obsessed with the former Yugoslavia and with its peace-dividend reductions of its military forces to get overly involved in central Africa. Were they in fact already betting that white Western nations had too much on their hands to attempt another foray into black Africa? Were the hard-liners playing us, and me, for fools? I think so. I believe they had already concluded that the West did not have the will, as it had already demonstrated in Bosnia, Croatia and Somalia, to police the world, to expend the resources or to take the necessary casualties. They had calculated that the West would deploy a token force and when threatened would duck or run. They knew us better than we knew ourselves.

5

THE CLOCK IS TICKING

I arrived back in New York on September 5, consumed with a sense of urgency. The first deadline of the Arusha accords was only six days away. The momentum of the peace process couldn't be allowed to dissipate: I believed the goodwill was there and those opposed to Arusha hadn't had time to consolidate their positions. The clock was running and the time to act was almost past.

The next morning, I met with Kofi Annan, Maurice Baril, Iqbal Riza and others in the DPKO to brief them on the situation in Rwanda. While they listened attentively and seemed to think I had a good handle on how to go forward, their response to my desire for immediate action was sobering. The process of mission approval and troop deployment could take up to three months or longer, they reminded me. This I already knew. What I wasn't prepared for was their near-impatience with the whole affair. Some of the people in the meeting made strong comments to the effect of, "Who let this irresponsible milestone of September 10 even get on the table?" It was clear that no one was looking forward to the work involved in manhandling the financial and administrative Goliath of the UN in order to launch another mission.

Over lunch that day, Maurice explained to me that we needed a committed "lead" national contingent of troops upon which we could set in motion the grinding slave work of UN bureaucratic procedures. Belgium had come forward, but as a former colonial power in Rwanda, its participation wasn't favoured by the UN. Baril told me that starting a mission from scratch, with only a few inexperienced but good-willed officers using their own paper, pencils and laptops in a borrowed conference room required extraordinary zeal, willpower, the patience of Job, and luck. But my sense of dedication survived even that brutal dose of reality. I debriefed Brent and Miguel Martin with these words: "They are skeptical of it ever coming off, the sense of urgency is not quite there, and we have a hell of a lot of work ahead. So let's get at it."

At a second meeting, the DPKO triumvirate directed me to complete the technical mission report and to include a recommendation calling for the immediate deployment of a small force in Rwanda. This document would form the basis of a formal report to the secretary-general, which in turn would form the basis for his report and recommendation to the Security Council, which in its turn (I hoped) would form the basis for a Security Council resolution mandating our mission.

I felt I had to find some way of accelerating the process, but this was to prove tricky. Brent and I had no access to models or any kind of doctrine covering the process for the development and approval of a peacekeeping mission at the UN, even though we asked repeatedly how it was supposed to be done. I was stuck in the tactical weeds just trying to put together a cogent, persuasive report to effectively argue the case for a UN-led mission, let alone spur it to a faster pace. As I'd suspected, when we got back to New York the other members of the reconnaissance team disappeared to their respective workplaces or went on leave. I was left with only Brent, the part-time help of Miguel and a lone political officer—but not Rivero, who had travelled to Rwanda with me. She, too, had taken leave.

Miguel continued to be a stalwart supporter of the mission. He was a commando officer with an unyielding sense of duty, which sustained him over months of fast-paced, pressured work with few clear victories. His usual frown reflected his true nature as a man who meant business; it said, "Stay out of my way." But Miguel believed deeply in justice and human rights, despite his tough exterior. I don't think he ever initiated a joke, but he sure enjoyed hearing them. We assaulted him daily with our questions and problems, and he gave unstintingly of his time and expertise—whatever he could steal away from the other half dozen missions he was responsible for.

Brent and I relied on him heavily as we finished the technical report, commenced the formal guidelines for troop-contributing nations and polished our rules of engagement and operational, logistics and personnel plans. Because I didn't have a permanent office, I had to continuously scrounge around for a phone to use. Brent and I were camped out in one of the large conference rooms on the thirty-sixth floor, as there was no place set aside for staff who were trying to mount new missions. We soon came to appreciate the silence, serenity and fresher air of very early mornings and weekends, compared to the chaotic noise and interruptions of the normal workday. Worn down by the constant swirl of people and noise in the DPKO, we usually stopped around six o'clock and took our work back to our hotel rooms for the evening.

I still felt that the "ideal" option of 5,500 troops and personnel was best, but there was no way to reopen that discussion. By the end of my first week back at UN headquarters, I realized that we had to go with the "reasonable viable" option. We needed to put together a small force of at most 2,600 soldiers, including a mobile reserve equipped with armoured personnel carriers and helicopters, which would be capable of quickly neutralizing violent flare-ups wherever they occurred in the country. A force of this size could handle monitoring the demilitarized zone and the Kigali area. I could cover the rest of the country with small, unarmed military observer teams instead of garrisons of armed peacekeepers. These military observers (MILOBs) could alert our small but highly trained and well-equipped rapid-reaction force to trouble. But I had to make serious compromises to achieve that force level and maximize the number of bayonets. I wanted a military headquarters and signals squadron, but Maurice told me that no troop-contributing nation would provide them. So I accepted the option of a small UN civilian communications section. This would mean that I would have no inherent headquarters support staff and communicators to run the command posts and operations centre. (This scenario would later cost me dearly.) The engineer and logistics companies would also be very weak and ill-equipped, which was risky for a force deployed in a mountainous country with limited hard roads and no infrastructure.

The questions that would haunt me later were, "Did I compromise too much?" and "Did I want the mission so badly that I took on an unacceptable risk?" In one of our chance encounters at the time, Maurice reassured me that missions in general, and especially small ones like mine, had to exist on a shoestring; you had to fight for what little you could get. He advised me not to use a shortage of resources as an excuse to back off. There were many officers who would give their right arms for the job, and not necessarily because they believed in the Rwandan peace process. From that point on, I was sure to make clear in all my conversations and mission documents that this was *my* mission and that I was the one who would lead and be responsible and accountable. Instead of quitting an impossible task, I was determined to do the best I could to secure peace for Rwanda.

We finished our technical report and sent it in for distribution and consideration by Kofi Annan's staff on Friday, September 10. Later that day, the president of the Security Council issued a lukewarm statement, suggesting that the UN was still reviewing the options. His attitude obviously set off alarm bells in Kigali. On Wednesday, September 15, a joint delegation of the Rwandan government and the RPF arrived in New York to goad the UN into action. Patrick Mazimhaka headed the RPF contingent, and Anastase Gasana represented the interim government. I had not met Mazimhaka in Africa, but he was usually the chief negotiator for the RPF in sensitive situations. He also had Canadian ties. He had immigrated to Canada, taught at the University of Saskatchewan and been part of the anti-apartheid movement before going back to Africa to join the RPF. His wife and children were still living in Saskatoon, where she was a doctoral student.

Coming to the UN was a gutsy move, and the Rwandans were savvy enough not to overplay their hand. At a meeting with all the key DPKO players, held in the conference room adjacent to Kofi Annan's office, Gasana went on at length about the necessity for rapid approval and deployment of the international force. Mazimhaka was more succinct but just as eloquent. By the time they had finished, you could have heard a pin drop in that room. Visibly moved, Annan immediately swung into action, making rapid annotations on his copy of my mission plan as he urged the delegation to meet with the ambassadors who sat on the Security Council.

Given that the Rwandans had seized the initiative in such a dramatic way and had received a fair amount of press coverage for it, I expected that the approval process would kick into high gear. Nothing materialized. I was never invited to speak with Boutros Boutros-Ghali or any of the members of the Security Council. I didn't sit back, either; I actively lobbied for the mission. The doors to the people who held the most influence on the Security Council, the Americans and the British, remained firmly closed. I did end up speaking with the U.S. under-secretary of state for Africa, but his sole concern seemed to be the projected cost of the mission. In fact, the Americans never took Rwanda or me seriously; their position continued to be that the job could be done with much fewer personnel. I talked to the French, remembering the very positive response I had had from Ambassador Marlaud in Kigali, but it seemed that the military attaché had greater influence: France thought a force of a thousand was sufficient. The only NATO country willing to step forward with an aggressive commitment of troops was Belgium, whose offer was on Miguel Martin's desk before I had even gotten back from Rwanda. But given the Belgians' colonial past in the country, their offer of support was a mixed blessing. Still, they desperately wanted this mission—I suspect a deal may have been struck with the French for Belgian troops to protect their countries' interests in Kigali after the French battalion was shipped out.

In the second half of September, Brent and I got down to the business of creating a shopping list of the men and materials the mission would need; guidelines for donor nations, in effect. This quite detailed document stipulated down to the amount and type of ammunition what was required for each formed unit or battalion. If I was going to make do with such a small number of troops, I wanted them well-equipped. But I guess the list was too extravagant; Maurice took me aside and explained as diplomatically as he could that UN force commanders—and I was not yet one—depended on the generosity of donor nations for both troops and equipment. There were never any guarantees on the quality or quantity of either. The best one could hope for was to attract the attention of a NATO member with deep pockets, and so far only Belgium had volunteered.

I approached Canada, hoping that if I could grease the wheels at home, maybe other NATO members would jump on board. Louise Fréchette, then the Canadian ambassador to the UN, was enthusiastic. I had first met her in 1992 in Cambodia at a supper hosted by my troops in their camp on the outskirts of war-ravaged Phnom Penh. I had about 250 soldiers stationed there, providing heavy lift transport for the massive UN mission in that country. Fréchette spoke to the troops as if she had been working with the army for a long time. She was friendly and keen. (Later she would serve as deputy minister of national defence and, later still, as under-secretary general of the UN.) I always considered her a friend at court and believed she would back me to the hilt. So I was doubly shocked by the response I got back from the Department of National Defence. It rejected my modest request for a movement-control platoon of thirty troops to load, unload and dispatch personnel and material from aircraft, and refused to supply any more staff officers or military observers. Its reason: the Canadian military was over-committed in the Balkans and on other missions.

Afterwards, I heard on the rumour net that the bureaucrats in the departments of foreign affairs and national defence were having a turf war. Defence supported a contingent for Rwanda: it is customary for a nation to provide a substantial military component when one of its generals is given the prestigious job of force commander. One simple reason is that other nations do not like to put their soldiers in harm's way under a foreign commander unless that commander's own country commits its troops to him as well. But foreign affairs opposed a contingent because it was in the process of reorienting Canada's diplomatic attentions toward eastern Europe and the Balkans and away from Africa. Foreign affairs wanted the prestige of the position without the cost of troops, and since it is the lead department, it won the battle.

It was hard not to be dragged down into futility. The administrative skirmishes were endless—Brent must have filed a volume of paperwork for the helicopters we needed, but it went around and around and around. (In the end, the helicopters did not arrive in Rwanda until late March 1994, and they abandoned the mission the day the war started in April.)

We continued to lobby and to work on the mission plan through

September. Many of my colleagues in the DPKO pointed out that there was still some question as to whether I would be selected as force commander; they probably wondered why I was so passionately interested in the job. It is an unwritten rule at the UN that, wherever possible, African peacekeeping missions are to be led by Africans. The front-runner was actually the Nigerian general who was commanding the OAU observer group monitoring the current ceasefire in the demilitarized zone. I had met him on the technical mission and was less than impressed with him as a soldier and as a leader. His own men had told my staff that when fighting had broken out in the demilitarized zone in February and the observer group had found itself in the middle of a war zone, the general had abandoned his soldiers to their fate and retreated to his compound in Kigali, refusing to offer direction or support.

The bulk of my time during the last ten days or so of September was spent briefing formal UN delegations and anyone else who would open a door to me. In addition to the under-secretary of state for Africa affairs, I also briefed a large and important delegation from Paris, the very influential department heads of political affairs, humanitarian affairs, FOD and human rights, and the lesser heads of offices in areas such as personnel, aviation, finance, transport and so on.

With Annan, Riza and Baril primarily focused on the Balkans, the key player on Africa in the DPKO was Hedi Annabi, who seemed to carry the woes of the continent on his back. His office resembled that of a medieval alchemist, with dockets and papers piled so high you wondered when one of the teetering masses would fall and increase the obstacle course already on the floor. You could not deploy a map in that office, since there was no horizontal surface on which to do it. Annabi was the only one at the UN who ever expressed any skepticism over whether the Arusha agreement would stand. He reminded me that the Hutu hard-liners had signed the accords under enormous pressure. I tucked his doubt away in some pocket of my mind and carried on.

The concept of operations that we developed under the direction of the DPKO stretched over a period of thirty months and called for four phases and a maximum force strength of 2,548, to be deployed only when absolutely needed.

Phase one, as outlined in Arusha, would begin on the day the Security Council approved the mission and would last for ninety days, requiring a buildup to 1,200 personnel. The immediate task would be to provide security for the city of Kigali and ensure the withdrawal of the French troops in accordance with Arusha. This was extremely important as the RPF viewed the French as a partisan force allied with the RGF and would not enter the city if the French were still there.

Then we would have to turn Kigali into a weapons-secure area, negotiating an agreement whereby the RGF and RPF would secure their weapons and only move them or armed troops with UN permission and under UN escort. As peacekeepers, we had to know where all the weapons were. With the French gone and Kigali declared a weapons-secure area, the RPF could move their political leaders and the battalion of soldiers necessary to protect them into Kigali, and the BBTG—whose members had already been negotiated in Arusha, though there was still much debate over the exact composition—could be sworn in.

In phase one we also had to take over the monitoring of the demilitarized zone and establish teams of unarmed military observers to roam the ten prefectures (provinces) within the country to keep an eye out for possible flare-ups.

Burundi, the country to the south of Rwanda, had just held its first democratic elections since independence and had seen the peaceful transition from a minority Tutsi military-run dictatorship to the installation of the first Hutu president to head a government in that country—I was not worried about security on Rwanda's south flank. The south was generally held to be the most moderate area of the country, and I was sure my small teams of unarmed MILOBs would be effective there. Eastern Rwanda, toward Tanzania, was also fairly peaceful, but the west, close to the border with Zaire, would bear closer watching—the hardline heartland was in the northwest, and there were reports of weapons being smuggled into the country from Zaire. Nevertheless I was confident that I could do the job with that first contingent of 1,200 troops.

After the transitional government was in place and Habyarimana was installed as temporary head of state, as directed by Arusha, we would roll out phase two, which would take another ninety days and require the deployment of the maximum 2,548-member force. I thought this would be the most dangerous part of the mission. A battalion group of about eight hundred, supported by an engineer company of another two hundred personnel, would be moved into the demilitarized zone to provide a buffer between the RPF and the RGF while each army retired from their defensive positions to demobilization centres. All weapons would be collected in cantonment points. I estimated that for this phase, I would need support elements such as eight helicopters equipped with night-vision capability to patrol the demilitarized zone (hence Brent's huge file on the matter). The Ugandan border was hard to monitor because of its altitude, its terrain and mist-filled valleys, and I suspected that the RPF was already sneaking all kinds of supplies into the country, using an old Viet-Cong ploy: loading up bicycles and taking the stuff over the tiny mountain paths that criss-crossed the border. My UNOMUR mission was supposed to get a handle on these potential supply lines; for the peace process to succeed, we had to shut them down. If I was going to be able to get troops out fast to contain hostile situations, the force would also need twenty armoured personnel carriers (APCs), since most of the roads outside of the immediate vicinity of Kigali were a mess.

I proposed a carrot-and-stick force structure to ensure that the climate of security would be maintained in the demilitarized zone. I would place the armed battalion between the belligerents. Then behind each force, I would station unarmed military observers. Both the battalion and the military observers would be non-threatening and would focus on building goodwill and good working relationships with and between the parties. The stick would be provided by the force reserve, which would intervene rapidly to deter aggression. The mission would need robust rules of engagement to give us the wherewithal to escalate force as required in support of our mandate.

Phase three would be the actual demobilization and reintegration process and would last ten months. This phase would see the creation of the National Guard, a new force that would integrate elements of the RPF, RGF, and Gendarmerie. We would follow the Arusha guidelines when constructing the new army; the majority of soldiers from all three forces would be given pensions and retrained for jobs in civilian life. As this process wound down, my own force would decrease to about a thousand personnel, a recommendation I made as a result of pressure from the UN to keep costs down, not because I was entirely comfortable that it was the best course.

The final phase of the mission would be the holding of the first democratic elections in Rwanda, bound to be an uneasy time within the country. My hope was that the thousand-member UN contingent would be reinforced by the new army and that it would have jelled sufficiently to withstand the potential return to ethnic conflict. Phase four was projected to last twelve months, after which we could pack our tents and go home.

In UN terms, the mission was to be small, cheap, short and sweet.

My technical report called for urgent deployment. To pull that off, we needed a commitment from a major Western military power with enough transport, or "lift," capacity to deal with the fact that Rwanda was landlocked, airports were limited and the nearest seaport, Dar es Salaam, was about a thousand kilometres from Kigali on nearly impassible roads. No one but the Belgians had stepped forward. At the time, I wondered about the real reasons. This was supposed to be a straightforward little chapter-six mission, a win for the UN, a win all around. So what held them back? The story of the day in the DPKO, as passed on by the white officers from the Western-based troop-contributing nations, was that these countries were "peacekeepinged out" and had no more stomach for far-off missions. All very well, except that Maurice and his staff had continued to obtain substantial troops and equipment with relative ease for the Balkans and Somalia.

When I'd met the diplomatic corps in August in Kigali, I had become familiar with other reasons. Rwanda was on nobody's radar as a place of strategic interest. It had no natural resources and no geographical significance. It was already dependent on foreign aid just to sustain itself, and on international funding to avoid bankruptcy. Even if the mission were to succeed, as looked likely at the time, there would be no political gain for the contributing nations; the only real beneficiary internationally would be the UN. For most countries, serving the UN's objectives has never seemed worth even the smallest of risks. Member nations do not want a large, reputable, strong and independent United Nations, no matter their hypocritical pronouncements otherwise. What they want is a weak, beholden, indebted scapegoat of an organization, which they can blame for their failures or steal victories from.

Worst of all, I suspect that these powerful nations did not want to get involved because they had a firmer grasp on the threats to the success of the Arusha accords than the rest of us. Certainly France, the United Kingdom, China, Russia and the United States, the permanent five of the Security Council, all had fully equipped and manned embassies in Rwanda, including both military and intelligence attachés. None of the means of communications used in Rwanda by the political or military hierarchies had encryption capabilities, except for a few communications assets within the RPF. Between human and signal intelligence on the ground and worldwide space- and air-based surveillance systems, these nations either knew in detail what was going on or they were totally asleep at the switch. I firmly doubt they were asleep. The French, the Belgians and the Germans had military advisers numbering in the dozens at all levels of the military and gendarme command and training structures in Rwanda.

However, since leaving Kigali in August, I had had no means of intelligence on Rwanda. Not one country was willing to provide the UN or even me personally with accurate and up-to-date information. One of the restrictions on a chapter-six mission is that it can't run its own intelligence-gathering; in the spirit of openness and transparency, it has to be totally dependent on the goodwill of opposing sides to inform the mission command of problems and threats. Our lack of intelligence and basic operational information, and the reluctance of any nation to provide us with it, helped form my first suspicion that I might find myself out on a limb if I ever needed help in the field.

So, despite the continued effort of the DPKO staff, out of all the developed nations, only the Belgians still wanted to sign up, with the French expressing political interest. The rest of the respondents came from several developing nations on three continents, and these troops had limited equipment capabilities and serious inherent logistic and financial problems. There was only a small list of peacekeeping nations who were capable of deploying units with all of the equipment and materials they needed to be independent of UN support while the UN built up its logistics base. These nations were primarily Western and First World. The slowly growing list of countries who were prepared to commit to a Rwandan mission came from a new generation of troop-contributing nations, who had large and untapped pools of soldiers but who were nearly completely deficient in *matériel,* sustainability and training specific to complex conflicts and vast humanitarian catastrophes. Furthermore, such troops sometimes came from nations that had little to no ethos regarding human rights, which raised a whole other set of problems.

As September wore on, I became aware that my presence and my aggressive manner were beginning to grate on many of the senior staff in the FOD and the personnel department. The FOD had total control of the equipment we needed. Personnel established manning priorities and had the final authority for deployment of UN staff in the field. I worried that by pushing so hard, on a mission that hadn't yet been mandated and of which I was not yet the force commander, I was actually hurting my cause.

While I had been obsessing about the larger mission, Uganda had finally signed the SOMA for UNOMUR, and the first observers were already arriving in the field. My place was clearly with them. I had to trust the future of the Rwanda mission to the experts in New York, though I still wanted eyes and ears at the UN. I decided to leave Brent in place for at least a month to keep working with Miguel. Brent's wife was due to give birth in November; by staying on in New York for a while, he could be closer to her.

At the end of September, the UN appointed Dr. Abdul Hamid Kabia, a career diplomat and political expert from Sierra Leone, with considerable field and UN experience, as the Uganda mission's political officer. I went to his office in the DPA immediately after the announcement to touch base with him. Expecting to find either a haughty, ambitious dandy or a crusty older politico who had seen it all and was not about to subordinate himself to a military chap, I encountered neither.

Dr. Kabia greeted me warmly. His office was relatively sparse, its accoutrements the familiar grey metal, and his desk layered with what seemed like a pell-mell collection of documents—but I had the sense he knew where everything was.

He confided that he was somewhat surprised to be chosen to go into the field, as he had been under the impression that he would finish his years with the UN at a desk job in New York. But he was neither reticent nor reluctant, and he was to become one of my most trusted advisers and colleagues. In mid-October he flew to Uganda and took up his post at the UNOMUR headquarters.

Somehow the mood had shifted on the thirty-sixth floor, and the best corridor intelligence that Brent could pick up had me as the leading contender for force commander of the Rwanda mission. One of my last duties before leaving New York was to create the name of the mission. The "United Nations" part of it was a given. Since our task was to assist the parties in implementing the Arusha agreement, "Assist" seemed a good term. And lastly, we were doing it "for Rwanda." "The United Nations Assistance Mission for Rwanda" seemed the perfect title, except that as an acronym, it fell short. UNAMFR did not sound right. So I decided to take the *I* from the second letter of "Mission." UNAMIR—the acronym was refined on a napkin in a Manhattan restaurant. For years I have heard UN officials, academics, bureaucrats— experts all—get the name wrong when they pontificate about the United Nations Assistance Mission *in* Rwanda. But that "for" was all important.

I met the DPKO triumvirate, along with Hedi Annabi, for my last instructions, and they told me to get the Uganda mission up and running and then be available for rapid deployment to Kigali should UNAMIR be approved. I was to keep in touch through Miguel and Maurice, and everyone wished me good luck. When Kofi Annan shook my hand, I felt a warmth and genuine caring from him that for a moment overwhelmed me. He was not a political boss sending off one of his generals with platitudes and the expected aplomb. Through the kindest of eyes and the calmest of demeanours, Annan projected a humanism and dedication to the plight of others that I have rarely experienced. It seemed clear to me from his very few phrases that my leader thought the mission was just, that I was the right choice as force commander and that we would help those Africans struggling for freedom and dignity.

I left New York in the late afternoon of September 30. The sun was wearing its new fall tint, painting all those glass panes of the skyscrapers of Manhattan with orange light. I was beside myself with energy, optimism and a sense of purpose. I was finally going to be tested in my profession. I had an operational command. All those years of reading about the strategies and tactics of the great generals of history came to life in my mind. All my experience, from playing with lead soldiers on the living room rug to commanding the 5ième Brigade Group, would culminate in this field command.

I headed for a brief leave in Quebec City to say my last goodbyes to my family and gather my personal effects and the enormous amount of equipment that the Canadian Army was issuing me for my journey to the tropical, disease-infested and dangerous place. I confess that when I visited my family, I saw what I wanted to see: they had settled into their new home and were managing well enough without me. I did not know that the atmosphere for Beth and the children at the garrison was already poisoned by jealousy over my getting an overseas command, and that only the highest-level interventions would improve their situation. During most of my time in Rwanda, Beth and the children were starved for real information about my safety and well-being and, fearful and isolated, ended up glued with the rest of the world to CNN.

At the airport, ready to leave for an indefinite stay in Africa, I leaned over to Willem and, instead of giving him the good, tight hug he needed, offered him the type of speech soldiers typically give to their eldest son: "Son, I'm off on operations, so seeing you're the senior male in the household, it's up to you to keep the situation in hand. I want you to live up to your responsibility and help your mother out." Little did I realize the effect those few ill-chosen remarks would have on my teenage son. As my plane took off, I mentally closed the door on family life to completely focus on my mission. This is what soldiers have to do.

• • •

A dozen hours later, I was halfway across the world and transported almost twenty years back in time. As we landed in Entebbe, the aircraft made a pass over the old airport and there, parked on the runway, was the Air France DC8 that Palestinian terrorists had hijacked back in the summer of 1976. The sight sent a shiver up my spine as I recalled the Israeli commandos' daring and successful raid all those years ago. I wondered why this eerie souvenir remained there untouched. Was it a memorial or perhaps a warning?

I liked Uganda. Kampala bubbled with life and, though less grand than Addis Ababa, appeared to be thriving. I was met by the UNDP resident representative, who had very efficiently organized my schedule of meetings with political and military leaders, including the Ugandan president.

We went to see Yoweri Museveni soon after I arrived. He received us at the former British governor general's home, a huge white mansion overlooking Lake Victoria. We were led through large, airy rooms crammed with African artifacts, and outside again to the place where the president was holding court under a huge tree. Museveni was tall, completely bald and had a sizable paunch—a powerful presence to say the least. Although he appeared to be well-informed, he offered no special insights into the situation in Rwanda. I was puzzled and more than a little disappointed. I'm not quite sure what I expected, but I had the impression that he accorded me no more and no less of his attention than he would the head of a multinational corporation trying to set up shop in his country.

The chief of staff of the Ugandan army was subtly unsettling. He was the soul of co-operation, assuring me that the Ugandans were very committed to UNOMUR, but I felt he was holding back some of the information I might need to do an effective job. That impression was borne out when I arrived in the Ugandan border town of Kabale, my mission headquarters. The very first item on my agenda was a meeting with the Ugandan army's southern region commander to discuss my operational plan. We met at my temporary headquarters in the White Horse Inn, a pretty little place tucked into the side of a hill. He was serious and professional, and seemed committed to co-operating with UNOMUR. Afterwards, the liaison officer from Uganda's National Resistance Army (NRA) who was assigned to my mission paid me a visit and informed me that all my patrols had to be planned ahead of time because he needed at least twelve hours' notice to arrange for troops to escort us. I looked at him in absolute amazement. The whole point of the patrols was to use the element of surprise in order to flush out any undesirable cross-border activity. He looked me straight in the eye and, in his polite, soft-spoken way, insisted that there were all kinds of unmapped minefields in the area, and for safety's sake, the UNOMUR patrols would have to be escorted by his soldiers. I told him we had to monitor five different crossing points twenty-four hours a day. He replied that he would try to have his soldiers there. I could protest, but it wouldn't do any good.

Even so, I was glad to be away from the UN headquarters and in the field, commanding troops and getting on with the job of surveillance along the 193 kilometres of unmarked border. Kabale is set amid rolling hills, a little bit of heaven on earth. There is one main street with a few shops and more churches than you can count. The local population seemed very appreciative of the U.S. dollars that we were pumping into the economy. We rented a large bungalow from one of the local businessmen to serve as our headquarters. It was on the edge of town and had enough land around it for us to construct a small heliport.

My second-in-command was a Zimbabwean colonel named Ben Matiwaza, a Zulu who had fought for several years against the Rhodesians in his country's war of independence and a veteran of the OAU mission to the demilitarized zone in Rwanda. As a former member of a rebel force, he knew how to sniff out RPF movements and offered terrific insights into their psychology. Willem de Kant, a young Dutch captain and a staff officer in the mission's operations room, briefed me on the status of the mission shortly after I arrived. I was immediately impressed by him.

The border was a sieve, riddled with little mountain trails that had been there for millennia. Given my tiny force of eighty-one observers and the fact that we had no access to helicopters with night-vision capability, the task of keeping the border under surveillance was at best symbolic. The troops, who were from the Netherlands, Hungary, Bangladesh, Zimbabwe and nine other nations, worked with great determination and courage for months with or without the support of the NRA and the RPF.

There was one other snag, and maybe I should have taken it as a sign of things to come. My mandate, signed by the government, permitted me to range a hundred kilometres into Uganda, which put the town of Embarara within my area of verification. The Ugandan army was now insisting on a twenty-kilometre limit. I kept on negotiating. Embarara looked like a town out of the Wild West, with its wide dusty streets lined with one-storey buildings, large warehouses and a few bars. It was a transportation hub, and key to stopping the cross-border arms traffic. Intelligence reports had alerted us to weapons caches in the area. If we went after them, not only would we go a long way to securing the border and helping President Museveni detach himself from any implication that he was aiding the resupply of the RPF, but such an action was well within the mandate and the competence of my troops. After much futile talk and many messages to the DPKO, I was ordered to back off. I would have to let Embarara go.

UNAMIR's mandate was approved by the Security Council on October 5, and I was officially appointed force commander. I had been told and told again that the UN usually took up to six months to get a mission on the ground *after* the approval of the mandate and *if* there was a reasonable infrastructure to work with in the field. That was certainly not the case with Rwanda: fuel, food and spare parts were in the hands of a few well-placed individuals who expected the UN to pay through the nose for what it needed. As far as I was concerned, we had already missed the first Arusha deadline by almost a month and this wouldn't do. I had spent time in Kabale, overseeing UNOMUR. I had a strong team in place and could rely on it to do what it was able to do within the limitations and with the few resources we had. It was time I turned my attention to Rwanda.

I had no headquarters in Kigali, no chief of staff, and the political head of the mission had yet to be appointed. With me in Kabale, however, were some fine officers already familiar with the players in the conflict and who would surely be a help to me. I thought that if I could get a few of us on the ground in Kigali, I might be able to force the pace at which the UN moved and get the mission up and running faster. Since I was already in theatre, I insisted that my DPKO superiors allow me to go in.

I booked a flight out of Kampala for the morning of October 21 and planned to take Captain Willem de Kant as my aide-de-camp, along with a few carefully selected, capable officers. Before heading to the hotel, we went to the airport to check on the schedule and our status and found out that we'd been put on some kind of standby list, even though we all had tickets in our hands. I searched out an airport chap and threw down fifty dollars, telling him, "We've got to be on that plane, make it happen!" Later that night, we got a phone call confirming that all four of us were on the plane.

When we got to the airport the next day, we were told that the flight had all kinds of room now. Overnight there had been a *coup d'état* in Burundi, and as a result, the plane was not going to continue on from Kigali. Everything had changed. Not only would the coup in Burundi shake the fragile political situation in Rwanda, but the stable southern flank, which I had relied on in my mission plan, had vanished.

On the plane, on the last leg of a trip that would change my whole life and that of my young family, I was neither melancholy nor fearful. I wanted this command and I would throw everything I had at it. As we landed at Kigali's bright and modern airport, I thought of my father and also of Beth's dad, the colonel, and I wondered about what must have gone through their minds fifty-odd years ago as they were about to land in England and enter their first theatre of war.

6

THE FIRST MILESTONES

At the airport in Kigali, we were greeted by the foreign minister, Anastase Gasana, a few other dignitaries and a sprinkling of press. We were hardly the focus of attention. Instead, everybody was anxiously following the progress of the coup in Burundi. The democratically elected government, headed by a Hutu moderate, had been toppled by Tutsi military leaders; the president and several cabinet ministers were already dead, and the nation was headed for an ethnic bloodbath. The fallout in Rwanda was immediate. Kigali was thick with rumours and suspicion, and the local media was full of hysterical talk of Tutsi hegemony. The contrast between the almost sunny optimism of Kigali in August and the sombre capital I returned to on October 22 couldn't have been more marked.

Amadou Ly had his hands full with reports of a sudden influx of refugees from Burundi, but as always, he did his utmost to help us get set up. The UN had finally appointed the head of mission, whose proper title was the Special Representative of the Secretary-General (SRSG); his name was Jacques-Roger Booh-Booh, and he was a former Cameroonian diplomat and a friend of Boutros Boutros-Ghali. But until he arrived, I was in charge of both the political and the military sides. That weekend, I scrambled to put together a temporary headquarters in the Hôtel des Mille Collines as well as keep abreast of the situation in Burundi. Amadou found us a few vehicles with local drivers to help us get around, as well as some much-needed cash. (Without his constant generous bending of UN regulations, we would never have made our phase-one objectives.)

Within a few days of my arrival, an advance party of officers from Uruguay, Bangladesh and Poland, who had been serving on the mission in Cambodia, joined us in Kigali. To a man these officers were magnificent. They were led by a handsome and resourceful Uruguayan, Colonel Herbert Figoli, who, until he was posted home three months later, served as the demilitarized zone sector commander. The others would be the backbone of the mission until the end. I took them into our conference room and gave them an extensive personal briefing on my concept of operations and our tasks. They paid close attention and asked interesting and insightful questions, and we seemed to bond immediately. I committed the essence of what we discussed to paper as "Force Commander's Directive Number 1," which laid out the plan that would guide us through phase one. I then issued our interim rules of engagement as "Force Commander's Directive Number 2," which I had drafted with Brent back in September. I forwarded both documents to New York and to the capitals of all the troop-contributing nations, asking for confirmation of my rules of engagement. Not only did I not get formal written approval of my rules from the UN, I never received any comment, positive or negative, from any nation, with the exception of Belgium, which had some concerns about its troops being used in crowd control, and Canada, which protested as too broad the sanctioning of deadly force in defence of all UN property. We eventually amended the rules to address these concerns and considered the silence on all fronts as tacit approval.

In these early days, I also met Per O. Hallqvist, a retired UN employee who had been recalled to serve as our mission's chief administration officer (CAO). He had arrived in Kigali a day or so ahead of me, along with a small civilian advance party, to begin building our mission infrastructure. Hallqvist made it abundantly clear to me that he was a stickler for process and that he expected it to take upwards of six months before UNAMIR's administrative and logistical support system was fully functional. He told me that the UN was a "pull system," not a "push system" like I was used to with NATO, because the UN had absolutely no pool of resources to draw on. You had to make a request for everything you needed and then you had to wait while that request was analyzed. If you did not ask, you did not get. For instance, soldiers everywhere have to eat and drink. In a push system, food and water for the number of soldiers deployed is automatically supplied. In a pull system, you have to ask for those rations, and no common sense seems ever to apply. If we asked for flashlights, we had better also ask for batteries and bulbs, otherwise they would likely arrive without them. The sheer fact that you have to make requests also puts you at a disadvantage. The civilian UN logistician, and not the operational commander, has the power of supply. If he judges that the item is required, the UN will supply it; if not, it won't.

We were soon to learn more of these hard realities, but at our first meeting, I was simply astounded by Hallqvist's dogged adherence to "process." We had to be fully operational in days, not months. I was determined to defy the rules, cut the red tape, bend the regulations and do whatever I had to short of illegal acts to achieve our first milestones.

January 1, 1994, was the last day of the interim government's mandate. We planned backwards from that date to include all of the tasks we had to complete in order to install the BBTG, upon which the entire Arusha peace process rested. I divided my staff into three working groups and subdivided the large meeting room into ad hoc cells set up around sets of rectangular tables. Coming in one morning, I was hit with a strong sense of déjà vu: the whole affair looked exactly like the command-post war-gaming that we'd undertaken back home before exercises, except here there was no clearly defined enemy and I wasn't so sure about the friendlies, either.

One group focused on the reception and logistics of troops, finding billets, equipment and figuring out how to pay and feed them. Those poor men had to fight the minute-to-minute battles with Hallqvist and his staff. The second group focused on operational plans, such as what we needed to do to make Kigali a weapons-secure area. The third group was largely concerned with information-gathering by way of reconnaissance throughout the country; for instance, we had to quickly assess what effect the situation in Burundi would have on our plans.

On Monday, October 25, Amadou Ly gave me his own reading of

the current state of affairs. I was already unsettled by the fact that President Habyarimana had not yet taken the time to meet with me or to formally welcome UNAMIR to Rwanda. I needed to know what stage the political process was at, but as of yet, I had no political staff to advise me. Amadou didn't mince words. The hardline radio station, RTLM, was building quite a following in Kigali with its African rock music allied with racist hype. We were expecting a Belgian army reconnaissance group of about fifteen officers and NCOs to arrive the next day, and Amadou informed me that RTLM was conducting a public opinion campaign against the arrival of the ex–colonial power's troops in the capital. He wanted me to understand that the political landscape was not as it seemed; the implementation of the transitional government was stalled and needed some deft coaching to get it back on track.

I knew this, but as far as politics was concerned, I was out of my milieu. I was hungry to grasp the political subtleties that were passing me by, but back home, generals were kept as far away from Parliament Hill and politics as possible. I had expected to have a skilled and knowledgeable diplomat at my side from the start. On the military and logistical front, I didn't yet have a chief of staff or deputy commander to back me up, though in less than a week, on October 30, the OAU peacekeeping contingent that had been patrolling the demilitarized zone was to come under UNAMIR's command. I was in uncharted waters—the geography, the culture, the politics, the brutality, the extremism, the depths of deception practised almost as a Rwandan art form—all were new to me. However, I knew about the sensitivities of minorities, of the weight of being different in style and attitude; by nature I was a moderate and a conciliator, and I burned with the desire to help fulfill the Arusha Peace Agreement—this best chance at a new social contract for the people of Rwanda. I was like an orchestra conductor who was supposed to put on a concert in five days and was determined to do so even though his musicians did not yet have any instruments. I was building my orchestra from scratch with a group of officers who not only adhered to different doctrines of peacekeeping but did not share a common language, and I was determined to put on the concert even though the UN seemed to have little capacity to respond to an urgent situation.

Those early days introduced me to begging and borrowing to a degree I'd never dreamed of. I spent far too much time trapped in the details of running the force, drawn into lengthy arguments with Hallqvist about everything from toilet paper to the form of official communiqués, while it slowly sank in that arguing with him was not worth the time, because even when he agreed with me, he had no discretionary power. My mind was constantly torn between military matters, mulling over what I could do to alleviate the political problems that were stalling the installation of the BBTG, and sorry details such as the fact that I couldn't pay the phone bills to New York, and my own line of credit was about to run out.

On top of it all, the mission so far was operating in total obscurity inside Rwanda. Most of the population seemed to be unaware of who we were and what we were doing, while at home, some UN-based reporters were already starting to snipe at our "inaction." I had to find a way to announce UNAMIR's presence, and I struck upon the idea for a flag-raising ceremony to be held in the demilitarized zone to mark the handover of the OAU contingent (from a commander who was still disgruntled that he had not been given the force commander's job). The UN flag was already revered in Rwanda, associated with such good things as education, health care and food aid. Our new role needed to be added to that list.

To patrol the demilitarized zone, which was about 120 kilometres long and about 20 kilometres at its widest point, I would have fifty-five unarmed observers, and a sixty-man contingent of lightly armed Tunisian soldiers limited by a lack of transport, basic equipment and cash. I was changing the mandate of these troops from monitoring a ceasefire in a limited area to participating in implementing a peace agreement for the whole country, which would increase the level of risk to them. I had no real idea of when I could improve their situation and capability, but I needed to send a strong signal to the UN that we were now fully committed—we were into "operational risk"—and the DPKO needed to step up the pace of deploying troops and logistical support. To be blunt, my flag-raising was also an attempt at brinkmanship.

I chose Kinihira as the location for the ceremony because a number of the protocols that made up the Arusha agreement were negotiated there, and the site was well-known both nationally and internationally. The village sits on the top of a small, rounded mountain from which you can see the juncture of two small rivers that feed the headwaters of the Nile. On the slopes down to those rivers, verdant rows of coffee alternate with the geometry of tea plantations.

Kinihira rapidly became one of my favourite places in Rwanda. The village school was a rectangular, mud-brick, one-room affair; sunlight streamed through holes that had been ripped in its corrugated roof by strong winter winds. The blackboard was a cracked patch of black paint on the wall, streaked with crude white chalk. Morning and afternoon shifts of fifty or so primary students sat on stones arranged in neat rows and scribbled their work on slates, under the care and direction of two teachers who had not been paid in months and had no paper and only one book at their disposal: a dog-eared teaching handbook from France. Out back was a dusty little playground that overlooked a green paradise that seemed to be perennially capped by the bluest of skies. It was one of the most serene spots I'd ever seen.

From my early days as a young captain, I had exhibited a flare for the Cecil B. DeMille productions of military life, showcase occasions put on to influence and impress people and bring home the symbolism of events. I have never had the capacity to "do lunch," but I have always been able to take full advantage of the opportunities of military display to regale, excite and sway a crowd. At the flag-raising, I wanted the Rwandan people to see us as a friendly force; at the same time, I wanted the belligerents to realize that we were here to do business. A symbolic flag-raising on a mountaintop that had been fought over, rendered neutral territory and then used as a place to negotiate peace seemed just the thing.

The day, November 1, was perfect: bright and sunny with a hint of a breeze, even though it was well into the rainy season. People from the surrounding villages turned out in droves. While the kids were running around having a grand time, at first the adults seemed exceptionally reserved, if curious. The Tunisian soldiers and unarmed military observers were kitted out in blue berets, which had taken two weeks of constant badgering for us to get. Obtaining 115 blue berets with UN badges didn't seem like much of a miracle to me, but old UN hands were impressed by the "speed" with which my staff officers, with Brent and Miguel in situ at the DPKO, had pulled it off. Still, it was worth the effort, for both the Tunisians and the military observers looked smart, disciplined and professional.

We didn't have a military band, so instead we hooked up a sound system and played the national anthem and lots of upbeat African tunes, which were a superb tension reliever and gave the whole occasion a festive air—somewhat hard to achieve, as armed troops from both sides of the conflict had accompanied the visiting dignitaries. For most of them, this was the first time they were meeting their former enemies, and my chief worry was how they were going to react to each other. I insisted that the troops stay by their vehicles, away from the bulk of the crowd, which they did, though their weapons were clearly in evidence.

Invitations had been sent out to the president, the RPF chairman and leaders, the government ministers, representatives from the different political parties, the diplomatic corps and military leaders. The RPF's civilian delegation, including Pasteur Bizimungu, was quite large and arrived twenty minutes late, looking sullen. I was pleased to see them become more lighthearted as the event went on. Madame Agathe, Faustin Twagiramungu and Anastase Gasana all attended. Once again, Habyarimana was absent, along with Paul Kagame; to be quite honest, I was somewhat relieved, because in this setting, I couldn't have provided the level of security they required. But I had expected the minister of defence, Augustin Bizimana, and key members of the ruling MRND party, and I was very disturbed when they didn't show up. Their absence didn't go unnoticed by the RPF, either. I took it as a deliberate slight to UNAMIR, the implication being that neither we nor the peace accord were important enough to them to warrant their time.

Still, the event was simple and respectful and passed without incident. The flag was raised and the constant breeze made it unfurl majestically; it was a rather big blue flag, and its communion with the blue of the Rwandan sky made quite a statement. The speeches, including my own, were laced with optimism, and UNAMIR received unequivocal support from the Rwandan leaders who attended. The major artisans of the ceremony, Colonel Figoli and his MILOBs, were quite proud of themselves and earned my admiration and gratitude.

After the speeches were over, the crowd pressed in, enjoying the scant refreshments we could afford—warm soft drinks—and mixing joyfully together in a situation that any security person would have regarded as a nightmare. The RPF were the first to leave—the situation was becoming a little too much of a carnival and their soldiers were getting tense—followed by the other dignitaries. After spending some time with a group of children, learning how to play soccer with a ball made of banana leaves and twine, I finally left for Kigali, my worries about the future of the mission and the country reduced to a dull roar, mostly confined to brooding about the slight by the MRND. The press, both local and international, left with great pictures and, for a change, a good-news story from central Africa.

When I got back to Kigali that night, I decided I needed to consult with Dr. Kabia, who was in Kabale doing adept political work for UNO-MUR, negotiating with Ugandan government officials for more freedom of movement for the troops as well as a much deeper area of surveillance. I wanted to know whether I should make an issue out of the absence of the hard-liners at the flag-raising, and Kabia quite wisely pointed out that if I complained publicly about it, the hard-liners would only say that they hadn't come because they hadn't been certain that UNAMIR could guarantee their safety. The mission would be embarrassed and I wouldn't have gained a thing.

Over the next weeks I consulted with Dr. Kabia often, as the political pace of the mission picked up. I knew him to be a square shooter, with solid contacts inside the department of political affairs back in New York, and he always gave me quality advice. When another suitable person became available to take over his duties in Uganda, he flew to Kigali to become my political adviser, and later became chief of staff for the SRSG.

The Belgian reconnaissance group had packed up and gone home, leaving a few staff officers behind to carry on with preparations for the main contingent. The Belgians had been visible all over town during their five days of information-gathering, and there'd been a few minor demonstrations against them that attracted some attention, especially from the radio station RTLM. My rationale for their presence, if anyone asked, was that although these troops were wearing Belgian uniforms, they were under UN operational command, and the badge of authority was the UN badge and the blue beret. Also, both the RPF and the Rwandan government had seen the list of troop-contributing countries that we had supplied for the approval of the Security Council, and neither of the ex-belligerents had objected to the presence of Belgian soldiers. I think they were resigned to accepting the Belgians because organizing another national contingent would have taken months; Maurice Baril had made it clear that no other First World country was remotely interested. As long as the Belgian troops behaved well and we continued to enjoy the goodwill of the Rwandans, I believed the situation was manageable.

We had roughly three weeks to get ready to receive the Belgian contingent, and increasing numbers of military observers were arriving every day. I spent much of the first half of November working flat out with my fifty or so officers, in order to get the force headquarters at least functional. We were less and less welcome at the Mille Collines; guests on vacation and soldiers on a mission do not mix very well. I set Hallqvist the task of finding us permanent headquarters that would house both the military and administrative sections. I also thought that planting the UN flag in Kigali would serve the same symbolic purpose as my flag-raising in Kinihira—demonstrate our commitment to helping the country move to a lasting peace.

We were still having endless administrative and resource problems. I remember sending a message over the radio to Colonel Figoli in the demilitarized zone, telling him I needed written situation reports on what was going on up there, and he radioed back saying that they had no paper or pencils to write with and that their request for more had been denied by Hallqvist for budgetary reasons.

The process of vehicle allocation was even more aggravating. The UN's workhorses for transport and communications were a hodgepodge of thousands of Japanese four-wheel-drive SUVs, which had been donated for the Cambodia mission. They were tough enough to survive the terrible roads and rough terrain, were equipped with decent radios (though not encrypted or secure) and were air-conditioned (which I actually viewed as a drawback because it was hard to start a conversation with the locals when troops were keeping their windows rolled up in order to stay cool). The dispersal of these vehicles was the province of the CAO, and Hallqvist distinctly left the impression that civilian needs came before military ones. MILOBs lucky enough to have vehicles were accused of wasting gas on short errands in Kigali, while some civilian staff were burning up fuel taking weekend jaunts to see the gorillas in Volcano National Park and other sights in Rwanda.

It maddened me that I was forced to fight a petty internal war over vehicles and office supplies. The lack of supplies and the delays damn near hijacked the mission. I had hundreds of troops arriving, and I had no kitchens, no food and no place to billet them. The unvarying official response to my complaints was that national contingents were supposed to come with a two-month supply of rations and to be self-sustaining. That was the rule. If they didn't, the UN didn't have the resources to make up the difference, and I would be left to improvise. Rich Western nations, such as Canada and Belgium, could afford these resources, but poor nations could not—often they were more or less "renting" their soldiers to the UN in exchange for hard currency. The result, which was terrible for building a united peacekeeping force, was that the Western soldiers were reasonably comfortable in the field while the Third World soldiers were living in near-destitution.

Under the pressure of events and the ever-retreating Arusha milestones, my staff was working night and day. Hallqvist and his civilian staff generally worked nine to five, Monday to Friday. The rationale was that he and his people were in Rwanda for the long haul, whereas the military personnel were passing through. They were soldiers and should expect to make do. However, because of my rank and secondment contract from Canada, Hallqvist seemed to expect me to take advantage of every possible perk and privilege: fancy car, big house, all the little luxuries. I believe a commander does his mission a disservice when he lives high off the hog while his soldiers are eating meagre meals prepared by cooks standing in the pouring rain in temporary kitchens. I think I may have actually shocked Hallqvist when I returned the Mercedes staff car he assigned me in favour of the UN standard four-by-four Land Cruiser and sent Willem de Kant out to rent us a small house, where I intended to house him and myself, and Brent and my personal driver when they arrived. I did not want one of the comfortable residences that so many of the UN staff were acquiring, because it sent a message to the Rwandan people that we put our comfort before their interests, and I couldn't stomach that. I loved the house that Willem found us: it was on a hill in Kigali and was cosy and clean behind its wall and single metal gate. Each morning I drank tea on the patio, staring out at the view of the city spread below me, and I sometimes struggled to find the resolve to leave that peaceful spot to take up the challenges of the day.

When I complained about the administrative situation to Maurice and Riza, they were sympathetic, but even they couldn't do anything to reform the system. Hallqvist was operating well within the UN guidelines. He and I were stuck with each other and with the battle lines that our differing sets of imperatives drew across the heart of the mission.

As my UNAMIR MILOBs arrived, we formed them into multinational teams. As vehicles and radios became available, I dispatched the teams throughout the country to conduct reconnaissance and locate potential team sites, meet political, security and military officials in the prefectures, show the flag and get the word out as to who we were and what we were up to.

When Colonel Tikoka arrived, he assumed overall command of the military observer group. Tiko had done many of the military assessments back in August with Brent. Anyone who has ever served with Tiko has many tales to tell about his bravery and daring. During his last UN mission, in Somalia, he had had so many vehicles shot out from under him that only the most gung-ho soldiers would ride with him. He is a fine soldier, fearless and big-hearted, a commander who adores his troops and is capable of winning their absolute loyalty even in the direst of circumstances. His only failing was an aversion to paperwork of any kind, which meant that my force headquarters sometimes went without the vital information we needed to get a good picture of what was going on in the area under his purview, which was almost everywhere outside Kigali. His men were travelling unarmed through country that had recently been at war; some were braver and more resourceful than others, and Tiko was excellent at figuring out this human calculus and deploying the best that he had into the most complicated settings. He even finally rectified his aversion to paperwork by instituting a rigorous set of standard operating procedures among the numerous observer teams around the country.

After a frustrating search, Hallqvist finally found a suitable permanent location for UNAMIR headquarters in the Amahoro (Peace) Stadium and attached athletes' hotel. The complex was in an excellent tactical location, off the major route to the airport in the east end of Kigali. The enclosed stadium could accommodate up to a battalion's worth of soldiers, vehicles and equipment. The hotel provided more than sufficient space for offices and conference rooms.

I set the official opening for the mission headquarters for November 17. I was pushing the pace—my Belgian contingent wouldn't arrive for another two days and I'd have to use MILOBs to monitor the proceedings—but we needed the exposure in front of the local and foreign press. We were falling behind in our phase-one objectives, and I wanted to show that I was prepared to make up for lost time. And at last President Habyarimana, who hadn't met with me since I arrived in Kigali, was willing to come out to express his support for UNAMIR in public. The RPF was also supportive, though they were only sending Commander Karake Karenzi, their liaison officer to UNAMIR, since I couldn't at that point offer much in the way of security in Kigali for a larger party of the former enemy.

I met President Habyarimana at the main entrance of the hotel complex, dressed in my Canadian general's uniform with UN insignia on the shoulders and wearing my blue beret. He was statesmanlike in an impeccable dark suit and black shoes so shiny they looked like patent leather. He shook my hand in a dignified fashion. Except for a few bodyguards dressed in civvies, he left his Presidential Guard escort out-side and walked with me to the main hall.

We were greeted by sustained applause, cheers and laughter. The atmosphere was celebratory, even though we'd been able to muster none of the pomp and fancy trappings of major international headquarters. People were seated on a couple of hundred borrowed folding chairs and wooden benches, and I led the president to his place at the front of the room, behind an ordinary six-foot-long folding table that we'd draped with some cloth. The UN and Rwandan flags were linked on the wall behind him in symbolic harmony.

I was the first to speak and attempted three or four lines in Kinyarwanda, which our few local staff had written out phonetically for me. Hearty laughter greeted me, but the attempt—and the rest of my speech, in which I reverted to French to explain UNAMIR's presence in the country—seemed to go over well with the crowd. Then the presi-dent delivered a heartfelt speech in French, full of high hopes for peace, co-operation and reconciliation, which surprised me because it broke with his party's usual dogma.

The media did its part, and many pictures were taken. The govern-ment even issued an official calendar poster of the event, with the president and me seated together, shaking hands under the Rwandan and UN flags. Habyarimana did not take questions, however, and soon I was ushering him back to his armoured Mercedes, through an enthusiastic crowd that sang and clapped as he passed by.

We had a small reception afterwards for those who wished to stay, but Hallqvist said he was unable to pay for the refreshments since he had no authority to spend money on social events. Once again Amadou Ly played the angel to the mission and dipped into his budget. Overall, I was pleased with the day. With this official opening, the headquarters and its commander were in place, the flag was up in Kigali and we seemed to be advancing our mandate. The atmosphere of peace and optimism, however, exploded in violence that same night.

At 0600 on November 18, the burgomaster of Nkumba commune called to inform the Kigali media and the government of a series of killings along the border of the ill-defined demilitarized zone north of Ruhengeri. He was able to supply details about each of the incidents, which he said had taken place at five different locations between 2330 and 0230 that morning. Two of these places were not even under his jurisdiction, and phone communication in the country was not reliable; we wondered how the mayor came into possession of all this information so quickly. The killings seemed to have been very well planned. The victims were men, women and children—twenty-one killed, two badly injured and two apparently kidnapped—associated with the ruling MRND party. Among them were people who had won local elections, and candidates for upcoming ones—elections that were being conducted with the assistance of Colonel Figoli and his troops in the demilitarized zone.

The local media leapt on the story, inflating the number of dead to forty and accusing the RPF of being the perpetrators. To my mind, the murders came suspiciously on the heels of government complaints, which had been brought to me by Augustin Bizimana and Déogratias Nsabimana, alleging that Ugandan troops and RPF reinforcements were massing south of Kabale and in the area of the Virunga Mountains. I had contacted Ben Matiwaza of UNOMUR to investigate, since his troops conducted constant patrols of the area. He said they'd seen no sign of large troop movements. When I confronted Bizimana and Nsabimana to ask where their information came from, they were vague, citing Washington contacts they refused to name.

Whether by design or not, the massacres were an immediate challenge to UNAMIR. We had just formally declared our presence to applause, song and cheers; now we were being tested on whether we could truly help to establish an atmosphere of security in the country. (Coincidentally, speculation and sensationalism about the killings filled the newspaper pages that might have been devoted to good-news coverage of our official opening.) If we investigated and found conclusive proof that the RPF had committed the murders, we'd be in tricky territory in which one of the ex-belligerents appeared to be deliberately destabilizing the country; if we investigated and were not able to point the finger at the RPF, the media and especially RTLM would view us as either in league with the RPF or totally incompetent.

I immediately launched a board of inquiry with as much noise as possible, though I was hamstrung by not yet having a civilian police contingent or a legal adviser (the UN never did post a legal adviser to UNAMIR, which would create enormous complications later on, when the world was arguing over whether a genocide was actually happening). The people who did the killing left enough evidence behind to suggest RPF involvement (pieces of clothing, the RPF's standard-issue rubber boots, even food) but not enough to dispel the notion that it had been planted. When our investigation proved inconclusive, we invited all sides to participate in an inquiry, but the government was slow to send a representative and the process dragged on well into the next year and was never resolved.

In a way, my bluff had been called. I'd taken a risk in opening our headquarters in such a public way before we had all the personnel in place and now our credibility was taking a hit. Our failure to find the perpetrators of the November 17 to 18 massacre became "proof" for the hard-liners that UNAMIR was biased against the regime and was a closet RPF supporter. My request for urgent deployment of personnel skilled in legal, media, investigative and political strategy in theatre went unheeded. No matter how sympathetic the DPKO was about the hits I was taking over this, they could not influence the already over-extended personnel branch of the UN to fill the positions. I had two comforting thoughts: Brent Beardsley, who had nurtured this mission with me, was scheduled to arrive on November 22 to take up his role as military assistant in my personal cabinet, and Jacques-Roger Booh-Booh was expected to land in Kigali the day after Brent.

On November 19, the first Belgian transport aircraft began landing and unloading their human cargo—about seventy-five members of the 2nd Paratroop Battalion, who we were putting up temporarily at the Amahoro Stadium. I can't say that the Belgians and I hit it off at the welcoming parade the next day. I gave my speech in French, not realizing that they were the advance party of the last remaining bilingual unit—Flemish and Walloon—in the Belgian army. The commanding officer, Lieutenant Colonel LeRoy, a self-confident, rather long-in-the-tooth parachutist, did not project any particular excitement about the mission.

The UN had requested an 800-man motorized infantry battalion, with one company (125 men) mounted in wheeled armoured personnel carriers, but it was not to be. Instead we had been told back in September that Belgium could send 450 para-commandos, with light weapons, few vehicles, only a handful of APCs, and a small logistical sub-unit, medical-surgical platoon and headquarters. (We ended up having to make up the difference in force strength with a 400-man half-battalion from Bangladesh; the two half-battalions never equated the strength and cohesion of a whole.) Many of the Belgian soldiers had completed a tour in Somalia, which was a chapter-seven mission, and they came to UNAMIR with a very aggressive attitude. My staff soon caught some of them bragging at the local bars that their troops had killed over two hundred Somalis and that they knew how to kick "nigger" ass in Africa. I was compelled to call a commander's hour when the bulk of the half-battalion arrived, in order to walk them through our rules of engagement and impress upon them that they needed to change their personal attitudes toward the locals and operate in accordance with a chapter-six mandate. I left them with no doubt that I would not tolerate racist statements, colonial attitudes, unnecessary aggression or other abuses of power.

Much of the Belgian equipment had been shipped directly from Somalia without being cleaned or serviced and was much the worse for wear. Even so, the Belgians would still be my best combat troops. Since in Rwanda, all roads lead to Kigali, and whoever controls Kigali controls the country, I planned to deploy them in the city. Standard UN practice is to name units for their countries of origin; the Belgians in this case would have been called BELBAT. I decided to pass on this custom, as I thought the best chance for melding my motley force was to keep them all focused on their mutual tasks, so the Belgians became KIBAT, for Kigali Battalion.

Our information gathering in southern Rwanda during this period was restricted to informal reports from Amadou Ly's field teams, moderate politicians, NGO personnel and the odd journalist. They all suggested tension was building in the region as a result of the coup in Burundi.

An estimated 300,000 refugees had crossed the border into Rwanda, and massacres inside Burundi had left the streams and rivers full of bloated bodies. The refugees were occupying makeshift camps and ravaging the small forests that decades of labour had re-established on the mountainsides to prevent soil erosion. The region was into a second year of drought and had suffered extensive crop failures, forcing many of the Rwandans in the area to depend on food aid. The UNHCR rapidly moved in to provide the essentials to the Burundian refugees, but since it is only mandated to look after refugees who cross borders, it couldn't provide for the displaced or hungry Rwandans. This meant that local people watched refugees eating while they and their children starved.

We were getting reports from NGOs that arms were going into the refugee camps in the south. There was an alarming increase in assaults and thefts in and near the camps, and also a report of arms smuggling. In order to put a lid on the violence, the Rwandan government decided to move the Burundian refugees into camps divided along ethnic lines. While this diminished the chance of ethnic violence, it provided fertile ground for radicals to move into the camps and stir up trouble. We could do little except maintain a thin presence in the area—hoping that it would help to cool tempers—diverting some of our precious MILOB teams south to conduct sporadic inspections of the camps.

On November 23, the SRSG arrived. I put together an honour guard of my Tunisians, who were becoming quite expert on the parade square, but I got the feeling that Jacques-Roger Booh-Booh had expected something more elaborate.

At our first meeting, my head of mission seemed impressive. A tall, heavy-set man with an assured walk, Booh-Booh was clean-shaven and dressed in a light blue suit. His grey hair was cropped close to his head, and he looked every inch the diplomat or man of business. And in fact, since his retirement from the diplomatic corps, he had become very successful in the world of banana production and sales (he once showed me a few pictures of his vast holdings in Cameroon and expressed regret about not being there to take care of things). Booh-Booh said that only a direct appeal from his friend Boutros Boutros-Ghali had brought him out of retirement to take up this post. With his background in politics, diplomacy, business and UN affairs, and his relationship with the secretary-general, he seemed like the right man for the job and certainly someone I thought I could work with. His presence meant that I was no longer the head of mission. I hoped he would be able to do an end run around the party infighting that was obstructing any movement toward installing the BBTG.

Dr. Kabia and I briefed him to the best of our ability. In September, two of the major moderate parties, the MDR and the PL, had fractured into moderate and extremist "Hutu Power" wings. Each wing had then laid claim to the ministerial positions and representative seats that had been allocated by party in the Arusha Peace Agreement. The RPF, of course, preferred the moderate candidates in each of these parties; the president's party and an increasingly visible Hutu extremist party, the CDR, preferred the Power candidates. These intrigues were only now coming to the surface and needed astute political handling. I knew I wasn't up to the task and could now hand it over to Booh-Booh and concentrate on the military and security sides.

Booh-Booh's arrival coincided with a worsening of the weather and an increased number of reports of shootings and killings around the country. Every afternoon, large purple clouds would darken the sky and we would hear the rumble of thunder; by nightfall, we'd be drenched with torrents of rain, and lightning would rip the sky apart, bathing the city in its eerie momentary glow.

The day after Booh-Booh landed in Kigali, we received a report that there had been an attack on a village in northwestern Rwanda by persons unknown and that a number of Hutu civilians had been murdered. This was followed rapidly by the news that some children had disappeared while fetching water in the Virunga Mountains. I drove to the area and, with an escort of Tunisian soldiers, confirmed the deaths. Rumours were spreading that the RPF had committed the attack, and I was determined to investigate and identify the perpetrators of these hideous crimes. We questioned local people and military personnel, who condemned the RPF without any proof or witnesses. I then led a patrol through forests of bamboo up a volcano called Mount Karisimbi.

We found some abandoned water cans but no sign of the missing children. As dark was coming down, I tasked the Tunisians to extend the search higher up the volcano the next morning and returned to Kigali to try to quiet flying rumours.

The Tunisians found the children the next day. They had all been murdered except for one young girl, who my soldiers carried to a nearby hospital. I dispatched Brent, another officer and a local translator to the site. After a long drive and foot march, they came to the place where a boy of eight and five girls between six and fourteen had been strangled to death. Deep violet rope burns cut into their necks. All of them had also suffered head wounds and the girls had clearly been gang-raped before they were murdered. Near one of the bodies was a glove in the colour pattern of the RPF uniform. Brent collected the glove, wondering why someone would leave such a distinctive signature.

A small party of civilians, who claimed to be relatives of the dead children, had also climbed to the site. Once Brent had finished his initial assessment, he turned to the group and, through his translator, asked who they thought had committed the massacre. The translator was from the public affairs office of our mission in Kigali and should have been reliable. But Brent noticed that the man repeatedly used the word *Inkotanyi* when he spoke to the group, which Brent knew was slang for the RPF. (The rough translation is "freedom fighter," a term the RPF meant seriously but opponents used sarcastically.) The translator turned back to Brent and told him that the villagers believed the RPF was responsible for the murders. Brent was sure the man was coaching the testimony. From that day forward, we did not trust that translator, and it was later strongly suspected that he was an RGF spy who had been ordered to infiltrate our mission. (After the war, the RPF identified six of our local staff as spies for the RGF. My first civilian driver turned out to be a militia member, and it was alleged that a francophone staffer in the SRSG's office was an informant to the MRND.)

By that time, it was late afternoon, and Brent wanted to get himself and the rest of his party off the mountain before it got dark. He turned to the relatives and asked for their help to carry the bodies down. Eyes wide with fear, they shook their heads, refusing to touch the dead children. Brent had to leave the bodies behind, assuming that the relatives would not touch them out of a reverence for their spirits or for some other religious reason. He later found out that the families thought the bodies had been booby-trapped, and preferred that someone else touch them first.

At the base of the mountain, Brent and his party were met by a large government patrol; the RGF soldiers had coloured ropes tied around their waists and carried large fighting knives in addition to other weapons. Brent briefed the commanding officer on what had been found, and said a UNAMIR patrol would return the next day to collect the children's bodies and return them to their families. Unprompted, the commander repeated the charge that the RPF had perpetrated a massacre. But Brent could still not figure out why the RPF would do such a thing. There was no tactical advantage in crossing forty to sixty kilometres of gruelling terrain into the Hutu heartland to commit such a brutal crime. Brent and his party took their leave and headed to the hospital in Ruhengeri to see the little girl who had survived the raid.

She couldn't have been more than six years old and was in a deep coma, shaking from severe brain damage. A few weeks earlier, back in Canada, Brent had been with his wife when she had given birth to their third child; now he was standing by a young Rwandan girl's bed, saying a prayer for her and puzzling over what he had seen and heard that day. He couldn't shake the feeling that there was something very odd about the crime scene. Why would the RPF leave behind a telltale glove? They were not known for stupidity. Was it possible that others had committed the crime in order to blame it on the RPF? Brent remembered the ropes dangling from the waists of the RGF soldiers, and their large fighting knives. He wondered if blows from the hilts of those knives could have caused the deep wounds he had seen on the children's heads. Brent was hoping that the girl would wake up and that she might be able to tell him what really happened; he stationed a guard by her bedside with instructions to inform him of any change in her condition. But the little girl never regained consciousness, and she died the next day. Brent returned to Kigali, troubled by what he had witnessed and frustrated by his inability to take the investigation further.

I was as stuck as I had been with the earlier killings, but I was determined to get to the bottom of this murder of children. I invited the RGF and the RPF to join UNAMIR in a joint commission of inquiry to determine who had committed the crimes. The RPF immediately named two lawyers to the inquiry. The RGF hesitated, saying they had to study the matter. Despite repeated pressure from me, months passed before the RGF finally appointed their commissioners, which left all of us chasing a cold trail. While the children's deaths became more fuel for the extremist propaganda machine, even RTLM had to recognize that we had invited both parties to participate equally in the investigation, and did not attack me personally. If we kept our wits about us and acted quickly, we could sometimes gain the initiative and counteract the damage being done.

To my surprise and chagrin, Jacques-Roger Booh-Booh turned out to be a proper gentleman who kept diplomatic working hours. He was not involved in helping me deal with the fallout of the massacres and the propaganda wars they were provoking. He was rarely in his office before ten, took a full two-hour lunch and left the office before five. He made it clear that he was not to be tracked down and disturbed on the weekends unless there was a dire emergency. He seemed to bring nothing new to the table in the way of expertise on Rwanda, knowledge of the conflict, familiarity with the Arusha accords, or skill at identifying and dealing with the political intrigues of the nation. He was not inclined to take the lead on the international political effort, even though the enormous power invested in him and his mandate by the UN Security Council made him the logical person to do so. While he met with the President, Prime Minister Agathe and the RPF within a few days of arriving in Kigali, the meetings were more in the nature of courtesy calls than discussions of real significance. Habyarimana unburdened himself to the SRSG, clearly more comfortable in this francophone African's presence than he had ever been with me. The session under the Cinzano umbrellas on the president's patio was cordial, with Habyarimana candidly revealing his distrust of the RPF; his perception that the MRND was the target of intrigue and unfair dealing; and his sense of injustice over the fact that the only political party that existed in Rwanda before the

Arusha accords did not seem to carry more weight in the proceedings. Booh-Booh asked no questions and made no promises, just told the President that he could be counted upon.

When it came to the RPF, it didn't help that Booh-Booh's English was minimal. At their first encounter with him in Mulindi, the RPF representatives pressed him to outline a program for pushing beyond the political impasses and getting them into their quarters in Kigali. Booh-Booh had no strategy to give them, and the RPF were not impressed.

I was rarely asked to accompany him or brief him, and he never offered to debrief for me after major political working sessions. He generally kept his own counsel or shared his thoughts with his close political advisers, who were all francophone Africans who also played things close to the vest. His grip on his political staff was unshakeable. After Dr. Kabia was appointed UNAMIR's chief of staff, he discreetly kept me in the loop as to what my head of mission was—or wasn't—up to.

The last of the Belgian forces arrived in the first week of December, bringing with them the final member of my personal staff, my military driver, Master Corporal Philippe Troute, who joined the ménage at my house. Troute had originally been a light-armoured soldier, but with the downsizing of NATO forces at the end of the Cold War, he had been transferred, somewhat reluctantly I think, to the para-commandos. He was an excellent driver, a solid, mature soldier with heavily tattooed arms and a stare that could freeze steam. He was a Walloon who prided himself on speaking only French, never Flemish, and he could not speak any English. He had never been away from home for longer than three weeks and was nervous about how his wife and child would handle the separation.

Colonel Luc Marchal, who would become the Kigali Sector commander, stepped off the plane on December 4, wearing his blue beret and looking fit and ready for action. He was a senior colonel with extensive African experience, and he had an intimate knowledge of the mission, as he had been the chef de cabinet in the office of the Belgian minister of defence. I was glad to have him in theatre with me, especially since the Belgians were becoming more of a problem than I had bargained for.

Unlike many of his countrymen, Luc carried no colonial baggage. He came to thrive within my ad hoc, multi-ethnic, multilingual force and had a special knack for working with troops from less sophisticated armies. He took a keen interest in Rwanda, building very positive relationships with the local leaders and the ordinary people. In our first meeting, I emphasized that the mission was there to support the on-going political process and therefore had to follow a strict chapter-six mandate. As soon as the weapons-secure area was negotiated—and Luc's major task as Kigali sector commander would be to maintain it—the RPF was going to send an armed battalion to the capital. I had wanted a rapid reaction force to deal with these kinds of challenges, but because Belgium had forbidden its troops to be used in crowd control of any sort, we had to build this force out of troops from Bangladesh. And he was going to help me.

Unfortunately, soon after he arrived, Luc became caught up in a nasty fracas over accommodations for the Belgian troops. I told the Belgian commanding officer that I wanted a significant portion of his contingent to occupy the airport as their garrison and their primary defensive location. In a landlocked country, where the only viable and efficient means in and out of the country is by plane, the airport is the vital ground. But I also needed troops to be a presence in the city to provide the atmosphere of security necessary for keeping the peace process on target as well as to allay the fears of the local population about the presence of an armed unit of the RPF in the heart of the city. To do this, I needed the Belgians to be prepared to live out of camp garrisons.

In the guidelines to the troop-contributing nations, I had directed that contingents bring camp stores (tents, stoves, ablution facilities and so on). But LeRoy informed me that not only had they not brought camp stores, they also had no intention of living under canvas. Belgian soldiers would only be accommodated in hard buildings as per national policy. I asked to see the policy and, over the next several weeks, had many discussions with Luc and the Belgian commanders about the issue. In the end, they did show me a national Belgian army policy directive that stated that in Africa, Belgian soldiers would never live under canvas but only in buildings, not necessarily for the sake of comfort or hygiene but because it was imperative that they maintain a correct presence in front of the Africans.

To add salt to the wound, once the Belgians finally found accommodation that suited them, in buildings scattered all over Kigali, they then wanted the UN to pay the rent. Luc was the one to deliver this message. He was caught between me and the operational requirements of UNAMIR—he knew it was potentially dangerous to have the Belgians scattered all over the city, which was proved beyond a shadow of a doubt after April 6—and the loyalty he owed his superiors, army policy and his government. We tried hard not to let the skirmishing over lodgings come between us and the mutual respect we soon developed.

My small force was operating at maximum capability. I still had no effective reserve with which to respond to unexpected violent clashes, and we were beginning to pick up the scent of a mysterious third force that seemed to be behind all the killings and assassinations. On December 3, I received a letter signed by a group of senior RGF and Gendarmerie officers, which informed me that there were elements close to the president who were out to sabotage the peace process, with potentially devastating consequences. The conspiracy's opening act would be a massacre of Tutsis.

Over the next few months I had several private meetings with Colonel Léonidas Rusatira, the head of the military school and senior member of this group. I wanted to determine the size and clout of this moderate group inside the military and keep a line open to them. I also ensured that the existence of these officers was passed on to Kagame so the RPF would realize there were moderates they could potentially work with inside the present security forces. To flush out who or what this force was, I set up a two-man intelligence unit, led by Captain Frank Claeys of Belgium, with the help of a Senegalese captain named Amadou Deme. Claeys was young, smart and self-assured without being arrogant. Born in Africa, he was an experienced para-commando and special forces officer and he was devoted to the mission, as was his equally efficient and multilingual teammate. According to my chapter-six mandate, I was supposed to rely on the goodwill of the ex-belligerent groups for all my information, but as mysterious deaths began to take on more political overtones, relying strictly on the warring parties for intelligence would have been foolish in the extreme. Because the team was not supposed to exist, I had to cover its expenses from my own pocket, and often Deme and Claeys themselves chipped in with funds.

Soon they were picking up information that suggested that the killings that had taken place on November 17 and 18 had been carried out by para-commandos from Camp Bagogwe, which was a big commando training base for the RGF in the northwest. This bit of news, together with information they uncovered about weapons caches in the president's hometown, caused me a number of sleepless nights. Something malicious was definitely afoot. I decided to approach Booh-Booh with my findings and suggest we search and seize the weapons caches. He was alarmed by the idea, saying that to launch such an operation might further jeopardize the political process—since the only targets I was offering were on the government side. I reluctantly obeyed his direction.

On December 7, Dr. James Jonah, the under-secretary general of the department of political affairs, visited Rwanda and held a series of meetings with President Habyarimana. I was not invited but noticed the sudden flurry of activity in Booh-Booh's office. The next day, I got a message from the SRSG, saying that he was going to hold a major gathering in Kinihira on December 10 to try to break the political impasse. The meeting was so hastily cobbled together I didn't have time to set up proper escorts or take adequate weapons control measures. Just when I thought things couldn't get any worse, when I got to Kinihira Dr. Kabia told me that there hadn't been time to put together a team to do translation work, and Booh-Booh was hoping he could count on me personally to pitch in and help. Because I had to translate for everyone, I was tied up with the meeting for five hours straight and was unable to keep an eye out for trouble. All of us on the military side were sweating buckets: the number of high-profile people on hand made the meeting an attractive target.

Even though there had been little advance notice, there was a large turnout, especially of the international press. But things did not go well. The room was set up for confrontation, not resolution, with the

RPF and moderate political leaders seated on one side and the government representatives on the other. Instead of trying to overcome their mutual distrust, Booh-Booh instead acted as a neutral moderator. What everybody in that room needed to hear was that the moderate parties were strictly non-aligned and had not affiliated with either the RPF or the regime. Someone had to say that all parties needed to put Rwanda first.

The best person to have done that would have been Faustin Twagiramungu, the prime minister designate, but for some reason, he chose not to. The only person to make this argument was Lando Ndasingwa of the Parti libéral, but nobody supported his bold stand. As the meeting dragged on and on, the representatives fell back on their old stories of oppression and marginalization. Booh-Booh, seeing the clock running down and the growing restlessness of the press, decided to take a few of the leaders into a back room, where they managed to hammer out a weak statement reaffirming their commitment to Arusha. I left the meeting very depressed. Once again, instead of grappling with the fundamental problems, the parties had chosen to paper over their differences for the public eye while stubbornly hanging on to their grievances.

The impasse continued through December as the political parties attempted to put together lists of the members they intended to put forward for the BBTG. Booh-Booh did not invite my counsel on this or any other political issue, though I made a point of seeking that information directly from him, in particular asking for his future plans. I stayed abreast of the political wrangling through Dr. Kabia and sought information from friends within Kigali's diplomatic circles. It was evident to me and others that hardline voices, pushing ethnic arguments and fears, were beginning to dominate the discussions, and there was an increasingly violent tone to political discourse, fed by the broadcasts of RTLM. The atmosphere in Kigali was becoming tense.

I had known the Bangladeshis would have little to no equipment or support, but I had hoped they would be well-led and well-trained. I was keen to get them on the ground so that the French paratroop battalion in Kigali could leave, as spelled out in the Arusha accords. The French maintained that their soldiers were in Kigali to protect the expatriate community, but with both the Belgian and Bangladeshi battalions deployed in the city, this excuse would evaporate and they could go home.

But when the Bangladeshis got off the planes at Kigali airport in mid-December, they had nothing but their personal weapons and their kit, and expected the UN to supply everything else they needed—from their first meal in the field to the canvas over their heads. The added logistical burden of caring for this force was a plague on the mission.

In order to accommodate them in the Amahoro Stadium, we had to move the last of KIBAT out. We commenced a rigorous training plan, half-heartedly implemented on the Bangladeshis' part. They harried me and their immediate superiors in the sector HQ on a daily basis with requests for everything from soap to ammunition, vehicles to sandbags. The Bangladeshis had agreed to first deploy their infantry battalion and then send the other units they had promised (an engineer company, a logistics company, a hospital, a military police section and a movement-control platoon) in phase two. This is what I had planned for and what I needed from them. But these four hundred soldiers were a mixed bag of each element, and officer-heavy to boot. A four-hundred-man unit would usually be commanded by a lieutenant colonel, if not a major. The Bangladeshis were commanded by a full colonel, with no fewer than six lieutenant colonels, dozens of majors and an unaccountable number of captains and lieutenants under him. I needed riflemen on the ground, not officers in the mess or headquarters.

After the French flew home in mid-December, the coast was clear to finalize the Kigali Weapons Secure Area (KWSA) agreement, yet another milestone on the road to installing the BBTG. The KWSA was an innovation I had come up with to deal with the unique problem of having an armed battalion of RPF soldiers located in the heart of the city, surrounded by thousands of their former enemies. Under the agreement, each party in the Kigali area would secure its weapons and only move them and armed troops with our permission and under our escort. When these conditions had been met, then and only then would the RPF send their political and bureaucratic appointments to the BBTG in Kigali, along with a security battalion. Once they were installed, the new government could be sworn in and that act would signal the end of phase one of our military objectives.

In the weeks before Christmas, I was totally engaged with preparations for securing the signing of the KWSA agreement and then moving the RPF delegation and battalion into Kigali. On December 23, I held an intense session that ended up running long into the night: I was determined that none of us would leave until all parties had agreed to the terms of the agreement. We held the meeting at a place we dubbed Kilometre 64, on the road from Kigali to Kabale, Uganda, exactly sixty-four kilometres from the capital. It was a perfect spot for a meeting: a couple of old shacks off the roadside in the demilitarized zone, surrounded by hills where I could deploy soldiers to keep an eye out for trouble. There was no electricity, so we had to bring in a portable generator. I had a table and chairs made cheaply by a local carpenter; I wanted the furniture to be rudimentary so that no one could get too comfortable. I wanted all parties to get down to the business of serious negotiations as rapidly as possible.

Colonel Théoneste Bagosora and Lieutenant Colonel Ephrem Rwabalinda, the RGF's liaison officer to UNAMIR, were there for the government side. The RPF had sent a delegation of senior officers who introduced themselves by first names only—Commander Charles, Commander Andrew and so on. The major stumbling point was that the RPF wanted all "private security firms" registered and included in the agreement. Bagosora refused, saying that these security firms were not part of the military. We all knew we weren't talking about private security firms but the growing militias and so-called self-defence groups at work in the country. I wanted them inside the agreement, where they'd be under our control. I pushed the meeting from three in the afternoon until three in the morning, until finally Bagosora relented.

We were all half asleep by the time we climbed into our vehicles for the long drive home. Luckily, Willem noticed that during the night somebody had covered the road with land mines. He was able to warn me and most of the others, but Colonel Bagosora had been in a greater hurry than the rest of us to leave, and he and Rwabalinda were already in their limousine and out on the road. We honked our horns to get their driver to stop, which he did just in time to realize the car was stuck in the middle of a minefield. I couldn't resist a chuckle at Bagosora's expense. The RGF had a bad habit of planting mines on their side of the demilitarized zone even though we had repeatedly warned them not to do so. We knew Bagosora's troops were bound to be nearby, and honked our horns and yelled to alert them, but it took more than an hour before a RGF soldier showed up on the scene and looked horrified to see Bagosora's car stranded among the mines. It would be dawn before we could get the mess straightened out. With the lights from my Jeep, I could see that he was stiff with fear and probably fuming over having been trapped by one of his own cat-and-mouse games.

Even after the KWSA agreement was signed, we ran into major problems with enforcement, and I can't say I was surprised. My troops reported that the RGF were moving heavy weapons just beyond the area covered by the agreement, and I was also hearing of militia training going on inside the KWSA. I got no satisfactory responses to my queries from the RGF chief of staff or the minister of defence, just shrugs and evasive answers. All I could do was to continue to monitor the situation with my MILOBs and report back to New York.

By far the most significant military task we had to accomplish in phase one was the operation we called "Clean Corridor"—preparing a secure route for the RPF battalion and politicians to travel into Kigali, and then a safe spot for them to stay once they got there. I had been after the minister of defence to help select a site for the RPF in Kigali since shortly after I arrived in Rwanda, but he had evaded my repeated requests, leaving this crucial decision to the very last minute. Though I had suggested four suitable options, both sides finally agreed to a site I considered the worst possible choice: the Conseil national pour le développement (CND), or the National Council for Development, which was actually the National Assembly building combined with a hotel complex and conference centre. He who controls parliament controls the nation: my fear was that extremists would say that UNAMIR was handing over the soul of the nation to the RPF. Imagine a rebel organization being given control of the East and West blocks on Parliament Hill, or a portion of the Capitol complex in Washington. The appearance was all wrong.

The CND buildings were located on a small hill in the heart of the city, overlooking the two major arteries leading in and out of Kigali and surrounded by a metal fence. On one side was the Rwandan National Assembly and government offices, a portion of which the Bangladeshis had taken over and were using for their quarters. The other side, the hotel complex of about two hundred rooms, had its own separate entrance and would be the new home of the RPF. Nearby on a low plateau was the Presidential Guard's headquarters; the two groups could keep a watchful eye on each other. From their hill, the RPF could cover and control major and essential arteries through the city. From the RGF perspective, lodging the RPF in the CND meant they were confined to a hill that was easy to fire upon; the RGF could surround, isolate and lay siege to their enemy if it came to that. Once the decision was made, I deployed my troops around the complex as a thin blue line between the former belligerents.

Both sides had agreed in August that the light battalion accompanying the RPF politicians would come equipped with machine guns with anti-aircraft mounts as well as light mortars. I had to admire the moxie of Major Paul Kagame, who must have seen the tactical advantage of such a site and seized the opportunity.

With the KWSA agreement signed on the morning of December 24 and December 28 set as the date on which we would escort the RPF to its garrison in Kigali, we set out to pass what we thought would be the worst Christmas of our lives. De Kant had gone on leave to Kenya to meet his girlfriend and spend the holidays on safari. I could tell that Brent and Philippe were missing their wives and young children—Brent was about to miss his new son's first Christmas.

On Christmas Eve, we came home at the end of a normal workday and had a spaghetti supper. Tiso, our cook, had given us a banana tree, and Major Arthur Godson of Ghana had given us a string of lights; Brent married the two gifts to produce the strangest looking Christmas tree I have ever seen. After supper, we exchanged some small presents and opened a number of letters from Canadian schoolchildren, along with Christmas gift packages, which people on the home front have been sending to troops on operations every year since the First World War. The maple syrup, fruitcakes, ham, cheddar cheese and other treats really boosted our morale. Still, we were all in bed by nine.

When we woke up, the Christmas tree was dead. Apparently banana trees do not like to be strung with electric lights. We spent a good part of Christmas morning trying to revive the poor tree, deeply embarrassed that Tiso would return from his short vacation and discover our carelessness. Philippe and I decided that there was only one thing to do in such a situation: blame Brent.

That night, Philippe went off to the Belgian contingent's Christmas service and dinner to pass the evening with his comrades. Brent and I were invited to the home of the Canadian consul, Denis Provost, to have a Canadian Christmas with his family, a number of Canadian expatriates and Rwandans with ties to Canada. At home, Beth and I would have been convening a big family gathering around our own table, and I would have been carving the turkey. I wondered how she and the children were doing without me, then immediately dismissed the thought—I had to make the best of what was in front of me, not long for what wasn't. I remember speaking at length with Hélène Pinsky, who was certain that the situation in Rwanda was taking a turn for the better and that there would only be bright days ahead as decency and respect for human rights took hold in the nation. Not one of the Rwandans at that party, linked by marriage or friendship to Canada, would survive the coming genocide.

We launched Operation Clean Corridor on schedule on December 28. Luc Marchal and his Kigali Sector contingents were to play a key role in this difficult and dangerous task, the biggest test UNAMIR had yet faced.

We were awake before dawn. I dropped Brent off at the CND to supervise the final preparations for the arrival of the RPF. With Hallqvist and his deputy away for Christmas vacation, the more professional and co-operative members of his staff, under the supervision of Phillip

Mitnick, had worked through the holiday, and we were ready. Philippe and I drove to the Ngondore refugee camp, near the demilitarized zone, where we checked communications and supervised the deployment at the camp of UNAMIR troops, RGF soldiers from the military police, and Rwandan gendarmes. Then we waited. The RPF convoy was supposed to depart from Mulindi at dawn, cross the RGF front lines around breakfast time and arrive in Kigali before lunch. Long after dawn, the code words for the movement had not yet been given; Luc called to tell me why there was a delay. The RPF soldiers had been exceedingly slow in loading their vehicles and getting themselves organized but that he expected them to be ready in an hour. An hour passed and he called again to say that they were now refusing to move because a suitable vehicle had not been provided by UNAMIR to carry the chairman of the RPF into Kigali. No one had ever asked us to provide a staff car, but they insisted they would not leave Mulindi until we sent a suitable vehicle. We hurriedly found a Mercedes and driver and sent it north from Kigali with an escort. By the time the car got there, it was almost lunchtime. With some prodding from Luc, the convoy finally started to move. It had to get into the CND before dark, and time was tight, but all went well and the convoy quickly passed through the RGF lines and moved down to Kigali.

At the refugee camp all was quiet. The CND was ready and the route through Kigali secure, with large and happy crowds of Hutus and Tutsis gathering along the way, turning out to welcome the RPF to Kigali. The extremists were nowhere to be seen. We were glad that the Interahamwe, in particular, was absent. The Interahamwe were a group of young men who had attached themselves to the youth wing of the ruling MRND party and were beginning to show up at a lot of political rallies dressed rather bizarrely, in cotton combat fatigues covered in fantastical symbols in the red, green and black of the Rwandan flag, and carrying machetes or carved replicas of Kalashnikovs. We had found them comical at first, because they looked and acted like clowns, but we soon learned that wherever they showed up, violence and mayhem were never far behind.

When the convoy arrived at the refugee camp, I joined it. There were no incidents along the route. It finally dawned on me why the RPF had procrastinated. If someone with inside information had laid an ambush, they would have expected the convoy by early morning. As the convoy was delayed for hours, any ambushers would have abandoned their position for fear of being discovered by our patrols or because they would have thought the operation had been cancelled. It takes a very disciplined soldier to hold still in an ambush position for many hours, and disciplined soldiers were in short supply in both the RGF and the extremist camps.

A single shot or grenade from the crowd that lined our way into Kigali could have been disastrous, but as we moved through the streets, there was only euphoria. The RPF soldiers were cheered and showered with flowers. By mid-afternoon, the convoy moved into the CND complex. I personally welcomed Colonel Alexis Kanyarengwe, the chairman of the RPF, to Kigali with a Rwandan flag to fly at the CND. Once the RPF troops unloaded, they began deploying into a defensive posture around the complex and taking over security from my soldiers. As these handovers were completed, my troops withdrew to the perimeter of the complex to interpose themselves between the RPF and the Gendarmerie, which was trying to hold the cheering mobs back.

I spent the evening at the CND with Luc, watching the RPF get settled. Ambassadors from the diplomatic community came to pay their respects to the chairman. I was surprised to see the French ambassador arrive, since no foreign nation had done so much to prevent this day from happening. Perhaps the French were reconciled to a new Rwanda.

Brent had spent the afternoon and evening studying the RPF soldiers and their deployment around the CND. The commanding officer—who went by his *nom de guerre*, Commander Charles—was only in his late twenties, but he was obviously an experienced and able leader. The occupation of the CND had been well-rehearsed: the RPF had deployed by company, platoon and section-sized groups in a direct and deliberate manner. The entire area was checked in minutes, commanders liaised and passed direction, troops were moved into defensive locations, and they immediately began to dig in. Once secure, they had dismissed the UNAMIR troops and assumed total control of the interior of the complex. Once the RPF began digging, they never stopped for the next four months. From shellscrapes or foxholes, they dug full fire-trenches, then roofed the trenches for protection from artillery or mortar fire. They then dug full communication-trenches between the individual trenches and built bunkers that developed into caverns. By the time the war resumed in April, they had built an underground complex under the CND. It was clear that while the peace process was progressing, they were also prepared for the alternative. I was determined that it would not come to that.

Earlier in December, Brent and I had sat down to draft our three-month review for Boutros Boutros-Ghali, which was to go to the Security Council on December 30. Overall, we were pleased, maybe even euphoric. Despite the world's lack of interest, the supply shortages, and the stonewalling from our CAO, we would achieve our phase-one military objectives by the deadline we had set. The ground was prepared for the interim government to step down and the BBTG to be sworn in.

However, the situation facing us was tough. With the RPF inside the capital and delays dogging the naming of the transitional government, I urgently needed all of the phase-two troops to deploy ahead of schedule. I had to concentrate troops in Kigali at the expense of the demilitarized zone, leaving me wide open with two possible fronts to worry about and only enough troops for one. I was very frank in outlining for the secretary-general how the lack of logistical support was placing my troops at undue risk. The fallout from the Burundi coup had also increased the demands on the military side of the mission. I had asked for more troops to deal with the changed situation in the south but had been told by the DPKO that I couldn't have them because I hadn't requested them in my technical mission report. How could I have, when the coup hadn't yet happened? Now I reported that I was making do by stretching my unarmed military observers to the limit so UNAMIR could at least maintain a presence in the south. We tried to frame it as optimistically as possible, urging the necessary backing instead of blasting the inadequate support provided to date. When we finished our report, we shipped it off to Booh-Booh to be included in his overall mission report.

When I eventually got a copy of the document that was presented to the Security Council, I was angry: where Brent and I had presented a realistic, if positively framed, picture of the overwhelming challenges facing the mission, Booh-Booh and his staff had watered it down, giving our masters back in New York a reassuring story of slow but steady progress.

In the last days of December, Faustin Twagiramungu became a frequent visitor to my office at the Amahoro. We would occasionally sit out on the balcony and talk well into the night. The balcony faced northwest, and as the sun dipped below the horizon, staining the sky blood-red, we would look out across the hills and valleys alive with the lights of hundreds of small wood fires. We could just make out the white cube of the CND and the silhouettes of RPF soldiers as they stood guard. The twilight hush was often punctuated by unexplained gunshots.

Faustin was another Rwandan leader who had been educated in Quebec during the Quiet Revolution of the sixties. He had been close to the radical students and intellectuals who would eventually migrate to the separatist cause of the Parti Québécois. One of the people he met during this period was René Lévesque, who became the PQ's leader. During our long conversations, he reminisced about his student days in Canada and the radicalism of his youth. I think he found that our shared history made it easy and natural for him to discuss the complex situation facing his country.

When he came to see me on December 30, it was late and he was on his way to another of the interminable meetings the politicans were holding to decide the final lists for the representatives in the transitional government. According to Arusha, the BBTG was to be a coalition of Rwanda's five signatory parties: Faustin's MDR; the ruling party led by Habyarimana, the MRND; Lando's Parti libéral; the PDC and the PSD (both moderate parties led by Jean-Népomucène Nayinzira and a triumvirate of Fréderic Nzamurambaho, Félicien Gatabazi and Théoneste Gafarange respectively); and the RPF. But the extremist CDR party, led by the likes of Jean Shyirambere Barahinyura, Jean-Bosco Barayagwiza and Martin Bucyana, whose ideology was blatantly fascist and racist, had refused to sign on with Arusha and as a result, was shut out of the transitional government. That did not prevent its members from infiltrating the official parties and whipping up public paranoia and hysteria in their propaganda rag, *Kangura*, and over RTLM.

In the Arusha negotiations, Lando's PL had been allocated the powerful justice portfolio, and the RPF had been given the interior ministry, which in theory would enable them to investigate, charge and try individuals for corruption, murder and other crimes. This ability undoubtedly worried many of the current power-holders in Rwanda, who had money in their pockets and blood on their hands. According to Faustin, the biggest fear of the former ruling party was that once the transitional government was installed, the PL and the RPF would see to it that the president and many of his entourage were clapped in jail for crimes committed during the regime. That night, Faustin also told me that President Habyarimana was trying to manoeuvre around the installation of the BBTG and that his direct interference was one of the major factors behind the political impasse.

I remember Faustin's voice rising with concern and anxiety as he described how that manoeuvring was playing itself out and why the lists of the representatives to the BBTG kept changing. A woman named Agnès Ntambyauro was agitating for a position in the justice ministry, an appointment that was being blocked by Lando, even though she was a member of the PL. Lando was also having trouble with his party president, Justin Mugenzi. Both Ntambyauro and Mugenzi were known to be extremists who had joined the shadowy group that called itself Le Power, or Hutu Power. There were rumours that Mugenzi was being paid off by Habyarimana's henchmen to stir up trouble within the PL.

I told Faustin I understood his worries but urged him to find some way to rally the moderates in other parties in order to get the political process on track. If the installation of the BBTG was further delayed, he risked losing the support of moderates inside the army, the Gendarmerie and the communal police, who we knew supported Arusha. Many of these military moderates were taking great personal risks by doing their utmost to co-operate with UNAMIR. He and the rest of the politicians had to do the same if we were to have any chance at success. I had hoped to inspire him, but he left me that night unpersuaded.

...

The holidays had passed in a blur of meetings, as everyone scrambled to make the last possible window for the installation of the BBTG. This last official round of discussions was held at the rotunda inside the Amahoro complex. I attended all of the meetings and even agreed to chair some of them. Booh-Booh, before he went on holiday, hadn't been able to get any forward momentum. By New Year's Eve, the rifts in the PL and Faustin's MDR were becoming even more marked, and a threatening tone edged the debate. As the clock ticked down on 1993, I could feel my energy and optimism ebbing. When the meeting broke up close to midnight, I was depressed and exhausted. I hadn't slept much in weeks and I just wanted to go home and crash.

As I was packing up, Brent slipped into my office with a twinkle in his eye and suggested that we go up to the New Year's Eve party that our officers had organized at the Meridien hotel. I didn't really feel like it but knew I should go. As soon as we entered the party room, the place erupted. The guys had hired a live band, which tore into a wonderful set of African tunes that started my blood pumping. I couldn't resist. I started dancing and didn't stop for a good two hours. At first, my troops couldn't quite believe what they were seeing and joined in a little nervously. As the night turned to morning, I felt the tension draining out of me as I danced out all the frustration and disappointment.

Whatever the future held, that night nothing could touch or interfere with the wonderful bond I shared with my men.

7

THE SHADOW FORCE

I went into the office at seven-thirty New Year's morning. The civilian staff were taking the day off, and all was quiet on the second floor of the Amahoro. As I looked around, my office seemed a symbol of everything that was wrong with the mission. I could use the phone on my desk only gingerly because the scrambling device attached to it never worked properly. We had begged, borrowed, scrounged and dipped into our own pockets to buy the furniture in the room. The fax paper was doled out by the CAO as if it were gold. Everything about this mission was a struggle.

I had pushed my small force to the point of exhaustion in order to meet the first of the ninety-day milestones set out in the Arusha accords, and yet where exactly had that gotten Rwanda or us? We were still bogged down in a political quagmire that threatened to hijack the mission. We had less than three days' water, rations and fuel; we had no defensive stores (barbed wire, sandbags, lumber and so on); no spare parts; no night vision equipment; and severe shortages of radios and vehicles. Staff officers worked on their bellies on the floor because there were so few desks and chairs. We had no filing cabinets, which meant none of the mission information and planning could be properly secured. Every week in our situation reports and almost daily by phone we begged for these shortfalls to be addressed; we knew there was equipment sitting at the UN depot in Pisa, Italy, but we were obviously a low priority, and everything seemed to go to missions such as the one in the former Yugoslavia. A commander seldom has all the resources he needs to conduct a mission and has to accept managing shortages, which themselves present risks. A leader manages risk. But *everything* we did in UNAMIR was a risk because we had next to nothing.

I walked out onto the balcony, where I lit a cigar and looked over toward the CND complex, already swarming with activity. For a moment I envied the RPF their organization, energy and resolve. We were three months into the mission and I still lacked a deputy force commander and chief of staff, which meant that all the day-to-day tasks and decisions about resources fell to me. I really didn't know how much longer I could sustain this pace and the administrative hassles, which were eating a black hole in my time.

That first week of January, I had a major row with Hallqvist, which must have been heard all over the headquarters. The CAO directly accused me of manipulating his staff while he was on Christmas and New Year's leave, in order to get them to approve the cleaning, repairs and equipping of the CND for the RPF battalion, as well as building the security perimeter. I shot back that as far as I was concerned he had left the mission without making sure our requirements had been met. He insisted that he had no authority to just make things happen and no money, either, and I yelled that it wasn't me who was setting the milestones, but the politicians and the accords—but still I was damned if we were going to let this country down. Somehow in this battle, which raged for one of the longest hours of my life, we cleared the air between us. While the UN administrative and logistics systems continued to frustrate us enormously, Hallqvist and I bashed out a way to work together.

A date had been set aside for the swearing-in ceremony of the BBTG: January 5. After the acrimonious debates of late December, there was still no consensus on the cabinet, but Booh-Booh suggested we go ahead on January 5 and at least swear Habyarimana in, and then sort out the problem of the ministers and the representatives later. I wasn't sure that was a good idea. Since the SRSG's arrival, I had sworn off direct involvement with the political side of things, so I was surprised, on January 2, to receive an unscheduled visit from Enoch Ruhigira, the former prime minister of Rwanda and now Habyarimana's chef de cabinet and a close confidant.

We sat in the little conference room beside my office and talked about the political impasse. Brent had put together a schematic of the BBTG on one of the white boards we'd put up on the walls, and I remember staring at it and actually having to agree with Ruhigira: for those inside the former regime, it looked like the cards were stacked against them. The moderates seemed to have cornered most of the important government portfolios; to Ruhigira, they weren't moderates at all but "RPF sympathizers." He suggested that once the BBTG was installed, the RPF and its "sympathizers" could send Habyarimana and those around him to jail for crimes committed by the regime.

And he was right. During the Arusha negotiations, the former regime, and especially Habyarimana, had wanted an amnesty provision. For the sake of making a lasting peace, they should have gotten it. Instead, the RPF had successfully argued for a process in which a two-thirds vote in the national assembly could impeach a president or minister. In the new government, the RPF believed that all the moderate opposition parties would support them; the moderates and the RPF would assume control of certain key ministries, open the books, no doubt find corruption, present such crimes to the National Assembly for a vote, have the individual impeached and charged, and be able to discredit and punish the MRND. It struck me that all the jockeying from Habyarimana's side since Arusha may have been dedicated to blocking the swearing-in of the BBTG until the Hutu Power factions had infiltrated the moderate parties and assumed control of at least 40 per cent of the assembly, thereby blocking any potential impeachments. If there had been an amnesty included in the Arusha Peace Agreement, none of this would be in danger of happening. But what could I say to Ruhigira? All I could offer was that because of the involvement of the international community, due process would have to be observed and any impeachment would take years to organize: there would certainly be a mellowing of attitudes as time went on and the political process matured. Besides, I added, the political landscape could change significantly when the scheduled democratic elections were held in two years. At that point it might prove to be counterproductive to put Habyarimana on trial.

After Ruhigira left, I sat alone in the conference room, looking at the chart of the BBTG and wondering if there was some way of getting the RPF to bend a little and offer some concessions to the former regime. But given the sweet deal they had cut at Arusha, the RPF had shown little interest in negotiating. As far as I was concerned, going ahead with the swearing-in ceremony in these circumstances was inviting disaster. But the SRSG insisted, and after meeting with all the concerned parties as well as the diplomatic community, the day of the installation ceremony was confirmed.

On the morning of January 5, large crowds swarmed around the CND, where the ceremony was to be held. The people were noisy but not particularly threatening to the UNAMIR soldiers who were providing security alongside the Gendarmerie. Then Habyarimana arrived in a high-speed motorcade of Presidential Guards, who drove so recklessly they almost ran down some of the spectators and blue berets. The guards leapt out of their transport, tough, arrogant and armed to the teeth. As Habyarimana was hustled inside the National Assembly, the Presidential Guard commander set up just outside the gate and began issuing orders to some of his troops, who were dressed in civilian attire. They dispersed into the crowd and, moments later, the situation turned ugly as spectators started to threaten the moderate delegates who were trying to follow Habyarimana through the entrance. Lando Ndasingwa and a busload of Parti libéral delegates were swarmed, blocked from entering and terrorized. When we asked the Gendarmerie to intervene, their attempt to control the mob was half-hearted. I did not want to create an incident by having armed UNAMIR troops wade in alone; we protected those who sought refuge with us on the perimeter of the mob. I was supposed to join Booh-Booh, the ambassadors and other VIPs to watch the ceremony, but something in me rebelled. I excused myself from the proceedings on the pretext that I had to keep an eye on the situation outside.

Meanwhile, inside the CND, Habyarimana was sworn in with much pomp and circumstance. Then the proceedings ground to a sudden halt when the list of ministers and delegates was distributed. The RPF delegation realized that someone had changed the document at the last minute. Members of the Hutu Power wings of the MDR and PL were now on the list and the names of the moderates had been omitted. The RPF delegation stormed out and the ceremony ended in failure. Nevertheless, the newly sworn-in president came out of the building and beamed for the waiting TV cameras; quickly surrounded by a cordon of Presidential Guards, Habyarimana climbed into his black Mercedes and was driven off at breakneck speed. Booh-Booh and his political staff melted away, leaving me alone to explain to the RPF and to the media what had happened.

In interviews and meetings the day after the botched swearing-in ceremony, the SRSG characterized it instead as a major step forward. The delay in installing the actual cabinet of the BBTG, he said, was a minor political problem that would soon be ironed out, especially since Habyarimana had shown his commitment to Arusha by agreeing to the swearing-in. Booh-Booh and the rest of the political types seemed persuaded that Habyarimana would be able to broker a deal to break the impasse. They couldn't have been more wrong.

Of even greater concern to me was the speed and skill with which the mob had been provoked by the Presidential Guard. This was the first time I'd seen just how well the extremists and the Presidential Guard were organized and how easily they could coordinate major operations—a new security challenge we had to overcome. That afternoon I held a meeting with Luc, Tiko and principal Force Headquarters staff officers, in which we drew up a security strategy for future installation ceremonies. We'd block the Presidential Guard in its camp, control the major routes to the CND and the entrance to the compound, escort the moderates to the CND and take down any barriers that might spontaneously appear in the way of the moderate politicians. The rest of the week was spent trying to hammer out an agreement on the representatives. At one point I stepped into the fray, telling the SRSG that after the meeting I had had with Enoch Ruhigira I had begun to believe that if the RPF and the moderates could agree to make some concessions around the issue of amnesty or even on the selection of the justice portfolio, there might be a way around this mess.

One night that week I got a phone call from Lando asking me to come to his house to discuss the situation. I headed over to his place with Brent and Philippe Troute. Lando and Hélène and a few other PL members were having an impromptu meeting in the living room; a couple of the deputies were pushing Lando hard to reach some sort of compromise with Justin Mugenzi, who had split the PL and now headed the extremist, or Power, wing. Mugenzi was quite an operator, smooth and charming, and up to his eyeballs in the dirt and corruption of the regime. He did, however, control many of the hard-liners inside the PL, so getting him onside was crucial if the impasse was to be resolved. Neither Lando nor myself were blind to the risks that such an alliance implied, but Mugenzi and his wing presented a much greater danger to Rwanda if they remained outside the process and continued to flirt with volatile elements such as the Interahamwe.

It was a difficult meeting, but I kept emphasizing that the installation of the BBTG was just a stage on the road toward free and fair elections and that stalling the implementation would send a negative signal to the international community, which Rwanda was depending upon. I think my argument made sense to Lando that night. In previous meetings, he had been extremely voluble, rarely giving way or really listening to what others had to say, but now there was a definite shift. He knew how serious the situation had become and how high the stakes were. We agreed among us to invite Mugenzi to the meeting, and I sent Brent and Troute to fetch him. Mugenzi's home was surrounded by militiamen who were either protecting the politician or preventing him from leaving home. When Brent argued his way into the compound, Mugenzi's wife told him that her husband was not at home. Brent suspected she was not telling the truth; he had heard male voices inside.

Even without Mugenzi, I still thought that we might get somewhere and suggested we call in the SRSG and get his input. This idea was not met with a great deal of enthusiasm, but I was uncomfortable mediating what was potentially an important political meeting without him and sent Brent to retrieve him from his suite at the Mille Collines. It was very late and Booh-Booh did not appreciate being disturbed, but he came anyway, and we went at it for another hour or so. Though nothing tangible was agreed to, I saw a crack in Lando's armour and I left feeling more optimistic than I had in days.

The political players—the president, the two prime ministers and the RPF—with the concurrence of the SRSG, decided to try again to swear in the representatives for the BBTG, on Saturday, January 8. We moved into high gear to ensure that the ceremony happened under the tightest possible security. But on that Saturday morning we were surprised by a series of violent demonstrations throughout Kigali. Many of the demonstrators were armed with machetes, and the focus of their anger appeared to be the moderate or non-aligned members of the PL, the MDR and the PSD parties. Angry crowds prevented the politicians from getting through to the CND where the ceremony was to be held. The mobs materialized rapidly, and again, a number of Presidential Guards in civilian clothes, men we recognized, were inciting them.

This swearing-in was also foiled by backstage manipulations of the lists of ministerial and assembly appointments, and the behind-the-scenes tug-of-war between the president and Faustin. At the last moment, the president decided not to attend, and when the politicians, the diplomatic community and the representatives of the RPF caught wind of the fact that he wasn't coming, the ceremony degenerated into a shouting match.

Late in the afternoon of January 10, Faustin came to my office and insisted on a private meeting. He was shaking with excitement and fear. I took him out onto the balcony where we could talk without being overheard. Almost breathlessly, he told me that he was in contact with someone inside the Interahamwe who had information he wanted to pass on to UNAMIR. I had a moment of wild exhilaration as I realized we might finally have a window on the mysterious third force, the shadowy collection of extremists that had been growing in strength ever since I had arrived in Rwanda.

After Faustin left, I immediately called Luc Marchal and asked him to meet me in my office. I briefed him on Faustin's news and suggested he try to arrange a rendezvous that night. Though I was as excited as he was, I cautioned Luc that the person who had come to Faustin might not be telling the truth and this might possibly be a set-up, and suggested that he take my intelligence officer along with him. I worked as long as I could and then headed home to the bungalow. Brent and I were both tense with anticipation and said little to each other. I made a pot of tea, sat down to watch some TV and tried to relax, but I just couldn't settle. Luc finally got to the bungalow with Claeys and Major Henry Kesteloot, the operations officer of Kigali Sector, at about 2200.

Drawing from the copious notes he had taken, Luc described his encounter with the informant we code-named Jean-Pierre. Jean-Pierre told Luc that he had been an officer in the commandos and the Presidential Guard. He said that he had left the army to become the chief trainer for the Interahamwe, and in 1993, he had begun drilling cells of young men in the communes (villages) of Rwanda, initially under the guise of preparing a civil-guard-style militia to fight the RPF if it resumed the offensive. Jean-Pierre said that his direct superior was Mathieu Ngirumpatse, the president of the MRND party. He reported to and received his orders from Ngirumpatse, along with a salary of 150,000 Rwandan francs a month (at the time, about $1,500 U.S.). He told Luc that in the past few months, the real plan behind the training of the Interahamwe had begun to be articulated.

He and others like him were ordered to have the cells under their command make lists of the Tutsis in their various communes. Jean-Pierre suspected that these lists were being made so that, when the time came, the Tutsis, or the *Inyenzi* as Rwandan hate radio called them—the word means "cockroaches" in Kinyarwanda—could easily be rounded up and exterminated. Jean-Pierre said he hated the RPF and saw them as the enemy of Rwanda, but he was horrified that he had been drawn into a plan to create a series of highly efficient death squads that, when turned loose on the population, could kill a thousand Tutsis in Kigali within twenty minutes of receiving the order. He described in detail how the Interahamwe were being trained at army bases and by army instructors in several locations around the country, and that on a weekly basis a number of young men would be collected and transported for a three-week weapons and paramilitary training course that placed special emphasis on killing techniques. Then the young men were returned to their communes and ordered to make lists of Tutsis and await the call to arms.

I was silent, hit by the depth and reality of this information. It was as if the informant, Jean-Pierre, had opened the floodgates on the hidden world of the extremist third force, which until this point had been a presence we could sense but couldn't grasp.

Luc told us that until now the only weapons the Interahamwe possessed were traditional spears, clubs and machetes, but Jean-Pierre had claimed that the army had recently transferred four large shipments of AK-47s, ammunition and grenades to the militia. These weapons were stored in four separate arms caches in Kigali. He offered to show us one of the caches to confirm the information he was giving us. For revealing all four arms caches and everything else he knew about the Interahamwe, including its leaders, financing, links to the MRND party, the civil service, army and the Gendarmerie, he wanted all his Rwandan francs exchanged for U.S. dollars and to be given passports for himself and his family to a friendly Western nation. He also warned us to be careful about who we told about him: not only was the local civilian staff of UNAMIR infiltrated, but the extremists had also recruited a civilian Franco-African on Booh-Booh's staff. Jean-Pierre said a stream of information about mission decisions at the highest level was being passed directly to Mathieu Ngirumpatse.

To demonstrate his authenticity, Jean-Pierre said that he had helped organize and control the demonstrations that had occurred the previous Saturday morning. He said the aim of these violent demonstrations had been to provoke UNAMIR's Belgian troops. At each location, selected individuals were to threaten the Belgians with clubs and machetes in order to push them into firing warning shots. Had this plan worked, as soon as shots rang out, members of the Presidential Guard, the Gendarmerie and the RGF para-commando regiment, already mingling with the crowd, would uncover hidden firearms. The roundabout near the Presidential Guards' compound had been littered with hidden weapons and radios. The ambush would be sprung for one purpose only: to kill Belgian soldiers.

Jean-Pierre told Luc that the trap was intended to kill some ten Belgians. The leadership of the Hutu Power movement had determined that Belgium had no stomach for taking casualties in their old colony, and if Belgian soldiers were killed, the nation would withdraw from

UNAMIR. He said that the extremists knew the Belgians had the best contingent in UNAMIR and were the backbone of the mission, and they assumed that if the Belgians left, the mission would collapse. Jean-Pierre warned that the leadership was about to make a decision to distribute the arms caches to every Interahamwe cell in Kigali. If that happened, he said, there would be no way to stop the slaughter.

While listening to Luc's briefing, I made the decision to go after the weapons caches. I had to catch these guys off guard, send them a signal that I knew who they were and what they were up to, and that I fully intended to shut them down. I knew that such a raid carried a high degree of risk and might incur casualties, but I also knew it was well within my mandate and capabilities. The spectre of the peacekeeping disasters in Somalia did not come to mind. These weapons caches were a violation of the Kigali Weapons Secure Area agreement; the arming of militias violated the Arusha accords and our mandate and presented a great risk to the safety of my force. My rules of engagement allowed the use of unilateral force in self-defence, in the defence of the force overall and the prevention of crimes against humanity. We needed to confirm the existence of the caches before we acted, just in case Jean-Pierre was baiting a trap for us. But if the informer was telling the truth, we had to act.

When Luc finished his report, there was a moment of absolute silence. I looked over at Brent to find his face flushed with what I can only describe as elation. Finally it looked like we could identify the third force, grab hold of it and wrestle it down. After months of frustration, of being forced to act after the fact, we had a chance to seize the initiative.

Luc's debriefing had gone on for nearly two hours, bringing us to midnight. I thanked him for a job well done and instructed Captain Claeys to keep meeting with Jean-Pierre for more information. I then led what amounted to a council of war. I ordered Luc to have his staff begin planning four simultaneous search-and-seizure operations on the arms caches within the next thirty-six hours, and to keep this planning on a strict need-to-know basis within his headquarters. There was to be another attempt at a swearing-in ceremony on Wednesday, January 12, two days from now. Jean-Pierre represented a fork in the road. By acting on his information, we would either galvanize the political process or reveal it as a sham.

After Luc left, I decided to inform the SRSG first thing in the morning—I was gravely concerned about the security of this information within the SRSG's staff—and also to put together for General Baril a carefully worded code cable, which I would send as soon as possible. By sending the code cable directly to Baril, I was breaking the usual protocol. The standard operating procedure was to route all communications on matters of substance between a force commander and the DPKO through the civilian political hierarchy—in this case, through Booh-Booh and his office. The only time a force commander was to deal directly with the military adviser or any other concerned department at the UN was in order to discuss purely administrative matters or requirements. My decision on January 11 to send this code cable under my signature directly to the military adviser—Maurice Baril—was unprecedented. I was opening a line of communication in an area where I had no authority to do so. But I believed that these revelations from Jean-Pierre had to be acted upon immediately.[1] I ended the cable with my high school and 5ième Brigade motto: *"Peux ce que veux. Allons-y!"*

Sending the cable was also a risk on several fronts. While the code cable to New York was secure from intercept, documents often travelled through many hands before they reached the desks of Baril, Riza and Annan. In one of those ironies of life, as of January 1, the Rwandan regime had a seat on the Security Council—the luck of the rotation that saw member nations take up temporary duties on the council alongside the permanent members. As a result, the Rwandans were now privy to many secure documents concerning the mission in their home country.

I needed New York to realize that, even though I wanted to move quickly, I was not blind to the possibility that this could be a well-laid

1. For the duration of the mission I continued to communicate information and intentions directly to, and to seek direction and advice from, the DPKO without reference to the SRSG or the authority of his office. Having been head of mission as well as the conceiver of the mission, I simply continued to use the channels that had been open to me before the SRSG arrived in Kigali. At no time did the SRSG or the DPKO advise me to stop this practice, although on occasion a response to a code cable of mine would go directly to the SRSG for action.

trap to force UNAMIR onto the offensive and jeopardize our role as keepers of a fragile peace. I also wanted to make it clear in the cable that I was not asking permission to raid the caches but was informing New York of my intentions, as was my responsibility as force commander. I was finally going to be able to wrest the initiative from the hard-liners. Brent and I fiddled around with the wording for over two hours. When we were satisfied with the document, Brent raced to the Amahoro to print it out and send it. I went to bed with the firm belief that we now had a handle on a situation that had been spiralling out of control.

When I woke up the next morning after a few fitful hours of sleep, I was still in seventh heaven. I was convinced that we were on the verge of regaining the initiative or at least of throwing the extremists off-balance, making them vulnerable to defections, to panic, to making foolish mistakes. Little did I realize as I waved to the local kids on the side of the dirt road on my way to work, that New York was already shooting my plan of action out of the water.

The code cable from Kofi Annan, signed by Riza, came to me and the SRSG; its contents caught me completely off guard. It took me to task for even thinking about raiding the weapons caches and ordered me to suspend the operation immediately. Annan spelled out in excruciating detail the limits New York was placing upon me as force commander of a chapter-six peacekeeping operation; not only was I not allowed to conduct deterrent operations in support of UNAMIR, but in the interests of transparency, I was to provide the information that Jean-Pierre had given to us to President Habyarimana immediately. I was absolutely beside myself with frustration. The November massacres, the presence of heavily armed militias, a rabid extremist press screaming about Tutsi *Inyenzi* and demanding that blood be shed, the political impasse and the resultant tension—all were signs that we were no longer in a classic chapter-six peacekeeping situation. Jean-Pierre simply connected the dots, revealing that the mission—and the Arusha Peace Agreement—were at risk. Something had to be done to save us from catastrophe. For the rest of the week, I made phone call after phone call to New York, arguing with Maurice over the necessity of raiding the arms caches. During these exchanges, I got the feeling that New York now saw me as a loose cannon and not as an aggressive but careful force commander.

My failure to persuade New York to act on Jean-Pierre's information still haunts me. If only I had been able to get Maurice onside, to have him as my friend in court to persuade Annan and Riza that I wasn't some gun-happy cowboy. I know now that the DPKO was still reeling in the wake of the American debacle in Somalia, in which eighteen American soldiers were killed while attempting to arrest a warlord in the streets of Mogadishu. But I was presenting a reasonable, carefully laid-out plan that was consistent with the approach I had adopted from the very beginning: to maximize our rules of engagement in order to ensure the atmosphere of security demanded by the peace agreement. The tone of the DPKO's code cable suggested a total disconnect between me and New York; they no longer trusted my judgment to conduct an operation that, while risky, was nowhere near as dangerous as Operation Clean Corridor, which we had pulled off without a hitch. In my view the inside information offered us by Jean-Pierre represented a real chance to pull Rwanda out of the fire. The DPKO's response whipped the ground out from under me.

The deaths and injuries suffered by the Pakistani Blue Berets and then the American Rangers in Somalia must have had a huge impact not only on the triumvirate in the DPKO but on many member nations. At the time there was simply no appetite for any operation that might lead to "friendly" casualties—the whole atmosphere within the DPKO and surrounding it was risk-averse. In my code cable I had pushed for a potentially high-risk offensive, diametrically opposed to the reigning climate at the UN. No wonder the reaction had been so rapid, deliberate and unequivocally negative. Still, as understandable as the UN decision was, it was unacceptable to me in the field. If we did not react to the reality of the arms caches, the weapons could eventually be turned against us and against many innocent Rwandans.

When I briefed the SRSG and Dr. Kabia on the situation on the morning of January 11, Dr. Kabia supported me fully and Booh-Booh was noncommittal. I hoped the SRSG might help me make a last appeal to New York, but I was mistaken. He had authority to go directly to

Boutros-Ghali to argue that the DPKO's decision be overturned, but he brushed aside any such idea and suggested we follow New York's instructions to the letter. Just before going to see Habyarimana on the morning of January 12, the SRSG, Dr. Kabia and I fully briefed the ambassadors of Belgium and the United States and the chargé d'affaires of France. All of them acknowledged the information we provided and stated they would inform their respective governments. None of them appeared to be surprised, which led me to conclude that our informant was merely confirming what they already knew. I pleaded with them to help us find sanctuary for Jean-Pierre and his family, but the Americans, the Belgians and the French refused to assist. We had been able to verify most of the information he had offered us at considerable risk to himself and his family; I knew the diplomatic community had helped other valued informants in tricky circumstances, and I could not and still cannot understand their refusal.

Usually when someone from UNAMIR requested a meeting with the president, Habyarimana would let us cool our heels for a couple of days before granting us an audience. Both the SRSG and I were rather taken aback when he agreed to meet with us immediately. He greeted us on his sunny patio, flanked by Enoch Ruhigira; Bizimana, the minister of defence; Major General Déogratias Nsabimana, the chief of staff of the army; and Major General Augustin Ndindiliyimana, the chief of staff of the Gendarmerie.[2] Of the five men present, four were hard-liners and Ndindiliyimana was an uncertainty. I trusted none of them, and we were about to hand over the best inside information we had received to date. Booh-Booh led off, giving the president a detailed summary of our knowledge of his party's activities, including the distribution of illegal arms inside the Kigali Weapons Secure Area as well as the MRND involvement with the Interahamwe and its attempts to subvert the Arusha accords. It was with some satisfaction that I

2. On January 1, 1994, according to the Arusha Peace Agreement, the military leaders of the RPF, the RGF and the Gendarmerie were all promoted to the rank of major general, and other officers' ranks adjusted so that the three faces shared equivalent ranks for the coming demobilization and creation of a new force for Rwanda.

watched the presidential countenance shift from weary indifference to outright incredulity—Habyarimana denied any knowledge of such caches. It was impossible to fathom whether he was actually surprised at the information or at the fact that UNAMIR had acquired it. The SRSG told Habyarimana that New York was expecting a complete investigation to be conducted within forty-eight hours and then went on to warn him that any subsequent violence in Kigali would be brought immediately to the attention of the Security Council. The president promised to take immediate action, and Booh-Booh was certain that Habyarimana had gotten the message. But I wasn't sure what message he had received. Had this come as a complete surprise to him? Was he part of it or was he losing control of his cronies? If he was losing his grip, who was actually in charge? Rumour had it that his wife and her brothers were at the heart of Hutu Power; they were called the "*clan de Madame.*" The one thing I was certain about was that this information would be transmitted to the extremists, and the arms caches would be moved immediately or, worse, distributed.

At the end of the session, Habyarimana spontaneously asked if the SRSG and I would personally brief the president of the MRND at party headquarters. This unusual request from the titular head of the MRND suggested that a fracture may have been in the making between the hardline MRND and the extremist MRND, as the rumour mill had been hinting. When we went to see Mathieu Ngirumpatse (whom Jean-Pierre had said was his boss) and the party's secretary-general, Joseph Nzirorera, we confronted them with the information about the training of the Interahamwe and the illegal weapons caches within the KWSA. Both tried to bluff, but when we protested that we had seen members of the Interahamwe participating in the violent demonstrations that had taken place on the previous Saturday, they conceded that some of their members had been in attendance. But they blamed the violence on infiltrators and bandits wearing MRND party insignia.

That night Jean-Pierre showed up late to a rendezvous with Claeys, delayed, he said, by an urgent meeting with Ngirumpatse. He said his boss had appeared rattled by our visit, demanded that the arms distribution be stepped up immediately. Jean-Pierre then drove with Captain Claeys and Captain Deme, the other member of our intelligence team, to show them one of the arms caches, as he had promised. Deme was Senegalese, fluent in French and dressed in civvies. There were two guards on the cache, so Claeys stayed in the car, and Deme went in with Jean-Pierre, who told the guards that he was an African friend. The cache was in the basement of the headquarters of the MRND, the same building I had visited earlier that day with Booh-Booh. The cache consisted of at least fifty assault rifles, boxes of ammunition, clips and grenades. The building was owned by Ndindiliyimana, the chief of staff of the Gendarmerie, who had portrayed himself as a moderate. However, he was seen in the company of extremists, his gendarmes had been implicated in extremist actions, and now it turned out that the building he rented to the MRND had an arms cache in its basement. Where did his loyalties really lie?

I was concerned that once Jean-Pierre learned we had relayed his information to Habyarimana and Ngirumpatse, he would stop talking to us, but he continued to feed us valuable and verifiable information. I wanted to secure him safe passage out of the country, but New York said it could not become involved in "covert" activities, such as providing him with travel documents.

Before Jean-Pierre finally gave up on us and broke off communication altogether, he passed on vital information that enabled me to more clearly assess internal threats to the mission. He told us that operatives were working under civilian contracts inside the mission headquarters at the Amahoro and that one of them had been my driver before being replaced by Troute. He told us that on at least four occasions he had been summoned to listen to tapes of interviews between an MRND party official and a non-Rwandan French-speaking African who was providing political and administrative information about UNAMIR. He also gave us the road map to the structure and planning process of the extremists. By mid-January, thanks to Jean-Pierre, we had all the information we needed to confirm that there was a well-organized conspiracy inside the country, dedicated to destroying the Arusha Peace Agreement by any means necessary. Jean-Pierre disappeared near the end of January. Whether he had engineered an escape on his own or was uncovered and executed, I have never been able to find out. The more troubling possibility is that he simply melted back into the Interahamwe, angry and disillusioned at our vacillation and ineffectiveness, and became a génocidaire.

The security situation continued to deteriorate in Kigali, with incidents along the border of the demilitarized zone and in the refugee camps in the south. Having been told by New York not to move on the arms caches, on January 18 I ordered all the sector headquarters and garrisons to improve their defensive postures and submit their requests for the necessary defensive stores within the week. We then consolidated these requests and passed them on to the FOD in New York, but they were not acted upon. As a result, we never received the stores with which to construct protective shelters in our camps, which would have devastating consequences in April. We had also expected to see the rest of the Bangladeshi troops and the Ghanaian battalion arrive in theatre in early to mid-January. But none of them had yet deployed (and in fact they would not arrive until early February). My current force was burning out as we attempted to stretch to deal with the increase in operational tempo.

In the meantime, Brigadier (Retired) Paddy Blagdon, the head of the UN de-mining program, completed his assessment of the mine threat in Rwanda and finalized his proposed de-mining plan. I was somewhat shocked when Paddy told me that Rwanda's mine threat of "only an estimated 30,000 land mines, most of which were anti-personnel" was a minor one. Since each mine had the potential to kill or maim a man, woman or child, I was shocked that thirty thousand of them was considered a minor problem; but when he explained the scope of the mine assessments in Cambodia, Angola, Mozambique, Bosnia and other hot spots around the world, I understood his terms of reference. He said he would attempt to obtain funding and arrange the contracting of the de-mining program, but that it would take time. Four months later, when the war resumed, we still had not seen one dollar or one de-miner in Rwanda, and soldiers and civilians continued to lose their lives or limbs on a daily basis.[3]

On the evening of January 18, I convened a rare social dinner at the Meridien hotel for my senior officers in honour of Colonel Figoli, who was departing the mission. Figoli had been with me since October and, more than anyone, had maintained the peace in the demilitarized zone, with just over a hundred MILOBs and soldiers and every conceivable logistics and equipment deficiency. He would be sorely missed. The SRSG attended and I also invited Per Hallqvist.

That day I had also said goodbye to half the Tunisian company, who had served under Figoli's command and who were now being relieved and rotated home. The Tunisians were all conscripts who had volunteered to extend their military service in order to serve in Rwanda, and they were the very definition of professional soldiers, led by an exemplary officer, Commandant Mohammed Belgacem. This small cohesive unit was (and remained) my fire brigade. Whenever I had a problem, whether in the demilitarized zone, at the CND in Kigali or later on during the war, I turned to the Tunisians, who never once let me down. As I said goodbye to thirty of these men on the tarmac at the airport, I praised them for their service and the sacrifices they had made during the very risky days of late 1993 in the demilitarized zone. With an entire force of such soldiers, we could have met any challenge in the Great Lakes Region.

---

3. I asked for de-mining equipment to be provided to my Bangladeshi engineers, as they had deployed without any. We were sent some old, ineffective equipment, and some new equipment that the UN wanted us to try out, which the Bangladeshi engineers did not have the skill to use and with which they showed no interest in training. When we asked for usable equipment, I was told yet again that there was no money in the budget to purchase it. My Belgian contingent had a limited de-mining capability, but it was under strict national orders not to engage in de-mining operations except in emergency situations where the lives of UNAMIR personnel were directly in danger or if mines were discovered in the immediate vicinity of Belgian quarters. As a result of the bureaucratic and financial limitations of the UN, and the restrictive national policies of the troop-contributing nations, we were never able to address the mine threat in the country.

Within days of their arrival, Commandant Belgacen had integrated the new soldiers into the unit, maintaining its high standard of operational effectiveness. The Tunisians remained my ace in the hole.

At this time I was beginning to be pressured by Paul Kagame over the snail's pace of the peace process. He told me he was running out of money to feed and fuel his force. As a result, his soldiers were making dangerous incursions into the demilitarized zone, looking for food and water. If he was already facing serious shortfalls, how were his troops going to survive until the time demobilization began, three months after the BBTG was sworn in? Kagame also told me that the fact that his army had been in the field for nearly four years was taking a toll on the unmarried soldiers in their twenties, who were becoming impatient to settle down. The common wisdom was that if they were not married by thirty, they would not live to see their grandchildren or reap the benefits of being elders in their society. It was an added and very real social pressure on his force.

I had to wonder how the demobilization process was going to begin when no one had stepped forward to fund it. Because everyone had been concentrating on the political impasse, no one outside of the military division had spent time planning for this very important phase. There weren't even any meagre UN monies allotted, and the only person still trying to drum up funding from the international community was Amadou Ly.[4] I went to Booh-Booh to present these urgent requirements, and as usual he heard me out, but he never seemed to realize that, as the SRSG, he needed to take responsibility for advancing this dossier.

UNOMUR's Ben Matiwaza had reported that refugees were making their way from Uganda into the RPF-controlled area of northern Rwanda. We also had unconfirmed reports that Radio Muhaburu, a station operated

---

4. On January 26, Ly convened a round table in Kigali of representatives from humanitarian agencies, the World Bank, the IMF, concerned UN agencies, the RPF, the Rwandan government, donor countries and UNAMIR to discuss the funding strategy for the demobilization and reintegration of surplus troops. This meeting became the basis of the donor-country round table in Europe in March.

by the RPF, was encouraging the Rwandan diaspora to take advantage of the right of return granted by the Arusha accords. It seemed to me that Kagame was using the return of the refugees and the incursions into the demilitarized zone by his troops to put the squeeze on UNAMIR to bring about the installation of the BBTG. On January 20, Kagame and I met in Mulindi at his request to discuss these and other matters.

I flew up to Mulindi in one of the two fifties-vintage helicopters that the Belgian troops had brought with them. I had arranged to use one of them whenever I had to make a snap visit to Mulindi or another location outside Kigali; there was only room for the pilot and two passengers in the old beasts, and they didn't have much oomph. Still, the trip to Mulindi was a flight I loved, low-flying (as always, to avoid anyone taking a shot at us) over the undulating emerald hills. We landed on a rough soccer pitch surrounded by a fringe of trees; it looked like it had been scooped out of the side of the mountain. RPF troops scattered every which way; they used the pitch as a drill area, and there were always at least a hundred or so men training there at any given time.

Escorts met me and walked me up to the RPF compound. Kagame had a modest bungalow set apart from the rest. Birdsong and the gentle sigh of the wind in the trees were the only sounds you could hear. I found him sitting on the little patio attached to the bungalow, and he slowly unfolded his long, angular body from one of the chairs as he stood to greet me. He has incredibly powerful eyes that lock on your own, probing, searching, testing, and he wastes little time on social niceties. When we sat down, he dived right in, addressing the situation of long-time Rwandan refugees in Burundi, which was rendered untenable by the October coup. He told me that many of these refugees had fled to the safe havens of schools and church missions to elude armed mobs seeking revenge for the killing of the Burundian president. Many had no other option than to escape back into Rwanda or face death at the hands of the mobs. He said that the Rwandan refugees inside Uganda were facing similar, although less extreme, pressures from their impatient Ugandan hosts. Recent land reforms had given squatters title to the land that the refugees had occupied for close to thirty years, and the refugees were being forced out. He and the other leaders within the RPF were trying to stem the flow into Rwanda, he said, but it was hard to do. After all, the RPF had fought the war so that the refugees could return to their homeland.

As he spoke of the plight of the refugees, he lost some of his customary reserve and dug deep into his own experience to emphasize or illustrate his points. At times he would get up and walk around restlessly as he described growing up in a refugee camp in Uganda, always the outsider, the minority, tolerated but never really accepted as an equal. He showed flashes of anger as he relived his struggle to maintain a sense of self-worth and dignity against the crushing defeatism of the refugee camps. In his case, he devoted himself to self-improvement. He told me how he had fought to help rid Uganda of the dictator Milton Obote by joining the NRA, training in Tanzania, and fighting in Uganda under the current president, Yoweri Museveni. Even though Kagame was a highly regarded officer, he told me he was never able to rise to his full potential in the NRA because no one ever forgot he was Rwandan.

I knew that the NRA had accepted Tutsi refugees such as Kagame in its ranks. They had fought for Museveni because they believed that when they defeated Obote and installed Museveni, he would treat them fairly. But Museveni had had to form alliances with other tribes and groups at the expense of the large Tutsi refugee population that had put him in power. I was reminded of a tale the RPF liaison officer, Commander Karake Karenzi, had told Brent to describe the Tutsi experience in Uganda. Karenzi had said that when the hunter and the dog are after the prey, they are equals. But once the prey is caught, the hunter gets the meat and the dog gets the bones. And that is how the Tutsis in Uganda, who had served under difficult conditions in combat for the NRA, felt after Museveni came to power. The realization that they would always be the dogs in Uganda had been the impetus behind the formation of the RPF. They wanted to go home and be treated as equals in their own country.

Kagame told me the only way to resolve the refugee situation was to jump-start the stalled political process. He looked me dead in the eyes and said that otherwise the situation would only deteriorate.

Desperate people were willing to take up arms in order to reclaim their birthright. Near the end of the meeting, he leaned toward me and said, with complete conviction, "If things continue as they are, we are going to face the situation where someone is going to have to emerge as a winner." In other words, if the impasse was not resolved quickly, Arusha would be swept aside and the RPF would resume the war, and battle it out until it achieved victory. It had nearly succeeded twice before, though each time the French had intervened on the side of the RGF.

I finally rose and, with some regret, explained that my helicopter had no night-vision capability and I had to be on my way. It had been amazing to see Kagame with his guard down for a couple of hours, to glimpse the passion that drove this extraordinary man.

The next day, Friday, January 21, I went to the airport in Kigali to welcome my deputy force commander and chief of staff, Brigadier General Henry Anyidoho of Ghana, who had finally been appointed. Anyidoho is an imposing man, well over six feet tall and weighing over 120 kilos. His impressive physical presence was matched by his voracious appetite for work. He was a born commander. Like myself, he was a graduate of the U.S. Marine Corps Command and Staff College in Virginia, and he had a tremendous amount of experience from being on many operations, from the Congo in the sixties to Lebanon and Cambodia, not to mention his own country. Henry was confident, aggressive, capable and committed to the mission from the start. We liked each other at first sight.

Later that day, one of the MILOB teams at the airport searched an unscheduled flight of a DC8 cargo plane into Kigali and found the aircraft to be loaded with tons of artillery and mortar ammunition. The paperwork on the plane—registration, ownership, insurance, manifest—mentioned companies in France, the United Kingdom, Belgium, Egypt and Ghana. Most of the nations on the list had troops in UNAMIR. Brent asked a Belgian officer what it felt like to be risking his life in Rwanda while his nation dealt arms that could be used to kill him. The officer replied that peacekeeping was peacekeeping, and business was business, and the business of Belgium was arms. I cursed the double standard of the supposedly ex-colonial powers. I ordered the munitions impounded and demand an explanation from the minister of defence. I sent Brent to deliver the message to impound the weapons at the airport to Colonel Marchal at his quarters at the Meridien hotel. Luc asked whether we were authorized to seize these arms. Brent confirmed that I believed it was part of the mandate and the KWSA agreement, and Luc issued orders accordingly.

On the way back to the Force Headquarters, Brent and Troute came across a mob outside the CND. Since the RPF had moved into Kigali, the RGF and the minister of defence complained regularly over the number of visitors to the CND, charging that the RPF was sneaking in reinforcements and ammunition along with them. The RGF, the Presidential Guard and the Interahamwe usually stationed people nearby to monitor the comings and goings, often stopping and harassing visitors, so it wasn't unusual to see an angry crowd gathered there. But as Brent and Troute drove past they could see that this mob was armed with machetes and was yelling at the RPF guards stationed inside the complex. Brent ordered Troute to stop so they could figure out what was going on. It quickly became apparent that members of the mob had attacked a couple who had been visiting the CND, and were now taunting the RPF guards to try to save them.

Brent, realizing how rapidly this situation could escalate, intervened, ordering the RPF to stay inside the compound and not respond to the provocation. Brent and Troute then plunged into the crowd, certain that they would be backed up by the eight-man Bangladeshi guard unit that was stationed at the entrance to the CND. As they got to the centre of the mob, they discovered a man sprawled on the ground with blood splattered everywhere. His face had been sliced almost in two, exposing the blue-white glint of bone. Close by lay a heavily pregnant woman, her arm sliced through the bone and broken. Brent lifted the man onto his shoulder and made directly for the vehicle. As he moved forward with his bloody burden, a man with a machete separated himself from the crowd and stood squarely in Brent's way. Without a second's thought, Brent drove his fist into the man's solar plexus, knocking him to the ground. Troute raised his assault rifle, and the crowd backed off, giving him room to pick up the woman and carry her to safety. It wasn't until Brent and Troute were both back at the vehicle that they realized the Bangladeshi guards were nowhere in sight. They were hiding in their bunker adjacent to the main gate.

Brent and Troute drove straight to the King Faisal Hospital, a magnificent medical facility that the Saudis had built in the early nineties as a gift to Rwanda. The trouble was the country had neither enough qualified medical staff nor the money to run the hospital, so the Rwandans basically padlocked the place and left it to gather dust. Given that I was stuck with no field hospital, I had come up with the idea of locating my medical staff in the King Faisal, and the government had leapt at the idea. The Bangladeshi medical platoon that I'd stationed there was headed by a lieutenant colonel who was known as a superb surgeon, grateful for the facilities of a first-class hospital.

When Brent arrived with his casualties, he was greeted with the usual emergency-room pandemonium. The pregnant woman, who had been talking incessantly in Kinyarwanda on the ride to the hospital, suddenly began to weep inconsolably. A young Rwandan boy, whom the Bangladeshis had hired because he spoke English, translated her anguished cries. It turned out that she had been carrying a baby in her arms when she was attacked and she had no idea where her child was or if it had been harmed. Brent turned around and, taking Troute with him, headed back to the CND.

By the time they got there, a few gendarmes had arrived and dispersed the crowd. The assailants were long gone, but crouched against a wall across the street was a woman cradling a baby. Brent asked her in halting French if the child perhaps belonged to the woman wounded by the mob, and she nodded. Brent and Troute immediately took the baby to the hospital to be reunited with its parents. When Brent visited the parents later in the week, he found them alive and well. The surgeon, famous at home for having saved the life of one of Bangladesh's prime ministers who had been shot during a coup attempt, had done a remarkable job of sewing the man's face back together and had also managed to save both the woman's arm and her pregnancy.

The attack at the CND was not the first time UNAMIR had witnessed the targeting of innocent civilians by machete-wielding mobs intent on killing Tutsis. But in the days that followed, these incidents accelerated at an alarming rate as the failure to install the BBTG led to frustration with Arusha and UNAMIR, and the militias grew openly aggressive. It was as if a signal had been given to them to start a cycle of civil unrest, injury and death.

Manfred Bleim, the head of the UN Civilian Police Division, had arrived in late December. I had hoped that he would work quickly to invigorate the existing civilian police in Kigali and persuade them to work more co-operatively with UNAMIR. I also hoped he would be able to root out elements within the Gendarmerie and the local police who were tacitly supporting, if not actively participating in, the growing ethnic violence. My technical mission report had called for the civilian police division to function under my command, seeing as how the parallel body in Rwanda, the Gendarmerie, was paramilitary in structure. However, instead of working with us, Bleim created a totally separate bureaucracy, which jeopardized the force's communication with the Gendarmerie. Bleim and his officers made little progress on the investigations into the November killings, which remained an example that the extremists liked to use to claim that UNAMIR was not only ineffective but pro-RPF. He and his people never developed a good working relationship with the Gendarmerie and the communal police, and they never managed to gather information on or to influence the moderates or extremists within Rwanda's police ranks. Bleim's aim instead was to build an independent UN Civilian Police unit, and to help him achieve that objective he nurtured a close professional relationship with the SRSG.

The morning after the couple was attacked outside the CND, we rose and drove to work at the Amahoro only to find all of the major intersections on our way blocked by machete- and club-wielding youths. At the roundabout by the Meridien hotel, we ran into a particularly hostile mob, which had surrounded a vehicle carrying some of our civilian employees. I immediately got out of our car, followed by Brent and de Kant. Leaving Troute standing by the vehicle with his rifle cocked, we waded into the crowd. I ordered the mob to let the vehicle through, which it did, now that its attention was focused on me. I harangued them about the violation of the KWSA agreement and told them that the Gendarmerie would deal with them shortly. We headed back to our vehicle amid a torrent of verbal abuse and physical posturing.

When we arrived at the Amahoro, reports were coming in from all over the city that all the major intersections were blocked. Brent took a UN bus and a local driver to collect some of our civilian staff who had agreed to work that Saturday morning. At one location he found a man with a severe machete wound and took him to the hospital. But no amount of negotiation could secure safe passage for the bus carrying our civilian staff through the mobs. Brent decided to drop the staff off at the Meridien, and then took a circuitous route back to the Amahoro, only to come upon a man and a woman being hauled from a vehicle by another mob. Captain Claeys also happened to be driving by, and he stopped too. Brent, Claeys and Troute rushed the mob and everyone ran, leaving the couple behind. They turned out to be a Tutsi doctor and his wife, a nurse, who had been trying to get to the Kigali hospital, as the radio was alleging that there were large numbers of casualties throughout the city.

Meanwhile, back at headquarters, many of my subordinate commanders and staff officers were recommending we intervene and clear the demonstrations, using force if necessary. But no one from UNAMIR had been directly attacked and we did not yet have confirmed reports that our civilian staff was being assaulted either. I did not want us to be dragged into this and then have a shooting incident that would create severe complications for the mission. I thought that clearing the intersections was a basic law-and-order task for the Gendarmerie, who should be assisted by Bleim and his team. But they were nowhere to be found. For the most part, the UN Civilian Police Division only worked the day shift, Monday to Friday. There was no one manning its headquarters on a Saturday. There was no sign of any gendarmes, either.

Luc Marchal was already onto this mess. He tracked down Ndindiliyimana and demanded that he intervene to enforce the KWSA agreement. By mid-morning the head of the Gendarmerie had agreed. By lunchtime, his men had deployed, the demonstrations had petered out and the mobs had been dispersed. I was glad that UNAMIR had not been dragged into a firefight with an angry mob of poorly armed civilians, and I was content that we had provoked the Gendarmerie to do its job.

Within a week I would find out how lucky I had been in taking this decision. Jean-Pierre told Captain Claeys that the demonstrations had been another attempt by the extremists to entice the Belgian soldiers into using force. Carefully laid ambushes had been in place near many of the demonstrations, and once again our restraint had saved the lives of UNAMIR soldiers.

Because of the deteriorating security situation, by the last week of January we had mounted UNAMIR guards at the homes of Madame Agathe; Joseph Kavaruganda, the head of the constitutional court; Faustin; Lando; and four other moderate ministers. Kigali Sector put five to eight men at each house, and they guarded these people twenty-four hours a day. Even though I could not afford the troops, the death threats were real and confirmed. Since these persons were so vital to the future of Rwanda, what choice did I have? At that time I had only three companies in Kigali that I could potentially draw from for guard duties: two Belgian and one Bangladeshi. One of them I couldn't touch because it was committed to protecting the airport. Each company could at most protect nine VIPs. Once I'd okayed these teams of guards, I'd used up a whole company of troops. Requests for UNAMIR guards began to pour in from other moderate politicians, from human rights activists, minor party officials, even branches of the UN civilian administration who had acquired offices away from headquarters but now wanted my soldiers to guard them. I knew that the guards were a credible deterrent except in the case of a deliberate sustained assault, but that providing the guards was undermining my ability to perform all the other essential tasks that UNAMIR needed to carry out. So I refused all further requests, except the one from the SRSG—Booh-Booh's residence had been fired upon, and he demanded a personal protection section. Once again, I felt like we were losing the initiative as we rushed to protect the targets of the threats, instead of dealing directly with the threats themselves, weakening our ability to achieve other aims. By the end of January, having not yet received the phase-two deployments, I had in effect one company in Kigali doing the work of four.

• • •

In the midst of all this turmoil, I received an unusual invitation. André Ntagerura, the minister of transport and the acknowledged dean of the MRND, wanted to see me. On January 24, I agreed to meet him for supper at the Restaurant Péché Mignon, a stone's throw from the MRND party headquarters. Perched on a hillside, the restaurant had a reputation for fine cuisine and a lovely courtyard that boasted a garden and fountain. When I arrived (with Willem de Kant, who would provide some discreet security) shortly after 2100, the place was almost empty. I found Ntagerura seated at a secluded table, a small pudgy man with a jovial air about him and an exceptionally round face. His features were unusual, with exaggerated curves, and he could overwhelm you with the power of his expressions, whether of joy or anger. Ntagerura had been involved with the Habyarimana regime for close to thirteen years and had occupied some of the most influential government ministries. He was a member of Habyarimana's inner circle, and I was curious as to why he wanted to meet with me, though I had worried that accepting his invitation could be misconstrued as a partisan gesture.

When Ntagerura did not order, or offer me, any alcohol, I realized how important he felt the meeting to be. It turned out that he was another Rwandan politician who had spent many years in Quebec. He could swear better in Québécois than I could and was extremely knowledgeable about the political culture of my home province and Canada. After he spent some time charming me, he got around to the point of the meeting. The president was no longer in charge, he said, and the MRND was operating independently of him. Faustin Twagiramungu's inflexibility regarding nominations to the BBTG within his own party was the source of much of the political impasse, he said. Leaning toward me, taking care to shut up when a waiter came near, Ntagerura insisted that pursuing Habyarimana for the solution to the impasse was useless. The better road was to persuade Twagiramungu that the nominations from his party to the BBTG should reflect the wishes of the party rather than his own. He went on to address the internal problems of the PL, saying that Lando and Justin Mugenzi should just agree to disagree.

As he warmed to his subject, his essential mean-spiritedness showed through. He said that the transitional government should reflect the country's real makeup and not the sudden resurgence of a minority ethnic entity seeking to dominate the majority. He suggested that the RPF was seeking to control the BBTG by wooing the majority of the cabinet over to its side, leaving the MRND isolated. To him, it all smelled like a return to the Tutsi-dominated pre-independence feudal system.

His eyes grew wild and his voice rose alarmingly as he insisted that the RPF was going to impose a Tutsi hegemony over the Great Lakes region of Africa. He claimed that the number of RPF soldiers inside the CND complex had increased since December to more than a thousand and that RPF agents were trying to influence the local population and distribute arms. I pointed out that under Arusha the RPF had the freedom to operate like any of the other parties, and that included holding political meetings and getting their message out to the local population. He threw me a skeptical look and said UNAMIR was being far too soft on the RPF, particularly the Belgians. Pursing his lips with disapproval, he said the Belgians had been observed running after women and causing fights in local bars and discos. Stabbing the air with his chubby finger, he charged that UNAMIR had not found out who had committed the November killings and seemed to be providing escorts and protection only to Tutsis and their supporters.

Things were coming to a head, he warned, and UNAMIR would no longer be able to sit on the fence. UNAMIR was not well understood by the local population, and unless we took the initiative, we would continue to be the brunt of misinformation. He hinted that the violence and the negative press would escalate if the situation remained unchanged.

By the time we finished talking, it was close to one in the morning. The fanatic in him disappeared and Ntagerura was all civility and charm. I thanked him for his candour and deliberately gathered up the many notes I had taken. As we stood, he reached, almost affectionately, to shake my hand, patting my upper arm with his other hand in obvious satisfaction at how the meeting had gone. As Willem and I headed home, I replayed the meeting in my mind. I determined that I had to improve security at the CND. Ntagerura's attitude confirmed what we had learned through Jean-Pierre: the regime felt that the tide was turning against them. I saw that a great chasm was opening up and the only way to bridge it would be through political involvement and diplomacy at a higher plane than the fiddling around that UNAMIR had been doing. We had to find a way of reaching out to the hard-liners while not pandering to their ethnic extremism. Ntagerura, for all intents and purposes, had asserted that the president was no longer in full control of the MRND movement. Who was running the show on the extremist side?

The following day I briefed Booh-Booh and a few of his staffers on my meeting with Ntagerura and handed him a written analysis and report of the conversation for his action. I told him that we had to start pushing harder, putting more pressure on the parties to solve their dis-agreements and get the BBTG installed. Booh-Booh responded with alarm. On the contrary, he said, we needed to *slow down* the process in order to build consensus. He pointed to the correspondence that was going on between Boutros Boutros-Ghali and Habyarimana and said that we should wait and see if the president's diplomatic efforts bore fruit. I couldn't believe what I was hearing: hadn't I just told him that the dean of the MRND had claimed that the president was no longer in control of his own party? I returned to my office furious.

The next day I received from Dr. Kabia a copy of the analysis done by one of the politicos who had attended my meeting with the SRSG. Instead of getting the point that one of the major powers in the MRND was saying the president was no longer in control, this adviser concen-trated his comments on the fact that it was inappropriate procedure for me to have met with Ntagerura: "According to UN practice and guide-lines, staff members are warned that in conflict situations as we do have in Rwanda, they should not have any close ties with individuals, organ-izations, parties or factions, so as not to raise any doubts as to their abil-ity to remain impartial and objective in discharging their duties."

Rwanda was adrift, and no one either wanted to or seemed to be able to do anything about it.

I was receiving reports from UNOMUR in Uganda of increased movements of food, fuel and young men into the RPF zone in northern Rwanda. Ben Matizawa and the others were certain that the RPF was gearing up for action. The government forces were equally busy. My MILOB teams were reporting troop movements from the southern sector to the area north of the KWSA, close to the RPF and the demilitarized zone. The army chief of staff had requested permission to reinforce Kigali with elite commando troops, at a meeting he called in the office of the minister of defence, using the lame excuse that the RGF had resupply problems and needed to concentrate their troops closer to their depots in Kigali. The minister of defence then intervened with a request to deploy the military police battalion of over four hundred troops inside the KWSA in static guard duties, to relieve the Gendarmerie of those tasks. The minister argued that the Gendarmerie was burning out and needed reinforcement. I categorically refused both requests, as the Gendarmerie, although stretched, was still able to deploy its two rapid reaction companies, and the balance of troops inside the KWSA was already overwhelmingly in their favour. Even after we lost contact with Jean-Pierre, we continued to receive reliable reports that the armed militias aligned with the MRND and CDR parties were continuing to stockpile weapons and distribute them to their supporters. Both sides were hedging their bets. If the political process failed, they wanted to be ready to fight it out.

The RPF battalion sequestered inside the CND complex was beginning to display a siege mentality. Recently they had broken out of the compound on a couple of occasions, firing their weapons and forcing their way through UNAMIR roadblocks. Both the troops and the political leadership showed an increasing tendency to vent their frustrations on UNAMIR, threatening my MILOBs if they turned up late for escort duty or flagrantly disobeying the rules of the KWSA agreement by showing up armed at the Amahoro headquarters. The battalion had been penned up in the CND compound for almost six weeks, often with hostile demonstrators on its doorstep, and I thought nothing good would happen if the political stalemate continued. During this time, Colonel Marchal visited my headquarters to inform me that, because the RPF had stepped up their meetings around Kigali in order to prepare for the BBTG, UNAMIR was being swamped by unreasonable requests by the RPF for escort parties. In his opinion, this was a ploy on the RPF's part to pressure UNAMIR to act more vigorously to break the political impasse.

For a while, Justin Mugenzi had seemed open to a political compromise on the makeup of the PL's representatives in the BBTG, but then his car was ambushed on the way home from a meeting on January 19, and one of his bodyguards was killed. He reverted to his hardline stance. We never found out who had tried to kill Mugenzi. When I confronted Paul Kagame about the attempt, he said that the RPF was not involved because if it had been, Mugenzi would be dead.

Even with our best efforts to enforce the KWSA rules, Rwanda was still awash in guns; grenades were readily available in the local market for about three U.S. dollars. In early January, you'd hear grenade explosions in Kigali every couple of nights. By mid-month it was every night, and by the end of January there were several a night. Attacks against our mission or against people closely associated with UNAMIR had now begun. On January 29, persons unknown had tried to assassinate Major Frank Kamenzi, the new RPF liaison officer to UNAMIR, with a grenade; the next day someone had thrown a grenade into the Kigali Sector headquarters. Luckily there were no casualties. All these factors were piling up like dry kindling waiting for a match.

I had to find some way of gaining an edge. As far as I could see, the only way to do this was to appeal to the DPKO again to allow me to launch deterrent operations aimed at recovering illegal weapons. This time I would propose that we share such operations with the Gendarmerie, or even with the RPF where appropriate. We needed to demonstrate that we were helping to create an atmosphere of security and abandoning our reactive, defensive posture.

On January 31, I sat down with Brent to draft a detailed security analysis of the situation for Booh-Booh's action. This was to be my third formal and comprehensive military and political analysis that month. The first was sent to the DPKO with Booh-Booh's endorsement on January 5; the second, on January 21, barely got a hearing from the SRSG and was sent on to the DPKO with only a cryptic covering note from Dr. Kabia, bringing it to the attention of the New York staff. I never received any direction from New York on either document. I concluded that either the DPKO was not receiving the documents or had no capacity left to deal with the information. I decided to implement any measures I could in Kigali, keeping Dr. Kabia and Maurice Baril in the loop.

In my third report I showed how we would conduct the weapons search and seizure operations in a transparent manner using a co-ordinated public relations campaign to inform the local population of our purpose. I requested that we set up a UNAMIR-run radio station with UN equipment that Brent had tracked down, which had been mothballed in Italy. We needed to circumvent the misinformation dished out by the local media. I supported my argument by referring to the Arusha Peace Agreement, specifically article 54, which tasked the neutral international force to "assist in the tracking of arms caches and neutralization of armed gangs throughout the country" and to "assist in the recovery of all weapons distributed to, or illegally acquired by, the civilians." Booh-Booh responded quite positively to my proposal and sent it off to the triumvirate in New York.

The response I got back on February 3, signed by Annan himself, was yet another body blow. Once again, he reinforced the passive posture of the mission. He wrote, " . . . we are prepared to authorize UNAMIR to respond positively, on a case by case basis, to requests by the Government and the RPF for assistance in illegal arms recovery operations. It should be clearly understood, however, that while UNAMIR may provide advice/guidance for the planning of such operations, it cannot, repeat, cannot take an active role in their execution. UNAMIR's role . . . should be limited to a monitoring function." They were tying my hands.

8

ASSASSINATION AND AMBUSH

February marked the tail end of the dry season. The freshness was gone from the air, and the landscape was coated with a film of fine, red dust, which sudden wind squalls would pick up and swirl into dust devils. The political atmosphere was heavy with anticipation. On February 1, the minister of defence invited me to a meeting at his office. Augustin Bizimana had always struck me as a man who was carrying around a pocketful of secrets. Though he tried to project an air of detached calm, he seemed propelled by internal forces that pushed his mobile features into absurdly dramatic scowls. No meeting I ever had with him was dull, because at any moment it seemed like he might let something slip.

But on that Tuesday morning, Bizimana decided to be uncharacteristically forthcoming. He raised issue after issue, as if he had gone through my list of security concerns for the Kigali Weapons Secure Area and was ticking off each one. He actually suggested that we work together on the problems: the banditry, the grenade attacks, the illegal demonstrations, the occasional riots. He said we needed to get the Gendarmerie to pull its weight in order to get things under control. He'd just come from a meeting with the MRND leadership, concerning the armed militias and how to get a grip on them, and he was planning similar sessions with the other political parties. He also offered to set up a meeting between UNAMIR and the leadership of the Interahamwe so that we could begin a dialogue with them and perhaps direct them to play a more constructive role in this very delicate transition period. I listened to him intently, sure my ears were deceiving me.

The door to his office was ajar, and both Colonel Ntwiragaba, the head of military intelligence, and Théoneste Bagosora, were lurking within earshot. I was very uneasy about Bizimana's sudden change of heart—just a few days earlier he had been slandering UNAMIR to the local media. However, I used the opportunity to press for an invitation for Luc Marchal and myself to attend a big security and public safety meeting we had heard about, a gathering of all the burgomasters and sous-prefects in the area, under the auspices of the prefect of Kigali. The minister seemed a little taken aback but agreed to arrange it.

On the drive back to headquarters, I puzzled over what could have precipitated Bizimana's dramatic change of attitude. The only recent event of any significance was the visit by Doug Bennett, the assistant U.S. secretary of state for international organizations. (It was customary for the state department official to visit the capitals of nations after they had taken up one of the rotating seats on the Security Council in order to brief their senior political and diplomatic leadership on U.S. policy and try to bring them onside with American interests.) Bennett had met the president, the interim prime minister, the prime minister designate, the foreign minister, the defence minister and others and, at each meeting, had stressed the importance of the Rwandans ending the political impasse and getting the transitional institutions into place.

On the following day, February 2, I had the opportunity to brief Bennett myself, in the Amahoro conference room, along with Booh-Booh and representatives from several NGOs. I was very frank about the problems plaguing Rwanda, but I wanted to get the message through to Bennett that UNAMIR still stood a good chance of succeeding if we received the resources that had been promised and the authority to act. He was a pleasant fellow who listened patiently to what I had to say and asked a few insightful questions. But then he was gone, and if he actually did communicate my message when he got back to the United States, nothing happened as a result. However, his visit and the message he delivered may have caused reverberations through the hardline community, to which Bizimana was reacting.

• • •

Later that day, I travelled up to Kilometre 64 for a meeting of the Joint Military Commission.[1] The one positive thing to come out of the political impasse was that it left me more time to work out the complicated process of demobilization. One of the first steps, and a critical one, was redrawing the demilitarized zone so that the two forces would be far enough apart that their longest-range guns no longer posed a threat to each other. As it stood now, at some points the parties were almost twenty kilometres apart, and in other places, within a few hundred metres of each other. The Arusha Peace Agreement gave the neutral international force the task of redefining the demilitarized zone and persuading the former belligerents to move their forces in order to comply with it; the area in between was to be controlled by UNAMIR troops. It was yet another example of the accords leaving a contentious issue deliberately vague, and UNAMIR had to sort it out.

I had thought out the problems of this process during the reconnaissance in August. Knowing any redrawing of the demilitarized zone would be controversial, I had kept the actual plan confidential until I had been able to build up a strong enough rapport between the RPF and the RGF to present it. I had only released it publicly on February 1, and this would be the first time that any of the men had seen it. The new line of separation that I had worked out required the RGF to pull back 75 per cent of their forces a few kilometres, since I couldn't push the RPF back any farther without shoving them into Uganda.

Gathered around the rough wooden table at Kilometre 64 were about twenty people: Major General Nsabimana, Major General Ndindiliyimana, Major General Kagame, and respective staff members—this was the first time these former bitter foes had actually met. Because Kagame spoke no French and Nsabimana spoke no English, once again I provided the simultaneous translation so there would be

---

1. This was a body that UNAMIR had set up back in November, according to the Arusha agreement and chapter six procedures. It brought together the heads of the RGF, the Gendarmerie, and the RPF with UNAMIR in order to set the agenda and plan and approve such things as the details of the disengagement, demobilization, rehabilitation and reintegration of the security forces as called for in the Arusha accords.

no room for misinterpretation, and a minimum of wasted time. Again the staffs mingled easily; I was also struck by the politeness and civility that each of the commanders afforded the others. However, as I laid the map out in our makeshift meeting-hut and traced the new line of demarcation, I saw Nsabimana's face fall. He had absorbed most of the blame for the military defeat of the RGF in February 1993, and he had barely managed to hang on to his job. Sitting across the table from him was the man who had defeated him. Lifting his eyes from the map to confront me, Nsabimana demanded to know why I was asking him to retreat. Kagame kept silent.

I told Nsabimana that I wasn't asking him to retreat but requesting him to reposition his force so that both armies would be beyond the range of each others' guns, and my troops could safely interpose themselves between them. The RGF had to move because Kagame's forces had nowhere to go. But if this scenario was unacceptable to him, there was another option. If each force consigned their medium- and heavy-weapons systems, including the RGF's helicopters, into UNAMIR's care, we would not have to conduct such massive troop redeployments. From the charged silence in the room, it was clear that no one was going to accede to this new plan today. I asked them all to take it home to their headquarters and come back to me within seven days, which they all agreed to do. That seven-day period for deliberation turned into weeks, and the new line of the demilitarized zone was never resolved.

As I left the meeting, however, I thought that we had achieved a breakthrough. If the highest military authorities on both sides were still willing to meet to discuss demobilization, there was a chance that we could continue to move forward in the peace process. But I had no way to leverage these small military advances into progress on the political level. The fact was that at any of my meetings with Kagame, Nsabimana or Ndindiliyimana, all three were far better briefed on the political situation than I was. The relationship I had been able to foster with Booh-Booh when he first arrived had been disrupted when he had gathered around him a group of Franco-African advisers who, with few exceptions, such as Dr. Kabia and Beadengar Dessande, were hostile to me. We were not a cohesive team.

Prime among the group was Mamadou Kane, Booh-Booh's chief political adviser and the leader of this clique. From the moment he landed in Kigali in mid-December, he manoeuvred constantly to increase his authority, his salary and his rank. In just two months, he managed to get himself promoted twice, until in UN terms he outranked me and just about everybody else in UNAMIR except Booh-Booh. In the end, Booh-Booh and the clique became isolated from the rest of the mission; the right hand never knew, let alone understood, what the left hand was doing.

The next day, Luc and I attended the town hall meeting on public safety and security in Kigali. It was packed. We were seated at a long table on the podium along with an impressive gathering of politicians, ministers and local officials. The meeting started at about ten in the morning and ran non-stop for six hours, with more people trying to squeeze into the room the whole time. UNAMIR took a lot of questions, some posed by ordinary citizens from the floor, which gave me insight into how the political stagnation was affecting their lives. People complained that the government was no longer really governing: a lot of salaries were not being paid, public schools were closed and government-sponsored medical care had been starved of resources. They were extremely disturbed by the increased banditry and lawlessness. Even so, the local leaders and the ordinary citizens had not given up but wanted to find solutions. They asked good questions and listened attentively when Luc and I explained the mission mandate, making it very clear why we weren't able to achieve all the objectives spelled out in the Arusha accords. They wanted us to do more to control the violence and hoped that we would take on the security of Kigali with the Gendarmerie working under our direction, and were disappointed in the limits set on our mission.

It was clear that the general public still did not know what all the blue berets running around in white vehicles really meant. I cursed the DPKO and the FOD in my heart for not understanding the vital need the mission had for a radio station or for a competent public information office so that we could build on the desire of the vast majority of Rwandans to reach out with both hands for peace. After the endorsement of UNAMIR by the crowd, the ministers at the table each pledged their support for UNAMIR, even encouraging us to go after arms caches in order to get a tighter grip on the KWSA. Ndindiliyimana appealed to me once again to ask the UN for non-lethal riot gear so that his gendarmes could control the violent demonstrations without having to resort to lethal force. One of the politicians even suggested that the minister of information and his office be utilized to help us get our message out.

Afterwards, I visited Booh-Booh to fill him in on the highlights of the meeting, and he seemed quite encouraged by the news. I then asked him point-blank once again when he expected the other components of his staff to arrive. We needed legal advisers to help work out solutions to the stalled investigations into the November killings and provide us with expert guidance. For instance, did our rules of engagement authorize us to defend an ex-belligerent who was attached to our force? I was thinking of the assassination attempt against Major Frank Kamenzi, the RPF liaison officer to UNAMIR. We also needed human rights workers to help us find solutions to the ethnically motivated violence and to liaise with the many activists and organizations in Rwanda, who had a wealth of information but would not share it with us. The NGOs for the most part treated UNAMIR as if it was one of the belligerents, and handed their excellent information over to the international news media, not to us.

Above all, we needed a humanitarian coordinator and workers to help manage all the different NGOs and UN agencies who were dealing with the various crises in the country and to handle the future challenge that returning Rwandan refugees would create when they flooded back into the country once the BBTG was established. I told the SRSG that we desperately needed these advisers and coordinators so that when the people had questions, we could actually answer them professionally. We had been in theatre for over three months, and we were still ineffective in these critical areas. Booh-Booh knew these issues were important, but seemed reticent to throw his weight around. I left his office believing that there was never going to be a way of moving forward.

I took it upon myself to lobby the French, German and Belgian ambassadors for riot gear for the Gendarmerie, but neither country would commit those resources. This unwillingness puzzled me, as these countries were the first to condemn civil violence and urge the Rwandan gendarmes not to overreact. But when they had the opportunity to actually commit some resources to match their words, they did nothing.

In the meantime, the bill was coming due for Rwanda. The political impasse was upsetting the country's principal creditor, the World Bank, which was threatening to cut Rwanda off from financing if the BBTG was not in place by March 1. Once the World Bank actually cut off funding, it would take six months for the institution to re-establish it; the chain reaction from other nations and organizations would be disastrous. It could lead to a total economic collapse in Rwanda, and the result would be more violence. We would find ourselves in a situation where ordinary people, such as the ones who had come to the meeting, would begin to wonder whether the oppressive but stable rule of Habyarimana was preferable to the current insecurity and hardship.

The other dire economic news came from a preliminary report on the demobilization process. The IMF and World Bank study on implementation wouldn't be completed before mid-March; that study would spark other planning exercises and studies. As a result, it would be another three to six months before the funding was in place and we could start demobilizing troops. The IMF and the World Bank also decided to off-load to us the first four months of taking care of the basic needs of the demobilized soldiers, at a cost they projected as close to $12 million U.S. But if all the potential troops—as many as forty thousand angry, hungry men—arrived at the demobilization centres at the same time, which was highly likely since neither the RPF nor the RGF would want to carry on supporting them once they could hand over the responsibility to us, we calculated that the cost would be more like $36 million U.S. We were supposed to carry this burden of demobilizing, retraining and integrating these forces over a nine-month period, when we couldn't even get our small peacekeeping force properly funded. The IMF and World Bank obviously did not understand the severe financial restrictions that UNAMIR was suffering under, and were in the middle of creating a plan that could never be successfully achieved.

Seeking to build momentum through the Joint Military Commission,

I once again proposed opening the major roadway that connects Rwanda with Uganda to commercial and humanitarian traffic. Except for the occasional aid convoy, the road had been closed since the hostilities in February 1993. It was well-built and still in good shape, though the bridge between Rwanda and Uganda had been damaged in the conflict and needed to be repaired, and the road would need to be swept clear of land mines. I was sure both tasks could be easily accomplished by the Bangladeshi engineers that I had stationed in Byumba near the demilitarized zone. Since the road sliced through parts of the zone controlled by either force, to open the road would require a major gesture of co-operation between them.

I planned for mixed RPF and RGF patrols, supervised by UN observers, to monitor the road; the larger aim was to build a rapport between the two forces. This time Bizimana readily agreed to my plan, but the RPF flatly refused, insisting that given the current political situation, they couldn't agree unless we opened the southern portion of the road first, from Mulindi to their compound in Kigali. I was angry at their inability to see beyond their own self-interest. Ordinary Rwandans were starving because humanitarian aid couldn't be properly distributed, and the bottle neck was not the section of road from Kigali to Mulindi. I was finally able to persuade the RPF to let me open the road to humanitarian convoys and UN staff, but they maintained their checkpoints along the route and refused to allow commercial or civilian traffic to flow freely through the area. Once again, the RPF proved how unwilling it was to give up any of its winning cards.

Things were coming to a head in Rwanda and also within the mission. On February 13, Per Hallqvist submitted his resignation. Mamadou Kane had pushed Hallqvist too far in ordering accoutrements. Booh-Booh's residence was already palatial, but Kane also insisted that the SRSG be ferried around the country in grand diplomatic style. At one point, Kane ordered the purchase of two Daewoo Super Salon vehicles and more furniture for Booh-Booh's residence, including oriental carpets and expensive easy chairs. Kane had also commandeered a Land Cruiser and driver so that Booh-Booh's staff could run errands and do shopping, even as my MILOBs made do with too few vehicles. Hallqvist refused to purchase many of these items and complained repeatedly to the SRSG about Kane. But Kane enjoyed Booh-Booh's patronage, friendship and confidence, and in exasperation, the SRSG told Hallqvist not to approach him on any of these issues but to speak directly to Kane. Hallqvist was furious. In a long and damning letter that itemized his problems with Kane, Hallqvist resigned, taking his complaints with him to New York.

His resignation couldn't have happened at a worse time. The Bangladeshi contingent had completed its deployment on January 30, and the Ghanaian contingent had begun to arrive on February 9; in the space of two weeks, roughly 1,200 soldiers arrived at Kigali airport, ready to be accommodated and absorbed into their new duties. I personally greeted most of the flights to welcome the troops and their officers. When the Bangladeshis had arrived at the end of January, their commanding officer, Colonel Nazrul Islam, invited me to address them at their quarters at the Amahoro Stadium. He and his soldiers were exemplars of the old British colonial standards of dress and deportment. When I entered the soccer pitch at the Amahoro to address the newcomers, I was rather astonished at the sight of more than six hundred troops sitting several rows deep on the field, impeccably dressed and perfectly aligned. As my words of welcome and inspiration were translated for them, I realized that none of these men understood French, English or Kinyarwanda; only the officers spoke any English at all. The soldiers demonstrated strong personal discipline, deportment and excellence in drill. But I soon found out that this was the extent of their skills; they were as fragmented a collection as their large advance party and equally reliant on UNAMIR for the necessities of life and of soldiering.

The Ghanaians were a different story. Since they were moving directly north to their place of duty in the demilitarized zone, I addressed them as they arrived at the airport. To the amazement of their officers and NCOs, I motioned for the whole group of two to three hundred troops to gather around me—I practically disappeared inside the circle of blue berets as I spoke to them about the importance of their mission to Rwanda and the major role that they would play in its success as my eyes and ears in the demilitarized zone. These men were generally tall, well-built and had a determined air about them. Though not as practised on the parade ground as the Bangladeshis, they bore the signs of a well-led, cohesive unit. They would distinguish themselves over the next couple of months and really come into their own during the war. They led the way on every new front and never wavered. They did not wait for supplies to come to them (if they had, they might have waited forever); they improvised, bartered and bent the rules, scrounging with the best of them. I felt a kinship with these men; after independence in the early sixties, the Ghanaian army had been trained by Canadians, and they shared our ability to make a military silk purse out of a sow's ear.

With them came a worthy successor to Colonel Figoli, the new demilitarized zone sector commander, Colonel Clayton Yaache, who was to become famous during the war. Sturdily built, bright, keen and unflappable, he brought the demilitarized zone under control in very short order and became a welcome addition to my group of immediate subordinates. He would distinguish himself during the genocide with his leadership of the emergency humanitarian cell within UNAMIR.

It was a good thing the Ghanaians were expert scroungers. Although a considerable staff effort had gone into identifying the interim requirements of these troops, Hallqvist and his civilian staff had not been able to arrange for their immediate needs for food and shelter. I felt we were being dragged backwards to the mad scramble of November and could ill afford the chaos. The Bangladeshis had nothing except their personal kit and weapons and weren't expecting anything to arrive from home. I didn't even have a proper kitchen for the eight hundred troops in the Amahoro Stadium, who had been making do with an outdoor affair and no proper sanitation. I had been begging Hallqvist for the funds to build a proper structure with basic plumbing facilities to no avail. Now he was gone. While Henry Anyidoho assured me that the Ghanaians would eventually be fully supplied, their equipment and stores were being shipped by slow boat from Ghana to Dar es Salaam and then had to travel by vehicle across eastern Africa to Kigali, a process that would take three months. I needed troops kitted and functional and deployed in the demilitarized zone as soon as possible.

With no facility to take care of them in Kigali, we shipped them out to Byumba, where they were accommodated in a school built by the Canadian International Development Agency (CIDA). We cobbled together what we could for them, undoubtedly breaking every rule in the UN book, with the help of Christine de Liso, a civilian staffer who became the acting CAO after Hallqvist left.

On the evening of February 13, we held another all-party meeting at the Amahoro; the next day was yet another deadline for the installation of the BBTG. We applied the code name "Grasshopper" to events such as these, which required a very high level of security. We provided UNAMIR escorts for most of the moderates and the RPF; the MRND was taken care of by the RGF; the PL, the MDR and many of the dissenting members or extremist factions had gendarmes. I would often wander off during a break in these sessions to watch the different groups of soldiers and militias milling around in the parking lot, all armed to the teeth and hyper-vigilant. We never had a shot fired in the numerous Grasshopper-coded events that we arranged, but the manpower required for these meetings put an added stress on my troops stationed in Kigali.

Near the beginning of this meeting, Booh-Booh announced that there were not going to be any more meetings: tonight they would solve the impasse. He then looked up from his notes to discover that the MRND representatives had not bothered to show up. There was an awkward pause and some stifled laughter before the politicians settled down and began marching out the same tired, circular arguments.

During the general discussion, an idea came up, which I had also been mulling over: why didn't we swear in those deputies and ministers on whom everyone had agreed, set up the transitional government, leaving the few positions that were so contentious unfilled, and then let the new government sort it out? At least then we could satisfy some of the conditions required for continued financial support from the international community, as well as send a message to Rwandans that we were advancing toward a solution instead of remaining stuck. The PL and the MDR shot this idea down in flames, worried that the Power wings would be given their parties' allotted portfolios and assembly seats. After a couple of hours of wrangling, Booh-Booh suddenly pounded the table, startling us all, and got up, knocking his chair over in his haste. This meeting was going nowhere, he announced emphatically, and he was not going to waste any more of his time. In fact, he refused to chair any more such meetings. He packed up his things and stormed out of the room, leaving the rest of us dumbfounded.

Even though it was evident to me and just about everybody else left in the room that there was no point in staging another swearing-in ceremony, Booh-Booh contacted me later that night to make sure I had all the security arrangements in place for the affair. The following day I geared up for another day of escort details and crowd containment, but this time none of the parties showed up. Even the RPF, who were just on the other side of the complex, couldn't be coaxed into making an appearance. The only people who were there were Booh-Booh, some ambassadors and the press.

Demonstrators crowded around the complex, egged on by the Interahamwe and the usual cadre of Presidential Guards dressed in civilian clothes. Denied the spectacle of the ceremony, they began to get ugly. The brief flash of candour and accommodation that we had witnessed at the beginning of the month had now vanished without a trace.

In the second week of February, my intelligence officers managed to recruit an informer from inside the Interahamwe who added details to Jean-Pierre's original revelations on arms caches and militia training. The informer told us that the MRND was behind a series of grenade attacks that had been carried out against Tutsi families, moderate businesses, Kigali Sector headquarters and Major Kamenzi. We also had gotten a report on February 7 from UNOMUR that several reliable sources from the NRA "had intimated to UNOMUR officers that resumption [of hostilities] between the RPF and the RGF could start this week, as a result of [the] stalled swearing-in" of the BBTG. Then we received information that death squads were being formed with the intention of assassinating both Lando Ndasingwa and Joseph Kavaruganda, the president of the constitutional court. When UNAMIR warned both men of these threats, neither of them was surprised, as they usually knew more than we did about the serious threats against their lives. The informant indicated that the masterminds behind the death squads were the brothers-in-law of President Habyarimana. Although we had no way of confirming the information, I was certain that there was more than a grain of truth in it—it was common knowledge among diplomats, moderate politicians, the NGOs and expatriates. I thought it was imperative to show in some way that UNAMIR was aware of the Machiavellian plots and was determined to shut them down, but how was I going to do it?

Since my last restricted code cable from Annan, I had kept pressing the DPKO on the issue. On February 15, I received support for deterrent operations from a totally unexpected source. Dr. Kabia passed on to me a code cable from New York, asking us to help the UN respond to a letter that the secretary-general had received from Willy Claes, the Belgian foreign minister. As a result of Luc Marchal's persuasive discussions with the authorities in Brussels, Claes was endorsing my call for deterrent operations, warning that if UNAMIR did not take a more assertive role, the political impasse could lead to "an irreversible explosion of violence." Finally, I had somebody on my side who might be able to persuade New York to give me greater leeway.

I quickly drafted a response to address Claes's concerns, adding public security measures to my existing plan for arms recovery operations, and walked it over to Booh-Booh's office. The SRSG seemed open to my suggestions, though I found out much later that he had sent my proposal to Annan's office but had not included it in his reply to Claes. Instead, Booh-Booh downplayed the information we had gathered on the distribution of weapons and training of recruits for the militias to Claes and emphasized in the strongest terms the strict limitations on the mission.

Two days later the triumvirate in New York, advised by Hedi Annabi, sent a code cable responding to my revised arms recovery and public security plans and again shot them down. The response stressed that "UNAMIR cannot and probably does not have the capacity to take over the maintenance of law and order, in or outside Kigali. Public security and the maintenance of law and order is the responsibility of the authorities. It must also remain their responsibility, as is the case in all other peace-keeping operations." I remember sitting at my desk, reading this reply as a particularly violent gust of wind whistled its way through the corridors at the Amahoro, rattling windows and slamming doors.

As the month wore on, I became even more concerned about the condition of my force. The armoured personnel carriers I had requested months ago had arrived from the UN mission in Mozambique on January 30. I had requested twenty. Only five of the eight APCs that actually arrived were in working order. They came with no mechanics qualified to operate them, no spare parts, no tools, and operating manuals in Russian. A hundred more vehicles, principally SUVs from the closing of the Cambodia mission, had been shipped to Dar es Salaam, where they had been vandalized while they were sitting in port; the Tanzanians would not let me send UNAMIR troops to guard them, and the UN had no capacity to provide security. The UN signed a transport contract with the lowest bidder, who hired inexperienced civilian drivers to convoy these vehicles over a thousand kilometres of African dirt roads to Kigali, and on the trip, about ten of the vehicles were lost. By the time the convoy arrived, just under thirty vehicles were functional, though they were missing everything from windshield wipers to seats, and many of them had been stripped of their radios. We could not find the spare parts or expertise in Rwanda to repair them.

Both Luc and I wanted to increase our firepower, particularly at the airport. I requested ammunition, some heavier weapons, mortars and the like—none ever came. The Belgians had used up a lot of ammunition in training exercises and never replaced it, since the UN and the Belgians could never agree on who would pay. The UN or Belgium should have resupplied me and quibbled about the cost later.

Though I had requested a further forty-eight unarmed observers in December in order to deal with the confirmed reports of recruiting in the Burundian refugee camps by both the RPF and the RGF, the SRSG had not supported my request, and I had not received them. As it stood, I had only six unarmed military observer teams available to search the camps; they could do little beyond verifying the reports. As well, the ceasefire along the demilitarized zone was increasingly fragile. On February 11, there had been a major violation about thirty kilometres northeast of Byumba at a place where RGF and RPF forces were stationed on either side of a river. Apparently, an RGF soldier had opened fire on a group of RPF troops collecting water. In the short firefight that followed, three RGF soldiers were killed and another five injured, and a number of civilians caught in the crossfire were wounded, and one of them killed. Colonel Tikoka produced a new deployment plan in order to reinforce the demilitarized zone, but the moves he suggested would come at the expense of the other sectors.

When I addressed these needs with General Baril, he told me that I shouldn't make such major requests on an ad hoc basis. Instead I should include these needs for consideration in the six-month mission report due in March. This meant that even if the increases were approved, I wouldn't see any new troops before the summer.

On February 17, General Uytterhoeven, the Belgian army's inspector general, and Colonel Jean-Pierre Roman, the Para-Commando Brigade commander, arrived in Kigali for a four-day visit. I was very happy to see these gentlemen. I needed to talk with the Belgian higher command and straighten out some problems I was having with their contingent. We had been told that in March, the UN intended to replace the battalion of para-commandos in Kigali with an ad hoc battalion put together from Belgian para-commandos and Austrian soldiers. I was determined to nip any such move in the bud, as it would destroy any nascent cohesion within the force at a time when our military tasks were becoming even more demanding.

With the full support of Luc Marchal, I broached the serious deficiencies in leadership, discipline and training of the Belgian battalion. Even after I had spoken to the Belgian leadership specifically about the change of attitude required to successfully conduct a chapter-six mission, the battalion did not change its approach. Belgian soldiers were often frustrated by the patient negotiations required of peacekeepers on a mission such as ours, where building a relationship of trust and co-operation with the local population was just as important as setting up roadblocks to check for smuggled weapons. They saw themselves as the *crème de la crème*, as vastly superior soldiers to their UNAMIR colleagues. They seemed to view the mission as a sort of Club Med assignment where their recreational and vacation needs were to be met and where any training they undertook was designed to help them meet the para-trooper evaluation they would face when they returned to Belgium. This serious deficiency in leadership, coupled with disciplinary prob-lems and the lack of mission-specific training, created conflicts between the mission, the RGF and the general population.

There had been dozens of incidents of disciplinary infractions. The Belgians were constantly being caught out of bounds in nightclubs that had been restricted for their own safety. They drank on patrol and got into barroom brawls, seeming to take their cue from the French troops who went dancing and drinking at Kigali Nights, the local hot spot, with their personal weapons. One night, several drunken Belgian sol-diers completely trashed the lobby of the Mille Collines, which was Kigali society's favourite watering hole. The Belgians often refused to salute or pay proper respect to officers of other contingents, especially officers of colour. There were Belgian soldiers who went absent without leave into Zaire and got up to heaven knows what until they were detained by the authorities. In one of the more serious incidents, in order to celebrate Belgian Airborne Day, the battalion commander, Leroy, held a party for the unit at the Meridien hotel, to which VIPs were invited. In the spirit of the occasion, the pilots of the Belgians' Hercules aircraft, which were parked at the airport for medical evacua-tion purposes, decided to buzz the hotel. While making a low pass over the Meridien, the plane overflew the CND complex, prompting an immediate reaction from the vigilant RPF battalion. After being cooped up for nearly two months, they were a little paranoid, and scrambled to the roof where they opened fire on the aircraft. In this case, as in many others, the culprits were formally charged by Luc Marchal and sent home to face punishment.

It was also brought to Luc's attention, and then to mine, that a few of the Belgian staff officers were fraternizing with Tutsi women. RTLM and the scurrilous extremist newspaper *Kangura* had gotten wind of this and exploited the story fully, accompanying lurid text with obscene cartoons that implied that I, too, was involved in such behaviour. As far as I'm concerned, there is no such thing as consensual sex between soldiers and the local civilian population in a war or conflict zone. The Belgians were also destroying the credibility of UNAMIR by giving fodder to the rumours that we were pro-Tutsi. Luc summoned these officers to his office, read them the riot act and confined them and the whole battalion to quarters. A few days later, a couple of the officers had the temerity to come to my office to protest Luc's action. I told them that Luc not only had my full support, but that I would personally write to their chief of staff.

Still, it seemed that no amount of censure and disciplinary action from me or from Luc could correct the rot that was eating away at this contingent. At the beginning of February, one of my Belgian patrols had roughed up Théoneste Bagosora at a checkpoint in Kigali. Bagosora was travelling in a clearly marked military vehicle and had presented his identity papers to the patrol, but the Belgians forced him, his driver and his bodyguard out of the car and proceeded with a humiliating search, all the time pointing their weapons at them. A Belgian officer finally intervened.

The *coup de grâce* came just before General Uytterhoeven and Colonel Roman arrived. A group of Belgian soldiers in civilian dress forced their way into the home of one of the heads of the extremist CDR party, Jean-Bosco Barayagwiza, and assaulted him in front of his family. The CDR had close links to RTLM, which often carried negative stories about the Belgians. The soldiers badly beat the politician on his own doorstep and, just before they left, one of them aimed a gun at his head and warned him that if he or his party or the local media ever again insulted or threatened Belgium, Belgian expatriates or the Belgian contingent of UNAMIR, they would return and kill him. Barayagwiza immediately went public and wiped out any of the hard-won public sympathy we had achieved earlier in the month. I ordered a full investigation to identify and charge the offenders, but a wall of silence descended over the unit, and we never did uncover the culprits.

It was with this thick file of incident reports that I confronted General Uytterhoeven and Colonel Roman. I told them that their troops were not only a discredit to the Belgian army but were seriously undermining the credibility of the mission. Their pre-deployment training must have been woefully inadequate for them to come into this chapter-six mission with such aggressive and destructive attitudes; worse, despite my clear instruction to their leadership, nothing had changed. I reminded them that through Luc Marchal, I had formally requested a copy of the training program that the Belgian replacement battalion was undergoing for the mission so as to avoid a similar situation with the incoming troops. I knew that by being so brutally frank, I risked damaging the relationship between myself and the Belgian military authorities, but I had no option—the Belgian para-commandos were putting the mission at risk.

Later, Colonel Roman came to my office on his own in an attempt to smooth things over and defend his troops. He thought he should explain to me the idiosyncrasies of airborne forces. They were trained to be very decentralized and inventive, he said, and therefore tended to be a little less responsive to their officer corps than regular infantry troops. They needed to spend time training in order to keep up their high level of efficiency. The undercurrent in all this was that I was over-reacting and "boys would be boys"—exactly the outmoded notion I was fighting in the Canadian military. I countered by telling Colonel Roman that his troops spent so much of their time keeping their skills up that they had gone through much of my valuable ammunition, and that his government didn't seem keen to replace these essential stocks, leaving us at risk. I told him what I had told General Uytterhoeven: unless these criticial deficiencies in training, discipline, attitude and leadership were addressed, I was considering the unprecedented step of recommending to New York that the Belgians be pulled from the mission. When I finished, the colonel was white with anger.

Coincidentally, Willy Claes was also in Kigali. I spoke with him on Sunday, February 20, as part of a round-table discussion among diplomats, NGOs, expatriates and the SRSG. I told him we had to get tougher and more active, both militarily and politically, to ensure that we could deliver a success within the time frame specified by the accords. I said that the leaders of Rwanda's nascent political parties had proven themselves incapable of rising above their own self-interest. There wasn't a statesman among them. In order to break the impasse, we had to raise the diplomatic stakes and get international partners such as Belgium to start applying real pressure, not only to Habyarimana but to all the political players, including the RPF. Claes listened attentively and complimented UNAMIR on what it had achieved to date. He left us with the impression that he was going to fight for our mission in Brussels and New York.

That same day, the Belgian politician had the opportunity to witness a couple of object lessons in Rwandan politics. Sundays were always the most difficult day of the week for my force, because that was when the political parties held their rallies. Little white Toyota pickup trucks chock full of drunk and belligerent Interahamwe and Impuzamugambi militia would zoom around Kigali, stirring up trouble. The streets were usually full of people milling around, looking for something to do, and it didn't take much to whip them up. This Sunday was worse than most. The MDR party was holding a huge rally at the Nyamirambo stadium; Faustin was still trying to sort out the split between him and the Power wing of his party, led by Froduald Karamira, the vice-president of the MDR. According to our informant, the Interahamwe was encouraging people to show up to the meeting armed with DDT "as medicine for the *Inyenzi*." By the time the rally began that afternoon, the stadium was surrounded by Interahamwe mingling with the raucous crowd, making it almost impossible for the MDR leadership to make its way into the building. When Madame Agathe arrived with her Belgian escorts, the crowd began to pelt them with stones, drawing blood. The Belgians fired into the air to break up the crowd.

That evening, at a supper given in honour of the departing Belgian delegation, Willy Claes had a front-row seat on the hair-trigger nature of Rwandan politics. The entire diplomatic community, the SRSG and myself from UNAMIR, and the leading politicians from the official parties, including the RPF, were invited. Extremists sat side by side with moderates. Still, the evening started well, with a lot of lighthearted chatter assisted by liberal quantities of food and alcohol. There was some political discussion, but it was all vague and optimistic. We were going to make another attempt at installing the BBTG later in the week, but the conversations flowing around me carefully avoided any real discussion of the impasse. I was struck again by the ability of the Rwandans to close ranks when the glare of the international community fell upon them, as if they were one big dysfunctional family conspiring to keep up appearances.

Then something quite unexpected happened. I was sitting next to Félicien Gatabazi, the head of the influential (and still united) PSD party, and a well-known Hutu moderate from the south who was very pro-RPF, who had a few too many glasses of wine and got into an intense discussion with members of the MRND about their extremist views. The more drinks Gatabazi downed, the louder and more confrontational he became, until he was almost shouting. He started to insult individual members of the MRND, accusing them of manipulating the political process and causing the deadlock, and the whole room fell silent to listen. Gatabazi had already publicly accused the Presidential Guard of training militias at the Kanombe barracks and had received a number of death threats; that night he was fearless. I tried to diffuse the situation by interrupting with a change of topic, but the damage had already been done. Staring into the eyes of the MRND extremists, I saw sheer hatred, which rose like a wall to surround Gatabazi and me. There is no doubt in my mind that Gatabazi wrote his own death sentence that night. Yet on the way home from the dinner, it was Faustin Twagiramungu's car that was ambushed. Faustin escaped but one of his bodyguards was killed.

It was as if some dark force had been unleashed. The next day, CDR demonstrators burst into Madame Agathe's office and took eight hostages. There was an uneasy standoff, but the Gendarmerie showed up to help my troops and, after a few hours of patient negotiation, managed to get the demonstrators to release the hostages.

That evening, Brent was attempting to enjoy some quiet time at home while de Kant and I were at an official dinner at the U.S. ambassador's residence. Brent had just got back from a two-week leave and was starting to unpack when the quietness of the night was shattered by the unmistakable crack of automatic weapon fire coming from behind the house. Believing our house was under attack, Brent shut off the lights and crept to the cupboard where he thought he would find Willem's pistol, but Willem had taken it with him that evening. Brent armed himself with a Canadian-issue machete (which had never been out of its sheath and wasn't even sharpened) and crawled to the phone to call headquarters. He hung up and moments later the phone rang. It was Félicien Gatabazi, who lived in our neighbourhood. He had been ambushed and wounded and was gasping, obviously in great pain. He had managed to get back to his house and wanted Brent to send help. Brent immediately called headquarters and reported the shooting, making sure that the message would be relayed to me at the dinner. De Kant, Troute and I raced back to the house just as a section of Belgian troops was pulling up. Once we knew that Brent was okay, we did a thorough sweep of the area. On the road behind the house, the Belgian patrol found a limousine riddled with bullet holes. The bodies of two gendarmes, the politician's escorts, lay nearby in a pool of blood. Gatabazi had died shortly after he had made the phone call to Brent.

This death may well have been the spark that set the whole country ablaze. The next day, February 22, we were once again supposed to swear in the transitional government. Fearing the worst, I ordered all off-duty troops to return to barracks, and cancelled all leave. Before first light, the force was on red alert and had deployed.

The next morning, moderates and extremists both took to the streets of Kigali. The extremist media immediately spun headlines celebrating the killing of Gatabazi as a victory against Hutu traitors; the Interahamwe was much in evidence. Political leaders of all persuasions literally hid from view, avoiding my attempts to contact them. The mob ruled the streets and only UNAMIR and the riot control Jali companies of the Gendarmerie were there to confront it. I restricted all unnecessary movement but increased our presence and patrolling in an attempt to calm the city. In the midst of this situation, Luc Marchal had to get Willy Claes to the airport. Once again, the swearing-in of the BBTG was aborted. Although the president did make his way to the CND, the prime minister designate and the RPF refused to attend in protest of Gatabazi's assassination.

Despite a determined effort on the part of the UN Civilian Police Division to finally solve one of these cases of political violence, not a single witness, other than Brent and members of Gatabazi's family, came forward. Kigali was alive with rumours that ran the gamut from the reasonable to the exotic. There was some talk that the assassination had been the work of a hit squad from Togo, but most people believed that extremists inside the CDR were responsible. (In fact, the case was never solved.)

In Gatabazi's hometown of Butare, in the south, there were huge demonstrations. Later that afternoon, we heard that a mob of PSD supporters had grabbed Martin Bucyana, the national president of the CDR, near Butare and had lynched him. When this news spread to Kigali, the Interahamwe militias retaliated by blocking all of the major intersections, and routes out of the city.

UNAMIR was overwhelmed by the vast numbers of hysterical and violent civilians who poured out into the streets. It was all we could do to move around. I wanted to avoid having armed UNAMIR soldiers use force against unarmed or machete-armed civilians, sure that if we fired on anyone, no matter the provocation, it would simply escalate the violence. Instead, I approached the government and the Gendarmerie to try to get them to do their jobs.

Prime Minister Agathe went on national radio to appeal for calm. It seemed like nothing would prod Ndindiliyimana into action. As well, the chief of staff of the army cleverly disappeared. When I eventually found him, he said he was compelled to abide by the KWSA agreement, which prohibited his troops from performing a task that was the responsibility of the Gendarmerie. Round and round we went as the violence increased. Over the next couple of days, 35 people died and a further 150 were injured—the majority were Tutsis and moderate Hutus. If there had been any doubt before, there was certainly none now: the poisonous pot of ethnic hatred had been well-stirred and was about to boil over.

At her request, I visited Madame Agathe in her office. She was close to tears. She told me that she understood that we couldn't do much more than what we were already doing, but she begged me not to take away the guards that we had stationed at the homes of the moderates. I assured her that until the situation was under control, I would continue to provide twenty-four-hour protection for all of the politicians who were in danger. She emphasized that my troops had to get a handle on the security situation inside the KWSA, because people simply didn't feel safe. Many abandoned their homes as soon as it started to get dark and made their way to church compounds to camp out overnight or until they felt safe enough to go home. Churches had always been a place of sanctuary in Rwanda and were increasingly becoming refuges for people who felt threatened.

She paced as she spoke, like a weary lion penned up in too small a cage. She told me that her hardline MRND cabinet ministers refused to attend the meetings she scheduled and even ignored her phone calls. She raged on about Habyarimana and how he was meddling with the political situation. She wasn't looking for advice or answers from me, just comfort and my assurance that no matter how difficult the situation became, I would not abandon her and the moderates.

As I rose to leave, tears spilled down her cheeks, and I felt a lump rising in my own throat as I pledged that whatever happened, I would never abandon Rwanda. It was hard to see her like that; she had been rock solid through all the troubled months in which I had known her. But Madame Agathe's courage and strength of purpose never wavered, and her absolute faith in her country and its people never failed to inspire me. I left her office with a renewed sense of purpose.

Later that day, accompanied by Colonel Marchal, I finally met with Bizimana and Ndindiliyimana. Faustin Munyazesa, the minister of the interior, a well-known MRND hard-liner, also joined us—I wasn't sure whether by chance or design. I asked them straight out why they weren't doing more to calm the situation. I told Ndindiliyimana that his gendarmes were not doing enough to help my troops get a grip on the riots. In defence, he confessed that he didn't really know what to do: his men were burnt out, their vehicles were breaking down, and they were almost out of fuel. Besides, he added with a significant glance at the minister of the interior, he wasn't getting any political direction on the use of lethal force. His men had no other way to disperse the crowds: no riot gear, no tear gas or water cannons. He also needed reinforcements to weather the crisis. Bizimana piped in at this point, suggesting that the RGF at Camp Kanombe could take over guarding VIPs and vital points and that he could move a battalion of military police into Kigali to beef up the depleted ranks of the Gendarmerie. With this increased force, they could impose an eight o'clock curfew in the evenings and start to shut down some of the more violent activity. This was essentially the same request I'd categorically turned down at the beginning of the month; I didn't believe that the safety and security of the citizens of Kigali was Bizimana's major concern. If I granted the request, it was quite possible that he would use those troops to reinforce Kigali, gain control of the city and potentially overwhelm the RPF battalion inside the CND complex, and the country would be back at war.

I countered by recommending that they go to the media and call upon the extremist parties to control their militias and stop the riots, then watched as the three of them fidgeted uncomfortably. Our inform-ant had indicated that the Interahamwe and Impuzamugambi militias were directly linked to the MRND and the CDR respectively. I knew as I sat there, that in the ministers of defence and the interior I was confronting extremists. Ndindiliyimana was still an enigma. I thought I could feel his ambivalence about his associates and their suggestions. I turned to him and proposed mixed patrols of gendarmes and UNAMIR troops. When he objected, saying that he didn't have enough vehicles, I sug-gested that his men ride with my troops. I told him that we had already had some success working together breaking up the demonstration at Madame Agathe's office earlier in the week. I left the three of them with the promise that I would work out a curfew patrol plan and that we would commence joint patrols as soon as I could sort out the troops and vehicles. For the time being, there was no need for the RGF to bring more soldiers into Kigali.

At about 1600, I returned to my headquarters. That morning, we had permitted the RPF liaison and supply convoy, under armed and MILOB escort, to conduct its regular administrative run to Mulindi to conduct liaison and pick up firewood, food and mail. The convoy made it out of Kigali with no problem, but later in the day, mobs again sealed off the city. After sending Tikoka to check out the current state of unrest north of Kadafi Crossroads, I decided the convoy would not be safe coming back that afternoon and issued an order for them not to return but to stay in Mulindi until the all-clear was given. But the Belgian escort deliberately disobeyed that order; they decided to risk returning to Kigali after dark with the whole convoy rather than spend an uncomfortable night camped out in their vehicles.

They had just entered the suburb north of Kadafi Crossroads, which had been a major flashpoint that day, when a grenade was tossed at the lead vehicle, followed by machine-gun fire. The Belgians returned fire and manoeuvred to get out of the ambush. One of the MILOB vehicles ended up in the ditch, and the two observers scrambled out and jumped onto one of the Belgian Jeeps; the other MILOB vehicle managed to do a U-turn to get out of there. The RPF soldiers, whose vehicle had been hit, could not. They returned fire, calling for help on their hand-held radios, and one of them was hit in the head. When the Belgians realized that the RPF had not escaped with them, they did not go back but headed for safety at the UNAMIR camp at Byumba in northern Rwanda. As soon as the RPF message was received in Kigali, two sections of RPF reinforcements burst out of the CND compound, easily overcoming the feeble protests of the Bangladeshi guards, and stormed through the city to rescue their comrades.

We were just finishing supper when the ambush was reported over our radio net. Moments later, I heard that the RPF had broken out of its compound. I called Luc to ask him to take action and then called more than a half hour later, asking for a sitrep: nothing was moving yet. I looked over toward Brent and Willem and said, "Let's go check it out." We piled into my vehicle, with Troute at the wheel, and drove like hell out to Kadafi Crossroads.

When we arrived, it was dead quiet. Although there was a scattering of houses nearby, there wasn't a soul to be seen. Not a person, not a light, not a sound. There was blood all over the road and the unmistakable grey matter we knew was human brain. We spotted the MILOB vehicle abandoned in the ditch, and near it, a trail of blood. Fearing the worst, Willem and Brent began to search around the vehicle for clues as to what might have happened. On their third pass, Willem suddenly yelled out to Brent to stop. Right beside Brent's foot was an unexploded grenade, pin out, hammer gone. A very close call.

Then Luc arrived with Kesteloot, followed some time later by a squad of Belgians, who secured the area. Brent and Kesteloot walked up the road and discovered a big old truck abandoned in the ditch. Brent looked over the tailgate and found himself looking at a dead male civilian whose skull had been split in two by a machete.

Not only had the Belgians disobeyed my direct orders to stay overnight in Mulindi and displayed outright cowardice in abandoning the RPF convoy they were charged to protect, they had put themselves before the mission, which was conduct that violated every code of the profession of arms. I demanded a full investigation and heads to roll. Luc, terribly embarrassed and shamed, agreed.

In breaking out of their compound, the RPF had demonstrated a complete lack of trust in UNAMIR, which at that moment I had to agree was justifiable. That night, I ordered the sixty-man Tunisian company to leave the demilitarized zone and come to Kigali to assume responsibility for the CND, and the Bangladeshis to return to their unit to take up less demanding tasks. I then proceeded directly to the CND to clarify the situation. When I got there, the wounded RPF soldier was being transferred to our hospital for emergency surgery. He had left a large portion of his brain at the site of the ambush. Commander Charles acknowledged that he had broken the KWSA agreement but only after my troops had failed to protect his men. I got home late that night, troubled by the failures of these troops.

That same night, the evening of February 22, Habyarimana had held a meeting at his office complex, inviting all of the political parties with the exception of the RPF. Dr. Kabia filled me in on the details. The diplomatic community, as well as Boutros Boutros-Ghali, were putting enormous pressure on the president to solve the political crisis. They didn't seem to understand that under the Arusha Peace Agreement, the president had renounced his authority over the government and had been moved over into the role of head of state. His only real power was persuasion.

At this point, many people were confused as to who really held the power. Who was responsible for governance? Was it Madame Agathe's interim government, whose mandate had expired at the end of December? Who held the final responsibility for finding a solution? Faustin Twagiramungu? Booh-Booh?

During the meeting, Habyarimana cleverly exploited this uncertainty by attempting to impose a solution. He laid out a plan whereby the warring factions within the PL and MDR would compromise by dividing up the ministerial and deputy-ministerial positions evenly. In the case of deputies whose fitness was being challenged, those positions would be decided by the courts. The proposal seemed reasonable, but Madame Agathe and the PL representatives rejected it out of hand, vociferously protesting that Habyarimana was manipulating the impasse to his own advantage although he no longer had the power to dictate such a solution. In the opinion of several of her moderate colleagues, Madame Agathe's fearless verbal abuse of the president at this meeting sealed her fate. Faustin Twagiramungu, perhaps chastened by his recent brush with death, seemed much more willing to accept the proposal. But because of opposition from Madame Agathe and the PL, this meeting, too, ended in failure, with no agreement on the lists.

On February 23, an eight o'clock curfew was declared in Kigali. With the increased presence of the Gendarmerie, the mobs disappeared and a nervous calm settled on the city. As the violence and mayhem seemed to just melt away, I couldn't get over the feeling that there was a hidden hand at work, orchestrating it all. I no longer questioned that there were direct links between the cadre of powerful ministers that controlled the interim government and the militias, but our informants suggested that there was another entity beyond them, one whose members didn't show up at meetings and whose motives we were just beginning to probe. On a number of occasions, I used Luc as a sounding board on these political–military issues and ambiguities. He and I spent hours trying to figure out where all the tracks led, but as soon as we thought we had come close to solving the puzzle, the tracks would disappear.

One thing was clear. We always seemed to be behind the eight ball, reacting to, rather than anticipating, what was going to happen. The reason for that was no mystery at all. Since January, the Rwandan ambassador to the UN, Jean-Damascène Bizimana, had had a seat on the Security Council and was not only privy to the inner workings of the mission but to the Security Council's attitude toward the mission and its many woes. All this information was obviously being fed back to the shrouded entity that seemed to be running the show in Rwanda. I remonstrated with Maurice about this situation in phone call after phone call; he told me that, yes, everybody knew it was a problem, but it would be impossible to remove him. There I was with my small team of intelligence officers who were risking their lives for crumbs of information while the extremists had a direct pipeline to the kind of strategic intelligence that allowed them to shadow my every move.

The following day I learned that the senior leadership of the RPF had been invited to attend Gatabazi's funeral in Butare. A soccer stadium had been set aside for the service, as it was to be a very large affair. I was shocked that the RPF had accepted the invitation without telling me; a high-level RPF delegation travelling the hundred-kilometre route to Butare would be an irresistible target for the extremists. We couldn't afford to lose any more ground with the RPF, so together with my staff, I built an operation to rival Clean Corridor in order to move the delegation safely to and from the funeral. There was a risk that we would be ambushed, but I was determined that this time we would use overwhelming force to respond, and I would lead the operation myself.

We embarked in a large, well-armed convoy, with the two Belgian helicopters overhead and APCs positioned along the route. At critical junctions, we passed UNAMIR soldiers who were confident and in control. All my troops were immensely impressive that day, especially the Belgians and the Bangladeshis.

It was a three-hour drive to Butare, and all along the route, word of our passage must have been announced, for both sides of the road were crowded with cheering Rwandan civilians. The RPF was delighted at the welcome; the fact that the ordinary people of Rwanda had left their schools and workplaces to spontaneously voice their support for all of us and what we represented also encouraged me enormously. At Butare, we arrived under tight RGF and Gendarmerie security and attended the funeral in the stadium, where the RPF delegation was cheered by the thousands of attendees.

The funeral went on for four hours and was quite moving, but my attention was fully focused on the security nightmare laid out before me. In the crowd were about eighteen of my unarmed observers, twenty-five to thirty Belgian para-commandos and twenty members of the RPF—and many more RGF troops and gendarmes. Behind every pillar in that stadium was a soldier, armed to the teeth either with AK-47s or rocket-propelled grenade launchers, and there were many others, equally armed, outside in the parking lot. All it would have taken was one gunshot—one overenthusiastic mourner to shoot his gun into the air—and there would have been a massacre. When the funeral was finally over, I almost wept with relief.

It was mid-afternoon when we reassembled the convoy, which meant that it might be nightfall before we reached Kigali. I stopped the convoy just outside of Butare and jumped into the RPF vehicle with Pasteur Bizimungu and Tito Rutaremara (a proposed RPF assemblyman). I wanted any potential assassin with his binoculars trained on the car to see me. We drove like that all the way back to Kigali. The trip home was as emotionally charged as the trip down; it was if the crowds of people had not moved, as if they had waited there all day for our return, and they were still wild with excitement when we passed. Pasteur and Tito were almost giddy with the joy that these ordinary Rwandans displayed as we made our way north.

After that trip, I became even more determined to launch a campaign to reach out to the local population and win their support. Luc was trying to build on our small success at the Kigali town hall meeting earlier in the month, and was conducting similar meetings in towns and villages within the twenty-kilometre radius of the KWSA. He met with local officials and citizens to explain who we were, what we were trying to achieve and how they could help; for the most part, he was warmly welcomed. I also tasked my MILOBs both in the southern sector of the country and in the demilitarized zone to not only patrol their areas of responsibility but to meet and talk with the population, to offer assistance and, where they were able, to solve practical problems, such as helping to repair a school damaged by grenade attacks. With the arrival of some old and trial de-mining equipment, we were able to clear small sections of the demilitarized zone, enabling many of the people crowded into the displaced persons camp that I had first visited on the technical mission back in August to return to their small farms and villages. These were such small steps, but at least they were positive ones.

I had been considering moving 225 Ghanaian troops from the demilitarized zone to Kigali to take over static guard duties in the city so that I could free up the Belgians for mobility and reserve tasks, while the Bangladeshi rapid reaction force trained. I had directed my subordinate commanders and principal staff officers to begin administrative preparations for such a move, when a final incident persuaded me that the decision was a proper one. On February 26, the entire senior political leadership of the RPF decamped unannounced from the CND and headed back to Mulindi, leaving only minor officials and the garrison behind them. Supposedly, they were leaving for a party congress, but they never came back. On February 27, I informed New York of my decision to move the Ghanaians before the end of the month, and we prepared a small tactical headquarters and logistics support group for the redeployment.

That day, Luc Marchal and I gave a major press conference to attempt to regain the initiative on the media side. I specifically attacked RTLM and its relentless anti-Arusha and anti-Tutsi rhetoric. I suggested that its broadcasts were nothing more than hate propaganda and as such constituted an unethical assault on the very idea of democracy and free expression. I told the crowd of journalists that the people of Rwanda were being manipulated by a well-organized campaign of fear to destroy the peace process by raising ethnic tensions. And then I launched an appeal to the people of the country to get together and, with the help of UNAMIR, hold a peace march to send a message to the forces of violence and extremism that such evil ideas did not have a place in the new Rwanda. This idea caught on, and in March we held a large and successful march through Kigali. Although our peace-building initiatives were generally successful and the situation seemed calm on the surface, ugly signs and incidents persisted.

At the tail end of February, one of our African MILOBs, who had been a teacher before joining the army, began visiting schools in remote parts of the country. At one school, he noticed the teachers undertaking an administrative exercise: they were registering the ethnic identities of their pupils and seating them according to who was Tutsi and who was Hutu. This struck him as bizarre, since children in Rwanda were not required to carry identity cards. As he visited other schools, he discovered that the same procedure was taking place. We mistakenly assumed that this was just another example of ethnicity at play in Rwanda.

9

EASTER WITHOUT A RESURRECTION OF HOPE

In March, the rainy season began—welcome, soothing. It seemed to extend the lull in the violence sparked by Gatabazi's assassination. The eight o'clock curfew was moved back to ten, and life returned to the city, but it was still clearly a time of covert preparations and hidden agendas.

The RGF was improving its defensive positions in garrisons just below the demilitarized zone and within the ten-kilometre radius of the KWSA. On a Sunday in late February, I had taken a helicopter to check up on an intelligence report. One of Tikoka's Southern Sector observers who had been scouting around the refugee camps south of Butare had seen two green Kigali city buses being loaded with young men and boys. He followed the buses for as long as he could and speculated that they were headed toward the RGF camp at Gabiro, on the eastern side of the demilitarized zone close to Kagera National Park, the most secluded government forces outpost in the area.

I told the pilot to land just outside the Gabiro camp gates. The major who opened up for me was especially nervous about the surprise visit as his commander was away. He led me on a relatively deliberate tour of the camp; the day was balmy and there was absolutely nothing going on. In the medical dispensary, the shelves were bare save for a few bottles of alcohol and rolls of gauze. There were used bandages on the floor, dirty and fly-infested. The major told me that the camp had received no medical supplies and that up to 20 per cent of his troops were succumbing to malaria every month and had to be rotated out. As we walked by the barracks, I noticed a group of about a hundred young men dressed in civilian clothes sitting off to one side. I asked the major who they were, and he explained with a shrug that it was Sunday and many of the troops elected to wear civilian clothes.

We proceeded to the camp kitchen, which was under a canopy of thatch. The facilities consisted of four open fireplaces; suspended above each one was a huge, dirty, black cooking pot. By this time, some soldiers had drifted toward the kitchen from the barracks. Unkempt and dressed in worn fatigues, they looked bored and listless. They watched as I peeked into one of the evil-looking pots to find it filled with a lumpy, grey-brown gruel. I made a face and they all laughed.

Behind the canopy, a hole had been dug for the kitchen slops and waste water, and I caught a glimpse of something moving. I gave the puddle a stir with my shoe, and the muddy water churned. Startled, I found myself on top of an enormous pig. I nudged it with my foot, and it let out a grunt before subsiding again to its comatose state. Turning toward the soldiers, I asked if they planned to have him for Sunday dinner, and again they laughed. But the funniest thing they'd ever heard was when I asked them if the pig had a name. "Charles, Henri or perhaps Pierre?" I asked, as they cracked up over the notion of any animal sharing the name of a human.

At the edge of the camp, I spotted two green Kigali buses.

There was increased activity on the RPF side as well. On February 28, I took one of the Belgian helicopters for an aerial reconnaissance of the RPF zone. As I flew over the green hills—sometimes low enough that I came eye to eye with startled RPF soldiers—I saw large concentrations of troops being trained, as well as evidence of defensive positions being dug on the northwest border of the demilitarized zone, near the presidential stronghold of Ruhengeri. In the middle of the zone, where it narrowed to less than a kilometre near Byumba, I spotted soldiers swarming around the rich sienna of freshly turned mounds of earth; they were like giant anthills bracketing the city on both flanks. It looked like Kagame was realigning his forces, pushing for a good secure start line from which he could launch an offensive.

I confronted Kagame with my findings, making the trip to his headquarters in Mulindi alone. When I raised with him the number of ceasefire breaches caused by his troops, their further incursions into the demilitarized zone and the movement of arms and ammunition between Uganda and Rwanda, obviously supplying his troops, he coolly explained that he was still having discipline problems due to the stagnant political situation. Until the BBTG was in place and UNAMIR began to play its part in sustaining his force, he would continue having problems. I responded that yes, he was in a tough spot, but that I thought the intransigence of his politicos was in part the cause of the impasse. He would have to keep a tighter rein on his troops, dismantle his defences and withdraw his incursions into the demilitarized zone. He agreed. But as a military man, he said, he had to be prepared in case the political process broke down completely.

I reminded him that I had close to a thousand soldiers scattered throughout the demilitarized zone and that if Kagame launched an offensive, they would be caught in the middle. He promised me that should the situation ever deteriorate to that point, he would give me a twenty-four-hour warning—he did not want to injure any UN personnel. But I knew that the Belgians' disgraceful behaviour during the Kadafi Crossroads ambush had broken a fundamental trust between Kagame's force and mine, and I wasn't sure if I could take him at his word.

The next day, I received a report from the new commander of the UNOMUR Sector, Colonel Azrul Haque, confirming that shipments of weapons and ammunition were going from the NRA to the RPF. At the same time, Claeys's intelligence team reported that Ugandan army officers had held meetings about supporting an RPF offensive to be launched at either Byumba or Ruhengeri. Claeys had also sniffed out information about a boatload of arms destined for the RPF that had been seized by authorities in Goma, on the Zairean shore of Lake Kivu. Apparently, Tutsi refugees living just inside the Zairean border near Gisenyi had approached the soldiers guarding the four-tonne shipment and tried to bribe them to release the arms. Local Hutus had foiled the attempt by making a counter-offer.

On March 1, I received a call from the president's office saying Habyarimana had some urgent security concerns he wanted to discuss. I could count on the fingers of one hand the number of times we had actually sat down and talked, and I decided to bring along Henry and Luc as ballast. We found the president seated on the palace patio with Bizimana, Nsabimana and Ndindiliyimana. He said he had heard I was moving some of my troops from the demilitarized zone into Kigali. I was a little startled. Henry, Luc and I had recently discussed relocating 225 Ghanaians from Byumba to Kigali, but we hadn't yet acted on it. I knew our headquarters was as leaky as a sieve, and here was another bit of evidence.

Habyarimana thought such a shift would leave my troops too thinly spread out in the demilitarized zone, and that this would be unwise considering the number of ceasefire violations there had been—all the fault of the increasingly aggressive RPF, according to him. I said I was more worried about the volatile situation inside the KWSA. If the RPF did launch an attack, my force had neither the mandate nor the means to stop them.

It was, however, within my mandate to provide security for the citizens of Kigali. Here Bizimana jumped in: he was receiving reports that the RPF were massively reinforcing the CND compound, turning it into a fortress. This was not only true but hardly a surprise given that everyone who was a party to the KWSA agreement expected that the RPF contingent would defend their compound once they moved into Kigali. Then Ndindiliyimana again tried to insist that since his Gendarmerie was overtaxed, I should allow him to beef up his force with RGF troops. That would breach the KWSA agreement, and I said no.

Bizimana thought he could persuade me to release to the RGF the air shipment of artillery and mortar ammunition that we had impounded at Kigali airport in January, insisting that the shipment had been ordered prior to the signing of the peace agreement and showing me the relevant documents. "No way," I said. Such an action would only further destabilize the ceasefire and, as demobilization was imminent, there was really no need. We were all supposed to be moving toward peace, not preparing for war.

A few days after the meeting, Nsabimana developed an uncharacteristic interest in my force. He and Bizimana began visiting Luc at his Kigali headquarters, something they had never done before, and dropping in on the Bangladeshi and Belgian battalions. Perhaps they were just countering my unannounced visits to their camps, or perhaps they were assessing the capabilities of my force. I didn't mind at all—I wanted to operate in an open and transparent manner. But this sudden interest after months of indifference was unsettling, especially when my unarmed observers were picking up information that the heavy weapon systems that we knew were located within the presidential compound near Ruhengeri were being moved (though we were not able to verify this, as Booh-Booh had specifically forbidden me to conduct searches there).

As both sides continued their military buildup, I reviewed our own capabilities. With the arrival of the Ghanaian battalion, I was able to cover the increased demands of the KWSA agreement by shifting the Tunisian contingent, along with the 225 Ghanaians, to Kigali full-time. But I continued to be plagued with transport and logistical problems and still couldn't fully equip the force. It was difficult to get messages to troops in the field. Most of the civilian staff were only capable of providing basic secretarial work, and the staff officers I could spare to oversee the headquarters were Bangladeshis who were fluent in neither English nor French.

Getting messages to headquarters was equally difficult. They either had to be hand-delivered—a problem when both fuel and vehicles were at a premium—or relayed over our radio net. Unfortunately, our Motorola radios (unlike those carried by both the RPF and the RGF) had no encryption capability. Though most of the troops were aware of this, there were times when sensitive information was radioed in and could have been overheard. Sometimes my observers were forced to borrow a phone from the RGF or the RPF in order to call in their positions to their command posts. Added to this security worry was the fact that a number of the local civilian employees weren't properly screened before they were hired and, as was clear from the president's familiarity with my plans, some of them turned out to be informers.

I still had only ten trucks for almost a thousand troops in the demilitarized zone. It took close to ten days to pull the 225 Ghanaians into the city. The vehicle squeeze meant that the bulk of my troops in the zone were forced into static guard posts, observation posts and checkpoints. And I had no way to make up for that immobility: my helicopters still hadn't arrived.

Then there was the ongoing problem of the lack of competency of the Bangladeshi troops. On March 8, Luc invited me to a demonstration of the Quick Reaction Force, which had been training since December in order to be able to smoothly extract VIPs from an armed and angry mob—the kind of situation most of my Kigali Sector forces had already confronted.

The Bangladeshis set up the exercise in a military training field not far from Kigali airport, even erecting a canopy on a knoll for me and Luc to sit under as we watched and were served iced beverages. The commanding officer described how the platoon of thirty-five soldiers (not the 120-man force I really needed, I can't help but point out) would rush in with our five functional APCs to surround the crowd (the eight promised APCs had arrived in February, but three of them were out of commission). When they were in position, the soldiers would leap out and form a tight cordon, confronting the crowd and pushing it back. They would isolate the VIPs, load them into one of the vehicles and then pull away. The idea was to shock and surprise the crowd with a show of overwhelming force but also to conduct the whole exercise without firing a single shot.

As Luc and I watched, the troops hesitantly drove toward the pretend mob of volunteer soldiers, taking far too long to position the vehicles. This was only the beginning of the comedy. The Bangladeshis were equipped with very long, outdated SKS rifles, and the APCs were not easy vehicles to get out of. Instead of streaming out of them in a river of force, they stumbled out, tripping over their equipment and each other. I didn't know whether to laugh or cry, but I knew at that moment that there was no way these soldiers would ever be able to perform in a real emergency.

I reflected bitterly on what the Bangladeshi army chief of staff had said to me when he'd come to Rwanda in February for an inspection: "You realize that your mission here is to see to it that all of my men get home safely." He said that he intended that their experience in Rwanda would help to "mature" his officers and NCOs. He was too proud to come out and say that he would prefer that his troops not be drafted for the Quick Reaction Force. He had shocked me to the core. Putting the safety of soldiers above the mission was heresy in my professional ethos, and his view confirmed for me that Bangladesh had only deployed its contingent for selfish aims: the training, the financial compensation and the equipment they intended to take home with them. I would have to rely on the Tunisians instead.

While the military situation was tense, there was some hope on the political front. Gatabazi's assassination had galvanized the international community into seriously trying to sort out the mess. Nobody backed Habyarimana's solution to the impasse; the diplomatic community in Kigali, seconded by New York, was convinced the president was simply trying to hang on to some vestiges of power if only to avoid jail or worse. Instead the diplomats focused their efforts on the RPF and also on pressuring Lando to sort out the rift in the PL. By the second week of March, there seemed to be some movement toward a political solution, which involved postponing the healing of the PL split until after the transitional government was installed. A new date of March 25 was set for the installation ceremony.

With this improvement on the political front, I decided to take two weeks' leave. I had been putting it off since Christmas, as one swearing-in ceremony after another failed or was postponed, knowing that if the BBTG was actually installed we would finally begin demobilizing close to forty thousand troops. Although all of the funds, plans and other resources were not yet in place, a contract had been signed to provide food for the demobilized troops, and shipments had already begun to arrive in Dar es Salaam. We had plans for temporary housing and areas for storing surrendered weapons. The actual reintegration process of pensioning and retraining was still at an embryonic stage, but once the BBTG was sworn in, I hoped the international community would start to invest. I didn't think either army would take any action if the political process continued to move forward, and I trusted Henry to keep the operation running smoothly in my absence—though I have to confess he was a little surprised when I handed him a list of thirty-nine action points to carry out while I was gone, including briefing the Belgian minister of defence, Léo Delcroix, who was arriving in Kigali the night I was flying out. I wanted Henry to confirm with Delcroix my written request that Luc stay on as Kigali Sector commander for another six months, even though he was due to be rotated out. Like Henry, Luc understood and lived the mission, and I couldn't afford to lose him now.

When on March 10 I stepped on the plane out of Rwanda, I felt I was being transported to another dimension, one of happy families and warm sunny beaches. In twelve hours I was hugging my wife and children, but I felt oddly artificial. Before leaving Rwanda, all I could think about was them, but when I was with them, all I could think about was Rwanda. I called Henry practically every day during my first week away, then finally gave in to exhaustion and stopped calling. I think I slept most of the second week, which I spent at home in Quebec City. My only Rwandan obligation was to walk five blocks from our apartment to hand-deliver a letter from President Habyarimana to his daughter.

I was to return to Rwanda by way of Ottawa and New York. In Ottawa I tried to drum up more Canadian support and lobby for the ten bilingual staff officers I desperately needed. On March 28, I addressed the daily executive meeting attended by the deputy minister of defence, Bob Fowler; the chief of the defence staff, General John de Chastelain; all of the three-star generals in Ottawa; the head of military intelligence; and the civilian assistant deputy ministers. I had ten minutes to make my case. As a symbol of Rwanda's poverty and spirit, I had brought with me one of the soccer balls that the Rwandan kids made out of banana leaves. I startled de Chastelain by tossing it to him as I started to speak. I explained that I wanted to take a Hercules-load of real soccer balls emblazoned with the Canadian maple leaf or the UN logo back to Rwanda for the troops to hand out as a gesture of goodwill. The current situation was stable though tense, I said, but if no political solution was found soon, I was sure that something catastrophic would happen: the peace agreement would fail and the civil war would resume.

They gave me my ten minutes, but I felt that my briefing was viewed as a sideshow to other crises. It was a difficult time for the Defence Department. A new Liberal government had just come to power with an aggressive cost-cutting budget and the Armed Forces were going to be hard hit. We also had major troop commitments to the former Yugoslavia, where the situation was very grave. And there were the soul-destroying details, which were just beginning to surface, of the murder of a Somali teenager, Shidane Arone, by Canadian peacekeepers in the ill-fated Somalia mission. However, before the meeting was over, I was told that my request for ten staff officers was finally being processed and that I would see them in the mission area by June.[1] I had to settle for this because it was clear it was all I was going to get. No one volunteered to send the soccer balls.

I arrived in New York on March 29, early enough to attend the morning briefing at the DPKO. I guess hope does spring eternal, because I went to the UN that day earnestly seeking real help in solving UNAMIR's perennial dilemmas and critical shortages—where were my helicopters, defensive stores, ammunition, medical supplies, spare parts, mechanics, and humanitarian and legal specialists? Even food, water and fuel was in short supply. But, as in Ottawa, my Rwanda mission was overshadowed by more familiar crises: the former Yugoslavia, Mozambique, Haiti, Cambodia and Somalia. As I looked in turn at the concerned faces of Annan, Baril and Riza, I knew that these were decent men who supported me as best they could, but that I was most certainly not the only game in town. And no one in the DPKO had ever been to Kigali to see for themselves the surreality of a headquarters infiltrated by spies, the lack of security, the unworkable mishmash of languages. In a private briefing with the triumvirate after the morning meeting, Maurice told me that the contract had finally been signed for the helicopters and that I should expect to receive the first four the following week. On the other fronts they were sympathetic and concerned, but offered me no firm commitment for resupply. In fact, they insisted, in UN terms the mission was actually moving quite swiftly, and they suggested I drop by the FOD to personally thank the desk officers there for their efforts in expediting my requests. This was not the message I would have chosen to deliver to the FOD.

---

1. Canada's decision to supply two Hercules aircraft for my mission during the war permitted us to stay in Rwanda, as they provided just enough transport for medical evacuation and logistical backup for my small force. Canada was also the only nation to reinforce my mission in April and May 1994 in the form of excellent staff officers and MILOBs.

I felt stymied on how to bring my plight home to them. For the past three months, I'd sent directly to the DPKO very detailed sitreps, special incident reports and periodic political and military assessments. I'd done media interviews. I had produced several comprehensive military and political analyses of the situation, with options and recommendations, which I had provided to the SRSG for his action. Rarely did I get any response. Who really read this material in New York and what did they do with it? Maurice told me over lunch that he had seen only one or two reports. Was the SRSG actually passing on everything I was producing? I was also sending some stuff to Maurice directly, breaching all the unwritten rules of DPKO etiquette, a practice no one ever called me on, but was the material actually making it to Maurice's desk? Or Miguel's? Or Hedi Annabi's? How much of it was getting through to the Security Council, where our mission mandate was being reviewed? Maurice assured me he would check up on the matter.

On all the big issues they shut me down. We were wildly overextended in trying to deal with the refugee situation from Burundi, and Henry and I had both supported the idea of a peacekeeping mission to Burundi that Henry would perhaps command. Annan told me the Burundian army had refused the offer of a UN force, and so there wouldn't be one. I wanted just forty-eight more MILOBs to help me stem the flow of men and *matériel* across all borders, which was feeding the not-so-surreptitious military buildup. At the end of February, a truck with a Burundian licence plate speeding through a routine roadblock set up by a Belgian patrol in downtown Kigali—the heart of the supposed KWSA—had overturned, spilling its cargo of guns and grenades. Maurice shut me down: there would be absolutely no more troops. When I mentioned the deterrent operations I was continuing to press for and the plan I'd worked out with Luc to train teams of gendarmes along with UN soldiers to take on these tasks, Riza once again reminded me of the limits of my mandate. We were planning our first raid for April 1: each individual raid, he said, would have to have prior UN approval.

As best as I can remember, it was Riza who filled me in on the political state of mind in the Security Council regarding the future of the mission. The unequivocal position of the United States was that if there was no BBTG in the next very short while, the whole mission should be pulled. However, both the French and the Belgians were adamant that they didn't want to be dragged back into Rwanda because the UN had left the place in a state of potential catastrophe. As a result, the United States seemed amenable to a sixty-day extension and both France and Belgium accepted this compromise.

That evening I joined Maurice and his wife, Huguette, for dinner at their spacious apartment on the forty-fifth floor of an elegant building close to the UN. We tried to catch up on our friendship, but it wasn't long before we drifted back to matters at the DPKO, with Maurice regaling me with horror stories from other missions. Later that night, as we walked his dog in a nearby park, he elaborated on the growing uneasiness at the Security Council about my mission, with France and the United States particularly active. Despite talk of a sixty-day extension, the council viewed the political impasse as a red flag, and if the situation dragged on much longer they would pull us out and let the country sink back into civil war and chaos, washing its hands of the whole situation. I told Maurice that we could not let that happen—it would be immoral. He said someone had to give in or something had to change—and soon. I couldn't argue with that.

I left New York the next day. My leave had passed in a blur of faces and sensations, some pleasant, some loving, some frustrating, some shocking, but none seemed to carry the depth and complexity of Rwanda. I had picked up one other disturbing piece of news on the trip, though try as I might I haven't been able to recall or uncover who it was who first delivered it to me. France had written the Canadian government to request my removal as force commander of UNAMIR. Apparently someone had been reading my reports and hadn't liked the pointed references I had made to the presence of French officers among the Presidential Guard, especially in light of the Guard's close links to the Interahamwe militias. The French ministry of defence must have been aware of what was going on and was turning a blind eye. My bluntness had rattled the French enough for them to take the bold and extremely unusual step of asking for my dismissal. It was clear that Ottawa and the DPKO were still backing me, but I made a mental note to keep a close watch on the French in Rwanda, to continue to suspect their motives and to further probe the presence of French military advisers in the elite RGF units and their possible involvement in the training of the Interahamwe.

Still, I did not regret for a moment leaving the bright lights of Manhattan behind in favour of night skies so dark the stars seemed close enough to be street lights. In the recycled cabin air of the long flight back, I physically longed for Rwanda, its rich red earth, the smell of its wood fires and its vibrant humanity.

I arrived in Kigali on Thursday morning, March 31. In my absence, the whole political landscape had changed. Henry met me at the airport, where he handed me a detailed report that he wanted me to read before verbally bringing me up to date. On the drive back to the bungalow so I could shower and change, Brent filled me in. There had been serious complications with the installation of the government, which was causing a further deterioration in the security situation. The president had insisted on the inclusion of the extremist CDR in the BBTG. All the foreign politicos, with the SRSG leading the pack, had agreed with this initiative in the spirit of "inclusion," and now, instead of tackling the extremists and the president, they were pressuring the RPF to compromise.

Shortly after I had left Rwanda on March 10, both the RPF and President Habyarimana had sought the assistance of President Mwinyi of Tanzania, the facilitator of the Arusha Peace Agreement, to arbitrate a solution. Mwinyi had sent his foreign minister to Kigali. If the only outstanding issue in the impasse was the split within the PL, he had suggested that the problem be resolved by sharing the ministerial and deputy positions between the two factions. He had then proposed that Faustin Twagiramungu should have final approval on the lists of ministers and that Prime Minister Agathe should have final approval on the list of deputies, but that they should consult everyone with an interest in the lists, including the president.

In a nationwide radio address on the evening of March 18, Faustin had read out the final list of ministerial candidates for the new BBTG and emphatically assured the nation that the political manoeuvring was now at an end. Nothing would stand in the way of the new government, he promised, which would be installed on March 25. On the following evening, Prime Minister Agathe had announced the names of the deputies for the assembly.

Prudence Bushnell, the U.S. deputy assistant secretary of state for African affairs, chose that very day to suddenly arrive in Kigali and meet with both Kagame and Habyarimana. What did she tell them? Was she simply delivering a warning that the international community was beginning to lose patience with them all? She also met with Booh-Booh and told him that the Security Council's forthcoming meeting to review the renewal of the mandate could be "difficult" if there was no progress toward the installation of the BBTG or if there was violence.

Habyarimana had been displeased with the lists and publicly chastised the prime ministers on national radio for not consulting him before their broadcasts. On March 21, he called Faustin into his office and told him that he had received a letter of complaint from members of the PL on the choice of the justice minister. He suggested that Faustin needed to continue his consultations with the party. Habyarimana said he had received letters from the CDR and the PDI (the tiny Islamic party) stating they were both now willing to sign the Arusha accords and the Political Code of Ethics and therefore wanted to claim their respective seats in the Assembly. In the spirit of reconciliation, the president said, the transitional government should go out of its way to include members from all of the official parties that were identified in the Arusha Peace Agreement. Faustin knew that including the CDR in the government was completely unacceptable. It was a blatantly fascist organization that espoused a radical pro-Hutu, anti-Tutsi agenda and was intimately linked with the Impuzamugambi militias as well as the infamous RTLM. And of course the RPF categorically rejected the inclusion of the CDR in the chamber of deputies and blamed Habyarimana for throwing insurmountable obstacles in front of an already stalled political process.

Considerable political effort had gone into the preparation of the March 25 swearing-in. There had been verbal assurances from the minister of defence and from Enoch Ruhigira that there would be no demonstrations to block the ceremony. But once again it had failed disastrously, this time because the RPF refused to attend. A subsequent attempt on March 28 failed too, touching off a significant increase in banditry and armed attacks against the more moderate elements of the population. The gendarmes had very limited transport and couldn't control the situation. Some people had sought protection in churches at night.

The Kigali diplomatic corps, jointly led by the papal nuncio and the SRSG, essentially endorsed the president's proposal that all parties acknowledged at Arusha should be included in the BBTG. They issued a joint declaration that was also signed by representatives from Zaire, Uganda, Burundi and Tanzania—in effect, the entire Great Lakes region. In one master stroke, Habyarimana had isolated the RPF as the sole party holding up the political process. The DPA in New York, the UN and the entire political and diplomatic community fell into his trap. We, the international community, caused the demise of Arusha the day all our diplomats, with the SRSG of the UN in the lead, accepted the president's gambit. In the Security Council deliberations on the future of the mission, the United States wanted to force the council into agreeing to a very stringent time limit for the swearing-in of the BBTG. The RPF would have little time to figure out a political countermove—but they were in a good military position for a swift offensive. No one at the UN had thought to fill me in on any of these events while I was in New York, and I had to wonder again whether anyone was paying real attention to Rwanda.

The security situation had deteriorated in concert with the political chaos, Brent told me. Many of the moderate politicians had received death threats. Henry now had UN troops camped out permanently in the backyards of five prominent politicians: Judge Kavaruganda of the constitutional court, who would have to rule on some of the contested deputy positions; the two prime ministers; Lando Ndasingwa; and Anastase Gasana. On March 15, in an incident reminiscent of the Gatabazi killing, Enoch Ruhigira's sister and her husband had been ambushed in their car and killed. Both were influential moderates. Chez Lando had come under grenade attack on March 19, a Saturday night when the hotel disco was packed. Eight people were injured.

There was also disturbing news from the south. Both my unarmed observer teams and aid workers with UNHCR reported that the RGF was continuing to recruit young men from the Burundi refugee camps of Ruheru and Shororo. The recruits were taken to a nearby forest, where they were being trained using dummy rifles and wooden grenades. In some northern areas of the demilitarized zone, the RPF was preventing my MILOBs from conducting patrols.

I had to tackle all these issues, but first I had to take on my political boss. The first piece of news I encountered upon arriving at headquarters that first day back was that Booh-Booh had accepted an invitation from the president to spend the Easter weekend at his retreat near Gisenyi. Not only that, the SRSG was requesting a UNAMIR escort. Dr. Kabia and I went immediately to confront him in his impossibly neat office. We tried to be diplomatic, pointing out that the only advantage to his trip was that he might be able to gain insight and intelligence. Of course, he said, that was entirely his intention. He'd known the president since he had been the foreign affairs minister of Cameroon, and he was well placed to penetrate Habyarimana's intentions. We quickly pointed out that any benefits he might reap were outweighed by the terrible optics: the RPF and the moderates would assume he was on the president's side. Booh-Booh shrugged and repeated that it would be a working weekend where he would continue to pursue strategies to bring about the transitional institutions. Nothing I nor Dr. Kabia could say would dissuade him, and he actually implied that our misgivings were the result of our imperfect understanding of the ethos of francophone Africa.

The next day was Good Friday, and I rose to the longed-for smell of charcoal fires and the cacophony of beautiful birds, but the first thought in my head was the fact that the head of mission would be leaving at noon that day in the service of a disastrous impulse. And sure enough, Booh-Booh went, with a UNAMIR escort and Kane in tow. The next morning we received a formal protest from the RPF questioning the SRSG's impartiality.

I needed immediate contact with the military leaders on both sides to see for myself where things stood. On Saturday morning, April 2, I met with the minister of defence, bringing Brent with me to take notes. I think Bizimana wanted to gauge UNAMIR's resolve after my trip to New York; he would certainly have known the status of the mission at the Security Council by way of Rwanda's ambassador. I came out swinging, rattling off his sins of omission and commission: Why had Bizimana done nothing to assist in the investigation into the Gatabazi assassination? Why had he not provided me with the list of those individuals who had special permits to carry self-protection weapons in the KWSA, or the lists of small arms that had been distributed in the countryside over the last couple of years? He had not had the mines removed from the Gatunda-Kigali corridor; he had obstructed further meetings of the Joint Military Commission that was attempting to plan the demobilization. I asked him, why were his troops preventing humanitarian traffic from getting through to the refugee camps inside the RPF zone? At this last question, he counterpunched: yes, he had promised to aid NGOs and humanitarian efforts, but some of this aid was being siphoned off to support the RPF troops, and he was not going to tolerate that. Neither the minister nor I received much satisfaction from the meeting.

I left him and, after lunch, flew up to Mulindi to see Kagame in one of our two mission helicopters, which had finally arrived. He seemed distant and a little withdrawn as I hit him with a similar long list of troublesome issues. Even when I told him that my helicopters had arrived and that we would be starting regular aerial reconnaissance over the whole country, including his operational area, he hardly reacted, which was odd considering his usual concern for keeping others in the strategic dark about RPF movements and capabilities. I chastised him about an increasing number of ceasefire violations on the east flank of the demilitarized zone where the sides were often separated by only one hundred metres. He had changed his local commander in the zone and, since then, there had been four altercations in which no less than six RGF soldiers had been killed and several injured. My UNMO investigation team had been on the site of the most recent incident in less than an hour and it appeared that the firefight had been started by Kagame's troops. He promised to investigate.

Finally I asked if he had any issues to raise with me. He wanted to know how the CDR and PDI proposal had come about. I looked at his face and it was as sombre as I'd ever seen it. Something cataclysmic was coming, he said, and once it started, no one would be able to control it.

As I flew back to Kigali, I realized I had seen two men that day who were both preparing for something I couldn't yet face: the whole Arusha experiment was about to collapse. I needed to see Luc—Kigali Sector would be key to our security if the worst came to pass—but I also needed to check in with all my subordinate commanders to assess our few strengths and our glaring weaknesses.

Later that day, Luc walked into my office as keen and confident as ever, though his eyes looked tired. I was happy to see him. The first joint deterrent raid on a suspected arms cache had gone ahead as planned on April 1, with UNAMIR troops providing the security cordon and gendarmes conducting the actual search. The gendarmes had come up empty-handed; obviously the plan had been leaked and the weapons moved. But Luc had not lost faith. He had been training the Gendarmerie and was certain of their good faith, and he thought that next time, if the intended location of the raid was more closely held, we might achieve some success. We picked April 7 for the next attempt.

But there were many matters troubling his sleep. We both knew how stretched the force was. Luc now told me that if either side launched a major action in the capital, his units simply couldn't defend themselves or protect UN civilians or foreign nationals. The 225 Ghanaians were still deploying. The new Belgian battalion hadn't yet adjusted to their area of responsibility or to the rules of engagement of a chapter-six mission. Then there was the Bangladeshi contingent. Their commanding officer was demanding that every order be delivered to him on paper and was resisting the use of his troops for operations. On the brighter side, the medical evacuation plan was well advanced, but we still hadn't received any medical supplies. Neither New York nor Brussels had solved the ammunition problem, and no one would pay for ammunition to replace what the first Belgian contingent had expended on training. The force had approximately two magazines, or forty to sixty rounds, per man—a pitifully inadequate amount. It could sustain a one- to three-minute fight and then we would be reduced to throwing rocks.

I went home that night exhausted and full of the warnings that were coming from all sides. But on some deep level, I was glad to be back. The people of Rwanda were not an insignificant black mass living in abject poverty in a place of no consequence. They were individuals like myself, like my family, with every right and expectation of any human who is a member of our tortured race. I was determined to persevere.

• • •

On April 3, Easter Sunday, I flew to Byumba to review the bulk of my forces in the demilitarized zone—the remaining Ghanaians and the Bangladeshi engineering company. We had a magnificent fifty-minute flight at very low altitude over the rounded mountaintops of central Rwanda. Below me that morning it looked like all the villagers in the country were dressed in their finest, walking in near-procession toward their places of worship. Here is what my experience in Rwanda has done: I am unable to remember the serenity, order and beauty of that scene without it being overlaid with vivid scenes of horror. Extremists, moderates, simple villagers and fervent worshippers were all in church that day, singing the message of Christ's resurrection. One week later, the same devout Christians would become murderers and victims, and the churches the sites of calculated butchery.

We landed in Byumba in a terrible cloud of dust. The site was a superb piece of modern architecture, a sprawling complex under the care of nuns, which was to open as a school the next year: an expression of the vast amounts of Canadian aid that had been invested in this small Franco-African country. Proportionally, Rwanda had been the largest recipient of Canadian aid in all of sub-Saharan Africa. The nuns had put the Bangladeshi engineers to work on various tasks and informed me that this would be our rental bill. There were discreet CIDA stickers with the Canadian flag on nearly every door. I wondered again why Brent and I constituted the entire Canadian military commitment to the country at this perilous time. A battalion or even a company of French-Canadian troops would have made more sense. The Department of Foreign Affairs and CIDA had a long history in the country, but there had been no contact between me and these agencies before my departure, no sharing of cultural and historical information as I prepared to try to secure a peaceful future.[2]

---

2. Canada did not have a coherent and integrated policy toward Rwanda, only isolated departmental initiatives that in a time of crisis did not come together. Howard Adelman, a Canadian academic, has written an excellent chapter on Canadian policy in Rwanda in *The Path of a Genocide: The Rwandan Crisis from Uganda to Zaire* (1999), which certainly reflects my confused experience of my country's relationship to Rwanda.

I was greeted by the sector commander of the demilitarized zone, Clayton Yaache, along with the Ghanaian and Bangladeshi company commanders. Since my last visit, more than a month ago, the Bangladeshi engineers had received about a third of the operational equipment they needed. Among the tasks facing them was building or repairing bridges to move troops and patrols and to serve the needs of Rwandans in the future. The Gatuna bridge was a priority, as I was still pushing to open the corridor between Kabale and Kigali. De-mining was also on their plate, along with preparing the camps for demobilizing soldiers. The Ghanaians were hobbled by all the usual shortfalls in their efforts to patrol the zone. The issue foremost in Yaache's mind was that he had no workable plan for medical evacuation from the area. There was a small medical team to stabilize the seriously wounded, but the trip to Kigali by road would take a couple of hours. There was no ambulance, though the recent arrival of the helicopters would help—I intended to dedicate one to casualty evacuation. Although suffering enormously from the lack of vehicles, equipment and supplies, both units remained keen and morale was high.

I attended Easter service in the chapel, amused at the transformation of the Ghanaian band, which I'd only heard belting out dance tunes or military marches, into credible church musicians. Briefly I let my thoughts turn to home. In Quebec, Easter Sunday is an important family day and it was almost over. No egg hunt with the kids, no sugar bush lunch with the family, just an imponderable distance.

I rose a little later than usual on Easter Monday and sat on the veranda for a while. I was to meet Henry for a long session later that morning, but I didn't have to rush—the headquarters was down to a skeleton staff since this was the first weekend in which my troops had been able to take some time off. The house seemed empty without Willem de Kant, who had rotated back to staff school in the Netherlands just before I had gone on leave. And the zoo of house pets that the animal-crazy Willem had acquired were obviously missing him. There was a goat named Gaetan (with Willem gone we had decided to fatten the animal up to serve at our Canada Day celebration on July 1—none of us except Willem had liked that goat); a rooster named Rusty, and two hens—Helen and Henrietta—who supplied us with fresh eggs.

The most demanding of the pets was a little black mongrel we affectionately called Shithead. He was incredibly dumb for a puppy, forever running after the goat or rooster and getting butted or pecked. Every morning when I'd get distracted with thoughts of the mission, he'd steal a piece of my toast. Willem had been replaced as my aide-de-camp by Captain Robert van Putten, who was eager to perform his duties but who had less experience than de Kant and also did not speak French, a serious disadvantage in Rwanda.

As I lingered there looking out over Kigali, I mulled my constant sense of unease and incomprehension. So many times back home when decisions were taken by an English-Canadian majority organization, I had witnessed the effect on the minority. Catching the linguistic and cultural nuances around how information or orders were conveyed and received could make the difference between acceptance or rejection. At home I had prided myself on being sensitive to these nuances. But in my mission, no one had that kind of insight into the Rwandans. Being bilingual, I understood the words the players spoke but not the meaning. Politically, militarily and diplomatically, the tension was undeniably building, and yet most of the time I felt as though I was swinging at phantoms in the dark.

This was the first chance Henry and I had had to sit down together since I got back, and in a long session, we sorted our order of business. My confidence in his grasp of command and of the situation was confirmed; he had handled matters very well in my absence. Troubling him was the fact that while I was away, the SRSG had kept him and the military side out of the political loop (no surprise there), and neither the Gendarmerie, the RGF chief of staff nor the minister of defence had met with him. He worried about the consequences of this loss of contact.

After Henry left, I went to the national holiday soiree organized by the Senegalese contingent, which was made up of thirty-nine officers, all of them military observers and most of them bilingual. Along with Moctar Gueye, the mission spokesman, they had arranged a buffet dinner with music and dancing at the Meridien hotel. Representatives of all parties, the government, the diplomatic community and a delegation from every contingent in UNAMIR were invited, and there was a large turnout. Some of the Senegalese officers had taken up a collection for needy Rwandans and literally dumped a large pile of bills in my hands. I thanked them for their generosity and handed the money to Brent, instructing him to find a suitable charity.[3]

I made it to the buffet through a flurry of dancing, often males dancing in groups, and noticed Luc sitting with Mamadou Kane and a few Rwandans. I was surprised to see that one of them was Colonel Bagosora, who was there with his wife. He welcomed me to the table. He had been drinking and was more loquacious than usual, though the band was loud and we had to yell to converse. As we talked about Arusha, Bagosora repeated the oft-told tale of the Tutsis attempting to form a hegemony over the Great Lakes region. Trying to distract him from his anti-Tutsi diatribe, I asked him if the president had ever anointed someone as his "dauphin." I was legitimately curious about the line of succession if something happened to Habyarimana. Given the events of the next few days, my innocent question must have been a bombshell to Bagosora. He responded no, it wasn't in the president's nature to think of such things. He then returned to his Tutsi hegemony theory, which I'd heard before. Luc remembers Bagosora telling him drunkenly that the only way to deal with the Tutsis was to eliminate them completely, just wipe them out.

The future of UNAMIR's participation in implementing the Arusha Peace Agreement was being decided by fifteen men sitting in a backroom beside the Security Council hall in New York, one of whom was a hardline Rwandan extremist. He represented a group in Rwanda that was against Arusha and now found himself allied with the Americans, Russians and Chinese, who all wanted the mission to end. On the morning of April 6, we received the Security Council's Resolution 909, which extended our mandate for six weeks. If the BBTG was not in place by the end of that time, the mission would be "reviewed"—UN-speak

---

3. Brent did not have time to see to this before the war started, and he gave the money to our Hutu and Tutsi servants to help them through what he thought at the time would be the difficult period before we regained control of the situation. Tiso and Célestin were both stopped at roadblocks and murdered, Tiso because he was a Tutsi and Célestin because he had a large amount of cash on him.

meaning it would end. How could we pull out? Would we have any credibility left? Would we have to evacuate all the UN civilians and expatriates? I read on. Although the resolution did not add any new restrictions on our modus operandi, it gave me no more room to manoeuvre in deterrent operations. And we were also being asked to find ways to reduce costs. This last point was absurd. The UN was spending millions of dollars a day in the former Yugoslavia. I had roughly $50 million for the year and had to fly everything in because there were no ports, only one airport, three roads to the border and no trains.

The report sent the wrong message, and the consequences were truly devastating. It confirmed for all Rwandans—the moderates attempting to hang on to hope and the extremists plotting extermination—that the world didn't give a damn about Rwanda.

April 6 would turn out to be the longest day of my life. The president was in Dar es Salaam meeting with the regional leaders, who were pressuring him to install the BBTG. I hoped against hope that this would make him deal—that is, if he could control the hard-liners and extremists in his party and the CDR. He still had a number of supporters, and he retained control of the army and the Gendarmerie through Nsabimana and Ndindiliyimana. I had to regard this diplomatic initiative as a last chance.

In the wake of Resolution 909, the DPKO wanted my withdrawal plans immediately. UNAMIR would be the central instrument, coordinating with any foreign forces that might arrive in Rwanda to evacuate their expatriates. Working on the withdrawal plan was anathema to my priorities. I thought, "Who evacuates the Rwandans?" The answer was no one.

I went home that evening still thinking about how to make Arusha work. I hadn't seen the SRSG since before his ill-advised visit with the president, and we absolutely needed to confer over the direction we had just received from the Security Council. We had an arms-cache raid planned for the morning: with luck, I could bring him news of a success. In Dar es Salaam, a plane was warming up at the airport to bring President Habyarimana back to Kigali. That plane and my hopes were on a collision course that would sink Rwanda into the abyss.

10

AN EXPLOSION AT KIGALI AIRPORT

At about 2020 hours on April 6, the duty officer relayed disturbing news from our UNMOs at the airport: "There has been an explosion at Kigali airport." At first the UNMOs thought our ammunition dump had blown up, but then we learned otherwise. A plane had crashed but no one could confirm that it was Habyarimana's. Presidential Guards and members of the RGF's Para-Commando Battalion from Camp Kanombe were running wild at the airport, threatening people with their weapons, and the observers had gone into hiding. I radioed Luc Marchal to send a patrol to find the crash site and to secure the area so we could conduct an investigation.

Our phone began to ring off the hook: Prime Minister Agathe, Lando Ndasingwa and others called seeking information. Madame Agathe said she was trying to get her cabinet together but many of the ministers were fearful and didn't want to leave their families. She said that all the hardline ministers from the other parties had disappeared. I asked if she could find out whether it was the president's plane that had crashed and if he was on board, and then get back to me. I called Booh-Booh to alert him to the situation. As soon as I hung up, Madame Agathe called back to confirm that it was Habyarimana's plane, and that he was presumed to have been on board.

She wanted any help UNAMIR could give her to get the political situation under control. With the president probably lost in the crash, she was legally next in line as the executive authority in the land. But some of her moderate ministers were already fleeing their homes for safer hiding places, and others, who had UNAMIR, Gendarmerie or even RGF guards, did not feel safe enough to meet with her and devise a plan. And where were all the extremist politicians?

By this point so many calls were coming in over the phone and by radio that we had to cut off conversations to keep the lines open. I needed to be able to receive accurate reports in order to act. We referred all these desperate callers to Force HQ, an option that was less than ideal considering that the Bangladeshi duty officers spoke no French.

At about 2200 I received a call from Ephrem Rwabalinda, the RGF liaison officer to UNAMIR. He told me that a crisis committee was about to meet at RGF headquarters and asked me to come. I called Luc and told him to meet me there as soon as he had ensured that Kigali Sector was on red alert. I also called Henry and told him to go to the CND and stay with the RPF. He needed to keep them calm until I could confirm what was going on. Just before we left, Riza called from New York. I filled him in as best I could and told him I was on my way to RGF headquarters.

Brent, Robert and I then headed out into the night. The city was frighteningly silent and the lights in most homes were off. Unless there was a curfew, Kigali was usually alive with people. But we didn't even see a police patrol. I thought that rogue members of the Presidential Guard might be on the move, and I didn't want an incident; they would exploit any confrontation involving UNAMIR for full propaganda value. We made our way cautiously through the streets.

The gates were overmanned by heavily armed soldiers. In the compound, troops in formation were moving around. I left Robert in the vehicle with the radio while Brent came with me into the headquarters. We were directed to the upstairs conference room. The overhead fans were off and the room was mostly in darkness, though a few long fluorescent lights fluttered; the ceiling seemed to press down on our heads.

Colonel Bagosora sat at the centre of the large horseshoe-shaped conference table. The fact that he was in charge didn't bode well. He impatiently waved us to sit down. On his left was Major General Ndindiliyimana, his chair pushed back and his expression noncommittal, accompanied by a few of his staff officers. On Bagosora's right was a senior RGF staff officer who we knew worked closely with the Belgian and French military advisers to the Rwandan force, but the advisers themselves weren't present. This worried me, because of all the foreigners in the country, these men best knew what was going on with the Rwandan military.[1] Rwabalinda was on the far right. There were about a dozen others, most of them senior army staff officers. Was this a well-planned *coup d'état* or were these officers simply maintaining order until the political leadership was sorted out? Bagosora's presence undermined my frail hope that perhaps this coup, if it was a coup, had been launched by the moderate members of the military and the Gendarmerie.

Bagosora welcomed us and explained that since the minister of defence was out of the country at an Olympic committee meeting in Cameroon, the group of officers in this conference room represented the senior leadership of the army and the Gendarmerie. The military needed to take control of the country because of the uncertainty caused by the crash of the president's plane. Bagosora looked at me with a straight face and said he didn't want the Arusha process jeopardized. He emphasized that the military only wanted to control the situation for the shortest time possible, then hand the situation over to the politicians. He wanted to keep peace with the RPF, he said. He acknowledged that elements of the RGF, especially the Presidential Guard, were out of control, but he assured me that every effort was being made to return them to their barracks. I didn't trust him for a minute.

He had just turned the meeting over to Ndindiliyimana when the fifties-vintage telephone on a small table behind him rang so loudly that we all jumped. A staff officer picked it up. He briefly listened, then calmly responded in Kinyarwanda. When he hung up, he said that not

---

1. Though they had never co-operated with UNAMIR in the past—insisting that they could not serve their home governments, Rwanda and the UN mission at the same time—perhaps they would have had a change of heart and given us their insiders' view. I had often wondered about the stance of the Belgian military adviser. I could understand that he needed to be loyal to his original mission of advising the inner core of officers in the RGF, but why did he refuse to help UNAMIR, especially his countrymen?

only had Habyarimana been killed in the plane crash, but so had Cyprien Ntaryamira, the president of Burundi, and Déogratias Nsabimana, the chief of staff of the army. He began to smile as he told us that the plane had crashed in the backyard of Habyarimana's own home near Camp Kanombe, but caught himself. Bagosora gave him a dirty look, then turned to me for a response.

I didn't even pause to offer condolences. I stressed that as far as UNAMIR and the world were concerned, Rwanda still had a government, headed by Prime Minister Agathe. All matters should now be under her control. Bagosora snapped back that Madame Agathe didn't enjoy the confidence of the Rwandan people and was incapable of governing the nation. This Crisis Committee had to assume control until a new group of politicians could form a government. He had summoned the senior military leadership of the RGF to meet the next morning in Kigali.

I referred him once again to the authority of Madame Agathe: she must be brought into this now. She should address the nation over Radio Rwanda, the government radio station, urging people to stay calm. UNAMIR and the Gendarmerie could work together through the night to conduct joint patrols to maintain order in Kigali. A secure Kigali was the key to controlling the situation.

Bagosora stood up then and leaned toward me, his knuckles pressed hard on the table. He vehemently insisted that Prime Minister Agathe had no authority. The officer next to Brent smelled of alcohol and muttered an insult in French at the mention of Madame Agathe's name. Here was Bagosora swearing his solidarity with the Arusha Peace Agreement, yet not a single officer in this room respected the prime minister's authority.

I turned to Ndindiliyimana, who said he wanted to place Gendarmerie guards at Radio Rwanda, the telephone exchange and the utilities and fuel complexes. These were sensible sites to secure, though I insisted that everything be coordinated with Kigali Sector under the rules of the KWSA agreement. Ndindiliyimana agreed. I had always found his loyalties an enigma. Until now I had assumed he was no friend of Bagosora.

I demanded that UNAMIR be permitted to secure the crash site so that a proper accident investigation could be conducted. Bagosora agreed so promptly I thought that either he had nothing to hide or it was already hidden. Since many of the questions we needed to discuss were of a political nature, I suggested that Booh-Booh be involved. I asked for a phone to call him, and they offered me one in the office next door.

It was around midnight and my call woke Booh-Booh up. I quickly briefed him on what had happened so far. Bagosora stuck his head in the door, interrupting me to see if Booh-Booh could see him right away. After a few words with the SRSG, I told Bagosora that I could take him straight over and hung up. Bagosora had another request: Would I approach the RPF to tell them that nothing that had happened or would happen should be interpreted as anything other than an attempt to maintain order?

I called Henry at the CND and directed him to tell the RPF that they must fully comply with the KWSA rules and stay calm. While I was talking to Henry, the Belgian and French military advisers arrived at the door of the office, insisting on an immediate investigation into the crash. The French had an aircraft accident investigation team in Bangui in the Central African Republic that could be here in twelve hours. I told them there was no way I could use a French team: the French were seen to be pro-RGF, and an investigation by them would not be perceived as impartial. I told them I was sure I could get a team here within twenty-four hours from either NATO forces in Europe or from the Americans in Somalia. They left in a huff.

Luc arrived as Robert and I were heading out with Bagosora and Rwabalinda to see Booh-Booh—I'd ordered Brent to remain behind to stay on the phone and keep a link to Force HQ. Luc told me that barricades were going up in the inner city, manned by the Presidential Guard, though the streets were quiet. His people were attempting to account for all Kigali Sector personnel. He had sent a section of Belgian troops to secure the crash site, but the Presidential Guards near the airport refused them access to the area and they were now in a standoff. I directed Luc to link up with Ndindiliyimana to work out the details of joint patrols and joint security of vital points, while I pressured the Crisis Committee to get the Presidential Guard back in their barracks—

we would minimize our own troop movements in order to avoid confrontational situations, and use negotiation to restore and maintain calm in the city.

We left to see Booh-Booh, with Robert driving and Bagosora and Rwabalinda dead quiet in the back seat. We took the most direct route through empty streets to the home of the SRSG and had no trouble until we came upon two Presidential Guard checkpoints on the main access road near their barracks—a direct violation of the KWSA agreement. A couple of cars were stopped and a few civilians were being questioned; in the light of a street lamp we could see one man lying on the grass in the median with his hands over his head.

I asked our back-seat companions to find out what these soldiers were up to and get them to let us pass. Bagosora rolled down his window and barked gruffly in Kinyarwanda at the Presidential Guard NCO at the second barrier. The corporal was clearly astonished at who was in the car shouting orders at him and stood to attention. No matter what he said to the contrary, Bagosora clearly had some control over the Presidential Guard, and we were waved through.

Back at the RGF headquarters, Brent and Luc were putting together other pieces of the puzzle. Brent noticed that the troops were being issued orders out in the compound and saw armoured cars leaving—more direct violations of the KWSA agreement. Each soldier carried an RF4 assault rifle, a weapon Brent had never seen before in the hands of a Rwandan government soldier. The rifles were brand new, some with the packing grease still on the barrels. Luc approached an officer of middle rank to protest the KWSA violations but was ignored.

At Booh-Booh's residence, all the lights in and around the compound were on but no one was outside. After we banged on the gate, the UNAMIR guards opened up and we entered the walled courtyard where we were met by Booh-Booh's bodyguard and ushered inside. The SRSG was in his bedroom, and we had to wait a few minutes before he came down to greet us. He led us into a large room on the main floor and took his place at the top of a rectangle of sofas. Bagosora placed himself on the sofa farthest from Booh-Booh and looked tiny on the large expanse of upholstery. He was convincing as he laid out the country's situation and asked for increased support from UNAMIR to help deal with this *débordement* by a few units close to the president, who were understandably unhinged by the loss of their protector. But his eyes contradicted his reassuring words. Booh-Booh heard him out and then reiterated that Prime Minister Agathe was the legitimate head of government and that she should be consulted on all matters. She was the one who should be issuing orders to the army, not the Crisis Committee. Bagosora protested, and for a time he and Booh-Booh politely debated the issue.

Then Booh-Booh abruptly went upstairs, and though he hadn't asked us to, we knew we were supposed to wait. Fifteen minutes later he returned and told us that he had consulted with certain diplomats and there would be a meeting at 0900 at the American ambassador's residence. Bagosora was invited to attend and he accepted immediately. Staring hard, Booh-Booh told him that this invitation was not recognition of the legitimacy of the Crisis Committee. The meeting was over.

As Booh-Booh walked us toward the car, I sent the others on ahead and asked for a moment in private. He approved of my plan for joint patrols and vital point and VIP guards with the Gendarmerie. He, too, had received calls from Prime Minister Agathe, who was staying put in her house. There was no word on the whereabouts of the MRND ministers. The prime minister was still planning to carry on with her address to the nation by radio the next morning, when most Rwandans in this radio-based culture would be tuning in for the day. The prime minister's speech was our best hope in stabilizing the situation. I told him I would provide an escort for Madame Agathe to get her safely to Radio Rwanda. Booh-Booh asked for an escort in the morning as well to take him to the American ambassador's residence.

Bagosora was becoming childishly impatient, sighing loudly and opening and closing the door to our vehicle. So I left the SRSG, and we made our way back to RGF headquarters. There were no new checkpoints or roadblocks. It was so completely quiet it reminded me of the minutes before an assault in a military exercise, when all your nerves are stretched and nothing can be done to change anything. You are committed, looking at your map for the last time, muscles taut and eyes straining in the dark. Your mouth is dry and your fingers are so tight around your weapon that your hands start to get very cold, you can't breathe and any noise sounds like a nuclear blast. I knew that the entire nation could explode.

It was about 0200 when we got back to the compound. Fewer troops were milling around but all of the defensive positions were manned and on full alert. Luc had worked out a comprehensive plan for joint patrols with Ndindiliyimana. The trouble was that the plan called for a lot of Belgian troops to be moving around town at night, which I thought would be a provocation. I asked him to cut back since that was the last thing we needed. I also told him to send an escort to Mme Agathe's home.

Brent and I needed to get back to Force HQ to report to New York and receive direction. The trip across the city was uneventful and we were back by about 0300. I asked Brent to draft our written report to the DPKO, then met with the chief and deputy chief operations officers, Colonel Moen and Lieutenant Colonel Ballis, who had left their billets at the Meridien with a few other officers and made their way here through back streets. Moen gave me the bleak news that fewer than a dozen officers were at work, of which three were the unilingual Bangladeshi duty officers. He was desperately trying to gain control of the radio nets and get situation reports from all six of our operational sectors, including UNOMUR in Uganda.

Henry had run the gauntlet back from the CND and had been lucky to make it through a short firefight between the RPF and the Presidential Guard: he stressed that the RPF had been responding to provocation. The weekly Belgian Hercules with its cargo of troops returning from leave—including many key staff officers and my driver—had been diverted to Nairobi. The Hercules had been scheduled to land before the President's plane but had been waved off to give the head of state priority. The air traffic controllers had closed the airport immediately after the crash under orders from the Presidential Guard. For the moment we were cut off from the world. The Belgian troops at the airfield were in a standoff with the Presidential Guard, and negotiations were underway to reduce the tension.

Moderate leaders, ordinary Rwandans and nervous UN civilian staff continued to call for information or to demand security. There were only so many troops to go around, and every soldier that was tied down on a guard post was one less we could put on patrol or have available for emergencies. We told callers to stay in their homes or go into hiding until the situation stabilized.

I finally placed a call to New York by satellite phone. It wasn't secure but it was the only means I had. Maurice was on leave. (Later I found out that around the time the president's plane had crashed in Kigali, Maurice and his wife had been in the living room of my home in Quebec City, visiting Beth to reassure her that I was fine.) I briefed Iqbal Riza. When I was done, he said, "UNAMIR is not, repeat not, to fire unless fired upon." I reminded him that our rules of engagement allowed us to intervene and use an escalation of force up to and including the use of deadly force to prevent crimes against humanity. He repeated that UNAMIR was not to fire unless fired upon—we were to negotiate and, above all else, avoid conflict. He said he fully appreciated the crisis we were in but that we must not create any incident that could be exploited. There was no persuading him. I told him that a written sitrep was on the way and we hung up.

Brent had left Robert's notebook of contacts and addresses behind on the Belgian military adviser's desk, and he and Robert decided to drive back to RGF headquarters to get it. They ran into an army roadblock manned by a group of angry, drunken soldiers who had an armoured car as backup. Brent got out of the vehicle and attempted to negotiate his way through, but when the soldiers pointed their weapons at him, including the armoured car's gun, he and Robert withdrew and drove back to Force HQ. When Brent told me what had happened, I tried to call Bagosora. But he was not in his office at the Defence Ministry; he was not at the army's headquarters; and he was not at home. So much for his promise to stay in touch. We couldn't locate any of the members of the so-called Crisis Committee.

Colonel Moen was trying to make sense of the radio nets, which had never really been operational let alone secure; our numerous outposts were cobbled together with hand-held Motorolas and too few repeater stations to boost the signals. Different contingents had brought their own radios with them, while the UN standard issue were the insecure Motorolas. From Force HQ to Kigali Sector, we operated on the Motorolas. Kigali Sector communicated with the Belgian battalion on the Belgian army's VHF radios, which were incompatible with our Motorolas. The Belgian, Bangladeshi and Ghanaian unit command posts also talked to their various subunits, patrols and outstations, such as the VIP guard posts, on a different set of VHF frequencies over incompatible radios. Every message of concern to the mission or to me could pass over four different insecure radio nets and between operators who had a wide variety of languages, accents and technical skills. At the moment it was all Moen could do to stay in touch with the few sector commanders who could reach us.

Prime Minister Agathe called regarding the radio address. We reached the station manager by phone, and I told him I was bringing the prime minister to the station within the hour. He said he'd have to get back to me. A few minutes later, he called and said he would only give the prime minister air time if I could guarantee that UNAMIR would provide security for himself and his family. I told him I would find out what was available and get back to him. I called him back in ten minutes, but this time he said there was nothing he could do. The Presidential Guard had arrived and was blocking the station entrances, not letting anyone in or out. I asked whether he could do a phone patch from Madame Agathe's home. In a nervous whisper he said he could do nothing more and hung up.

I called Madame Agathe to tell her the address was off and urged her to stay inside her walled compound, protected by the extra Belgian troops. She agreed. I counted off the men designated to protect her: the five original Ghanaian guards, several gendarmes who were loyal to her personally, and whoever Luc had sent to reinforce and escort her. There could be as many as twenty well-armed men with her by now. She was as safe as we could make her.

There was no sleep that night. As the sun came up over the mountains, the phone calls pleading for help and protection dramatically increased. Brent fielded these calls without a break for the next twelve hours, sometimes as many as a hundred an hour. Moustache, the security officer for the UNDP, called by radio to tell us that an "important figure" had sought refuge with them, but he wouldn't say who it was over the radio. Brent relayed the message to Kigali Sector, which directed two Bangladeshi APCs to the UNDP.

We began to get ever more disturbing phone calls reporting that elements of the Presidential Guard, the army, the Gendarmerie and the Interahamwe were going from house to house with a list of names. Shots and screaming had been heard. It was terrifying and surreal to be talking to someone, sometimes someone you knew, listening to them pleading for help, and being able to do nothing but reassure them that help was on the way—and then to hear screams, shots and the silence of a dead line. You'd hang up in shock, then the phone would ring again and the whole sequence would be repeated. Help might or might not be arriving, depending on whether Kigali Sector received the message and had a patrol to dispatch and if the patrol was not held up at a roadblock.

Information was sketchy, incomplete and hard to collate. This difficulty was compounded by poor radio discipline. Everyone from UN civilians to military staff was speaking in English—which was their second, third or fourth language—and everyone was trying to speak at once.[2] Of the 2,538 UNAMIR military personnel on the ground on April 7, Brent was the only one who spoke English as his first language. Panic was erupting and only the direct intervention of senior officers maintained any discipline whatsoever on the radio nets. Users lost their tempers, yelled louder and became incomprehensible; less and less information was getting through. Even the most vital messages had to be repeated time and time again as a Bangladeshi tried to relay it in broken

---

2. Even though we were in a francophone country, English was the mission language, as is usual in UN peacekeeping operations. Some exceptions had been made (in Western Sahara the mission had used French, and in Central America, Spanish) and I had strongly recommended French for UNAMIR in my technical report. I was turned down by the DPKO, the rationale being that we would not find enough French-speaking civilian personnel to staff the mission. I now regret not insisting on French.

English through a Uruguayan who in turn had to relay it through a Ghanaian who in turn had to relay it through a Flemish-speaking Belgian.

Early that morning I received a call for help from Hélène Pinsky. I told her to remain with her guard in her home until we could arrange transport to bring the family to Force HQ. There were already five UNAMIR troops and at least two gendarmes who were loyal to the Ndasingwas with her family. I believed that they would be safer at home than to try to move on their own. She was very fearful for her husband and two children; she'd heard that some of their moderate politician friends were being attacked in their homes. I assured her that we would get there as soon as we could, and Brent passed the message to Kigali Sector. Even as I was telling her this, she stopped me to say she could hear people in the street outside her home. Her voice became indescribably calm, as if she had no choice now but to be resigned to her fate, and she hung up. I found out the next day that her husband had then called Luc Marchal and while still on the phone with him, the Presidential Guard arrived, overwhelmed the guards and killed the entire family. Hélène, like so many others, trusted UNAMIR to protect them. Luc had heard them being murdered over the phone.

I can't bear to think of how many Rwandans were told that help was forthcoming that day and were then slaughtered. In just a few hours the Presidential Guard had conducted an obviously well-organized and well-executed plan—by noon on April 7 the moderate political leadership of Rwanda was dead or in hiding, the potential for a future moderate government utterly lost.

The senior leadership of the RGF and Gendarmerie were meeting that morning but I didn't know where. I needed to find them, and I asked for Major Peter Maggen, the senior duty officer, to come with Robert and me to take notes since he was the only other officer available at Force HQ at that time who was fluent in French. A slight, reserved air-defence artillery officer, Maggen was steeped in the mores of the NATO Central Front in Europe. When he'd heard what was going on, he'd made his own way to the headquarters through Kigali's dangerous streets. My thought was that if it was only the units close to the president that had gone rogue, why shouldn't my force intervene with the Gendarmerie and help nip this thing in the bud? If it was a Bagosora-led coup by the hard-liners, aimed at derailing the Arusha accords, I had no more mandate. Civil war would surely break out.

Booh-Booh called to complain that the APC had not yet arrived to take him to his meeting at the American ambassador's residence. I told him I would see to the missing APC myself and sent out the request over our shaky radio net. Booh-Booh called back about ten minutes later. The APC still had not arrived, he was going to miss the meeting and he was furious.

Before I left, I phoned Riza in New York. We now knew that moderates were being targeted, that people under the protection of UNAMIR had been attacked—and God knew what was happening to our guards. It was difficult to get through roadblocks. Soon we might have no choice but to use force. Once again Riza instructed me that UNAMIR was not to fire until fired upon. (From the sitrep sent to New York later that day, I quote, "The Force Commander discussed Rules of Engagement with Mr. Riza and the Rules of Engagement were confirmed that UNAMIR was not to fire until fired upon.")

At about 0930 the SRSG called to say the diplomatic meeting had been cancelled because the ambassadors couldn't be safely escorted there. It was a lost opportunity to try to sway Bagosora. I had to get to the RGF military meeting as quickly as possible.

At 1000, I met with the few officers who had made it to Force HQ. The standoff at the crash site hadn't changed; a platoon of Belgian troops at the main terminal of the airport was still being held prisoner, but they still had their weapons. It was hard to move around the city; we had neither the authority nor the firepower to force our way through roadblocks. There was little our patrols could do other than try to find an alternate route, which inevitably led to another roadblock. The situation outside Kigali was relatively quiet.

I asked Henry to round up the remaining staff any way he could and to bring order to the chaotic situation in the operations centre. I broke the news of Riza's new limit on our ROE, emphasizing the need to avoid any incident the extremists could exploit to turn the army,

the Gendarmerie, the militias and possibly the population against us. I
directed that the change of rules be passed to all sectors down the chain
of command. I sent Ballis to the CND and asked him to remain with
the RPF, who for the present were holding up their side of the KWSA
agreement. He was to assure them that I was in contact with the Crisis
Committee and intended to stay with Bagosora for as long as it took to
get control of the situation. What I really didn't need now was for the RPF
to break out of the CND. The ceasefire and the whole peace process were
hanging by a thread. Brent was to finish the written report to New York
but hold off on sending it until I got back. He was also to answer my
phone and maintain the link with the DPKO, relaying messages to
myself or Henry as required.

Robert, Major Maggen and I left to try to find the meeting. We had
a hand-held Motorola radio in addition to the one in the vehicle.
Robert had the only weapon, a pistol. There was the sound of sporadic
gunfire around the city, but the main streets were still empty except for
the occasional Presidential Guard vehicle. Maggen was at the wheel,
Robert was in the back seat, and I was in the front with my ear close to
the radio. We had to make a long detour to the southwest of the city in
order to avoid the firing that had broken out again between the RPF and
the Presidential Guard around the CND. I hoped Ballis had made it
through. As we approached the city centre, there were people in the
streets and in doorways, and groups were gathering around the roadblocks. Interahamwe, in their distinctive baggy, clown-like suits, some
soldiers and ordinary civilians were manning the roadblocks, armed
with machetes. Some of them had guns. Youths half-dressed in army
uniforms swore at us before reluctantly letting us through.

Near the Hôtel des Mille Collines in the centre of Kigali, we met
two Bangladeshi APCs held up at a roadblock manned by Presidential
Guards. A French-made armoured reconnaissance vehicle had its sev-
enty-six-millimetre-cannon aimed at them. When I got out, the
Bangladeshi lieutenant pushed his head out of the turret. He and his
men were very uneasy, he told me. They hadn't been able to get to the
UNDP compound to extricate the Rwandans stranded there. I told him to
stay put until I could get the APCs through. I walked up to the corporal

who was running the roadblock and told him to let my vehicle and the APCs by. He refused. His orders were that no one, especially UNAMIR, was permitted into the city centre and that if we tried to cross his roadblock he would open fire. I wanted to drive right over his roadblock, but I remembered Riza's directive. I turned in place, absorbing the situation around me, and noticed that the cannon on the turret and its coaxial medium machine gun were now aimed at me. I walked back to my vehicle and told the Bangladeshi lieutenant to keep the APCs in place until I ordered them to move forward. This did little to allay the fear so explicit on his face. The five working APCs were our last line of resort and if they couldn't get through a roadblock, nothing we had could. I had to get Bagosora or Ndindiliyimana to open the roadblocks.

I decided to proceed on foot. I told Robert to back up and find a road to the west; he might be able to negotiate his way through a roadblock there and link up with us. I told Maggen to join me as I walked toward the roadblock. The corporal watched as we went by him, then yelled at me and gave orders in Kinyarwanda, which were followed by the sound of weapons being cocked. I told Maggen that we would keep walking. Other orders were yelled but no shots rang out.

We now had to walk about half a kilometre through the deserted government and business district. There were a few bursts of small arms fire coming from northwest of the city, but there was no sign of life here, as if all the people had fled or were in hiding. The Presidential Guard was doing a fine job of containing the relatively small city centre, but who was issuing the orders? Why was the rest of the city starting to resemble anarchy while the Gendarmerie was apparently sitting on its hands?

We stopped at the gates of the UNDP office compound. It was deserted. The important person, whoever it might have been, was not here now—there were no signs that anyone had been here all morning. We returned to the Boulevard de la Révolution and kept walking. Our pace was brisk. The only sounds we heard were birdsong, the echo of our footsteps on the pavement, and the pounding of our hearts. Maggen kept his own counsel as I was deep in thought. Should I use force regardless of the direct order from Riza? Given our resources, I couldn't magically transform us into an intervention force, but how far could I go? I still had a mandate—the RPF was still following the rules and we were only facing rogue RGF units. The key to re-establishing a secure situation was Bagosora. He was in charge. He and Ndindiliyimana had to demonstrate to me that this was not a coup.

The Ministry of Defence was only about a hundred metres from the UNDP office compound and was guarded by a platoon of about forty personnel, mostly army troops wearing no regimental insignia, along with a few gendarmes. I asked the lieutenant in charge—who had made it clear that he was not disposed to let me inside—where Colonel Bagosora was. He responded that he wasn't there. I turned around and carried on walking with Maggen, heading west to the main gate of army headquarters at Camp Kigali, about four hundred metres farther down the avenue. As we walked along the edge of the Ministry of Defence compound, a major called out from the wall. He yelled that he did not think it wise for us to proceed on foot—he would drive us the rest of the way. I told him not to bother, but he came running to join us, trailed by a small military car. At his insistence, we climbed in. I told him I had to find Bagosora and Ndindiliyimana.

The army headquarters was just inside the main gates of Camp Kigali. When we arrived, the place was still in full combat readiness. All the bunkers were manned and medium machine guns covered the entrance. Several rows of spiked barriers were set up to deter wheeled vehicles. There was a large bunker about twenty metres inside the gates with a direct line of fire down the long, straight boulevard. An armoured car was parked outside the entrance in a semi-hull-down position, partially hidden, its gun aimed down the street. Several troops and some Presidential Guards were manning the gates. The major leapt out of the car and approached the guards. After a few minutes he came back and told us that the meeting was being held at the École Supérieure Militaire.

We backed up and drove south along Avenue de l'Hôpital, past the second gate to Camp Kigali, heading for the military school entrance. Inside the gate, I got a glimpse of what looked like two Belgian soldiers lying on the ground at the far end of the compound. It was a brutal shock. How had they been captured? I ordered the major to stop the car, telling him I thought I had seen some of my own soldiers on the ground. Instead, he sped around the corner and drove directly into the college parking lot. It was only a matter of moments, but those moments seemed to last a lifetime, the small car carrying me farther and farther away from the second gate. The major told me emphatically that I could not go into Camp Kigali. The troops inside the camp were out of control.

I got out of the car, Maggen behind me. Sizable numbers of fully armed troops and gendarmes, some with bandoliers of bullets across their chests, were sheltering from the noon-day sun in the shade of several mature trees. All talk amongst them abruptly stopped as they stared at me. Suddenly a UNAMIR military observer, Captain Apedo Kodjo of Togo, stepped away from the soldiers who had been holding him and approached me. He was fearful and whispered in my ear, pointing out five Ghanaian soldiers who were being held nearby. They had just been brought here from Camp Kigali, where a group of Belgian soldiers were still detained. These Belgians, he said, were being assaulted—the verb he used was *tabasser*, which means "beaten" or "roughed up." I looked over at the Ghanaians, who should have been armed but had no weapons with them. They waved nervously. Murmurs were rising from the RGF soldiers, but none of them changed position.

I told Captain Kodjo to stay put and await my return. His eyes grew wide at this order but he obeyed. I judged that the Ghanaians and my military observer would be safe for the moment and rapidly headed along a short path to the amphitheatre where I suspected Bagosora was holding court.

I entered a small anteroom that was in total darkness. Opening the heavy curtains on the other side, I burst out into a well-lit room full of people in uniform. I could see the shock and surprise on Bagosora's face. I seemed to have caught him in mid-speech, with one arm raised for emphasis. I advanced a few steps toward the small platform where he stood. Ndindiliyimana was sitting at a table to his left. The hall was silent and no one moved. Then Bagosora lowered his arm and came toward me, extending his hand and saying that I was most welcome, and how fortuitous it was that I had arrived when all the army and Gendarmerie senior leadership were in one location.

A third chair was quickly placed on the podium for me. I looked around the room, spotting some of the moderate senior officers with whom I had had several discussions in the past about the political future of the nation. Overall though, it was a less than sympathetic crowd. Carrying on with his speech in French, Bagosora defended the creation of the Crisis Committee and said that it must put together a communiqué by two o'clock that afternoon to calm the nation and inform the people that the security situation was well in hand. Bagosora received support for this plan, and Colonel Léonidas Rusatira, the senior colonel in the army (a moderate I had met with several times), was made the chair of the subcommittee that was to draft the communiqué. Bagosora emphasized that it was essential that the RPF understand what was happening. He hoped that I would relay this information to them.

At this point I still did not believe that Arusha was irrevocably lost. However, with the Belgian soldiers being mistreated in Camp Kigali, as well as other troops still not accounted for, we were moving rapidly toward confrontation. How could I protect the unarmed civilian and military personnel? And there were other UN staff in remote locations around the country who would become targets for retaliation if I met violence with force. In addition, there was a diplomatic and expatriate community of about five thousand, scattered all over Rwanda, who were vulnerable.

Bagosora turned to me and asked if I would address the commanders— I discovered a completely new set of stomach muscles that were attempting to bend me in two as I stood. The hall was silent. "I regret enormously the loss of your president and the chief of staff of the army in the crash last night," I began. "I realize that some units very close to the president have been overwrought with grief, fear and anger and have conducted over the last twelve hours the gravest of crimes, which must be stopped now by you, the senior and unit commanders. We in UNAMIR are staying put. I will continue to support you in avoiding the destruction of the Arusha accords and will assist you in preventing another civil war with the RPF. It is the duty of the commanders of units in the KWSA to regain control of their units and return immediately to their garrisons to abide by the rules of the KWSA. It is crucial that you, the commanders of sectors and units around the country, maintain a state of calm in your units and in the populations in your areas of responsibility until the political and the security situation is resolved."

There was scattered applause at the end of my short speech. They'd heard from my lips that UNAMIR was staying; the implementation of Arusha was still my mission. I couldn't abandon the people who had trusted the international community to help them. I made the decision to stay in the final split second before making the most consequential speech of my life. As a result I had to accept that UNAMIR would be threatened and at risk.

I have been severely criticized in some quarters for the decisions that I took on April 7, 1994. I accept responsibility for every decision I made that day, on the days previously, on the days after—for my conduct during the entire mission. I will try to tell the story so that you understand that this was a day not of one or two isolated incidents and a few decisions. It was a day that felt like a year, where there were hundreds of incidents and decisions that had to be made in seconds.

I didn't raise the issue of the Belgian soldiers in that speech because I wanted to discuss it with Bagosora alone. I needed to assess its impact on the entire mission, and I wanted to talk to the senior army leadership, who I hoped might be able to save the situation. It was that decision, in part, that contributed to the deaths of ten soldiers under my command. I wanted to proceed by negotiation, as I realized I could not use force without the certainty of more casualties. I did not have the offensive force to take on a dug-in garrison of more than a thousand troops. I considered a rescue option irresponsible. If we used force against the RGF compound, we were then a legitimate target and we would become a third belligerent. My aim that morning was to do everything in my power to avoid a confrontation, regain control of the rogue units in Kigali and keep the dialogue and the prospects of the peace accord alive.

Commanders spend their careers preparing for the moment when they will have to choose between lose-lose propositions in the use of their troops. Regardless of the decision they make, some of their men will most certainly die. My decision took sons from their parents, husbands from their wives, fathers from their children. I knew the cost of my decision: I was risking the lives of the Belgians in Camp Kigali, men whose names are listed on the dedication page of this book. They were and remain heroes of Rwanda.

It was clearly the fulfillment of the plot Jean-Pierre had told us about months earlier. The Belgian soldiers were being deliberately targeted by extremists to create fear. The aim was to secure first a Belgian, then a UN withdrawal. The extremists had taken their cue from the grim farces of Bosnia and Somalia. They knew that Western nations do not have the stomach or the will to sustain casualties in peace support operations. When confronted with casualties, as the United States was in Somalia or the Belgians in Rwanda, they will run, regardless of the consequences to the abandoned population.

I remained standing for a few minutes as Bagosora resumed centre stage. I heard him express his relief that UNAMIR was staying to help them through this terrible crisis. As the meeting ended, he disappeared through the mass of officers who rose from their seats and gathered at the front of the stage to greet me. A group of senior officers endorsed my stand. Among them were my RGF liaison, Ephrem Rwabalinda, and the head of the military college, Colonel Rusatira. Since I couldn't spot Bagosora, I confronted Ndindiliyimana: What was happening to my men in Camp Kigali? He didn't know for sure, he said, but RTLM had been broadcasting that the presidential plane had been shot down by Belgians, and soldiers and veterans were rioting inside the camp. He and the others insisted I let them try to secure the release of the Belgians. At the time I didn't realize that these were the soldiers who had been the escort and guard for Prime Minister Agathe. The officers asked me to attend the sub-committee that was drafting the communiqué to the nation while others intervened on behalf of my men, and we proceeded to a classroom on one side of the amphitheatre. I wondered whether Rusatira was going to make a move to coalesce the moderates. As the meeting began, Ndindiliyimana seemed to sink into a sullen lethargy and didn't take part in the discussions. The only men who were not morose and uncertain were two RGF lieutenant colonels whom I had never met, who kept urging Rusatira to make haste—obviously hard-liners planted there to keep an eye on things. If the moderates in this room actually had the will to attempt to reverse the manipulations of Bagosora, they would have a difficult time of it.

It was around noon. Though I'd dismissed the idea of a rescue mission, I kept running scenarios in my head. The RGF units, particularly the Presidential Guard, had taken up defensive positions, set up barricades throughout the inner core of the capital, and were restricting movement as far away as the airport. The Presidential Guard had been reinforced by elements of the Reconnaissance Battalion and the Para-Commando Battalion. They were well-armed, experienced and well-trained. Camp Kigali was a walled and sprawling area, home to the Reconnaissance Battalion, the artillery unit, a maintenance and transport unit, the senior military academy, the military hospital and convalescent centre, and the RGF national headquarters. Hate radio had led everyone inside its gates to believe that our Belgians had killed their president.

To have any chance of success at storming a well-fortified camp, I'd need several hundred men, supported by light armour and mortars. My Quick Reaction Force was still woefully inadequate. Most of the Ghanaian contingent was in the demilitarized zone far to the north without vehicles or heavy weapons, let alone ammunition. They, too, were vulnerable. The Ghanaians we had moved into the city were dispersed on protection jobs all around Kigali. They and the Tunisians at the CND who were guarding the RPF were lightly armed, possessed no transport and already had essential duties. The Belgians were also spread all over town. Any attempt at taking the camp or even part of it would have been an irresponsible mission. Even if we had been able to assemble an intervention force, fight our way through several roadblocks and get into and out of the camp with our men, we would have had to withdraw through the city, past more roadblocks, and gain the airfield, as we had no place of retreat where we could realistically withstand the inevitable RGF counterattacks and bombardments from their 105- and 120-millimetre guns. I thought of Mogadishu, where a few months earlier the Americans—the most militarily capable force in the world—had botched the abduction attempt of a couple of aides to a Somali warlord and had suffered eighteen dead and more than seventy injured. The Malaysian and Pakistani peacekeepers who tried to rescue the American troops took ninety casualties. And these forces were large, well-trained and well-equipped.

I had to keep the pressure on the RGF leaders to go in and retrieve the Belgians. The work session on the communiqué was going nowhere. It had been at least an hour and a half since I'd left the vehicle with Robert at the barrier. I had to get out of there. I told the group to be sure to include our commitment to Arusha in the communiqué, made my apologies and left.

I sprinted up the path to the parking lot. Captain Kodjo and the Ghanaian soldiers, still under guard, were relieved to see me. I told them that they had to get back to our lines right away. I spoke to an officer and asked him for transport to take my men back to Force HQ, and he agreed without hesitation, even providing a small escort. The major was still waiting in the car. He drove me and Maggen to the Ministry of Defence. The route he chose did not pass by Camp Kigali. I didn't have a radio and I had to get to a phone. When we arrived, I told Maggen to go find Robert and our vehicle and bring them both back to meet me.

The ministry was almost deserted. A few guards gave me curious looks but let me pass. Inside one of the buildings, I asked a lieutenant if there was a phone and an office I could use. After some hesitation, he led me into the building that housed Bagosora's office and directed me to the room next to his. Where were the leaders? Where was the staff? The ministry along with army headquarters should have been the hub of action. There were no couriers bringing in up-to-date information, no staff officers or civilian bureaucrats at their desks, no telephones ringing. Except for the new guards and the manned defences, the place was nearly asleep. Was there an alternate command post, and if so, who was in charge? The minister of defence was in Cameroon, conveniently out of the picture. I sent for the duty officer and asked him where everyone was. The last thing I expected was the answer he gave me: they had all gone for lunch.

I called the Force HQ and got through to Henry. He had horrifying news. The UNAMIR-protected VIPs—Lando Ndasingwa, Joseph Kavaruganda, and many other moderates—had been abducted by the Presidential

Guard and militias and had been killed, along with their families. Missing or captured in and around Kigali were at least thirty-five of our military personnel, many of whom had been on duty with the kidnapped VIPs. There was one politician being held at Force HQ, who had been saved by Luc and whose name Henry wouldn't reveal over the phone. The important people who Moustache was harbouring at the UNDP housing compound were Prime Minister Agathe, her husband and children.

Henry had heard there were Belgians in trouble at Camp Kigali— eleven men, he thought, maybe as many as thirteen. I told him that I had seen two Belgian soldiers on the ground in Camp Kigali. He had no more news from Luc because Kigali Sector headquarters was being overwhelmed with requests for help. Tiko and his military observers had abandoned Kimihura and moved in convoy to the Amahoro because a noose of barricades had been slowly closing around them. Prior to their withdrawal, they had witnessed Presidential Guard and Interahamwe members going from house to house with lists, breaking in and executing families. His unarmed observers had no way to stop this gruesomely efficient series of murders. Tiko wasn't going to risk any of his men, and I would not have ordered him to do so.

Dozens of civilian staff couldn't be accounted for because they had no phone or radio, and we couldn't get to their homes. The standoff at the airport and the situation at the crash site hadn't changed. Henry was trying to rescue Rwandans and expatriates who were in danger, bringing them to UNAMIR compounds such as the Amahoro Stadium, the Meridien, the King Faisal Hospital, the Hôtel des Mille Collines, the Belgian camp at the Dom Bosco school, and several smaller Belgian and UNAMIR compounds around town. These locations had become UN-protected sites for persons at risk, and the volume of people seeking our protection was growing exponentially. I asked Henry about Booh-Booh and the political front, and he responded that he hadn't heard any more from the SRSG since the morning.

Henry was totally frustrated with the Bangladeshi troops. Their APCs were either mysteriously breaking down (we later found out that the crews were sabotaging the vehicles by placing rags in the exhaust pipes) or they couldn't be reached (a confirmed tactic by some of the crews was to move a short distance from the headquarters, shut down the radio and return later, claiming they had been held at a roadblock.) Those who actually arrived at the place to which they had been sent exhibited a lack of zeal in pursuing their missions.

A mob of angry locals, fired up by extremists, were blocking the entrances to the Amahoro Stadium complex to which thousands of Tutsis and moderate Hutus were attempting to flee. Henry kept urging the Bangladeshis to clear the area, but their commander was not responding to his orders and was seeking direction from Dhaka. The couple of APCs that had returned to the stadium were sitting idle while Kigali Sector was pleading for them to respond to calls for help from other UNAMIR personnel and Rwandans at risk. I ordered Henry to inform the Bangladeshi commander that he was contributing to the potential deaths of Rwandans and UNAMIR personnel and that he would be held accountable. That night I found out that he had received direct orders from his chief of staff in Dhaka to stop taking risks, stay buttoned down, close the gates and stop carrying Rwandans in the APCs. He did exactly as he was ordered, ignoring the UNAMIR chain of command and the tragedies caused by his decisions.

I told Henry to keep trying to account for our personnel, to secure our locations and get rescue patrols out to as many people as we could in Kigali. Luc would be the sole decider on whether a particular mission was worth the risk, as he was the one who owned the Kigali area troops and had the best network in the KWSA. I would stay close to Bagosora and Ndindiliyimana. Henry would stay close to the RPF, and we would keep each other fully informed.

Robert and Maggen arrived with the vehicle soon after I'd hung up. There was no time to grieve for the Rwandans who had already been lost. Robert had been monitoring the Force radio net and had two new pieces of information: UNAMIR had been able to rescue Prime Minister Faustin, who was now at the Force HQ. His was the name Henry hadn't mentioned over the phone. The second, ominous piece of news was a message to me from Paul Kagame: "I have just learned many homes of our supporters are surrounded by RGF soldiers. The intentions certainly clear. Informing you that our forces have to react to protect ours. I'm very serious and want to info you before [*sic*]." I immediately called the Force HQ and, after several attempts, got through to Henry again. I told him to contact Ballis at the CND and relay in no uncertain terms that the RPF must stay put in the CND and in the north until I had been given a full opportunity to try to contain the situation with Bagosora.

It was after 1300 by the time I got off the phone. There was still no sign of Bagosora or Ndindiliyimana, so I decided to go with Robert to the UNDP housing compound, where Madame Agathe and her family may have fled. There might still be a chance of helping them out. We continued to hear sporadic gunfire coming from the direction of Camp Kigali. Leaving Maggen behind to monitor the vehicle radio, Robert and I set off down the Boulevard de la Révolution. We stopped at the fourth or fifth compound on the left and banged on the blue steel doors. We identified ourselves and were let in.

To my astonishment, Captain Diagne Mbaye, a Senegalese MILOB, was standing there with a UNAMIR vehicle. As the gate closed behind us, a rush of fifteen to twenty civilians appeared, all speaking at once. Captain Mbaye got them to calm down and then described for me the morning's horrible events. He had made his own way here from the Hôtel des Mille Collines as word had filtered in about Madame Agathe from civilians seeking shelter there. By the time he got to the UNDP, the prime minister and her husband had been captured by men from the Presidential Guard and the army. They had surrendered in order to save their children, who were still hiding. Madame Agathe and her husband were murdered on the spot; there was blood on the wall and signs of grenade explosions at the entrance of one house as well as in the living room. For some reason, the killers didn't search the compound, and the four children remained safe. I was brought to a dark room where they were hiding in a corner, behind clothes and furniture.

Since the killing of their parents, the compound had been relatively calm. Mbaye had taken over from Moustache, who had gone out to rescue other UN personnel. Still, the Senegalese captain was worried that the Presidential Guard would return and find the children. I promised him that UNAMIR personnel would return later in the afternoon with APCs to get UN staff and the prime minister's children to safety. Moving them in an open UNAMIR vehicle would be too risky at roadblocks manned by the Presidential Guard. He said he would stay until the children were safe. (No APCs made it to the compound that day, but Mbaye and Moustache saved the children by sneaking them away in their own vehicles.)

I was heartbroken at Madame Agathe's death. She loved her nation and her people and wanted a democratic future for them. And for that she was dead. I could not even stop to feel her loss—too many others were at risk, including my troops at Camp Kigali and elsewhere. Robert and I walked back to the Ministry of Defence, hoping the leaders were back from lunch.

No one had shown up yet. Maggen passed on another message from Kagame: UNAMIR should immediately move to protect all of the disappeared or arrested politicians and the sooner the better. I called Force HQ again. We had troops in dangerous situations and, although limited by the ROE change, I could have overridden the prohibition on intervention and used force where crimes against humanity were being committed. I did not exercise that option for I could not have sustained combat operations nor guaranteed the safety of civilians or my troops if UNAMIR were to have become the third belligerent. I did not receive a request from Luc to mount a rescue of the Belgians in Camp Kigali because he understood the reality of our situation as well as I did. If I had received such a request, I would have categorically refused because of the high risk involved. In the end, the strategy of non-intervention did limit the chances of my troops being targeted, but it also meant that force was not effectively used to protect persons at risk.

Bagosora got back at about 1400, with Ndindiliyimana close behind. I stopped them in the hall, and yes, it turned out that Bagosora had taken a lunch break—but, he said, only after he had unsuccessfully attempted to get into Camp Kigali to save my troops. Ndindiliyimana chimed in: Every senior officer who had tried to calm the camp down had been threatened or assaulted by the mutineers. Bagosora told me that he was putting a force together to stop the chaos in the camp. Frustrated and angry, I told him that I would go into the camp myself.

He stopped dead at the door of his office, turned around and with his eyes fixed on mine told me that I was not to approach that camp. I was to leave the situation in his hands. I told him he had no authority over me, and I made it clear that I held him personally responsible for my soldiers' safe return.

I went back to the phone and called Brent to alert him to what was going on. He put Henry on the line. There was a third message from Kagame, a straightforward ultimatum. The killings throughout the city had to cease immediately or he would order his troops to intervene. The message had six brief lines:

A. RPF is prepared to secure Kigali;
B. Force Commander should not rely on his Belgian Staff;
C. UNAMIR should pull its forces out of the DMZ to reinforce Kigali;
D. RPF prepared to assist UNAMIR; and
E. If CND is attacked RPF will move on Kigali; and
F. If situation is not secured by last light 7 April, definite RPF attack.

This last point was Kagame's promised warning to us to get out of the way. Henry told me that Kagame and his senior staff had just moved out of Mulindi and were suspected of setting up a tactical command post closer to the demilitarized zone so that they would be in a location where they could launch their offensive. This was no bluff.

Last light in Rwanda fell at about six o'clock, which meant I had less than four hours to bring the situation under control, or the nation would sink back into civil war. I told Henry I would call the CND and try to arrange for the RPF and Bagosora to speak to one another to negotiate an end to the rogue units and civilian killings. It was the only way I could think of to prevent the RPF from advancing south. No sooner had I put down the phone than Robert came in with another message from Kagame. He was offering to immediately reinforce the RGF with two of his battalions to assist them in getting the rogue units under control, especially the Presidential Guard. He needed an answer right away.

Relaying an offer of help from Kagame finally got a rise out of Ndindiliyimana and pushed a definite wrong button in Bagosora. He stood behind his desk, a portrait of the late president looking down on him from the wall as if Habyarimana were still watching his every move. His face contorted as he tried to maintain his facade of reasonableness. He told me to pass on his thanks to the RPF for the offer but he couldn't accept. It was his problem to solve. I looked to Ndindiliyimana, the fence-sitter, for a sign of hope that he might consider using the RPF troops with subordinate elements of the RGF to conduct a counter-coup within the RGF against the hard-liners. There was none. He agreed with Bagosora. It was becoming clear that the moderates had no units in Kigali that were favourable to them. There might be some in southern Rwanda, but it was doubtful they could link up with the RPF and overwhelm the elite extremist RGF units. (Later I found out that the southern units themselves were thoroughly infiltrated with extremists.) I forwarded their refusal to Force HQ and asked again for the RPF to stay in the CND and behind the demilitarized zone.

If Bagosora was genuinely committed to Arusha, surely he would want to tell the RPF directly and make the necessary guarantees to prevent a resumption of hostilities. If he was opposed to Arusha and peace, he would have no interest in speaking to the RPF. Or he would continue to follow his usual path: appear to be co-operative as part of a deception to mask his true intentions. So I confronted Bagosora again on the issue of moving the rogue units back to their barracks and getting rid of the roadblocks. He was shuffling papers and signing them at his enormous desk, looking every inch the bored bureaucrat. Sunlight was pouring through the window onto the freshly painted walls, no phones were ringing, there were few visitors. He waved me over to the sofa where Ndindiliyimana was sitting, apparently relaxed, but I didn't want to sit. He offered me tea or coffee, as if this were an ordinary visit on a slow day at the office.

Prime Minister Agathe was confirmed dead, I said, killed by the Presidential Guard. Bagosora responded that he was sorry, that this was just another example of the difficulties he was facing in trying to regain control of the rogue troops still reacting to the death of their beloved leader. I asked why he hadn't resolved the standoffs at the airport and the crash site or been able to secure the release of my Belgians. I told him he had to guarantee freedom of movement to UNAMIR. Bagosora pleaded for time; both he and Ndindiliyimana were having logistical and transport problems. He had called and given orders to sort out the airport problem. As for the crash site, he said the Presidential Guard was operating on its own. The Guard appeared to be behind all the altercations and killings around town, I said. Bagosora claimed he was negotiating with their commanding officer to get them back into their garrison. There was no panic, no sense of urgency animating this man. Bagosora was either the coldest fish in Africa or he was the ghost of Machiavelli executing a subversive plan.

I told him that in order to prevent a full-scale civil war he should talk to the RPF directly, outlining the measures he was taking to calm things down. Bagosora sat back, unimpressed with my suggestion and returned to his papers. But Ndindiliyimana thought this might be a good idea and asked me if I could arrange a meeting. I told him I would do everything in my power to make it happen.

I left to make the calls, but the phones were jammed at the Force HQ and the CND. While I was trying to get through, I watched a large, ugly RGF colonel enter Bagosora's office and close the door behind him. I had never seen him before and didn't see his face again until years later, when the International Criminal Tribunal for Rwanda (ICTR) showed me his picture. He was one of the military leaders of the genocide, and one of the most ruthless characters in the slaughter that was about to unfold.

When I finally got through to Ballis at the CND, he said that the RPF had been under direct fire from the area of the Presidential Guard compound and that they were taking down the fences and preparing for military action. The Tunisians were in a very precarious situation, sitting between the two forces, and had spent most of the day holding the gate closed and digging their trenches deeper. I told Ballis to inform their commander to reduce their presence around the perimeter and consolidate most of his force in their protected area inside the CND offices and in trenches outside. If the RPF decided to punch out, all of the Tunisians were to withdraw without confrontation to their safe area.

I then asked Ballis to bring any one of the RPF's political leaders to the phone. Major figures, such as Pasteur Bizimungu and Patrick Mazimhaka, had gone to Mulindi several weeks earlier, leaving three second-string politicians behind in Kigali. There didn't appear to be a well-defined hierarchy among them: none of them ever claimed to be in charge. The one I negotiated with most often was Seth Sendashonga, who was also the most vocal of the three. A Hutu who had fled Rwanda and joined the RPF in Uganda, Seth spoke fluent French and a little English. He was extremely self-confident, ambitious and aggressive. It was Seth who came to the phone, and he was quite cold to my suggestion of talking directly to Bagosora. He said that he would consult first and get back to me. This was typical for the RPF political leaders, who always needed to consult with their peers. The clock was ticking on Kagame's deadline.

I called Force HQ and dictated my responses to Kagame's six points to Brent, spelling out extensively my response to point F: "UNAMIR wouldn't conduct any offensive operations as it is mandated for defensive peacekeeping tasks only. UNAMIR with the Gendarmerie and elements of the Army loyal to Rwanda are attempting to stabilize the situation. UNAMIR is not in an offensive posture and if the RPF initiates action at the CND and/or RPF offensive in the DMZ tonight, this will be deemed to be a serious ceasefire violation. UNAMIR's peacekeeping mandate will be totally violated. Request you reconsider these actions as loyal forces and UNAMIR are attempting to establish order and control on aggression in Kigali."

I asked Brent to send this message to Kagame as soon as possible with a copy to the DPKO. Since it didn't look like I'd be back at the Amahoro any time soon, I also asked him to forward the written sitrep to New York. There had been no movement on the political front and no word from Booh-Booh, though with the shooting increasing near the SRSG's residence, Henry was planning to escort Booh-Booh and his staff to the Meridien hotel, which had become a safe haven for UN personnel.

I returned to Bagosora's office as the huge RGF colonel was leaving, after receiving some last words of instruction in Kinyarwanda. Again I harangued Bagosora and Ndindiliyimana over the violence that was breaking loose throughout the city, over the release of my soldiers and over their seeming detachment from the whole catastrophe. I asked when the Crisis Committee would hand over control to the politicians. And who were the politicians, since many of the ministers named to the BBTG were unaccounted for? All the hardline ministers had disappeared before midnight last night. Madame Agathe was dead. Who would be the chair? Bagosora responded that the politicians were gathering to take over the situation within the next day or so. I demanded that Booh-Booh be invited to assist. Bagosora refused to answer and returned to his papers. Ndindiliyimana was nearly asleep beside me.

Out of the blue, Bagosora suddenly volunteered that there was something I should think about: it might be best to get the Belgians out of UNAMIR and out of Rwanda because of the rumours that they had shot down the presidential airplane. What had been happening in Camp Kigali might happen to the rest of the Belgians if the Crisis Committee continued to have problems regaining control of the situation.

Was he hoping that the best combat unit in UNAMIR would desert the field? This was the first time I had ever heard a senior leader of the Habyarimana government even mention that they did not want the Belgians here. If the Belgians withdrew, New York would surely order UNAMIR's departure.

A short time later, the phone rang in the little office I had been using. It was Seth confirming that he would talk to Bagosora. I told him to call back on Bagosora's number and headed for his office. His phone was ringing as I entered the room, and Bagosora picked it up. If he was a man intent on saving his country from civil war, there was no sign of it in his voice. After a few words, he passed the receiver to Ndindiliyimana. That conversation was a little longer and more amiable. When Ndindiliyimana hung up, he said that there was nothing to be done—the RPF insisted that the Presidential Guard be arrested and jailed and the killings stopped immediately. Ndindiliyimana had told Seth that they were doing their best to regain control, but from Seth's negative reaction, he concluded that the RPF would most likely attack soon. Bagosora was nonchalant in the face of this new crisis. He told me that the interim chief of staff of the RGF, Colonel Marcel Gatsinzi, would arrive in Kigali in time for a meeting of the Crisis Committee at army headquarters around 1800 and invited me to attend. I said I would, but I wondered why Bagosora had chosen to appoint Gatsinzi, a southern Hutu from Butare, a known moderate and an honest man.

There were about two hours left until twilight and the only chance to avoid a civil war had just been lost. When hostilities broke out, we could expect that large numbers of innocent people would be slaughtered, as had happened in Burundi after the coup in October. I decided to stay for the upcoming Crisis Committee meeting. Maybe Gatsinzi's presence would encourage Ndindiliyimana to try to wrestle control from Bagosora. Half an hour later, Ballis called to say that the RPF battalion had just broken out of the CND at company strength and were advancing toward the Presidential Guard's camp.

I needed some political advice on how to move this situation out of the hands of this military clique as soon as possible. I decided to send Maggen and Robert to pick up Dr. Kabia and bring him here. I waited outside in the compound in the cool breeze of the early evening. There were long shadows cast by the tall trees, and a disarming serenity barely touched by the echo of distant gunfire. A sense of despair suddenly overwhelmed me; the path to war and slaughter was now open. It was high time to consolidate my troops to ensure their safety, do what we could to keep our safe havens open for civilians from both sides and try to flush out the nature of the politics at work behind Bagosora. What was I going to do if the 450 Belgians had to withdraw under pressure from the RGF, or were pulled by their own government? I would be left with a very lightly armed, nearly useless Bangladeshi contingent of about 1,100 soldiers, an excellent Ghanaian battalion of about 800, mostly deployed in the demilitarized zone with no operational equipment or vehicles, 300 or so unarmed military observers scattered around the country, and a ragtag Force HQ, undermined by the loss of the Belgian staff officers and manned by Bangladeshis who listened to their contingent commander and not to me. My headquarters support group as well as my logistics group were made up of civilians, and they would surely be evacuated for safety reasons. And what of the thousands of civilians under our protection? Our food, water and medical supplies were barely enough for my force, let alone these displaced persons. The dispassionate professional side of my nature was telling me to cut my losses and get all my troops to safety. My gut, my emotions—my sense of the right thing to do—was telling me to do everything I could to stop the coming onslaught.

I was still struggling with my thoughts when Dr. Kabia, Robert and Maggen drove into the compound at about 1730. They had been threatened and had turned back on their first attempt to get through the roadblocks and had commandeered a Gendarmerie escort to try again. Hundreds of barriers were now going up all over the city, manned by militia, military, gendarmes and civilians, all of them angry and armed with clubs, axes, machetes, Belgian FN rifles and even the odd AK-47. The radio in the vehicle was crackling with descriptions of the RPF assault on the Presidential Guard—a vicious firefight in which the RPF was being held just short of the Presidential Guard's camp.

It was almost 1800, so we drove to the Crisis Committee meeting. For the first time that day, we were allowed inside the gates of Camp Kigali, passing through a gauntlet of steel barriers, past an armoured car and a large group of guards with machine guns. Where were the mutineers? I left Maggen and Robert with the vehicle, and Dr. Kabia and I headed for the same conference room as the previous night. As we reached the top of the stairs, the newly promoted Major General Gatsinzi came forward to welcome us, with Ndindiliyimana close behind. It was good to see Gatsinzi and we exchanged regards. Bagosora was nowhere around.

As the meeting began, I wondered if Gatsinzi and Ndindiliyimana were simply Bagosora's puppets. Of the two, I was certain that Gatsinzi was more at risk from the hard-liners: he had been a member of the group of moderate army officers who had warned me of the third force in their open letter of December 3. Could he actually be in control of the army? Why would Bagosora countenance it?

The briefing was sombre. The Presidential Guard had captured and, as far as Gatsinzi knew, executed all of the moderates in the government who hadn't been able to escape. He read the list of persons who were killed or missing. Two survivors were Faustin Twagiramungu and

Anastase Gasana, the foreign minister. Faustin was at Force HQ, and Gasana was in Dar es Salaam after Habyarimana had unceremoniously kicked him off his plane to seat the president of Burundi. Gatsinzi also confirmed that command of the RGF had broken down, particularly in Kigali. He assured me that he was committed to Arusha and would do all he could to get the Presidential Guard under control and the RGF units back in their barracks. He urged me to inform the RPF that he wanted peace but needed time to exert control over his forces.

I believed him. Here was my hope. The forces in southern Rwanda were mostly moderate. Gatsinzi could perhaps rally these elements and suppress the Presidential Guard, the Interahamwe and the third force. I had to talk to Kagame and get him to wait.

Then Ndindiliyimana took over. The first item on his agenda was to tell me that with the hate RTLM was spewing, and the mood of the army and the citizens of Kigali, it would be prudent to withdraw the Belgian contingent as soon as possible. I told him I would take the recommendation under advisement but first had to get my Belgian soldiers back. The camp was quiet now. Why hadn't they released my soldiers? Ndindiliyimana sent one of the officers to get me an answer.

The meeting droned on and on and the officer didn't come back. The Crisis Committee still hadn't issued the press communiqué that was supposed to calm the nation. Rwandans were listening to the non-stop hate and lies put out by RTLM. The only concrete sign of the committee's good faith would be the detention of the Presidential Guard in its garrison, the return of all units to KWSA rules, and an end to the killings. But no one in this group, well-intentioned though it might be, seemed to know just how to achieve all these objectives and prevent the looming war.

Suddenly everyone was standing up, stretching and collecting their papers, behaving as though this were a normal meeting on a normal day. It was then that I lost my temper. I banged on the table. "Enough is enough," I yelled. No more time, no more excuses, no more discussion. I told them to either turn over my Belgian soldiers to me now or I wouldn't leave this headquarters and they would get absolutely nothing more from UNAMIR or me.

Ndindiliyimana got on the phone again and dispatched several more staff officers. After twenty minutes of silence, with me sitting immobile and furious, the phone rang. Ndindiliyimana picked it up and, after a murmured conversation, turned to tell me that my soldiers had been found in the Kigali hospital nearby. I announced that we were all going to the hospital, right now, and together we would secure the Belgians' release.

The hospital was only two hundred metres away. Several soldiers, including a number of wounded, were milling around the entrance. Ndindiliyimana took the lead at that point and got us through the crowd and inside. We nearly plunged into an operating theatre where the doors were open to let in fresh air. There was screaming, moaning, blood on the tables and floors, and staff in red-stained medical gowns. The room seemed full to overflowing with wounded, both military and civilian, lying on cots and even on the floors. The nearest doctor growled angrily at us to get out.

At the back door, an officer told Ndindiliyimana that the bodies of the Belgians were at the far end of the large courtyard in front of the morgue. The word *bodies* hit me right in the heart and shocked me for a moment. I heard gasps and other sounds of disbelief all around me. They were all dead. We made our way down the dark path toward a small hut with a twenty-five-watt bulb over the door. There were more injured in the yard, along with dozens of bodies. I could not believe that this scene was unfolding so close to the meeting room where I had sat all evening.

At first, I saw what seemed to be sacks of potatoes to the right of the morgue door. It slowly resolved in my vision into a heap of mangled and bloodied white flesh in tattered Belgian para-commando uniforms. The men were piled on top of each other, and we couldn't tell how many were in the pile. The light was faint and it was hard to identify any of the faces or find specific markings. We counted them twice: eleven soldiers. In the end it turned out to be ten.

I wanted to take justice into my own hands, an eye for an eye—the first time I had ever felt the toxic pull of retribution. I ordered Robert to photograph the bodies, and he went about the task numbed and silent. I asked the commanders who had done this. They said renegade soldiers and amputee veterans in Camp Kigali. I asked them what they were going to do about it. Gatsinzi assured me he would investigate the incident and that all of those responsible would be brought to justice. I told him that these murders would be immediately reported to New York and that Rwanda could expect the wrath of the international community to descend upon its head. He and Ndindiliyimana were genuinely distraught. They apologized profusely, offered their condolences and sympathies—and pleaded with me that these deaths should not deter UNAMIR from helping their country.

I told them to have the bodies cleaned and properly laid out and demanded that a guard be put on them. UNAMIR forces would pick them up at first light. I said I would hold each of them personally responsible for my dead soldiers.

When I finally turned away, I nearly bumped into Dr. Kabia, who appeared to be praying. I made my way back up the path to the hospital, where the moans of the wounded and the shouts of the doctors and nurses seemed much louder than when we had arrived. Maggen had pulled up in front of the hospital, and there was a small crowd of injured soldiers and some civilians waiting near the vehicle. I looked at him and couldn't remember whether he had been with us at the morgue. What a day of fear and courage he'd been through.

Ndindiliyimana offered me his escort of six men and a vehicle to get us safely back to the Amahoro, giving his orders to them in French, no doubt for my benefit. He told them to defend me with their lives. We drove forward into the pitch-black night. Many of the street lights weren't functioning. Still I could see Robert's face in the back seat, bone white and motionless. Maggen, shaken by the deaths of his countrymen, was concentrating hard on the driving. In the distance we could see a few fires burning and could hear light weapons and the odd grenade explosion. The mobs were retiring to their homes, but a number of barriers were manned by aggressive militiamen.

The RPF and the Presidential Guard were still engaged in sporadic firefights near the Meridien hotel roundabout. To take the curve at a major intersection, we had to reduce speed, and we drove straight into an ambush. Several fusillades of machine-gun fire and red tracer bullets streaked over our heads. The para-commando unit from Camp Kanombe had moved out and were controlling this intersection. The crack of bullets was piercing as they whizzed by our heads. My white vehicle, with UN painted on it in large black letters and flying both a large, blue UN flag as well as my smaller UN commander's flag, was distinctive. Clearly, we were now a target. Bullets struck the car. The gendarmes in the vehicle behind us returned feeble fire. I yelled and hit Maggen to push the gas pedal to the floor and race through the ambush site. The diesel engine didn't respond quickly, and we felt like sitting ducks for what seemed an eternity. Despite the bullet holes in the car, no one was hit. It was the first time I had ever been shot at. It had been twenty-four hours of terrible firsts. No one in the vehicle uttered a sound as we sped toward our headquarters.

The mob had been cleared away from the entrance to the Amahoro, and the gates were closed and well-guarded by Ghanaian troops. Once we were safe, my Gendarmerie escort did not want to risk the trip back to Camp Kigali to pick up Ndindiliyimana and decided to remain with us for the night.

As we entered the building, the noise from the operation centre was very loud. I told Maggen to carry on to his place of duty and get a grip on his duty officers. Dr. Kabia and Robert followed me up the stairs to the command offices, where Brent and Henry were hard at work and the phones were still ringing off the hook. Both of them were tired, red-eyed and nearly talked out. I told them to get an orders group together and I would brief them in the conference room beside my office. I spoke to Henry alone for a few minutes while Brent assembled the few officers at Force HQ. I had not radioed in the information that the Belgians were confirmed dead; this was news I needed to deliver in person. Henry grimaced at the realization of his worst fears. I told him I was not about to give up. I may have failed to prevent civil war so far, but I was not about to run for cover, leaving the country in this state. We were going to salvage whatever we could of Arusha. I emphasized the point that Bagosora and the RGF senior leadership wanted the Belgians to leave as soon as possible. If the Belgians left and we were not reinforced, the weight of the mission would certainly fall on the Ghanaians' shoulders. Henry stood before me listening intently. He was my deputy force commander and chief of staff, but he was also the contingent commander of the 800 Ghanaian soldiers in UNAMIR, the majority of whom were dispersed in the demilitarized zone and at this moment extremely vulnerable. Without any hesitation and with a fierce scowl on his face, Henry said the Ghanaians were staying. It was not we who had failed, he said. He had always doubted that there was enough genuine good will and desire for peace on either side for anyone to succeed.

Next I called Luc at his Kigali Sector headquarters and told him that I had seen the bodies of his men at the morgue, that they had been mutilated and that I had counted eleven bodies. He uttered a short, cryptic, "Oui," showing his distress only by the raggedness of his breathing. But no, he said, there must be ten. Ten soldiers were sent out to protect Prime Minister Agathe, a mortar section commanded by Lieutenant Thierry Lotin, and these were the only men not yet accounted for. He had been told earlier in the day that some of them were probably dead but not all. He couldn't believe the news I was giving him now. I offered my condolences and told him that the bodies were now under guard and should be picked up the next morning with an escort from the Gendarmerie.

Luc regained his composure and briefed me. I congratulated him on saving Faustin, and then I passed on my instructions for the next day. We all had to help Gatsinzi and Ndindiliyimana gain control of the Presidential Guard and stabilize the city. I was going to continue to pressure Kagame not to move south and pull his troops back into the CND. Luc said he would work closely with Ndindiliyimana so that his troops and the Gendarmerie could help each other with the escalating demands for assistance. I warned him about what Bagosora and Ndindiliyimana had said about the wisdom of pulling his contingent out, and Luc said the Belgian ambassador was demanding a lot of his time concerning the needs of the Belgian nationals and diplomatic corps. He was to consolidate his troops as much as possible, improve defensive postures and continue to provide support to those in peril. But one thing was certain: We were not pulling out. As we finished the phone call, I once again offered my condolences to him, to his troops, to his government and to the families of the soldiers who had died.

Then I went in to talk with the orders group: the same officers I'd left in the morning were still running the show because the rest were stuck at the Meridien hotel, trapped by the firefights between the RPF and the Presidential Guard. I directed that all staff were to be at their place of duty just after dawn. Henry would coordinate this effort. And then I told them that the Belgian soldiers were dead. The news hit these tired men and knocked the last vestiges of energy out of them. Moen reiterated that all the rest of the missing men were now accounted for. The Belgians were freed at the airport but still could not get near the crash site. The RPF had no objection to having an outside investigation of the crash, but there was no answer from the RGF side. I moved on to instructions for the next day. I wanted Kigali Sector to consolidate its troops, with the airport as a priority, and we should do the same with our Force level unit troops, such as the logistics company. We were to continue helping Rwandans seeking refuge, supporting our own UN staff and any others in emergency situations. I closed the meeting by urging all of them to get some rest.

I took a walk around the HQ. There were a few hundred Rwandan civilians—men, women, children— asleep on the floor in our cafeteria and the hallways. Earlier in the day Brent had ordered the gates be opened to these people, but stipulated that they all be searched before they came in. He told me that Henry was quite angry at him for committing this breach of security and wanted him disciplined (nothing ever came of it). These people were among the thousands of Rwandans who had fled to UNAMIR compounds all over the city. Most were Tutsis, some were moderate Hutus, but all feared for their lives.

Some of our rescue attempts were successful, as with Prime Minister Faustin, but most were not—our patrols had been blocked time and again by drunken militia and hostile youths. In the midst of all this, Ottawa's National Defence Headquarters had called to demand bi-daily reports. They had never shown any particular interest in our mission and for the past six months had not responded to a single one of our weekly reports. I thought it was a little late for them to be showing an interest now.

We had no food stored at the Force HQ, but somewhere Brent had found some chocolates for sustenance. He'd also located an old mattress in a storage room out back and had torn down some curtains for blankets, making a bed for me on the floor of my office while I called New York. It was past midnight in Kigali, and about 1600 at the UN.

On the line were Kofi Annan, Iqbal Riza and Hedi Annabi. I went through the failures of the day: the deaths of my soldiers and the moderate political leaders, the systematic killings, the failed political meetings, Kagame's offers and threats, Bagosora's actions, the resumption of hostilities—but they had no suggestions on how to put the evil genie that had been released back in the bottle. I told them we had thousands of Rwandans from both ethnic groups in all of our compounds and that Prime Minister Faustin was in the Force HQ, and that we would not give him or any of the others up without a fight. They all reassured me that such an action was within my mission mandate.

I raised the possibility that the moderates might coalesce overnight and give us some opportunities to get things under control, at least on the military side. This would require me to show support and give them some sense that the international community would provide security. They told me no, I was to let the moderates come forward first. I was not to offer UNAMIR up as a protection force for a faction within one of the two belligerents. I was confused by this direction. The moderates wouldn't show their hand without me showing mine first. I said if we had a chance to put Rwanda back on the Arusha path, we must not let this opportunity slip by. Otherwise we would again be surrendering the initiative to the extremists and become nothing more than witnesses to a human catastrophe. The answer came back loud and clear: I was not to take sides, and it was up to the Rwandans to sort things out for themselves. I said that as long as the RPF did not cross the demilitarized zone I felt I still had a mandate. No one objected to that, and I was reminded to stay within its strict parameters.

They told me not to risk UNAMIR troops, to help with the security of all UN civilians and dependants, to keep in close touch with the expatriate and diplomatic communities and to update my withdrawal plan and be ready to implement it. I hung up feeling angry, empty and in a state of moral and ethical conflict.

It was 0100 but, before going to bed, I went to see Faustin, who after he'd been rescued had spent the day listening to the radio. All day long RTLM had been reporting the murders of his moderate allies and their families. The station encouraged its listeners to kill Tutsis and called for the death of all moderate Hutus, calling them traitors. The statements were accompanied by taped music from popular singers, violence-provoking songs with lyrics such as "I hate Hutus, I hate Hutus, I hate Hutus who think that Tutsis are not snakes." As far as Faustin was concerned, we had entered the apocalypse. What could I tell him? Only that he was safe at the Force HQ and we would try to find the members of his family who had fled. I left him in a state of mourning.

As I lay down, the window was open and there was the sound of gunfire and grenades coming from the east side of the city. My head was filled with sounds and images: The mangled bodies of my Belgian soldiers. Hélène, Lando and their beautiful children crying for help and then resigning themselves to their fate. The congealed blood and screams in the Kigali hospital compound. Bagosora's deceptive smile. The Presidential Guards and Interahamwe militiamen at the roadblocks, their faces filled with blood lust. The enigma of Ndindiliyimana. The voice of Prime Minister Agathe as she realized she could not get to the radio station to speak to her nation. Her children cowering in a dark corner of the bedroom, expecting the next footsteps to be those of their executioners. The shock in Robert's luminous face at the morgue.

My mission had failed. I, the stubborn lobbyist for and commander of UNAMIR, had failed. There was no chance of sleep.

My troops had died, not in the defence of their respective nations and citizenry but in the defence of decency and human rights. Was this the true price of peace? Was it an expense that the families, friends and governments of my blue berets were prepared to pay? The loss of the ten Belgian soldiers would be the defining factor: either the international community would give me more support and possibly stop this lunacy or, as in Somalia, they would use these deaths as an excuse to desert in the face of calamity.

Today would most likely be much worse than yesterday. If the killing continued and the RPF decided to engage the RGF below the demilitarized zone, we would either be ordered out or reinforced. However, I might be asked to stay in place with only what I had. I wasn't going to run from this mess. Between Luc, Henry, Tiko, Moen, Yaache and myself, we would reposition the force, try to support the moderate RGF initiatives, seek help from the UN to stop the killing in its tracks, and launch ceasefire initiatives to get the RPF back north. I got up and scribbled some notes about this in my agenda, then lay down again and finally fell asleep.

It was the end of the first day of a hundred-day civil war and a genocide that would engulf all of us in unimaginable carnage.

11

TO GO OR TO STAY?

I awoke at dawn on April 8 to the sound of heavy gunfire. Brent had scrounged a cup of tea for me, and after I drank it, I washed and shaved using a glass of water. This would be my morning routine for the next hundred days. The city water supply had already been cut off, and we had to conserve as much as we could of our bottled water for drinking. None of us would see a shower or bath for months, and we were rationed to a single glass a day for keeping ourselves clean. We began to save rainwater in order to wash our uniforms—by hand, often without any soap—and all of us soon carried a very distinct and unpleasant odour.

With the dawn, the mobs were back on the streets, and firing was being reported across the city. The RPF's attack on the Presidential Guard compound had been repulsed, and the RPF was consolidating their positions around the CND complex. Elements of the RGF and the Gendarmerie had joined the Presidential Guard and the Interahamwe in the rampages of the previous day, and it appeared that the power of the Third Force now extended well beyond the known extremist units.

All UN compounds were sheltering thousands of fearful Rwandans. I needed clarification from New York as to what authority I had to protect these people, whose plight posed both a moral quandary and a logistics nightmare. How could I possibly keep them safe? In the meantime, we continued to open our gates to all those seeking sanctuary. At the first morning prayers of the war, I directed that everyone entering the compounds be searched and disarmed. I also directed that the few hundred Rwandans already in the Force HQ be escorted to the Amahoro stadium as soon as possible. The lack of water and food would take a toll over the next days and weeks. We protected these citizens from certain death at the hands of the extremists or the RPF, but then had to watch helplessly as some of them succumbed to dehydration, disease and ultimately hunger. Many of my troops living among them would also fall ill: they simply could not eat what little rations they had in front of starving people, especially children, and gave what they had at the expense of their own health. Humanitarian assistance was still a long way off.

I also directed that all staff officers be moved by convoy from the Meridien to Force HQ that day. If I could drive around the city with no escort, they could find a way here under guard. This was a priority: we needed to be fully staffed and as functional as possible. All sectors were to account for their people and to launch patrols to rescue any missing military and civilian personnel. I wanted to know that by nightfall everyone associated with UNAMIR was in a guarded UN compound. We were still faced with the restriction on our ROE that Riza had outlined, which made these rescue efforts a matter of luck and persuasion rather than of force. To make things even more complicated, just as my officers began these tasks, the telephones in the Force HQ went dead.

The day before, along with the killings of the Belgians, two of our Uruguayans, one Bangladeshi and one Ghanaian had been wounded, and I knew we were bound to suffer more casualties. Despite all our requests for resupply, even the field hospital's cupboards were bare; only the Belgian contingent had any medical supplies. The Belgian Hercules that had been denied landing on April 6 was sitting on the ground in Nairobi. The airport in Kigali was under RGF control and remained closed to traffic. Our two contracted helicopters had disappeared yesterday—with the country exploding, the pilots had fled to Uganda. They were both civilian contract employees, so who could blame them? But the result was that we were confined to Kigali with no ability to evacuate casualties. In all likelihood any seriously wounded would die. In every decision I was to take over the coming weeks, I had to balance the risk of the operation against the fact that we had no medical safety net, and a lack of ammunition.

Robert and I left for the home of the SRSG. The CND was taking fire from several directions, and the RPF were returning as good as they got.

Once again we drove through a battle in our four-by-four. Driving under a firefight is unnerving to say the least, especially in an unarmoured vehicle, but it would become a daily experience.

When we got to Booh-Booh's house, he and his staff were in a state of shock. I recommended that they all move to Force HQ where Booh-Booh could better control the situation and have satellite communications with New York. Clearly he had already been in contact with the UN by phone, and heaven knows what he had said or if the wrong people had been listening. He insisted on staying where he was, even though he was obviously overwhelmed and uncertain about what to do. I didn't understand why he was unwilling to move to a location where he could stay abreast of what was happening, especially as I thought we could guarantee his safety on the journey. Later that day, his house was caught in a crossfire between the RPF and the Presidential Guard, and the Belgians moved him and his staff to the Meridien hotel. It was an awkward command post, and Booh-Booh relied on his political adviser, Mamadou Kane, to shuttle between Force HQ, his rooms at the hotel and any political meetings we arranged.

I left for the CND. I wanted to get Kagame to halt his resumption of hostilities. We drove through what was now the no man's land between the RGF and the RPF. Ballis met me at the entrance to the CND building and whispered in my ear that the RPF was not listening to reason; it was sticking unwaveringly to its preconditions to negotiating any ceasefire and was preparing for military action. Many Tutsis, including members of the RPF's families, were being hunted down and slaughtered—a compelling argument for taking up arms. If the RPF went on the offensive, however, it would lead inevitably to civil war.

I met with what remained of the RPF political leadership in the grand hallway that separated the assembly building from the hotel complex, formally greeting Seth Sendashonga, Tito Rutaremara, Dr. Jacques and Commander Charles, who stood like dignitaries in a reception line. I followed them into a small, poorly lit conference room. The heart of my argument was that if the RPF resumed military hostilities, the moderates wouldn't be able to rally elements of the army and Gendarmerie to their cause. I urged them to keep the peace and permit me to organize a meeting with the RGF moderates of the Crisis Committee. "What moderates?" Seth wanted to know. The prime minister and the other leaders had all been killed, and the extremists were obviously enacting their long-anticipated plan. If there were moderates still alive and in a position of power, Seth insisted that they show their hand, and quickly. Commander Charles would soon implement Kagame's orders, and UNAMIR better not get in his way. Seth left a small door open. If I could arrange it, the RPF would agree to meet with the Crisis Committee, which was a creature of the army, not the government. I pushed them to commit at such a meeting to negotiate for the resumption of the ceasefire status that existed under Arusha. As usual with this group, they told me they had to refer all decisions to the RPF high council. At least, I said, they could clarify their preconditions. Seth rhymed them off: (1) the slaughter of innocent civilians must stop; (2) the indiscriminate shooting by the RGF on the CND must stop; (3) the Presidential Guards must be disarmed, returned to their camp and arrested; (4) the Crisis Committee must openly condemn the actions of the extremists, particularly the Presidential Guard; (5) the telephone system must be fully restored; (6) the Crisis Committee must identify its leader; (7) the Crisis Committee should produce a joint communiqué with the RPF regarding the true state of affairs and broadcast it to the nation; (8) the Crisis Committee had to fully account for all the officials who had died or disappeared. Then and only then would the RPF be open to negotiating a ceasefire. The meeting came to an abrupt halt when some glass from the skylight came crashing down, the result of heavy machine gun-fire.

I had left my vehicle at the entrance with Robert, who despite all the shooting was still sitting in it. After a quick goodbye to Walter Ballis—he was a dependable, solid senior officer and I told him I still needed him to stay put with the UNMOs and wished him luck—we headed through the line of fire on a direct route to the Ministry of Defence to see if I could connect with Bagosora and the Crisis Committee. It took over half an hour to manoeuvre through the various roadblocks, many of which had now attracted spectators; it was as if each barrier had turned into a theatre of cruelty. Power was in the hands of vigilante groups. Closer to the Ministry of Defence, in the inner city, the Presidential Guard and the Reconnaissance Battalion were still manning the roadblocks—we saw no civilians past the Mille Collines checkpoint. Soldiers stopped us at each one, glanced in at us and let us pass. I had the impression that instructions had been given to permit me to move freely and I hoped that such freedom would be extended to all UNAMIR personnel. I was mistaken.

I surprised Bagosora again, as he sat at the head of the minister's conference table talking to politicians from the different parties. The men I recognized were all known hard-liners. He got up to greet me and told me he was chairing a meeting of the political parties in order to advance the transition from the current military control to political control. He was clearly nervous: he was fidgeting and all the while trying to steer me toward the door. He couldn't have made it any plainer that he didn't want me at this meeting. Before he shooed me out and closed the door in my face, he said that the government would be sworn in the next day, April 9, probably at the Hôtel des Diplomates. Most of the surviving politicians had moved there with their families for security reasons.

Fuming, I went directly to the RGF's headquarters to find Gatsinzi and Ndindiliyimana to see if I could figure out what direction Bagosora had given them. Soldiers opened the defensive steel barriers and the gate for us. There were Presidential Guards in all controlled locations, and the RGF soldiers appeared to be deferring to them. I met General Gatsinzi near the entrance of the office complex. He seemed relieved to see me, as were all the officers in his entourage, but he looked anxious and tired. He apologized again for the deaths of the Belgians and for the fact that he still hadn't gained control over the army. Some units refused to communicate with him at all; others listened but then ignored him. He had some units in the south that had not engaged in any skirmishes, but they were extensively infiltrated by hardline officers from the north and were too far away to influence the situation in Kigali. He was despondent that the moderates were unable to rally a cohesive force. He said Ndindiliyimana was attempting to reconstitute the quick-reaction companies to bring his gendarmes under control. Both he and Ndindiliyimana suffered extensive command and control problems: their radios weren't reliable and the phone system was down.

Since Bagosora hadn't given me a chance to speak, I relayed the pre-conditions to Gatsinzi and told him that the RPF would only negotiate with the military Crisis Committee, not with any politicians. He agreed to meet with the RPF, but because he wasn't in control of the army, I knew the RPF wouldn't find him very credible. I wanted to re-establish liaison officers between our headquarters to increase direct communications and promised I would dispatch an UNMO team for that purpose. I wanted the same from him. I then asked him where the abducted politicians were. He didn't know, though I suspected Bagosora did. Gatsinzi walked me to my vehicle and watched me drive away with a look on his face I recognized: that of a commander in the throes of an impossible mission.

On the way back to the Amahoro, I decided to stop by the Mille Collines, where a number of expatriates, Rwandans and UNAMIR personnel had sought sanctuary. The lobby, patio and rooms were filled with terrified civilians, who crowded around me begging for information and protection. I told them all to remain calm and tried to be encouraging, but words were all I could offer.

I was discreetly trying to spot Captain Mbaye when he appeared out of nowhere and pulled me aside. Yesterday, when no APC had shown up, he had gathered Prime Minister Agathe's children, put them under a pile of clothes in the back of his vehicle and driven them to the hotel. There had been no incidents along the way, and for the moment the children were safe in a room upstairs. I told him I would do what I could to get them out. Without a doubt, there would be informers in the hotel—he was to keep the kids hidden in the room.

Outside, a group of Interahamwe was erecting a roadblock in front of the hotel. I stopped and demanded to know what they were doing. They said there were traitors in the hotel and they were not going to allow anyone to leave, but that anyone who wanted into the Mille Collines could pass through their barrier. Shivers went up my spine. They were herding people into the hotel, which would be a convenient place to kill them. I told them the hotel was now under UN protection and that they were not to enter. They laughed at me. I waved over the group of MILOBs who had taken refuge at the hotel under the leadership of a Congolese major, Victor Moigny. I ordered the major to permit any unarmed person to enter the hotel and to deny entry to any armed person. He looked at me in disbelief—how was he going to stop an armed person from going in? My order put him and his team at extreme risk. His only weapon was his ability to bluff until I could get armed troops and possibly APCs to the hotel, in the heart of the extremist-controlled area of Kigali.

On the way back to Force HQ, we could hear sporadic firing from several directions. Chez Lando was in flames. It was early afternoon by now and the mob had increased to thousands, again blocking the entrance to the stadium. As we drove through them, all I could think about was the possibility of widespread massacres breaking out, as they had done in Burundi after the October coup. We absolutely had to find a way to stop the killing from spreading.

Inside I received an update. Kagame had launched his offensive and had crossed into the demilitarized zone almost twenty-four hours after his original warning. Before the attack, all of our forces in the demilitarized zone had been able to withdraw from forward or isolated locations and were now consolidated in their camps. Fighting had broken out near Ruhengeri in the northwest, Byumba in the centre and Gabiro in the east. Our MILOBs reported a three-pronged attack: Kagame obviously wanted to keep his enemy guessing as long as possible as to where the main effort would be coming from. He had massed his forces for a direct assault on Kigali while fixing large concentrations of enemy forces on the opposite flanks—Ruhengeri and Gabiro. If he launched a determined attack he could overwhelm the garrison in Kigali, link up with his unit in the city, seize the capital and control the country in record time. This time there were no French intervention forces to stop him, and UNAMIR was not mandated to stand in his way.

While more of my officers were at their desks, and Tiko had hastily organized a new MILOB group headquarters in a room adjacent to my operations centre, many staff officers were still missing. Apparently the order to convoy them to Force HQ had gotten lost somewhere between Kigali Sector and the Bangladeshi headquarters. Too many of my orders seemed to disappear in the Bangladeshi battalion. I directed Henry to personally ensure that another convoy was conducted the next day and that all of the staff officers were brought into Force HQ. They were not doing anyone any good sitting in their rooms at the Meridien. As we had no food or water left, Henry was organizing a convoy to bring us a reserve of water, fuel and food from the Bangladeshi logistics company, which couldn't bring the supplies to us since it refused to move without an armed escort. Electrical power had now gone down in Kigali, to join the water and the telephone systems. If we had no fuel to run our generators, we would lose both our satellite communications system and our mission radio net and be completely isolated from the outside world.

We now had about 15,000 Rwandan civilians taking shelter in our compounds, with the highest numbers at the King Faisal Hospital and the Amahoro Stadium. The Bangladeshis, from experience with natural disasters in their nation, knew that dehydration and the risk of cholera and dysentery were imminent. They ordered latrines to be built and their use strictly enforced. But even so, we did not have lime for the pits. No matter what we did, in the present circumstances people would start to die within days.

I went to the operations centre to get a feel for the overall situation in the country from Moen and the duty officers. While I was being brought up to date, Brent reported that the UNDP security officer had accounted for and secured all of the UNDP staff without casualties. The acting CAO had located most of her people and essential civilian support staff in the headquarters. There were no reports of any expatriate casualties—it appeared that UN and diplomatic staffs weren't being targeted by the extremists. Our local staff was not faring as well, however. Brent reported that patrols sent to the staff's homes had found families murdered or that they had disappeared. Our Rwandan contract workers, most of them Tutsis, had provided the link in language from us to the local people and had been crucial to the functioning of the Force HQ. In the coming hours we were able to rescue some of the workers, but the majority were killed as priority targets in the early days of the tragedy.

Armed with this dismal information, I called New York and talked to Annan, Riza and Maurice Baril. For all intents and purposes, my mandate was over. I needed direction on what to do with what I had. I didn't control the airport, which was the only link to the outside world.

While my troops still held their positions there, the RGF controlled the perimeter, and the tower and runways remained closed. The RPF had informed me that it considered the airport closed and would fire on any plane attempting to land, in order to ward off any attempt by the French to intervene in support of the RGF.

I told the triumvirate of the humanitarian disaster that had been dropped into our laps as thousands sought our protection in Kigali. I asked for two battalions, and I urgently needed logistics support. I was going to attempt to expand UNAMIR's control beyond its current isolated garrisons, as this was the key to any evacuation, or any expansion of the mission. By this point, I had already made an extensive verbal report to the DPKO as well as two written reports.[1] I was confident that my superiors were fully informed of the state of my force and the situation in the mission area and had as clear an understanding of the crisis as I could provide them. They directed me to prioritize my logistics requirements and they committed to meet them. Kofi Annan offered words of encouragement and promised to support me, urging me to stay in touch with the parties and to try to negotiate a ceasefire.

By evening prayers, the situation had worsened. Kagame had left Mulindi with a tactical headquarters, and our MILOB sector commander was accompanying him. The RPF soldiers were moving out of their camps, loaded for war, their morale and discipline high. It was as if they were just off on a well-planned and rehearsed exercise. There were no reports of any outbreaks of violence in the RPF sector.

In the demilitarized zone, the Ghanaian battalion, the Bangladeshi engineer company and the MILOBs were moving into defensive positions in their camps. In the Northern Sector there were reports of killings, especially in Ruhengeri and Gisenyi. I directed Tiko to keep his teams in place as long as he could. If they felt their lives were threatened by the fighting, they were

---

1. "Outgoing Code Cable 8 April 1994 Supplementary Report on UNAMIR Humanitarian Activities" and "Outgoing Code Cable 8 April 1994 An Update on the Current Situation in Rwanda and Military Aspects of the Mission."

to head to our garrisons in the demilitarized zone, to Kigali or to the nearest border. All was quiet in the south, where the army and Gendarmerie were out in force. The situation there was tense but calm, and our MILOBs were in close contact with the political, military and police leadership, all of which claimed to be committed to law and order and to Arusha.

In Kigali all members of the Belgian and Bangladeshi battalions—the logistics company, the movement control platoon, the military police section and the hospital—had been accounted for and were in guarded locations. The Belgian and French ambassadors were pressuring Luc for help in securing the expatriate population. I told Luc that UNAMIR tasks came first and that the integrated evacuation plan, which included the expatriates, would be implemented when ordered. Until then we had a responsibility to all of the people of Rwanda. The militia was now blockading whole areas of the city and Luc's Belgian troops were being physically harassed and occasionally fired on. The situation with the Bangladeshi battalion was worsening. Luc felt that this unit was almost useless. The Bangladeshis had either ignored his orders to conduct missions or told him they had complied when they hadn't. The commanding officer offered nothing but excuses, and most of the contingent had gone to ground inside their compounds in a state of fear.

After evening prayers, I had a cup of tea with Faustin in my office. His family hadn't yet been located and he had again spent most of the day listening to the propaganda being broadcast by RTLM—a stream of commentators were exhorting violence, playing provocative songs and even reading out the names and locations of those who must be killed. In Rwanda the radio was akin to the voice of God, and if the radio called for violence, many Rwandans would respond, believing they were being sanctioned to commit these actions. The killing songs Faustin had been listening to must have been taped, which meant that RTLM had known for a while what was coming and was a key player. A call from the RGF ordering up reservists had also gone out over the radio. Even so, Faustin thought that the RPF would win this war. Its soldiers were fighting for a cause they believed in, whereas the RGF soldiers were killing for the sake of killing, not knowing or caring why. In this type of conflict, the men fighting for principles they believed in would inevitably win.

When Faustin left, I summoned Colonel Moen and asked him to explain the Bangladeshi contingents' performance over the last twenty-four hours. He stated that the Bangladeshi commander had no problem risking the lives of his men to save foreign nationals but did not want to put them on the line to save Rwandan civilians. He told me that the commander had referred the matter to Dhaka for direction and that his superiors had ordered him not to endanger the troops by protecting Rwandans or to risk carrying any Rwandans in their vehicles. Looking uncomfortable, Moen told me that if I issued any order that the contingent commander felt unnecessarily risked the lives of his men, I would have to provide the order in writing.

This stance made me furious. I told Moen that I was tired of the Bangladeshis' lack of courage and unprofessional behaviour. I expected orders to be obeyed. I assured him that I would not unnecessarily risk the lives of the Bangladeshi troops, but I expected them to take the same risks as the other UNAMIR soldiers. They were not here for a free ride. I directed Moen to order the unit commander to launch in force at dawn, clear mobs from the area around the stadium and the Force HQ and open the crossroads to traffic. I wanted this forward posture maintained. Any time a crowd formed to block a route, it was to be cleared immediately. This operation was to be conducted in overwhelming force with every man the unit could muster, with all the APCs they could put in the streets. It was to be led personally by the unit commander. Moen agreed and assured me he would speak to the unit commander. I felt sorry for him. He was an experienced officer, a graduate of the U.S. Army Command and General Staff College in Leavenworth. I knew he was ashamed of his compatriots' performance. As a UN commander, I could not fire any national officer over the rank of lieutenant colonel, and especially not a commanding officer, without permission from New York, but pressure from a countryman of equal rank might prod the contingent commander into action.

After Moen left, Brent encouraged me to call Beth and let her know I was fine. I'm glad I did. Earlier that day the regimental padre had been in touch with her to offer whatever help she might need, and she had immediately assumed the worst. She told me that she and the children were praying for me and were holding up. Every day I was in theatre she and so many other wives and children of UNAMIR soldiers would live on a knife-edge, waiting for a phone call or a visit that would tell them their loved one was dead or injured. In this era of live twenty-four-hour broadcasting from war zones, our families had to live the missions with us—a new phenomenon that haunted them and haunted us.

I finished more written reports to New York before midnight and, still restless, left my office to walk the dark corridors. The Ghanaians had taken over the security of the Force HQ that day, and I decided to take a look at what they had deployed. I went onto the roof of the causeway to the rotunda and met with two Ghanaian soldiers who were manning a machine gun overlooking the parking lot. They had also been given the short-range anti-tank rocket, the M72, but were uncertain how to use it. I ran a short weapons lecture in the dark, then went to the roof of the hotel, where an observation post had been set up. I startled the lone Ghanaian observer so badly he soiled his pants. I sat down beside him to try to ease his embarrassment and reassure him he was all right and then sent him to change his pants while I replaced him at his post. The city was largely quiet. Sitting there in the dark, I studied the fence surrounding the compound and visualized hundreds of extremists swarming our headquarters, intent on getting to Faustin. The image made me think of the movie *Khartoum,* when swarms of dervishes rush the stairs to kill General Gordon and his men. Would my soldiers fight under a UN flag to defend Faustin? For the first time that day I felt truly hopeless and trapped, a feeling I determinedly shunted to one side when the young Ghanaian came back to relieve me.

Sometime after midnight, an RPF officer and a platoon of soldiers arrived at our main gate, and Brent was summoned by the Ghanaian guards to talk to the officer, who was cockily wearing a UN blue helmet like a war trophy and demanding to see Faustin. Brent told him to take off the helmet and leave his weapon and troops outside the gate. The officer said he had come to escort Faustin to safety, and we relayed the offer to the prime minister designate. Faustin refused to leave, saying he had to keep a distance from the RPF if he was to maintain credibility with the moderates and the people of Rwanda. He preferred to remain under our protection.

It was around two when I drifted into a fitful sleep. At about a quarter to three I was awakened by a phone call from Maurice to tell me that in forty-five minutes—around 0330—the French, followed by the Belgians, would begin landing a military force at the Kigali airport to conduct an evacuation of expatriates. I was livid, and not only because of the short notice. I reminded Maurice that I no longer controlled the airport. What if the RGF (or as they had threatened, the RPF) shot down the aircraft? Why was I only being informed when the planes were already in the air and possibly even entering Rwandan airspace? Maurice insisted that he had only just been told himself and directed me to help with the evacuation.

Since the phones were out, I had to use our insecure radio to get Luc to warn the airport company of the imminent arrival of the French. Luc himself had just gotten a call from General Charlier, the Belgian chief of staff. I radioed Ballis at the CND and told him to assure the RPF that the French forces were being deployed only to extract the expatriate community, and to request that they take no action.

With the lights off to avoid making a tempting silhouette, I stood by the small open window in my office, waiting for the call from Luc that would spell disaster or inform me that the planes had landed safely. A light breeze was blowing in through the screen. For a time I thought I heard human moaning, as if hundreds of distant voices were being carried on the wind. I do not recall how long I stood there, uneasily listening, but at last I heard the distinctive roar of aircraft landing at the airport, and to my relief there was no answering sound of gunfire or explosions.

Ignoring my pallet on the floor, I decided to rest in my armchair for a while while I tried to sort out how the various parties would perceive this action. The RGF would be suspicious, angry and concerned about the new Belgian troops. The RPF would be suspicious, angry and concerned about the French. UNAMIR would be caught in the middle. But perhaps it would also turn out to be an opportunity to assert my influence over both parties, as each would have to go through me as a conduit to the French and the Belgians. I prayed that there would be no confrontation between the French and the RPF in this already chaotic situation—or between the Belgians and the RGF. The RPF had anti-aircraft guns, mortars and possibly surface-to-air missiles in the CND, which was only four kilometres from the airport—well within range. The tension was too much, and despite myself I fell asleep in my chair.

The Bangladeshi contingent never faced the test I'd set them. That night the RPF moved into our area. By dawn on April 9 there were no crowds, no mobs, no militia, only disciplined and co-operative RPF soldiers who had secured our area either to protect us (they later claimed they had intercepted a radio message ordering the para-commando unit at Camp Kanombe to assault the Force HQ and capture or kill Faustin) or more likely, to safeguard the thousands of terrified people in the stadium.

In the operations centre, the duty officer confirmed that three French aircraft had arrived, that there were already about three hundred French paratroopers on the ground at the airport, and that more aircraft were landing. Were the French going to get involved once again with the fight or were they really only here to evacuate their expatriates?

Luc arrived a few minutes later and jubilantly told me that Willy Claes, the Belgian foreign minister, was lobbying New York for immediate reinforcement of UNAMIR and a massive logistics resupply. If we were given a new mandate and the necessary force, we might be able to get the two parties back to the negotiating table. At morning prayers, I told Kigali Sector to carry on with as many rescue missions as could be managed and also ordered that our gates be kept open to anyone seeking asylum. I was told that the resupply route for our troops in the demilitarized zone was now cut; we would have to figure out whether we should, or even could, move them to Kigali. Given our resources, there was no way we could accomplish moving these troops in one lift. We'd have to shuttle them in over several days, and the effort would require most of our vehicles and fuel.

My first stop that morning was the CND. I knew I would be in for a cold reception. On top of the French landing at the airport, the radio had announced that RGF reserves should report for duty, and word was also out that the new government was being installed and the names of the ministers announced. To the RPF, these actions were an overt declaration of war. Seth stated categorically that there would be no recognition whatsoever of this illegitimate and clearly extremist government: this crisis was not an overreaction to the sudden death of the president but a coup. The RPF would be prepared to open discussions with the military representatives of the RGF in areas related to stopping the killings and arresting the Presidential Guard, but only after the Crisis Committee had complied with their preconditions. I raised the possibility of local truces that would permit the foreign troops and UNAMIR to conduct humanitarian activities including the evacuation of the expatriates, and Seth was grudgingly open to the idea. He was clear, however, that this humanitarian effort had better not turn into military assistance to the RGF. If the French, the Belgians or UNAMIR got involved in such a way, the RPF would use force to stop us. I told him I wanted a forty-eight-hour truce to be in place in Kigali by 1600. Our goodbyes were sullen, suspicious and without pleasantries.

I headed for the Ministry of Defence to find Bagosora and get more information on this new "interim government." The city was descending into chaos. Large numbers of people were moving toward the outskirts of Kigali carrying bundles of belongings. There were bodies on the street, surrounded by large pools of blood that had turned black in the heat of the sun, which made the corpses look burnt. Groups of Interahamwe and RGF soldiers were roaming between roadblocks, which were often simply a few stones or empty plastic crates. The guards at the barriers were aggressive, more like animals that have had the taste of blood than security officers legitimately seeking supposed RPF "infiltrators." At each roadblack, portable radios blasted the music and exhortations of RTLM over the heads of Rwandans of all ages paralyzed with fear who were lined up to have their papers checked. Clearly more and more people were being drawn into acts of violence, as if a blood frenzy was multiplying exponentially.

There were only a few guards at the Ministry of Defence, and they told me that everybody was at the Diplomates. At the hotel, I encountered a number of ministers and their families packing their suitcases and belongings into vehicles. No one wanted to stop to talk to me, since they were concentrating on getting out of town. I found out later that they were heading for safety in Gitarama, which was about sixty kilometres west of the capital. The scene reminded me more of the fall of Saigon than of the supposed installation of a government determined to take control of the country. Bagosora was nowhere to be seen.

Gatsinzi, Ndindiliyimana and others on the Crisis Committee were still at army headquarters. They told me that the mobilization of the RGF reserves was a terrible mistake and that they had sent messages and telegrams to all units instructing that it was to cease. I could not see a way forward and neither could they. They couldn't guarantee the RPF preconditions. With the interim government now supposedly in place—Bagosora's doing, I was certain—the Crisis Committee was likely to dissolve. And what government? The ministers had decamped and there was no infrastructure left. Still I asked them for a truce so that the French and Belgians could evacuate their expatriates, another futile gesture since no one on the Crisis Committee controlled the elite units of the RGF. Bagosora did, and without his co-operation, the evacuation operations would be in jeopardy, especially when the Belgian troops Luc was expecting arrived later that day.

Returning to Force HQ, I saw more dead bodies discarded like piles of rags beside the road as displaced people streamed past them, looking to escape the same fate.

Brent and a team of MILOBs had spent the day conducting rescue missions in one of the APCs. On the first effort, he'd picked up several UN civilian staff and their families and also the Canadian chargé d'affaires, Linda Carroll, who was able to provide him with a list of addresses of Canadian expatriates in Kigali.[2]

---

2. Linda Carroll was the epitome of what a diplomat should be in a crisis. Since the president's plane went down, she had warned her area wardens, calmed everyone by radio, located most of the Canadians she knew to be in Kigali and managed to gather them in key locations. With assistance from our embassy in Nairobi and others, Brent and his team conducted dozens of missions over the next two weeks to rescue and evacuate not only Canadians but also Rwandans and other nationals. There was one large complicating factor. From her records, Linda believed there were only about 65 Canadian citizens in Kigali, but we evacuated over 195. Many travellers and expatriates do not take their security seriously and feel under no obligation to check in with their local embassies or consulates—which causes enormous effort and grief among the men and women who must try to save them when conflict breaks out.

With Brent that day were Marek Pazik and Stefan Stec, both Polish officers who had briefly been billeted in the Gikondo Parish Church, known as the Polish Mission because it was run by priests from Poland. Pazik and Stefan had not lasted long under the austere regime at the mission, but two of their fellow Polish MILOBs had stayed on. That morning, a faint radio call had come from the men at the mission begging for help. The batteries on the radio were dying and all Brent could make out was that there had been killings at the church.

Not knowing what to expect, Brent, Pazik and Stec armed themselves and, hatches down, set off to Gikondo in the APC with a Bangladeshi officer and three men. Along the route, they passed through fighting between the RGF and the RPF, through Gendarmerie roadblocks and through the ever-increasing and chaotic militia roadblocks. They saw the bodies of men, women and children near these roadblocks. So many civilians were on the move, it looked like the entire population was abandoning Kigali.

At the church, they came to a halt and dismounted. Pazik and a Bangladeshi soldier went to the rectory to find the Polish MILOBs, while Brent and Stec confronted the first evidence of wholesale massacre. Across the street from the mission, an entire alleyway was littered with the bodies of women and children near a hastily abandoned school. As Brent and Stefan were standing there trying to take in the number of bodies, a truck full of armed men roared by. Brent and Stefan decided to head for the church. Stefan went inside while Brent stood by the door to cover him and to keep the APC in sight. They confronted a scene of unbelievable horror—the first such scene UNAMIR witnessed—evidence of the genocide, though we didn't yet know to call it that. In the aisles and on the pews were the bodies of hundreds of men, women and children. At least fifteen of them were still alive but in a terrible state. The priests were applying first aid to the survivors. A baby cried as it tried to feed on the breast of its dead mother, a sight Brent has never forgotten. Pazik found the two Polish MILOBs, who were in a state of grief and shock, hardly able to relate what had happened. The night before, they said, the RGF had cordoned off the area, and then the Gendarmerie had gone door to door checking identity cards. All Tutsi men, women and children were rounded up and moved to the church. Their screams had alerted the priests and the MILOBs, who had come running. The priests and officers were seized at the church doors and slammed up against the wall with rifle barrels at their throats. They were forced to watch at gunpoint as the gendarmes collected the adults' identity cards and burned them. Then the gendarmes welcomed in a large number of civilian militiamen with machetes and handed over the victims to their killers.

Methodically and with much bravado and laughter, the militia moved from bench to bench, hacking with machetes. Some people died immediately, while others with terrible wounds begged for their lives or the lives of their children. No one was spared. A pregnant woman was disembowelled and her fetus severed. Women suffered horrible mutilation. Men were struck on the head and died immediately or lingered in agony. Children begged for their lives and received the same treatment as their parents. Genitalia were a favourite target, the victims left to bleed to death. There was no mercy, no hesitation and no compassion. The priests and the MILOBs, guns at their throats, tears in their eyes, and the screams of the dying in their ears, pleaded with the gendarmes for the victims. The gendarmes' reply was to use the rifle barrels to lift the priests' and MILOBs' heads so that they could better witness the horror.

Killing with machetes is hard work, and sometime in the night the murderers became fatigued with their gruesome task and left the church, probably headed for some sleep before they moved on to the next location. The priests and MILOBs did what they could for the few survivors, who moaned or crawled from underneath the corpses that had sheltered them.

Both of the MILOBs were overwhelmed by emotion as they recounted the night's events. One fell completely silent while the other admitted that though he had served in places, such as Iraq and Cambodia, this was it, he was going home. The men needed to get out of there, to get back to the security of headquarters and regain their equilibrium, and they urged the priests to join them. But the fathers refused, saying they had to stay with the wounded, who were too many to carry in the APC. Brent and the others gave the priests a radio and a charged battery, what water they had and a small first aid kit, and promised to report the incident and mount a rescue mission. They warned the priests that since it was already mid-afternoon, it was unlikely that a large armed escort with ambulances or heavy transport could be mounted and then negotiate the dozens of roadblocks before nightfall, but the priests were confident they could hide overnight, as the militia and gendarmes had surely finished with them.

Feeling like deserters, the UNAMIR group returned to Force HQ, and the Polish MILOBs were put to bed. Kigali Sector was directed to conduct a rescue mission, but as Brent had suspected, it couldn't comply until the next day—dozens of missions were already underway. Early the next morning, the priests called on the radio and reported that the militia had returned during the night. Our APC had been spotted at the church, and the killers had returned to destroy the evidence of the massacre. They had killed the wounded and removed and burned the bodies.

The decision to leave the priests and the victims had had disastrous consequences, but such are the decisions that soldiers make in war. Some days you make decisions and people live, other days people die. Those innocent men, women and children were simply Tutsi. That was their crime.

The massacre was not a spontaneous act. It was a well-executed operation involving the army, Gendarmerie, Interahamwe and civil service. The identity card system, introduced during the Belgian colonial period, was an anachronism that would result in the deaths of many innocent people. By the destruction of their cards, and of their records at the local commune office, these human beings were erased from humanity. They simply never existed. Before the genocide ended, hundreds of thousands of others would be erased. The men who organized and perpetrated these crimes knew they were crimes and not acts justified by war, and that they could be held accountable for them. The Interahamwe returned to destroy the evidence. The faceless bureaucrats who fed the names to the militias and destroyed the records also played a part. We were not in a war of victors and vanquished. We were in the middle of a slaughterhouse, though it was weeks before we could call it by its real name.

• • •

I got to the airport that day at about 1400, avoiding firefights between the RPF and the RGF para-commando battalion to the northeast of the airport, less than a kilometre from the Force HQ. On the way to meet the French commander, I really had to wonder about what the speed of this effort to evacuate foreign nationals meant about the UN commitment to stay in place. Were they getting the foreign civilians out of the way of a future military intervention in the conflict or were they intending to abandon Rwanda?

My conversation with Colonel Poncet was curt, and the French commander showed no interest in co-operating with us. This unhappy exchange was an indication of how the French evacuation task force, Opération Amaryllis, would continue to behave with UNAMIR. Poncet said his mission was to evacuate the expatriate community within the next forty-eight to seventy-two hours. We had heard from the MILOBs at the airport that the French had already evacuated a number of Rwandans and that twelve members of the presidential family were part of this group, but Poncet insisted to me that he was only here to evacuate expatriates and "white people." I told him that within two hours there should be a truce in place but that there was no guarantee from the RGF that they could observe it. At that Poncet asked to be excused and, without waiting for a response from me, simply turned his back and walked off. I decided then that Luc would handle all future dealings with this rude Frenchman.

Late that afternoon I went to the Meridien to meet with Booh-Booh. The Belgian battalion command post was now set up at the entrance to the hotel, and I stopped to talk with Lieutenant Colonel Dewez, whom I hadn't seen since the murder of his men. I offered him my condolences and commended him for maintaining restraint and discipline in his unit.

In the lobby I was swarmed by hundreds of UN civilians and Rwandans wanting information. I addressed them, saying that the Belgian battalion command post had moved into the hotel to provide security. There was food and water in the hotel and they should be rationing it. I told them that some evacuations had started and that my MILOBs would continue to assist in co-ordinating lists of people in order to be prepared for evacuation when it was judged relatively safe. I asked them to be calm, to rest and to stay away from windows and balconies.

The SRSG's suite was on the top floor, and since the elevators weren't working, I arrived slightly out of breath. His wing was empty save for him and his staff; he'd asked the hotel manager to clear all civilians from the floor for security reasons. Booh-Booh was seated in a large chair surrounded by political officers, including Mamadou Kane. My welcome wasn't particularly warm. A bullet had come through one of their windows and they were scared. I told them that, for one thing, it wasn't wise to be on the top floor—if they insisted on staying there, they needed to be very cautious near the windows. We discussed the installation of the interim government. Booh-Booh insisted that neither the UN nor the international community should recognize this illegitimately established extremist regime, though he agreed with my suggestion that it would be wise to maintain contact with it, if only to find out its intentions. I told him that the RPF would only negotiate with the military leaders of the Crisis Committee and that I had encouraged both Ndindiliyimana and Gatsinzi to obtain such a mandate from the new government. Augustin Bizimana, the minister of defence, was due back from Cameroon tomorrow, and he would most likely be their political master once again.

Back at the headquarters, the news wasn't great. Many observer teams were off the radio net and had either become hostages, casualties or had decided to run. We could do nothing for them except ask New York to contact bordering nations to offer asylum. I was also informed that a large U.S. convoy, escorted by UNAMIR military observers and RGF troops, had left the American ambassador's residence that day and headed south to Burundi. The night before, Brent had received a telephone call from a man who claimed to be a U.S. Marine officer with an American force in Bujumbura, Burundi. He told Brent he was just checking whether he had the right number for my office. We never heard from him again, but we later discovered from a number of sources that about 250 U.S. Marines had been flying into Kigali when they were diverted to Burundi and that they had believed they were being sent to reinforce UNAMIR and protect U.S. nationals.

That evening I called New York and described the situation. They had my reports in hand: along with political assassinations and indis-criminate killings, we now had an example of systematic ethnic killing in the Polish Mission massacre, and twenty thousand Rwandans under our supposed protection. But even though Kigali was crawling with elite foreign forces, no nation was interested in reinforcing us except the Belgians and a few non-aligned Third World states. By now there were five hundred French para-commandos working out of the airport, and a thousand Belgian paras staging in Nairobi. To that I could add the 250 U.S. Marines in Bujumbura. A force of that size, well-trained and well-equipped, could possibly bring an end to the killings. But such an option wasn't even being considered.

As I toured Force HQ during the evening, it was obvious that every-one was exhausted but that morale was improbably high. You have to know where your people are morally, mentally and physically, and how much more you can ask of them. That night I was convinced that we could carry on. When I retired to my office, Brent surprised me with a plate of rice and curry he had scrounged from the Bangladeshis, and a promise that Belgian rations were coming the next day. Robert had also conducted a run to our home in Kigali and had grabbed whatever he could, including a change of uniform for me and more toiletries. The final treat was a sink full of hot water, already an unimaginable luxury.

On Sunday, April 10, I awoke to reduced gunfire in the city and the odour of death in the air. I directed the Ghanaians to sweep the area for corpses and to remove them in order to minimize the risk of disease to us and the Rwandans sheltering with us. They found eighty dead people within a few hundred metres of the Force HQ, behind a slope in a local slum. They put the bodies into a pile, poured diesel oil onto them and burned them. The terrible smell lingered in the heat. I wondered whether these were the people whose moans I had heard through my window while waiting for the French to land. If so, they had been real moans and not the wind.

I had to control the airport; it was the only way to sustain or even-tually reinforce the mission. The French and the Belgians were there now, but they would soon withdraw. The one incentive I could offer both the RPF and the RGF was the hope of humanitarian aid, which could only be forwarded if UNAMIR secured the entranceway to the nation. That realization was the beginning of the Kigali International Airport Security Agreement. But first I would have to get the parties to actually agree.

I embarked on my daily attempt to meet the political and military leaders, shuttling back and forth between the RGF and RPF, looking for ways to negotiate. The trip to the heart of Kigali was a road into hell, with thousands and thousands of people on the move, even more checkpoints and even more bodies at those checkpoints. What shocked me was the resignation of the people who stood patiently in line, waiting to be identified as victims.

At the RGF headquarters, I was told that Bizimana was now back from Cameroon, so I headed over to the Ministry of Defence to speak with him—another man not so happy to see me. I told him I was here to expedite a truce within a broader ceasefire negotiation. As I had suspected, he told me that the interim government was now in charge of the military and that the Crisis Committee had been disbanded. He felt that by noon the next day the government and the local authorities would bring the situation under control. He told me he was meeting with Jean Kambanda, the newly declared prime minister, in a couple of hours. I asked him to eliminate the roadblocks and told him I wanted the airport to remain open so that humanitarian aid could enter and the expatriates could leave with less risk. Bizimana didn't like the signal sent by the sudden departure of the expatriates but told me that he, too, wanted a ceasefire and a return to the KWSA rules.

I left him and went to the CND, running the ever more dangerous gauntlet of roadblocks. There was an exchange of fire going on when I arrived, and I had to leave my vehicle and walk up the hill to the complex. I was ushered into a dark room where the three politicos were waiting for me. I passed on Bizimana's reassurances and congratulated them on their restraint regarding the French forces, but floodgates of resentment were then opened. Seth angrily told me that the French had been using UNAMIR vehicles to move Rwandans of known extremist background to the airport, where they were flown out of the country.

He also alleged that the French had opened fire on a number of occasions from these vehicles. It was absolutely unacceptable for the French to use UNAMIR this way, putting my troops at risk and confusing everyone about what our blue helmets meant, and I told them that Luc was arguing this point with the French commander. I moved on to the truce and airport negotiations, and they said they'd pass the request to Major General Kagame immediately. I hadn't seen Kagame since the Easter weekend and offered to travel anywhere in Rwanda in order to meet with him. The RPF wanted the terms of the truce to be clearly laid out on paper and signed by both parties and were justifiably outraged about the continued widespread killings.

I left the complex by a safer route, passing by the ad hoc surgery area where RPF soldiers and some civilians were being treated. The room with its dark green walls, black furniture and poor lighting, the screams and the blood, was like a scene out of Dante's *Inferno*.

I went directly to the American ambassador's residence nearby, arriving just in time to see Ambassador Rawson and his staff put the last piece of their luggage into their vehicles. The ambassador was pleased to be able to say goodbye to me and thankful for the support of my MILOBs in their evacuation. Rawson had worked hard to try to break the political impasse during the preceding months and was one of the most influential members of the country's small band of ambassadors. I have to confess that his departure extinguished one more ray of hope in my heart.

I decided to check on the Belgian ambassador, who had been named the coordinator of the expatriate evacuation plan. While climbing the hill to his residence, I passed by an assembly point where French soldiers were loading expatriates into vehicles. Hundreds of Rwandans had gathered to watch all these white entrepreneurs, NGO staff and their families making their fearful exits, and as I wended my way through the crowd, I saw how aggressively the French were pushing black Rwandans seeking asylum out of the way. A sense of shame overcame me. The whites, who had made their money in Rwanda and who had hired so many Rwandans to be their servants and labourers, were now abandoning them. Self-interest and self-preservation ruled. Large numbers of Belgian blue berets were in the area of the ambassador's residence, and inside the building, military personnel were working the radios and charting the evacuation. I told Ambassador Swinnen that we hoped to have a truce in place by noon the next day, which would make his convoys much less vulnerable.

I headed to Kigali Sector headquarters to find Luc in the midst of a satellite conversation with the Belgian chief of staff in Brussels. As I waited for him, I wandered throughout the headquarters, where the radio nets were squawking and a flurry of staff officers, tired and jumpy but obviously still effective, were in constant motion. After Luc finished his call, he briefed me on the status of his sector as well as his work with the French. Basically the new Belgian forces were going to secure the airport and, for obvious reasons, stay as much as possible off the streets of Kigali. UNAMIR would organize the convoys to and from the airport, and French troops would guard the assembly points and provide escorts. The evacuation would start in earnest the next day at 1000.

I raised with Luc the issue of his airport company having been unilaterally ripped from my command and given to Operation Silverback, which was the Belgian portion of the expatriate evacuation. He told me it was a direct order from Belgium and he was unable to do anything about it. The DPKO hadn't been able to do much about it, either. A good number of my Belgian staff officers had never come back from leave, including Frank Claeys, my intelligence officer. Luc had heard that these men wouldn't be coming back to UNAMIR at all and had been reassigned to the Belgian evacuation force. Tactically this made all kinds of sense from the Belgian perspective, but to take these important officers away from me at this critical time in the mission struck me as irresponsible and dangerous. Luc assured me that the rest of his Belgians were still under my command, but he was at the receiving end of a lot of my frustration over the coming days as the situation regarding the Belgian forces was played out.

It was getting dark as I arrived back at the Force HQ. My new chief intelligence officer, Captain Amadou Deme, was ready with a detailed briefing on events outside of Kigali. The RPF noose around Byumba was closing in on between five and seven battalions of RGF. Byumba was

Bizimana's hometown, and the minister had extensive economic and property holdings in the area. The town itself was indefensible, and clearly Bizimana was sacrificing the lives of his men to try to secure his own wealth, a stupid move that Kagame would not fail to exploit. Deme also reported that the RPF appeared to have withdrawn from Ruhengeri and were focusing on strangling Byumba and opening a land link to Kigali. An RPF column that had left Mulindi by foot on April 8 had arrived, singing, at the RPF garrison in the CND this morning. Two days of walking over sixty kilometres through enemy territory, carrying heavy packs and weapons, and they got to Kigali still singing. They were kids—young, tough and dedicated. There was no doubt in my mind that they would win this war. But could they save their people?

The other offensive, in the east, through the Kagera region and toward Kibungo, had gained momentum—the RGF troops were running for their lives. Gabiro had fallen, and UNOMUR reported that the entire Ugandan-Rwandan border in the east was now held by the RPF. I thought Kagame would avoid fighting in Kigali until the French left because he wouldn't want to provide them with an excuse to intervene. He would strangle the RGF in Byumba and seize the Tanzanian border area while closing in on Kigali from the east. He was possibly one of the greatest practitioners of manoeuvre warfare in modern military history, but his brilliance exacted a toll. As he conducted his time-consuming manoeuvres, the killing of civilians only escalated.

Jean Kambanda and the new foreign minister, Jerome Bicamumpaka, wished to see me at the Diplomates. We drove to the hotel in almost complete darkness; there was little movement in the streets and a number of the roadblocks were unmanned. A dozen fires burned around the city, and the acrid smell of smoke filled the air. It was past seven by the time I got to the hotel. I was led into another darkened meeting room, where Kambanda and Bicamumpaka were waiting. It was just the three of us, and despite the polite handshakes, they didn't bother to mask their hostility. I warned them not to mistake my presence for recognition of their government. I was there simply to listen. They raised all the old political issues, as if Arusha wasn't derailed, as if a massacre wasn't happening in the streets. In their skewed universe, the RPF had initiated hostilities by attacking the Presidential Guard, and UNAMIR was to blame, too, for letting the RPF out of its compound. And where, they wanted to know, was Faustin? I told them I didn't know. The meeting ended abruptly. My last shot was to warn them to make no mistake, UNAMIR was not pulling out. I left them with surprise in their eyes.

That night an adviser to the Secretary General called me to find out what was going on. I told him if I had four thousand effective troops I could stop the killing. I called the DPKO around 2230. Maurice was wondering where my options analysis was—what options analysis? Were they pulling me out, were they reinforcing me or was I staying? He said that six APCs were on their way from the UN force in Somalia to provide more protection and mobility, and that the FOD was working diligently on our logistics problems. I hit him with all my anger over the French and Belgian actions, including the fact that the French were shooting from my vehicles, which they had stolen from the airport. Once again the call ended with words of encouragement that couldn't have seemed more futile. Maurice promised to call Beth. After I hung up, exhaustion finally caught up with me, and I slipped between my curtains on the mattress on the floor and fell into a deep sleep.

April 11, the fifth day of slaughter. The Security Council and the office of the secretary-general were obviously at a loss as to what to do. I continued to receive demands to supply them with more information before they would take any concrete action. What more could I possibly tell them that I hadn't already described in horrific detail? The odour of death in the hot sun; the flies, maggots, rats and dogs that swarmed to feast on the dead. At times it seemed the smell had entered the pores of my skin. My Christian beliefs had been the moral framework that had guided me throughout my adult life. Where was God in all this horror? Where was God in the world's response?

Two thousand Rwandans had lost their lives that day as a direct result of the Belgian withdrawal. They had taken refuge after April 7 at the Belgian camp set up at the Dom Bosco School, joined by a few expatriates. That morning, French troops had come to the school to evacuate the foreigners, and after they left, the company commander, Captain Lemaire, called Lieutenant Colonel Dewez, his CO, to request permission for his company to consolidate at the airport. He didn't mention the 2,000 Rwandans his troops were protecting at the school. When Dewez approved the move and the troops pulled out, the Interahamwe moved in, killing almost all of the Rwandans.

Despite our verbal and written reports of the worsening scenario, and episodes such as this, reinforcement wasn't being discussed in New York. Maurice had made it clear to me on several occasions that no one was interested in Rwanda, and now, because of the escalating risks, they were even less interested. If the reinforcement option was off the table, as New York indicated, then I wanted to ensure that abandonment was also off the table. There was a void of leadership in New York. We had sent a deluge of paper and received nothing in return; no supplies, no reinforcement, no decisions.

In order for UNAMIR to participate in the evacuation, that night I signed a new ROE that permitted my troops to disarm belligerents and to intervene with force after warning shots. The new rules also permitted local commanders to decide on the level of force they needed to use. The question remains as to whether I had the authority to change my own ROE for the duration of the evacuation mission. I was on the ground, I was in command, I had been given the mission and I took the decision.

My first priority was the truce agreement. But Bizimana didn't have much clout in the interim government. Bagosora had the skills and the lust for power, but he was hard to find. That day, I left the Force HQ at 0700 to try and negotiate a truce. It took eight separate meetings, travelling back and forth past the increasingly angry, drunken militiamen at the barriers, but I finally secured the signatures of the RPF at 0230, and at 0600 the next morning, the RGF also signed. The truce meant that we were able to safely evacuate 650 expatriates from 22 nations on 10 French flights. Two hundred and eleven UN personnel left on three Canadian Forces Hercules flights. A company of French Marines arrived and more paratroops were standing by in Bangui. Eight flights brought in half of the Belgian para brigade, along with motorbikes and three armoured vehicles.

I mark April 12 as the day the world moved from disinterest in Rwanda to the abandonment of Rwandans to their fate. The swift evacuation of the foreign nationals was the signal for the génocidaires to move toward the apocalypse. That night I didn't sleep at all for guilt.

Kagame's forces had ceased to squeeze and were now mounting an assault on Byumba. The major-general had given me twenty-four hours' warning to get my forces out of the Byumba pocket in the demilitarized zone. After I informed the DPKO of the standoff in the zone and of my contingency plan for a possible withdrawal, New York sent us a little reminder that only the secretary-general could order a withdrawal—we had to stay until further orders. On the one hand, I was being told not to take unnecessary risks, and on the other I was being ordered not to take timely tactical decisions. At that point, I decided that I would take upon myself the decision to move my troops or not.

Kagame's chief of staff sent a formal response regarding my intention to stay in place in the demilitarized zone: "We have done everything possible to protect UNAMIR. Up to now, we have not shelled Byumba despite the shelling from the enemy. We have lived up to our commitment." Well that was that.

The battle around us escalated that day. There were several exchanges of artillery and mortar fire, the fighting more intense and determined to the north and east of the city. A few bombs exploded around my headquarters and Luc's Kigali Sector command, and a few of the thousands of civilians cowering at the Amahoro and the King Faisal Hospital sites were wounded. Reports from the UNMOs still in-country carried fresh horror stories. In Gisenyi, a tourist town on Lake Kivu, an Austrian MILOB reported a festive spirit on the part of the killers, who seemed oblivious to the sheer horror and pandemonium as they cut down men, women and children in the streets. In Kibungo, government soldiers were running a scorched earth policy against Tutsis and Hutu moderates. In parts of Kigali, bulldozers had been brought in to dig deeper trenches at the roadblocks to reduce the piles of bodies. Prisoners in their pink jail uniforms were picking up corpses and throwing them into dump trucks to be hauled away. Think of that for a moment: there were so many dead that they had to be loaded into dump trucks. Whole sectors of the city were deserted except for wild dogs.

Kagame was bringing about three more battalions of troops into the north of Kigali. There was a lot of movement to the east of the demilitarized zone, toward the Kagera National Park and the main north-south road along the Tanzanian border. Butare was tense because some Presidential Guards were in the area. Cyangugu, Kibuye and Gikongoro were scenes of ethnic killings by suspected CDR supporters and RGF soldiers. MILOB teams had established contact with an International Red Cross vehicle convoy of humanitarian aid coming from Burundi. The French had nearly completed their evacuation operation and were beginning to withdraw, with Luc's troops taking up the French positions at the airport. France's ambassador had closed the country's embassy and flown out.

That evening, Brent brought me a copy of a *communiqué commandement des forces armées Rwandaises*. It pleaded for a face-to-face meeting between Gatsinzi and Kagame under UNAMIR auspices, and it was signed by Rusatira, Gatsinzi, five colonels and three lieutenant colonels of the RGF, including our liaison officer, Ephrem Rwabalinda. They stated that there had been too much killing, and they were submitting to an unconditional surrender as of 1200 tomorrow, April 13. They wanted to establish the BBTG. I wondered why Ndindiliyimana's signature was not on the communiqué, but I found out from him the next day that he had been stuck in Butare helping some Tutsis escape from the country and hadn't been able to get back in time to sign. Of course the offer was next to useless, as the moderate politicians had been killed and there was no political structure to build on. How could the officers even guarantee that anyone would surrender? As naive as the offer seemed, I applauded the courage it took to make it, and their desire to stop the war and the killings. And if Kagame would give them the recognition and the support they needed to create a moderate countermovement within the RGF, they might ultimately emasculate the extremists.

It turned out that the communiqué was the last whisper of hope. Just as it was sent, Gatsinzi was demoted, and the minister of defence announced that Lieutenant-Colonel Augustin Bizimungu, from the Ruhengeri garrison, would be promoted to major general and confirmed as the permanent chief of staff of the army. Bizimungu was a brutal, hard-drinking tyrant who commanded through fear. He had successfully fought the RPF in earlier conflicts and hated them with a passion; his appointment was definitely a sign that any noises the interim government made about wanting to put an end to the killing were just noises. It was clear he was meant to kick-start the lethargic government army in the field. From that point on, when I attempted to negotiate with the government side, I faced three known extremist leaders—Bizimana, Bizimungu and Bagosora—and Ndindiliyimana, who was somehow hanging on to his job and was no match for the hard-liners. Within days, all the officers who had signed the communiqué were transferred to symbolic positions and replaced by known extremists. The last chance of the moderates to gain control of the government side had been lost.

Later that night I received a telephone call from Europe, a Mr. Gharekhan on the line, who was a special assistant to Boutros Boutros-Ghali. He told me that the Belgian government had just decided to withdraw its peacekeepers from Rwanda. Between his curt questions on the status of UNAMIR and the country, and my equally curt answers, he conferred with someone in the background—I believe it was the secretary-general himself. I had never met with or spoken to Boutros-Ghali, and clearly he wasn't about to talk to me that night, though his assistant was obviously moving me toward the thought of withdrawing UNAMIR completely. He asked me to consider future options and terminated the call.

Within the hour, Luc called me, his voice distraught. He had just finished arguing with General Charlier against the withdrawal of the Belgian contingent from Rwanda. Luc hoped that he had persuaded his chief of staff that a withdrawal would be a grave error, but he knew that Charlier was only a conduit of information to and from the Belgian government. I told him that we needed to meet with all contingent commanders the next morning to discuss the position of their governments. Though the last I'd heard was that Willy Claes was urging that the mission be reinforced, the Belgians had obviously shifted their position. They had no doubt communicated this intent to Boutros-Ghali, who in turn had directed Gharekhan to sound me out.

It was late and I went up to the roof to watch the tracer bullets and small explosions in the sky around the city, trying to appreciate for a moment the coolness of the night air. Bagosora and the extremists had expected me to withdraw. Their man was still on the Security Council, privy to all discussions on the status of my mission. Since I hadn't yet withdrawn, maybe my fantasy of the fence might yet come true, and they might be tempted to come at us in order to capture Faustin and inflict more casualties that might cause us to run home. Our defences were paper thin, but we would not hand over Faustin without a fight.

That night, Maurice confirmed the scenario I'd guessed at. The secretary-general, after consultations with the Belgian foreign minister, was going to inform the president of the Security Council by letter the next day that the Belgians intended to unilaterally withdraw from Rwanda. Boutros-Ghali thought this withdrawal would put the whole mission in peril. I asked why the turnaround on the part of the Belgians, especially Willy Claes, but Maurice had no reason. I made my stand very clear. I would not leave. We could not abandon the Rwandans in this cataclysm, nor could we desert those thousands of people under our protection. Booh-Booh had been holding separate conversations with Riza and possibly Annan that same evening. I wondered what had been said, for over the following few days Booh-Booh also shifted to support a complete pullout.

The next morning, I informed my staff of the Belgian about-face. We had to produce a summary of contingency options in the event of the Belgian withdrawal. The contingent commanders needed direct communication with their home nations to determine which countries intended to stay, which intended to leave and who was on the fence. The United States, France and Belgium had proven with their evacuation exercise that this mission could be reinforced. It was certainly not a lack of means that prevented them from reinforcing my mission or even taking my mission under their command to stop the killings.

Later that day, I went to my first negotiation with the RPF regarding the RGF moderates' offer of unconditional surrender. As I'd predicted,

Seth and the other politicos dismissed it outright. Seth was particularly arrogant during the meeting, his stance reminding me of the inflexible position the RPF took during much of the BBTG negotiations. Once more they were going for the extremists' jugular. The RGF insisted on a ceasefire so they could redeploy forces to stop the killings. The RPF insisted that the killings had to stop before they would agree to a cease-fire. Round and round we went, day in and day out, both sides defending their positions stubbornly and neither side willing to bend.

Back at the Force HQ, I sent New York another report, this one on the contingency options after the Belgian withdrawal. You can imagine how bleak they were, but the critical point I made was that in some incarnation we had to stay in place to be a witness to events and to pursue ceasefire negotiations. At 0612 on April 14, I received a new code cable from the DPKO requesting that we examine two new options. The first was to tell both sides that the secretary-general would consider leaving the force in place for three weeks, minus the Belgians but with the benefit of the bulk of their equipment, in order to permit the parties to resume the Arusha process—but only if there was a ceasefire for the whole period and the airport became neutral territory. If no agreement could be reached by April 30, UNAMIR would be completely withdrawn by May 7.

The other possibility? If no progress was possible, both sides should be informed that UNAMIR could not stay in Rwanda and would leave in concert with the Belgian withdrawal. Booh-Booh and I would stay on, along with a small security force of approximately 200 to 250 troops, to carry on with mediation efforts. The cable specified that the Belgians could be counted on for just four more days. It gave us eight hours to consider this direction, to provide a complete list of the equipment we needed from the Belgians, and my assessment of the viability of the two options.

I scanned the attached transcript of the Security Council meeting of the day before to find that Riza had raised an even more disconcerting point. On the issue of protecting the civilians in our care, Riza noted that, "the [Security] Council should consider whether PKOs [peacekeeping operations] should be assigned such tasks." On humanitarian and moral grounds, I had taken the safeguarding of civilians as a given, and here my superiors were questioning the whole concept.

Even though we had absolutely no means to defend them except our own presence, so far the security at the sites had been working fairly well. There had been just one incident at the Amahoro Stadium, when RPF soldiers had forced their way in with no resistance from the Bangladeshis and had taken away about a dozen civilians who had been singled out by other Rwandans in the stadium as having committed atrocities. They were summarily executed outside the stadium.

At prayers, when I announced the imminent withdrawal of the Belgians, the Belgian staff officers felt embarrassed, betrayed and angry. They had been with me since November, and now that things were desperate they would be ordered to abandon Rwanda to its fate. The military ethos of loyalty to the chain of command was sorely tested that morning. I tasked Henry to produce a reorganization plan for staffing Headquarters minus the Belgians and then drove all of us near to despair by outlining the thinking in the code cable about what would happen to UNAMIR when the Belgians were gone. The one bright spot was that the Belgian staff officers could be replaced by Canadians, three of whom would be redeployed from Somalia to UNAMIR over the next couple of days. There was a promise for another eight or nine Canadian Forces officers over the next few weeks. While others were abandoning Rwanda, Canada had taken the unique decision to reinforce the mission.

That was also the day that a Belgian magistrate arrived to investigate the murder of the ten para-commandos. I gave instructions that he was to receive full support in getting testimony from witnesses and that I and any other member of UNAMIR would be available upon his request. I had already ordered a board of inquiry to be conducted by Lieutenant Colonel Dounkov of Russia and that all material of the board be made available to the Belgian military investigation.[1]

---

1. I found Dounkov's investigation incomplete. On July 14, however, I signed off on the board of inquiry, since it ultimately provided sufficient information to be used as the basis for UN compensation of the Belgian soldiers' families and the Belgian government. I added the caveat that the board required a follow-up investigation.

I met with the minister of defence that afternoon. Bizimana was over-joyed that the Belgians were pulling out; he claimed it would reduce tensions amongst his colleagues, the Rwandan military and the popula-tion as a whole. We took a new route back to the Force HQ after the meeting because of heavy weapons fire around the CND and sporadic fire in different quarters of town. When I got back, there was a call from Katz Kuroda at the UN Department of Humanitarian Affairs, offering his expertise for my fledgling humanitarian section. He asked me for a rough assessment (a word I would learn to despise coming from the aid organizations) of the general humanitarian situation to share with his department and the Security Council. He gave us authority to use all material and food in the UN humanitarian warehouses (supplies origi-nally intended for internally displaced Rwandans and Burundian refugees). The trouble was how to take advantage of his offer. We tried on several occasions to get control of the warehouses and were fired upon by both sides, who were engaged in plundering these supplies for themselves. We returned fire on a few occasions. Sometimes we were able to escape with a few truckloads of food. Bravery was called for and was the order of the day. I remember one APC making it back with sup-plies despite hundreds of bullet hits and a flat tire.

The hospitals remained operational throughout the genocide, thanks to efforts by Philippe Gaillard and the International Committee of the Red Cross, backed up by Médecins Sans Frontières and the Canadian doctor and Somalia veteran James Orbinski. But at what a cost. Fifty-six Rwandans working for the Red Cross would be killed before the conflict was over, a few white doctors and nurses would be injured and hundreds of Rwandan casualties would be pulled out of ambulances and slaughtered on the spot. On one trip to the city centre, I saw a white Red Cross van, angled on the road, riddled with bullet holes. Smoke was coming out of the engine compartment and all the windows were smashed. The passenger door was open and a Rwandan in a Red Cross vest was hanging down, facing us, with blood oozing from his head in a slow, steady stream. The back doors were open and a body on a stretcher was still inside, with another held up on the bumper. There were three other casualties, their white and bloodied gauze dressings spun

around them. One body had no head. Five blood-spattered youths sat
on the curb, smoking cigarettes beside the ambulance. Their machetes
were stained red. At most they may have been fifteen years old.

On April 15 I awoke at four-thirty in the morning. A code cable from
New York had just arrived; our cables were criss-crossing over the
Atlantic and confusing the discussion. This cable informed me that the
two proposals about how to withdraw had been approved by Boutros-
Ghali and had been presented to the Security Council. The DPKO had
added a third option, a finessing exercise: in this plan we'd start with the
larger force of 2,000 troops and then slide down to the 250-troop level
if no ceasefire was in place at the end of three weeks. Boutros-Ghali was
standing by option one: an immediate ceasefire as a precondition of
2,000 troops staying in place for three weeks, and France supported
that plan as long as a reassessment of the situation occurred in five to
six days. The British essentially took a similar position to that of the
French. Nigeria, speaking for the non-aligned members of the Council,
said none of the options met their concerns and that the possible withdrawal of UNAMIR would send the wrong message. Nigeria wanted more
time to make a proposal. The United States wanted to pull UNAMIR
right away: "The Security Council should adopt a resolution providing
for the 'orderly evacuation' of UNAMIR, since it is unlikely that a cease
fire would be established in the near future."

Only New Zealand's Colin Keating, the president of the Security
Council, thought they should move to stop this catastrophe. He actually
proposed that the UN should *"increase the strength of UNAMIR and . . .
revise its mandate to enable it to contribute to the restoration of law and
order and the establishment of the transitional institutions within the framework of the Arusha Peace Agreement."* In case my heart lifted too high,
Riza pointed out in the cable that neither the language nor the resolution had been agreed upon.

Later that morning I was handed another cable from Riza. I had
requested clarification from his office as to the Standing UN
Operational Orders in regards to persons under our protection. His
answer: it was my call on the priority, feasibility and level of response to

these demands. "In the abnormal circumstances prevailing," he wrote, "these orders may be overridden at the discretion of the SRSG and FC [force commander], for humanitarian reasons." I felt sickened as I read. On the morning of April 7 Riza ordered me "not to fire unless fired upon." Now he was saying that all along it had been the Force Commander's prerogative to take offensive action for humanitarian reasons.

Ten days into the killing, Captain Deme summed up the state of the war as far as the belligerents went. In an intelligence report to me, he wrote, the "general intention seems that [the RPF] are conducting a deep penetration to control the main RGF supply routes, to surround the main targets and to make assaults only once they are ready. They have no interest in the airport at this time. They are slowly, calmly and coolly gaining terrain. Many important targets like Byumba are surrounded. They are installing Tutsis in areas already under their control." When pressed on that issue, Seth and the other RPF politicos simply said that they were letting the Tutsi refugees come home—surely there was nothing wrong with that since it was one of the aims of the whole Arusha exercise. But once the Tutsis were in place, the RPF guaranteed some humanitarian NGOs safety behind the front lines, and the NGOs—hotheaded and undisciplined in my view—moved in to feed and aid these supposedly displaced people. Of course, the RPF controlled all the aid distribution points and "recuperated" their share from the people the NGOs were pledged to help. This was a flagrant instance of NGOs providing aid and comfort to a belligerent, and as far as I could see, there was no way to stop it except by making the issue part of the ceasefire negotiations.

Deme's assessment of the RGF was revealing. The troops were receiving very little tactical information or direction at the front; soldiers were deserting, while others looted to feed themselves. Some troops wanted peace and had confidence in UNAMIR (once the Belgians were gone), and a rift was starting between some military units and the Interahamwe. As anticipated, the RGF front-line troops and recruits, undisciplined and disorganized, would not put up much of a fight.

I went back and forth between the RPF and RGF, trying to arrange a meeting to discuss the terms of a ceasefire. They all finally agreed to meet at the Meridien hotel. On the government side, the delegate was supposed to be Ndindiliyimana, but when I arrived with an APC and some Bangladeshi troops to pick him up, the RGF had decided to send Marcel Gatsinzi instead, telling me that the head of the Gendarmerie would be saved for the next, more senior round of discussions. It was a very nervous Gatsinzi, charged with pleading for an unconditional ceasefire, who joined me in the APC. He would hold his breath each time we hit a roadblock and I would pop my head up through the hatch to help argue us through. Getting out of the RGF and Interahamwe zone was really slow, but in the RPF-held areas we were flagged right along. I got the driver to run the APC right up the stairs at the front of the hotel to get us as close to the doors as possible and got out first to cover Rusatira's exit from the vehicle.

The meeting was being held in the spacious hotel dining room, flanked by two walls of windows. When we walked in, the curtains were wide open, and my first move was to get help pulling the drapes. With the curtains closed and the doors shut, it made for a hot, uncomfortable afternoon. Mamadou Kane was there and took charge of the formalities, but the RPF was late, as was Booh-Booh. Gatsinzi's face fell when he saw that the RPF delegation was indeed very low-level, just Commander Charles from the CND and Frank Kamenzi, the RPF's liaison to UNAMIR. When Booh-Booh arrived, flanked by his personal security detail and accompanied by Dr. Kabia, it was clear he was also disappointed in the RPF showing.

Booh-Booh turned to Gatsinzi first, and Gatsinzi did his best to make an impassioned plea for the immediate cessation of hostilities and of the massacres. The soldiers who were killing civilians had received no orders from him or his headquarters; they were rogue elements that must be stopped. And he closed by saying he regretted the terrible loss of UNAMIR personnel and thanked us for staying on in Rwanda.

In response, Commander Charles did not budge an inch but simply restated the RPF's preconditions for the ceasefire, that inexorable chicken-and-egg scenario of having to stop the killing before they could stop the killing. I quote: "All these conditions are not negotiable and must be executed immediately." He even handed out copies.

Booh-Booh in his capacity as chair summed up. Both positions reflected a desire for peace, he said. Well, yes, but the RPF was the intransigent party. It had the RGF on the run and had just essentially demanded that the moderates conduct a *coup d'état* of their own. We'd then have a three-way civil war on our hands in addition to the massacres. I felt pity for Gatsinzi, and something close to disdain for the smug Commander Charles, who was clearly willing to countenance all the killing while his side remained cloaked in bogus superiority. At that moment, as if on cue, gunshots sounded behind the hotel. A glass door behind the drapes opened with a crash, and all our hearts skipped a beat. Then a Belgian officer fought his way through the curtains to report that the shots had been fired by a single trigger-happy RPF soldier. We resumed our negotiations in an even tenser state and got absolutely nowhere. After the meeting ended, I drove a morose Gatsinzi back to army headquarters. He was a man fighting a losing battle with the extremists, and after sticking his neck out to attend this meeting and being rebuffed so firmly, he had become more vulnerable. The lack of progress at this first formal ceasefire negotiation would only give weight to the option of total withdrawal at the Security Council.

When I got back to the Amahoro, I found out that the Security Council deliberations had ended that day with a split between those supporting option one (the non-aligned nations, as well as China, France and Argentina) and those supporting option two (the United Kingdom, Russia, and the United States under duress). Colin Keating had concluded the discussions by saying that it wasn't necessary to reach a final decision that day. Seeing as it was Friday, we would have to wait until at least Monday for word on our future. We were in limbo. There would be no cavalry coming over the hill. How many thousands of Rwandans would die that weekend?

Each new day there were new rounds of ceasefire negotiations and discussions aimed at an agreement to bring the airport under UNAMIR control. The killings were accelerating. More and more Rwandans were coming to us for protection. There were continuous ambushes, firefights and shelling that resulted in casualties in most of our protection sites. Lost or forgotten expatriates called every day asking to be rescued from impossible and dangerous circumstances. Every day we scrambled for food and water and tried to get simple items like paper from a support base a thousand miles away, in Nairobi, Kenya. My people were edgy and exhausted, and nothing was more wearing on them than the endless bickering of diplomats.

On April 16, I received a letter from the manager of the Mille Collines saying there were now over four hundred people, mostly Tutsis, taking sanctuary in his hotel. The Tunisians and some MILOBs had done an excellent job in bluffing the militia and keeping the hotel safe, but the manager thought it only a matter of time before the militia assaulted the hotel and asked that the people be moved. I ordered Bangladeshi troops to reinforce the hotel but received a formal letter of protest from their commanding officer, stating the mission was too dangerous and informing me he had passed his protest of the order on to Dhaka. I retracted the order. What was the use? If they'd obeyed the order there was a good chance they would have fallen apart in any confrontation. For the time being there was nothing we could do. Moving four hundred people would be more dangerous for them than maintaining the uneasy détente with the militia.

I can't say enough about the bravery of the Tunisians. They never shirked their duty and always displayed the highest standards of courage and discipline in the face of difficult and dangerous tasks. That morning at the King Faisal Hospital, for instance, Tunisian troops were confronted by a platoon of RPF soldiers desperately low on medical supplies, who argued that whatever was in the hospital was theirs as spoils of war, and then broke in with two sections of infantry. The head of the Tunisian contingent, Commandant Belgacem, stopped them in their tracks with his small reserve force. He had his men in a solid position to defend the medical supply section of the hospital and made it clear to the RPF that he would open fire—the few supplies they held had been flown in for the over seven thousand wounded Rwandans in the hospital compound. The Bangladeshi field hospital commander then came forward and worked out a deal with the RPF, and the troops retreated with not a shot fired.

A couple of hours later, I stopped to congratulate the soldiers and toured the facility. Every room and corridor was filled with sick, injured and dying Rwandans. Families were huddled with children, who were crying, hungry and dehydrated. The operating area was dispensing what care and bandages they had amid the smell of unwashed bodies, congealed blood, and death. With no water supply for washing, they risked a cholera epidemic. In the back of the building, a large fenced area held thousands of people of all ages and a collection of small tents, clothes, latrines and garbage. It was like a concentration camp. Here the elderly suffered a slow death, and newborns brought anguish to their mothers, who couldn't feed them.

There was no water and very little food, with nothing to cook it in and next to no wood to heat it. As I walked among the sick they were begging on their knees, pulling at my clothes, holding their babies up to me. I had nothing to ease their plight. I was guided by a few of the leaders to the site where a large mortar bomb had exploded the day before. The ground had been only lightly disturbed because the impact fuse most likely hit some humans first and exploded instantaneously, spreading a maximum of shrapnel at surface level. There were traces of flesh, brain and blood in the immediate area. Dozens of shredded bodies had been moved and buried. There were over a hundred people still alive who had horrific gashes from the shrapnel. There had been a panic to get inside the hospital itself, and children had been trampled to death. Fights had broken out for space, but in the end everyone had settled down again because they had nowhere else to go—if they went beyond the compound fence they would be killed. Death was all around them, and now death had started to invade from the sky. I wanted to scream, to vomit, to hit something, to break free of my body, to end this terrible scene. Instead I struggled to compose myself, knowing composure was critical with so many despairing eyes upon me. I thanked the medical teams for their efforts and promised them all supplies as soon as I could get them.

Before he left, Colonel Roman, the Belgian para-commando commander, gave me a phone number in Tanzania where he was deploying his brigade for the next couple of weeks. He told me he and his soldiers would remain in Tanzania just in case we needed help extricating ourselves once we were ordered to withdraw. He phoned twice over the next ten days, asking me if I was withdrawing and if I could use any help, and both times I said no. I suspected that the Belgians didn't want UNAMIR to take any casualties that could be directly associated with the Belgians' abandonment of the mission.

The first three Canadian officers arrived that day from Somalia, and I barely let them unpack before I put them to work. I asked Major Michel Bussières to take over the personnel branch in the Force HQ. Though I'd been told that all our people had been accounted for, the branch had not been able to provide me with even a nominal roll. Within twenty-four hours, Major Bussières had it sorted, and he went on to provide sterling service as we downsized the mission. I gave Major Jean-Guy Plante the job of media officer, escorting and coordinating all journalists in and out of theatre. I told him I wanted at least one report a day to appear on international news networks, and with BBC reporter Mark Doyle, that is what Major Plante accomplished, trying to spark the world's conscience. The naval officer, Lieutenant Commander Robert Read, I tasked with building from scratch a logistics base at the airport to unload, sort, store and disperse the supplies that were now starting to flow in on the two Canadian Forces Hercules shuttling back and forth from Nairobi. Read did have to ask Brent, "What's a logistics base?" But once he knew, he settled to his task and within days had created it. That first day, Brent was overwhelmed with rescue missions and tasked Plante and Read to go with a Bangladeshi APC to rescue a Rwandan-Canadian hiding at the Mille Collines. He and his family had been vacationing in Rwanda on April 7 and had fled their relatives' home. His wife and daughter had been caught and killed by a mob, but he had saved his two sons and hidden them away. Plante and Read sneaked him out of the hotel and back to the Force HQ, where he revealed the location of his sons. Plante and Read then went back out again and rescued his boys. What remained of the family was evacuated to Nairobi and then home to Canada the next day.

That night the fate of the Rwandan refugees at the Mille Collines kept me awake. I knew that an attack could occur any minute. I wanted to use force to defend all the sites under our shaky protection, but I knew I didn't have the military capability—I could only hope the militia did not call our bluff. I called Moigny (the Congolese MILOB who commanded the site) and asked him to call me directly to check in every night, especially if an attack started. For many nights to come I talked to him over the radio, offering encouragement if nothing substantive. Over the next weeks he would prove himself to be a magnificent leader of men, fending off with his Tunisians three large force attacks against the hotel, as well as a couple of bombardments.

There were more requests for assistance as the rogue elements of the RGF and Gendarmerie overtly allied with the Interahamwe and other militias. This alliance was fuelled by a call over RTLM from the interim government for all ordinary citizens to take up arms nationwide and mount barricades or roadblocks to protect themselves against what RTLM billed as a rebel army bent on infiltrating and killing Hutus. It was a sort of mass mobilization of the population, and the result was that there were now three belligerents in the fight, one fanatically dedicated to exterminating an entire ethnic group.

Our blue-beret neutrality was under fire. It was only a matter of time before my troops would be engaged in battle with the murderous hordes of militia, or even with one or both of the warring parties. We were entering a new phase of the conflict, where our bluffs would be called.

At the roadblocks throughout Kigali, there were more youths with machetes and spears. Ten days into the genocide (a word I had yet to start using to describe what was going on around me, for reasons that still elude me: maybe simple denial that anything like the Holocaust could be happening again), most streets were vacant except for the patrols of prisoners from the Kigali jails who were loading corpses into dump trucks for disposal in mass graves outside the city.

The memory of those trucks is indelible. Blood, dark, half-coagulated, oozed like thick paint from the back of them. One day I saw a young Hutu girl in a light dress, wearing sandals, lose her balance as she slipped on the blood beside the truck. She landed hard, and though she got up immediately, it was as if someone had painted her body and her dress with a dark red oil. She became hysterical looking at it, and the more she screamed, the more attention she drew. Soon we were surrounded by hundreds of people, many carrying weapons. In seconds, such a crowd could lash out at any target. I rolled down my window and greeted them in Kinyarwanda. Some of them started to hammer on the vehicle. I kept my open palms quite visible in the traditional expression of friendship. People in the crowd recognized me and called my name, even smiled, and I was able to ease the vehicle forward until we were clear of the mob. The scene took only fifteen minutes but felt like an eternity.

For the last four days we had been forwarding our radio logs to the UN at the end of the day, as requested by the DPKO, a practice we carried on until the end. I thought that if the UN knew what we were dealing with day to day, someone might still come to our aid. Instead, the log was used to inform troop-contributing nations of the state of risk to their national contingents, effectively scaring off the timid. We finished the newest military assessment late that night and sent it on: by now one would have had to have been blind or illiterate not to know what was going on in Rwanda. In this report, I informed my superiors that, with all of these hard-liners now in positions of authority in the RGF and the Gendarmerie, we were witnessing the death of any desire on the RGF side for a ceasefire. Over the last few days while the Security Council considered, the extremist movement had been emboldened. Was it possible, I asked, that the interim government had concluded that there would be no international intervention and that they had carte blanche to exterminate the Tutsis?

I also reported that Kagame was obviously achieving his goal, though his campaign was slowing down even further. Three days ago the RPF could have overrun Kigali in a matter of hours, if not days. They didn't, and that was either Kagame's intention or perhaps he was slowed because they encountered stiffer resistance than they expected because of the mass mobilization of the population sparked by RTLM, or possibly because they were running out of supplies. If supplies were the problem, the RGF might potentially produce enough defensive capability to stop the RPF and turn this into a protracted war. As it stood, I wrote, the killings were increasing in scale and scope "just ahead of the RPF advance" and under the eyes of the RGF and the Gendarmerie.

I was pushing the NGO community, the humanitarian agencies and the UN Department of Humanitarian Affairs to link up with my nascent humanitarian branch in response to the immense effort needed in Rwanda, but we faced a huge quandary in the risks we were required to run. "Rapidly UNAMIR is being dragged into a peace enforcement scenario for humanitarian reasons," I reported. "If this mission is to be changed into a peace enforcement scenario to stop the massacres and rescue threatened civilians then a change in mandate will be required and the mission must be reinforced with men, weapons and equipment." I added, ". . . the [Bangladeshi] contingent's junior officers have clearly stated that if they are stopped at a roadblock with local people in the convoy, they will hand over these local people to the inevitable killing rather than use their weapons in an attempt to save them. . . . UNAMIR must be prepared to defend the airport with one battalion as it is our and the humanitarian agencies' lifeline."

In conclusion, I wrote, "The force simply cannot continue to sit on the fence in the face of all these morally legitimate demands for assistance/protection, nor can it simply launch into Chapter 7 type of operations without the proper authority, personnel and equipment. It is thus anticipated that over the next 24 hours or so, the Force Commander will either recommend a thinning out of the force down to a responsible level needed for security of airport, political process, humanitarian support tasks . . . a force of 1,300 personnel, or the FC will recommend . . . the 250 men force."

On Sunday I received another of Riza's cables. He provided some surprisingly direct guidance on the intransigence of the RPF. "It should be impressed upon the RPF that without some quick agreement on a cease-fire—even a limited one—by Wednesday [April 20] at the latest, the Security Council can be expected to decide to withdraw UNAMIR from Rwanda. At that time the RPF could be blamed for not accepting the cease-fire to allow discussions to begin. Only once a durable cease-fire has been established, [can we move on to] the creation of a framework for the resumption of the Arusha [process] . . . Please stress to them that without a cease-fire, humanitarian assistance operations cannot begin."

There was disturbing news in the cable as well: "Your plans to start sharp reduction of UNAMIR personnel is approved. This also will demonstrate imminence of withdrawal of UNAMIR if cease-fire is not achieved." I had given them an argument for pulling out, and they jumped on it, though that hadn't been my intention. Henry and I, talking late that night, mulled over how little the massacres and the plight of the Rwandan people seemed to inflect the instructions we were receiving. Maybe they believed a ceasefire would automatically stop the killing, which was naive in the extreme given what was happening behind RGF lines. I felt helpless and frustrated by what I viewed at the time as my inability to make the horror sink into the minds and souls of the people in the DPKO, the security council, the secretary-general's office, the world at large.

Before going to sleep, I went downstairs to spend some time with the six civilian communications staff who had insisted on staying with us after the rest of their colleagues had been evacuated. Although they were living in squalor in the back of what had been the Amahoro hotel kitchen, their morale seemed to soar with each passing day. They had scrounged some Primus beer and offered me one, and we sat together in a fug of fatigue and cigarette smoke and a whirl of their loud commentary on where I could stick the Security Council and all its dithering, along with our gang in the "Club Med" in Nairobi. On a serious note, their manager brought to my attention the fact that the main satellite and control system, located near the operations centre, was not sufficiently protected against heavy fire from either party. I made a mental note to cover the communications system in sandbags the next morning and then headed off to try to sleep. Two days later, a bomb exploded no more than five metres from the new sandbag barrier around communications central. The system was damaged and went down for nineteen long, isolated hours, but it wasn't destroyed. I scrounged a bottle of whisky as a thank-you present to those men for their prescient advice.

On April 18, I awoke to machine-gun fire and the sound of exploding grenades. The Force HQ was under bombardment. Today was the day that Luc was leaving with the Belgian contingent. He had been one of the first on the ground, and his steady nerves and professionalism, his rock-solid moral sense, had provided me with a certain feeling of confidence, even security. He was handing over airport security to Colonel Yaache, the Ghanaian commander in the demilitarized zone, and Yaache and I met with Luc at 0800 to discuss the last details. Luc did not look well. The fatigue, the stress, the physical and mental pain and the crushing weight of his Kigali Sector command had finally worn him down, and he stood before me slightly hunched and short of breath. I could see the shame, sorrow and uncertainty of his position reflected in his eyes. But he soon straightened his back and got on with the job at hand, conveying the necessary information.

I had wanted to have a little leave-taking ceremony for Luc at the airport, but the RPF had vetoed that, so we made do at the Force HQ, presenting Luc with the UNAMIR VIP gift of a wooden statuette of a traditional Rwandan warrior. (We had bought a few of these impressive statuettes before the war; we later found the bodies of the Tutsi carvers slaughtered in their shop.) I know my words were inadequate to thank him for the services he had performed for the mission and for the people of Rwanda.

The Belgian government had offered Faustin sanctuary, and Luc had already stashed the prime minister designate in the APC. Before Luc left, I took him aside to try to express privately how sorry I was about the loss of KIBAT and to thank him for leaving us with Belgian equipment, weapons, supplies and ammunition. I was about to tell him how proud I was of him and how sad I was at his departure when several artillery and mortar rounds landed inside the Force HQ compound and the stadium. Glass broke all around us, and for a moment panic reigned. More than a dozen people were killed, and more than a hundred were wounded, including a Ghanaian blue beret, but the drills we had practised served the situation well and things calmed down.

Then Luc said his quick goodbyes and was gone.

As I sat down amongst the crowd of military and civilians waiting for either a direct hit or an end to the bombardment, the full realization of his departure struck me with a potent sense of loss, and something more bitter. Dewez and his two hundred paras would be gone tomorrow, as well. The former colonial masters were running from this fight with their tails between their legs.

People were huddling in every corner of the main hall. I'd been able to come up with enough sandbags to protect the satellite system, but we had not been able to reinforce the doors and windows. Around me were young children with tears in their eyes, trying to be brave; poorly clothed men and women, using their bodies to make human shields to protect their kids; soldiers smoking nervously, flinching slightly with each explosion. If a round were to hit the front or the back of the building, there would be a horrific mess of human arms, legs and brains.

The bombardment lasted an hour. When it stopped, Brent and I made a quick survey of the damage: broken windows, a part of the outside kitchen wall blasted away, a number of vehicles in the compound damaged but most still workable. As we made our way back to the office, Brent looked through a broken panel on the roof and saw an unexploded 120-millimetre mortar bomb wedged between some pipes. He passed on the job of safely removing it to one of the Polish engineer officers who had witnessed the Gikondo Parish Massacre. We found out later that he had simply picked up the unexploded bomb and carried it through the building, out of the compound and across the street where he set it down. It could have exploded at any time. Brent suspected he had suffered psychological damage and had a death wish after witnessing the Gikondo massacre. The officer was repatriated shortly afterwards, not the last psychological casualty of UNAMIR.

RGF troops were still billeted at the airport and in Camp Kanombe nearby, but during the French and Belgian evacuation operations, they had been prevented from engaging in any military action at the airport by well-armed foreign troops. We now had neither the mandate nor the muscle of these troops, and when the Belgians flew away, the RGF moved back into the airport. If the RGF didn't sign the airport neutrality agreement by the next day, April 19, we would have to cohabit with them in a worsening security situation. Their presence at the airport would also draw RPF fire, leaving us and any humanitarian resupply or evacuation flights much too vulnerable for comfort.

I had meetings with the RGF that day to move them toward turning the airport completely over to UNAMIR as neutral ground so that we could support our force and bring in humanitarian aid for Rwandans. The RPF would agree with the proposal only if the RGF complied with airport neutrality. Meanwhile, I was worried about the last two convoys of our Ghanaians coming in from the demilitarized zone. They were terribly exposed, driving slow-moving vehicles that were prone to breakdowns along a route that was open to ambush. An overnight stop would bring them in too late to arrive before the departure of the last of Dewez's Belgian battalion.

At a ceasefire meeting late in the day, Gatsinzi and Ndindiliyimana took a new hardline stance. Previously they had both agreed on making the airport a neutral zone, and had even accepted participation by the RPF on a joint commission to supervise the application of the agreement. Now they rejected the neutrality proposal and objected to the RPF being part of the discussions. The airport was a national infrastructure, they argued, and must be under RGF control. They became particularly defensive about the RPF precondition that demanded the outright condemnation and imprisonment of all Presidential Guards; some weren't involved in the massacres, they said. Ndindiliyimana even insisted that the slaughter had dramatically declined—a ridiculous statement. I suspected they were now being forced to dance to the extremist tune.

The possibility of a ceasefire started to recede. Someone had obviously got to the two generals. As for the RPF monolith, it was absolutely plain that they didn't want a ceasefire. But why? They knew the slaughter was escalating. They knew that we were diminished by the departure of the Belgians and even more limited in our movement and interventions because of the militias. They knew now that the moderates had lost all possibility of influencing the outcome. Why destroy the ceasefire negotiations? It meant the killings wouldn't stop, and any humanitarian aid would be in jeopardy. I had to confront Kagame.

Late that afternoon, I received a message from Dewez. He had been ordered to accelerate the departure of the remaining Belgian troops. To buy time for the Ghanaians to get down from the demilitarized zone, for three days Luc Marchal had ignored direct orders from the Belgian chief of staff to get out. Now Dewez was having to pull out and the Ghanaians had not yet taken over all of the Belgian positions at the airport. I was afraid that if there was a gap in occupation, the RGF would move in and take total control. The last aircraft would leave sometime early the next morning. Then we would be alone.

Code Cable 1173, signed by Riza for the triumvirate, arrived that night under the heading "Status of UNAMIR." In essence, the message was simple: If the RPF and the RGF wouldn't agree to a ceasefire by nine the next morning New York time, UNAMIR was to start its withdrawal. There was no discussion of any of the other options. The cable went on to ask for our assessment of the consequences of the withdrawal on those who had "taken refuge" at our sites. I noted the use of the phrase "taken refuge" as opposed to "under UN protection." The cable stated, "We feel that appropriate handover arrangements should be negotiated with both sides." I could not imagine how anyone at the UN could believe that these desperate Rwandans would be safe in the hands of either of the belligerents. I wondered about information Booh-Booh was sending to New York over his satellite phone.

I had no choice but to set Henry, Brent and our staff to the task of preparing for our evacuation, and turned my mind to producing a risk assessment for the DPKO on the consequences of total withdrawal. But I needed to know whether Booh-Booh and his staff had anything to do with this new turn and headed off in the pre-dawn with Dr. Kabia to the Meridien hotel. There was considerable shelling going on around the airport, mostly directed at Camp Kanombe by the RPF. All was quiet in the hotel lobby; people were still sleeping or simply too weak to get up. We walked up to the top floor through crowded corridors and stairwells to find ourselves in the clean, dark solitude of Booh-Booh's emptied floor, where a lone UN security officer stood guard at his door.

Booh-Booh looked troubled. When I started to review the cable with him, it was clear that he was already aware of its content. I told him that total withdrawal was out of the question—we needed to keep the UN flag flying in Kigali, even if only to bear witness. He replied that I was to stop arguing and prepare to withdraw as ordered to Kenya, where UNAMIR could operate out of Nairobi. What followed was a *va-et-vient* of opinion, spiced by Mamadou Kane's interventions on the side of his master, including the charge that I was fear-mongering. Exasperated, Booh-Booh turned to Dr. Kabia and asked him point-blank to state his position on the matter. I suddenly saw that the future of UNAMIR hung totally on what Dr. Kabia would say.

It seemed to take an eternity for him to speak, but when he did, he wholeheartedly supported my proposal to retain a skeleton force of 250 inside the country. We could not totally abandon the Rwandans. To give him credit, Booh-Booh agreed without flinching, but Kane shot looks at me that could have killed. Dr. Kabia knew just how crucial his support had been, and over the roar of the car engine as we drove back to Force HQ, he told me that he had no regrets. We were doing the right thing, or as right a thing as we could do given the circumstances.

As if to drive home the stakes, before I left that morning for a last-ditch attempt to persuade both sides to agree to the ceasefire, Tiko asked to meet with Henry and me to brief us on the situation in Gisenyi, the tourist town on Lake Kivu that had been the killing ground of Hutu extremists since the night of April 6. These are notes from that briefing, taken for me by Major Diagne, an officer from Senegal and a new addition to my personal staff:[3]

> . . . by noon on the 7th, they were going house to house . . . they killed some people on the spot but carried others away to a mass grave near the airport where they cut their arms and legs and finally massacred them, as observed by the UNMOs. The Army and Gendarmerie did nothing to stop these killer-groups

3. Major Diagne attended nearly every meeting with me after the war started, taking detailed notes and then rewriting the minutes so that they would be legible. One evening as he sat at his desk transcribing, he felt the sudden need of prayer and slid off his chair to his knees on his prayer carpet, his head toward Mecca, as required by his Islamic faith. At that exact moment, a huge piece of shrapnel smashed through his window from a mortar explosion, flying through the space he had just vacated, bouncing off the walls and landing still red-hot near his feet. He came within a hair's breadth of certain death. Always dignified and composed, Diagne reported the damage to his window and then returned to his desk to complete his tedious but essential transcribing.

. . . they closed the border with Goma, Zaire. The UNMOs were threatened and they regrouped at the Meridien hotel where foreigners were massing for protection. Stories of massacres all over the region were reported by these eyewitnesses. A priest assembled in the church with about 200 children for protection, after prayers the killers opened the doors and massacred all of them . . . another chapel was burned with hundreds of people inside. Children between the ages of 10 to 12 years old killed children. Mothers with babies on their backs killed mothers with babies on their backs. They threw babies into the air and mashed them on the ground. At Rsumbura, 3 Belgian teachers, 2 males and 1 female, and 3 local priests were killed. On the night of the 8th, an expatriate convoy was allowed passage to Goma. On the 10th, Madame Carr, famous because of the movie *Gorillas in the Mist* left her house for the first time. She has been in Rwanda for more than 45 years. The 85-year-old woman said that what she saw was terrible. Madame Carr and 68 Americans, many students, left the country. UNMOs provided food and aid to those Rwandans, mostly Tutsis, at the Meridien. Were able to conduct some patrols but streets too littered with roadblocks and dead people. Ordered to evacuate on the 13th, spent two nights between Rwandan and Zaire border posts. Finally made way to Mkumba and moved to Kigali. Communications very bad.

I listened to the report without moving a muscle. It wasn't shock any more at the horrific descriptions. Instead I now entered a sort of trance state when I heard such information; I'd heard so much of it over the past two weeks that it simply seemed to pile up in my mind. No reaction any more. No tears, no vomit, no apparent disgust. Just more cords of wood piling up waiting to be sawed into pieces in my mind. Much later, back in Canada, I was taking a vacation with my wife and children, driving down a narrow road on the way to the beach. Road workers had cut a lot of trees down on either side of the road and piled the branches up to be picked up later. The cut trees had turned brown, and the sawn ends of the trunks, white and of a fair size, were stacked facing the road. Without being able to stop myself, I described to my wife in great detail a trip I had had to make to the RPF zone, where the route had taken me through the middle of a village. The sides of the road were littered with piles upon piles of Rwandan bodies drying in the sun, white bones jutting out. I was so sorry that my children had no choice but to listen to me. When we got to the beach, my kids swam and Beth read a book while I sat for more than two hours reliving the events reawakened in my mind. What terrible vulnerability we have all had to live with since Rwanda.

I got to the Diplomates at about 1130. I was not optimistic about the chances of making any headway with the RGF on the ceasefire, since Bizimungu had finally taken up his appointment as army chief of staff, replacing Gatsinzi, and no one would ever call Bizimungu a moderate. Bagosora was usually ensconced in an office at the hotel that had a clear view of the lobby, where petitioners and business people lined up to see him, but he was nowhere in sight.

Bizimungu, a short, well-rounded man with an aggressive expression and a well-kept uniform, came into the lobby to greet me. His eyes were bright, even shining, but they did not project confidence nor mastery of the situation. We shook hands and spoke niceties to one another as we headed to the conference room to the left of the lobby. We settled on separate sofas; at my back was a wall of windows giving out to the hotel gardens, where Presidential Guards were patrolling. I was surprised that he met with me alone, but nothing he said to me was the least bit surprising. Sitting on the edge of the sofa in order to maintain a certain height advantage over me, he launched into a litany of complaint. He was quite annoyed that the international media and press were being manipulated by the RPF propaganda machine, making the RGF and the interim government out to be the bad guys. Why was no one reporting the fact that the RPF had initiated considerable massacres behind their lines, a case in point being the wholesale slaughter of all the RGF officers' families in the Byumba zone, including the family of the minister of defence. Bizimungu wanted to be interviewed and soon, as he had things to say. (And in fact the next day I brought the media with me to my meeting with him, but the only thing he showed himself to be was a hawk and a fighter and hardly a credible source of information that might change anyone's mind about who might be the good guys in the situation.)

When I pressed him on the issues of stopping the atrocities, the ceasefire and airport neutrality, he said he was not totally *au fait* as of yet but that he would get me an answer from the government soon. I returned to the Force HQ full of an unreasonable disappointment. Bizimungu had merely confirmed the scenario I had already expected: he was going to fight, the massacres would continue, and between the self-interested powers dominating the Security Council and the gun-shy secretariat, the UN would do everything in its power to pull us out.

When I got back, Tiko called me on the net to brief me about the fate of the MILOBs and the nuns under their protection in Butare. A recent visit to Butare by Jean Kambanda and the Presidential Guard had stirred up the nastiest of fervours for eliminating the moderates and the Tutsis. The local (moderate) prefect had been fired and was probably already dead. The Interahamwe, under the supervision of Presidential Guards who had stayed on after the prime minister left, were killing indiscriminately. The MILOBs had been warned by some locals that their lives were in grave danger, and finally the MILOBs were asking to be pulled out. But they had about thirty Rwandan religious and locals under their wing and couldn't leave them behind.

In the middle of the phone call, Brent waved at me urgently to tell Tiko that a Hercules aircraft was on its way to Butare. It would be there in an hour, so the MILOBs and their charges must make it to the short, grass runway at the edge of town. Tiko acknowledged this and ended the transmission.

Here is the resulting scene in Butare: Three UN SUVs, jam-packed with people, speed through town, crashing through a few minor barriers, and make it to the end of the runway. An angry crowd has given chase, hastening to the airfield clearly intending to slaughter everyone in the SUVs. With fear getting the better of them, the small unarmed band is scouting the sky desperately, looking for the Hercules. No sooner has the mob broken into the airport than they hear the sound of the four turboprop engines of the Herc, and the aircraft comes into view low to the ground, lining up for an emergency landing. The huge transport aircraft touches down, screaming to a grinding and slippery halt about two hundred metres from the UNMOs and their charges. With dust and dirt filling the air, the ramp is lowered, the engines loud and unforgiving to the ear, and the near-crazed troop—the MILOBs pulling, even carrying, nuns and children—rushes to the back of the plane.

At the other end of the airfield, the MILOBs can see that the crowd has grown significantly and can spot flashes of machine guns spitting bullets. The plane is taking some hits, and the loadmaster, vigorously waving for the passengers to hurry up, is ducking as the sharp crack of bullets surrounds him. The MILOBs want to bring their vehicles with them, but there's no time to set up that ramp, so their furious drivers disable them. The aircraft is already turning and about to roll down the short grassy runway directly toward the crowd and the guns, with the last of the evacuees struggling to grab the ramp and be hauled into the plane. That the Herc could take off in the heat, with the increased load, on a shortened, unprepared runway, is a miracle. It was Stanleyville in the early sixties all over again. These scenes of heroism were happening all over the country.

Just before the sun set that evening, I made my way to the airport to see off Dewez and the last of the Belgian blue berets. The airport grounds were strewn with litter, and even cars vandalized by the Italian forces that had flown in to "help" with the French and Belgian evacuation. In the terminal itself, all the shops had been vandalized and destroyed. Windows were smashed and garbage was all over the place. Only European soldiers had used the terminal since the start of the war, along with the mostly European expatriates who had transited through, and I was struck by the blatant banditry and disdain they had demonstrated toward what was a national treasure to a poor country such as Rwanda.

Dewez and I spoke for a bit to confirm that all handover and military technical matters were sorted out. He was in terrible emotional straits as he described his overwhelming feeling of abandoning the mission in the face of the enemy. I did not make his departure any easier as he saluted for the last time and walked away from me to the Belgian aircraft, its engines already turning. The ramp closed as he entered the belly of the aircraft, and in no time the plane was moving. It lumbered its goose-like way along the runway and became airborne, climbing into a picture-perfect Rwandan sunset sky. The sounds of battle, for a while lost to me, became more and more loud as the plane escaped into the horizon.

I was beside myself with anger, and the gunfire only exacerbated it. Images of my father and father-in-law wearing their Second World War battledress seemed to leap out of the darkening sky. They looked tired, muddy and haggard and were in the midst of fighting for the liberation of Belgium. As Canadian soldiers fought tooth and nail against the Germans, King Léopold III of Belgium and his ruthless lackeys kept millions of black Africans in Rwanda and all of the Great Lakes region of central Africa under subjugation, raping these countries of their natural resources. And here I was, in the heart of one of the Belgian king's former colonies, watching Belgian troops abandon us in the midst of one of the worst slaughters of the century because they had lost some of their professional soldiers to soldierly duties.

I stood watching the sky for a long time. Fifty years after my mentors had fought in Europe, I had been left here with a ragtag force to witness a crime against humanity that the Belgians had unwittingly laid the spadework for. With the noise of gunfire and grenades in the background, and the pitch-black night closing in around me, I gave myself over to hate of a nation that had not only lost its nerve to stay in the fight but that was prepared to sacrifice the names and reputations of its own soldiers to soothe its conscience. Marchal, Dewez, Ballis, Van Put, Kesteloot, De Loecker, Deprez, Puffet, Van Asbroek, Mancel, Podevijn, Maggen, Dupuis, Claeys, De Weghe, Yansenne and other loyal Belgian officers and NCOs to the mission would ultimately be the saving face of the Belgian government and people. And soon enough they would also become targets of disdain for those who should have given them medals, accolades and respect. They had single-handedly maintained the dignity and social conscience of a nation that, after being bloodied, turned its back on the plight of 8.3 million Rwandans in peril and the 800,000 women, children, elders and men who would die at the hands of extremists.

I finally returned to the Force HQ through the RGF para-commando lines, where a few bullets hastened my pace. I was determined not to go down in history as the commander who ran. Why send soldiers in at all if at the first casualties we are told to abandon the mission to protect our hides? I had to make sure the Ghanaians, the only truly organized force left to me, would not waver. I salute Henry Anyidoho, who at great personal risk, kept his government at bay for the rest of the war and genocide and kept the Ghanaian troops with us. He was a fine leader and a loyal servant to the mission. It was Henry on the night of April 18 who steadied my resolve not to withdraw.

Brent had been impatiently awaiting my return so that he could put my last comments into the Military Assessment of the Situation (MIR-19) in order to counteract the code cables ordering us to withdraw if there was no move toward a ceasefire. Once again I laid out the terrible situation as clearly as I could, along with all the tactical and moral reasons for keeping at least a small force inside the country. A total withdrawal of the force would be both dangerous and fraught with obstacles: "UNAMIR does not have the heavy weapon systems, ammunition, let alone secure transport to force its way out. Options like an internationally imposed truce or a guaranteed military supported extraction may have to be considered if UNAMIR is to successfully withdraw its personnel with safety from Rwanda." Our withdrawal would clearly imperil the displaced persons in our safe sites. The best we would be able to do in such cases would be to gather lists of the names of the people and have Philippe Gaillard and the Red Cross oversee their handling by both sides. Since the Rwandans would be maltreated and possibly killed at the hands of the other side, we'd open up even more grounds for animosity and recrimination between the belligerents.

"The safety of our withdrawal is directly related to our keeping a foot on the ground in Rwanda for at least the short while," I argued. "FC cannot stress this point emphatically enough. We await your decision on this matter." I signed off and Brent sent it.

Just hours later, my strings were jerked yet again. In the early hours of April 20, I was woken up in order to read two code cables from the DPKO. One summarized the Security Council's deliberations of the day before and contained a stunning fact: once again Colin Keating had delayed the decision on pulling UNAMIR by telling the members that UN-led negotiations between the belligerents would soon begin in Arusha, and that no decision should be taken before the results of this consultation were in. What UN-led negotiations in Arusha?

The other cable essentially ordered me to *stop* the withdrawal of my troops until further orders. Laying out three options in yet another draft to the Security Council, the report read, "One alternative that could be considered would be to reinforce UNAMIR and expand its mandate to attempt to coerce the opposing force into a ceasefire, and to attempt [to] restore law and order and put an end to the killings. If this scenario is to be considered, it must be kept in mind that it would require several thousand additional troops (Note: perhaps 10,000— figure being requested from UNAMIR) and UNAMIR may have to be given enforcement powers." I, of course, had never requested ten thousand reinforcements. Reading between the lines, and catching the red flag of the suggested "enforcement powers," which no Security Council member would wish to grant to UNAMIR, I suspected that the option may have been included only for the archives.

The other point in the draft report that caught my eye was this line: "Ultimately, it is only the parties who signed the Arusha Agreement, namely the government of Rwanda (or its successor) and the RPF, who must bear the reponsibility whether their country and people find peace or suffer violence." The trouble was that the "successor" government in Rwanda was in no way a signatory to Arusha, being an expression of an extremist coup, but that distinction was becoming very fuzzy, considering among other factors that a Rwandan hard-liner was sitting on the Council in New York. But the secretary-general knew full well that the RPF would never recognize this government. And the extremists were not about to give up their power positions to a moderate or even mixed moderate-extremist government, so what was the UN political solution to the impasse? There wasn't one. It behooved the Security Council to get off its butt and provide me with a mandate and the means to stop the killing and establish an atmosphere of security. I had to get on the phone with the triumvirate before it finalized this draft. Here I was sitting in the slaughterhouse of Kigali, parsing the bureaucratic entrails of misbegotten reports.

By mid-morning the next day I was fully informed about the plans for Arusha negotiations, which were set for April 23 and energetically supported by the secretary-general of the Organization of African Unity, Dr. Salim Salim. It turned out that the RPF vice-chairman had gone to Dar es Salaam to ask the president of Tanzania to get the parties together. I was incredulous when I learned this news. What was the RPF expecting, when it had been the most inflexible in the ceasefire negotiations? Since Booh-Booh was invited, I decided I would send Henry to provide military input and be a witness and note-taker for me. We also had to provide transport for the RGF delegation as they had no means of getting there. Two significant points, among others that would be worked on: stopping the massacres using a combined UNAMIR and sub-regional observer force, and re-establishing the rule of law to find and prosecute those committing the massacres.

In the meantime we had to figure out how to restore the airport to some semblance of functionality. Neither the French nor the Belgians had left behind their air-control assets, so the search was on to find some qualified staff. With an RPF agreement in my pocket to respect the neutrality of the airfield, I sent another note to Bizimungu and the interim government in Gitarama to hasten their response. Meanwhile my MILOBs found the former airport manager at the Mille Collines and put him to work immediately—under heavy guard, for he was scared for his life. And quite rightly, since he was a Hutu helping UNAMIR to prepare (possibly) for the arrival of an intervention force.

On the morning of April 21, I held a special meeting with my subordinate commanders and senior staff about the holding of our position. The points raised varied from logistics to the size of force that would remain and the ability of the troops to sustain their security duties. All of them felt that we should try to keep more than 250 troops on the ground. I told them that the DPKO had left me with the task of deciding this once we were down to about six hundred of all ranks. At that point we had twelve days' worth of food and water supplies at minimum rations. The last convoy of Ghanaians from the north had finally arrived, seriously starved and thirsty, and a number of them were suffering from malaria as their pills had run out.

On the military front, the RPF was still advancing and capturing substantial amounts of RGF equipment, including rockets left behind by the fleeing troops. All forces were converging on Kigali for a major battle, and the heavy exchanges of artillery and rocket fire in the city during the last two days pointed to a major confrontation on the way. Having taken Byumba, the RPF was conducting repeated ambushes on RGF troops trying to make it back to Kigali. The RGF was reporting heavy losses, and Mount Kigali and Mount Nianza near the city were the scenes of heavy fighting.

So there we sat, with new talks about to commence in Arusha; the humanitarian aid structure set to join the mission; the carnage continuing to spread unabated throughout the country; and both sides gearing up for a difficult and possibly decisive fight for control of the capital. The situation was normal.

After the meeting I prepared a code cable to the DPKO, stressing yet again the need for a final decision regarding the future of my forces on the ground. I received no solace when I raised the reinforcement option. Maurice and the other two simply responded that I should not expect anyone to wade into the mess in Rwanda. The reinforcement option would never see the light of day, and that was it. Many nations had turned toward Belgium, as the ex-colonial power, and its persuasive foreign minister for guidance. And Willy Claes put forth that the whole force needed to be evacuated before we were all massacred. Early on the morning of April 22, Brent brought me a fax from Riza, to which was attached Security Council Resolution 912. The Council had finally voted for the skeleton force option. The resolution's phrases were pure UN-ese: ". . . having considered . . . express regret . . . shocked . . . appalled . . . deeply concerned . . . stressing . . . expressing deep concern . . . condemns . . . strongly condemns . . . demands . . . decides . . . reiterates . . . reaffirms . . . calls upon . . . invites . . . decides to remain actively seized of the matter."

As I write these words I am listening to Samuel Barber's Adagio for Strings, which strikes me as the purest expression in music of the suffering, mutilation, rape, and murder of 800,000 Rwandans, with the help of the member nations of the only supposedly impartial world body.

Ultimately, led by the United States, France and the United Kingdom, this world body aided and abetted genocide in Rwanda. No amount of its cash and aid will ever wash its hands clean of Rwandan blood.

With Resolution 912 now in writing, I ordered the accelerated withdrawal of about one thousand troops to Nairobi to be held there no more than three days so that I could perhaps get them back if a ceasefire was agreed upon in Arusha. By mid-afternoon, I was informed that the UN staff in Nairobi was redirecting the troops toward home as the Kenyan government refused to permit them to leave their camp at the airfield, and conditions there were appalling. Once they were sent home, even if still earmarked for UNAMIR, they would disappear in their garrisons and we would have to start again from scratch.

Some fine pickle I was in with my depleted command. I had to explain to my troops—many of whom were very tired and sickly because of the lack of proper food and medicine, while others were in a zombie state after living horrific and traumatic experiences in this cesspool of guts, severed limbs, flesh-eating dogs and vermin—that although acts of heroism had been performed by many of them, the world had decided not to support us in our efforts but instead to pull most of us out to safety. I told their commanders to stress to them that there was no shame in this withdrawal and that they should remain ready for a potential return.

To my great displeasure, later that afternoon I received a call from Riza asking me what was going on with the withdrawal. He said that the *Washington Post* had just published on its front page a large picture of UNAMIR soldiers rushing an evacuation aircraft like a scared herd of cattle. Some, he said, were actually kissing the aircraft while others were dropping belongings on the tarmac as they raced to the plane.

I asked Brent to look into this, and within fifteen minutes he confirmed that during the first airlift of the day, the Bangladeshi officers and NCOs—leaving their troops to wait for the next plane—had conducted a very embarrassing rush on the plane. All the other flights had gone smoothly and over six hundred troops had been airlifted out. What could I say? The harm had been done. The picture of a UN rout in Rwanda after the resolution to withdraw had been signed had already been flashed around the world. We were portrayed as scared rats abandoning a sinking ship. Even in their departure, the Bangladeshi contingent was able to bring my mission even further down in the eyes of those who saw us as a joke in the first place.

I had to bring the RGF and RPF leadership up to speed on the troop reductions and explain my new mission. I could not hope to bluff any longer concerning our ability to protect the roughly thirty thousand people now being held by us behind each belligerent's line. The solution I was going to propose was to begin transfers of these people to safety on their own side and thus eliminate our need to keep our sites open and protected.

First I met with Seth at the CND. He wanted us not only to start the transfers but also to rescue the Rwandans in hiding. I replied that though I couldn't intervene in the war, we would attempt to help. Second, I met with Bizimungu at the Diplomates, where Bagosora was again holding court with anxious and well-dressed men carrying briefcases. Bizimungu had no problem with the truce at the airfield to cover the UNAMIR withdrawal. But he had to get approval from the interim government about the transfers of refugees and the ongoing neutrality of the airport, which he indicated might be forthcoming. He recommended that I take up these matters with the prime minister himself the next day in Gitarama. Kambanda was not going to Arusha but was sending Colonel Gatsinzi, a powerless figure who would agree to nothing that would restrict the interim government because if he did, his life and the lives of his family would not be worth a nickel. The extremists were obviously emasculating this new attempt at a ceasefire although they overtly insisted they wanted it. And the RPF would not budge an inch. Once again the belligerents were set to outwit the regional and international diplomatic efforts to sort the situation out. Bizimungu ended the meeting by demonstrating considerable emotion about the RPF in the CND, and he asked me to remove all MILOBs and liaison officers from that site. I replied that I would not do so before I got a firm indication of when any artillery or ground attack would be conducted; my personnel were crucial in keeping me in touch with the RPF authorities.

I left him and headed for Mulindi, where Paul Kagame had finally agreed to meet with me.

The main road to Mulindi was still a battleground. On the back roads running through very small villages and over hilltops, I encountered ample evidence of the disastrous state of the countryside. Most of the area had recently been in RGF hands, and signs of fighting, including military casualties on the roads and in the ditches, littered our way. A few villages had been burnt to the ground, and bodies formed a carpet of rags in all directions. We took turns walking in front of my vehicle to make sure that we did not run over any of them. Even to this day, if I encounter an article of clothing dropped on the street, I go around it and must control the urge to check if it is a body.

Thousands of people of all ages, carrying what they could, lined dirt paths, huddled beside streams, built small shelters among the banana trees or simply sat in total despair. Everywhere one looked, children were crying, their mothers and sisters trying to console them. The putrid smell of decaying bodies in the huts along the route not only entered your nose and mouth but made you feel slimy and greasy. This was more than smell, this was an atmosphere you had to push your way through. Attempting to move bodies out of the way of the vehicle without touching them with our hands was impossible. With no real protection and amongst a population that had epidemic levels of HIV/AIDS, with every body that we moved, our hands became more covered in dried blood, in pieces of flesh. It seemed that traces of this blood stayed on my hands for months.

We finally reached the main road, about twenty kilometres south of Mulindi. We had forded streams full of bodies and passed over bridges in swamps that had been lifted by the force of the bodies piling up on the struts. We had inched our way through villages of dead humans. We had walked our vehicles through desperate mobs screaming for food and protection. We had created paths amongst the dead and half-dead with our hands. And we had thrown up even when there was nothing in our stomachs. My courageous men had been wading through scenes such as this for weeks in order to save expatriates and members of religious orders. No wonder some of them had fallen off the face of the world and had entered a hell in their minds. We had absolutely no medication to help them.

It was getting dark by the time we reached Kagame's office and residence in the Mulindi compound, its defences orderly—nearly impregnable unless you had considerable heavy fire to support an assault. Kagame looked fit and impeccable amongst the magnificent tropical flowers of his garden. He had no time for small talk, so I quickly covered the issues of the troop reductions, the ceasefire, the neutral airport, the civilian transfers. He told me several times that he would not tolerate UNAMIR conducting any actions that could be interpreted as interventions. I told him that not only was intervening in the war not my mandate, I had been stripped of any capability to carry out such offensive operations. I told him in return that I would not tolerate any actions from his troops or the RGF that would endanger those Rwandans under my protection. He promised to make all the necessary preparations for the transfers to commence as soon as possible. He said that he had delayed his offensive on Kigali specifically to let the civilians leave the capital before the battle. He had refugee sites already marked out and asked for my help in getting aid to those locations. I told him that I would consider this request only if the aid did not end up in the vehicles and mouths of his forces. He said we should let our staffs work that out, which did not reassure me.

We then entered into a discussion of the situation on the battle-field, and I laid out my commander's operations map on the ground between us. There was no doubt that Kagame had pinned down, with minimum effort, a number of RGF battalions defending the Ruhengeri Hutu heartland. This permitted him, after seizing Byumba and the main road in the east, to proceed south as far as the Tanzanian border and seal it up at the river. Concurrently, he was moving his assault forces west, below Kigali, on the main axis of the paved road to the capital. Kigali was clearly being surrounded for a showdown. With one more hint about possibly consolidating along a north-south river, he abruptly ended the map exercise and moved on to discuss the Arusha meeting that was to start the next morning. He had not gone because it was up to the political wing to sort that out. He was not optimistic at all on the potential outcome, however, and basically thought that the Arusha accords I'd been mandated to support served only "to save the lives of the military and not those of the civilians." When we finished our session, he invited me to sleep over as it was too risky to head back to Kigali after dark. We shook hands firmly and wished each other well, and then I was escorted away.

The diplomats would posture tomorrow in Arusha, but the die had already been cast: we were moving methodically on one side, and at best haphazardly on the other, to a major fight for Kigali. During our meeting I had asked Kagame why he wasn't going straight for the jugular in Kigali, and he ignored the implications of my question. He knew full well that every day of fighting on the periphery meant certain death for Tutsis still behind RGF lines.

I found my escort and officers having a drink at a small cantina in the camp. Pasteur Bizimungu (who, after the RPF victory, would become the president of Rwanda) was there with a few politicos, and I sat down with him at the edge of the cantina as my guys and the RPF soldiers had a good time together, as soldiers will always find a way to do. Pasteur and I spent about an hour talking about his past, the present catastrophe, the SRSG, the international community, and the future of the country if the RPF won. We then walked up the hill and entered the house where we had held our formal meetings. There was a small fire in the fireplace, since it had gotten quite chilly when the sun went down. On a small rickety table, surrounded by four equally uncertain wooden chairs, we sat down to eat as two bowls, one of beans and the other of starchy and bland miniature bananas, were placed between our cracked plates.

The warm food and the fireplace took a toll on me, and I was nearly delirious with fatigue by the time Pasteur led me to a small guest room. On a little night table was a candle already half burned. There was a military cot with clean white sheets and a magnificent bulging pillow under a mosquito net. I got undressed, did the usual field bath with not much water, and climbed into bed, feeling a bit guilty about my troops and Brent in Kigali but so overwhelmed with the smell of clean sheets, the feel of a warm blanket and a decent meal in my stomach that I fell asleep in what seemed that night to be a brief heaven on earth. I do not remember dreaming.

12

LACK OF RESOLUTION

I got up at first light to head back to Kigali. The return route was a little shorter but no less ugly. Morning fires of wet banana leaves and a few lumps of hoarded coal added an acid sting to the omnipresent putrid smell of death. By 0700, I was in my HQ for morning prayers. Moen presented the troops-to-task plan under the reduced force, and it was immediately evident to all of us that the original target of about 250 personnel would be drastically insufficient for us to render any humanitarian assistance such as transport, surveillance, distribution of aid or the transfer of persons between the lines. I ordered the Ghanaian battalion to hold back as many qualified drivers as possible from the withdrawal. Orders went out, and over two hundred Ghanaian soldiers who had originally been scheduled to leave stayed behind with the rest of us. My force, by the end of the day, would be 454 of all ranks, along with our dozen UN civilians.

Peter Hansen, the UN under-secretary for Humanitarian Affairs, was due that day with his group of analysts—he was the first senior UN executive to visit us since the war began. The major point I made to him, after he had toured the protected sites and had been briefed by our humanitarian section under Yaache, was that UNAMIR had to be the conduit on information to the NGOs and agencies coming into Rwanda, and that we had to control their movements. I could not tolerate individual aid organizations wanting to do their own thing in ignorance of the overall situation and possibly jeopardizing ceasefire negotiations or the security of the mission. The best thing Hansen could do was send me a solid emergency team to marry up with my humanitarian section.

Hansen was courageous, determined and quick to grasp the situation. He left a team behind with orders to integrate with the Force HQ and promised to convey my plan and directives to the aid agencies, though he could not guarantee that they would all fall in line. I told him to pass on a simple message: if any one of them aided and abetted the belligerents by even inadvertently allowing aid resources to end up in the hands of troops, I would expel them from Rwanda and answer questions later.

I set off for Gitarama to brief the interim government members and the RGF on the new mandate and troop reductions. The trip was yet another descent into the inferno. You can handle such scenes for a while, but as we once again became engulfed in a slow-moving, suffering human mass, my tolerance for the brutality waned and I see-sawed from rage to tears and back again, with brief interregnums of numbed-out staring. I could not look away. All those eyes staring back at us. Tired, red, sad, fearful, mad, bewildered pairs of eyes.

I was late for the meeting, and as we drove into the compound where the interim government was holed up, the contrast between the site and the scenes along the road really got to me. The compound was a peaceful modern schoolyard. A large number of well-dressed gentlemen and a few middle-aged women milled aimlessly about under the avocado trees amid a large flower garden. The prime minister and a particularly aggressive minister of information seemed to be at work in small offices, but no one else was doing much and there was no apparatus of government to be seen—the interim government had been here for over a week and still looked as if it was sorting out the seating plan for a meeting that was not about to convene any time soon.

Kambanda was uneasy, and no one looked particularly pleased to see us, so I got right to the point. The prime minister had no reaction one way or the other to news of the reduction of my force and the new mandate. He said he would support the secure transfer of people between the lines and would confirm with the minister of defence a militia truce for such transfers. When I mentioned the relentless killing at the barriers, Kambanda insisted that the "self-defence personnel" had an important security job to perform in weeding out rebel infiltrators.

We ticked off a few more items on the list, and then he singled out the fact that UNAMIR was "cohabiting" with the RPF at the Amahoro complex: How could he go along with a neutral airport when we would fold up if the RPF decided to take over the airport? I said that I was not cohabiting with the RPF: my headquarters area had been overrun and was now behind their lines. I said I would move the Force HQ to the airport as a guarantee that my actions were independent of the RPF, which caused the minister of information to scoff loudly.

Then the minister surprised me by requesting a public funeral for the murdered president. I replied that unless I could get access to the presidential residence and the crash site, I could do nothing about it—international inspectors had to be allowed in to do an independent investigation. He and Kambanda agreed and asked when the inspectors could come. I said they were waiting for my call. Lastly, I firmly decried the verbal abuse and disinformation being broadcast about UNAMIR and the Tutsis by RTLM. I wanted to go on air and tell my version of the situation. To my surprise, the minister agreed and said he would set it up for the next day.

Shaking hands automatically, I left the small office and walked among the ministers and others on my way to my vehicle. As I walked, I brooded on their complacency, on how clean and at ease they all seemed; either they were outside the decision loop or they had ulterior motives in this catastrophe befalling their homeland. And where was Bagosora?

We arrived back at the HQ by 1800 and held prayers soon after. The news from the Arusha meeting was that the RGF delegation hadn't shown up. The RPF had sent their secretary-general, Théogène Rudasingwa, as head of a small delegation, and he presented a ceasefire proposal that still included the demanding preconditions. In the words of Booh-Booh in his report to UN headquarters: "Having waited in vain for the arrival of the Government delegation and with the departure of the RPF delegation, I plan to leave Arusha for Nairobi. . . . I however took advantage of the presence of the OAU Secretary-General and the Tanzanian delegation (President) to exchange views on our efforts to help the peace process and also to prepare a cease-fire proposal which I believe could form the basis of ending the present hostilities." Not only did Booh-Booh decide to leave for Nairobi, from that point on he mostly stayed there, as did his politicos, making only brief visits to Kigali. So the political wheel went spinning into a vacuum, and everyone could say on their way home that they had tried their best.

The last of the six troop flights was leaving Kigali airport as we wrapped up prayers, and the HQ was readjusting for the second time in two weeks. I retained a Force Headquarters, a reduced Military Observer Group, a little more than a platoon of Tunisians and a small battalion of Ghanaians. The MILOBs were with us at the Amahoro Hotel in our familiar headquarters, protected by the Tunisians. I based the Ghanaian battalion at the airport, as my alternate headquarters, with the medical section, the service support element (which would run the logistics base) and one rifle company to defend the airport. The other rifle company I based at the Amahoro Stadium to protect the refugees.

I had also placed small detachments at the other sites throughout Kigali where we were protecting persons, with mobile MILOB teams travelling between them. I gave the APCs to the Tunisians, who without tools, spare parts or mechanics, managed to increase the working number from three to five within hours. The "deadheads" (an old military term for unserviceable vehicles), which had arrived in February from Mozambique, could not be redeemed, and we hauled them to the gates of our camps and employed them as bunkers.

Despite the best efforts of the Tunisians, the vehicles progressively broke down—eventually all of them did. After much wrangling, the United States authorized its mission in Somalia to "loan" UNAMIR six old, stripped-down (no guns, no radios and no tools), early Cold War–era APCs in mid-April. Brent had taken a call one night from an NCO at the Pentagon, who asked why we needed the APCs. With some eloquence, Brent described our substantially reduced force structure, our desperate logistics state and our precarious situation on the ground, ending his explanation with: "It gives a whole new meaning to the word 'light forces,' doesn't it?" The good old boy in Washington responded, "Buddy, you'll get your APCs, good luck to you and God bless." We got more and faster support from that one sergeant than from the rest of the United States government and armed forces combined.

How could I spark the conscience of the world? We were diminished but determined to stay put and continue to tell the story of what was happening in Rwanda. I had to press the right buttons and I had to do it as fast as possible. Since my reports seemed to keep vanishing into the abyss of non-action in New York, I stepped up the media campaign. For those politicians and generals who distrust and avoid the free media, I can assure them that the media can be an ally and a weapon equal to battalions on the ground. With the Belgian departure, it appeared that Mark Doyle of the BBC might also leave. I called him into my office and made him an offer he could not refuse. He could live with us, be protected by us, be fed and sustained by us, and I would guarantee him a story a day and the means (my satellite phone) to get that story to the world. I did not care if his story was positive or negative about UNAMIR as long as it was accurate and truthful. The key was for him to become the voice of what was happening in Rwanda.

Mark agreed and in the coming days he did become that voice. Other news agencies noticed, and journalists began to flow into Rwanda to cover the slaughter. Jean-Guy Plante was on the case, helping them in any way he could. He loved to be around people, and he organized the reporters already in country, establishing a system of rotation of media between Nairobi and Kigali with the help of the Canadian movement staff in charge of the Hercules flights. Plante decided how long reporters would stay in theatre in order to permit a maximum of different media outfits and journalists to report what was going on in Rwanda. I wanted no stupid casualties. Plante had UN vans, rooms in the Meridien, food cards, and electronic hookups in the Force HQ ready for them. He guaranteed them security, at least one story every day and delivery of their stories to Nairobi. This was achieved on occasion by UNMOs driving to the Ugandan border and handing the material to UNOMUR, who would take it by helicopter to Entebbe and beyond.

I also directed Brent to ensure each night that any journalist calling for an interview was given access to me. With our own national broadcasting network, the CBC, Brent exercised his initiative, with very positive results. The producer of *As It Happens,* an internationally well-regarded radio interview show listened to at home by hundreds of thousands of Canadians, finally secured our phone number and called to set up a live interview with the show's host, Michael Enright. Brent refused to put me on the line unless the producer provided the scores of the NHL (National Hockey League) playoff games. We had no news at all from home but knew the playoffs were on. Brent, a confirmed Toronto Maple Leafs fan at the time, and I, a resolute Montreal Canadiens fan, were grateful for this news. In the weeks that followed, we always got our scores, and Enright got his live interviews. In our conversations, Enright became the voice of home to me.

The media was the weapon I used to strike the conscience of the world and try to prod the international community into action. I would even risk the lives of my UNMOs to ensure that the stories got out every day.

As far as I have been able to determine, on April 24 the NGO Oxfam became the first organization to use the term "genocide" to describe what was happening in Rwanda. Calling it "ethnic cleansing" just did not seem to be hitting the mark. After numerous telephone conversations with Oxfam personnel in London, we queried New York if what we were seeing in Rwanda could be labelled genocide. As far as I am aware, we never received a response, but we started to use the term sometime after April 24 in all of our communications. Little did I realize the storm of controversy this term would invoke in New York and in the capitals of the world. To me it seemed an accurate label at last.

April 25. Tiko briefed me with a big smile on his face. He had made contact with and regained control of all the valorous UNMOs forced to escape to Tanzania, Uganda, Zaire and Burundi. He had chosen the officers he wanted to keep in Rwanda and concentrated the rest in Nairobi until further orders. That was the one good piece of news I was able to pass on in my assessment cable to New York that day.

The rest of the report: Bizimungu had made it quite clear that he would take no action except under instruction from the interim government, which I was having a hard time keeping track of, since it had refused my liaison officers (which I ultimately sent anyway). He also did not want to ask the militias at the roadblocks to open the gates for the transfers of RPF supporters. He and the prefect of Kigali demonstrated real uneasiness when speaking of the militias, as if they had to defer to a body more powerful than either the RGF or the interim government.

I had a report from Gatsinzi that Ndindiliyimana was in the south actually helping people escape, and that there existed a number of RGF officers who were disgusted with the way things were going and felt that Bizimungu did not have control of the military. I recommended to New York that, if required, we should provide these moderates with protection as they could prove to be useful in the post-crisis period. The humanitarian side continued to be bleak, bleaker in fact after a huge massacre in Butare. Both Médecins Sans Frontières and the International Committee of the Red Cross had had people severely threatened, and local Red Cross staff had been killed. Médecins Sans Frontières had decided to get out of the country to regroup, and, I wrote, "Due to the Butare massacre, the withdrawal of Médecins Sans Frontières, the pillaging of the Red Cross refugee supplies by the militias, the security situation and the lack of guarantees from both sides, the ICRC shut down operations in Rwanda for today and is only staying put for now at their hospital."

With the airport drawing fire from both sides, planes had stopped coming in, and Canada was going to repatriate its Hercules in five days. Add to that the fact that the Amahoro complex was being fired upon by both sides with mortars, and this was neither a good start to my new mandate nor an encouragement to my troops to carry on.

Lastly, it looked very much like we were heading for a scenario resembling the Cyprus green line. The capital could even end up split in two. The RPF was deliberately slowing down its advance from the east, and with Bizimungu in Kigali overseeing the battlefield personally, the RGF were putting up a better fight. The crux of the problem remained the militias and self-defence forces behind the RGF lines and figuring out who was pulling their strings. But with the RPF ceasefire proposal and some help from the moderates, or by putting the fear of death into the interim government in some way, we could offer up the idea of a temporary stop to the fighting along a well-defined line. If we could get that agreed to, I wrote, it just might develop into something more stable. I went to sleep to the sound of Brent at the computer typing up a cleaner version of the assessment.

The next day was frittered away with more meetings about a potential ceasefire, and more accusations from both sides as to who was the recalcitrant party. That night at about 2200, I was standing on the balcony of my office with Brent, taking brief advantage of the night breeze, when we heard the sound of a small cowbell on the street in front of the HQ. Straining our eyes in the direction from where the bell had jangled, we saw the most surreal scene. Earlier in the day the RPF had warned our humanitarian cell that they intended to move their people from the Amahoro and the Meridien to safety behind their lines. What Brent and I were witnessing was the movement of over twelve thousand people of all ages in the dark in order not to draw RGF fire. We barely heard a shuffling as they went by. The RPF guards gestured their directions and people obeyed without a word. It was like a parade of ghosts, heads bowed, burdened with their few possessions, moving in the dark of night to an unknown destination where at least they would be safe. I watched with an undermining feeling of helplessness but with such deep respect for these people. They had been without food and water for the best part of two weeks yet were able to move with discipline and order. Not even a baby cried as they went by.

With our reduced force, we had to do a lot of toing and froing to fit personnel to tasks. Henry became the enforcer of good order and all matters of staff and military discipline. I spent my time with the humanitarian buildup and negotiations, and meeting with both sides to come to grips with the massacres and the ceasefire. We were often only one-deep on any task. Fatigue, poor eating, traumatic experiences, long hours and no time off required us to keep a close watch on our people. I started to send some of them by air on three-day leaves in Nairobi (my request to Admiral Murray, the Canadian deputy chief of defence staff, that the Hercules not be withdrawn had made its way up the chain of command and to the prime minister, who okayed it, so we still had our flights). Good food, clean sheets, a few beers, no stress and a taste of normalcy would bring them around fairly quickly. Some would feel guilty about having some time off outside Rwanda and would want to return faster: that was a no-no. My office would regularly get calls from the CAO asking that my troops stop harassing the staff about poor support. By the time the last Canadian officers arrived in a week's time, the force would be 463-strong with a dozen civilians, including my mission secretary Suzanne Pescheira, who had escaped Nairobi to be with us. She demonstrated considerable spunk in coming back to join us and worked to all hours, even under fire.

By the end of April, twenty-three days into the slaughter, the situation continued to grow nastier in the rural areas as well as in the cities. Neither side was putting any serious effort into the unilateral ceasefires, and the airport was now a major battleground. The Ghanaian battalion there had become quite vulnerable and we had taken minor casualties. The lone battalion doctor was swamped. The interim government and the RGF were constantly complaining that I must be a reconnaissance party for the RPF since the war seemed to follow me. I explained to Bizimungu himself that his troops were continuously withdrawing, providing little or no fight to stop the RPF. As I shuttled between the sides, I could be considered either a spy for one side or an advance party for the other.

As the RPF advanced, it all too frequently captured killing fields of corpses. The eastern rivers were packed with bodies that flowed into Uganda and Lake Victoria. So far, an estimated forty thousand bodies had been recovered from the lake. The crocodiles had had a feast. And in a matter of days, 500,000 refugees spilled across the lone bridge at Rusumo into Tanzania, creating the largest dislocation of a population ever witnessed by the UNHCR as well as one of the largest refugee camps in the world. In those camps, a pattern that would later reappear in Goma and Bukavu was established. The refugees were organized by village, commune and prefecture and placed under the same génocidaire leaders who had led the killings in Rwanda. Remy Gatete, the prefect of

Kibungo, established control of the whole camp, threatening and, if required, killing anyone who testified to journalists or human rights activists about what the génocidaires had done in Rwanda. He also executed anyone who tried to go home. In addition, he began siphoning off humanitarian aid to support his thugs in the camp. The Tanzanian government was reluctant to use force to dismantle this network of terror, and with no alternative, the aid agencies reluctantly reinforced the abuse.

The UN Rwanda Emergency Office (UNREO) personnel left behind by Hansen were doing stellar work, however, under the direction of Lance Clark. He and Yaache integrated their efforts with little problem and made good headway with the RPF to get the aid effort moving. Clark himself had been hit with insurance hassles—no insurer wanted to gamble on the scene of a genocide—but stayed in the field anyway, serving as the critical link with the bigger UNREO office in Nairobi. We were pushing hard to get the same things from the RGF, but it was so splintered by now it was difficult to figure out what information was getting to the authorities and who the authorities even were. Bizimungu seemed to be letting the militia and its leaders run the show, though he still had somewhat of a grip on the army and the Gendarmerie.

Late in April I received a message from Gatsinzi. He said that the Kigali garrison had become demoralized and vicious in the wake of strong RPF advances, and some young officers were planning to conduct killing sprees at our protection sites. I deployed more MILOBs and troops to reinforce our presence, but there was little else I could do.

Bagosora had been avoiding me, even when I showed up while he was in his office at the Hôtel des Diplomates. I finally managed to meet, instead, with Bizimungu, around noon on April 28. He was irritated that the U.S. under-secretary of state for Africa, Prudence Bushnell, a woman at that, had called him directly to order him to stop the massacres and sign the ceasefire document. He told me he had informed her that he was not mandated to sign anything and was outraged by what he viewed as her brazen act of calling him to impose her will. He spent some time pointing the finger at Booh-Booh and the diplomats: what was up with the ceasefire and the political efforts in Nairobi? He went on to say that all the problems—airport neutrality, refugees and transfers—had to be resolved within the ceasefire discussions. I agreed but asked what he and his government were offering in order to move the negotiations along. He rhymed his answer off: (1) return to positions before April 6; (2) stop the massacres; (3) arrange the return of the displaced persons and refugees; (4) accelerate the installation of the BBTG; (5) respect a ceasefire under the auspices of UNAMIR.

I asked him what he thought the RPF was attempting to do with this war. He replied that the RPF wanted to conquer the whole country. Since he and the government would not let that happen, there would be lots and lots of dead. His side, he claimed, had never refused to share power with the RPF; it was the RPF that was now refusing to negotiate with the interim government.

That night I received a draft copy of a president's statement to the Security Council calling for an end to the appalling slaughter and massive displacement of people in Rwanda. The non-aligned members of the UN, supported by the OAU and the Red Cross, were now insisting that too much emphasis had been placed so far on the fighting and not enough on the killings. The U.S. representative informed them that the RGF was buying new arms and that an embargo was beside the point. The non-aligned members wanted some strong action-oriented language in the presidential statement and they wanted my comments immediately.

I brooded over the fact that the United States knew exactly what was happening on the ground in Rwanda. Once in a blue moon, Americans would even share some information. A few days earlier Brent had received a telephone call from Colonel Cam Ross (who had led the first technical mission to Rwanda for the UN), the director of Peacekeeping Operations in Ottawa. He told Brent that a friendly foreign power (we later confirmed it was the United States through the American ambassador in Nairobi) had received information that I was to be assassinated in the next few days and recommended that I bring adequate security with me when I had to leave the force compound. Brent told Henry, who hand-picked two Ghanaian sergeants and a section of troops. One sergeant had taken a special driving course and had driven the president of Ghana for a time and the other was an excellent marksman. The assigned troops were the biggest, baddest, meanest-looking gentlemen I had ever seen, especially when their eyes were hidden by sunglasses, which was more or less all the time. This team latched on to me and was my constant escort until I left the mission. I guess I should have been grateful for the tip, but my larger reaction was that if delicate intelligence like this could be gathered by surveillance, how could the United States not be recording evidence of the genocide occurring in Rwanda?

As the staff, largely led by Brent, prepared responses for New York, Henry and I finalized the requirements for the technical mission to Burundi, which had been sent to us a few days earlier. The situation there had worsened—that country was experiencing a more subtle type of genocide. The Tutsi-dominated army had commenced operations against Hutu rebels, and many villages were going up in smoke. It was felt in New York that we should go take a look. I did not object, and I placed Henry, Tiko and four members of the HQ and MILOB group on twenty-four-hours' notice for the trip; Henry had thought a lot about Burundi and would do a good job on the reconnaissance. But I told the triumvirate that no resources that were destined for my mission could be diverted to this possible new venture.

Rescue missions continued throughout this period, with us successfully picking up a family here, a few nuns there, a lost expatriate here, a missing person there. For much of the time, Brent was in charge of rescue missions, and each morning he would take the requests that came in from foreign capitals, embassies, the UN and other agencies in Nairobi, and by rumour, and pick which ones could be conducted and which ones could not be given the limited resources we had to spare for these tasks. I particularly detested the way world leaders or foreign government bureaucrats would try to contact me directly and attempt to order, threaten or otherwise intimidate me into rescuing some individual Rwandan whom they knew. Why should an acquaintance of a VIP be more important than any other individual at risk? I left the selection to

Brent, who became particularly adept at rescuing nuns, to the everlasting gratitude of many orders around the world. These were extremely stressful and emotional missions. It was never worse for Brent than when he delayed a mission a day or two for lack of resources or because of the particular level of risk in the area, only to mount it and find the persons in question recently killed. As men, we do not play God well, but the situation demanded that in some cases we had to choose who lived and who died.

Booh-Booh arrived with his political team from Nairobi early on the morning of April 30. Dr. Kabia and I met with him in his office at the HQ, where he briefed us on the regional political events over the last week. He showed us the formal response to the Arusha ceasefire proposal, which was signed by Bizimungu for the interim government. It was the same old rhetorical merry-go-round, with Bizimungu insisting that the ceasefire had to be signed by the interim government, which he knew was a non-starter with the RPF. We had not advanced a step. The RPF, winners on the battlefield so far, would never agree to these RGF points.

That morning I lost Brent. The day before, I found him lying down on his mattress in the afternoon. Brent never rested during the day. He told me he had a headache, but by suppertime he could no longer move his fingers to type and he was sweating profusely with a fever. My new aide-de-camp, Captain Babacar Faye Ndiaye, said he recognized Brent's illness as malaria and took him to the airport to see the Ghanaian battalion doctor. Brent and I had both lost our malaria medication when we abandoned our home on April 6. The doctor diagnosed Brent with malaria, gave him an enormous amount of drugs and told him to rest. Brent returned to the HQ and went to bed, watched over by Major Diagne.

Brent was awoken routinely during the night to take his drugs, but at dawn he looked like death warmed over. I ordered him to go to Nairobi for examination, expecting him to be back in a few days. In Nairobi they figured out that it wasn't malaria that had made him ill in the first placec, but he then had suffered an allergic reaction to the anti-malaria drugs. He was ordered to rest under observation for a couple of days, and he opted to stay at a hotel so he could get a good meal and a shower.

Two days later, his wife called and found him nearly paralyzed with pain and delirious. She contacted the Canadian Forces Operations Centre in Ottawa, which contacted our air force detachment in Nairobi, which picked him up and took him to the hospital. The next day he was evacuated to Canada. He had nearly died and would take almost a year to get healthy again. First from Nairobi and then from Ottawa he called to say he was being replaced. I felt like I had lost my right arm. After all that we had been through together, we were now split without even a proper goodbye. His replacement would be Major Phil Lancaster, an officer I knew very well since Phil and I had been junior officers together early in our careers. He was fluently bilingual, staff-trained, experienced and extremely skilled. Somehow I'd have to get along until he got to Kigali.

In the afternoon of the day Brent was shipped out, I had a chance to meet with Kagame regarding the ceasefire and the airport. He had promised to keep his guns clear of the airport, but not only had some of his rounds fallen on the runway, but the terminal housing the Ghanaian battalion had suffered deliberate artillery and mortar assaults, and we had established that the firing had come from RPF positions.

On the way up to Mulindi, taking a new route through the bush and swamps north of the city, the two vehicles of my convoy came under directed mortar fire at a prominent crossroads. Not only did the initial rounds come close enough to spray the vehicles with dirt, a couple more nearly hit us as we hastened to drive through the ambush. In this case, either side could have been the culprit, as fighting had not ended for control of the crossroads.

Kagame was waiting for me not far from his quarters. Our greetings were curt and we got right down to business. I wanted him to deal with the airport situation. He said he would instruct his troops to be careful of UNAMIR but that the RGF were well dug in en masse at Camp Kanombe, right at the end of the runway, and the airfield was inevitably going to be the focus of a big fight. I reminded him that the airport was the principal source of aid and the humanitarian buildup, and if the airport got thoroughly blown up, I had no engineering capabilities to repair a runway.

I shared the points in the letter Booh-Booh had obtained from Bizimungu, which echoed Bagosora's enumeration of conditions for a ceasefire. Kagame surprised me by saying that the idea of the belligerents returning to the pre–April 6 positions was an invention of the French. He said that last week, the diplomatic corps in Uganda had met under the auspices of the French ambassador in Kampala. President Museveni had also attended. Kagame had sent a representative, who made it quite clear that such a return was a no go. He was surprised that I raised it again today and that I was so obviously in the dark about the Kampala meeting. As far as Kagame was concerned, I was the UN representative in Rwanda and I had to sort this out.

He had one more subject he wanted to discuss, out of the blue it seemed to me at that moment. He was not going to be happy with any reinforcement of UNAMIR that looked like an intervention force. With the ceasefire going nowhere fast and his successes mounting on the battlefield, it was obvious why he wouldn't be.

I told him outright that there had been no discussion of an intervention force coming from UNAMIR and that if a force was being considered, it was to help stop the massacres and then work on the ceasefire and its potential application.

But Kagame contradicted me. "The UN is looking at sending an intervention force on humanitarian grounds, but for what reason?" he asked. "Those that were to die are already dead. If an intervention force is sent to Rwanda, we will fight it. Let us solve the problem of the Rwandans. This force is to protect the criminals in power. The international community cannot even condemn the massacres of poor innocent people. It is presenting the Rwandan problem as an ethnic one, which is incorrect as the massacres were against Tutsis and the opposition. All my soldiers that I command have individually lost family, starting with myself. My idea is not to divide the country but to hunt the criminals everywhere they might be."

He berated France and world indifference and blamed the UN for not giving me an appropriate mandate when the time was right. And then, as a final shot, he banished Booh-Booh: "The SRSG is not welcome anymore in Rwanda. We do not recognize him, and if he stays we will cease to collaborate with the UN." After politely offering me and my party beds for the night, he excused himself.

It was already past 1700. With direct death threats uttered against me, I knew it would be dangerous to try to get back to the city in our unmistakable white SUVs with the blue UN flags after nightfall, but I decided I had to pass on this pronouncement to Booh-Booh that night as well as touch base with the triumvirate. I also had to review the first draft of our response on the future of UNAMIR.

Dark descended on us as we wove our way back over the hills and down into valleys, our headlights picking out the roadblocks manned by drunken militia and half-asleep RGF soldiers. Around one curve, out of the pitch-black we fell into what looked like a swarm of fireflies, an entire cosmos. For as far as we could see, on the mountain slopes and seemingly high into the sky, thousands upon thousands of small fires and candles flickered in the perfectly still night. We had driven into a displaced persons' camp. We cut our speed drastically to manoeuvre through crowds of people still moving on the main route, hardly able to make out their dark shapes against the night. We crept along, our hearts in our mouths, hoping that we wouldn't attract the wrong kind of attention, for what seemed like endless kilometres, and then, just like our sudden stumbling into this unusual carpet of stars, we were out of it and back into utter blackness.

When we made it to the Force HQ, Henry was very relieved to see us. I spoke separately to Dr. Kabia, confiding to him alone Kagame's comment about Booh-Booh. I then called the triumvirate and briefed them on my session. Since Brent was gone, the draft notes to the secretary-general's report were not ready for my review. For a time I slept in my big chair by the window in my office-cum-bedroom. An hour later, I was awoken with the news that my new aide-de-camp, Captain Ndiaye, had gone to the Meridien hotel to bring some papers to Booh-Booh and had been ambushed about five hundred metres from the hotel. One of the bullets had creased the left side of his head, giving him an awful headache. The RPF soldiers controlled the area and were undoubtedly the culprits. Kagame's troops were getting more and more trigger-happy, and it was time for him to sort them out. So far, his troops had handled themselves quite well. There had been a case of rape that was dealt with summarily—the guilty soldier was shot. We had witnessed no looting per se. Bizimungu had told me that all the families of the senior officers in Byumba had been killed outright after the fall of that city. An RPF non-commissioned officer had come across his own uncles, aunts and cousins who had all been slaughtered by machete in Ramagana. He had gone on a rampage, killing Hutus until he was stopped.

The next morning I met with Bizimungu at the Diplomates, in our regular place looking out on a magnificent garden now full of artillery and mortar shell holes. A window was cracked and splattered with mud from the explosions. Once I briefed him on my meeting with Kagame, Froduald Karamira, the vice-president of the MDR, slipped into the room and joined us. I had a proposition for them: I wanted them to arrange for me to meet the Interahamwe leadership. If I was going to approve humanitarian efforts and civilian transfers I wanted to form a personal impression of the militia's willingness to let this happen since it would be impossible to get through all those barriers, back and forth, without having a firm commitment from the militia leaders. I needed their personal agreement in order to hold them accountable if things went wrong. I also wanted to talk to them directly about the refugee transfers between the lines because Bizimungu refused to do so. He and Karamira told me they could arrange such a meeting for later in the day.

I then made my way to the airport to see Lieutenant Colonel Joe Adinkra and his battalion in the air terminal. The Ghanaians had done a first-class job of reinforcing the interior with the sandbags and revetting that had finally commenced to come in with our twice-daily Hercules flights. Although the battalion had been bombarded on two separate occasions, there was little damage to their area of the massive building. They had established good defences from any ground assault, had excellent observation and fire positions over the tarmac and had laid land line (to link field telephones) to the support troops on the other side of the airfield.

I then moved on to tour the rest of the positions with Lieutenant Colonel Joe, a fine young battalion commander, solid and straight as a metal rod, whose troops were very loyal to him and responded to his orders with energy. The support troops, many of whom were members of the regimental band, had built themselves a veritable fortress, which would sustain artillery fire without any doubt. The problem was that they had poor observation and fire control around the site. They did not like digging in and so they had few people posted outside. I took Joe along with a few of his officers and NCOs to the old Belgian trenches. Although well-disposed, they needed to be expanded and connected by either open or covered communications trenches. A media crew joined us as we went, though I didn't realize it at the time. The newscast the next day showed Joe and me standing on the old Belgian trenches, binoculars in hand, as I pointed farther afield. I am saying, in the most collegial of fashions, "If you don't dig in here and place a heavy machine gun under cover there, the f-----s are going to be right on top of you before you can even fart." The comment was followed by footage of extensive scurrying about with orders at top voice and troops with shovels and picks leaping into holes in the ground followed by dirt flying in the air. It felt good to do some classic soldiering.

Later on the afternoon of May 1, I had my first meeting with the leaders of the Interahamwe. Not only was Bizimungu present, but so was Bagosora, who had deigned to come himself. I had made my way to the Diplomates, jostling through the ubiquitous roadblocks, drunken and downright mad militiamen, and hundreds of children jumping around, all excited among today's kills. These kids were being egged on to throw stones at our vehicles and yell at us as we stopped for the militiamen to open the gate. I had tried to anaesthetize myself to the ethical and moral dimensions of meeting with the génocidaires, recognizing that if they refused to assist in the transfers I might not ever get anyone out. Arriving at the hotel, I took the bullets out of my pistol just in case the temptation to shoot them was too extreme, and went inside.

The three young men Bagosora introduced to me had no particularly distinguishing features. I think I was expecting frothing at the mouth, but the meeting would be with humans. Until now, these men had never figured in any official discussions. They had been perceived as gang leaders, punks, criminals. However, today they had been asked to meet me for formal discussions on security. They had come of age, and they conveyed a certain cockiness as they greeted me. I remember smiling at them, with my heart beating so hard I was sure they could see it. I nearly lost my composure when I noticed that the middle guy's open-collared white shirt was spattered with dried blood. There were small flecks on his right arm as we shook hands. I moved on before I could think. They were Robert Kajuga, president of the National Interahamwe; Bernard Mamiragaba, representing the National Committee Interahamwe, and Ephrem Nkezabera, whose title was special councillor. At the end of the receiving line, Bizimungu was polite. We all sat down at once. Bagosora presided as Kajuga, the most senior of the three, whose mother had been Tutsi, began with words of respect, admiration and support for UNAMIR and its efforts with the Arusha peace process—at which point Bagosora excused himself and was out the door so fast we barely had time to respond.

Kajuga continued, offering to help UNAMIR. He proposed putting some of his youths with us as we patrolled our different protected sites. He said he had passed the word to all the barriers to let the Red Cross through while on humanitarian activities. What other kinds of activities did the Red Cross do? I wondered to myself. "We are at your disposal," he insisted and then was interrupted by the chap to his right, who said they were ready to work on the details of the transfers. He also said that they had "sensitized" all their people to stop the massacres. I could not believe my ears. He had actually blurted out the fact that they were doing the killing. Kajuga took over again, a little put out. He repeated that the Interahamwe had absolutely no problems with UNAMIR.

I thanked them for their support, for demonstrating such a sense of co-operation. I said I was overwhelmed with their positive attitude and promised that in the future I would be consulting them on matters of security. They nearly burst their shirts with pride. Whether they were telling me the truth regarding their intentions I could not be sure, but it was clear that they responded well to flattery. After about twenty-five minutes of this, I had had enough. Delighted with the turn of events, Bizimungu thanked me and I returned the compliment, shaking all of their hands.

What a sick event. I walked out of the hotel and passed by the RGF guards without even looking, at odds with myself about what had just happened. I then proceeded to the Mille Collines hotel to meet separately with the vice-president of the MDR party, Froduald Karamira who, due to his extremist loyalties, had survived the fate of his party colleagues. He gave me the same story as Bizimungu, only from the stance of a political person from the interim government, not a military man. At least I now had proof that they were all singing from the same song sheet. The links between the army, the militia and the interim government were real.

On the way back to the Force HQ, I felt that I had shaken hands with the devil. We had actually exchanged pleasantries. I had given him an opportunity to take pride in his disgusting work. I felt guilty of evil deeds myself since I had actually negotiated with him. My stomach was ripping me apart about whether I had done the right thing. I would only know when the first transfer happened.

The Sainte Famille church is a reference point on the Kigali skyline. The compound surrounding it is large, open and on a slope halfway up one of the hills in the city core. For artillery and mortar observers, it is an ideal target—impossible to miss if you're trying to hit it and easy to avoid if you're not. After I got back from my sickening encounter with the Interahamwe leaders, I had been trying to deal with the deluge of paperwork at my desk, already badly missing Brent and his ability to triage my workload. I had left my radio on as I worked, monitoring the force radio net, and at about 1645 I heard a call go out for medical support at Sainte Famille, as mortar rounds had fallen in the protected site at the compound.

It took almost half an hour to get there. The scene was chaos. Several thousand panicked people were either trying to seek refuge in the school and chapel, cowering against the walls or trying to get away from the area, even though that would likely mean falling into the hands of the militias. I could see the blue berets of the UNMOs in the thick of things, surrounded by the dead and the dying. Civilians, some obviously from the Red Cross, were working on the dozens upon dozens of casualties. As I got out of my vehicle, I was swamped by hysterical men and women demanding answers, comfort, rescue. I ended up having to push and fight my way through them to meet with my UNMOs. Breaking out of the mob, I approached the sites where the bombs impacted. Severed limbs and heads, children ripped in two, the wounded turning their bewildered eyes toward you at the moment at which you can actually see the life expire from them, the smell of burnt explosives mixed with burning blood and flesh. And amid the carnage, a glimpse of dignity in the face of an elder resigned to his approaching and inevitable death. The MILOBs and Red Cross staff were working feverishly. Covered in blood, the MILOB chief told me that one of his team was finishing the calculations on the crater analysis in order to determine where the bombs were fired from. He had taken his measurements among the bodies and gore in the shell holes.

Meanwhile, some of the informal civilian leaders were having some success in calming parts of the crowd, and I waded over to talk to as many people as I could. They could not understand why I did not have more soldiers to protect them. They appreciated the mobile patrols that checked in on them during the day, and the fact that some of my unarmed men stayed with them at night, but that simply was not enough. Squeezed in by hundreds of frightened people, I remember trying to explain to one group all the reasons why my troops were unable to fight to protect them. Puzzled at the complexity of my answer, they pressed me to sort it out. What could be so complicated? They were under fire and I was their only hope.

At prayers the next morning, it was confirmed that we finally had a team that could visit the presidential crash site, and an agreement in place allowing an international investigation. Thus commenced a process that to my knowledge has never brought a definitive answer to the mystery of who shot down that plane and why.

The report on the Sainte Famille bombing was in: over 120 casualties with 13 dead, 61 evacuated to the Red Cross field hospital and 15 to the King Faisal. I couldn't help thinking, "Too bad this slaughter was not in a market in Yugoslavia—maybe somebody outside Rwanda would have cared." As it happened, the Rwandan genocide was having a hard time knocking the South African elections and American figure skater Tonya Harding's criminal troubles off the front pages. The crater analysis indicated that the mortars were eighty-one-millimetre projectiles and they had been fired from the RPF positions. I would see Kagame tomorrow and formally expose this to him for action and, in the daily sitrep to New York, lay the atrocity at the RPF's doorstep.

Finally my request to be interviewed by RTLM came through, and I drove to the Diplomates around noon. Despite an attempt by the RPF to shut down the station by shellfire a few days earlier, it was back on the air, more virulent than ever, and we suspected it had a mobile capability.

The three RTLM staffers were set up in a room in a lower level of the hotel—a white man, George Ruggiu (who claimed to be Italian, but was actually a Belgian), a very aggressive female announcer and a technician. The interview was taped, not live as I had wished, which meant that they would chop it up to use as they liked. I decided to get some value out of the encounter and started asking them questions. What did they think the RPF was really up to? With venom, the woman replied, "Divide the country in two, which will not happen. No Tutsis will be secure in their villages. Arusha has been buried by the RPF." I'd heard that illogic before, but what was behind it? I asked about the impact of Habyarimana's assassination and got a surprising answer. As far as these extremists were concerned, Habyarimana had been protecting the Tutsis. He was pro-RPF, and they had not wanted him to stay in power. It was as close as I could get to a confession that the extremists wanted to get rid of Habyarimana.

I went a little further and asked them about the massacres. They immediately responded that the RPF was responsible for the downing of the plane and starting the war, and the Presidential Guard had merely reacted "to liquidate certain elements who had dabbled in the conspiracy." Clearly, in their minds this was a pro-Tutsi RPF conspiracy. The session ended with them making more accusations against the Belgians, but at least I'd gained some information.

...

That afternoon I received a letter from the interim government, signed by Bizimungu, agreeing to the transfers from the Mille Collines and the Amahoro. The UNAMIR staff led by Henry, with Yaache and two members of his humanitarian action cell, Major Marek Pazik and Major Don MacNeil (a new officer from Canada), were concurrently meeting with the militia and RGF staffs to iron out the details for the transfer we had scheduled for the next day: we were going to move some pro-RPF people from the Mille Collines to behind the RPF lines outside Kigali. It would be a first test of whether the Hutu belligerents were actually on side and in control. There were considerable exchanges of artillery and mortar fire, including medium-calibre rockets, all over Kigali that third day of May. More rounds ended up in Sainte Famille, though this time there were few casualties. Later in the afternoon the hangar area at the airfield received four to five hits. Three Ghanaian soldiers were wounded in the attack and required evacuation, but the Hercules could not get into Kigali because of bad weather, and the wounded would have to wait for a flight at first light.

That wasn't the worst of it. The attempted transfer ran into trouble just outside the Mille Collines and nearly cost the lives of the seventy Tutsi leaders in our trucks. To protect them, Don MacNeil put himself between the threatening militiamen and the trucks and came within inches of being killed, as did most of the Ghanaians attached to his part of the convoy. Over the force radio net I reminded MacNeil that he could use deadly force. He stated that he was going to negotiate them out of harm's way. (For this action MacNeil was awarded a mention-in-dispatch decoration from the Canadian government.) They had to retreat back to the Mille Collines, which as a result was even more insecure because the identities of some of the prominent persons inside were now known to the RGF and the militia. I feared that an assault would come that night. The hotel was shelled at sunset, but apart from broken windows and the smashed-up pool area, that was the extent of the damage. I kept my line open all night to Major Moigny, who was stationed there with his half-dozen UNMOS and the Tunisians.

The Force HQ also came under attack. The shells that landed in our compound destroyed a few vehicles and smashed several windows in the operations rotunda. The word went out that flak jackets and helmets were *de rigueur* for the next while. I was surprised at the quantity of artillery and mortar ammunition being expended by both sides to little tactical advantage. Not much of the fire seemed to be coordinated with infantry actions. Instead, the belligerents were posturing for better positions in and around the city, the RGF reinforcing their positions around Camp Kanombe and the eastern part of the airfield. The RPF was manoeuvring around the north. The fighting had intensified in the area between the HQ and the airport and we were being hit with peripheral explosions. The platoon sleeping room at the end of the top corridor of the HQ, just under the machine-gun position on the roof, was hit by an anti-armour rocket. The five Ghanaian soldiers who hot-bedded there had left the room barely minutes before the impact. A four- to five-foot hole was blown through the rooms, and no one would have survived.

It struck me that I was in the dark regarding the evolving situation in New York. Before morning prayers, I went through the cables that came in during the night and had to stifle white-hot rage when I read a copy of a May 2 letter from Rwanda's permanent representative at the UN, stating that his government wanted immediate action to stop the killing and bring the fight to an end for humanitarian reasons, and "offers its full cooperation for the success of the operation, which should be envisaged without delay, *with respect for the principle of the sovereignty and institutions of the Rwandan State* [my emphasis]."

The other code cable was a summary of the previous afternoon's deliberations in the Security Council. The play at the table between members left me perplexed. The French were for intervention either by neighbour states, the OAU or the UN. The United Kingdom said that the Security Council should avoid terms such as "forceful action" and "intervention." China supported the United Kingdom's position. Russia said the only way forward was to get the OAU more involved. New Zealand insisted that the words "forceful action" be retained. The United States proposed that a group from the Security Council go to Rwanda and get the needed information first-hand. Nigeria shot that down because such a trip would delay any decision by at least a week. All members supported cross-border humanitarian action and an arms embargo. Someone raised the fact that Boutros-Ghali's May 3 letter to the president of the Security Council (as requested in response to the president's report of April 30, which was prepared with lots of information from UNAMIR) had "infelicitously" suggested that the Security Council had made the wrong decision about the troop withdrawals. What really stuck in my craw was that now they were wasting time on finger pointing. What were they thinking? Why even think of passing the buck to the OAU when its troops had little equipment and no strategic lift?

The Hercules arrived at dawn to pick up the injured Ghanaian soldiers, and I went to the terminal to send them off. As the Hercules was turning back onto the runway, several rocket rounds hit the big hangar that housed the support company. A frantic call came in over the radio to hold the Hercules because another Ghanaian had been seriously injured. I told my aide-de-camp to get the plane to hang on for a few minutes.

The pilots were very uneasy on the ground, as they had already had so many narrow escapes. They kept the engines running and the ramp open as they waited in front of the terminal. A UN vehicle bounced across the open fields and then raced toward us. The soldier was brought inside so that the doctor could look at him and stabilize him enough for the trip. The plane had been on the ground for over twenty minutes when a couple more rounds landed across the airfield. I pressed the doctor to get the patient to the plane—Canadian air-evacuation nurses were on board to tend to him, and we simply could not let the other injured soldiers perish with the aircrew in a burning ball of fire. I was moving toward the doors to wave the plane on, leaving the terribly injured Ghanaian behind, when a hodgepodge of medical assistants in white, the doctor and troops ran for the plane with the cut-up soldier on a makeshift stretcher, nearly dropping him twice before they got him on board. The plane was on the runway before the ramp was totally up. All the wounded men pulled through.

I went to the other side of the field to look at the damage. It was obvious that the hangar had been specifically targeted with rocket fire and that the projectiles had come from the sprawling Camp Kanombe at the end of the airfield. What was Bizimungu trying to prove? Or perhaps more likely, what were Bagosora and the para-commando battalion based at that camp trying to achieve? Did they want us out, and if yes, what was yet to come? Bagosora would know better than I did the state of play at the UN, that the Security Council was once again discussing increasing my force. Was he trying to scare us off before the UN took the reinforcement decision?

The rest of the day was devoted to routine patrols to the safe sites, assisting the Red Cross in its distribution of some aid, licking our wounds from the transfer fiasco of yesterday, composing letters of protest to all the transgressors and getting up to speed with the DPKO about our future. To my great delight, after the second Hercules flight of the day managed to land and take off safely, a very large box was delivered to my office from Quebec City. Beth and the wife of one of the new Canadian officers, Luc Racine, had bought us a few hundred dollars' worth of peanut butter, Cheez Whiz, jams, crackers, chocolate bars, jujubes (my favourite) and other goodies. Then Beth had tracked down a resupply Hercules that was leaving the base in Trenton, Ontario, and after all the expected runarounds, got the box on that plane. It had made its way from home to Kigali without mishap. I spent a few hours distributing the goodies all around. My military wife knew that we would share, so she had tucked a smaller box inside for me—my own personal care package of peanut butter. (The Canadian Army kept its troops rolling on peanut butter.) We savoured every spoonful.

May 5 was the fiercest day of artillery, rocket and mortar fire throughout the city so far. At about midday, the shells were flying in all directions from both belligerents—at the CND, the airport terminal (causing one flight to return to Nairobi without off-loading), the Mille Collines and Sainte Famille—and none of our sites were sufficiently protected because of the lack of defensive stores. My troops' nerves were being frayed to levels of considerable concern, worn down by their powerlessness to help the people they were protecting from these threats from the sky. I set off again to meet with the manipulating leaders and protest,

protest, protest. We were being targeted by both sides, yet both sides said they wanted us here. I did not want to abandon the field nor those under our protection, but unarmed military observers could not intimidate bombs.

Later that day I learned that José Ayala Lasso, the high commissioner for human rights, and an investigative team were coming to Kigali on May 9. That was excellent news. I instructed the commanders and staff to make available to him all personnel who had witnessed any crimes against humanity, and that he should be taken to see Kagame and, on the government side, Bizimungu at least. Ayala Lasso was going to get an earful.

I was also handed a copy of a letter from the foreign minister of Belgium—sent on to me by Riza, possibly as an expression of black humour. In the letter Willy Claes reminded the secretary-general that the UN had to provide protection for Rwandan hospitals and NGO staffs, as well as ensure that those who were responsible for the massacres did not go unpunished. Was there no decency at all in either Claes or his government? They certainly missed a good opportunity to remain quiet.

By late afternoon I was finally able to sign our "Proposed Future Mandate and Force Structure of UNAMIR," which was an in-depth option analysis of what we needed if the Security Council decided to reinforce us on the military, humanitarian and political fronts. I could lay it all out here; experts have studied the plan since and have agreed that if enacted, it would have stopped the killing and even allowed stability to reappear in central Africa. All I can say is that forwarding the plan briefly allowed us to live again in hope that the world would do the right thing, but nothing I outlined in it ever happened. At the time I thought, "Now they cannot procrastinate anymore. My troops are under fire on a daily basis, the politicos have a detailed concept of operations and a plan, and all we need is approval from the Security Council."

But I sent it in on a Thursday, the next day was Friday and then came the weekend. The fastest they would get to it would be Monday, and tens of thousands more Rwandans would be dead, and hundreds of thousands would be on the move to another possible campsite in the mountains, in the rain, the mud and the horror. We did not have another week to fiddle. When I expressed some of my despair to

Maurice, he told me to keep my head down and hope for the best. He had no power in the UN. He was the secretary-general's military adviser in an organization swamped and sinking under the dead weight of useless political sinecures, indifference and procrastination. Between the buildup of the former-Yugoslavia mission, the Somalia debacle and the near-total absence of funds and support from the UN Fifth (financial and budget) Committee, UNAMIR ended up being just another catastrophic failure that was simply getting worse.

I knew Maurice had seen first-hand the suffering and destruction caused by this new era of conflict, and at one point he had come very close to dying of malaria picked up in a war zone. How was it possible that he had not become jaded? I still held him in high regard even though we had had our serious differences over these many months. But where could I find the means to prod the world into action? Living with the constant stink of death in my nose, carried on the breezes I had once found so seductive, I was forced to keep thinking: What was the spark that lit the fuse that blew up into all this degradation and perversion? And why were we so feeble, fearful and self-centred in the face of atrocities committed against the innocent? I woke the next morning with my head on my desk, pulled out of my stupor by birds singing in the trees inside the compound, and with one thought in my head: more Rwandans would die today.

Booh-Booh sent a report to Annan on the status of the ceasefire meetings in Arusha, with a copy to Dr. Kabia (not me). What a circus. It turned out there were two copies of the ceasefire agreement. Tanzania and the OAU had signed both, but the interim government and the RPF had signed different copies. Booh-Booh and the diplomats had tried to get the RPF to sign the copy that had the interim government's signature on it, but of course the RPF stormed out. Why did all these fine people in authority not understand that they would never persuade the RPF to deal with the interim government? The RPF might sign such an agreement with the military directly, but Bizimungu was far too much of a Tutsi-hater, even killer, to give up on the interim government and negotiate with Kagame directly.

In the second part of the report, Booh-Booh complained bitterly about being accused by the RPF of being an ally of the interim government. He blamed me for not defending him to Kagame and argued that the RPF was framing him. I passed the news back to Annan that when I raised Booh-Booh's name with Kagame it inspired a torrent of expletives. That was an opinion of Booh-Booh that no one would be able to change.

It was Saturday, May 7. The RPF had now bypassed Kigali to the south and were consolidating. The RGF, still madly recruiting, had held off repeated assaults in Ruhengeri and the north side of Kigali. The fighting around the airport and the terminal was extremely heavy, and I had had enough of hollow promises from both sides about their attempts to "avoid" my positions. All of the helicopters with UNOMUR in Kabale were broken, and the wrong parts had been sent to repair them. With the NRA still feigning that they had no escorts available, my force there was limited to surveillance of the five main crossings. The RPF and the NRA were now in overt cahoots in prosecuting this war.

I decided to drive out to the airport to bring encouragement to the Ghanaians. The firing was so heavy that the morning cargo of much-needed water, medicine and food was still on pallets in the middle of the tarmac. On the way back to Force HQ, we ran into a new roadblock put up by some very scraggly militiamen. I was getting very tired of this; by signed agreement the road to the airport was supposed to be kept open. After slowing down to get a good look at the layout—a dozen youths milling about with a few plastic crates set up on the road—I pressed on the gas and smashed my way through. The crates flew into the air, and the militiamen jumped back in complete surprise. Back at the HQ, Tiko was looking for some action, and I decided to give him charge of my escort to go sort out the problem. The outraged militiamen became very subdued when Tiko approached, backed by my squad of burly muscle-men. Tiko sat down on one of the plastic crates and held court with the AK-47-toting kids, who were no older than sixteen. He was obviously quite persuasive, as the youths decided to withdraw, after shaking hands and promising not to come back to the area. They never did. I enjoyed the story, but it reinforced for me what we could have possibly done with even 5,000 troops and officers of this calibre.

• • •

Once more I returned to the Diplomates, this time to meet with Augustin Bizimana, the minister of defence, who had been conspicuously absent from Kigali for most of the month. He told me he had been wrapped up in cabinet affairs, but I knew he had been dealing with his personal losses of family and property in Byumba.

After what now seemed like a ritual of complaints and promises all around, I told him of the plans for the new UNAMIR. Though I was looking for major reinforcements, I said, we were not to be an intervention force. His immediate response was to announce that there would be only one Rwanda, not a country divided into Tutsi and Hutu territories. Where did he get that idea? Not from me and certainly not from Kagame. The only other people who knew of my musings on a Cyprus-style future for the country were in the DPKO. Had they shared that prospect with the Security Council, which still included the extremist Rwandan representative? I let it lie.

I promised Bizimana that when I was reinforced I would deploy a battalion to protect a neutral airport. He said this information would help him with the cabinet. He ended the meeting, heading for cover when a few mortar rounds started to fall in the area. Once again I was left with the feeling that the extremists were better informed than I was about what my superiors were planning.

Not long after, I was heading for my meeting with Kagame, rolling through the countryside with my escort, avoiding piles of clothes and abandoned household goods. We were in newly held RPF territory, and the scenes were as horrific as elsewhere. Several ambush or killing sites were old, not attributable to the RPF, but some huts were smouldering here and there. We arrived at a ford across a creek. There had once been a small bridge here but it had been blown up. For a minute I actually wondered why the RPF soldiers guarding the ford were fishing with long poles but no string. I then noticed large piles of bloated blue-black bodies heaped on the creek banks. The soldiers had been given the task of making sure the bodies would not block the passage, as the creek was very shallow here. The stink was suffocating, and my undigested lunch was soon added to the mess. The soldiers, either tired or having run out

of room, were poling the bodies past the ford to float their putrid way
to the nearest river and possibly on to Lake Victoria. Mentally retreat-
ing behind the protective shield of command, I plunged my vehicle
into the water and carried on along the trail to my objective: Byumba,
where Kagame had set up a tactical headquarters that was much easier
to reach than his compound in Mulindi.

I raised with the general my worries about the fate of the Tutsis and
the moderate Hutus still marooned in the Mille Collines; Bizimungu
had threatened to kill them if the RPF didn't stop shelling RGF positions
in the city. Kagame was pragmatic, the complete portrait of the cool
warrior: "They are practising their age-old blackmail methods and it
will not work anymore. There will be many sacrifices in this war. If the
refugees have to be killed for the cause, they will be considered as having been part of the sacrifice." I instinctively asked if his forces would
conduct any reprisals on the Hutus we were protecting in our sites. He
told me to get those civilians out of Kigali because the fight would only
get worse. On the airport problem, he said that he had given me all the
time he could to sort out the neutrality agreement, but he could no
longer hold up or change his operational plans. He was not targeting
UNAMIR positions per se, but in the fog of the battle, my troops could
get hit. In fact they already had been hit. I told him I had no choice but
to stay at the airport to protect the field for humanitarian purposes and
the Canadian mercy flights. He did not respond, just sat there impassive, so calm his thin chest barely moved with each breath.

I then explained the concept of the new UNAMIR. He listened attentively even though he probably had already been briefed in detail by his
representatives at the UN. His reply stunned me. "No objection," he
said. "I suggest however that it be strong enough and ready to fight."
He promptly rose, shook hands and departed.

The sun was going down fast, and we sped off, hoping to get to the
HQ before darkness fell completely. Although we arrived way past sunset,
the trip back was without a wrong turn or a close shave. I finally sat
down that night at a table in the operations room in the rotunda with
a cup of tea from somewhere. My job was to study a draft of a "non-
paper" being prepared for the secretary-general on the way forward for

UNAMIR. A non-paper is essentially a means by which the UN considers a subject without treating the process as official business that has to lead to an official resolution. Here I was up to my armpits in bodies, and the DPKO was reduced to presenting a non-paper in order to garner possible support for a mandate debate. How in hell did they find themselves in such a position? They'd had my sitreps and assessments and military estimates and more staff analyses than they could shake a stick at. But still they wanted my input on the non-paper by early tomorrow.

Call me a wide-eyed optimist, but the draft of the non-paper looked good. It looked, in fact, very much like what I had been recommending (so much so that one of my staff had sarcastically noted on the draft, "This is excellent so let's get at it"). In my response, I approved the fact that they were proposing my "minimum viable" option of 5,500 troops, yet describing its function with the action verbs I'd attached to the 8,000-troop model. I congratulated them on essentially taking as a package my concept of operations, my plan and my layout of tasks and reported that both belligerents accepted the idea of the reinforced UNAMIR. I insisted that the non-paper stress the sense of urgency—there were still a lot of people at risk and we had to save as many as possible. It already went part of the way by recommending that the normal process of getting troops should be put aside and that nations should provide troops in operational brigade formations. There was no room for untrained and ill-equipped units from developing nations, even if some were ready to send them. The non-paper also endorsed reinforcing the mission even without a signed ceasefire or airport neutrality agreement: music to my ears.

I insisted that the first task of the new UNAMIR would be to address the humanitarian crisis. Their non-paper spoke of a mandate to provide safe conditions for people and safe delivery of humanitarian support, based on self-defence against persons or groups who threatened the safe corridors and areas we would establish, as well as our already protected sites. This read very much as if they would endorse an active defence by strong, highly mobile forces. I pushed for levels of clarity on the risks these troops were prepared to take. I'd asked not for a chapter-seven mandate but for my chapter six and a half, which would allow us to take aggressive action to prevent crimes against humanity as well as in self-defence. I wanted the term "safety assured" attached to our safe sites in Kigali and the churches, stadiums and schools around the country where people were sheltering. I would be able to provide "significantly enhanced security" to the two million internally displaced. I grew elated as I worked. Yes, it was a non-paper, but it finally looked as if the DPKO wanted to give me the right mandate and tools. I signed the code cable the next morning after passing a copy through Dr. Kabia to Booh-Booh for comment.

My spirits had risen and stayed that way even after writing a detailed tactical analysis of what would happen if the RPF attacked the airfield in the next few days. But I could not shake my fears of waking up in the morning to be told that everyone at the Mille Collines had been slaughtered during the night. I called Moigny, who had proven his worth several times already, fending off RGF soldiers, gendarmes and Interahamwe. The militias had only breached the building once, kicking down doors in search of Tutsis. But Moigny and his unarmed officers, supported by some very determined Tunisian soldiers, were able to persuade them to leave before any harm was done—aided by the hotel manager's deft and generous gift of many bottles from the hotel wine cellar.

Drafts of the UNAMIR 2 mandate were flying between New York and us. On May 9, I had to cancel the Hercules flights, one of which was supposed to bring in Ayala Lasso and the investigation team, because heavy artillery and machine-gun fire in and around the airfield were simply too intense. The RPF shelled several parts of the city that day, including my protected sites. At the Amahoro Stadium, a Ghanaian private was about to enter his room when a mortar shell exploded inside the stadium. Fragments flew through the window and hit him under the armpit where there was no protection from his UN flak jacket, and one struck his heart. He was dead before he hit the ground. Several civilians were injured as well. Henry was on the phone to his bosses in Accra right away, defending the need to keep the contingent in place and to augment it as soon as possible.

Late that afternoon, I was called to meet with the minister of social welfare at the Kigali hospital. He was absolutely hysterical by the time

I got out of my vehicle at the main gate. Before me was a scene of chaos and horror that simply seemed to explode in my face.

The RPF had fired three to four artillery rounds into the hospital compound. Fumes and smoke still hung over the site, filtering the brightness of the sun and turning everything into a dreamlike image of atrocity. One bomb had landed in the middle of a large tent erected as shelter for about thirty injured persons. Staff were cleaning up pieces of charred bodies and trying to put the tents that had surrounded it back up. Inside the nearby walled compound stood the pharmacy and dispensary. It had a wired service counter in a doorway; people would line up along the front wall waiting for their prescriptions to be filled. The yellow-painted, one-storey building was still standing although all the windows were smashed. After a closer look I was aghast. On the wall there were outlines of people, of women, of children, made of blood and earth. It was like a scene out of Hiroshima. There had been over forty people standing against the wall, caught between the shell blasts and the solid building. A medical person said that some people just exploded into the air. None survived.

I could not absorb the carnage. As an artillery officer, I had seen the effects of explosions on all sorts of targets, but never could I have imagined the impact of such hits on human beings. The age of abstract "exercises" was over for me. Hundreds of people of all ages were crying and screaming, and staff ran every which way trying to attend to all the wounded. With tears and crazed gestures, the minister of social welfare screamed at me that UNAMIR and I were accomplices to this savagery and that he hoped I would never be able to erase this scene from my mind. Then my aide-de-camp came up to me with the Motorola. It was Henry. The Force HQ was under heavy artillery attack.

We raced back through town with little patience for the barriers, rage welling so hot in me that the militiamen must have taken one look and decided the risk of stopping me was not worth it. As we approached the HQ, the smoke of explosions was still billowing and a round landed about three hundred metres away as I drove through the gate, a pillar of earth flying up and then in all directions. A few vehicles were destroyed. Many of the windows in the rotunda were shattered. As I walked into the headquarters, two rounds landed on the edge of the compound near the street. All the staff and civilians were huddled in the central lobby. As I was being briefed by Henry, another round exploded in the compound right outside the doors. Later I watched media footage of the attack and was quite surprised to see that when a bomb exploded, everyone around me flinched but I was so focused I remained immobile, impatient in fact for them to get up and back into the briefing. About an hour later I gave the all-clear. There was a huge mess to clear up but luckily this time no one was injured.

I spoke a few words of encouragement to the staff and sent people back to their duties. I then asked Frank Kamenzi, our RPF liaison officer, to come with me outside. Away from prying ears, I lit into him. Threatening an immediate pullout and world scandal in between curses, I insisted on seeing Kagame the next day. I was not going to bring more forces into this cesspool unless such scandalous and dishonourable actions stopped right now. And I told Frank not to return to my headquarters unless he successfully set up the meeting

The next day in Byumba, Kagame met my outrage over the assault on UNAMIR and the killings at Kigali hospital with his own horror stories, including the mass extermination of young Tutsi students in Gikongoro. He agreed to apply more discipline to his troops and said he would personally brief the liaison team to my HQ and provide them with the necessary communications to be able to call off misbegotten attacks on us. I left after about an hour, wanting to believe his word but still concerned.

Henry had formally written to me reminding me that Kagame had warned us that he was implementing his tactical plan to take the airport. It seemed to Henry that holding on to our positions at the airport in the face of that threat was of no great benefit to the mission. When we met later that day, I argued that if we withdrew from the airport, the RPF would make it nearly impossible for us to return. Henry agreed with me but let me know that he was under pressure from Accra to get his troops out of there. He spent a good part of the next day with his Ghanaians.

The last of my Canadian reinforcements arrived that day, led by Lieutenant Colonel Mike Austdal as contingent commander. Phil

Lancaster arrived that day as well, a sight for sore eyes. The other Canadian officers were Major John McComber, Captain Sarto LeBlanc, Captain Jean-Yves St-Denis, Captain André Demers and Captain Nelson Turgeon. Within hours I put them to work in my headquarters where they rendered sterling service for the duration of their tours with UNAMIR. I released two of the three officers who had come from Somalia—Major Plante opted to stay—sending Bussières and Read home with my thanks for a job well done. Major Don MacNeil and Major Luc Racine had arrived from Canada in late April, just before Brent got sick, and both of them would provide excellent service for the next year in Rwanda.

That day the high commissioner for human rights, Ayala Lasso, made it in, and we all briefed him. He did his rounds as best he could on all sides and saw the horrific sites. This was his first trip into a human rights disaster since he had been appointed, and he could not hide his fury nor his disgust. At the end of his fact-finding tour he declared that what he saw in Rwanda was a genocide. The report he eventually made was an accurate account of events as we knew them thus far. He also wanted to send in human rights observers as soon as possible but was well aware of the risks. Kagame encouraged him to do so and said he would provide support. The RGF was less enthusiastic and said it would get back to him on the matter.

As we crept further into May, more extremists in the government, including ministers, were encouraging the arming of the Hutu population and demanding more action at the roadblocks to weed out Tutsis and rebel infiltrators. UNOMUR reported that the RGF was being supplied by boat over Lake Kivu and by land from Goma and Bukavu in Zaire. Reports were coming in of new massacres in towns around the country. Philippe Gaillard called in with news that thousands had been murdered at the great religious centre of Kabgayi, which was next door to Gitarama, where the interim government was set up.

Dr. Kabia came to see me with the news that Booh-Booh had left again for Nairobi and then Paris to meet with Boutros-Ghali. I asked what that was all about, and he said that such consultations were not out of the ordinary. I told him I needed his comments on the most recent version of the non-paper, especially as the United States was working diligently to shoot it all down. Instead of establishing safe sites based on concentrations of displaced persons in Rwanda, as I had called for, they wanted me to set up a Kurdistan-type of large safe zone on the periphery of the country, arguing that troops would be safer that way. But there the concept had worked because the bulk of the Kurds were already in that general safe-zone area, whereas in Rwanda the people at risk would not be able to get to a safe zone on any border since the militias and armed civilians would simply set up a cordon some distance away and massacre anyone foolhardy enough to try. On top of that, the British representative argued that a more formal report was required before any decision could be taken, and the report also needed to include a budget assessment. The DPKO had to write the report and then the Security Council would look at it. Ambassador Keating was insisting that my chapter six-and-a-half wasn't good enough—we needed a chapter-seven mission. I did not want to intervene in the war or become a third belligerent—I wanted just enough authority and firepower to move the humanitarian agenda safely. In a conversation with the triumvirate, it was clear we had to step up the fight for the new mandate.

For four more days, the Americans put obstacle after obstacle in our way, with the British playing a coy supporting role. The French backed UNAMIR 2 but with conditions; the non-aligned countries were furious at the delays; and the RPF published a statement to the Security Council that looked very much like a manifesto against us, arguing that UNAMIR 2 was too late to stop the killing and could potentially destabilize the RPF's struggle for power. In fact it was not too late; the massacres would continue for weeks. If I had been a suspicious soul, I could have drawn a link between the obstructive American position and the RPF's refusal to accept a sizable UNAMIR 2. In the pre-war period, the U.S. military attaché from the American embassy was observed going to Mulindi on a regular basis. In addition, a large Tutsi diaspora in North America backed the RPF.

Meanwhile the smell of death continued to permeate the real world in central Africa. We prepared and sent updates on the situation, clarifications of the concept of operations, lists of acceptable troop-contributing nations, vetted by both the RPF and the RGF, and still it was not enough. I increased my media interviews, and Mark Doyle poured articles into the BBC, but nothing seemed to prod the Security

Council into motion. I ordered an attempt to get humanitarian aid into the RGF zone under the protection of UNAMIR in order to respond to the accusation that we were favouring the RPF but also to prove how vulnerable we were. UNREO organized the attempt, under the direction of its brilliant coordinator, Arturo Hein, and brought along four journalists. It headed to Runda and the displaced camps there (there were ninety-one such camps around the country). They ran an ambush on the outskirts of Kigali, were searched at several roadblocks, and the journalists had their film confiscated twice. After they unloaded the trucks at the site, the locals, armed with machetes, clubs, grenades and stones, surrounded the vehicles and threatened the whole team. The mob had started to pull the aid persons off the trucks when the local sous-prefect finally arrived to put a halt to it. The UNMOs had done their best, but the size of the crowd and its state of frenzy had flummoxed them. On the way back to Kigali they barely squeaked through a rocket attack. We sent a detailed report of this foray to the DPKO for promulgation. The bulk of the civilians were behind RGF lines. If we did not get to them, thousands would continue to die by the road and in the displaced persons camps. I hoped this account would prove exactly why the humanitarian effort needed muscle.

There were so many life-and-death decisions swirling in my head that I needed to find a stable reference point so I could get my bearings. I decided one morning to go to Kinihira in the former demilitarized zone. After warning the RPF liaison officer of my intentions, my escort and I drove north on the main route to Gatuna for about eighty kilometres and then veered off onto a dirt track at the edge of a small village where children still waved at us as we bumped by. The trail was broken up due to the heavy rains, and I was doing quite a job of trying to leap from one hole to another in my SUV. We drove for about thirty more kilometres like this. My aide-de-camp, ever polite, and the Ghanaian sniper sitting in the back seat didn't complain but were rather shaken up by the time we arrived at the commune office at the top of the third long ridge in the paint-by-number series of valleys. I badly needed to stand in the little school on the spine of that ridge, where nearly a hundred children had studied before the killing started.

And the place did not seem touched by the war, except that there were no children playing in the schoolyard. We noticed only a few very timid adults peering at us from their doorways. As I walked around, under the watchful eyes of my African escort, in my mind's eye I could see the children wearing their bright blue-and-beige uniforms, the overworked but smiling teachers, the little brothers and sisters dragged to school by the older kids in order to let their mothers work in the fields, the boys racing after a banana-leaf soccer ball at recess. I sat at the end of the schoolyard and looked at the scene below. Tea and coffee fields, once precisely groomed, looked scraggly and in need of tending. The hundreds of small garden plots running up the sides of the hills were now overflowing with weeds. The landscape used to feature spectacular splashes of colour from freshly washed clothes, laid out neatly in the sun on green patches of grass beside brown huts with thatched roofs. They were all gone. I looked out over burnt huts, some still smouldering, carrion birds overhead, black lumps in rags moving ever so slowly downstream as others piled up on a curve in the river. I was filled with a sense of gross ineptness. I had come to paradise in full bloom and now, on my favourite hillside, I saw myself walking these hills and valleys, crossing streams and sitting in the shade of banana trees, talking without anyone being there, ripped apart by failure and remorse. I had come to Kinihira looking for a little peace, but peace had been murdered here, too.

I was brutally brought back to the moment by my aide-de-camp, who handed me the Motorola radio. The DPKO wanted our response ASAP and I was required to review yet another document before it was sent. We drove back in silence.

Back at headquarters, Yaache had news for Henry and me. That day the RPF had held a humanitarian coordination meeting with the UNHCR and sixteen NGOs at Mulindi. I had not been informed, and our military observers with the RPF were also kept in the dark. "The bastards," I said. With huge problems delivering aid to the RGF zones, efforts in the RPF area had to be absolutely transparent. In no way could aid resources be siphoned off to Kagame's troops. Thus started a running battle between me and the UNHCR, which lasted right through the over-aid crisis in the Goma camps that was still to come.

At that moment, Phil Lancaster stuck his head into the office to inform me that we had an unannounced visitor. I was in no mood. Before Phil could say anything more, Bernard Kouchner—a former French minister of health, a founder of Médecins Sans Frontières and now the president of a humanitarian action group based in Paris—came through the door. I asked him to return to the hallway before he could even introduce himself. After Henry and Yaache left my office, Phil came back in with one of Kouchner's handlers, who in very rapid French explained to me who the man was and why he was here. I said I would be happy to receive him now.

Though he had blown his top while waiting out in the hall, he came in now with a smile and a most courteous manner and immediately cut off my excuses so that he could apologize himself for barging in and expecting preferential treatment. We got along famously after that. He was here on his own initiative, he said, to get a better feel for the situation and to provide whatever help he could over the next few days. I called Henry back in and we spent the next couple of hours together, mapping out his schedule. I asked him to meet with the RGF leaders and also with the interim government and beat them down as regards to the killings, the insecurity for humanitarian aid, and the forced movement of nearly two million civilians. I told him I suspected that the RGF and the interim government had taken a hard look at the situation and realized that they should conduct a strategic withdrawal into the Kivu area of Zaire and be ready to fight another day. I needed them to stop scaring the populace by portraying the RPF as devilish child-eaters. He told me he had already met with the RPF as he had come into the country through its lines a day or so ago. He had not succeeded in making their position more flexible.

I asked him what he wanted from this trip. The answer was straightforward: he wanted to save a bunch of orphans in Interahamwe-held territory. He wanted to fly them out of the war and then bring them back when things were calm. He said the French public was in a state of shock and horror over the genocide in Rwanda and was demanding action.

I told him that I was totally against the export of Rwandan children, orphaned or not. They were not a means for some French people to feel a little less guilty about the genocide. He asked me to give the matter some more thought and said that while I did, he would take on the extremists and visit a few of the orphanages. He travelled with a coterie of journalists to help him make his point.

The following day I sent Tiko with Kouchner to go and meet the interim government in Gitarama. Tiko did not speak French, but he was fearless and I believed that their travels would go well. Kouchner would then come back and join me in a meeting with the military heads. As I was preparing for the meeting with Bagosora and the two chiefs of staff at the Diplomates, I got a call from UNOMUR telling me that the Dutch minister for development had entered the RPF zone through the Katuna border post and had gone to Mulindi to discuss humanitarian activities. What was this about? I asked that he come to Kigali for a meeting.

At the Diplomates, we rode the usual merry-go-round of issues. But at the end, Bizimungu said he wanted to start the transfers again the next day and Bagosora claimed he had made arrangements with the Interahamwe, which was ready to help. When Kouchner arrived at the hotel, we all sat down together. Kouchner pulled no punches. Though he was in Rwanda on his own hook, he told them that France and the world were beside themselves with disgust at what was happening here. The killing had to stop. The UN was about to approve a new mandate for UNAMIR and was clearly going to identify the catastrophe as genocide, not as an ethnic war. Kouchner would report on this trip directly to the secretary-general himself, who had personally facilitated his visit. (That explained why neither I nor the DPKO had known he was coming.) Bagosora and Bizimungu made the usual protestations, and only Ndindiliyimana finally said that they needed to stop the killing but that a ceasefire was an essential first step.

Kouchner interrupted. Do not wait for the ceasefire, he said. Show good will and change the psychology of the situation. As an example, let him pull out orphans from the militia-controlled areas and take them to safety in France. I admired his chutzpah. I volunteered that UNAMIR could help but I needed firm guarantees of security. If such an attempt failed, it would be a disaster for the children.

The meeting ended with Bagosora and the chiefs committing to help evacuate orphans, Kouchner at the front of such a procession with lots of media. I hated Kouchner's argument that this action would be a public relations coup for the interim government. I already didn't like the idea of exporting Rwandan children, but to do it to give the extremists a better image made me ill. However, if such an exercise inspired the RGF and the interim government to sign the ceasefire, including the neutrality of the airport, I was willing to co-operate. Kouchner was a very experienced internationalist and had seen many other such situations. This manoeuvre to assist the RGF and the government had not been in the cards he'd displayed when I'd met with him the day before. I made a mental note to keep a careful watch on Kouchner's motives and actions.

Since I had some time before my next meeting at the hotel with the Interahamwe leaders, I decided to deal with a problem at the Red Cross hospital. Militiamen were barring the entrance to those seeking help. I arrived at the gate at a fair speed, the powerful diesel motor of my SUV grinding loudly as I made my way up the hill. My escort was very close behind, and by the time I leapt out of my vehicle, three of them had come running to my side. Two more aimed the barrels of the machine guns on their Toyota pickup trucks right at the militiamen, who observed my guys very closely while trying to feign cockiness. I marched up to the one who looked like the leader and threatened him with grave consequences if they continued to obstruct the entrance or tried to get inside. Though my Ghanaian escort did not understand a word of French, they relished the moment and moved to separate the thugs from the onlooking crowd. A near-instantaneous change of atmosphere came over the scene. Respectfully, the Interahamwe said they would not take any action here and, in fact, would leave the area. After a few words with the Red Cross people at the gate, I headed back to the Diplomates.

This time as I was removing my pistol, which was the etiquette for such meetings, I hesitated, certainly long enough to be noticed, then let my gun drop on the sofa. I don't know what the three Interahamwe leaders made of the gesture, but I was fighting a terrible compulsion to shoot them on the spot. This was no fleeting urge. I had to consciously take my weapon off and put it away from myself. Why not shoot them? Wouldn't such an act be justified? They spoke their words of welcome, and I let the chance go. I still debate the choices of that moment in my head.

The three riders of the apocalypse were all smiling at me, apparently proud of the fact that I had come to see them again. Kajuga, Mamiragaba and Nkezabera were confident and neatly dressed—no blood spatters this time—and very attentive to every nuance of my opening comments. Kajuga read my eyes more than he listened, I believed, trying to discern any sign of weakness or doubt. I said that I wanted to operate with all forces in Rwanda, including them. I told them that UNAMIR 2 would be a humanitarian-focused mission, not an intervention force. Kajuga assured me again of the movement's co-operation. The Interahamwe pledged to work diligently for the halt of the massacres and the return to peace. I told them the transfer exercises were going to start over the next days, and the world would be watching. We parted as politely as we could.

In the next couple of days, I learned that Yaache and his team had stopped the Kouchner orphan rescue because the Interahamwe had continued to raise problems, arguing that UNAMIR was simply helping the RPF to empty the RGF zone of Tutsis preparatory to an attack. The militia told Yaache that it wanted me to be present at the loading site. Then Bagosora asked Yaache to come and explain why he had cancelled the transfer when it was so important for his government's image. When Yaache told him of the militia's intransigence, Bagosora apologized for the problems the Interahamwe had raised and said he had not been aware of them before. He assured Yaache that the government was committed to the orphan transfers and asked if the problems could be resolved within twenty-four hours, obviously before Kouchner left town with all his journalists. Yaache said he would have to have another meeting with these seemingly fickle militia leaders. I agreed with Yaache that we had to go slowly. Yaache said Bagosora seemed desperate for the transfer to take place right away. By losing the chance to use Kouchner to show that the extremists were really trying to sort things out, he would lose a major opportunity in the eyes of the French authorities and population, and in front of the world.

I was running on adrenalin that evening and decided to take another look at the concept of operations for UNAMIR 2. With the diligence for which I was always grateful, the staff stayed with me in the operations room to help me put a further response and assessment together. The interim government, the RGF, the Gendarmerie, even the Interahamwe, were suddenly co-operative and speaking with one voice, under the apparent leadership of Bagosora: it had to mean that something or somebody had changed the extremists' strategy. Had they realized that the RPF was not going to settle for half of the country and then decided to show a supportive attitude to the UN and the international community while bargaining for time? Did Kouchner's sudden appearance have some effect? He was close to the government in France, and perhaps France had some plan in motion that I didn't know about.

I needed to rethink the deployment of UNAMIR 2, as every passing day brought more chaos and change. I had to come up with alternate deployment sites that would concentrate the new forces more quickly if I was still going to have a chance to influence the situation. I made another plea for a sixth battalion and for my UN bosses to consider peripheral airfields and new secure operations and logistics centres. Finally I called it a day. I remember someone brought out a case of beer and we all had a cold one. Where did the beer come from? It was not the horrible Rwandan Primus. The Ghanaians must have brought it; they loved their beer and once in a while arranged for an emergency supply to come in on the Hercules.

I went to bed and prayed for a better day.

On May 17, Henry chaired the first ceasefire Standing Operating Procedures meeting at the Hôtel des Diplomates. The RGF officers were led by the operations head, a known hard-liner. The RPF did not attend, claiming it had not had enough time to review the proposed procedures. As far as headway went, Henry concluded that the next meetings had better take place inside Force HQ—relatively neutral ground. Kouchner left that morning, still confident of having made a difference in Rwanda but furious that the orphan evacuation had failed. I had appreciated his efforts and his courage in attempting to come to our aid.

Later that day, I received an important code cable from Annan himself. It included a copy of the Security Council resolution that would govern our future, complete with the last-minute changes imposed by the United States. Annan's covering letter described its heavy-handedness. The morning of the final debate, the Americans had visited the DPKO seeking clarifications "on the nature and concept of operations of the expanded UNAMIR, its deployment schedule, the availability of troops and the consent of the parties.[1] Based on this discussion, the U.S. wished to suggest the attached changes." Maurice lost his temper and vehemently accused the United States of unconscionable stalling. Nonetheless the Americans had forced through some changes, as Annan's cable laid out: "Please note that paragraph 7 of the resolution implies that, while preparations for the second phase of the expanded operation will proceed, its implementation will not take place until the Security Council has had the opportunity to review the situation and take the further decisions that may be required, on the basis of the report to be submitted by the Secretary-General. This provision leaves open the possibility of a revision of the concept of operations on which, as you know, the U.S. continues to have doubts."

The resolution called for the redeployment of nearly two hundred UNMOs from Nairobi and the buildup of the Ghanaian battalion to full

---

1. Some U.S. politicians wholeheartedly supported UNAMIR 2. On May 5, senators Paul Simon and Jim Jeffords contacted me in Kigali and got first-hand the information they needed to draft a letter to the White House seeking a change in policy from the administration in regards to Rwanda and UNAMIR. In the months to come these gentlemen became my greatest allies in the U.S. government until finally the administration was so embarrassed by the media and by the senators' lobbying that it finally mounted a humanitarian mission. That mission did save the lives of millions—including most of the perpetrators of the genocide—but it did not assist the victims nor did it arrive in time to prevent or stop the genocide. I owe a great debt of gratitude to Simon and Jeffords for at least trying to get Rwanda on the radar screen of the White House.

strength and mechanized capability. This meant training those troops on APCs before we could finally commit them to operations. That would take longer than seven days. As for the phase-two battalions, I would not see them until after the assessment of phase one was studied by the Security Council. If the Western nations continued to refuse to commit mechanized and well-equipped troops for phase two right from the start, then the process of deployment of troops and armoured vehicles, including the marrying-up of both these components for training, then I would not see them in two months or more at best. With that timetable, phase three wouldn't be deployed for three to four months. In that case, the need for any new troops at all would be enormously diminished, as the RPF would have probably won the war and overrun the country.

I went for a walk around the compound that night and wondered what I would do with this lame mandate. I would not get my troops. Should I even attempt to carry on? I listed in my head all that we were up against as I paced. The RGF and the interim government were speaking from both sides of their mouths and showed no real desire for either the ceasefire or the cessation of the massacres. The RPF was opting to go it alone, and wanted to limit UNAMIR to the status of a token observer. The Security Council, under the overbearing weight of the United States, had once again sold us out. The French seemed to be on the sidelines, ready for their cue.

I decided to wait for the morning before making up my mind. I didn't want to give up, but how could I justify staying?

13

ACCOUNTANTS OF THE SLAUGHTER

On May 17 the Security Council approved a watered-down version of my plan as Resolution 918, which officially created UNAMIR 2. While the resolution approved the concept of operations, the force structure and the phased thirty-one-day deployment, it was vague on the genocide and the role the force should play in stopping it. Colin Keating later publicly admitted, "The United States has gutted this resolution." Even so, I was prepared to accept vagueness as permission to execute my plan so long as I was given the required troops—the resolution authorized an immediate change in UNAMIR's mandate and the rapid deployment of 5,500 men. After nearly a decade of reliving every detail of those days, I am still certain that I could have stopped the madness had I been given the means.

But as the days went by and no troops arrived, it was clear that the Security Council had once again passed a resolution that did not truly represent the intentions of its member states. In this case, while most nations seemed to agree that something had to be done, every nation seemed to have a reason why some other nation should do it. So there we sat, waiting for a promise to be kept, reduced to the role of accountants keeping track of how many were being killed.

Madeleine Albright, the U.S. permanent representative to the UN, and Sir David Hannay, her British counterpart, had for some time resisted the use of the term "genocide" in UN debates, but now that their objections had been swamped in a deluge of factual reports out of Rwanda, the United States fell back on the argument that African security problems should be solved by African troops. A number of African states were willing to contribute: Ghana, Ethiopia, Malawi, Senegal, Zimbabwe, Tunisia, Nigeria, Zambia, Congo, Mali and others. But none of them had the logistical capacity to deploy and sustain their forces without help. The burden of sending troops eventually fell to Ghana, Ethiopia, Zambia, India, Canada and Nigeria. With the exception of the Canadians and, to a lesser extent, the Indians, these forces were logistically too weak to deploy themselves without First World assistance. None of the nations that eventually stepped forward had the capacity for the massive reinforcement that might have bought the UN credibility in the eyes of the belligerents.

The United States and the United Kingdom committed other acts of sabotage on deployment to Rwanda. For instance, I had long been arguing with New York that RTLM had to be shut down, as it was a direct instrument in promoting genocide. The UN did not have the means to stop the broadcasts, either through jamming, a direct air strike on the transmitter, or covert operations, but it made a formal request of the United States, which had the means to try all three. The issue was studied by the Pentagon, which in due course recommended against conducting the operation because of the cost—$8,500 an hour for a jamming aircraft over the country—and the legal dilemma. Bandwidth within a nation is owned by the nation, and jamming a national radio station would violate international convention on national sovereignty. The Pentagon judged that the lives of the estimated 8,000–10,000 Rwandans being killed each day in the genocide were not worth the cost of the fuel or the violation of Rwandan airwaves. The death toll, which was estimated at 200,000 by the end of April, reached 500,000 by the end of May and 800,000 by the last day of June.

I had judged that we needed one hundred APCs to be effective on the ground. The DPKO approached forty-four nations to give, lend or lease APCs to the troop-contributing African countries to equip their forces. The United States, with its vast unused Cold War stocks of APCs, eventually supplied fifty. As soon as the United States offered anything at all, the DPKO stopped searching for other donors. And then the stalling began: staff with the Pentagon were reluctant to put their vehicles into central Africa and seemed content instead to let them rust in

German depots. They badgered the DPKO with questions, and staff there passed the questions on to me. Then the United States decided that the APCs could not be given to the mission but would have to be leased and that the lease would have to be negotiated. Eventually they came up with the price of $4 million, which they insisted had to be pre-paid. When the issue was raised of transporting the carriers to Kampala to link them up with the Ghanaians who needed to be trained to oper-ate them, the United States insisted upon another $6 million to cover the cost of air transport. After the funding was secured—another time-consuming exercise—the APCs were airlifted to Entebbe; after much negotiation with Uganda, they arrived stripped of machine guns, radios, tools, spare parts, training manuals and so on. The United States, in effect, delivered tons of rusting metal to Entebbe. We were without trucks to transport the APCs to Kigali and had no drivers trained to operate them.

Not to be outdone by the Americans, the British offered fifty Bedford trucks—again for a sizable amount to be paid up front. The Bedford is an early Cold War–era truck, which in 1994 was fit only to be a museum relic. When I was told of this "most generous" offer, I sar-castically asked, "They do work, don't they?" I was answered first with silence and then: "I'll check and get back to you." The British later quietly withdrew their request for payment and provided some of the vehicles, which broke down one at a time until there were none left. There were many more transactions like these, and they were not iso-lated to the great powers.

While the UN and the international community were dithering about the fate of UNAMIR 2, on the ground in Kigali we were picking up signs that the interim government was getting ready to launch a coherent counteroffensive in the city. The Interahamwe leaders had told my military intelligence officer, Deme, that they had been having exten-sive meetings with Bizimungu. They said they had made a deal with the RGF chief of staff that would allow the militias to carry on as they liked at night, but that required them to work with the RGF on local security operations in the daytime. Taking their cue from Bizimungu, the militias were continuing the genocide after dark with a free hand.

Apart from the inner core of the city, where Presidential Guard units were still running the show, on the barriers we saw more gendarmes working with the Interahamwe. Deme's deduction was that a decision had been made to synchronize all the forces—the military, Gendarmerie and militias—in order to launch a counterattack in the city. A significant number of government forces were still inside Kigali: the army had seven battalions—four thousand troops—as well as the para-commandos, the artillery, the military police battalion and the reconnaissance battalions, who were the most highly trained troops and had heavy weapons systems.

The Interahamwe leaders told Deme that the militia was now split into two factions. The CDR-affiliated Impuzamugambi (in Kinyarwanda "those who have a single aim") would offer no mercy to the Tutsis. The Interahamwe, represented by the leaders I had met with, described itself as the legitimate third force and as "more considerate of the situation." The leaders also admitted that the chances of our transfers succeeding were very slim because they couldn't guarantee that the other faction would respect any agreement they had made. Even if Bagosora said that the transfers would work, they couldn't promise that they would. They advised UNAMIR not to negotiate with the government or the military because we wouldn't get the real answer. "Co-operate with the people," they told Deme, "and avoid the politicians and the heads of the military, for they are telling only lies." I gave this report from my intelligence officer a lot of credence. It confirmed for me that there was going to be a last-ditch effort to save Kigali, and the Interahamwe were in on that plan. Negotiating a ceasefire was a secondary concern: we were about to see these bastards continue the fight, even as they were making nice noises at the negotiating table. Stopping the killing had to be UNAMIR 2's primary mission.

Deme also had news about the other side. The RPF was heavily recruiting Tutsis behind its lines. After basic training, these men were deployed as rear security in the areas that had already been captured. Our UNMOs started to encounter these new troops behind the RPF lines and noticed that some of them spoke only a dialect of Swahili, which meant they came from the Ugandan diaspora. Reports of massacres of Hutus who were former government agents and employees, along with their families, continued to come in. These massacres were mainly conducted in the areas of Byumba and Ngarama. Deme also passed on the news that there was a huge number of Hutu orphans in Byumba, whom Kouchner had gone to check on. To make matters more interesting, the RPF had put heavy restrictions on where our UNMOs could go. The last line of Deme's report read, "It has been established that the restrictions imposed on us are done to conceal their [RPF] activities especially massacres."

Throughout May the RPF continued to pursue their campaign of turning Kigali into a pocket in order to slowly strangle the RGF. They advanced from the north and east and in a large southernly hook, which on May 16 cut the road between Kigali and its large RGF garrison and Gitarama, where the interim government was located—effectively separating the head from the body. Increasingly the morale and discipline of the RGF forces were faltering, as the appearance of RPF patrols on their flanks or in their rear would bring wholesale retreats. Retreats cause defeatism and inevitably a breakdown in discipline; we received an increasing number of reports of RGF troops assisting in the genocide, looting, deserting and mutinying. This process was accelerated when the RGF conducted mass recruiting and conscription campaigns, gave the recruits three to four days of training and then threw them into battle against the seasoned and skilled RPF, which only resulted in the RGF's inevitable defeat and a further deterioration of morale and discipline. At Gitarama, the liaison team of MILOBs that I had finally established with the RGF's consent, was often threatened by drunken and dispirited soldiers.

Around this time, I found out that Mamadou Kane had commandeered an APC to go meet directly with the chief of staff of the RGF. I had no idea what he thought he might achieve by talking with Bizimungu on his own, since we usually went together. When I confronted him about the visit, he denied that he'd even gone.

The pressures on all of us were beyond extraordinary. The fighting around the airport, with the RGF and the RPF firing on each other and anything else that raised its head, curtailed the Hercules flights, cutting drastically the emergency supplies that could get in. We had little food, little medicine and much stress: the result was a sapping of will and commitment among my troops. On a daily basis I saw the increase in sick parade, as more and more soldiers went down with disease, especially malaria. I can't tell you how disgusting daily life could be; the corpse-eating dogs that we shot on sight now had no qualms about attacking the living. One day while I was driving in Kigali, a lone dog attacked my side window while the vehicle was on the move. If I had not had the window up, the dog would have ripped off my arm. Another time, several officers taking a short coffee break saw a strange-looking dog wandering in the compound, then realized it was a rat that had grown to the size of a terrier. One of the officers, who was from Ghana, said that he had seen this after natural disasters back home: the rats fed and fed on an inexhaustible supply of human flesh and grew to an unbelievable size.

We had completely run out of water and were unable to find a source inside the country. I called the new CAO in Nairobi, Allay Golo from Chad, and asked him why there was no water.[1] Golo was a career UN civilian administrator, and he responded that he was bound by UN rules. Even though we had had no water for days, he still had to conduct a call for proposals and then do an analysis of the three best bids. The minimum estimate was a million litres, but securing that much water would take weeks, and we didn't even have days. I told him that even twenty thousand litres would tide us over, but he insisted on following procedure. I couldn't wait, and instead arranged to bring water in from UNOMUR. Even so, all of us, including the people we were sheltering, went without water for two more days.

RTLM was escalating its personal attacks on me. I already knew that I was the target of "third force" death threats. But what brought the

---

1. Christine de Liso, our acting CAO, had been relieved of her duties in early May. A fine human being, she had done everything humanly possible to aid UNAMIR despite the enormous restraints placed on her by the FOD.

hostility out into the open, I think, were my continuing efforts to negotiate safe passage for Tutsis trapped behind RGF lines—combined with the lie that I was plotting to export orphans from Rwanda. It didn't seem to matter to the hate-mongers that I was also trying to transfer Hutus in the other direction. On May 18, RTLM broadcast propaganda against what it described as the Canadians' desire to deport orphans, portraying it as an RPF-inspired attempt to put the extremist government in a bad light. It claimed that Bernard Kouchner and I were part of a cabal working to release the Tutsi refugees from the Mille Collines and the Meridien, ignoring the fact that most of the people in the Meridien were Hutu. The radio recommended the usual culling: "We do not oppose the principle of the release of these refugees, but we must first sort out the RPF sympathizers, who will not be allowed to leave." The extremists were also incensed about Canada's role in pushing for a UN Commission on Human Rights investigation of the genocide.

With hate propaganda targeting us directly, no water and little food, relentless killing all around, military buildups happening on both sides, and clear preparations being made for the escalation of the war, Riza sent me a message on May 20 announcing that he and Maurice Baril aimed to arrive in Kigali in three days for their first visit to UNAMIR. Their stated purpose, Riza said, was not political but humanitarian, to explain the new mandate and advance the ceasefire negotiations. My immediate job was to arrange a two- to three-day truce so that Riza and Baril wouldn't get shot in my company.

The threats got even more personal on May 21, the day that RTLM first openly exhorted its listeners to "kill Dallaire," describing me as the white man with the moustache. If I was seen, the broadcasts said, I was to be stopped and killed immediately. At that point I became the target of any Hutu with a machete. I recognized the escalation of danger to myself, but what this threat also did was put all my white MILOBs in jeopardy, particularly the ones with moustaches. I immediately ordered them to stand down from operations, but even so, a couple of them narrowly escaped from roadblocks with their lives. If I sent them out again, they would run even more than the ordinary risk of being killed.

The RPF forwarded a communication it had intercepted between Bizimungu and his head of operations, in which the chief of staff told the officer that "the order was to eliminate Dallaire." I had no way of corroborating this intercept, and I didn't move on the information since I didn't have definitive proof. Also, with the broadcasting of the command to kill me, the damage had been done.

Whatever stress Mamadou Kane was under did him in around this time: he totally lost it one afternoon. I was in my office when I heard screaming and the sound of running footsteps on the floor above. Kane had gone berserk in the halls, apparently from fear, and locked himself in one of the rooms. His colleagues from political affairs had to break the door down and Beadengar Dessande, a large man, had to sit on him to physically restrain him. The next morning, we flew him out to Nairobi, where he was treated for his breakdown.

The day the death threat went out over hate radio, the HQ came under sustained artillery attack. A few of our troops were injured, vehicles were destroyed, windows were broken, strewing glass all over the place, and the operations centre was damaged. Our crater analysis confirmed that the attack had come from the RGF at Camp Kanombe.

It seemed like another unending marathon. Before the attack, I had met at the Hôtel des Diplomates with Ndindiliyimana, who had finally reappeared earlier in the month at a political session in Gitarama. He had approached me to arrange to meet with him alone in Kigali. And so Ndindiliyimana and I sat together, ostensibly to resolve some Gendarmerie operational concerns with the transfers between the lines. He seemed terribly ill at ease but determined to speak his mind. He warned me that the prefect of Kigali was not to be trusted, and confided that Bizimana, the minister of defence, was despondent due to the failures in the field, the loss of his properties in Byumba, and the deaths of his relatives there. He told me that the moderate faction in the RGF, including Gatsinzi and Rusatira, was growing in strength, yet he could give me no specifics except that most of its members had left Kigali and were now in the south. (Later Deme found out that Gatsinzi had left after he had proposed to the high command that the RGF withdraw to southern Rwanda, and his own troops had threatened him with death.)

The meeting continued for about an hour with Ndindiliyimana doing nearly all the talking. He confided that he had become the protector of a large number of persons in danger in and around Butare. He said that many people had been hiding in the ceilings, the walls and even the latrines of their houses and were now dying of starvation, thirst and worse because we could not get to them. He stressed that it was essential to create a force or a movement that was neither ethnic- nor military-based to govern the country. He gave me names of prominent Tutsis in the Mille Collines who had to be saved from certain death. Yes, I said, the people in the Mille Collines were like live bait being toyed with by a wild animal, at constant risk of being killed and eaten. Yet until the mission was reinforced, I was doing all I could. The militia cordon around the site, the harassing of my UNMOs and blue berets to give the refugees up, the deliberate bombardments, the sniper fire through the windows, the random RPF rounds through the hotel walls, were enough to wear on anyone's resolve. It was admirable, I said, that the Red Cross still made it through the cordon to patch up the injured and help the sick while bringing in water and food.

Ndindiliyimana had one last piece of advice for me. He said that the roadblocks would disappear if I used the threat of force: the local bullies would abandon the barriers when they realized that the risks of being attacked by a reinforced and bolder UNAMIR 2 were high. He believed that if UNAMIR 2 came on strong, the hard-liners would melt away, and he did not think they could readily organize a reappearance. I had sat through most of our session taking in what he said with a healthy skepticism. But he was now essentially confirming the rationale behind my argument for UNAMIR 2. If he was being candid with me, I was saddened that he had never once offered to take on the mantle of leader of the moderate movement. With support from Kagame or even just from us, we might have helped the moderates create another front, confounding the extremists' belief that they were acting in the name of all Hutus. The moderates' ineptness, and lack of courage and commitment would cost them dearly after the RPF victory. As we said our goodbyes, Ndindiliyimana looked like a man who had been to confession but had not received absolution.

Late that afternoon, I had to return to the same hotel to meet with Bizimungu. Because of the now-explicit death threats, I was usually moving around the city in the slow and unreliable APCs. The Tunisians had done wonders to keep them mobile, keeping the engines and other moving parts running with wire and even cloth. They assured me that the main weapon, a heavy machine gun, worked and that they knew how to use it. They never hesitated to point the weapon at the person who controlled a barrier, aiming at his upper thorax and keeping the gun on him no matter where he moved. It was enough to intimidate many of those gangsters of the so-called self-defence forces.

As Diagne and I arrived at the hotel and got out of the APC, we were faced with more than sixty militiamen who were set up in trenches and bunkers replete with heavy weapons, including armour-piercing rockets. My pleasant "Good afternoon" did not erase their scowls, though they let us pass. As I entered the lobby, I saw Bagosora to my right, talking to an officer I did not recognize. Spotting me, Bagosora launched into a tirade, blaming me for the failure of the evacuation of the orphans. His body was spastic with hostility. He accused me of stalling for time in order to make him and the interim government look bad in the eyes of the world. He demanded to know why I was "deliberately" preventing these transfers from happening.

When he finally paused for breath, I told him that I was not totally convinced that the extremist branch of the militias had agreed to the orphan transfer. His face was about a foot from mine, but he screamed his response. He had made sure, he yelled, that the real authorities in the militias had been present at the meeting to arrange the transfer and they, in front of him, had given their word to support this exercise, and that was that. He stomped away. I had seen him angry in the past, but this time he bordered on the berzerk. I had to wonder what was really eating at him.

Despite everything that was going on, I slept rather well the night of May 21. Maybe I was somehow relieved that the death threats against me were now out in the open. I had protested the extensive bombardment of the HQ to Bizimungu and the minister of defence, and I was scheduled to meet them again the next day about the three-day truce we needed for the safe passage of Riza and Baril. Bizimungu could explain to me in person what his troops hoped to accomplish by bombing UNAMIR.

Phil Lancaster woke me up at about 0615 to pass on to me a report from the UNMOs at the airport: during the night the RGF had totally abandoned its positions there and at Camp Kanombe. They had thinned out through a hole in the RPF ring surrounding the camp. I asked him if there had been significant fighting in Kigali overnight or early this morning, since the RPF liked to leave openings for their enemy and then ambush them in the open or on the run. Phil said no, but told me that Tiko had reported that an observer had spotted artillery guns in the western part of the city.

I decided to head to the airfield. I had to ensure that we held our positions there, since my rapid deployment plan for UNAMIR 2 rested on the Kigali airport being open and under our command. I got there in fifteen minutes, moving quickly through checkpoints that had been held by militia and government forces the day before and were now manned by the RPF. When I pulled in, the hazy morning sun was just above the horizon and mist was slowly rising over the edges of the plateau where the runway lay.

Lieutenant Colonel Joe Adinkra was outside the main terminal with a few troops, assessing the situation. We spoke about the adept withdrawal of the RGF forces and the necessity of maintaining our present positions. I told him to be ready to defend his ground. I was surprised that the RPF was nowhere in sight as yet, and thought that it might be concentrating on Camp Kanombe.

The logistics and infantry company were stood-to in their defensive positions across the field. I went directly to the old control tower and looked out over the airfield. I couldn't see Camp Kanombe—it was below the edge of the plateau at the end of the runway. While reports over the Force radio net confirmed that the RGF artillery and reconnaissance battalions were indeed gathering in the west end of the city, the situation here was unnervingly quiet. I was back at my vehicle at the foot of the tower, sending instructions regarding morning prayers, when an observer called out to me that there were people—or were they apparitions?—at the end of the runway.

Scrambling to the top of the nearby defensive earthworks, I looked east and there they were: thin black silhouettes that seemed to rise out of the earth and the morning mist as they crested the lip of the plateau, the sun at their backs, like illustrations out of *Don Quixote*. Lieutenant Colonel Adinkra broke the spell by asking, "What are those things?" I jumped in my vehicle and, followed by a couple of four-by-fours carrying UNMOs, sped down the runway, weaving around chunks of shrapnel that could puncture a tire. The hundreds of wavy silhouettes took clearer form as we drew near. Moving slowly toward us were a number of RGF soldiers, some with their rifles above their heads, others hanging on to the hands of their wives and children, all with their heads down, along with Hutu civilians who had been left behind when the bulk of the troops moved out of Camp Kanombe. When their first officer reached me, he stated in impeccable French that they were the remnants of the RGF battalions from Camp Kanombe and wanted to surrender to me and to UNAMIR. The major added that he hoped his men and their families would be treated as prisoners of war. More of my Ghanaian soldiers had now arrived and, in rather quick time, seized their weapons and escorted them to an area near the main terminal.

I had a problem. These troops and civilians—nearly eight hundred men and their families—had just given themselves up to a neutral force. Technically I couldn't protect the soldiers against their enemy, even though I believed there was a very good chance they would be slaughtered by revengeful RPF troops if I didn't. I told Adinkra to provide tight security for the groups and to have his battalion doctor look to their medical needs, as some of them were severely wounded. He and his Ghanaians were to count them, record their names and wait for further orders. They were not to let the RPF take these people away under any circumstances. The new UNAMIR 2 rules of engagement were to be applied without hesitation.

I left the site as RPF patrols were approaching the airfield. I was not sure of the status of the prisoners, but I was determined that the RPF would not get them without a fight. After consulting with Gaillard,

Henry reminded me of the Geneva Convention statute that allows prisoners of war to be accounted for under Red Cross auspices. Later Gaillard went to the site with a team and conducted official registration procedures as well as providing medical help and sustenance. It took several weeks and the withstanding of threats and bullying from the RPF, but in the end, the soldiers and their families were formally put in the hands of the Red Cross and then handed over to the RPF, with due process observed. Gaillard said we had to trust the RPF in this and that is what I agreed to do.

On May 22 Yaache and his humanitarian team held an important meeting at the Diplomates with Bagosora and the Interahamwe, to discuss the transfers. The meeting was caught on film and is definitive proof that Bagosora controlled (as well as anyone could) the genocidal militia. I was more and more certain that he had some other card up his sleeve but couldn't yet figure out how he would be able to use the transfers to his advantage.

That same day Bizimungu improbably explained to me that he had withdrawn from the airport in order to give it to us as neutral territory. Of course he had never told us he was withdrawing. Since the RPF had moved right in, RTLM soon billed the airport incident as another UNAMIR scandal—we became the ones who had handed the airport over to the enemy. I taxed Bizimungu on the artillery attack on the HQ, though he insisted he had never ordered such an attack.

I had to find another airhead: I didn't trust the RPF to respect my operations. Kagame's forces would now be calling the shots at the airport, and we had found them very uncooperative and single-minded when they wanted to control a situation. My options for a new air base were Bujumbura, Entebbe or Goma, which meant I'd have to undertake negotiations with the governments of Burundi, Uganda and Zaire. These weren't the best prospects. Establishing the airhead at any one of these places would mean that all of the incoming troops and supplies would have to travel significant distances overland. That morning at prayers I had given orders to prepare a thinning out of the force. Henry's Ghanaians had come under fire at the airport; our HQ had been bombarded the day before. Because the airport situation was so dicey, I instructed my commanders to start sending troops out overland. Even with the new mandate, we wouldn't necessarily be able to stay. We were already running the risk of having to fight our way out.

And here I was, expecting Riza and Maurice in the morning. The RPF did not want to guarantee them safe passage on the direct road from Kabale down to Kigali. Instead we had to move them by a circuitous route to the northeast of Rwanda and drive them in the long way. If the RPF had wanted to, it could have opened up the road. I did not buy the argument that it was so beset by the RGF it couldn't do it. But the good thing about Riza and Maurice having to come into the country by such a route was that they would have a snail's-pace tour of the areas ravaged by the slaughter.

Still, that night, for a change, I-didn't feel alone. I was looking forward to seeing Maurice. I also hoped that Riza, a diplomat with the ability to cut through to the heart of matters, would bring some light to the negotiations. I had run out of silver bullets and needed any sort of magic that the two of them could provide.

When Maurice and Riza drove into the compound the next day, I was overjoyed to see them. It was nearly seven weeks into the genocide, and for the first time I felt as though I could let my wildly mixed emotions show. As the commander, you just can't vent on your subordinates and, with Maurice's arrival, I suddenly had a peer in whom I could confide. Riza, by nature more formal, was still a welcome colleague. In a sense, they had not been shocked by the scenes that had greeted them. These gentlemen were running sixteen other missions. They'd been in Somalia during the worst of the killings and the famines. They'd been in Cambodia, Central America, the former Yugoslavia. To a degree they were inured to horror, experienced with it. They weren't neophytes as I had been.

We welcomed them as best we could. We had a supper of the terrible demobilization rations—canned sausages, sardines and beans. Over the next two days, May 24 and 25, I stayed with them all the time. What became noticeable to me as I looked at the city through their eyes was that Kigali had become a ghost town. At most there were maybe twenty to thirty thousand people still living here, clustered in the worst of the shantytowns. Nobody was coming into the city, and no one was escaping it any more. Around us was not a scorched-earth scenario so much as a scorched-human scenario. The RPF was conquering an empty country and conducting its own exactations against any enemies stranded behind the lines. Bizimungu said it this way: "They may gain the country but not the people."

Yet killings were still going on in the city. People who had been hiding for so long were trying to escape to the RPF, who were now as close as the airport. The Interahamwe and the Presidential Guard were going around in the streets presenting themselves as RPF. People would come out to them seeking their protection and instead would be killed. The RPF advance inspired the extremists to get back to work in a ferocious way.

The advance was also concentrating the population in the west, creating a new humanitarian catastrophe of displaced persons and refugees. Hutus, scared to death by hate radio accounts of RPF atrocities, were moving ahead of the withdrawing RGF—vast numbers of them, at least two million. If they continued to move west and into Zaire through Gisenyi and Goma in the north and Cyangugu and Bukavu in the south, it would be a total disaster—those regions were rugged, forbidding, unfriendly, impoverished. In the northeast, where Kagame was securing the countryside, members of the Tutsi diaspora were starting to come back, taking over the lands, even cultivating new crops. It was a very complex humanitarian problem. There was no such thing as an isolated incident. Every event, even the smallest, had ramifications for one side or the other.

I needed Riza and Maurice to be more conscious of the vulnerability of the Kigali airport and my tattered outfit. I wanted them to support me in finding an alternate airhead. I needed a place where the new equipment and the troops could marry up before coming into theatre. Training in front of the belligerents wouldn't exactly impress them with our new ability to use force. A logistics base outside of Rwanda was critical.

I also briefed them on all the ways in which the RPF was conducting a deliberate campaign to undermine us. In meetings the leaders would say yes to all our reasonable requests, but then they would restrict our movements, prevent my people from attending meetings and run independent humanitarian discussions with NGOs. At the same time, the NRA in Uganda was blocking UNOMUR from doing its job, which I was sure was no accident. And, I reminded them, the RGF was still firing on UN installations, the argument being that the RPF had positions around us and we were in the way.

I deeply appreciated Riza's straightforward approach. He led Maurice and me through the night of May 24, reasoning that negotiating the ceasefire directly was an excuse for it never to happen. The strategy he hit on was to create a "declaration of intent to negotiate a ceasefire" that everyone could sign on to as a way to deal with cleaning up all the troublesome preconditions. Once that impasse was broken, we could move on to the ceasefire proper.

I organized four sets of meetings over the two days, since there were really four sets of players—though the thought of counting the interim government as one of those parties made me deeply uneasy. My argument was yes, there were two sides, but one of the sides had partially disappeared. The interim government bore no relationship to the original government, even though Rwanda's representative on the Security Council reported to it. The majority of the members of the original Arusha-bound government were either dead or in hiding because they were moderates. If you acknowledged the interim government, you were acknowledging the power of the Hutu ethnicity. And that was exactly what the ministers of the interim government in Gitarama told Riza when they met. They bluntly said that the war was an ethnic war. The RPF insisted it was a political war—a fight for democracy in Rwanda. But the RPF refused to recognize that the RGF's strings were being pulled by the politicians in Gitarama. Riza was being drawn toward negotiating with the interim government even though we had not resolved how to recreate the political side of the RGF so that it *could* negotiate under Arusha rules. Apart from my attempts to support the moderate members of the RGF, no one was working on how to establish a moderate political voice in this killing zone.

My superiors' other brief was humanitarian. The RPF insisted that it had to control aid distribution in its zones, and the result was that the NGOs were directly sustaining the war effort: quantities of aid ended up feeding RPF troops on the front lines. On the RGF side, humanitarian aid was limited to what could be provided by the Red Cross, whose special immunity generally allowed it to move reasonably unimpeded in RGF zones. But other NGOs attempting to help were attacked, injured or robbed at the roadblocks and there seemed to be no way to guarantee their safety. Riza and Maurice believed that the way to move forward here was the way outlined in my concept of operations for UNAMIR 2: create safe sites where people could congregate, be protected and receive aid. (This gave me great satisfaction because Maurice told me he was still fighting the Pentagon regarding the effectiveness of my operational plan.)

Their final report, shaped by what they saw, was written in UN-ese by people who were far more skilled than I at expressing themselves in terms that the institution would accept. There was nothing new in the report, but it was presented by a senior authority within the echelons of the organization. And it finally recognized (in Riza's words and presented to the Security Council on May 31 as a report from the secretary-general) that "[i]t would be senseless to attempt to establish a ceasefire and to allow deliberate killings of civilians in the RGF zone to continue. There is the danger that if not stopped this would lead to the setting off of a prolonged cycle of violence. I repeat that a halt to the killings of civilians must be concomitant with a ceasefire. . . . The immediate priorities are to relieve the suffering of the displaced population and the fears of civilians under threat." This was music to my ears because it brought to the fore the potential mass movement behind the RGF lines of millions of people scared insensate by the spectre of RPF retribution. "This requires organized humanitarian relief operations, which cannot be launched on the scale required unless adequate security conditions for them can be established. UNAMIR has already prepared its plans to provide these conditions, which encompasses the second priority, the security of concentrations of civilians in peril." That was another major breakthrough: I now had the offensive authority to actually, finally, be able to do something to stop the killing.

The trouble was (as Riza, Maurice and I all knew) that the UN did not have the capacity to achieve this aim by itself: the international community had to step in. "Our readiness and capacity for action has been demonstrated to be inadequate at best and deplorable at worst. . . . the entire system requires review to strengthen its reactive capacity. It is my intention that such a review be conducted." The report became the catalyst for Security Council Resolution 925, passed on June 8, to authorize the concurrent advance of the phase-one and phase-two troops. I was amazed that Boutros-Ghali and the Security Council were able to secure that change so rapidly after the visit of the senior UN officials and the delivery of their report. It is a travesty that no one came sooner.

Over those two days with me, Riza and Maurice experienced nearly all the dangers UNAMIR encountered on a daily basis; despite the supposed three-day safe passage, we were fired upon. I still remember the look on their faces when we all climbed into an APC in the UNAMIR compound for the trip across Kigali to meet with Bizimungu at the Diplomates—a journey that would last thirty to forty minutes. As we settled ourselves as best we could, Maurice and I commented on the poor internal design of the old Warsaw Pact–APC but Riza stayed quiet. Maurice told me later that Riza suffered excruciating pain from a very damaged back that plagued him, to varying degrees, most of the time, and that the APC ride was almost more than he could take. We were reasonably safe for a while as we travelled through RPF territory, but when the crew commander informed me that we were approaching the RGF zone, I took my pistol out of its holster and chambered a bullet, and the Tunisian escort nearest to the door did the same with his light machine gun. Maurice and Riza clearly wondered why I felt such measures were necessary inside a supposedly secure if elderly APC. I explained over the vehicle noise that the Interahamwe and self-defence groups regularly stopped the APCs and looked inside. The escort and I wanted to be ready if somebody recognized me and decided to be a hero and "kill Dallaire."

The trip to Gitarama and back brought them face to face with the true dimension of the displaced population inside Rwanda. We left my

HQ mid-morning, travelling in my four-by-four, an escort vehicle with my protection squad behind us, along with two functioning APCs. The road was packed with tens upon tens of thousands of Rwandans fleeing the RPF. It took us three tense hours to reach our destination, slowly edging our way through the crowds, witnessing up close the suffering of old people too tired or sick to put one foot ahead of the other, men stooped under the burden of carrying the remaining family possessions on their heads, women in despair because their children could not walk any farther and they hadn't the strength left to carry them. My Ghanaians stuck close, but the APCs, underpowered and much larger than our four-by-fours, were left far behind.

We had our meeting but also knew that we had to be back in Kigali before dark or face the consequences. We were just heading out of the compound when the APCs lumbered into view and I had to tell the crew commanders to turn right around and follow us back.

The usual afternoon deluge had started, the rain beating down so hard at times that the wipers could not keep up and we'd have to stop. We lost the APCs, even though we were barely inching along the winding road with its endless procession of lost souls. Maurice made a comment about the missing APCs. The fact that there were still another fifteen or so barriers of half-drunk, ruthless and totally unpredictable Interahamwe between us and Kigali may have been bothering him, along with the fact that every extremist of whatever kind knew my face and was aching to shoot me on the spot. Then, in the midst of this drenched, tired and unfriendly human serpent of suffering and death, I hit a long-horned cow.

Though I had only been creeping along, the cow had been knocked clean over. I could only imagine the reaction of the person who had managed to get the animal this far along the road. The cow was a very precious commodity as well as a sign of standing in the community in Rwanda. If I had killed it, it would be very bad news.

The crowd that surrounded us stopped moving and stared at us menacingly: we were three non-African gentlemen, in dry clothes, sitting in an air-conditioned vehicle. As far as they were concerned, we had been elbowing them off the road down a rather steep slope or squeezing them against the side of the muddy hill. And now we had hit a cow.

But before I could open the door (still debating if I should), the cow staggered up in front of us, shaking its head and leaning slightly on the hood. It then dragged its owner off to the ravine side of the road, to the sudden laughter of everyone around.

I took a few very deep breaths before pushing on. My colleagues had been silent throughout the incident, but soon similar war stories from other conflict zones came pouring out of both of them, laced with black humour.

One last note on that visit: Riza and Baril had to leave as they had come, circuitously by road, because I still couldn't guarantee their safety on the main route north to Kabale. They were picked up by helicopter at the Ugandan border and flown to Entebbe. There, a UN plane was supposed to carry them to Nairobi and beyond. Booh-Booh was now established in Nairobi and was hopping all over the continent, contacting African governments to ask for troops, even though that was a job that needed to be coordinated out of the DPKO. He had demanded that staff in Nairobi rent him a house so he could live in proper ambassadorial style but was ordered to make do on his various trips with only one aide. Riza and Maurice were temporarily stranded in Entebbe because Booh-Booh had commandeered the aircraft that was supposed to be seconded for their use.

Heavy negotiations were in full swing in New York regarding the problems of scrounging equipment and finalizing the troop-contributing nations. Ethiopia was still in, though I was very surprised that the Ethiopians were capable of sending a peacekeeping force, given that they were just finishing their own civil war and were not trained in peacekeeping—in fact, they were a rebel army, not a professional one. (Moen also passed on to me his concern that Rwandan Hutus might take Ethiopian peacekeepers the wrong way, as they were viewed as being genetically linked to the Tutsis, though neither the interim government nor the RGF ultimately raised any objections.) But the days of calling upon the dozen or so veteran troop-contributing nations were over and, in desperation, complete neophytes were being thrust into some of the most complex operations ever managed by the UN. I thought this was not only technically wrong, but ethically wrong in some cases. Booh-Booh had even gone looking for troops in some nations where I'd be surprised if the politicians could spell the words "human rights."

Between the visit of Riza and Maurice and June 6, I sent the DPKO three separate assessments regarding the way events could unfold and how that might affect the mission and future deployment. For days on end I sent reconnaissance teams out in large numbers to gather any possible field intelligence. I even created a small fifth column of four UNMO teams chosen by Tiko, who received orders from me personally. They were exceptionally courageous officers who became precious assets in my search for operational information. They also conducted delicate missions between the various players, including the RGF moderates, Kagame and me.

I again reported to the DPKO my fear that the RGF, faced with defeat, might receive instructions from the interim government to commence a slow thinning out and withdrawal of military and militia forces west into Zaire in order to fight another day. By making a strategic withdrawal westward, they could pursue their policy of scorched humans while moving the bulk of the Hutu population ahead of them into exile in the surrounding provinces of Zaire. Many powerful members of the extremist regime were alive and well in France and even Belgium. They were in touch with the interim government as well as the Rwandan ambassador to the UN and could be tapped to come to the aid of extremists at home. Half a million Rwandans had already flowed into Tanzania, where they lived under the tacit control of the extremists; I thought we could expect four to five times that number to move into the Kivu province of Zaire. I needed up-to-date information on the movements of large numbers of internally displaced persons in the western part of the country in order to help them in situ and prevent this massive human exodus. Repeated requests to Western nations for aerial photographs and satellite pictures fell on deaf ears. (Later, the Russians were prepared to sell me satellite images, but I had no budget for such an expenditure and could persuade no one to give me one.) I had no choice but to employ my UNMOs, putting their lives at risk every day, in order to keep up with the interim government and the state of the masses of displaced Rwandans, who were dying in droves from hunger, fatigue and sickness along the escape routes or were being weeded out and executed by the machete strokes of the extremists. If the refugees made it to Zaire, the extremists most likely would be running the camps in no time, preparing for revenge. If such a scenario came to pass, it would not only guarantee instability in Rwanda for years to come but destabilize the entire region.

Still, for a brief time I felt as if we were on a bit of a roll. The day after Maurice and Riza left, carrying with them a report that basically endorsed everything I had been saying about how to proceed, I got a copy of the report of the UN Human Rights Commission's Special Session on Rwanda in Geneva. The session recognized without hesitation that this horror show in Rwanda was a human rights violation and that the world should be acting to stop it. The session agreed to send in a team, which would arrive in early June, to begin the investigation to determine who the perpetrators of the genocide were.

I was fascinated to find out that at the Geneva meeting (which happened at the same time as Riza and Maurice were with me in Kigali), the United States, France, Germany and Australia had all issued statements that acknowledged the horrors taking place in Rwanda, but none of them offered concrete help. Geraldine Ferraro, who led the U.S. delegation, actually announced that she supported UNAMIR's efforts. The French claimed that the word "genocide" was not too strong to classify the events in Rwanda. Lucette Michaux-Chevry, the French minister of human rights, declaimed to the assembled diplomats, "As requested by France, the Security Council had significantly expanded UNAMIR." She patted her nation on the back shamelessly: "Without delay, France had provided exceptional assistance to the victims of the conflict." Yes, I thought, to the French expatriates who wanted to flee and to members of the Habyarimana family.

Around this time we received a fax from the Canadian Association of African Studies in Montreal informing us that members of Faustin's family were still alive in Kigali and asking if UNAMIR could do something. This request may seem unusual seven weeks into the genocide, but during the last week of May, General Kagame also sent word to me that ten members of his extended family were still in hiding in the city. How was it possible that he, the bitterest foe of the extremists, still had surviving family in this extremist-controlled ghost town? We sent UNMOs to the places where Faustin's and Kagame's relatives were hiding. We managed to save Faustin's brother-in-law with help from the Red Cross. In the case of Kagame's relatives, my MILOBs went to the house, knocked on the door, checked around and found no one. They decided to try again the next day, but when they returned they discovered only bodies lying on the floor. Somebody had obviously noticed the MILOBs' visit and had staked out the house, flushing out the family. These were the kind of situations that absolutely haunted us: by going to help we sometimes imperilled those we hoped to save.

As I had guessed from my private session with Ndindiliyimana, late May marked the last gasp of the moderates. One day at the HQ I received a letter from Rusatira and Gatsinzi, passed to me in secret. They told me they were living in the south with some former students of the military school, and they wanted me to tell Kagame that when the RPF got to them, they would not resist and did not want to be attacked. When I conveyed the message, Kagame was not impressed. As far as he was concerned, these men should have publicly resisted the extremists right from the start and now had to accept the consequences for themselves, their few living supporters and their families.

The first successful transfer happened on May 27, organized impeccably by Clayton Yaache and the humanitarian cell. We moved RPF sympathizers from the Mille Collines to a town southeast of Kigali, and Hutus from the Amahoro to a drop-off point outside the city, which was still in RGF hands—about three hundred people in total. I wanted to be part of the first transfer and joined the RPF convoy because we thought it might run into the most trouble. I made sure that everyone knew I was part of that convoy, and we passed through checkpoints without incident. When we got to the town where the refugees were to be handed over, crowds were waiting to greet them. There was such an explosion of pent up emotion—so much hugging and crying—that these hungry people hadn't even touched the meal that had been laid out for them as I headed back to my headquarters. (On my way back to Kigali that day, I met the little boy who so deeply tested my resolve about orphans, an encounter I described in the introduction of this book.)

The transfer the other way was also successful, though the convoy was fired upon at the Kadafi Crossroads. The RPF held the hills on the east side, overlooking the bridge, and the RGF was dug in on the west. There was no welcoming party to greet these souls when they reached the drop-off point, which was just a spot on the road to Gitarama, about seven kilometres outside Kigali. The RGF personnel simply told the people to start walking.

We had another transfer planned for the next day, but we decided to postpone it. We needed to improve protection on the trucks and arrange for RGF observers to scrutinize the selection of their people at the Amahoro Stadium so that they could be sure the transfer was done fairly and freely. I found it ironic that we had gotten the undisciplined Interahamwe to observe the transfer truce only to have the other transfer fired upon by the RPF.

I kept my UNMOs busy trying to fill in all the blanks regarding what was happening in Rwanda and making regular rounds to all our protected sites. There were two areas of the country where information was really sketchy. One was in and around Gisenyi, close to the Zairean border. That area was significant because I had been told that the interim government was moving its members there. The second area was in Cyangugu, on the western side of the huge southern forest. We'd heard that large pockets of Tutsis were hiding out in the forest and that others had been massacred. I needed to know where the government was moving to and what was happening at the border at Goma because I'd also heard that large quantities of arms and ammunition were coming through the border. In the south I was concerned mostly about keeping some kind of handle on the humanitarian situation, though I also wanted to check out a rumour that there had been some French-speaking white males spotted in Cyangugu. I wondered whether we might see an increase in white mercenaries being brought in on the RGF side. In order to get more hard data, I sent two large reconnaissance teams of UNMOs to both places. Later I would find out that the gang going to Gisenyi encountered thirty-eight major roadblocks where the militia members were barely able to restrain their hatred of all things UN. The team headed to Cyangugu had to negotiate through fifty-two roadblocks.

We didn't have the manpower to guard most of the sites around Kigali where people were gathered in an effort to be safe. I sent patrols several times a day to the orphanages, schools and churches to check on security and drop off food and supplies, but finally the need was so dire, especially at the orphanages, that I ordered MILOBs to start spending the nights with the most-threatened refugees. My hope was that the MILOBs' presence would deter the killers and, just as at the Mille Collines, it seemed to work. We also safely evacuated some seven hundred Zaireans and Tanzanians who had been holed up at their embassies and had run out of food.

On May 30, at our headquarters, we held the first ceasefire negotiation meeting aimed at gaining consensus on Riza's idea of declaring an intent to reach a ceasefire. Like old times, it was a security nightmare, but at least we had finally gotten the belligerents to meet face to face and to profess good intentions. The most surprising development of the day came from Ephrem Rwabalinda, the RGF liaison officer to UNAMIR, who asked whether UNAMIR could help find ways to reduce the tensions between the factions, including taking action against hate radio. He said he wanted all radio broadcasts toned down, which was an incredible statement to be uttered on behalf of the RGF. (Later, Rwabalinda was killed in an ambush while going over to the RPF.)

That day I also received word that Brian Atwood, the U.S. under-secretary for foreign aid, was in Nairobi, and I insisted that he needed to meet with me. His schedule was tight, but I arranged to see him for a couple of hours in the VIP lounge at the airport in Nairobi. I flew out early on the morning of May 31, climbing aboard a Hercules aircraft for the first time since being in Rwanda. My uniform was relatively clean and pressed but did not smell all that wonderful. About the rest of me, all I can say is that I'd washed my neck and my arms up to the elbows.

At takeoff, instead of climbing into the air, the Hercules immediately swooped off the edge of the plateau and down into a valley. The passengers, all from UNAMIR, were crammed in the aircraft and sitting on flak jackets and blankets; some even wore their steel helmets to protect them from stray bullets. Sitting up in the cockpit, I got my initiation in nap-of-the-earth flying. We followed valleys and skimmed the tops of mountains, nearly picking bananas off the trees, until we hit the Tanzanian border. We then flew northeast to Kenya at a normal altitude. I was queasy, and the people in the back were throwing up. The pilots were clearly proud of themselves—I hope for their flying skills and not for how many of us got sick as a result of their evasion tactics.

At the airport in Nairobi, I nearly had to fight my way into the VIP lounge because I was apparently missing certain papers I hadn't known I needed. The mix-up only reinforced my opinion of the airport staff—the same ones to whom I had paid several U.S. dollars the previous October to be able to board an aircraft to take over command of my mission.

Atwood arrived about fifteen minutes after I did, trailing a large entourage. I launched into him, laying out on the table between us my commander's tactical map. There was no substitute for U.S. logistical capacity and no doubt in my mind of the dominance of the United States in the Security Council, I said. I insisted that the United States should provide the equipment and the airlift capability for UNAMIR 2. I then proceeded to describe my concept of operations in detail, and for one of the first times in public, I warned that if the millions of Rwandans on the move to the west pushed into Zaire and Burundi, the world would end up with a cataclysmic regional problem, not a Rwandan problem. I needed immediately the means to prevent that vast exodus. I told him that the fighting in Kigali was not over and that heavy ammunition was still coming into Rwanda, particularly on the RGF side—the embargo that had been established on May 17 was useless, as it was not being implemented. Atwood was a friendly, easygoing chap, but the keeners travelling with him kept pushing me for "clarification."

Finally Atwood asked me for my bottom line, as Americans are wont to do. I replied, "Send the equipment to put the peacekeeping troops effectively on the ground last week. Without the equipment, UNAMIR can do nothing. Without the strategic lift of the United States, no one will ever get there."

We shook hands, and as he left, he told me he would do his best. I sat for a time in the dark, wood-panelled lounge, feeling as if I had just been interrogated by the court and was now awaiting my sentence. One of my UNMOs had gone down to the canteen and bought me a sandwich—I had not tasted fresh bread for nearly two months. I got on the Hercules and flew back to Kigali willing that sandwich to stay down.

Mid-afternoon that day, to the now usual cacophony of small-arms fire and artillery noise, I completed my thirty-four-page reassessment of the situation and sent it off to New York. And then I found out that Captain Diagne Mbaye of Senegal had been hit by mortar fragments fired by the RPF at an RGF roadblock while he was bringing back a message for me from Bizimungu. Diagne was dead before he hit the dashboard. He was the MILOB who had saved Prime Minister Agathe's children, and in the weeks since, he had personally saved the lives of dozens upon dozens of Rwandans. Braving direct and indirect fire, mines, mobs, disease and any number of other threats, he eagerly accepted any mission that would save lives. In our HQ we observed a minute of silence in his honour, and on June 1 we held a small parade for him at the airport, behind sandbags, with the sound of artillery fire in our ears. His body was flown home, wrapped in a blue refugee tarp, another hero of Rwanda. As one of his fellow MILOBs said, "He was the bravest of us all." The BBC's Mark Doyle, who considered Diagne a friend, recently wrote to me, "Can you imagine the blanket media coverage that a dead British or American peacekeeper of Mbaye's bravery and stature would have received? He got almost none." (Doyle did write about him much later in *Granta* magazine.)

June 1. I decided to enlist the help of the Gendarmerie to go look for a safer westward route out of the city, one that would avoid the RPF gauntlet and the RGF no man's land. We took a fairly large loop through some pretty rough trails. The rain fell so hard during the rainy season that it didn't have time to sink in, eroding the roads and leaving behind inches of slippery mud. On our trek we reached a washout on the slope of a hill and tried to run it. One of the vehicles slid and tumbled away down the hill. Luckily, nobody was injured.

We abandoned the vehicle that had tumbled, taking the distributor cap out of it so it couldn't be easily appropriated. About a week later, one of my UNMOs saw the truck in the hands of the RPF. The vehicle had been smeared with mud to try to camouflage the UN markings. The RGF also spotted the vehicle and concluded that this was simply another way that UNAMIR was favouring the RPF. Eight of our vehicles had been abandoned in various parts of the country by this point, and I had to commence a campaign of negotiation to get the RPF not to use them.

We continued along lanes and paths that often took us through the middle of villages that did not appear on any map. In one village, we stopped to wait for all the vehicles to catch up to us. The path we were on had been one of the exit trails used by people fleeing Kigali. There were remnants of a barrier here, and many people had been killed and thrown in the ditches and on the sides of the road. As I got out to wait, I looked at the bodies, which seemed relatively fresh. Just as I glimpsed the body of a child, it moved. I wasn't sure if it was my imagination, but I saw the twitching of the child and wanted to help. I leaned down to pick the child up, and suddenly I was holding a little body that was both tingling and mushy in my hands. In a second I realized that the movement was not the child but the action of maggots. I was frozen, not wanting to fling the child away from me but also not wanting to hold it for a second longer. I managed to set the body down and then stood there, shaky, not wanting to think about what was on my hands.

We carried on with the reconnaissance of the road. In the early afternoon we crested a hill and before us stretched a huge encampment of the internally displaced, people who had managed to pass through all the roadblocks out of Kigali. The sky was lowering with dark rain clouds, and a blue wave of refugee tarps rose up to greet it; it was as if we were looking out at an ocean of the displaced. We drove very slowly down the hill and up through the camp, heading for the aid station that was set up near the top of the next rise. There were so many people jammed together on these hills that every little motion caused ripples of movement in every direction. The masses were so great it was hard to perceive the individuality of the people—there were so many faces, so many eyes. Clothing that had once been bright was drained of colour and smeared with dirt so that everything was a uniform brown.

The Red Cross workers here were locals, and they were overwhelmed by the demands on them. I told them how courageous they were and how impressed I was that the Red Cross was able to deliver some assistance in all parts of Rwanda. One of the elders in the crowd surrounding us began to speak. He told me that many of them had had to leave in such haste that they had left behind essentials. Since they'd arrived here, he said, they had received aid in the form of maize, and he held out a bit to show me. It was cattle corn, recognizable by its large, hard, jagged kernels. He said that they did not have the tools they needed to grind the kernels. They did not have the pots to cook the corn in to make it softer. They didn't have the water to put into the pot or the wood to build a fire to heat it. The uncooked maize was not edible, yet some of the children were so hungry they ate it. The jagged kernels ripped their digestive tracts and caused internal bleeding. The children were dying of it, bleeding through their bowels. With an ineffably sad face, this man asked me what I could do. I couldn't find an answer. In shame, I went back to my vehicle and we drove back to Kigali.

The road back was just as difficult and circuitous as the road in, but it did provide me with time to think with bitterness about how slow the humanitarian response had been. Rome, Paris, Geneva and New York were still demanding assessment upon assessment. Instead of coming to the aid of roughly two million people, the international community and aid groups were still conducting analyses of what was really needed. That night at evening prayers, I received Yaache's report on the situation, along with one from the new UNREO representative, Charles Petrie. Petrie was in despair about the continuous demands for assessments. I turned to him and said that in his next assessment, he could quote me: "Tell them to send me food, fuel, medical supplies and water for two million people, and we will work out the details of distributing it, but for God's sake tell them to start sending it!"

A couple of years later I met some of those decision-makers and assessment-demanders, who took the opportunity to tell me that I had been looking at the situation in a "simplistic fashion."

June 1 was also the day that the number two man in the Canadian Defence department, Bob Fowler, and the number three man in the Canadian Forces, Admiral Larry Murray, arrived for a twenty-four-hour visit. Fowler had taught English at the University of Butare in the 1960s and had a warm spot for this small, tortured country, huddled amongst the big boys of Africa. As chief of operations, Admiral Murray wanted to check out the situation in person before making recommendations to his boss in Ottawa regarding Canadian military participation. As time was short, we ran them through a series of briefings at Force HQ, and then I sent them out to see the protected sites, the Red Cross hospital and as much of the city as possible, and also to meet for a brief session with Bizimungu at the Diplomates. In order to make the whole affair complete, several rounds landed near the hotel while Fowler and Murray were there.

That evening, we had a supper of canned sausages and beans, with water to wash it down. We sat on mismatched chairs in a small conference room off the main hall, crowding around tables that were too large for the room, so that there was barely space to move, though we had plenty of fresh air and bugs thanks to the previous artillery bombardments and a lack of plastic or plywood to cover the holes.

The conversation was lively and the atmosphere warm. One point raised several times was our regard for the exceptional work being done by the Canadian aircraft and crews. I explained to Fowler and Murray that it had gotten to the point where the mere sound of the aircraft engines gave a tremendous boost to our morale. The sense of both isolation and vulnerability that we all suffered from every now and again was totally alleviated when we heard those planes. I almost didn't care if the planes came in empty, as long as they came in, and I thanked Fowler and Murray for leaving me these aircraft and their crews, who risked their lives on a regular basis and had the bullet holes in the frames of those old Hercs to prove it.

We made speeches to each other. At the end of Admiral Murray's remarks, he asked me to stand up, and then and there he awarded me the Meritorious Service Cross. He pinned it on my uniform in front of my closest brothers in war, and I could barely stay upright and composed. I was proud to be honoured in this way, yet ashamed that I was being decorated ahead of so many of my troops. I had had soldiers and officers die in theatre, and had several others evacuated because of injuries sustained in the line of duty, or because of sickness due to lack of medical supplies, and yet they had not been recognized in such a fashion. One more bittersweet memory of Rwanda.

That night our guests slept in the discomfort of our HQ. We had planned a visit to the RPF for the next day, but in the morning we couldn't secure the clearances, and the route was under considerable fire. So we went up to the roof and I pointed out a number of sites in and around Kigali. They got to see an assault by the RPF in a quarter of the city less than two kilometres away.

On June 2, I received a message from Kofi Annan, asking me to provide extra protection at a place called Kabgayi. It was a huge Catholic mission not far from Gitarama. The Red Cross had reported that there were about thirty thousand people there, as well as a large number of prelates and priests. The RPF had surrounded the place, and Annan told me that the Pope himself had requested extra security for the people there. I responded, "I will continue to send UNMOs to visit Kabgayi as often as I can spare them, but I can do no more until I get more troops."

At the ceasefire meetings, which Henry had been chairing, both sides agreed again to respect a truce for the continued evacuation or transfers of refugees. On June 3, we decided to try another one. I thought it would be wise for Henry to go along with the RGF convoy and to be conspicuous in the area of Kadafi Crossroads to see if the RPF was still going to fire. Even with Henry and a UNAMIR APC planted there, mortar fire still came from the RPF zone.

I decided that I would wait for the returning convoy in plain view at the crossroads, with Phil, my escort, and a couple of APCs. As I was standing there, out in the open, chatting with a few of my men, an RGF soldier appeared from the ditch behind us. He was a sergeant, clearly in rough shape, tattered but armed to the teeth; he was the RGF guard in this no man's land. He talked with us a little and then pointed up the hill to show us where the RGF was positioned. I reached for the binoculars around my neck to check it out—I'd brought them so I could spot from the smoke where the mortars were situated if the RPF fired. The soldier was intrigued by the binoculars. I took them off and let him look through them, and it was clear that this was a first for him. With my binoculars in hand, he eyed my flak jacket and asked what it did and how it felt to wear it. I took it off and helped put it on him, and I wrapped the binoculars around his neck. For a brief moment he was in heaven.

I asked for my flak jacket back, and just as he was handing it to me, a mortar round fell and hit the hard asphalt about ten metres from where we were standing. It sprayed chunks of the road and hot metal in all directions. Instinctively everybody dropped to the ground, including the RGF soldier. I didn't move. I had my flak jacket in one hand, and everybody else was on the ground. As soon as they realized they weren't hit, they all scrambled for the protection of the APCs. I noticed a piece of hot metal stuck in my trouser leg, but I stayed put and calmly put my flak jacket back on. I then turned toward the RGF soldier to get my binoculars back, but he was nowhere to be seen. And I thought, "That's okay, he liked the binoculars so much, he can have them."

Phil urged me, in not very tactful language, to take cover in an APC. Instead I walked to where the crater was, and he followed me, and we undertook a crater analysis. It had been a light mortar round and it had come from the RPF lines. The crews moved the APCs away from the crossroads, but for the five minutes or so before the convoy got there, I stood my ground, naked to incoming fire. The empty convoy finally moved by me, and there was no more shooting. Over the course of the mission, we rescued ten thousand people in this fashion, never knowing whether we would be fired upon.

• • •

That night, Yaache sent me a formal letter, drafted by Don MacNeil, informing me that the Ghanaian soldiers as well as the UNMOs considered these high-risk missions unessential and thought they were being exposed to danger unnecessarily. I understood their complaint, but I didn't agree. Not only were the transfers one of the few positive acts we could perform, they were also helping to reduce the numbers of people we had to shelter and feed. Still, coming on top of the events at the crossroads, I welcomed the letter because it helped me to decide to put an end to the transfers until the RPF came to its senses. I was also troubled as to what the RGF was doing with its people once they were dumped on the road; their zones were totally chaotic. And there was another complication we had to contend with before we could proceed with more transfers: not everybody sheltering with us wanted to leave. Some did want to seek the safety of their own sides. Some wanted to get out of the country altogether, though in order to accomplish that, we had to ensure they had the right documentation, or Nairobi would send them back. But a surprising number wanted to stay, and I had to admit there was logic to that. With us they were receiving some assistance and minimal protection, and they were not keen to throw themselves into total uncertainty.

That night I wrote a sharp letter of protest to Kagame over the mortar fire at the crossroads. I made it quite clear that his senior liaison officer to UNAMIR had okayed the whole operation and that we had received confirmation from his side that everything was a go. I reminded him that my ROE permitted retaliatory fire. I closed with, "I must insist on your personal response on this matter. I will, once again, personally deploy to Kadafi Crossroads when and if we resume the displaced persons exchange to monitor the situation."

Less than twenty-four hours later, I had a contrite written response from the general. He wrote that the local battalion commander had not obeyed his orders and that serious disciplinary action was being taken. Later, we heard two rumours about what may have happened to that battalion commander. One was that he was severely chastised and sent to take up an ignominious command in the rear. The other was that this particular battalion commander was a fanatical Hutu-hater, that he had already been in trouble with Kagame for taking too many losses, and that he was taken away and shot.

Since Bernard Kouchner had left Kigali, he had often been in touch with the humanitarian cell regarding the Rwandan orphans. In his capacity as the president of a French NGO, he asked our permission and aid to evacuate a group of very sick children to Paris. We finally said we would get them out if Kouchner could negotiate an agreement from both sides.

The evacuation of over fifty children went ahead on June 4. The plan was that the Canadian Hercules would arrive in the morning in Kigali with Canadian military nurses on board, and after off-loading, would pick up the children and fly to Nairobi. There, a French military hospital aircraft would be waiting to take them directly to Paris. Our end of the operation went well. Early that morning the children were loaded on board, where the nurses stabilized them for the flight. Some of the children were coping with severe injuries, and many were terrified because they'd never been on an aircraft before.

The flight arrived just past midday in Nairobi. But there was no French aircraft waiting, and the Kenyans didn't want the kids to get off the plane. It was a sweltering day, exacerbated by the heat from the asphalt runway. The children were stuck in the plane for over nine hours, and their health suffered badly—one of the children was reported to have died. That night the hospital aircraft finally arrived, and the children were loaded and taken to Paris. The flight landed the next morning in France at a time of day that guaranteed the maximum exposure in the press.

The batch of code cables I was handed on the morning of June 5 informed me that the battalion being considered for the phase-three deployment was from Bangladesh. What could I say?

Henry was away in Nairobi, sitting in on a meeting that Booh-Booh was chairing as a run-up to a summit in Tunis, organized by the OAU, which was determined to broker a ceasefire. That morning at prayers, I asked for a status report on our resources—I particularly wanted to know how many vehicles were functioning and how much food and fuel we had left. It turned out we had about a dozen trucks and forty to fifty working four-by-fours, depending on how ingenious the UNMOs could be. We had a small amount of fuel to keep the generators at the Amahoro, the King Faisal and the Mille Collines running, but we were down to next to nothing for the vehicles. Even if I thought the situation was safe, I couldn't send out a transfer convoy for fear of running out of gas. (I asked Kagame the next day if he had a bit of fuel I could borrow, but in that crisis, it was the Red Cross who came through, lending us the fuel for one more transfer.)

When it came to my troops, I was constantly worried about how far I could push them and how I could keep them motivated to the point where they would risk their lives, especially in the transfers. Henry's steadfastness went a long way in propping up the morale of many of the African UNMOs and, of course, his own Ghanaians. He had also forged a strong bond with Tiko, who was considered a saint by the UNMOs. Tiko had never once left an UNMO in a precarious situation. Henry and Tiko together were able to keep the vulnerable and overtaxed UNMOs going flat out.

The surprise of the day was the sudden visit of the Italian foreign minister, who was scheduled to arrive that morning at the airport and was expecting me to greet him. We quickly drew up a schedule for him, and at about 1000, I arrived at the main terminal to wait for the plane. Finally we heard the engines and all moved outside to watch the landing. The Hercules was used to coming in under fire and had developed a routine where it would land, circle in front of the terminal, letting its ramps down and laying pallets in a line as it moved in front of us, like a goose laying eggs. This time the plane had turned and the crew chief had lowered the ramps, when heavy mortars hit just behind the tower. The roar of the plane obscured the sound of the explosion, but when I saw the plume of smoke that billowed up, I gave the sign to the pilot to get out of there. The pilot reacted immediately, turning up the engines and starting to move. But the crew chief was on the ground, connected to the plane by the line from his headset, and as the plane started to move, he was pulled along. The big goose of a plane rolled forward, and he was trying to lift the ramps back into the plane. One of my

Canadian UNMOs, Captain Jean-Yves St-Denis, instinctively ran to help. They got one ramp up and then tried for the second—the plane was now moving so fast that the crew chief was running behind, with us cheering him on. Finally they got the ramp up, the crew chief jumped in, and the plane was able to move. Just as the Herc made it to the runway, another round fell right where it had been unloading.[2]

I ordered everyone inside the terminal. In my mind I was certain the plane was going to blow up. I thought our luck had run out, that I would see a massive explosion and that fifty or sixty lives would be lost, including that of the Italian minister. But though another round landed much too close, the Hercules made it safely into the air. There was no doubt that the rounds had been aimed at the plane, because the bombardment stopped as soon as it cleared the field.

Just after the incident, Frank Kamenzi came to me to say that it had been the RGF that had targeted the plane. His people had intercepted the order from the RGF head of operations to shoot on the aircraft. When I confronted Bizimungu that morning, he flatly denied it, though he did admit that the RGF had not been warned of the Italian minister's arrival and had not been thrilled with the unannounced visit.

I had no choice but to order the airport closed until further notice, leaving us exactly where I had most feared to be: stranded in Kigali with no quick resupply or evacuation route.

That night before I fell asleep, I realized that the next day was the fiftieth anniversary of D-Day. The week before the war in Rwanda had started, I had targeted June 6 as our own personal D-Day to be ready for demobilization. I lay sleepless on my mattress, taking stock of where we were instead: out of food, being shot at, the slaughter in full flood, and still no cavalry coming over the hill.

June 6. At morning prayers, Yaache informed me that the numbers of people who were entering our compounds, including the Mille Collines, had increased by thousands in the past few days. He was

---

2. St-Denis received a Chief of Defence Staff commendation.

having a tough time creating lists of people for the transfers because more kept arriving and others kept changing their minds about whether they should go or stay.

That same day the RGF attempted one of its only offensives to open the road from Kigali to Gitarama and was easily defeated by the RPF (leading to the fall of Gitarama to the RPF by June 13 and causing the interim government to flee first to Kibuye and then on to Gisenyi, in the extreme northwest, on the border with Zaire). I had to make another trip to see Kagame that day, this time travelling not to Mulindi but to a temporary headquarters in newly won territory. I made my way through the usual horror show to find Kagame sitting on the patio outside a small cottage with easily twenty to thirty soldiers deployed around him. Patrick Mazimhaka, Kagame's senior adviser on political matters, was also there. It struck me how serene they both were as they sat in their wicker chairs in the shade of the patio, and what a contrast their situation seemed to the life I was living with my troops at the Amahoro. Kagame's clothes were pressed and clean, and he greeted me with warmth and composure. Inside the cottage, the furniture was thrown around and on the floor was a picture of Habyarimana amid broken glass. We sat down on a long sofa with a fairly large coffee table in front of us. And I, as always travelling with my battle map, laid it out on the table. We proceeded to talk informally about the evolution of the campaign, with me trying to intuit his future moves from the little he'd say. When I told him of my concern about the human wave that was sitting just this side of the southwestern forest near Butare, he gave me the same old line, that his aim was to stop the killing wherever it was happening.

I asked Kagame what his estimate was of the RGF's situation. He was sanguine. The road between Kigali and Gitarama was now a very risky route. He had the best of the RGF troops locked up in Kigali so they couldn't fight him elsewhere; he could close the gap any time he wanted and wipe them out. My distinct impression was that he was toying with his enemy.

I mentioned Ephrem Rwabalinda's initiative to reduce tensions between the warring parties: he thought a meeting between Kagame and Bizimungu might crack some of these hardened differences. But Kagame saw no value in that. Why would he meet with the enemy when he held all the cards?

June 7. I was wracking my brain, trying to think of a way to give the troops a brief respite from the constant stress. Henry was stranded in Nairobi when I had to close the airport; we all felt his absence, and our isolation. That evening, I was asked by the staff at prayers whether it would be possible to find a television and an antenna so they could watch the World Cup soccer final on June 17. (UNOMUR had sent me a personal invitation to join them in Kabale to watch it; the Dutch and the Brazilians, two of the countries who were part of that mission, were in the finals.) This was one small thing I could do. I authorized my staff to scrounge up a TV and go, taking as few risks as possible, to my former residence to see if the antenna there was still intact. If it was, they were to bring it back and install it on the HQ. Having the TV was a great boost to morale, though as it turned out, by the time June 17 arrived, no one in UNAMIR was thinking about soccer.

When Henry discovered that I had closed the airport, he diverted to Kampala and took on the Herculean task of organizing an overland logistics route from Nairobi to Kampala by air and then by road to Kigali. In three days, he negotiated and secured agreements from the Kenyan and Ugandan governments, the UNDP in Kampala, UN headquarters in New York, our UN administrative staff in Nairobi, and the RPF to open a route. He borrowed trucks from the UN World Food Programme and then personally led the first convoy with the Ghanaian reinforcements—about fifty soldiers—to Kigali.

When they entered our compound on June 8, we clapped and cheered. This was the first signal that UNAMIR 2 might actually unfold (albeit fifteen days late and with soldiers who did not have the requisite training, equipment and troop carriers), and it created the logistics route that would have to sustain the refugees and us in the weeks and months to come. The co-operation of World Food Programme in this operation was crucial: it provided us with heavy lift trucks, and we in turn provided it with a route, coordination and security to deliver humanitarian aid into Rwanda. (This was a classic example of what can be achieved when aid organizations co-operate with a peacekeeping force instead of frustrating it.)

Ironically, that same day, the UN Security Council voted on Resolution 925, extending the mandate of UNAMIR until December and authorizing the phase-two deployment of UNAMIR 2 concurrently with phase one. What a farce. Twenty-three days had passed since the mandate had been approved, and we should have been nearing full strength for rapid intervention. Much as we'd cheered to see the Ghanaian reinforcements arrive, fifty men were nowhere near enough.

The day that Henry returned with the Ghanaians, June 8, Major Luc Racine led a small team of UNMOs, accompanied by a French journalist, into Nyamirambo, a suburb of Kigali, to do a reconnaissance of a French-run orphanage called St. André's. The orphanage was one of the places that Bernard Kouchner had on his radar, and the situation there was desperate. The children, mostly Tutsis, were crammed into the building with little food or water and they could rarely even venture safely out into the yard. The orphanage was surrounded by unfriendly people, including militiamen.

To get there, Racine had to negotiate past twenty-one barriers. Nyamirambo was one of the few densely populated areas left in Kigali and was full of militia. All the barriers there were set up close to drinking joints, and the people at the barriers were boozed up on homemade banana beer. Huts were so jammed together on the sides of the road that driving along it was like going through a tunnel. As Racine drove deeper and deeper into Nyamirambo, he seemed to be penetrating the heart of the Interahamwe. The people of the suburb were so poor it was hard for them to imagine a future and they had been receptive to the Hutu hate message.

The orphanage was a square building surrounded by a fence, and jammed up against the fence on all sides were more huts. When Racine and his team drove into the orphanage compound and parked near the one big tree, the French missionary who ran the place burst into tears. But the arrival of the UN vehicles had drawn attention, and soon hundreds of locals had climbed onto the roofs of the surrounding huts, and some even hopped down to stare in the orphanage windows at the children.

Inside the building, a couple of the adults who had been attempting to care for the children had lost it and become near-crazed with fear. Racine knew there was no way he could bring the children out that day. The crowd was getting ugly, and the UN's evacuation of orphans was a potentially explosive issue. But he decided to try to move the adults who had suffered breakdowns. With the occasional militiaman now firing his weapon toward the orphanage, getting anyone out was going to be tricky. They managed to dodge the bullets and reach the cover of the tree, but on the way to the truck, the French journalist was hit in one buttock, and they had to grab him, fling him inside and make their escape.

Racine stepped on the gas and started ramming his way through the barriers, making it past each one just ahead of the word being passed on to stop them. Before he headed back to the Force HQ, he dropped the wounded journalist off at the King Faisal Hospital, leaving him in the care of Dr. James Orbinski. In Racine and his team's wake, Nyamirambo exploded—the Interahamwe had no compunction about firing at their own people when denied a target. The suburb became so chaotic, we weren't able to get back into the neighbourhood until Kigali fell to the RPF three and a half weeks later—even Kagame's troops had trouble taking control of the area.

That failed mission was exactly the nature of the tasks I had to ask the UNMOs to do in order to try to deliver medical supplies and save, protect, feed and possibly evacuate innocent people. That night Yaache brought me up to date, as he did every day, on the humanitarian work being done. By this point we had received 921 requests from the outside world to go in and save Rwandan individuals or entire families, and 252 requests to rescue expatriates. All of those people had connections pulling strings for them through New York, or even calling us directly. Even though Racine and his team had made it out of St. André's orphanage alive, Racine was devastated by the thought of not being able to rescue the children. He knew that after he'd left there was a good chance that all the kids would have been murdered—people had been looking in the windows waiting to pounce.

It took every ounce of our effort, resources and courage to produce tiny results, yet all around us hundreds of thousands of human beings were being ripped apart and millions were running for their lives. Sometimes we did more harm than good. After each and every mission, failed or "successful," I had to wonder whether it was ethical for me to keep my men at such a level of operational intensity and risk. After I got home from Rwanda, and the years slowly revealed to me the extent of the cynical manoeuvring by France, Belgium, the United States, and the RPF and the RGF, among others, I couldn't help but feel that we were a sort of diversion, even sacrificial lambs, that permitted statesmen to say that the world was doing something to stop the killing. In fact we were nothing more than camouflage. When I hit my personal rock bottom in the late nineties, after I testified at Arusha for the first time, it was because I had finally realized the extent to which I had been duped. I had pushed my people to do real things that ultimately saved human lives, but which in the scheme of the killing seemed nearly insignificant, and all the time I had thought I was leading the effort to try to solve the crisis.

We eventually received word that there had been a large massacre in Kabgayi, the place the Pope had asked us to protect. A group of RPF soldiers who had been part of the force that had secured the area had gone into the monastery and killed an archbishop, three bishops and ten priests. The rebel troops had been travelling for weeks and encountering everywhere the effects of the Hutu scorched-human policy, and they were well aware that the church was very intimate with the Habyarimana family and members of the former government. Quite simply, they killed the princes of the church out of vengeance, their discipline frayed to the breaking point by the atrocities they'd witnessed. At the ceasefire meeting held on June 9, the RPF acknowledged a total breakdown of military control at Kabgayi and that it was a group of its soldiers who had viciously slaughtered the clerics, all of whom were Hutu. Henry took on the job of co-ordinating between the RPF and the RGF the logistics of retrieving the bodies and handing them over to the interim government for burial. That night, when Henry sent a code cable sitrep to Maurice, he signed off, "Would appreciate the arrival of the cavalry soon."

• • •

That morning I had left Henry in charge in order to go to Nairobi. I needed to talk face to face with Golo, the new CAO, and see if I could persuade him and his staff to respond to our needs more expeditiously. I also wanted to meet with the unruly gaggle of NGOs and aid agencies who were fetching up in increasing numbers in Nairobi, and who presented themselves as knowing better than anyone else how to solve the humanitarian crisis in Rwanda. While a few of the more reputable agencies, notably the Red Cross and Médecins Sans Frontières, continued to carry their enormous burdens quietly, others seemed caught up in assessment missions and photo opportunities. I wanted to persuade them to think twice about their dealings with the RPF and see if I could build a fire under them to stop their eternal "assessments" of the crisis and take action. As for the UN humanitarian family, with the exception of World Food Programme, as far as I could see its members were few on the ground.

The loyal and unflappable Amadou Ly thought it was about time I came and spoke to the international community directly. I also had a personal incentive for the trip. When he had got back to Canada, Admiral Murray had decided that it would be good for my state of mind to have a few days with Beth, and he had made arrangements to fly her to Nairobi to meet me.

I made my way north by four-by-four through RPF-held territory without any incident. The countryside was deserted, the fields were brown and without crops, and a number of villages had been completely destroyed by fire. The RPF refused to let our vehicles across the Gatuna bridge, so I walked across the small river into Uganda and felt as though I was stepping into a zone of peace and sunshine. I was picked up on the other side of the river by UNMOs from UNOMUR. We stopped briefly to see Colonel Azrul Haque, my local commander, who was waiting for me with a warm cup of tea and a succinct report on the state of things along the border. For a time, the UN had wanted to disband UNOMUR entirely, arguing that with the arms embargo in place, there was no more need for the mission. The day before I'd left on this trip, I sent the DPKO a report arguing strenuously that the arms embargo was a joke and that I needed the mission to stay put. Haque told me that the NRA remained uncooperative and was preventing observer operations. But he had deployed our UNMOs not too far from the major border checkpoints, even leaving them there at night to keep watch, and they were seeing significant traffic between Uganda and Rwanda.

I climbed aboard a helicopter for the flight to Entebbe, where I was to rendezvous with a Hercules for the last leg to Nairobi. Soon I was flying over the old Entebbe airport, doing a visual inspection before landing at the new air terminal. Entebbe would be my main staging base for UNAMIR 2; the old airfield was still reasonably serviceable, and it and the tarmac could be transformed into the site of a tented city for training and for the maintenance and repair of incoming equipment. (In the weeks to follow I would end up competing with humanitarian organizations for precious cargo transport and buses to get the new forces from Entebbe to Kigali, a full day on the road if the trip was smooth. Word of our needs had made it as far as Mombasa and even Dar es Salaam, and rental prices of heavy transport skyrocketed. Was that the capitalist system of supply and demand at work or was it the hovering of vultures?)

I had an hour or so before the flight to do my rounds at the airport, and I headed out to see the few UNMOs from UNOMUR who had already been moved here to set up shop. But I soon forgot all about that: coming down the tarmac toward me from the waiting Herc was Beth. I wanted to run toward her as people do in the movies, but I was too stunned at seeing her. Home had seemed so far away. We climbed into the Herc and were given seats up front with the crew. I found I could say very little during the flight to Nairobi, but I remember noticing tears falling onto my hands even though I wasn't aware I was crying.

Of course I had no time with Beth once we arrived in Nairobi. I was immediately whisked away from the airport to a major information and coordination meeting with all the humanitarian groups and diplomats. I gave a detailed briefing on the military situation and the genocide, and described the UNAMIR 2 concept of operations and my mission's new roles, which included providing support and protection to the aid agencies as well as to Rwandans in danger. I forcefully warned them about freelancing in the RPF zone and told them how much it was aiding and abetting one of the belligerents; as long as they continued to deal directly with the RPF, the RGF would never allow the groups to claim neutral humanitarian status, which meant they would not get access to the displaced camps in the RGF-held territory. I left that meeting feeling uncertain about whether these strong-willed aid workers would get the message and play by my rules.

I then spent almost an hour with the international media, accusing them fairly candidly of dropping the ball. As far as I was concerned, their mission was to report the truth and to embarrass the fence-sitting political leaders in their home countries without reserve, to never let them off the hook for the Rwandan genocide. "I need troops and I need them now," I told them. "So get out there and help me sell the Rwandan cause." At least they listened.

By the time I got to the UN headquarters in another part of town, it was well past 1700 and most of the staff had gone home. Their nine-to-five attitude nearly made me blow a gasket, and I was only restrained by the ever-sensible Amadou Ly. Even so, after describing once again the dire situation in Kigali and receiving bureaucratic answers from Golo and the few staff who had stayed behind to meet with me that evening, I found myself threatening my CAO: "I have more rifles than you, Mr. Golo, and you don't want to see them here." After calming down a little, I realized that no amount of telling would demonstrate to the administrative staff the conditions we were living in, and I resolved to put on the pressure to bring them on field trips to Kigali so they could smell first-hand the acrid odours of death and starvation, and experience what it was like to eat expired tinned rations and to cope with the resultant diarrhea without toilet paper or running water. Then they'd know how serious I was when I said that the loyalty of my troops was being pushed beyond decent limits by the conditions they were forced to endure.

By this time I was long overdue at the Canadian embassy, where Ambassador Lucie Edwards had made arrangements for Beth and me to have quarters and some good cooking. I can't tell you what being inside a comfortable house again felt like, though I have to confess it took me three complete scrubbings to feel clean enough to pretend for a while to be normal.

For the next two days I went into hiding with Beth at an isolated British colonial-style hotel in one of Kenya's game parks. On the second night, I was called from dinner with my wife to take an urgent phone call. I immediately assumed something terrible was happening in Kigali. But no, to my considerable ire, it was the French ambassador to Kenya on the phone. How he got the number is still a mystery. His pressing business was orphans—he wanted to meet with me when I got back to Nairobi. As I returned to Beth, I wondered what it was with the French and their obsession with orphans: what did it mean that they were now approaching me directly rather than going through Kouchner? When I sat down again, I told Beth that I thought the French were up to something and I needed to figure out what. I never would have guessed at the time the extent to which the interim government, the RGF, Boutros-Ghali, France and even the RPF were already working together behind my back to secure a French intervention in Rwanda under the guise of humanitarian relief. But what was new about that? I was truly the pawn in the field, expected to simply react to the higher political game that bigger people than I were playing.

When we got back to the city, I saw very little of Beth as I was rushed from meeting to meeting, though I never did meet the French ambassador, who did not follow through on his request to talk about orphans. Before Beth left, Ambassador Edwards had us over for a quiet dinner on June 14 with her husband and some of the diplomatic staff. I was in total culture shock: I found normal human interactions— pleasant chat, good food, the world outside Rwanda—surreal. Plagued with the raw experiences of genocide, I rolled with the evening as best I could. Beth was lovely and did a superb job of hiding her concern about what might still happen to me, what had already happened to me. Later she told me that she could tell that serious trouble was brewing inside me—I did not seem to be really there with her and the others. The one light note I remember about the evening was Edwards suggesting a cure for my relentless insomnia. She offered up a recent book written by her husband on the history of the Canadian forestry industry as a perfect soporific. He looked on good-naturedly as I accepted the book from his wife. And she was right—I cracked it open on several desperate occasions and never got past the introduction.

As I said goodbye to Beth and the bustling city of Nairobi, I was caught in an emotional mental battle that pitted what I now considered the "real" world—genocide in Rwanda—and the "artificial" world—the detachment and obtuseness of the rich and powerful. I asked myself again and again, "Why stay? Why ask my troops to stay? Why ask for reinforcements?" But every time I answered in the same way: it was a moral duty to stay and help, even if the impact of our actions was small. On the way back, I took more time at Entebbe to do a more thorough reconnaisance. I walked the old airfield, past the wreckage of the hijacked airliner, visualizing the heroism of the Israeli assault and thinking of the selflessness of the people I'd left in Kigali.

While I was away, Henry juggled demands on all fronts. The special rapporteur of the UN Commission on Human Rights, René Degni-Segui, arrived to begin his formal investigation of the genocide. We did everything we could to help him in his work, facilitating meetings with witnesses and all the political and military players. He and his team stayed with us at the Amahoro, the safest place for him we could find, which on some days was not saying much. One of the first documents he asked us to pass on to the belligerents was an absolute blast from him regarding the killings of the churchmen at Kabgayi. Media all around the world picked up the story, which was embarrassing for the RPF. And Degni-Segui warned Kagame off the top that he was going to be conducting that investigation as a priority. At the ceasefire negotiations, which Henry kept trying to push along, all the parties were clearly worried about what the special rapporteur would find, and with good reason the Interahamwe and the RGF were really tense about the scrutiny.

On June 13, Henry and the humanitarian cell transferred 550 people from the Sainte Famille church, the King Faisal, the Mille Collines, and the Amahoro Stadium to their respective safe zones. The transfers were becoming more and more crisis-prone. People tried to board the vehicles without going through due process, though due process was hard to achieve when refugees were flooding into our sites and we weren't able to keep the lists up to date and complete. Then once people were properly boarded, some got scared for the simple reason that the Interahamwe set up roadblocks within view of the gates of our sites. They didn't stop any convoys, but the militiamen were a clear threat. RTLM was continuing to claim that UNAMIR was only rescuing Tutsis, even though witnesses knew that the Hutu transfers were just as large, and that there were even some Hutus who were refusing to leave the security—however inadequate—of our sites. And then, on June 14, the Interahamwe entered the St. Paul church site, collected about forty children, took them out into the street and killed them, just to show they could. Our UNMOs who had been stationed there were outnumbered and, of course, unarmed, and had to watch as the kids were hauled away. Maybe the massacre was a response to the large and successful transfer we had pulled off the day before, or maybe it was an act of defiance directed at René Degni-Segui.

Whatever the explanation for this latest atrocity, by the time I got back to Kigali late on June 16, Henry was glad to see me. Catching up that night on not only what had been happening locally but what was going on at the international level, I discovered that Booh-Booh had tendered his resignation on June 14 and that the UN had taken him up on his offer the very next day. And once again the interim government of Rwanda was trying to get me fired, protesting to the secretary-general that my "deficiencies and overt partiality [to the RPF] have largely contributed to the failure of UNAMIR." It was perhaps a symptom of how far gone I was that I was glad to be back.

14

THE TURQUOISE INVASION

The battle for Kigali raged through the month of June with no respite. Kagame was a master of psychological warfare and used it to overcome the imbalance in weapons and numbers between his forces and those of the RGF. After the initial lightning attack to link up with the RPF battalion already based in Kigali, he had begun a more deliberate operation of encirclement and reduction of the defending forces. He was not the least bit intimidated by the elite Presidential Guard, artillery and armoured units, civil defence forces and militia who were determined to defend the capital. He believed they did not have the discipline needed to fight a clever and determined foe and that they were wasting their resources on killing civilians instead of concentrating their efforts on defence. From the first, he focused on what he saw as the main task: defeating the RGF in the field.

The story of the Sainte Famille raid illustrates the level of competency and daring of the RPF troops. Thousands of Tutsis had taken refuge in the Sainte Famille church, on the eastern side of central Kigali. One night in mid-June, the RPF sent a company two kilometres inside what was enemy territory, recovered six hundred Tutsis from Sainte Famille, and pulled them out to safety through RGF lines. The mission began as a clandestine operation and ended as a fully supported running battle with carefully planned artillery support—and, by the standards of any military force, ranks as a first-class rescue.

As the June battles chewed off ever-larger bites of RGF territory, the defenders' morale dropped. And once again, RTLM stepped up its personal campaign against me, airing more accusations from the interim government about me being the architect of Hutu misfortunes. But the extremist forces were about to receive a boost from an unexpected source.

On the afternoon of June 17, the day after I got back from Nairobi, I was in my office attacking paperwork with a vengeance, when Phil appeared at my door. Behind him were Bernard Kouchner and another Frenchman, introduced by Kouchner as a representative of President Mitterrand's crisis committee on Rwanda. I thought that they were not especially smart to be here, with the RPF in Kigali and not fond of the French. Still I was in some ways pleased to see Kouchner, a man of great energy and presence, even if I never knew when or if his humanitarianism masked the purposes of the French government.

Unlike the first time we had met, when he had just barged in, Kouchner asked politely if I could spare him an hour or so, explaining that he was acting as an interlocutor for his government in the field and had been sent specifically to see me. At least this time his role was clear. Kouchner opened the conversation by recapping the horrendous situation and deploring the lack of action by the international community—it was easy for me to agree with that. But then he floored me. The French government, he said, had decided that in the interests of humanity, it was prepared to lead a French and Franco-African coalition force into Rwanda to stop the genocide and deliver humanitarian aid. They would come in under a chapter-seven UN mandate and set up a safe haven in the west of the country where people fleeing the conflict could find refuge. He asked me for my support. Without a pause, I said, "Non!"—and I began to swear at the great humanitarian using every French-Canadian oath in my vocabulary. He tried to calm me with reasons that probably sounded high-minded to him but, considering the track record of the French in Rwanda, struck me as deeply hypocritical: surely the French knew that it was their allies who were the architects of the slaughter. Just then Phil Lancaster opened the door, cutting Kouchner off. Phil needed me outside right away. I excused myself and went to see what the crisis was. It wasn't one crisis, but two.

An UNMO patrol had either hit a mine or been ambushed on the outskirts of Kigali—the picture wasn't yet clear. Phil had received a report that one of our officers was probably dead and another injured.

The ambulance that had been sent to retrieve them—"ambulance" in this case a fancy word for a van with a stripped interior, a rudimentary first-aid kit and one stretcher—had run into trouble.

At the same time, the ceasefire negotiation meeting being held that day at our headquarters had just erupted into a potential hostage crisis. It turned out that while the meeting was in progress, the RGF had shot at a transfer convoy of Tutsis, preventing the transfer from taking place. When the RPF representatives at the meeting heard the news (via radio) they arrested the whole RGF delegation, including Gatsinzi. My officers intervened but were now caught in a Mexican standoff. Phil asked me to look out the window: in the compound was a melee of yelling officers, ringed by the armed escorts of both sides. I saw Henry down there, and Tiko, but even so it was clear that panic reigned and mayhem was only a split second away. Phil said, "General, you better get down there or you are going to lose this command."

I don't actually remember how I got to the compound, it just seemed that I was suddenly in the thick of it. I ordered my senior officers out of there: they were to meet me in the operations centre immediately. I spotted Frank Kamenzi off to one side talking on his Motorola. Interrupting him, I told him to tell his bosses to call off this absurd action at once: any attempt to remove or harm hostages from my compound would spark a forceful response from my troops, as well as his own arrest. Kamenzi rarely showed emotion, but he stepped back from me with his eyes wide and got back on his radio.

In the operations centre, I asked Henry and Tiko, who was clearly having a hard time restraining his anger, what was going on with the patrol. I was told that at about fifteen minutes to noon the report had come in that the MILOB team—an Uruguayan major, Manuel Sosa, and Major Ahsan from Bangladesh—had seemingly hit a mine about twenty-one kilometres north of Kigali. Our only doctor, an officer from Ghana, hopped into the van-ambulance with a MILOB team and headed out, accompanied by an APC, to rescue the wounded UNMOs. They successfully negotiated fifteen kilometres of bad roads and roadblocks, then the van got a flat tire. The doctor and crew abandoned the vehicle and continued on in the APC, but the APC was leaking oil and also broke down.

Meanwhile, the two-man MILOB team that had been travelling just behind Sosa and Ahsan managed to report in that they had picked up both casualties but were now being held up by the RPF.

The situation was extremely ugly. The RPF soldiers were refusing to believe that the wounded Ahsan was actually an unarmed peacekeeper, despite the fact that he was wearing his Bangladeshi uniform and UN insignia. Furthermore, Ahsan and Sosa had not actually run over a landmine; they had been targeted by a rocket, and when Ahsan had tried to pull Sosa out, they were fired on again. The troops took the money Ahsan was carrying, and then the sergeant leading the party told his soldiers to drag the Bangladeshi officer away and kill him. When Major Saxonov, one of the UNMOs from the second team, rushed forward to plead for Ahsan's life, he too was placed under guard. What ultimately saved Ahsan was that the RPF soldiers stopped to squabble over how they would split the stolen money. Throughout the confrontation, no one had been allowed to touch Sosa, who was badly wounded but still alive. After almost an hour, the RPF decided to let all of them go.

Along with their wounded colleagues, Saxonov and his partner, Major Costa, reached the spot where the APC was broken down at about 1310. But it was too late for Sosa, who had died on the way in Saxonov's arms. When they found the ambulance, they had to spend tense minutes fixing the flat tire. By this time, Tiko had launched a second rescue team, led by Lieutenant Colonel Mustafizur Rahman, but their APC, not to mention the drawn-out haggling to get through every roadblock, slowed them down terribly. North of the Kadafi Crossroads, they were fired on constantly and had a close shave with a mortar bomb. When they finally met up with the ambulance and the UNAMIR four-by-four heading south, Rahman sent part of his team to try to recover the broken-down APC and led the rest of them directly to the Red Cross hospital.

Upstairs at Force HQ, Phil had gotten in touch with the Hercules detachment in Nairobi to request an immediate medical evacuation. They agreed to come even though the airport was closed, and said they would arrive in about three hours. The hostage standoff was not yet completely resolved, but Phil got the RGF and the RPF liaison officers to call for clearance for the Hercules to land.

In the operations centre, I asked Henry to take over negotiating the RGF's way out of here, and told Tiko to get his observer headquarters back under control. We had suffered a terrible blow, but losing our heads was not going to help anything. Even so, I could not blame my officers. They were obviously affected by the stress and strain of the impossible situations they faced each day and their living conditions. I announced that I would deal with the RPF. Kamenzi was still on his Motorola in the compound, talking with great passion to whomever was on the other end. When I approached him, he told me that the RPF was backing down.

Kouchner and his colleague, who were settled uneasily in two springless armchairs, were still waiting for me in my office. I told Kouchner I could not believe the effrontery of the French. As far as I was concerned they were using a humanitarian cloak to intervene in Rwanda, thus enabling the RGF to hold on to a sliver of the country and retain a slice of legitimacy in the face of certain defeat. If France and its allies had actually wanted to stop the genocide, prevent my UNMOs from being killed and support the aims of the UN mission—something France had voted in favour of twice at the Security Council—they could have reinforced UNAMIR instead.

But Kouchner and his compatriot clearly wanted me to stop arguing. They did not say that my mission should be subordinated to the French one but nonetheless left me with that impression. They said that I should concentrate on getting UNAMIR 2 operational in the RPF zones over the next four months, while they sorted out the RGF-held territories and their supposed safe area. I concluded that they had come to see if I would voluntarily agree to subordinate UNAMIR to the French force. There was no chance of that.

I ended the meeting abruptly when I heard the sound of the Hercules overhead. Kouchner wanted some support from us when he went to meet with the RPF; I told him we would do our best to help despite my complete disapproval of the French course of action. I thought he was positively nuts to try to argue his position with a rebel army who hated the French. What I did not know at that point was that the French government and military had already held high-level meetings with RPF representatives in Europe about this plan, and that members of the RGF, including Ephrem Rwabalinda, my RGF liaison officer, had been to Paris to discuss the coming French intervention. I had been kept in the dark like a mushroom—and fed plenty of fresh manure.

At the airport the Hercules kept its engines revving while we loaded the injured officer onto the plane and into the care of a Canadian military nurse. In the airport VIP lounge, we performed a solemn, if short, ceremony of remembrance and respect for Major Sosa. He was the twelfth UN soldier to be killed in Rwanda and to my chagrin he would not be the last. I grieved for him and for his family. Once again one of my officers was being shipped out wrapped in a blue refugee tarp while my small and tattered force tried to absorb the meaning of his loss—and the world's indifference to the risks we had to take.

That night, French media reported France's plan to deploy troops to Rwanda, news that was soon picked up by RTLM and the other local stations and broadcast to the nation. The defending forces in Kigali went mad with joy at the prospect of imminent rescue by the French. Their renewed hope and confidence had the side effect of reviving their hunt for genocide survivors, which put in further jeopardy those who remained in refuges in the few churches and public buildings that had been left untouched. The génocidaires believed the French were coming to save them and that they now had carte blanche to finish their gruesome work.

I had not been able to reach the triumvirate in the DPKO by phone before I'd gone to bed, but I'd made sure that full sitreps describing the chaos of the day—including Sosa's death, Ahsan's being wounded and Kouchner's reappearance—were sent to New York. Among the overnight batch of code cables was one from Riza. In short, he told me to keep my head down. "In what appears to be an increasingly dangerous situation, you will take the operational decisions necessary," he wrote. "Our general advice would be that you adopt a defensive posture in order to [avoid] risks and casualties until a clearer picture emerges." My mandate for the last month had been to do exactly what I had been doing. Now Riza was advising me to isolate the mission in Kigali and stop trying to maintain contact with the RPF and the interim government. He told me that until the reinforcements arrived, which could take two to three months, I should limit UNAMIR to passive guarding of our sites in and around Kigali.

In the same cable he officially informed me of France's desire to send troops into western Rwanda, and told me to sort out what my role would be in relation to the intervention. Riza confirmed that the French were mounting a separate operation that would not fall under my command, and said it would resemble the U.S.-led Operation Restore Hope in Somalia. Riza advised me that the new mission could be on the ground even before the Security Council authorized it. "You should ensure that only the cooperation absolutely necessary is provided by UNAMIR and that cordial relations are established," he wrote. In UN-ese this was a circumlocution designed to let me know that I should cover for the DPKO and the secretary-general by not being *too* co-operative with the French before their mandate was approved. The trouble was that this meant I should not be in touch with the French force until they actually landed. The humanitarian disaster was huge and growing, the need was urgent, and I was the one with the most current information on the ground, yet I was to observe the niceties and not try to enlighten the French.

Much as I resented the mission that the French would dub "Opération Turquoise," I thought that not sharing the picture on the ground was a mistake. I later realized that a number of officers who became part of Turquoise had been French military advisers to the RGF until the start of the war. How would their presence strike the RPF, who had to suspect that the French were not on a purely humanitarian mission? And how much encouragement would the presence of their former advisers bring the RGF and the extremists of the Presidential Guard, who were already ecstatic in the streets of Kigali? The appearance of UN-sanctioned French soldiers was going to make it even tougher for UNAMIR to deal with the RPF. Riza wrote, "RPF perceptions of the operation itself will determine their attitude and we hope that this will not strain relations with UNAMIR." If I hadn't felt so grim, I would have laughed. Of course, all my remaining Franco-Africans would be at even greater risk.

I passed the cable on to Dr. Kabia and to Henry, asking them both to study our options under this Orwellian scenario, in which a UN force under chapter seven and a UN force under chapter six would have to function in the face of a determined belligerent. The French troops were reputed to be aggressive, and the RPF was pushing to conquer the whole country. Would we by default become a peacekeeping force between the French and the RPF?

The follow-up phone calls between me and the triumvirate were somewhat reassuring. Annan, Riza and Maurice also thought the scenario beyond belief, and they were not keen on the French initiative. But I should make no mistake: it was going to happen.

How would we carry on? Yesterday's ambush hit me very hard—it was a blatant overreaction of the RPF toward my mission, even before the French took the field. It was as if the RPF were sending me a blatant message to stay out of the way. Tiko, who had lost a man from his close-knit group of observers, approached me that morning to tell me that although the UNMOs were still willing to serve, the situation had finally become too dangerous for them to carry on with reconnaissance and information-gathering. Tiko was the bravest of the brave, with years of experience in some of the world's worst war zones, and he always got the job done. That such a soldier had decided to pass on the feelings of his men lent them even greater weight. They had had enough. They had been living in the midst of a raging battle for months; there had been fatalities; they had been taken hostage, caught in the middle of fire-fights, shot at, menaced by drunken or drugged Interahamwe, asked to share their accommodations and rations with thousands of displaced people, and generally abused by the fortunes of war. It was hardly surprising they felt as they did.

As far as I was concerned, the ambush had also been a result of my judgment. Until yesterday, every time one of our patrols was sent through the lines, we had warned the belligerents in advance through our liaison officers. But the night I'd got back to Kigali, neither

Kamenzi nor his assistant was anywhere to be found and we needed to send out patrols for airfield reconnaissance and contact with the interim government. Though I ordered that the UNMOs were to stop and turn back at any point where they judged there was too much risk, I had agreed that the patrol needed to go. The UNMOs suffered the consequences of my poor operational decision.

That afternoon I met with a group of senior officers. I told them that, yes, I *had* been asking them to take extraordinary risks because we needed the vital links they could provide with the belligerents and the information only they could find out. I told them that from here on in, they would not be asked to perform any operation that hadn't received the consent of both sides. I don't know where they found the strength to recommit to the mission, but I left that meeting having been told that they had the confidence to continue to serve with me.

I met separately with the officers of the Uruguayan contingent. I shared in their grief and offered the solace of a brother officer. I told them that they had served bravely and that the mission still needed them to stay dedicated to it in the aftermath of their loss. I also told them that if they wished to return home they could count on my full support—no stigma would be attached to their decision to pull out. The next day three of the officers requested to go back to Uruguay. I was encouraged that the number was so small.[1]

Before I met with Tiko and the UNMOs, I had gone to see Kagame. Setting off with my usual escort, we took a route north from the city and then circled around to the east before heading south and finally turning west on obscure dirt roads toward the Nyabarongo River. We drove through village after deserted village, some still smouldering. Garbage, rags and bodies intermingled at places where either an

---

1. Little did I know the impact that the death of Major Sosa would have on the political situation in Uruguay. When elections were held, the incumbent president almost lost power. Voters could not understand why the government would send its officers to such a far-off place to die.

ambush or a massacre had occurred. We drove by abandoned check-points ringed with corpses, sometimes beheaded and dumped like rubbish, sometimes stacked meticulously beside neat piles of heads. Many corpses rapidly decayed into blinding white skeletons in the hot sun.

I don't know when I began to clearly see the evidence of another crime besides murder among the bodies in the ditches and the mass graves. I know that for a long time I sealed away from my mind all the signs of this crime, instructing myself not to recognize what was there in front of me. The crime was rape, on a scale that deeply affected me.

We saw many faces of death during the genocide, from the innocence of babies to the bewilderment of the elderly, from the defiance of fighters to the resigned stares of nuns. I saw so many faces and try now to remember each one. Early on I seemed to develop a screen between me and the sights and sounds to allow me to stay focused on the work to be done. For a long time I completely wiped the death masks of raped and sexually mutilated girls and women from my mind as if what had been done to them was the last thing that would send me over the edge.

But if you looked, you could see the evidence, even in the whitened skeletons. The legs bent and apart. A broken bottle, a rough branch, even a knife between them. Where the bodies were fresh, we saw what must have been semen pooled on and near the dead women and girls. There was always a lot of blood. Some male corpses had their genitals cut off, but many women and young girls had their breasts chopped off and their genitals crudely cut apart. They died in a position of total vulnerability, flat on their backs, with their legs bent and knees wide apart. It was the expressions on their dead faces that assaulted me the most, a frieze of shock, pain and humiliation. For many years after I came home, I banished the memories of those faces from my mind, but they have come back, all too clearly.

We were in newly conquered RPF territory, which was deserted except for the corpses and rebel soldiers. The RPF guide who was taking us to Kagame moved along at a fair clip, seemingly oblivious to the impact on his vehicle of the cratered and scarred dirt trail. The RPF had mechanics and spare parts, but I had neither. My four-by-four had to see me through the war and I deliberately slowed the pace.

When we reached the river, across which Kagame had made yet another temporary headquarters in his advance, the opaque earth-coloured water was high and fast. The RPF engineers had constructed a pontoon-type bridge that light pickup trucks could cross gingerly. Getting out of my vehicle, I noticed a number of soldiers with long poles upstream, pulling bloated bodies up on the bank. To me this was now such a commonplace sight it did not penetrate my protective screen.

I did not want to risk our vehicles on the bridge. As we made our way across on foot, I noticed that clothes were caught between the struts of the floating base and I stopped to look over the side. Staring up at me were the faces of half-nude corpses, stuck under the bridge. There were a lot of them. In some places they had accumulated to the point that we were actually walking on a bridge of dead bodies. On the far bank, soldiers were trying to pry them loose for fear that their weight would pull the bridge apart. The screen shattered, my stomach heaved and I struggled for composure. I couldn't bear the movement of the bridge, up and down on the slaughtered hundreds.

The first thing I raised with Kagame when I reached his small command bungalow was the ambush on my UNMO team—it was out of my mouth even before the news of Turquoise. He expressed sincere condolences. His only excuse for firing on my men was that too many of our vehicles had been abandoned after breaking down and were being used by the RGF; he said his soldiers did not trust any unannounced travellers in UNAMIR vehicles. In that case, I countered, he should make efforts to return the UN vehicles his own troops had commandeered, since the RGF surely felt the same way. I insisted that from now on, his liaison officer and his assistant had to remain at my headquarters and not disappear at night, as they had both done on June 16. If they hadn't gone missing, the clearances would have been dealt with. Kagame said that going forward he would guarantee a response from the RPF the night before we launched any mission.

We moved on to the French. I asked him about meeting with Kouchner; Kagame was inscrutable on the subject. I told him I was becoming concerned that I, and my mission, were being used as a kind of public relations front to distract the world from others' hidden agendas. He denied this wholeheartedly. I said I was definitely not looking for a fight. Though I expected the RPF to react to the French and to be confrontational, the triumvirate had told me over the secure phone that the United States was putting considerable pressure on the RPF to cooperate. I told Kagame that I would handle the French proposals to firm up their area of operations and that I'd be a conduit between him and Turquoise. I would insist that the French not deploy in Kigali; ultimately the capital should be under my control to prevent the French getting anywhere near his forces. For a moment Kagame just looked at me. Then in a very confident fashion, he told me that I shouldn't worry about that. The French would not be entering Kigali. As to the reason why, his assessment was blunt: "Tell France that Kigali can handle more body bags than Paris."

I dreaded the return trip over that bridge of death. As I picked my way back across, I was careful not to look over the sides or down through the slats, but I could not get out of my mind the fact that I was walking on bodies.

I had little to add to the sitrep that night except for my concerns about the bigger game going on to which I was not privy. That evening at prayers, I asked Henry to assess the risk of conflict in and around Kigali and to once again draw up plans for a possible withdrawal. The capital could soon become a major battle zone.

On June 19, the date that UNAMIR 2 should have had 4,600 soldiers in Rwanda, my troop strength stood at 503, and we were still living with all of the problems and shortages that had plagued and undermined us in April. The secretary-general wrote to the president of the Security Council on that date to say that the phase-one deployment was about to go ahead, but that because no nation had provided a fully equipped and trained battalion, UNAMIR 2 would not be operational for at least three more months. In these circumstances—combined with an exponential increase in humanitarian problems and the fact that UNAMIR was taking casualties as it attempted to provide a modicum of support for Rwanda—Boutros-Ghali suggested that the Security Council consider a French-commanded multinational operation under a chapter-seven mandate to assure the security and protection of displaced persons and civilians at risk in Rwanda. He also asked that governments maintain their troops until UNAMIR 2 was up to strength.[2]

Since Booh-Booh was officially gone, I had to formally assume his political duties. On June 20, I forwarded a document called "Assessment of the Proposed French-Led Initiative in the Rwandese Crisis." In the clearest, most objective and rational terms I could muster, I described all of the reasons why the French should not deploy and what I estimated would happen if they did.

I proposed three options to the UN. The first was to withdraw UNAMIR outright and hand over the entire situation to the French. The second option was to secure the agreement of both parties to the French deployment but to keep UNAMIR as an independent mission and interpose it between the French and the RPF. The third was to redeploy UNAMIR into a country near Rwanda, develop UNAMIR 2 and return once the French had completed their operation. "It is strongly recommended that the French-led initiative be encouraged only if the RPF agrees to French troops on the ground, or if this force comes with personnel and equipment but not with any French troops. Should this option not be possible," I wrote, "in order to avoid an escalation of the conflict, both inside Rwanda and in the region . . . the French-led initiative should be let to run its course alone and permit UNAMIR to build itself up in a secure environment . . . after which the Mission could redeploy with the effective forces planned for in its mandate." If French troops were coming in, and we could not secure the belligerents' approval, I recommended the third option. New York now knew exactly where I stood. The final salutation in UN messages is always "Best regards." For the only time on this mission, I closed the document with "At this point, FC finds regards very difficult to express."

---

2. UNAMIR 2 did not complete its deployment until December 1994, fully six months after the genocide and the civil war were over and when it was no longer required.

I raised grave concerns about what area the French were in fact going to occupy. Was it their intention to support the RGF right into the capital, or were they looking to avoid confrontation with the RPF? Nobody could tell me. Boutros-Ghali's letter to the president of the Security Council simply stated that the French wished to help "displaced persons in Rwanda," which could mean anywhere. For the next six days, my discussions with New York, Paris, Kigali, the RPF and the French force (I don't remember the RGF being a party to these negotiations) concentrated on drawing a single line in the western part of Rwanda to delineate the French zone.

On June 21, I sent them all a drawing of the tactical layout of the RPF positions as of that day. After the French announcement, the RPF had accelerated its campaign, and the RGF had also sped up its withdrawal toward the west, with an estimated two and a half million Rwandans moving ahead of them. Even while the French awaited final authorization from the UN, the RGF-held territory was shrinking, mostly in the south. I ended up negotiating the final line that the RPF and the French would accept as the French zone of operations. I subsequently sent UNMOs to liaise with both sides to confirm the line on the ground. And so, as I had predicted, above all the other tasks my small force still had to perform, we were turned into a chapter-six peacekeeping force between a UN chapter seven force and the winning side of the civil war.

When news of the French intervention was broadcast in Rwanda, the RPF, as I had feared, retaliated against my Franco-African officers from Togo, Senegal, Mali and Congo. They were robbed, insulted and roughed up to the point where I had to confine them to camp. I negotiated their withdrawal from the mission area for their own safety and informed New York of my decision. On June 21, I said farewell to these magnificent Franco-African officers, who had served the mission well since the previous November. Being the only francophones in the mission, they had had to conduct most of the tasks in the RGF sector and had been exposed to more than their fair share of danger. Some of their comrades had been killed and others wounded. Most of them had fallen ill at least once, and they had witnessed scenes that would haunt them for the rest of their lives. But they had all stayed on through the frustrations and dangers, and it was an emotional farewell.

Because of the risks of altercations with the RPF in the rear areas where the troops were less disciplined than in the front lines, I tasked Henry to personally lead the convoy to Uganda. Tiko, wanting to be with his UNMOs to the last, went as well. About a dozen kilometres outside Kigali, they were turned back by the RPF and brought to the airfield. Under the eyes of Frank Kamenzi, who did not intervene, RPF soldiers proceeded to conduct a complete "customs" inspection of each one of the forty-two men. Their belongings were thrown about, and their electronic equipment—radios, tape recorders and the like—were confiscated. The inspection lasted about an hour. When it was over, they were told to pick their stuff up off the runway and get back on the buses, and then they were sent on their way. This humiliation, which they endured after so many months of putting their lives on the line to help Rwandans, created such anger in them that Henry was concerned they might take matters into their own hands with every delay at the checkpoints. When I protested their treatment to the RPF, I was told that it was entirely normal that the occupying force would search anyone attempting to leave the country since, they claimed, there had been considerable looting in the past.

The departure of the Franco-Africans stripped me of most of my French-speaking staff officers. For the third time in the short history of this mission, I had to rebuild my headquarters from the bottom up, all the while continuing with operations. The weight and the complexity, the sheer urgency, of demands related to the coming mobilization of UNAMIR 2 hit us right in the face, swamping us in the organizational details of how to secure resources, logistics, infrastructure, training, the Entebbe theatre reception and logistics base, the troop carriers, the rations and the water we would need. I sent a message to the DPKO that I was bringing in forty-eight UNMOs from Nairobi to replace the departed officers.

The Canadians stepped into the breach to become the sole French speakers in my headquarters, but their effectiveness was somewhat limited by the fact that all Canadians were under attack on hate radio, because of me and because of Canada's initiative to launch the full-scale human rights investigation into the Rwandan war. In my note to the DPKO about bringing in the new UNMOs, I warned that "FC will be forced to move [the Canadian] contingent out also, if situation does not improve. At this time FC is about to restrict their movement to RPF territory only." I concluded: "This Mission will not be able to sustain its rhythm of activities, let alone see any increase of work. . . . FC cannot make this point more emphatically." In those days after the announcement of Opération Turquoise, I came very close to saying, "Pull us out, we capitulate, we can't go on." My soldiers were being tested under conditions that never would occur in a standard peacekeeping operation, and they survived circumstances we wouldn't even have wanted to read about. Serving with them, I was a constant witness to extraordinary displays of commitment, determination and raw courage.

On June 21 the RPF's New York office issued a press release and a letter to the new president of the Security Council, Salim Bin Mohammed Al-Khussaiby. If the council approved the French mission, the RPF requested that it should "simultaneously authorize the withdrawal of the existing contingent of UNAMIR. The Rwandese Patriotic Front is concerned that its personnel may not always be in a position to make a clear distinction between UNAMIR and other foreign forces in the event of an escalation of hostilities. We have, regrettably, come to the conclusion that it is necessary that UNAMIR personnel be withdrawn to safety, at least on a temporary basis." The powers-that-be ignored the RPF position and carried on. The next day, the UN Security Council approved Resolution 929, which provided France with a chapter-seven mandate to assemble a coalition and intervene in Rwanda. The OAU initially opposed the intervention but, under pressure from the Franco-African states, changed its mind. At the vote, New Zealand, Nigeria, Pakistan, Brazil and China had abstained. The council tied its approval of Opération Turquoise to two conditions: the mission was limited to sixty days, and the secretariat had to make every effort to get UNAMIR 2 deployed by then. From his refuge in Belgium, Prime Minister Designate Faustin Twagiramungu issued a public statement condemning the French intervention, but then added that since the French *were* going in, he hoped that they would attempt to achieve the ends outlined for UNAMIR 2.

That night I got a code cable from the DPKO giving me some very limited guidance. The French had promised to avoid the conflict lines between the RGF and RPF. The cable read, "We don't expect the French to propose a presence in Kigali, but if they do please inform us immediately and we shall try to persuade them, given RPF sensitivities and other problems such a presence may cause." To me it looked like the French were still thinking about coming into Kigali, and I imagined what it would be like if French paratroopers landed here. I had to get our withdrawal plans finalized. Reading between the lines of the code cable, with its reiteration that I should sit tight in Kigali, I saw that the DPKO was under enormous pressure from nations with troops already serving in UNAMIR, and that the recent casualties we'd suffered must have been making it even harder to come up with enough troops for the new deployment. (In the cable, Maurice Baril also asked me in a very diplomatic way to curb the enthusiasm of my media liaison officer, who in his attempt to respect the transparency I had mandated with the media, was causing problems with both the RPF and the RGF by much too accurately describing the ebbs and flows of the front lines.)

And here was my superiors' attempt to improve my morale: "Nevertheless you are likely to face unanticipated problems and we shall depend on your good judgment to deal with them, along with the assurance that we always are available for consultation at any hour."

The last paragraph of the code cable informed me that Booh-Booh's replacement, a Pakistani career diplomat named Shaharyar Khan, was "stopping in various capitals for consultations" at the request of Boutros-Ghali while on his way to UNAMIR.

By now French flags draped every street corner in the capital. *"Vive la France"* was heard more often in Kigali than it was in Paris. RTLM was continuing to tell the population that the French were on the way to join them to fight the RPF. It seemed to me that for every life that Opération Turquoise would save, it would cost at least another because of the resurgence of the genocide.

On June 22, the attitude of the RPF changed dramatically toward all of us. Hostility, rudeness, threats and direct attacks were the order of the day as the RPF accused us, as the representatives of the UN in

Rwanda, of co-operating with the UN-mandated French intervention. Kagame's position was that we should immediately withdraw because he could not guarantee our safety. It took several tries to arrange a meeting with him at which I explained the stated purpose of the French operation as loyally and directly as I could. I thought I persuaded him we were not part of some diabolical conspiracy to deny the RPF its victory or protect or promote genocide. Of course, I found out later that while the RPF publicly opposed the French intervention, privately it had reconciled itself to the French deployment while Kagame completed his campaign.[3] It is extremely Byzantine that two former enemies had closer coordination and co-operation and better information than I had from either of them.

I've spent much time since wondering why Kagame was happier to tolerate Opération Turquoise than a fully mandated UNAMIR 2. I can only assume that since the intention of UNAMIR 2 was to stop the genocide and establish protected sites that would keep the displaced millions from fleeing the RPF, I would have inevitably argued that the RPF's advance should not exacerbate the humanitarian crisis, and that we would step in to provide protection until the situation stabilized. He knew that I regarded that task as my primary objective. But Kagame wanted all of the country, not parts of it. I came to believe he didn't want the situation to stabilize until he had won.

Operating in a void of information, I had to guess how the French would enter Rwanda and how they would conduct their operations. I knew Burundi had denied French transit and that Uganda would do the same. Tanzania had no infrastructure in the west that the French could use. I had denied entrance through Kigali. I told New York that if the French were permitted to enter that way, I would resign my command; if French planes appeared at the airport, I'd shoot them down. I also shot my mouth off on the subject to the media. To a certain extent, I meant it: if French troops

---

3. At a conference in 1997, the RPF ambassador to the United States, Théogène Rudasingwa, confirmed to me that he and the RPF representative in Europe, Jacques Bihozagara, had been invited to Paris and had been fully briefed on Opération Turquoise before I had even heard of it.

landed in the middle of Kigali, it would set off a gigantic battle with the RPF and permit the RGF and the interim government to continue to function. I was assured by the DPKO that Kigali was out of the question.

That left only Zaire (today the Republic of Congo). Goma, at the northern end of Lake Kivu, had a modern airport that needed repair but could support the French. There was also an airfield at Bukavu at the southern end of the lake. I decided that if they went only through Goma and Gisenyi, just inside the Rwandan border, that would confirm that they were really coming in to support the RGF. If so, I could expect them to enter combat operations against the RPF, which by default would drive a direct reprisal against UNAMIR and force our withdrawal. However, if the French entered through Bukavu, across the border from Cyangugu, to the west of where the vast majority of persons at risk were congregating, then their motives might be solely humanitarian and we could continue our mission.

Even before the Security Council had taken its final decision on June 22, the French were already landing in Goma, which I found out through media reports on the morning of June 23. So much for the argument that the international community did not have the means to rapidly deploy UNAMIR 2. On the same day, the RPF announced that it was not opposed to a French operation if it was confined to humanitarian aims. And with our Franco-Africans gone, hostility toward UNAMIR immediately subsided, and we again began to push our patrols out from Kigali. Unfortunately almost all of the Hutu population, driven by RTLM, the RGF and the Interahamwe, were now moving to the west. Even more tragically, as the population moved it was again subjected to Interahamwe roadblocks, where not only surviving Tutsis were killed but also those without identity cards. Even a suspected "cockroach" had to die.

On June 24 the French entered Rwanda in patrol strength and were reported in the media to be in Gisenyi in the north and Cyangugu in the south and pushing beyond those locations. I was sure that if the French got too close to the RPF, a firefight would ensue; I had to get to the French commander, General Jean-Claude Lafourcade, to confirm his intentions and exchange liaison officers with his force. I wasn't going to wait for him to come and see me.

I contacted New York to ask the DPKO to determine, through the French Mission staff, where the Turquoise headquarters was in the field and to secure a meeting for me with its commander. Again, the DPKO directed me to co-operate with the French, be patient and understand the *realpolitik*. I replied that I expected no good to come of Opération Turquoise. From my perspective it looked like a cynical exercise in furthering French self-interest at the expense of the ongoing genocide. I failed to get anything from my bosses but tepid promises to consider my views.

With the RPF apparently calmed down about the French presence, I briefed Henry on the need to get the civilian transfers going again and to arrange for the moving of RGF prisoners of war from the Red Cross and King Faisal hospitals. I also told him that we had to regain contact with the interim government to restart the ceasefire negotiations that had come crashing to a halt after the hostage-taking in our compound, and keep an eye on its relationship with the French. We also needed to liaise with the interim government wherever it was in order to keep up our humanitarian efforts; the aid groups, with their increasing burden of displaced people, needed a conduit to the shrinking RGF zones.

That afternoon, Don MacNeil chaired a meeting in the HQ between Frank Kamenzi and Dr. James Orbinski, the Rwandan team leader of Médecins Sans Frontières and the head of the King Faisal Hospital.[4] Armed RPF soldiers kept invading the hospital to take medical supplies, despite the fact that the site was UN-protected. The blue berets stationed there were itching to sort these guys out with "minimum use of force," and the situation was becoming very dangerous.

Orbinski protested to Kamenzi that under the Geneva Convention, which Rwanda had signed, armed troops were not allowed in any hospital, let alone in one operating under the overarching protection of the Red Cross. Kamenzi replied that he had reason to believe there were militiamen and RGF personnel among the eight thousand or so protected civilians at the

---

4. Médecins Sans Frontières returned to Rwanda in late May, led by the Canadian doctor, James Orbinski. By mid-June, James and his team had the King Faisal Hospital operational.

King Faisal, and that the RPF troops needed their weapons to protect themselves. At a checkpoint search during a recent transfer of injured persons, under the banner of the Red Cross, the RPF had discovered grenades. As far as the RPF was concerned, the hospital belonged to them and the people of Rwanda. They were at war, and were justified in taking what they needed.

MacNeil then pointed out that everyone needed the medical resources, but that the displaced persons at the hospital were getting nervous about a possible massacre at the hands of the RPF. Using the Faisal to house thousands of displaced people hampered the medical staff's efforts to treat the never-ending flow of casualties. He proposed making a new compound for the Faisal refugees on a nearby golf course, which would give us the opportunity to conduct a total weapons check when they were moved. This would eliminate the need for the RPF to come into the hospital armed. Once UNAMIR 2 was up and running, we would have more medical supplies and a dedicated field hospital, and the RPF could take over the Faisal. This solution was acceptable to everyone.

Don MacNeil achieved such results constantly in his humanitarian duties. He showed no fear (as the incident with the first disastrous transfer showed) and had imagination and a solid dose of common sense. His call sign on the radio net was MamaPapa One, and he lived up to it with his dedication to others and the example he set.[5] He was

---

5. The MamaPapa moniker was the creation of Marek Pazik. As the first Humanitarian Assistance Cell (HAC) officer, he was tasked with checking on the aid agencies still in Kigali and providing them with Motorola radios. Not familiar with the phonetic alphabet used by Western military forces, he translated his initials *MP* into MamaPapa (it should have been MikePapa) as the radio call sign for the aid agencies to reach him. Radio traffic during the failed evacuation attempt from the Hôtel des Mille Collines on May 3 was heard by all UNAMIR personnel who had tuned in on the frequency to monitor the situation, and everyone heard the MamaPapa call sign—the Ghanaian troops in particular thought it was great. Attempts were made to change the call sign to standard military form, but the Ghanaian troops wouldn't hear of it and continued to call all members of the humanitarian cell MamaPapas, to the particular consternation of Colonel Yaache. The name stuck throughout UNAMIR and UNAMIR 2, with many aid workers throughout the world using their assigned MamaPapa call sign to check in with UNAMIR.

committed but also fun-loving, and his spirit, along with the steady resolve of his commander, Clayton Yaache, welded the humanitarian action cell of UNAMIR into a unit where others hoped to serve, no matter how dangerous and thankless the tasks. MacNeil got along particularly well with the Polish officers, including the hardbitten Marek Pazik, who carried an AK-47, which he had lifted from a militiaman, wherever he went. Pazik's room became the focal point for entertainment and discussion, usually organized by MacNeil. Those gatherings were an escape valve for our humanitarian warriors. They faced down the militias to help people to safety. They risked their lives every day in tense confrontations, any one of which would have weakened the resolve of most other people. They carried blood-soaked elders, women and children to aid stations. As with Pazik, who witnessed one of the first instances of the genocide at the Polish Mission, they were haunted by what they'd experienced, but they carried on.

The RPF was mounting its assault on Kigali with renewed vigour. I hadn't seen too much of Ndindiliyimana lately, but Kouchner and the Gendarmerie were doing good work in moving and protecting some of the orphans caught in the RGF zones of Kigali. Other moderate RGF leaders had disappeared from the capital over the last week. They must have been worried about what might happen to them given the renewal of purpose that the French arrival was inspiring in the extremists.

Henry's father died, and as a result he needed to go on compassionate leave to Ghana for much of July. On June 26, I sent him to meet with Bizimungu at the Meridien hotel to lay the groundwork for resuming the ceasefire negotiations. I also wanted Henry to raise again the issue of how to stop RTLM from inciting the militias and the population to kill me. I was not directly blaming Bizimungu or the RGF. But they had to know the threats weren't working. I was not leaving. No one in New York was calling me back. If we were to go forward, the threats had to stop.

Henry filled Bizimungu in on the reasons why we had sent the Franco-Africans to Nairobi, and also on the status of the bodies of the churchmen killed by the RPF at Kabgayi. The RPF had buried the bishops and the priests themselves, and were not in favour of releasing them to the interim government. He also requested that Bizimungu and the defence minister meet with me as soon as possible after I had seen the French commander, to clarify exactly what our roles were to be. Henry also informed Bizimungu that because of his father's death, he would be gone for a while, and that I would take over the ceasefire negotiations.

When he got back to Force HQ, Henry told me that Bizimungu had been in exceptionally good spirits and was serene and even friendly. (This was a major shift from the week before, when Bizimungu had behaved as though his cause was totally lost.) His condolences to Henry seemed genuine, which struck Henry as truly bizarre considering the army chief's apparent indifference to the hundreds of thousands of deaths all around him. Henry had also finally confirmed through Bizimungu that the interim government was holed up in Gisenyi, with some ministers possibly even in Goma; Bizimungu had told him that my upcoming trip to Goma to see General Lafourcade was an excellent opportunity to meet the minister of defence there.

Things were bustling in my headquarters now as reconnaissance parties from the various UNAMIR 2 contingents began to arrive by the long land route from Entebbe to Kigali. The RPF border guards were not making life any easier on these incoming troops, insisting on inspecting them and all their gear as though they were tourists, not UN peacekeepers. UNOMUR was helpful in guiding and assisting these convoys through the hills and through the Ugandan side of the border; and after more interminable negotiations, we worked out a protocol with the RPF that smoothed the way. With the APCs and other force and humanitarian resources starting to move down the pipeline from Kampala, another company of the Ghanaian battalion arriving in a week or so, the Canadian Signals Regiment and the Ethiopian battalion reconnaissance parties already on the ground, the British Para field hospital and the Australian field hospital and protection force recce teams set to come in quick succession, and a possible Canadian field hospital also in the wings, Force HQ was absolutely awash with new people. We were no longer alone—which was both exhilarating and impossibly draining, since we had become used to being the embattled few.

Nothing was easy, of course. The CAO and UN bureaucratic procedures were still obdurate in the face of our needs. All kinds of logistics and infrastructure problems required extensive negotiations with both the RPF and the RGF. The mission was still without supply and transport contracts or an increased budget, let alone enough food, water and fuel. The Canadians, under Colonel Mike Hanrahan, would arrive fully equipped, as was the norm for developed countries with professional armies. For the next six to eight weeks at least, we would have to rely on the engineers, logisticians and support personnel of this experienced and professional contingent, and on the British as well, to tide the whole mission over.

The Ethiopians were at the other extreme of preparedness. They had just finished a protracted civil war, and the reconnaissance party, which included the chief of staff of the Ethiopian army, was clearly ill at ease in brand new uniforms. As I wrote earlier, this was their first experience in peacekeeping and they had no equipment to sustain themselves, let alone conduct operations. (However, these soldiers were incredibly resourceful. I once watched them use only long wooden switches to restrain a crowd that was trying to surge across the bridge at Cyangugu into Zaire. The switches were the kind that might have been used to herd cattle. The soldiers also had no compunction about getting into the fields to help local farmers harvest the rare planted field.) Most of the other African units were not much better off.

My days started to fill up with innumerable administrative demands, and we had even fewer HQ staff than we had had last November. We were in the centre of an ongoing genocide, and we could not let up at all. As the reconnaissance parties came through, I emphasized over and over again the sense of urgency in the acrid, often putrid, air. They were already late, I said—and we had been late all along. I know that Mike Hanrahan at least carried the urgency of my plea back to Canada; instead of deploying slowly by ship, as his commanders had intended, the Canadian contingent took commercial flights to Nairobi in order to get here faster.

Two troubling incidents had already occurred between the French and the RPF. The RPF had ambushed a section of at least ten Turquoise soldiers who had moved too far into the Butare prefecture. No one was actually hurt in that ambush, but French pride suffered a blow—special forces had to negotiate the troops' release. The other incident happened on the road from Kibuye to Gikongoro. Shots were fired and two French soldiers were saved only by their flak jackets. Both patrols had been outwitted by the RPF and shamed in the process. This did nothing to dissuade the French from wanting to support their former colleagues and put the RPF in their place.

The mission medals finally arrived, and on June 26 we held a mission medals parade in the courtyard near the Force HQ's main entrance, surrounded by a pile of shot-up, broken-down and cannibalized UN four-by-fours. I had sent word home asking that either the Canadian chief of defence staff or the minister of national defence present Brent's medal to him in person.[6] Henry, Tiko and I proceeded to pin the mission medals on sixty HQ staff, UNMOs and the Tunisian contingent, who lined up in three rows, as spit and polished as they could manage while dressed in flak jackets. We had to keep the ceremony short in case of stray fire, but as we worked our way along the rows, looking in the eyes of every man and shaking his hand, I think all of us were reliving the darkest parts of the mission. I pinned medals on Henry and Tiko, and then they both pinned mine to my jacket.

The next day, I met Henry at the airport for the Ghanaian battalion's medals parade. Before we got started, he passed on the disturbing follow-up to his session with Bizimungu. Headquarters staff had made inquiries at the Kigali prefecture about resuming the transfers of displaced persons and orphans. A meeting had been held with the sous-prefect, who very matter of factly stated that the interim government did not see any value in carrying on with the transfers: the French forces would be in the capital soon and they would be able to provide proper protection for all. The sous-prefect also said he thought that when the

---

6. That didn't happen. Brent's mission medal was first handed to him by his commanding officer. Later I arranged for Louise Frechette to present Brent's medal to him at a small reception in the DPKO conference room at the United Nations in New York.

French arrived and saw people in the camps, it would prove to them that the Kigali authorities had seen to their welfare. Clearly the interim government and its underlings believed the French were actually making their way toward Kigali. As Henry said to me in a very low voice, these were "a very sick-in-the-head group of people."

We proceeded along the ranks, pinning medals on the Ghanaian officers, NCOs and troops. The battalion sergeant major found recorded music to play, but I missed the sounds of the Ghanaian regimental band, whose members had been evacuated to Nairobi. Lieutenant Colonel Joe Adinkra promised me they would be on one of the first flights back in.

That day I spent time with the operations team and Henry, as well as the two Rwandan liaison officers, to come up with the most accurate demarcation line between Turquoise and the RPF. We had sent a few UNMO teams to scout the main routes and bring us news of the RPF front line. It was evident that Kagame was finally moving with speed— but not recklessly—into the western part of the country along two principal axes, one running to Butare and the border with Burundi, and the other aiming directly at Ruhengeri, to link with his forces there (soldiers who had kept many RGF battalions tied up in the heart of the extremist country). The fighting was getting stiffer by the day in Kigali; as Kagame had indicated to me, he aimed to take the city before any possible intervention from the French. We were losing the battle to keep displaced people inside Rwanda in the north; they were fleeing in front of Kagame's advance. The potential Turquoise area was becoming quite limited in that part of the country.

Overall I felt as though we were finally moving, or at least staggering, ahead. The same phrase kept running through my head: *we aren't alone anymore.*

The morning of June 28 was filled with finalizing the last-minute details on Turquoise and the front line of the RPF. There was a lot of action in the city and, whenever I could find the time, I went to the roof to check out our surroundings through my binoculars. All I was able to spot were plumes of smoke and a few RPF troops moving in the open. I left Kigali around 1300, heading under escort for the Merama border and crossing into Uganda. I then flew by UNOMUR helicopter to Entebbe and caught a Hercules flight to Nairobi, arriving after supper. My aide-de-camp and four members of the media came with me, and on the trip to Goma we would be joined by the four-person UNMO liaison team who were to be our eyes and ears on the French force.

Tensions and confusion were building regarding UNAMIR's authority to coordinate humanitarian and peacekeeping efforts throughout Rwanda. Yaache and MacNeil had complete faith, as did I, in Charles Petrie, who was now working in the Nairobi office of UNREO, and they recommended I bring him with me to Goma because of his extensive experience and his ability to swiftly analyze a situation. Humanitarian support was still at a minimum in the RGF zones, where most of the people in need were trying to survive amid constant moves west. June 29 in Nairobi was an arduous exercise in patience, posturing and repeating myself to deaf ears. I had already alienated the French defence minister, François Léotard, who was on an inspection visit to his troops and had asked to meet me the same day in Cyangugu. I hadn't been able to go because I was supposed to be in Nairobi, and he was quite put out. I, however, was just as glad. He was travelling with an entourage of media, and any sign that I had rushed to his side would have given the RPF cause to question my neutrality.

My meetings in Nairobi were with the diplomatic community, the UN civilian administration support staff, the media and the NGOs. As usual, the diplomats promised support without making specific commitments. The media was focused on Turquoise and wanted me to threaten the French again so they could grab a punchy news clip (which I declined to do). The administration staff offered excuses instead of results, and the NGOs renewed their demands for independence and non-involvement with the military for reasons of neutrality, at the same time as they called for an "atmosphere of security" to allow them to do their work. UNREO was making headway in getting the NGOs and agencies to agree to hold daily information sessions not only in Nairobi, but also in Entebbe, Kabale, Goma, Bujumbura and Kigali. And Petrie promised to set up shop again in Kigali over the next weeks in order to shift the aid groups away from Nairobi and into the heart of the action.

Before I left for Goma, I held a medals parade for the mission's eighty or so Franco-African and other UNMOs and military staff who had been evacuated to Nairobi. We performed the ceremony on the front lawn of the expansive UN regional headquarters. This time, with no worries about mortar attacks or stray fire, and with the media in attendance along with some diplomats, UN senior staff, and NGO personnel, I spoke my mind and my heart. I stressed that the medals were well-deserved but that the job was certainly not finished; I took my listeners through the heroism and the horror, and the world's indifference. Even as I spoke, the carnage was continuing in Rwanda. I did my best to leave an impression that would survive for at least a few hours, maybe until the next news deadline, and then tried to enjoy the post-parade gathering.

The city of Goma looked as though it had been painted in blacks and greys. At about 1000 on June 30, I was sitting up front with the crew as we made our final approach to the single airstrip. We had stopped to pick up our liaison teams and their vehicles in Entebbe and then had flown on over the Volcano National Park, which was the home of the endangered mountain gorillas. Dian Fossey was buried down there among her great apes, having given up her life to a butcher with a machete in that thick bamboo mountain forest. One of the seven volcanoes we flew over was in a state of instability, spewing out steam and ash.

Goma was depressing. Before the genocide, Gisenyi, across the border in Rwanda, had been a beautiful tourist town, but Goma struck me as a dreadful, dark backwater, even though it was the capital of Kivu province.

I could see the sprawling Turquoise main base spread out before me. As we came down, I noticed hundreds of children playing chicken with the large cargo aircraft as they took off and landed. A misstep or a stumble and the children would be under the wheels of those monsters. No one had thought to put up fencing to keep the children out of danger. It was an inauspicious start to the first of my many visits to Turquoise.

Still, the French had obviously not skimped on their own logistics, billets and military requirements, and had carefully deployed around

the airfield and in the town. Witnessing the size and level of the outfit-
ting of the camp vividly put into relief my own lack of support. Money
and resources were no problem when the full weight of a world power
is put behind the effort. Opération Turquoise included over 2,500
members of elite units such as the French Foreign Legion, paratroopers,
marines and special forces. They were equipped with state-of-the-art
weapons, command and control communications HQ assets, over one
hundred armoured vehicles, batteries of heavy mortars, a squadron of
light armed reconnaissance and medium troop-lift helicopters, even a
dozen or so ground-attack and reconnaissance jet aircraft. They were
being deployed to Goma by an armada of very large cargo aircraft—
Boeings, Airbuses, Antonovs, Hercules and Transalls delivering supplies
of all sorts. Large bladders of fuel and water were already functional,
and a tent city to house troops and equipment was receiving final
touches. All that capability was mustered under a command team that
had worked together for years and was familiar with African conflicts.

A small group of tall, fit French senior officers was waiting for us at
the edge of the airfield, looking very smart in grey-green field dress.
Brigadier General Lafourcade introduced himself and his principal officers. He had a low voice, a generous handshake and an engaging
demeanour. I introduced my team, which included Charles Petrie, the
liaison officers and the journalists. Lafourcade invited us to climb into
jeeps for the ride into the centre of town, where he had established his
HQ. We made small talk as we drove along near-impassable streets
carved out of lava-covered ground, bouncing in all directions and trying not to hit any of the crowd in the streets. Everything was filthy from
falling ash.

About twenty minutes later, we entered a low-walled compound
with an unfinished building at its heart. The communication vehicles,
antennas, satellite dishes, and land lines going every which way were the
classic signs of a well-equipped HQ, even though doors and windows
were missing and the rooms were still unfinished.

We convened in small, straight, military field chairs in the middle
of a Spartan briefing room. Lafourcade's staff had taped a few area maps
on the wall, marked with minimal tactical information about troop

deployments. Lafourcade was very interested in my opinion regarding the RPF front line and confirmed that he had sent out troops toward Butare and Ruhengeri. Over the past few days, his force had set up a secondary airhead in Bukavu, across the river from Cyangugu. His mandate, he said, was to protect people at risk but not necessarily to disarm the RGF. He was, however, going to take down the barriers and disarm the self-defence forces and the Interahamwe. He stressed that he was only in the region until UNAMIR 2 was operational—at most for two months. Overall his briefing on his plan of action was rather skimpy, considering all the means he had at his disposal.

I walked Lafourcade and a couple of his senior staff officers through the mandate, concept, plan and operational status of UNAMIR 2. I then showed them a map marked with the five deployment sectors covering the country and the proposed force structure. I briefed them on the status of the battle for Kigali, and our picture of the massive movement of displaced persons and the major locations of camps. I then went to Lafourcade's map and drew the line that I saw as the outer limit of the French-protected area inside Rwanda. He was aghast. He could not believe the RPF had moved so fast in the last week. I told him that there would be no room left for him to operate east of Gisenyi if the displaced persons moved any closer to the Zairean border. In the southwest, the RPF was about twenty kilometres from Karama, east of Gikongoro, holding a front straight down to the Burundian border, though I did not know in what strength. The line I had drawn on his map left a narrow margin of no man's land between his forces and the most forward RPF positions. I made it clear that Butare was in essence in RPF hands. Still mulling what I'd revealed, Lafourcade proposed that we break for a light lunch and come back to the map after we had eaten.

Over lunch I found him to be much more genuine and level-headed than his officers. While I was talking about stopping the ongoing genocide, his staff were raising points about the loyalty France owed its old friends. (I had been told the Habyarimana family had close ties to President Mitterrand; one of his sons had serious business interests inside Rwanda.) They thought that UNAMIR should help prevent the RPF from defeating the RGF, which was not our job. I tried to alert

Lafourcade to be on his guard when it came to the interim government, which I thought would likely do everything in its power to bring about a confrontation between his forces and the RPF to try to bring the French firmly in on its side. I told him that the extremists were very astute and desperate, as well as in shock because so far the French had been taking down some barricades and seemingly doing nothing to help their cause. But my French interlocutors weren't convinced and continued to express their displeasure with UNAMIR's poor handling of the military aspects of the civil war. They refused to accept the reality of the genocide and the fact that the extremist leaders, the perpetrators and some of their old colleagues were all the same people. They showed overt signs of wishing to fight the RPF.

Some of these officers came from the colonial tradition of military intervention in the domestic affairs of former client states; they saw no reason to change their views over what they billed as one more inter-ethnic squabble. Other French citizens, such as Bernard Kouchner, seemed genuinely motivated by humanitarianism. I believe the French never did reconcile which attitude was supreme in Turquoise. To be fair, I do not think that at that point many of the Turquoise troops had a clear idea of the scale of the massacres or the degree of complicity in the genocide by the Habyarimana regime. While I feel no inclination to be generous in interpreting the motives of the French military, I honestly believe that their subsequent face-to-face encounters with the reality of the genocide brought most of them to their senses.

The French media very soon would start to report interviews with French soldiers who were shocked that it was their allies who were conducting the massacres and not the RPF, as they claimed to have been told by their superiors. Some of them soon came to understand the horrible responsibility of peacekeepers in a genocide. Despite its humanitarian aim, Opération Turquoise had arrived extremely light in trucks, which are essential to relief operations. At Bisesero, hundreds of Tutsis came out of hiding to be saved by a French patrol. The soldiers told them to wait while they went to find transport, and left them out in the open and on their own. When they got back with the trucks, they found the Tutsis massacred by the Interahamwe. As Opération

Turquoise continued, more and more French soldiers experienced similar incidents and became disgusted with their role in Rwanda.

When we returned to the briefing room after lunch, I informed the French officers that the RPF had asked that I be the link between them and Turquoise, and that UNAMIR be the arbiter and monitor of the demarcation line. We confirmed that Lafourcade would disarm all non-combat troops he encountered and also any persons who committed crimes, but he had no mandate to disarm the RGF in Rwanda. The French-led force would actively stop the killing in the Humanitarian Protection Zone (HPZ)—the term we agreed on to describe the Turquoise-secured area of Rwanda. Lafourcade agreed that his forces would never go beyond the demarcation line. He would include UNREO in the planning and execution of humanitarian efforts in the HPZ, which would keep us all in the loop. My mission would pursue its mandate even in the HPZ but in full coordination with his forces on the ground.

I asked him to concentrate on preventing the 2.5 million displaced persons from running through the western forest from fear of the RPF, pointing out what would happen if they spilled over the border into Zaire. Lastly, I asked that his public affairs people get the message across in the HPZ that Turquoise was *not* there to reinforce the RGF.

The meeting ended on a friendly note, but I was certain that Lafourcade would have to confirm many of my points with Paris. And even though he struck me as a competent and decent commander, I did not leave his headquarters with the warm and fuzzy feeling that we were totally on net.

My team and I took off at about 1500 for Entebbe, where we overnighted beside Lake Victoria, not far from the presidential palace that used to belong to the British governor general. The next morning, Canada Day back home, I inspected the movement control and liaison teams at the airport. Our transition camp for the contingents coming into Rwanda was still only a dream, even though in less than seven days the rest of the Ghanaian battalion was expected to be coming through and would need training on how to operate the APCs. So much for the power of my motivational speeches in Nairobi.

We then proceeded by helicopter to Kabale and stopped there for a session with Azrul Haque and UNOMUR, a meeting with the NGOs that were setting up advance transition points in the town, and not least, the final mission medals parade at the White Horse Inn. I warned the troops in my speech of praise and thanks that things would get more difficult before they got better, and I asked them to continue their effective cat-and-mouse games with the NRA. Then we flew by helicopter to the Mirama hills and crossed into Rwanda to link up with my escort.

The road trip through the Kagera National Park was beautiful despite the fact that at this time of year bush fires were burning, and in some places enormous clouds of smoke filled the sky. It was ghost country—though the RPF had the area firmly under control, there were still no civilians in the desolate and garbage-strewn villages.

We got back to the Amahoro that afternoon just in time for Canada Day celebrations: frivolity in the middle of hell. My Canadian contingent had determined that since everyone in the world knew we produced the best hockey players, a field hockey game was the right way to mark the holiday. For a field we would use the HQ parking lot, and Henry had agreed to assemble a Ghanaian team to play against us. My overconfident Canadians gloated about how they would trounce the Africans. Due to the possibility of shelling, the game would be played in flak jackets.

We adhere to a tough brand of hockey back home. As play started, the Canadians dominated for about a minute—until one of the Ghanaians floored Major John McComber. John was a solid, firmly planted infantry officer who took to competition like it was combat. His fall was a sign of things to come. I joined in for the first few minutes, but after being bodychecked onto my stick, which broke immediately, and landing on the unforgiving asphalt, I surrendered my place and limped off. When Henry, who is over six feet tall and weighs in at close to three hundred pounds, stepped onto the lot, the Canadian team revised its tactics and played a more European style of hockey. As the game progressed and the score went up, not in our favour, we realized that we had been had. The Ghanaians play field hockey as a national sport, and Henry had assembled a high-calibre team of fit, talented young men to counter the older and somewhat less fit Canadians.

Even so, it felt to us as if we had managed to put aside the troubles of the mission for an hour or two. Later, Colonel Hanrahan, who was in Kigali leading the Canadian Signals Regiment team recce party, wrote, "On the evening of 1 July 1994, the reconnaissance team asked MGen Dallaire and six Canadian UNMOs for a beer, which was carried in by us from Uganda to celebrate Canada Day. It was a surreal celebration. MGen Dallaire and his team were 'zombies.' They were in the same room as us, but their minds were elsewhere. Hollow eyes lost in thoughts of what they were experiencing. The stress was taking a huge toll."

That same day in New York, the Security Council passed Resolution 935, which requested that the secretary-general establish a committee of experts to investigate "possible" acts of genocide in Rwanda. The world could still not bring itself to call this slaughter by its proper name. RTLM wasted no time in denouncing the resolution. In its view, the Rwandan Supreme Court was both competent and impartial enough to handle the task. The station relentlessly pumped out lies to all Hutus able to find batteries for their radios. Even a month later, amid the horrors of the refugee and displaced persons camps that I would visit in Zaire, I saw people with small portable radios at their ears, listening to this vile propaganda. The radio remained the voice of authority, and many could not detach themselves from it. Because of its accusations against Hutu extremists, Médecins Sans Frontières joined white men with moustaches and Canadians in general on RTLM's hate list, having been pronounced pro-Tutsi; as a result I ordered more security around the King Faisal Hospital where James Orbinski (the head of the Médecins San Frontières team *and* a Canadian) and his team were working.

As predicted, the creation of the HPZ lured masses of displaced people out of central Rwanda and into the French zone. This was the terrible downside to Opération Turquoise. Having made public pronouncements about their desire to protect Rwandans from genocide, the French were caught by their own rhetoric and the glare of an active international media presence, and now had to organize the feeding and care of them. Realizing the news potential in the HPZ, many of the journalists who had been with me for weeks moved on to Goma or Cyangugu.

Still, we were guardedly optimistic in Kigali because the arrival of some more UNAMIR 2 troops was finally imminent. My staff officers were busy coordinating flight schedules, visiting donor nations for briefings on the mission, organizing troop reception and the thousands of other things that have to happen if a military deployment is going to work. My plan was to send troops out soon after they got to Rwanda to the most likely points of contact between the French and RPF. I tried not to think too much about the irony of having to devote forces intended to serve the cause of peace in Rwanda to preventing confrontation between one of the belligerents and another UN-mandated force. This stands as one of the crueller twists of cosmic irony foisted on the long-suffering Rwandans.

The only way I saw to avoid a total slide into absurdity was to effect a relief-in-place of French forces by UNAMIR 2 as my troops became available. The trap the French had rushed into would inevitably begin to close. Either they would pull out as soon as they could—even before the sixty-day limit to their mandate—or they would be cast in the role of protectors of the perpetrators of one of the most severe genocides in history. Given the large numbers of terrified displaced people who were moving into the HPZ, and the difficulties the RPF would almost certainly have in controlling victorious troops who knew all too well the dimensions and horrors of the genocide, it had become absolutely critical to get UNAMIR 2 troops onto the ground in the HPZ well before the French forces left. I emphasized to my staff that a relief-in-place of the French could not be delayed. But it would be a delicate and dangerous task: the Rwandans who had fled to the French zone, mostly Hutu, did not have as much faith in our ability to hold off the RPF as they had in that of the Turquoise forces. Their minds had been filled with lies about UNAMIR's collaboration with their enemy, and they themselves knew the level of their own complicity in the deaths of their neighbours.

• • •

The fighting was still intense in the city. Despite our warnings to stay inside, a reporter went out on his balcony at the Meridien hotel to watch the explosions and the arc of tracer bullets in the night and got shot in the leg (our second, and last, media casualty). He had been foolish, but even being cautious was inadequate protection at times.

Around this time I had a final, memorable encounter with Théoneste Bagosora. I had gone to the Diplomates to see Bizimungu, and was waiting for him at the front desk, when Bagosora opened his office door and spotted me there. From almost ten metres away, he started to shout, accusing me at the top of his lungs of being an RPF sympathizer. I was undermining the very important transfers from the Mille Collines and Meridien, he yelled, and he continued to berate me and UNAMIR for having failed the Arusha peace process as he passed me and started to climb the long stairway that swept in a curve up to the second floor of the lobby. When I mildly responded that it was his side that had been failing to keep truces for the transfers, he ratcheted up to an even more intense level of rage, and paused to lean over the metal railing in order to look me in the eye. With menace in every line of his face, he promised that if he ever saw me again he would kill me. Then he resumed climbing the stairs and carried on ranting even as he moved out of sight. Everyone in the hotel lobby had stopped to listen, and for several minutes after Bagosora's voice faded from hearing, all of us, civilians and soldiers alike, stood speechless and rooted to the spot. That was the last time I was to see Bagosora, who is now about to stand trial in Arusha as the chief architect of the genocide. When I see him again, it will be in the courtroom as I testify against him.

During those long nights in early July while the RPF fought to control the city, I sometimes let myself think about the evil that men such as Bagosora wrought—how the Hutu extremists, the young men of the Interahamwe, even ordinary mothers with babies on their backs, had become so drunk with the sight and smell of blood and the hysteria that they could murder their neighbours. What did they think as they were fleeing the RPF and stepping through blood-soaked killing fields and over corpses rotting into heaps of rags and bone? I rejected the picture of the génocidaires as ordinary human beings who had performed evil acts. To my mind, their crimes had made them inhuman, turned them into machines made of flesh that imitated the motions of being human. The perpetrators on both sides had their "justifications." For the Hutus, insecurity and racism had been artfully engineered into hate and violent reaction. In the RPF's case, it was willing to fight to win a homeland at all costs, and its soldiers' rage against the genocide transformed them into machines. And what of the witnesses—what drove us? Had the scenes we'd waded through frayed our humanity, turned us into numbed-out machines too? Where did we find our motivation to keep going on? Keep on going is what we had to do.

We were solving problems from dawn to dusk and long into each night. When Hanrahan went back to Canada, he left two members of his recce team behind so they could help establish an APC driving school for the Ghanaian contingent, which was supposed to be deployed by mid-July. The Ethiopian and Zambian battalions were due by the end of the month—we had to locate some English-Ethiopian translators. The Canadians under Hanrahan would arrive in the next three weeks. We were supposed to reach a troop strength of about 2,800 by late July, just in time to implement my aggressive plan to relieve the French forces in the HPZ and subsequently open the zone to the RPF in phases.

Lafourcade soon sent me a memo confirming his (and his government's) interpretation of our discussions. He wrote that he had no mandate to disarm the RGF, though he would prevent it from taking action in the humanitarian zone. His memo stated that Turquoise was not going to disarm the militias and the RGF in the HPZ unless they posed a threat to the people his force was protecting. As a result, the extremists would be able to move about freely in the zone, safe from any interference from the French, and also safe from retribution from or clashes with the RPF. Before we took over, I would have to persuade Lafourcade to disarm the whole bunch or our task would be risky to say the least. While the RGF and the militias were unlikely to shoot at the French, they might be tempted to shoot at us.

Lafourcade's description of the demarcation line between him and the RPF was still slightly to the east of the one I'd presented to him in

Goma, but was far less ambitious than the one France had originally proposed to the Security Council. When Kagame received his copy, he made it clear that he already had troops to the west of Lafourcade's line and certainly wasn't rolling them back. I had to intervene, and what a day that was. I lost track of the number of meetings and faxes and phone calls, but by the end of it, we had an agreed-upon zone that didn't include Ruhengeri or Butare or Gitarama or even a whisper about Kigali. We also had a working plan with Turquoise.

That night the mood in Force HQ was almost festive. Beth and the Canadian wives had sent another huge air transport carton of goodies from home, and we divided up the spoils. There was a small nook with a counter in the hall outside my office, left over from the building's incarnation as a hotel. While I stood there chatting with Henry, someone—possibly Tiko—produced a bottle of Scotch and set it on the counter. I went to my office and found a bottle of wine donated by a grateful NGO, and a few beers appeared from somewhere else. I supplied my small yellow radio and tape player and I blasted out our limited repertoire of Frankie Lane and Stompin' Tom Connors. We smoked cigars and kept everyone in the building, maybe even the compound, awake until past midnight. We were celebrating our success with the demarcation line, but even more than that, I think we were celebrating the fact that we had survived. Henry, Tiko, Phil, Moen, Racine, McComber, Austdal, the complete humanitarian cell and the rest of my ragged band—we had lived to see the cavalry. The night was shot through with jolts of pure sorrow, but it was also full of laughter and an intensity and joy I've rarely experienced since.

Of course, both Kagame and the French had to test the line, and two major incidents nearly blew into open combat between the new belligerents, as I took to calling them.

First, the RPF ambushed a French convoy that was returning from Butare with a couple of expatriates and a large number of orphans. The transfer had been approved, but a local RPF commander let the convoy through a couple of barriers and then fired on them. The French fired back. Luckily no one was injured, and that mess was sorted out within hours.

The second event was far more damaging to Turquoise's semblance of neutrality. A French officer named Colonel Thibault, who had been a long-time military adviser to the RGF, was in charge of the southwest region of the HPZ. Thibault publicly announced that he was not in Rwanda to disarm the RGF or the militias and that if the RPF made any attempt to come near the HPZ line, he would use all the means at his disposal to fight and defeat them. This kind of talk was exactly what the extremists wanted to hear from the French. It also made superb copy for the voracious media. RTLM put the colonel's posturing to immediate use. Lafourcade had to rein Thibault in and, to his credit, he did, publicly rebuking his subordinate commander. He clarified Turquoise's position in an unequivocal media statement: "We will not permit any exactations in the HPZ against anybody and we will refuse the intrusion of any armed elements." He sent a letter to Kagame through me explaining the situation, and Kagame received it with his usual skepticism. The question did remain: Which man best expressed Turquoise's underlying sympathies, Lafourcade or Thibault?

This was a political question that the new SRSG, Shaharyar Khan, would have to deal with; he was due to arrive in Kigali on July 4. Khan had a reputation as a well-respected crisis manager; Maurice assured me he was competent and well-briefed, a hard worker who had put in serious time in such complicated places as Afghanistan. I looked forward to handing over the political and administrative functioning of the mission to him.

By first light on July 4, reports started to come in that the RGF had withdrawn from Kigali and made a clean break toward the west. (From the evidence we later found in and around their defensive positions, it looked like they had run out of ammunition.) By morning prayers, the battle for Kigali was over and the city was unusually quiet.

We would devote most of the day to receiving the new SRSG. Khan flew to Entebbe and then on to the Rwandan border by helicopter. Dressed in a blue UN bullet-proof vest and surrounded by an impressive number of UNMOs and UN vehicles, he carried on to Kigali by road. He arrived around 1800 and was greeted by a Ghanaian honour guard at the stadium, while the roughly ten thousand displaced persons still behind protective razor wire looked on with curious eyes. From our first handshake, he struck me as a leader to be relied upon. He did not blanch at the sight of his office-cum-bedroom in the Force HQ, and he greeted everyone he met with warmth and sincerity. Over the coming weeks he dined with us on the usual terrible German rations, and experienced our ongoing privations and rationing. Khan was a man of ideas and initiative who rapidly put his imprint on the political team. For the first time in a long while, Dr. Kabia looked happy.

15

TOO MUCH, TOO LATE

July 5 was the start of a new phase in the civil war and genocide. Kagame wanted to meet me as soon as possible, but I spent a good part of the morning briefing the SRSG and then taking him on an orientation tour of our sites in Kigali. Shaharyar Khan described his first encounters with the genocide in his book *The Shallow Graves of Rwanda*: "As General Dallaire drove me past places where massacres had taken place, there were corpses and skeletons lying about picked bare by dogs and vultures. The scene was macabre, surrealistic and utterly gruesome. Worse was to follow. We went to the ICRC hospital where hundreds of bodies lay piled up in the garden. Everywhere there were corpses, mutilated children, dying women. There was blood all over the floors and the terrible stench of rotting flesh. Every inch of space was taken up by these patients. The day before, as government forces (the RGF) left, they had fired mortars indiscriminately and one had hit the casualty ward in the ICRC hospital, killing seven patients." (In fact, when we got there, the staff were still cleaning up body parts.) Khan continued: "I have never witnessed such horror, such vacant fear in the eyes of patients, such putrid stench. I did not throw up, I did not even cry: I was too shocked. I was silent. My colleagues who had lived through the massacres were hardened: they had seen worse, much worse."

The scene was essentially the same at the King Faisal. That hospital tour, however, included a locked ward. When Khan asked James Orbinski why, James explained that these casualties had been identified by the RPF as having participated in the massacres, and the RPF wanted them to live to face the courts instead of lynch mobs. Khan considered this an extraordinary example of discipline from a victorious rebel force.

Khan had been in Afghanistan during the worst of Soviet and mujahedeen conflict. As a child he had lived through the Hindu-Muslim riots of 1947. In his book he wrote, "The fact is that never in living history has such wanton brutality been inflicted by human beings on their fellow creatures [as in Rwanda]. . . . even the killing fields of Cambodia and Bosnia pale before the gruesome, awful depravity of massacres in Rwanda." He chose one example from among many others to make his point. "The Interahamwe made a habit of killing young Tutsi children, in front of their parents, by first cutting off one arm, then the other. They would then gash the neck with a machete to bleed the child slowly to death but, while they were still alive, they would cut off the private parts and throw them at the faces of the terrified parents, who would then be murdered with slightly greater dispatch." Khan was wrong when he wrote that the veterans of the genocide had become hardened to such things. We were simply putting off our feelings until later.

Kagame had moved his command post into a cottage inside Camp Kanombe, and after winning Kigali was trying his best to be magnanimous. He told me he now fully supported the total deployment of UNAMIR 2 to help move the French out of the HPZ; he promised that the airport would be opened in a few days; and he was ready to announce a unilateral ceasefire. If the RGF didn't accept the ceasefire, Kagame vowed to push the fight to the Zaire border.

He informed me that he and his political advisers would soon be setting up a broad-based government founded on the Arusha framework—with some modifications, of course. No one who had had any part in the genocide would be included, and despite the fact that the RPF was calling for a ceasefire, it would not enter into negotiations with the interim government. The country, as he saw it, was now divided in three: the RPF zone; the Turquoise humanitarian zone, which UNAMIR 2 needed to monitor and then take over in order to evict the French as soon as possible; and in the northwest, the relatively small RGF zone, which he would have no scruples about attacking if the former regime's forces didn't lay down their weapons. There we had it, the victor's map.

I asked Kagame to wait until he could meet the new SRSG before going public with his plans so that UNAMIR could have some time to react to the new circumstances, and he agreed.

I can only dream of what Shaharyar Khan might have done for Rwanda if he had been the one who had led the mission from the start. He had the valuable leadership trait of being able to anticipate. Two days into his mandate, he already understood that the most crucial issue facing us was the need for action in order to bring the refugees home. When he had his first meeting with Kagame, at the damaged VIP lounge of the airport on the morning of July 6, he quickly grasped the implications of the RPF's position—we had to get to the interim government and Bizimungu as soon as possible because it was up to us to persuade them they should agree to the ceasefire. Otherwise Kagame would push right through the remaining RGF territory in pursuit of total victory, and the humanitarian disaster would be complete.

Khan managed to set up his first meetings in Goma and Gisenyi for the next day, and took off with Tiko and a mixture of civilian staff and UNMOs by road to Kabale and then by helicopter to Zaire. (Tiko accompanied Khan on this and other risky early missions of shuttle diplomacy since Henry was finally in Ghana seeing to the myriad details of burying his father. Tiko would never allow anyone to come close enough to injure Khan.)

Lafourcade met Khan at the airport and gave him a short briefing on Turquoise. A French escort accompanied Khan and his team across the border to the Meridian Hotel in Gisenyi, where they met with the interim government's minister of foreign affairs, Jérôme Bicamumpaka, whose job was clearly to size up this new player. To be effective, Khan had to persuade both sides of his complete neutrality. Over the next few days, he met the other major figures of the interim government in Gisenyi, as well as Bizimungu, the head of the RGF. (The Gendarmerie's chief of staff, Ndindiliyimana, was nowhere to be found, and I was never to see him again.) The ministers were calling their flight to Gisenyi a strategic withdrawal rather than a rout, and while they ultimately agreed to the ceasefire, I suspected they were brokering deals with the local Zairean authorities (possibly even colluding with sympathetic senior French officers inside the camps) in order to retain their weapons and political structure, thus setting up to come back into Rwanda in force within a couple of years and start the war all over again.

The RPF was certainly aware of the use to which its foes could put the refugee camps in Zaire and the Turquoise HPZ. On July 8, Frank Kamenzi asked if I would consider forwarding a letter from a new group, "les forces démocratiques de changement," to the president of the Security Council. Though I didn't recognize the names of the signatories, the group was composed of moderate political leaders who claimed to represent the MDR, the PSD, the PDC and the PL parties. The letter expressed vehement opposition to the HPZ, which they described as a protection zone and escape route for criminals. The fact that they'd come forward so quickly after the fall of Kigali was a sign that the RPF was helping to build a coalition of most of the old Arusha signatory parties. UNAMIR's efforts to identify politicians who could speak for the Hutu population after an RPF victory—and therefore had the moral right to sit and discuss the future political structure of this disembowelled nation—had been sporadic at best. True to form, the RPF took the initiative. I informed Khan and agreed to forward the letter immediately.

The RPF also stuck rigorously to their position that they would not deal with any people who had played a role, no matter how reluctantly, in the command structure of the old regime. The next day I received a copy of an open declaration by the RGF moderates, who were now holed up in the town of Kigame just southwest of Gikongoro. (I had lost touch with them and had assumed they had already fled to Zaire.) The document was an unequivocal disavowal of the extremists and a total commitment to ceasefire, peace and the reconstitution of the nation according to the terms of the Arusha accords. Nine moderate officers, headed by Rusatira and Gatsinzi, had signed it. I sent the declaration on to Kagame with a covering note stating that accepting their return to Rwanda would be a significant act of reconciliation that would help the cause of international recognition of the new government. But I got no substantive response. Kagame, and those around him—figures such as Pasteur Bizimungu, the RPF's hardnosed political negotiator—still had no time for these officers.

Meanwhile, the ebb and flow of contingents was picking up momentum. On July 9, we held a small farewell ceremony at the airport for the Tunisians. Earlier in the mission I had given this stalwart contingent the large UN flag we had raised in Kinihara on November 1, 1993, to mark the official start of the mission. The Tunisians were the only troops on the ground when we boldly took over the monitoring of the demilitarized zone and the flag had stayed with them as they fulfilled all the dangerous duties I had assigned them. On the tarmac in front of the gaping hold of a Hercules, we saluted each other and shook hands for the last time. At their request, I signed the flag. I'm told it still flies today in a garrison somewhere in Tunisia.

The first small batch of Ghanaian reinforcements had been dropped off at Entebbe only to find that our supposed reception and training site was non-functional (we still had no budget for it, just a million administrative excuses from UN staff). They were eventually bused to Rwanda and we put them up in the military school in Camp Kigali, where they dug themselves in.

Later that day, Lafourcade sent me an urgent message that he wanted me to deliver immediately to Kagame. He had serious concerns about the northwestern part of the country, essentially the RGF area from Ruhengeri west to the Zairean border. There were hundreds of thousands of displaced people in that area and they were fidgety from fear of the RPF. He wanted Kagame to stop his advance. An exodus to Goma would complicate things with the Zaireans and make it impossible for the belligerents to reach a political accord.

Kagame reacted as if Lafourcade's letter confirmed every suspicion he had of Turquoise's agenda—clearly it was political, not humanitarian, he charged. He told me to remind Lafourcade that all the RGF had to do to stop his advance was agree to the unilateral ceasefire—unlike his opponents, Kagame said, he was not targeting civilians. As far as he was concerned, the movement of displaced persons was a reaction to extremist propaganda and therefore not his responsibility. Lafourcade was furious.

Kagame did acquiesce to the request to move a French liaison team into Force HQ, perhaps realizing how much more effective it would make me as intermediary between himself and Turquoise. Lieutenant Colonel Francis and Commandant Pierre arrived on July 11 on a Canadian Hercules flight with their vehicles and equipment. They were immediately escorted to my HQ, where they set up shop not far from my office. Although they received curious looks from the heavy RPF presence at the airport and along the route to headquarters, all went smoothly. The two officers were friendly, cooperative and respectful, but since my Force HQ was in RPF territory, the officers agreed to be confined to the headquarters for the time being, both to keep them safe and because I did not want them to conduct intelligence operations against the RPF that would violate UNAMIR's neutrality. Within hours of their arrival, we had a dependable and secure communications link between Turquoise and UNAMIR 2.

As the RPF had moved in, Kigali had been nearly abandoned, save for the militia-populated communes in the poorest suburbs of the city. Now increasing numbers of displaced persons were starting to enter the city. Some were coming home but others seemed to be squatters. It was not unusual to see RPF soldiers evicting people from an abandoned home and then moving others into it. (We didn't know whether they were original owners who had survived the genocide, or whether they were merely friends of the RPF movement.) As the days went by, a large number of Tutsi refugees and diaspora came to Kigali and settled in.

The influx worried Khan, who thought it would destabilize the country. I took him on an extensive tour of all the nearby hellholes. Neither he nor I enjoyed swerving around corpses and bundles of rags left on the streets, but the vestiges of the barbaric handiwork of the militias was everywhere. Though the Amahoro Stadium was still full, several of our protected sites were now empty or occupied by only a few hundred people still in dire need of aid. One orphanage in the Butare area still harboured over six hundred children along with a makeshift hospital that had thirty-five casualties confined to beds and a large number of ambulatory patients. One German doctor and two nurses were running the place with assistance from some of the healthier adults. Yaache and the MamaPapas had been in contact with UNICEF to arrange deliveries of food and water. Many of the kids were so psychologically damaged that they were immobile, sitting here, there and everywhere and reacting to nothing, even the hundreds of flies that clustered at every orifice of their bruised, dirty and frail bodies. The eyes in their thin faces seemed to blaze at you like lasers, projecting beams of energy that burned right into your heart.

Around this time the little sleep I got at night began to be completely invaded by nightmares of these children's accusing eyes, or gruesome scenes that I'd blocked out of my mind shortly after I'd witnessed them, or the ugly consequences of decisions I'd taken. My dreams often brought back in ghastly detail the ten dead Belgian soldiers piled in a bloody heap by the morgue door in that terrible hospital courtyard.

July 12 began with a major political statement from the RPF, the "Declaration of the RPF for the Installation of the Formal Institutions of Government." The three-page document laid out modifications to the Arusha Agreement that generously favoured the RPF. Those ministerial and legislative positions previously held by the extremist parties would now accrue to the RPF. There would be no amnesty for members of the old regime or the military implicated in the genocide—they would face the full penalty of the law. Faustin Twagiramungu would be the new prime minister. Since the leaders of the other political parties had been murdered, it would be up to Faustin to propose suitable replacements in consultation with the president, who would be nominated by the RPF. The leaders of the RPF were moving very rapidly to build a government and a national army that would be instruments of their movement. Although they professed the new institutions would not be ethnic-based, it was becoming harder and harder to accept that line of argument when some of them quietly expressed disdain for the millions of Hutus now being pushed into living as both refugees and potential pawns to another round of war.

Faustin, back from Belgium, had made contact with the UNAMIR liaison team in Nairobi and asked for transport into Kigali. He came home on July 14 on one of our Hercules flights. We had cleaned out a couple of the floors in the Meridien for the new mission staff. When Faustin said he had no accommodations in the capital and that the RPF had nothing to offer him, we set aside a suite for him, which he had to use as an office as well as living quarters for a while. We provided him with office supplies, typing support, long distance phone calls, food and even some transport. His surviving family was still scattered and he had to scavenge to survive, because the RPF was not yet supporting him in any way. His situation was not unique. As more of the surviving Rwandan officials came back to the city, we found ourselves putting up several of them in the Meridien. Everything in Kigali was either burned or otherwise destroyed, or had been looted, and with the RPF still sorting itself out, these officials needed help to open up their offices. Even the Supreme Court justice was operating out of his bedroom at the Meridien hotel.

Things were hopping on all fronts. Yaache and the humanitarian team were meeting with the bigger NGOs and agencies such as UNICEF, WFP, MSF and the ICRC to sort out how to restore the water system in Kigali. The civilian humanitarian staff moved to the UNDP building downtown, as space and communications were at a premium in the Force HQ. MamaPapa teams were moving over two hundred Hutu displaced persons from the Byumba camp into our Kigali safe sites for protection. Our UNMOs in Entebbe were having a hard time getting support from the airport authorities, who threatened to throw us out of the main complex because we were not paying our bills. The UNMOs were also having arguments with Brown and Root regarding the state of the American APCs and the contractor's logistics support plan for our battalions to be deployed across the country. A bright note was that the Australian recce party was still here, and busy considering where to put their field hospital. Since we agreed they had to serve the force but also be of maximum aid to the civilian population, they were looking at the main Kigali hospital. I immediately requested that the head of the recce party, Colonel Ramsay, contact his leaders back home and ask that he be given authority to take on—in fact, create—the position of UNAMIR's chief medical officer. Ramsay was keen. For the first time since the departure of the Belgian medical field hospital, we would have a professional medical plan with the assets needed to support the force. The Australians were also bringing a company of infantry for close protection.

On July 14, my intelligence officer reported at morning prayers that the RPF was running two interrogation centres in Kigali and that summary executions were being conducted all day long. He could not get close to the well-guarded centres himself but believed his informants were reliable. Also, new recruits were being trained in Camp Kanombe—we were seeing more and more of them at the checkpoints. In eastern Rwanda, soldiers speaking only Swahili were conducting security checks and patrols. My intelligence officer believed they were NRA soldiers from Uganda.

On a trip that day to Bukavu and Goma, I met with five of the RGF moderates who had signed the "Kigame Nine" declaration, among them Gatsinzi and Rusatira, whom I was relieved to see again. They and their families had been evacuated to Zaire by the French after their declaration made them even more of a target for Hutu hard-liners. But the French were not supporting them, and they asked if I could give them some cash so they could buy food. They wanted to come back to Kigali and work on the reconciliation of the country; they insisted that they were not defectors to the RPF, but men who loved Rwanda. I promised to speak with Kagame about them. This time I offered my services as their guarantor if he let them back into the country. A couple of weeks later we brought them to Kigali, and the RPF set them up in the Milles Collines, where we fed them and provided security. The RPF left them to stew for a while, but finally integrated them into the new national army.

As we flew over Goma, I could see the massive movements of people flowing across the border (technically Gisenyi fell to the RPF on July 17, but it had already been under attack by the RPF). Lafourcade and I met for an hour or so in his logistics base. He estimated that about 300,000 people had already crossed into Zaire—Gendarmerie and militia groups among them—and were being directed to camps just north of the city. Neither he nor the government of Zaire had the capacity to aid them, and Lafourcade thought the number of refugees would soon hit one million.

Back at my helicopter, I was told that we could not take off from the airport unless we paid a landing fee of $800 U.S. UN aircraft were supposed to be exempt from such fees, and I went into the tower building to negotiate with the manager. He told me to pay up in cash or we wouldn't be allowed to leave—and there were enough Zairean guards around the airport, armed to the teeth, to indicate his threat was very real. We pooled our money, but the bulk of the cash came from Phil. He was never reimbursed—the manager gave us no receipt and the UN did not accept our explanation of the expense, insisting that we should have refused to pay.

Late that night Khan and I received a code cable from the DPKO describing the Security Council deliberations on the new humanitarian catastrophe that was upon us. The French had requested that pressure be put on the RPF to stop its campaign and sign a ceasefire immediately, for humanitarian reasons. From the briefing notes prepared by Boutros-Ghali's senior adviser, Chinmaya Gharekhan, they all seemed to think that there was still a fight going on. But by now Ruhengeri had fallen and the RGF were on the run. It was too late to stop the debacle but more support for building up UNAMIR 2 could prevent the same refugee scenario from happening in the south. The French had agreed to close the only road through the southwestern forest and mountains to try to stem the movement toward Cyangugu. I thought to myself that night that the way things were going, we were doomed to fail this operation as totally as we had failed the last one.

By this time the pressure of my absence and the nature of my mission were weighing far too heavily on my family and they hoped to see me before the end of summer, at least on leave. Boutros-Ghali did not want to change force commanders at this critical juncture, and wanted me to stay on until my scheduled end date in October. I proposed to go on leave near the end of August, so that I could have time with my kids before they went back to school, and then return to Rwanda until late September, when I'd hand over my job. I wanted Henry Anyidoho to replace me, and the DPKO was unanimous in its support of his candidacy. In the meantime, I proposed that a new deputy force commander and chief of staff be recruited in order to understudy Henry just before I went on leave.

Three days after I made my request, having first run it by Maurice, General de Chastelain approved my proposal, and supported my recommendation that Henry take over from me. I passed on the news to Khan, who was aware of my request to leave Kigali a few weeks early. He regretted my departure, but certainly understood the reasons, and thought that Henry would make a fine replacement.

Word arrived from our liaison team in Goma that the situation was very tense and the flow of refugees was increasing. The Zairean army had moved a parachute battalion to Goma to increase security. The French reported that the RPF were shooting into their advance positions east of Gisenyi with heavy weapons including artillery, and that the French had responded with a show of force using their close-attack fighter jets. The Zaireans were finally disarming the RGF at the border, stripping some of them of items such as machetes and rifles, but large weapon systems—artillery, heavy mortars, anti-aircraft guns and anti-tank systems—were being waved through and escorted north of the city. Neither the Zaireans nor the French were taking any measures to separate the militia, gendarmes or soldiers from the civilians as they crossed the border. Yaache spent the day in Goma with the HAC team, UNREO and the Turquoise humanitarian cell, attempting to coordinate efforts. UNREO formally passed the task of caring for the refugees outside Rwanda to the UNHCR, which bothered me. As media cameras were being drawn to the massive movement across the border, even less attention would be paid to the survivors of the genocide inside Rwanda.

The worsening picture finally seemed to prod the U.S. administration into making some public noise. On the morning of July 16 I got a cable from the DPKO to which was attached a "White House Press Statement Concerning Rwanda." The statement announced that "the Clinton Administration has closed the Embassy of Rwanda and ordered all personnel to leave the country. Representatives of the so-called interim government of Rwanda must depart within five working days." The Clinton administration announced that the U.S. government would "begin consultations with other UN Security Council members to remove representatives of the interim government from Rwanda's seat on the council . . . [and that the U.S. has] denied access to any Rwandan government financial holdings in the United States. The United States cannot allow representatives of a regime that supports genocidal massacre to remain on our soil, President Clinton said." The last set of surprises: the U.S. "has taken a leading role in efforts to protect the Rwandan people and ensure humanitarian assistance. . . . [It has] provided $9 million in relief, flown about 100 Defense Department missions . . . strongly supported an expanded UNAMIR, airlifting 50 armoured personnel carriers to Kampala . . . [and is] equipping the UN's Ghanaian peacekeeping battalion."

Clinton's fibbing dumbfounded me. The DPKO was still fighting with the Pentagon for military cargo planes to move *matériel*. The Pentagon had actually refused to equip the Ghanaians as they felt the bill was too high and that Ghana was trying to gouge them. And *who* exactly got the $9 million?

Luc Racine and his small team were back from their reconnaissance of the HPZ, where they had been looking for suitable sites for our battalions and firming up handover procedures with the local Turquoise commanders and civilian authorities. They had got around in French vehicles with armed Turquoise escorts, and had kept signs of their UN affiliation to a minimum. Most of the people in the area were either hostile to UNAMIR or fearful we wouldn't have the will to do the job of protecting them after the French left. Luc recommended that all UNMOs going into the HPZ travel with French units for protection; he judged that it was crucial that they be French-speakers in order to help build trust in the people. There was little aid coming in, so Luc also recommended that we couple our deployments with major food distributions, which would prove we had something we could offer. Lastly, he said the RPF had to stop their advance and quit probing the HPZ line so that people inside the zone would feel safer.

Luc confirmed that, in all areas inside the HPZ, the RGF were still moving about with their weapons. In only one of the three sub-zones of the HPZ were the militia unarmed. In another, they wore special bandanas and were assisting the French to maintain order. There were still roadblocks all over the place, generally manned by the Gendarmerie. The best estimate was that there were over two million people in the zone, two thirds of them internally displaced persons; of those, about 800,000 were already on the west side of the forest, though still a good distance away from Cyangugu. Tutsis were being held in large numbers in at least three sites. The French had three light battalions in the zone and were patrolling vigorously day and night.

I was to meet with General Bizimungu in Goma at 1100 on the morning of July 16. I also wanted to touch base with the provincial governors of Goma and Bukavu districts to find out for myself what they planned to do about the refugees, and especially with the Rwandan military and militia in their midst. I was met at the airport by Lafourcade, who asked me to be discreet about how the meeting with Bizimungu had been arranged—it might not look so good that the RGF chief was inside the French military camp.

A French staff officer led me and my aide-de-camp, Babacar Faye Ndiaye, through the labyrinth of the Turquoise tent city and then left us alone to see the general. Bizimungu had just crossed the border that morning and he looked terrible. He was haggard, his left arm was injured, his uniform was dirty. He was incensed with the RPF for not stopping before Ruhengeri and proclaiming the ceasefire, which would have prevented the exodus. He had nothing with him—no kit, no money, no food—and he asked whether UNAMIR might assist him. I told him to stay in touch with my liaison team in Goma and to produce a list of what he needed. As we were leaving, he asked my ADC to send him cigarettes and soap.

We headed into Goma proper under French escort, driving past ash-covered squalor, dead bodies abandoned in the street, and suffocating crowds. We waited at least twenty minutes outside the governor's office before he was free to see me. The governor was a gracious man with a no-nonsense air about him. I asked him what he thought of this onslaught of refugees, militia and Rwandan army personnel. He said that he needed massive support from the NGOs and the UN; the influx had taxed the local infrastructure beyond its capacity and there was suffering among his own people. Food and water were already scarce. Starvation and disease wouldn't be far behind.

Regarding the RGF, he said that their small arms and major weapons were being moved to secure compounds several kilometres north of the camps and the city, and that Zairean troops would provide protection for the refugees and the NGOs in Goma. I informed him that UNAMIR might find itself obliged to assist in the return of the refugees as well as escorting convoys of aid. He was not favourable to my forces entering his country.

As we made our way back to the helicopter, the sky seemed to darken though it was only early afternoon. The nearest volcano was spewing more ash, which was blocking out the sun. I suddenly felt claustrophobic, as if this scene were about to swallow me up. We escaped the airport without having to pay a landing fee.

In Bukavu, the governor had similar concerns about UN troops crossing the border. He said he could handle the 300,000 refugees so far who had fled into his province, but he hoped the French could hold the others across the river. I was surprised at the lack of NGO or UN agency presence in town, but I already knew that Turquoise did not have a solid humanitarian plan. There had been major looting in Cyangugu under the noses of the French. This was not looking good at all.

After Gisenyi fell on July 17, RPF artillery rounds began to land on the outskirts of Goma, principally along the escape routes among the foothills of the volcanos. Both Lafourcade and the Zairean authorities were outraged. A few rounds landed at the airport where the runway area was chockablock with a steady stream of incoming and outgoing aircraft. Panicked, some of the refugees started to move farther away from the border. What was the RPF trying to prove? I ordered Frank Kamenzi to inform his headquarters that they had to stop the shelling. A day or two later it did stop, but the psychological effect on the refugees was debilitating.

Ironically, the unilateral ceasefire—another name for total RPF victory—was announced the next day, though there were no crowds cheering the peace in the streets of Kigali. I don't think any of us except the humanitarian gang felt much relief, but Yaache and the MamaPapas were happy that at last they would be able to deal with only one over-all authority to coordinate emergency relief, and that the rebuilding of the nation's judicial, financial, medical, policing and government infra-structures could begin in earnest. And the atmosphere in the HQ eased a little. The fighting and the killing were officially over, but the exact nature of the horrors that were soon to afflict the Goma camps and the displaced people in the HPZ were waiting just around the corner.

On July 19, Khan and I set off to attend the official swearing-in of the new Broad-Based Government of National Unity at the CND. Having seen so many failed attempts in the months leading up to April 6, I felt a little strange sitting at the end of the front row of dignitaries on the lawn by the main entrance to the CND, under a canopy in the sun, with no responsibility except to be a witness. The RPF was taking care of security; the well-armed soldiers who stood between the hundreds of spectators and the dignitaries under the canopy, as well as all around the perimeter of the CND, detracted from the serenity or hope the swearing-in of a new government might have inspired. As a general rule, I thought, the larger and more overt the security precautions, the less safe one should feel.

So I watched as the ceremonial necessities were undertaken with solemn decorum. Rwanda's new president, Pasteur Bizimungu, a Hutu who had been tortured by the Habyarimana regime, was sworn in, fol-lowed by the rest of the eighteen-member cabinet. Khan and I didn't understand a word, as all the speeches were in Kinyarwanda, but Bizimungu looked almost regal. Then Paul Kagame took his oath as vice-president and minister of defence, followed by two more Hutus: Faustin as prime minister and Colonel Alexis Kanyarengwe as vice–prime minister.

As the ceremony ended I thought, "So now they are the ones in charge, after nearly four years in the bush." I wondered again about the nature of this less-than-perfect unilateral ceasefire and victory, and of Paul Kagame, so dignified as he accepted his new office. Was he haunt-ed by the human cost of his victory? He and the rest of the RPF leader-ship had known what was going on behind the RGF lines. He and the movement had been relentlessly inflexible about any concession that might have eased the tension in the country, both before the civil war broke out and later, when they had the RGF on the run. He had been reluctant to support UNAMIR 2, whose specific duty was to stop the killing and the mass displacement of the population. Increasingly we could see the immaculate cars of Burundian returnees or the ox carts of the Ugandan Tutsi refugees in the streets of Kigali, as members of the scattered diaspora took up residence throughout the better parts of the capital, sometimes even throwing out legitimate owners who had survived the war and genocide. Kagame seemed to be doing little about it. Who exactly had been pulling his strings throughout the campaign? I found myself thinking such dire thoughts as whether the campaign and the genocide had been orchestrated to clear the way for Rwanda's return to the pre-1959 status quo in which Tutsis had called all the shots. Had the Hutu extremists been bigger dupes than I? Ten years later, I still can't put these troubling questions to rest, especially in light of what has happened to the region since.

Unsettled by my reflections about the RPF victory, I met with Vice-President Kagame in his walled bungalow at Camp Kanombe the next afternoon to discuss the pressing issues that faced his newly-won country. He agreed to all my UNAMIR 2 deployments and to the force structure I envisioned, though both he and I recognized it would be tricky to achieve my tasks when the pace of UN deployment was still so slow. I also suggested that we move some of our forces into the Gisenyi area in order both to secure transient camps inside Rwanda for returnees and to be ready to go into Goma to help out. On stopping the outflow of displaced persons, Kagame agreed that there should be a major aid effort inside Rwanda, which could act as a magnet to draw people back into the country. He raised the idea of sending some of the new government ministers into the HPZ to start explaining to the populace what was going to happen and to encourage them not to flee to Bukavu.

He needed our help to repair the airport in order to persuade a commercial airline to start regular flights into Kigali. He wanted normalcy as fast as he could get it. He asked us to make every effort to meet the planned July 31 date for entry of formed units into the HPZ, and was adamant that the French leave by August 22; he wanted us to work with the French to set up the bureaucratic infrastructure in the HPZ before the handover in order to avoid creating a vacuum of civil authority. He wanted Canada to provide a technical mission to help reconstruct his army because of our reputation for being able to accomplish such tasks and the fact that our forces were bilingual. He had yet another delicate job he wanted me to undertake: could I persuade Turquoise and the Zairean government to return all the heavy weapons and vehicles they had let into Zaire? I could hold onto them until things stabilized, he said, but he wanted them back. In the hands of his enemies they were a constant threat to Rwandan security. (That did not happen before I left.)

In that two-hour meeting over soft drinks in his bungalow, we built a program for the next two to three months at least. All I needed was my troops and the promised resources. I reinforced with Kagame that I was receiving reports that starvation and disease were beginning to cut a swath through the refugee camps. There was not a moment to waste.

After the installation of the new government, we were in a race against time, which was nothing new to me because UNAMIR had always been running to catch up to the situation on the ground. The French were making noises about seeking the authority to stay past August 22. As the RPF caught wind of those noises, they began to up the pressure on UNAMIR to replace the French and get them out of Rwanda. Our logistics situation was still erratic: we periodically ran out of water or food or fuel, and we never seemed to have enough working vehicles, radios or equipment to do anything the way it should be done. In many areas, we were regressing, not progressing.

The situation in Goma was truly desperate. As the media converged to cover the refugee influx, world public opinion began to pressure governments to act. The NGOs, broken free from UNREO now that camps were overflowing in Zaire, cast co-operation and coordination aside, followed the cameras to Goma and began what can only be described as an exercise in over-aid. Meanwhile, a hundred kilometres to the south, almost as many people still inside Rwanda were under-aided and there was little to no media coverage of that situation. Nothing we could say was able to shift any of the attention south.

New York still waffled on providing my minimum requirements. Except for national reconnaissance parties, UNAMIR 2 had still not deployed sixty days after mandate approval and thirty days past the deployment date. I got tired of asking where my troops were.

Life began to return to Kigali. The Amahoro Stadium and our other protected sites slowly emptied after the government was sworn in as at first one person and then a family and finally all of our companions left us to find out what had happened to their relatives and their homes. Too often the news was bad. Everyone had lost someone in the genocide. With almost ten percent of the pre-war population murdered in a hundred days there were very few families who did not lose at least one member. Most lost more. It has been estimated that ninety percent of the children who survived in Rwanda saw someone they knew die a violent death during that time.

As far as homes and businesses went, first the RGF, the Interahamwe and ordinary civilians had stripped the city of anything they could lay their hands on. In my pre-war house the only items left were a set of golf clubs I had borrowed from the Belgian military attaché, and a single copy of *Maclean's* magazine. Sinks, faucets, windows, light fixtures—everything was gone.

Some of the more recent recruits to Kagame's army also engaged in looting. Kagame had promised that they would receive their back pay after they had won, but he did not have the money—no government cash reserves were left in the capital (they had evaporated along with the interim government). His troops began to pay themselves with whatever they could find; genocide survivors and diaspora returnees also scrounged what they could. I am told that for years afterwards you could buy the material goods of Kigali on the street markets of Uganda.

I believe Kagame tried his best to control his new recruits who were lusting for revenge and the returnees who were scrabbling for what they could find, recognizing correctly that word of their excesses would leak out of Rwanda, draw unwanted media and political attention, foil his attempts to acquire loans and aid to rebuild his country and most importantly fuel RGF propaganda and Hutu fears about returning to an RPF-controlled Rwanda. The myth of the "double genocide" was now in full swing—some people actually bought the line that the racial war had cut both ways. The last thing Kagame wanted was to legitimize these claims in any way. Unfortunately, we could not ignore the reports we received of revenge murders, looting and rape, as undisciplined rear elements of the RPF and returnees sought their own retribution. Rumours of secret interrogations at checkpoints for returnees were making people nervous. We investigated and publicly denounced these atrocities just as we had condemned the genocide. The only chance for reconciliation in Rwanda was for everyone to drop their machetes and focus on true justice against the planners and perpetrators of genocide.

The country also had to focus on rebuilding. Water, that most essential life-sustaining requirement, was not potable, as the waterworks had long since been sabotaged. Wells were dry or tainted and the only other sources were the creeks and rivers that flowed through Kigali, and they didn't bear thinking about. Food was scarce. All over Rwanda, crops had rotted in the fields because no one was left to harvest them and bring them to market. The city's sewage system, not even close to acceptable before the war, now presented a significant health hazard. There was no fuel, no electricity, no telephone or other communications—the list of nothings increased by the day. The infrastructure of government, which should step in at such times, did not yet exist, even if the ministers had been sworn in. Kagame used all the resources he had to guard the border with Zaire in the northwest and to build up against the French in the southwest, and who could blame him? We continued to offer what little we had to try to get the government running. But the UN would not authorize us to loan or give any of our resources to the Rwandan civilian administration. Even as millions in humanitarian aid flowed into Goma we could not get a few thousand dollars to help in Kigali. We often ignored the bureaucrats and helped anyway, digging into our own pockets when we could, embarrassed that we couldn't do more.

Life for Rwandans trying to survive inside Rwanda seemed impossible in those days of late July and early August. However, the people demonstrated a lack of self-pity and admirable resilience. Slowly, small markets began to appear on street corners, people could be seen working the land and harvesting the rare late crop, small businesses reopened and occasionally even some laughter could be heard in the streets if you listened hard enough. Immense problems remained but with a little help we hoped the survivors would endure to rebuild their nation.

But I had to wonder about the kind of help on offer from the outside world. As it became safe to venture into the country, the tourists inevitably arrived. On a daily basis, delegations of politicians, bureaucrats, NGO staffers, celebrities, actors, singers and any Tom, Dick or Harry who could manage it (if my tone seems harsh, I have to say that's what it felt like to us) came to Rwanda requesting that we coordinate their visit, their accommodations, their transportation and their itineraries. They tied up our staff, our time and many of our precious resources. While I recognized that the visitors were absolutely essential in the political fight to obtain aid for Rwanda and to get the troops of UNAMIR 2 deployed, I wasted more hours than I care to remember explaining the unspeakable situation over and over and over again. Every word began to rip at my soul. The one humorous aspect of these visits was that Khan and I would make a point of inviting our distinguished guests to a supper of expired German rations. Maybe it was adolescent of us, but we truly enjoyed the amazed looks on people's faces at the sight of these "state" dinners, along with their pained gulps as they attempted to eat the hideous fare that had been our staple for months. As time went on I begged out of these endless briefings and visits, and Henry filled in for me.

In Goma, on July 21, the United States began a massive and magnificent airlift of humanitarian aid that amazed any who saw it. Within three days of the presidential order authorizing the aid, the first U.S. planes were landing. In order to hasten food distribution, the Americans even tried bombarding areas with large loads of aid using low-flying transport aircraft, though they called a quick halt to this initiative as too many people on the ground were wounded by these enormous bundles of food. Such a practice had worked in Somalia, but here, between the jagged and unforgiving terrain and the swarming masses, there was no spot where such drops could be made safely.

I awoke that morning to the now familiar sounds of hammers, saws and shovels as the advance party of the 1st Canadian Headquarters and Signals Regiment were on the job repairing and setting up the place for the main force. Riza had sent a code cable to Khan asking for UNAMIR's sense of "broader anticipated tasks" in the "emerging situation." We had already produced operational directives to cover the HPZ mission and the exercise we were calling "Homeward Bound," to bring people back safely from the camps in Zaire. I was glad the SRSG was now the one to lay out the mission's broad political strokes, and the one who would have to travel to Dar es Salaam and to Kampala to try to engage the neighbouring countries in the political and diplomatic efforts to shore up Rwanda and the region. Khan agreed to provide an aircraft so that President Bizimungu could visit Zaire and Tanzania on his own to test the waters and also to discuss with his fellow African leaders the presence and effect of extremists in the camps.

My own operational priorities were clear. One, we had to move the UNMOs under Luc Racine into the HPZ to prepare the way for our takeover; two, we needed to get our MamaPapas into Gisenyi and the Gikongoro area to help the displaced persons still on this side of the border and to link up with the French, Zairean and RPF forces to calm the situation there; three, we needed to carry on monitoring the HPZ line and to discourage the RPF from probing the zone; four, staff had to work flat out to coordinate the arrival, training and deployment of new contingents with equipment and vehicles. Our chief of plans, Mike Austdal, was not only working feverishly on all these fronts, he also took on the job of head of training. Instead of conducting paper exercises, he took the new officers and NCOs as they arrived out to role-play situations that would test their comprehension of our rules of engagement. I cannot praise enough the way my tiny headquarters staff kept rising with great invention to meet the urgency of the situation.

The international community was hedging its bets on the legitimacy of the new government. The Human Rights Rapporteur not only harshly criticized those countries who were harbouring the génocidaires, but also condemned the looting, revenge killings and summary executions inside Rwanda, which not even Kagame could prevent. This did not help the new government's image and, as Kagame and Pasteur Bizimungu had feared, kept a number of nations on the fence about offering help. The cholera epidemic now raging in Goma continued to be a bigger draw on the world's compassion than the starving displaced persons in the HPZ or the survivors trying to stitch back together a civil society in Kigali. I found myself in the disgusting position of mentally comparing magnitudes of horror: how could the world allow 3,000 deaths a day in Goma to overshadow the effects of the genocide inside Rwanda and let the toll on the 1.7 million people inside the HPZ go on unnoticed? (In the end, as I suspected, the cholera epidemic, which would kill about 40,000, did pale in comparison.) Yet the men who witnessed cholera at its height were beyond such calculations. On July 25, Major St-Denis took a trip to Goma where he was to liaise with the French. Years later, he wrote me a description of what he had seen. "As I was moving through the streets I could not take my eyes off the hundreds of bodies that were littering the roads. All of them . . . had succumbed to cholera. The air reeked of putrefaction, and all I wanted to do was to throw up. For a while we followed a dumptruck filled with bodies that had been picked up by French soldiers. . . . I remember the soldiers' eyes; they were lifeless and full of sadness. . . .

"On the return trip, I drove in front of a hospital and saw one of the most gruesome scenes. . . . A pile of bodies at least twenty feet high stood in front of that hospital. . . . Some of the people still had their eyes open and I felt that they were looking at me with an intensity I could not bear. I had to turn my head away." Nearby, St-Denis saw a mother tending to her young son in a group of exhausted women and children. That day happened to be his own mother's seventy-fifth birthday, and the scene struck him with incredible force. "I wanted to stop and see if I could provide them with assistance, but I had been forewarned that the UN was not overly welcome here and that I should not stop anywhere until I crossed back into Rwanda. I left the scene wondering what would happen to this family, would they survive?" When he got back to the Force HQ, he was able to get a line out to call his mother, but "I could not shake this image of the young boy and his mother. I did not talk for long. [When] I hung up, I drank from a bottle of scotch, something I had never done before, but I had to do something to remove the stench of death from my mouth."

Radio Rwanda, now in the hands of the new government, was broadcasting to the refugees in Goma, telling them to come back. Its announcers quoted a letter, dated July 19, from Boutros Boutros-Ghali that promised that the big UN agencies would assist the homeless and the have-nots. Boutros-Ghali also announced that he was calling for a UN inter-agency appeal for victims of the crisis in Rwanda, and that the head of the DHA, Peter Hansen, would chair a conference on August 2 in Geneva to bring about a coordinated response from all donors. But first Hansen would have to head to Rwanda to do his personal assessment on the ground.

Hansen was an old hand at humanitarian crises and his visit was a professional piece of work. He had at least twenty people with him, including senior representatives from the other UN agencies. At a meeting with Khan and myself, he acknowledged the wisdom of immediate repatriation and even accepted the idea of aid coming from within Rwanda. He and Khan visited the president and other members of the new government, and then toured the camps in Goma and Bukavu (but not the displaced persons camps inside the HPZ). By this point Lafourcade's support troops, stationed principally at the Goma airport, were totally overwhelmed, even paralyzed by scenes such as St-Denis described. Lafourcade had come into the country heavy with combat assets and light on the tools of humanitarian relief. Frozen in its tracks by the spread of cholera and by the knowledge of the health risks its troops would be exposed to due to the high infection rate of HIV/AIDs among Rwandans, Turquoise remained limited.

UNAMIR 2 was still engaged in a scramble for resources and equipment. Belgium had at last agreed to equip a Malawi company once they got to Kigali; the old colonial powers were fearful that equipment might be hijacked en route and used for coups or to outfit palace guards to reinforce the new government. The site at Entebbe was still all too basic and

I redirected more UNOMUR personnel and assets there to assist in improving it (UNOMUR was to close down and I'd soon lose their valuable assistance). Our facilities were too limited to hold troops for any length of time before deploying them. But the reinforcements were still not coming. By the last week of July, I had at best six hundred personnel of all ranks in the mission.

My Kigali staff, still living in terrible conditions, were visibly tiring, now partly from the stress of dealing with all the parties who wanted to come in and help us. I nearly had a second mutiny over food when another batch of German rations was opened and it smelled to high heaven. These rations, so generously provided to us when we had nothing left to eat, were now well beyond their best-before date. (The crisis was resolved when the Canadian contingent arrived, bringing with it a hefty supply of hard rations that we all could share.)

I had a mission headquarters staff of fewer than thirty officers, with varying levels of skills and knowledge, trying to keep a multitude of operational tasks moving: I had made a vow that UNAMIR would never be the stumbling block to peace and stability in Rwanda, and the staff worked themselves ragged to fulfill that promise. I had not allowed my principal staff any leave time, with only a few exceptions, since the start of the war. A couple of people had become zombies, blank and unresponsive, and we'd had to send them home. Others were over-irritable and would become very emotional over conditions that we had been living with for some time. It was as if a line had been crossed and they began to interpret everything as if they were Rwandan, wholly identifying with the victims. Once they started inhabiting the horror they could not handle any serious new work. We started to send them off to Nairobi on the Hercules for a couple of days' rest. Their fatigue was a recognized medical state. After seeing a doctor in Nairobi, they would move to a hotel room and then wash, sleep, eat and somehow attempt to relax. Since there was no budget to handle the walking wounded, such bouts of rest and recuperation were at the expense of the injured person.

What really began to wear us down was the constant raising and then dashing of hopes. Watching the world support Turquoise, with all the ambivalence that engendered in us, was one thing. But believing that we were finally to be aided by the Americans—and then being utterly let down—was another.

The first American officer to arrive in Kigali was Brigadier General Jack Nix, every inch the image of a solid U.S. Army combat one-star general— the only way he didn't fit the stereotype was that he didn't smoke cigars. As the field commander of the U.S. Joint Task Force (JTF) to Africa, Nix came to me to discuss the U.S. concept of operations in the region. He said the Americans would first operate out of Entebbe and then trans- fer all *matériel* to cargo planes, then onto trucks to move to UNAMIR in Kigali, and then on to Goma and all regions of Rwanda. I told him our most urgent requirement was off-loading equipment and personnel at the airport—he wouldn't be able to send anything more than a Hercules into Kigali until we had the infrastructure to deal with it. As far as he knew, his mission was to help the UN efforts in Goma and in Rwanda, but before he initiated anything he had to await confirmation from the overall JTF commander, Lieutenant General Daniel Schroeder, who was due in theatre in a couple of days. We parted with me reminding him that Goma had to remain a temporary exercise. For the Americans to be part of the solution, the aid effort had to be from within Rwanda.

The UN did its bit at the airport. Within twenty-four hours of receiving the call from the DPKO a group of about twenty Canadian Air Force air traffic controllers had been assembled from all the bases back home and were in the air. When they arrived in Kigali they went directly from their Hercules to the air-control tower and complex. They removed the bodies they found (no abandoned building in Kigali was without its dead), washed the place down, set up their old manual-and-visual air control apparatus (which looked like something out of the Battle of Britain), and slapped a large Canadian flag on the tower underneath the Rwandan and UN flags. They were open for business before nightfall.

A few days later, when the U.S. ground and off-loading crew arrived with media crawling all over them, the Americans unabashedly announced that they had "opened" the Kigali airport. But the picture that made it to newspapers around the world caught a gaggle of our air controllers hanging out of the tower pointing to the large Canadian flag. The Americans had to take a lot of ribbing after that as they worked hand in hand with Canadian and other UN troops to get the airfield functional and the much-needed aid, contingents and logistics on its way.

I had to drive north toward the border of Uganda in the last week of July to meet with Baroness Chalker, the British minister for Overseas Development, who had just been to Goma and Mulindi but had not had enough time to complete the leg of her trip to Kigali. (She was a "tourist" I immediately warmed to. She did not stand on protocol and travelled with a tin of homemade tea biscuits, which she shared with everyone.) I met up with her at Kilometre 64, and we carried on northward, crossing into Uganda at the Gatuna bridge, while I pointedly explained why we needed the promised British trucks, engineers, maintenance platoon, field hospital, small headquarters and UNMOs. She sent the colonel who was travelling with her to do a recce in Kigali and told him to forward the list of our needs to the British ministry of defence. In parting, she promised me what I requested, though she reminded me that she had only a six-month commitment from her government to support Rwanda and UNAMIR.

At Entebbe the American presence was already strong—the Stars and Stripes flag was flying from the roof of the main terminal. I visited my team in their minuscule ground-floor office and then proceeded to my transient camp. The Ghanaian platoon had set up tents and portable latrines, benches and tables, but they had no cots. There was no electricity and no running water, no cooking facilities and no phone lines. The APCs were standing in silent rows by a pile of junked parts. The Brown and Root mechanics were working hard, swearing about the lack of spare parts, and the repainting of the vehicles in UN colours had begun. Even with the exceptional efforts of the UNDP resident representative and our UNOMUR civilian support staff, the camp was going nowhere fast. I went back to the UNMOs in charge of troop movement and told them to alert the mission and New York to the fact that the Entebbe base was not functional and that all incoming troops should fly directly to Kigali, where we'd manage as best we could. They needed to get the word out quickly since the large Canadian contingent under Mike Hanrahan was due the next day.

I then headed to the top floor of the new terminal, where at least a hundred military personnel were going in all directions putting the American headquarters together before Schroeder arrived. Nix was in Goma doing a reconnaissance. Not wanting to burden the junior staff officers, I headed back to Kigali, wryly smiling about how comfortable the furniture in the American headquarters looked—a demonstration of the priorities and capabilities of an imperial force.

Of course, Hanrahan did not get the word in time, and the next day 170 personnel landed in Entebbe. The unit was up to strength, operationally current and ready for a rare deployment as a full unit (usually only individuals were sent to augment missions). They got to the theatre exactly fourteen days after official notification of the mission, and were proud of their speed. Hanrahan took one look at the camp at Entebbe airfield and rented a large warehouse and a bunch of hotel rooms until they could fly into Kigali. This was the kind of despatch and flexibility I desperately needed from contingents, but which only the "have" nations could afford.

The night before I was to meet General Schroeder for the first time the DPKO sent us some pertinent news clips from the U.S. media. The *Washington Post* was reporting that the U.S. government was planning to put at least 2,000 troops inside Rwanda "to set up a relief network to encourage Rwandan refugees to return home from their horrific camps in Zaire." A Lieutenant General John Sheehan, director of operations for the Joint Chiefs of Staff, was quoted as saying that "the operation would be done in concert with UN forces in Africa and several nations would be taking part." Their mission, according to officers interviewed in Entebbe by the *Post*, "would be to establish relief stations with food and water that would tend to refugees on their walk home." According to Sheehan, "U.S. military teams would fan out from Kigali airport on roads leading to the Zairean border" and establish way stations as the proposed support structure for a reverse trek. "Establishing a multinational HQ in

Kigali is also intended as a statement to Hutu refugees that there will be no reprisals." The triumvirate had done a fine job, because it seemed as if, this time, the United States had accepted my entire concept of operations. We were elated. It looked like we now had the means and a plan that would end the Goma catastrophe and enable the return home of the displaced persons in the HPZ.

Reality struck again at morning prayers with a report from our liaison officer in Goma. Some refugees trickling back into Rwanda in order to escape the hellhole of their disease-infested camps had been attacked by extremists. A few were killed but most were mutilated and returned to the camps to serve as examples—the favoured punishment was using a machete to chop the Achilles tendon, which prevented the victim from walking. The news sent me spinning into a tirade against every nation and body who could have assisted us in preventing this, most especially Turquoise. My ranting was beyond the bounds of decorum, and rendered my own staff and the French liaison officers noticeably ill at ease. When I stopped, the orders group headed quietly off to their duties.

It has never been my way to rant and rave like a cartoon general. In fact, even at the height of any crisis, a model Canadian headquarters was low-key, restrained, efficient. I remained alone for a time, staring at the big map of Rwanda tacked to the wall. I had to recognize that I was exhibiting the signs and symptoms that caused me to send others to Nairobi for a rest. I could rarely sleep, and could not bear to eat anything other than peanut butter from Beth's last care package. I was moody and overtaken at the most inopportune times by spontaneous daydreaming. I resolved to speak to Maurice about my condition soon, then pulled myself together to meet the American commander.

Schroeder was preceded by a small military police detachment led by a very tense colonel. They were given space in the terminal to set up their preliminary HQ. The general arrived in a small twin-engine commander's aircraft. When I laid eyes on him for the first time it looked to me like real help had finally arrived. His introductory words to me were, "General, I am here to help you in whatever way I can."

We spent some time together in my HQ going over the concept of operations for both Goma and the HPZ, my status of forces in theatre, my future capabilities, the priority of effort I needed from his troops (airfield handling; transport for *matériel* and men between Entebbe, Goma and Kigali; mine clearance, logisitics and security elements for the way stations; water and electricity in Kigali; if possible, the restoration of the hydro dam near Cyangugu); and the humanitarian and political situation as of that day. He and his few staff officers took notes. When Schroeder left, the only outstanding question about the imminent arrival of American help was some political posturing in Washington.

The next morning, July 29, I was reading the Washington clips sent overnight by the DPKO, this time accompanied by a note from the triumvirate warning me that our plan was now running into serious opposition. Schroeder was quoted as saying that the U.S. deployment would take place despite hesitation voiced in Washington, but he added that he would proceed cautiously because of difficult conditions in Kigali: "The one thing you do not want to do is to overwhelm an already overstressed infrastructure." What kind of doubletalk was this? His resources were the solution to the stress. Clearly between the time he left me and the time he gave an interview to the media in Entebbe he had been told off by his superiors. Apparently the State Department and the Pentagon were at odds, and the State Department viewed it as premature to speak of a large-scale U.S. presence in Kigali, or of the capital as the proper hub for relief efforts. I scanned the clippings to discover that U.S. Defense Secretary William Perry along with the chairman of the Joint Chiefs of Staff, General John Shalikashvilli, were to tour the region on the coming weekend; no policy decision about Kigali would be reached until after their visit.

The root of the issue was expressed by an unnamed State Department official, who said that the Clinton administration did not want the U.S. military presence in Rwanda to be seen as a de facto recognition of the new Rwandan government, which had not yet satisfied Washington of its commitment to protecting human rights. They also did not want to station any U.S. military personnel in Rwanda until their safety was "absolutely" assured. While the U.S. military thought it would be more efficient to operate out of Kigali, General Shalikashvilli told reporters that U.S. officials had concerns about how they would ensure the security of participating American forces if they were inside Rwanda. As a possible alternative to the way-station plan, Shalikashvilli offered that "Pentagon officials also are considering a system of airdrops to provide food and other basic supplies to refugees on their way home." The great humanitarians in the U.S. administration wanted no part of anything inside Rwanda that could lead to American casualties.

Schroeder had been too transparent and committed during our briefing to have been sitting on the fence. I phoned his HQ in Entebbe but he was already en route to Goma. An aide assured me he would get back to me later that day. But the fact of the matter was that once again UNAMIR was on its own.

The Canadians started to pour in and were sent to quarters in the Amahoro Stadium. The place had not been touched since our last Rwandan refugee had left and it resembled an overflowing sewer. Within hours of his arrival, Regimental Sergeant Major Lebrun, who had been a signaller in my old regiment, had the troops in full cleaning mode. (They did such a good job that a week later the new Rwandan minister of youth, Patrick Mazimhaka, wanted to move into the Amahoro and displace them. Golo said no—we were the ones who had cleaned the place and, futhermore, we were the ones paying rent.) Those who weren't on duty setting up communications and HQ assets carried on scrubbing, building and sandbagging. It seemed as though we had been invaded by carpenters, plumbers and electricians. For a time I had the impression that my tiny band of veterans were in the way, but the Canadians soon won us over with their efforts to make us more functional than we had ever been.

The support assets who came in with Hanrahan at my request—a construction engineer company, a logistics and admin group, and a solid transport platoon—would soon take over the whole of the force logistics and administration role and would be the coordinating link with Golo and the UN civilian staff and also with Brown and Root. Chatting with the burly construction engineers in their canteen, I complimented them on the enormous amount of work they had accomplished in a short time. But they were not impressed with themselves. On the way over someone had off-loaded all their power tools at the last minute in lieu of something else. They had been working with hand tools, and though they were proud of their old-fashioned blisters, they felt they were wasting too much time.

The Canadians had decided to send a complete 200-bed field hospital, not under my command but as an independent humanitarian support to the Goma UNHCR exercise—though I wasn't informed of that little wrinkle until they started to arrive in Rwanda. However, after they discussed the matter with me and UNAMIR HQ staff, the Canadian hospital ended up exactly where I had planned for it—along the return route between Gisenyi and Ruhengeri. The Brits were assigned the hospital inside Ruhengeri and, as planned, the Australians were given the Kigali hospital.

More and more contingents were being processed through the UN system, and the U.S. finally offered something useful: it would move our troops and equipment to Kigali by air. Infantry companies and units from Ethiopia, Zambia, Malawi, Mali and Nigeria were prepared to deploy; Kagame had approved a plan whereby Turquoise would hand over its Franco-African soldiers to my command so that I would have enough French-speaking troops in theatre when we began to take over the HPZ. I had the usual UN macédoine to deal with, with all its inherent complexities of command relationships, languages, skill sets and the roulette of assigning tasks to troops whose capabilities were a mystery until they landed. I was starting to get embroiled in the same frustrations, delays and lost operational opportunities of the initial UNAMIR buildup of the previous October. But this time I also had to weather more complex emotions.

Even now I have trouble sorting out my own reaction to the mostly well-meaning people who came into Kigali to help. Perhaps it was their apparent detachment, the ease with which they ignored the imperatives that I thought critical. Perhaps it was the attitudes of some of them or the photo ops they arranged of themselves beside mass graves or the way they were able to step over bodies without seeming to notice those people had once had names. Speed, innovation, imagination and understanding operational priorities were fundamental ingredients of success. Too many of the support staff who arrived once the genocide had ceased brought with them rules, regulations and procedures that weren't tied in any way to achieving our urgent aims.

More troubling than this conflict in views was the feeling that the new people were outsiders. They had not been with us when we needed them most and had not shared the danger or hardship. I felt as though they were contaminating something private, that they had trespassed on a family gathering. Our experience of the previous few months had separated me and my small band of warriors from the world and, in some senses, had made us all into prisoners of memories too personal to share, and too difficult to express outside of the context of a time that had already passed. The fact that few of the newcomers seemed to show much interest in what had happened—and many were anxious to brush it all aside in their haste to impose a new order on things—did not help. It is also possible that we had been running on pure adrenalin for so long that we couldn't function as well once the danger passed and help arrived.

Nor can I completely discount the possibility that my own ego had grown unacceptably large during the time I was the focus of all that media attention. Perhaps, like the generals of Roman times, I needed someone to whisper in my ear, "Remember Caesar, thou too art human." Is the human condition not defined by an endless struggle to control the ego's subterfuges?

On the other hand, I wasn't immune to the criticism that whispered its way into my consciousness. Naturally the French had an interest in laying blame for the collapse of their allies and in making it appear that the genocide was in no way connected to them. What better way than to suggest that the whole thing was somehow the fault of the United Nations? As I was the commander of the UN forces on the ground, it was an easy thing for the French to imply that I had somehow failed. Add to this the horrified reaction of the swarm of people involved with NGOs who appeared within hours of the danger passing and who may have been unable to deal with the emotional trauma of what they saw without finding a scapegoat. I do not blame the NGO community, nor was their criticism entirely misplaced. We could have done more. But who are "we" in this case? To ears made oversensitive by self-doubt, the whispers cut like hot knives.

I remember co-chairing with Charles Petrie one of the first NGO aid-coordinating meetings in the UNDP conference centre. Yaache and MacNeil were reeling under the horrendous tower of Babel the humanitarian relief world had quickly become. The meeting lasted forever. There were so many interventions, so many divergent agendas and so many demands on the resources of UNAMIR that the minutes of that one meeting became a brick of paper. What got under my skin was the way the aid community so unthinkingly rallied behind its first principle: no matter what, they had to protect their neutrality. It was my opinion that, in this new reality we had all inherited, they were defining their independence so narrowly it often impeded their stated aims.

An example of this misguided independence was the time doctors and nurses from the Canadian field hospital, which regularly sent out emergency teams to pick up the injured and the sick, came across a small NGO aid station where hundreds of people were waiting to be treated. Many of the patients were lying in the sun and even dying at the doorstep of this inundated facility. When the military doctors and nurses in their Red Cross armbands offered to help, the NGO staff actually refused. They feared losing their neutrality more than losing the lives of the patients at their door. The Canadian medical teams brushed aside their objection, scooped up the whole stranded group and transported them to the waiting staff at the field hospital.

That the Red Cross remains staunchly neutral, to the extent of refusing to give testimony at the International Tribunals on Genocide, is a fixed point of ethical reference as well as its careful interpretation of *realpolitik*. But in conflicts where the military have had to become intimately involved with the humanitarian crisis, the neutrality that NGOs cling to needs to be seriously rethought. A man like Philippe Gaillard had had no trouble understanding the new roles.

In these last days of July, Khan and I, along with a small group of staff, entertained the head of the UNHCR, Sadako Ogata, at a supper of expired rations at our headquarters. Ogata's agency was at the centre of the arena in Goma, directing traffic and dealing with cholera and starvation. Ogata had a keen intellect, and she demonstrated her grasp of the situation during the briefings and discussions we held. By the time she left, both Khan and I thought that she supported our plan to repatriate the refugees without delay. But when she got to Goma she announced that such a plan would be foolhardy. The refugees might export cholera into Rwanda when they returned and spread it through the hills. Militia men might infiltrate with them and destabilize the new government, or the old regime's burgomasters might sneak back in and wreak havoc. As far as she was concerned, the refugees should stay in place until there was a partial return to normalcy inside Rwanda. Khan was fuming, and once again I totally lost it. Was it a sense of turf that informed the UNHCR's decision to maintain the camps? The crisis was apparently providing the first real test of their new command and control structure out of Geneva. The decision to wait for a "partial return to normalcy" left more than a million pawns in the hands of the extremists who, as predicted, eventually took control of the camps, even evicting NGOs who displeased them.

After I had cooled down again, Phil approached me. He had been watching me like a hawk, and trying to diffuse situations when he saw me getting too emotional. Phil told me I had to consider my own state and the state of the mission—and soon. That night I spent many hours silently wondering just how far gone I was, and what I could still get done before I needed to get out of there, for the sake of the mission and myself.

On July 31 four hundred men—Henry's Ghanaians, under Colonel Joe—were scheduled to leave Kigali as the first UNAMIR troops to take over from the French in the HPZ. I drove out to the large parking lot near Kadafi Crossroads with Phil and my aide-de-camp at about 0630 to send them off. The vehicles appeared out of the orange glow of the dawn, lined up and parked. The troops disembarked and I gathered them around me. I spoke to them of the significance of their mission and the difficult demands I was making of them individually to ensure that their part of the HPZ remained calm. They were eager and their energy was overflowing. I told them that just as I had relied upon them through the heart of the genocide, I was calling on them once again to be the vanguard of this new mission. I wished them luck and told them that I expected nothing from them but the kind of success they had had in the past.

Then, with a call from the regimental sergeant major and a salute from the officers, they clambered back onto their totally overloaded vehicles and set off like a gypsy caravan. Troops lay on mattresses on top of some of the trucks, holding onto pots and pans. Some soldiers perched on a load of everything from steel beds to wicker chairs. Canvas covered some truck beds, while others were open to the elements and had a few goats and chickens along for the ride. I silently prayed that they would take no casualties—the unit had suffered enough death and misery. As they disappeared over the hill, I congratulated Yaache and said that Henry would have been proud to have witnessed this gutsy unit setting off to take on the HPZ.

I'd had to keep a hundred of the Ghanaians back for security and staff duties in the capital, but in this one move I had essentially emptied my garrison of formed troops. It was a gamble, but I had to take it now or face impossible pressure from the RPF to oust the French.

As August began—the fifth month of this grotesque exercise in human destruction and paralysis—we got a report from Goma that Lafourcade was moving troops out of the HPZ faster than we had planned for. The French were now having clashes with the Interahamwe as well as struggling with all the humanitarian challenges, and things were still tense between them and the RPF. At the same time, the prime minister of France announced that the peacekeepers of Turquoise should stay on even after we had taken over all of the HPZ. Who was calling the shots?

The French prime minister's visit to Goma and Rwanda on July 31 had been an ill-timed comedy of errors. He had invited both Pasteur Bizimungu and me to come see him in Cyangugu at such short notice and with such a lack of respect for the new political reality of Rwanda that neither of us felt in the least compelled to accept. Bernard Kouchner, who was now a deputy of the European Union, had been in and out of Kigali recently and had gone public to criticize his home-land's heavyhanded disdain for the new Rwandan government.[1]

Rwandan politicians such as Seth Sendashonga (now the minister of the Interior) were travelling to Gisenyi with increasing regularity to try to persuade the refugees to come home. Khan was working closely with the government to get them access to the UNAMIR-held parts of the HPZ as soon as possible. We were providing helicopters, ground transport, fuel and minimal humanitarian aid to the Rwandan government, which was working throughout the country as best it could to support the populations who had remained and to help those who were coming back.

Having fulfilled his duties as a son, and having seen his children, Henry was back and fresh for the fray. On the evening of his return, he and I sat down together and discussed our future with the mission. If I had to go, then my soldiers and officers deserved the best replacement commander I could get. That person was Henry Anyidoho. He knew the ground, the players, the situation, the plan, and what tasks had to be accomplished—and despite all the deprivation we had suffered and the scenes we had witnessed, he had not been worn down. I showed him the recommendation I had made to my chief of defence staff as well as to Maurice, and told him that the triumvirate backed his appointment. With permission from his government in hand, all that remained was the final confirmation and the handover.

---

1. Kouchner had shown up with his own usual lack of warning, leading an E.U. delegation that had come to Rwanda to offer us a hundred human rights observers to start conducting the investigations that had been called for by the International Human Rights Commissioner. A special investigation had already begun under the auspices of the UN, and I wondered why the E.U. wanted to launch this effort, and told them I thought their efforts would be misguided. I told Kouchner that what Rwanda needed at this delicate point was not another hundred human rights investigators (who would not easily be able to get to the perpetrators inside the Goma camps) going through the entrails of the RPF, but rather a hundred qualified policemen to come and help train the nascent Gendarmerie and bring law and order to the capital.

On August 2, I made my way to Entebbe to meet Schroeder in his HQ. The visit from Defense Secretary Perry and General Shalikashvilli and their large entourage had changed nothing, though Khan and I had taken our best shot at explaining the region's imperatives. Once again, General Schroeder was most welcoming and he immediately had his staff bring me up to date. More of his forces were moving into Goma and he had sent Nix there semi-permanently. He would be sending a total of three hundred military police and airfield staff with off-loading equipment to Kigali over the next few days, and I could expect the C5 military cargo planes to start carrying in my troops by August 6.

We then spoke privately as there were far too many busy people and boards and charts and crackling communications systems arrayed around us. When we were alone together in his office, I didn't even have to ask the question. His orders, he said, were to operate out of Entebbe with his main effort concentrated on Goma. His people at the Kigali airport would not be allowed to leave the airfield perimeter. The political heat was on for him not to take any risks that might lead to the injury or death of his troops. When I left him to go visit my UNMOs in their unassuming quarters I was incensed, and Schroeder, who had criticized the course his bosses had decided upon, was ashamed. His political masters were being suckered into Goma and into a no-risk approach— shades of Mogadishu haunting us still. Such actions helped ensure lasting conflict in the area.

I climbed to the top of the decrepit old terminal and looked out from the bullet-riddled tower. My camp at Entebbe looked like a tiny, amateur operation against the bustle of the American enterprise here. I could not believe that the outside world was finally coming into the Rwandan catastrophe en masse and screwing it up so totally—and for the same reasons that had prevented them from reacting properly to the genocide in the first place. I flew back to Kigali that night, knowing that without the Americans' support for the Homeward Bound plan the road ahead was near-impassable.

And so for the last weeks of my command the Americans, with all their resources, sat inside the perimeter of the Kigali airport, and though they helped us bring our troops in and out, they did little else.

There were still casualties in Kigali as a result of crime (our UN civilian police were working hard with the new government, but there was a ways to go yet) and people were stumbling across land mines or other unexploded ordinance. The Americans had several well-equipped ambulances on the ground with medical staff, while we were making do with vans, pickup trucks, four-by-fours and sometimes even dump trucks. But when we asked the Americans if they could do emergency casualty evacuation to the hospitals in Kigali, they refused, evoking their standing orders.

Then there was water. With the help of British and Canadian engineers, we were able to establish water purification points around the city but we did not have any bulk-water carriers to move the water to our locations or to the civilian population. As a result, we had to make endless water runs, which ate up fuel and time. Rwandans had to walk long distances to the water points each day to fill up buckets and cans. One day an American C5 landed at the airport and unloaded several huge bulk-water carrying trucks, some even painted in UN colours. Even though we knew about their restrictions, we asked if they could please drive the vehicles, under our escort and protection, and begin moving potable water to distribution sites for the population and UNAMIR within Kigali. They refused. We then asked if we could "borrow" the vehicles, as we suspected they were destined for us. They again refused, stating they had no authority to loan the vehicles and no, they weren't coming to us, but were destined for Goma. Apparently, the water carriers had landed in Kigali by mistake.

The original U.S. assessment for UNAMIR 1, which the Americans committed to pay to the UN but never did, would have been no more than $30 million. The cost of UNAMIR 2 would have been only slightly more. By deciding to support the refugee camps in Goma, the U.S. paid ten times that amount—$300 million—over the following two years. If we reduce to the petty grounds of cost effectiveness the entire argument over whether the U.S. should have supported the United Nations in Rwanda, the United States government could have saved a lot of money by backing UNAMIR. As to the value of the 800,000 lives in the balance books of Washington, during those last weeks we received a shocking call from an American staffer, whose name I have long forgotten. He was engaged in some sort of planning exercise and wanted to know how many Rwandans had died, how many were refugees, and how many were internally displaced. He told me that his estimates indicated that it would take the deaths of 85,000 Rwandans to justify the risking of the life of one American soldier. It was macabre, to say the least.

A solicitous Canadian signals officer had found me a cot to replace my flimsy old mattress on the floor, but I found it difficult to sleep the night I came back from seeing Schroeder. I was haunted by the feeling that no matter how fast we moved we would never be a match for all that was required of us. Morning prayers that day showed that the rhythm of activity had increased exponentially. My daily list of things we had to accomplish had gone from an average of fifteen to a high of forty-nine. Looking back now at those daily lists, I see that I was often repeating myself and becoming unrealistically demanding. I was also continuing to lose my temper.

Near the end of prayers I exploded again over our continuing difficulties in securing the basics for the mission, especially the water supply. Major John McComber, our harried chief logistician, had already solved so many problems so unobtrusively some of us had taken to calling him "the silent miracle worker." He and his young partner, Major St-Denis, had worked hard to meet impossible milestones, but since the Canadian logisitics base was just opening up and contracts were still being negotiated, there were some problems we still couldn't adequately fix. McComber felt I was attacking him directly, but he said nothing. Looking at my orders group, I realized that my manners and my sense of humor, two essentials of leadership, were fading fast.

After prayers I climbed into my vehicle and took off without telling anyone. It wasn't the first time. I had begun to suffocate in the headquarters, with its endless stream of problems and demands. I had been inventing trips to get me away from it, deciding that I had to see the troops in the field or just tour the country. In every village, along every road, in every church, in every school were unburied corpses.

My dreams at night became my reality of the day and increasingly I could not distinguish between the two.

By this point I wasn't bothering to make excuses any more to disguise my quest for solitude. I would just sneak away and then drive around, thinking all manner of black thoughts that I couldn't permit myself to say to anyone for fear of the effect on the morale of my troops. Without my marking the moment, death became a desired option. I hoped I would hit a mine or run into an ambush and just end it all. I think some part of me wanted to join the legions of the dead, whom I felt I had failed. I could not face the thought of leaving Rwanda alive after so many people had died. On my travels around the country, whole roads and villages were empty, as if they'd been hit by a nuclear bomb or the bubonic plague. You could drive for miles without seeing a single human being or a single living creature. Everything seemed so dead.

On one of my solo wanderings, I ended up at the modern convent that belonged to the Soeurs du Bon Pasteur from Quebec City. I found it full of looters. Drawing my pistol, I ordered everybody out—and they went. I rescued the small wooden cross from the chapel to take back to the sisters. Though a lot of the doors were kicked in, the built-in beds and the nuns' personal effects were still there, and the water and sewage systems and most of the windows were intact. I went back to my vehicle and called the Canadian contingent headquarters and requested that Mike Hanrahan meet me there. He arrived less than fifteen minutes later with Lebrun. I asked them to take care of the convent. Hanrahan called the order's Mother Superior in Quebec and got her blessing to use the building as a rest area for his troops. Her only caveat was that the troops not establish the bar in the chapel. The signallers completely refurbished and protected the convent, and handed it back to the order some months later in a very emotional ceremony of mutual appreciation. One happy ending.

Toward the end of July I had asked my Ghanaian escort to buy us a few goats—a ram, a nanny and a couple of kids—to bring some life into my days. I took immense pleasure in watering them, feeding them and watching them roam the Amahoro. The goats were not appreciated by the staff, as they left droppings all over, even inside the operations centre. One day my Ghanaian batman came running into my office and said for me to come quickly—a pack of wild dogs was attacking my goats. Without stopping to think I grabbed my pistol, raced outside and started shooting at the dogs as I ran across the parking lot. I fired my entire clip at them. I missed them all, but still the dogs fled and I felt satisfied that I had saved my goats. When I turned to go back to my office, I saw at least fifty pairs of surprised and concerned eyes staring at me intently: Khan, the civilian staff, my staff officers and my soldiers. They said nothing but the message was clear: "The General is losing it."

I informed Maurice on the night of August 3 that I needed to be relieved of my command sooner than planned. He checked with Annan and Riza, and they recommended that Maurice pursue the matter directly with the Secretary-General. He told me later that he warned Boutros-Ghali that if I wasn't replaced, I would be dead in less than two weeks. Unknown to me, Phil had been laying the groundwork for Maurice's swift response by keeping him informed as to my deteriorating state of health. Phil did this out of love and loyalty to his old friend and commander. When close subordinates realize that their commander is becoming a liability, the act of passing such information to the chain of command is not disloyal, but the epitome of loyalty. To have subordinates with the courage to act in such a way is a reward in itself.

The next morning I told Khan I had to leave. He was sorry but also not surprised. The guilt I felt was incalculable.

On August 4 I was given a copy of a code cable received in the night from the DPKO, which contained notes from the Security Council deliberations of the day before. Sometime during the meeting, the U.S. representative announced that General Dallaire would shortly be replaced by another Canadian of equal rank. This was the first I'd heard of it. Back home, Beth was on a trip to Halifax and when she returned to Quebec City with our two youngest children, the answering machine was blinking like a Christmas tree with messages from family and friends telling her how happy they were that I was finally coming home. None of the calls were from official channels, however, which didn't impress Beth. She called the CDF operations centre herself, and they confirmed the news.

I was extremely upset at hearing that Henry, who was away visiting the Ghanaians in the HPZ, would not be getting the command he so richly deserved. I called Maurice to find out what had happened and he told me that the DPKO had fully supported my recommendation, but that the Secretary-General's office had rejected Henry. He quietly confided that they wanted a bilingual general from a Western nation. What type of criteria were those? While Henry could not speak or understand French, he worked extremely effectively through interpreters. And why should it matter where Henry came from when he had all of the requisite skills and more experience than anyone else in the world? The decision was final. The UN had turned to Canada for a replacement. Complimented by the unique opportunity to appoint back-to-back force commanders, Canada had readily agreed and named Major General Guy Tousignant to replace me.

When Henry got back, I told him the bad news. He was stoic about it, and said he would carry on serving the mission loyally as deputy force commander if he was still needed. He was only sorry and embarrassed that he had already gone to his government to sound out whether Ghana would support his appointment and the required promotion.

The next day, I headed to the HPZ for a last tour with my aide-de-camp, a driver and a guard. It was beautiful out, bright and cloudless. When we slowed down at the final RPF barrier before the HPZ, I noticed a truckload of people travelling back into Rwanda being waved to a dirt side road that led behind a hill surrounded by trees. I stopped my four-by-four, got out and asked where the truck was going. I got a mumbled and evasive answer. I decided we would follow the truck.

I don't think we had even edged our front wheels off the highway and onto the dirt road before we were stopped by RPF soldiers practically stuffing their AK-47s up our noses. The soldier who had his weapon trained on me yelled that we were to go no farther, and I yelled right back telling him with gestures to get his boss. We stayed like this until an NCO appeared. I asked him why I could not go and inspect what was around that hill. He told me his troops were conducting a security check of returnees, looking for weapons, ex-militia and RGF soldiers, and he refused to let me through. He warned me that, blue beret or not, he was authorized to use force if necessary.

I withdrew. I now had personal proof that Kagame was allowing the security checks of returnees to go beyond what had been discussed with me, and I could only think the worst. I was putting my people at risk in the HPZ so that his troops could conduct purges as Rwandans tried to return home.

We continued on our way to meet with Luc Racine and the local French commander, who were waiting for us by the side of the road near Gikongoro. In their opinion security was still very tenuous here. The Ghanaians were settling in with the locals and their patrols were generally well received. But many were worried about who else was coming to replace the French. Racine took me aside and emphasized that we had better get a lot of aid into this zone fast, as word was going around that the people in Goma were being well treated. I promised that Yaache and the HAC team would concentrate their efforts here as soon as trucks were available (we were still waiting for the fleets to be airlifted in).

I then carried on with an escort party to visit the Ghanaians. The battalion HQ was in an abandoned school in a hilltop village, with one company quartered around it. They were making do, but the supply line from Kigali was still quite deficient and they were forced to buy on the local market. Most of the APCs were standing in a neat row and when I asked about them I was told that the newly trained drivers were not quite sure of themselves in these winding and hilly trails. Pressing further brought out the real reason. To navigate in the hills they needed armoured jeeps or one-ton section trucks.

On our return trip through the HPZ, I stopped in a village and waited for a group of journalists who had found out I was in the area and wanted to interview me. I wandered about twenty metres away from my vehicle, and elders from the village approached me. We started talking. Within minutes, the crowd grew to more than a hundred and its size soon attracted even more. The elders were concerned about the departure of the French and the eventual arrival of the RPF. The discussion at first was friendly, with a few people asking questions and the others listening intently. The rings of people around me kept increasing and the questions went on and on. The reaction of the crowd was starting to veer wildly. One moment there was laughter and in the blink of an eye things turned nasty. New interlocutors who were anti-UNAMIR and anti-RPF started to shout. I did not pull out my pistol but I was reaching for it when my ADC, with my vehicle on his heels, started to make his way toward me through the crowd. No one budged. With not very convincing thank-yous and goodbyes, I suddenly pushed toward him. When I reached him we both turned and forced our way back to our four-by-four. Once inside we beat a tactical retreat. I was still catching my breath when we met the gang from the press. We signalled for them to follow us and when we judged that we had reached a safe enough distance from the crowd we stopped and held the conference. For years afterward, I could not bear to be pressed close in a crowd.

On August 6 I was invited to meet with President Bizimungu. He seemed to have grown into his new job and the trappings of head of state. We discussed a rainbow of subjects from how to conduct political visits in the HPZ to water for the capital to fixing the hangars at the airport to old times. Top of my mind was the encounter I had had at the security checkpoint at the exit from the HPZ. I told Pasteur there was considerable pressure from the human rights people and New York for his government to ease off and be much more transparent. He acknowledged the bad position they were in and also the danger to his government if there were considerable delays in official recognition because of such practices. I made it clear that if UNAMIR ever had to declare RPF-held territory unsafe due to exactations without due process, then the people in the HPZ would head west by the fastest means possible. And UNAMIR would have no choice but to stop the RPF with force, in accordance with our mandate to protect people in danger. The Security Council would then most likely ask the French to stay on and the exiled interim government and its forces would gain some sympathy internationally.

He had heard I was leaving soon and said he was sorry and hoped to see me before I left. Though he and I both remembered our sessions at Mulindi, talking as friends into the night, we ended our last session formally, as there were staffers all around.

Lieutenant General Gord Reay, the commander of the Canadian Army, came to Rwanda from August 6 to 8 to visit the troops, bringing with him an old friend of mine, Lieutenant Colonel Ralph Coleman, the army's public affairs officer. In private conversation General Reay confirmed that my replacement would be Guy Tousignant. I knew Guy as a bilingual logistician whose skill set and experience would certainly help Rwanda and UNAMIR 2, but I told Reay that I still supported Henry for commander. Reay informed me that when I got back, my posting would be that of Deputy Commander of the Army and Commander of the 1ˢᵗ Canadian Division. I was pleased, as this would mean that I would stay in a command appointment. However, the former Deputy Commander had retired in late June, and the post had been vacant since, with the Chief of Staff doing both jobs. Reay wanted me back at work in Canada as soon as possible. He then spelled out a host of problems I'd have to deal with, including the need to handle the Somalia fallout, army reorganization driven by severe budget and personnel cuts, and an ever-increasing tempo of operations. I admit I wasn't as pleased at the end of the conversation as I had been at the beginning. I was physically and mentally exhausted and I needed a break. I asked for leave before I assumed my new duties and he readily agreed, but he gave me a look that implied "just not too much."

Tousignant would arrive in Rwanda August 12 for a week's handover. I would relinquish the command of UNAMIR to him on August 19.

Until then, I stayed immersed in our non-stop work. By August 8, we had grown from 600 to about 1000, but we still had only a half-battalion and a company of line troops, the rest being UNMOs, staff and support. Every now and again I would break out in a cold sweat over the looming deadline of August 22, when my bluff might be called. Games at the Security Council continued apace. We had filed a three-month report the week before, and Madeleine Albright was leading the strong resistance to the wording of a new mandate that would include our "ensuring" stability and security in the provinces of Rwanda. "In her view, it would be more practical to describe the task as the 'promotion' of stability," the code cable read. How far does one go up the scale in the use of force to achieve "promotion" without getting into "ensuring"? How would a junior officer understand the resultant new ROE in the field? Once again, we could end up with soldiers injured and dying, and more innocent people sacrificed, because of nuances in mandate that the politicos did not even fully comprehend. I had terribly mixed feelings about my departure but all it took was a code cable such as this or another frustrating session with the administration gang to reaffirm my total incapacity to accept any more excuses, delays or budget limitations.

I went to see Lafourcade to bring him up to speed and assure him we were still on net with the handovers and withdrawals of his forces. He was feeling the squeeze of getting all his people and equipment out in time, and still hearing some noises that his government might ask him to stay a bit longer. I told him that staying was out of the question—if he did, the RPF would break through the zone and confront him. I told him I would be back next week to personally introduce my replacement, and we parted amicably.

Lafourcade provided transport and escorts for me to go and meet Augustin Bizimungu, who had asked to see me. The former RGF chief of staff was now living in a comfortable bungalow on a hill overlooking Lake Kivu, and seemed totally at home. He was surrounded by a few senior Zairean officers, a couple of French officers and, to my surprise, the same huge RGF lieutenant-colonel who had come into Bagosora's office on the afternoon of April 7 (his G-2, or intelligence officer, a man said to have been deeply involved in the genocide).

Bizimungu met me at the top of the long staircase up to the house. Both he and the lieutenant-colonel were in impeccable RGF uniforms down to their shiny boots, and Bizimungu looked relaxed, even ebullient, as we sat down to talk. Soon he had launched into his usual tirade against the RPF, accusing them of genocide and of targeting RGF officers and their families for execution. He did not ask me how things were inside Rwanda but gave me an earful about his desire to go back and sort out the RPF once and for all. Before he had worked himself up to a complete lather—and perhaps before he could reveal anything more of their future operational plans—the lieutenant-colonel stepped in and effectively ended the meeting. We stood up to make our farewells. With a wry smile, Bizimungu told me that things were fine for him and he didn't need to meet anyone from UNAMIR anymore. Neither of us offered to shake hands.

When I got back to UNAMIR headquarters, after a brief stop in Entebbe and a visit with President Museveni (who gazed at me kindly and said, "Well, General, you have certainly aged during this last year"), I saw that a copy of a letter sent by the Secretary-General to the President of the Security Council was on my desk. My eye went to the crucial sentence: ". . . his government has decided to reassign [Dallaire] to national duties . . . [Guy Tousignant] will assume his duties on 15 august 1994." There it was, now official.

On August 13, Khan got a call from the DPKO asking him to go to the new government and ask to delay the departure of Turquoise by up to two weeks. I had argued against it, but New York was getting very nervous that my bluff was only a bluff and we would be too thin on the ground to safely conduct our mission. Kagame had at first agreed in principle, but Pasteur Bizimungu was adamant—no delay would be tolerated.

Guy Tousignant had arrived on schedule and we did the rounds and the prayer sessions and the decision meetings together. Another Canadian came with him; Colonel Jan Arp, a fellow gunner who made a real difference to the mission as its first dedicated chief of staff. At prayers a couple of days before I was to leave, a problem with lack of water came to the table again. I was about to be very nasty to the administration staff but Guy jumped in and said he would like to look into it. I realized then that I was truly out of a job.

When I took Guy to meet Lafourcade, the French commander broached the subject of keeping a small logistics component in Goma in order to ensure support for the Franco-African battalion. I emphatically replied that the UN would allow no remnants of Turquoise to remain in the area. He was a bit taken aback by my forceful manner but Guy backed me up.

I was invited to have lunch with Kagame on August 18 in his new home in Kigali where he was living with his wife and children. It was a bit more formal than we had been used to, the conversation was light, and the menu actually included meat. All in all, it was a pleasant two hours. Kagame wished me well and thanked me very kindly. He said that he hoped I would return to Rwanda someday.

I do hope to return to Rwanda very soon, after I have finished my duties as the UNAMIR force commander by testifying for the prosecution at the International Tribunal on the Rwandan Genocide in Arusha, Tanzania, in the spring of 2004. The place where the Arsuha Peace Agreement was signed—the very same building in fact—is now the place where the tribunal meets to deliver justice to the extremists who destroyed that agreement.

How do you say goodbye to people who have bravely travelled through the inferno with you? On the night of August 18, all of the old gang, including Henry, Tikoka, my brave civilian secretary Suzanne, Yaache, Khan, Golo and the rest of the staff organized a farewell party for me in the damaged restaurant at Chez Lando. I won't think of what they had to do to clean it up given that the place had been closed since Hélène, Lando and the children had been killed. They plugged a large hole in the roof with some blue refugee tarps, and the CO of the Canadian logistics base had found a caterer just setting up shop in town who produced a meal the likes of which none of us had seen in Kigali in a number of months. Some of Lando's surviving relatives had come back, and the party was also designed to help them relaunch the business.

We drank a lot that night. We sang songs and even brought out the Stompin' Tom Conners tape for a while. Some of us quietly cried our hearts out. It was a rare celebration, and the emotions it unleashed ranged from deep hurt and anger to exaggerated laughter and even love. It is not too strong a word.

The next morning, I said a formal goodbye to my staff, and then in a slight rainfall we conducted a change-of-command parade in front of the main entrance to the HQ building, as Henry insisted was proper. A proud contingent of Ghanaians was waiting for me, joined by many of the staff officers. While Guy, Khan and I inspected the ranks and pinned UNAMIR medals on everyone, my favourite band from the

Ghanaian battalion played for us. I cannot remember my speech, though I know I was grateful that the rain shortened it. Following Ghanaian military tradition, Guy and I exchanged a white baton of command.

Then I was escorted off the dais into an open four-by-four. Two long ropes were stretched before the vehicle and all the officers took up positions along them. They pulled me out of the compound to the music of "Auld lang syne." I called to Tiko, hauling on the rope, to come and join me, because I would need his support one last time when I reached the end of this ride. He climbed in with me and propped me up like a brother. We laughed and yelled to the men on the ropes and waved to the crowd who'd gathered to see me off. When we came to a halt, Tiko helped me out of the four-by-four for the ride to the airport. After a flurry of fraternal hugs all around I was gone.

Phil had flown ahead to Nairobi to sort out the terrible mess the UN staff had made of my tickets. I was to travel to Amsterdam before going home for some leave with my family, walking the old battlefields where my father and Beth's dad had fought.

The next morning Phil took me to the airport. It wasn't necessary for me to say much to Phil. He understood how guilty I felt abandoning my troops before the mission was over, how guilty I felt that I had failed so many people and that Rwandans were still dying because of it. Phil would have none of it. I had to accept that I had become a casualty, he said. Just like other casualties, I needed to be evacuated. There was no guilt in that.

I left Africa on August 20, 1994, nearly a year to the day from when I had first arrived in Rwanda, full of hopes for a mission that would secure lasting peace for a country that once had been a tiny paradise on earth.

CONCLUSION

In the introduction to this book I told the story of meeting a three-year-old orphan on a road lined with huts filled with the Rwandan dead. I still think of that little boy, who if he lived would be a teenager as I write. What has happened to him, and the tens of thousands of other orphans of the genocide? Did he survive? Was he reunited with any members of his family, or was he raised in one of Rwanda's overcrowded orphanages? Did anyone care for him and love him for himself, or was he raised with hate and anger defining his young life? Did he find it in himself to forgive the perpetrators of the genocide? Or did he fall prey to ethnic hate propaganda and the desire for retribution and take his part in perpetuating the cycle of violence? Did he become yet another child soldier in the region's wars?

When I think about the consequences of the Rwandan genocide, I think first of all of those who died an agonizing death from machete wounds inside the hundreds of sweltering churches, chapels and missions where they'd gone to seek God's protection and ended instead in the arms of Lucifer. I think of the more than 300,000 children who were killed, and of those children who became killers in a perversion of any culture's idea of childhood. Then I think of the children who survived, orphaned by the genocide and the ongoing conflict in the region—since 1994, they have been effectively abandoned by us as we abandoned their parents in the killing fields of Rwanda.

When we remember the Rwandan genocide, we also have to recognize the living hell these children inherited. My work after the genocide has intimately acquainted me with the circumstances in which the children of genocide and civil war are forced to survive. In December 2001, as part of my duties as special adviser on war-affected children to the minister responsible for CIDA, I conducted a field visit to Sierra Leone to get first-hand information on the demobilization and reintegration of child soldiers and bush wives—children who had been abducted from their families and had then fought for several years as part of the once powerful rebel force, the Revolutionary United Front (RUF). I travelled deep into the heart of rebel territory, near the towns of Kailahun and Daru in the far eastern sector of the country. I remember a visit that my small team, which included retired Major Phil Lancaster, made to the local demobilization centre. Sitting down with a group of the boys, all around thirteen years of age, we were soon discussing tactics, bush life and the brutality of civil war. They were only a few days into the retraining process, and they fervently hoped—now that they were permitted to hope—that they had a promising future in a country that could sustain peace. But, talking with them, it was clear that if things did not work out in the camp, they would return to the free and violent life of terrorism in the bush, where they would carry on taking what they wanted by force. The rehabilitation and reintegration period was scheduled to last at best three months, and they wanted to know what would happen next. Who would pick up the ball? Certainly not their families or communities, who had yet to accept them back, nor their devastated country in which teachers and other educated persons and potential leaders had been a favourite assassination target. Abducted at nine or even younger, a number of these boys had become RUF platoon commanders, and in terms of experience they were thirteen going on twenty-five; if laying down their weapons meant they had no future except to join thousands of others in displaced and refugee camps that dotted the countryside, they would not countenance it. Some of them were running camps within the camps for the younger children; if these combat-tested leaders were not specifically targeted for advanced education and social development programs, they would surely lead the children back into the bush. Simple, well-intentioned Dick-and-Jane schooling was not going to be enough to meet their needs.

Even worse off were the girls, who were much shyer about coming forward for help. Many of them had serious medical problems caused by rape, early child-bearing and unassisted births. Their state of health was appalling. A high proportion had been infected with HIV/AIDs by the male adults in the rebel army, and were so emotionally scarred and so inexperienced with "normal" life that it was difficult for them to care properly for their children. Where would they find the necessary love to give their babies when they could not remember ever having received it themselves? In time, the boys were generally accepted back into the community, but the girls were often shunned and abandoned, since in this male-dominated culture they were considered to have been permanently sullied by the uses to which the soldiers had put them. If they tried to go home, they and their children became outcasts in their communities; if they went to the displaced and refugee camps, they again became the prey of adult males. Some of the girls had fought or held considerable responsibilities in the rebel formations; if properly supported, there was a chance they could become leaders—the forerunners of change on the gender-equality front. The demobilization and re-integration camps were their best chance, which was nearly no chance at all, especially if the aid community didn't get behind them and help.

This was the fate that may have awaited the boy on the Rwandan road, the fate all the children of the Rwandan genocide would have been lucky to avoid. These disordered, violent and throwaway young lives—and the consequences of the waste of these lives on their homelands, and inevitably on the rest of the world—are the best argument to vigorously act to prevent future Rwandas.

Too many parties have focused on pointing the finger at others, beyond the perpetrators, as the scapegoats for our common failure in Rwanda. Some say that the example of Rwanda proves that the UN is an irrelevant, corrupt, decadent institution that has outlived its usefulness or even its ability to conduct conflict resolution. Others have blamed the Permanent Five of the Security Council, especially the United States and France, for failing to see beyond their own national self-interest to lead or even support international intervention to stop the genocide. Some have blamed the media for not telling the story, the NGOs for not

reacting quickly and effectively enough, the peacekeepers for not showing more resolve, and myself for failing in my mission. When I began
this book, I was tempted to make it an anatomy of my personal failures,
which I was finally persuaded would be missing the point.

I have witnessed and also suffered my share of recriminations and
accusations, politically motivated "investigations" and courts martial,
Monday-morning quarterbacking, revisionism and outright lies since I
got back to Canada in September 1994—none of that will bring back
the dead or point the way forward to a peaceful future. Instead, we need
to study how the genocide happened not from the perspective of assigning blame—there is too much to go around—but from the perspective
of how we are going to take concrete steps to prevent such a thing from
ever happening again. To properly mourn the dead and respect the
potential of the living, we need accountability, not blame. We need to
eliminate from this earth the impunity with which the génocidaires were
able to act, and re-emphasize the principle of justice for all, so that no
one for even a moment will make the ethical and moral mistake of rank-
ing some humans as more human than others, a mistake that the international community endorsed by its indifference in 1994.

There is no doubt that the toxic ethnic extremism that infected
Rwanda was a deep-rooted and formidable foe, built from colonial dis-
crimination and exclusion, personal vendettas, refugee life, envy,
racism, power plays, *coups d'état* and the deep rifts of civil war. In
Rwanda both sides of the civil war fostered extremism. The fanatical far
right of the Hutu ethnicity was concentrated in the MRND and its
vicious wing in the CDR party, and was nurtured by an inner circle
around the president, Juvénal Habyarimana, and his wife. The Tutsis
also had their hard-liners, in the persons of some of the embittered
refugees of the 1959 revolution, and sons and daughters raised in the
poverty and double standards of Uganda, permanently gazing across the
border to a homeland denied to them until they took it by force; among
them also were vengeful Hutus who had been abused by the
Habyarimana regime.

Together these extremists created the climate in which a slaughter
of an entire ethnicity could be dreamed up—an attempt to annihilate

every Tutsi who had a claim on Rwanda, carried out by Rwandans on Rwandans. The violent extremism was nurtured over decades of an armed peace, but it could have been controlled or even eradicated before Hutu Power enacted its "final solution." Through our indifference, squabbling, distraction and delays, we lost a great many opportunities to destabilize the génocidaires and derail the genocide. I can easily delineate the factors that might have guaranteed our success, beginning with having the political and cultural savvy from the start to ensure an effective military and civilian police presence on the ground in Rwanda as soon as the Arusha Peace Agreement was signed; providing UNAMIR with hard intelligence on the ex-belligerents' intentions, ambitions and goals so that we didn't have to fumble in the dark; providing the mission with the political and diplomatic muscle to outmanoeuvre the hard-liners and also to push the RPF into a few timely concessions; reasonable administrative and logistical support of the mission; a few more well-trained and properly equipped battalions on the ground; a more liberal and forceful application of the mandate; and to bring it all off, a budget increase of only about US$100 million.

Could we have prevented the resumption of the civil war and the genocide? The short answer is yes. If UNAMIR had received the modest increase of troops and capabilities we requested in the first week, could we have stopped the killings? Yes, absolutely. Would we have risked more UN casualties? Yes, but surely soldiers and peacekeeping nations should be prepared to pay the price of safeguarding human life and human rights. If UNAMIR 2 had been deployed on time and as requested, would we have reduced the prolonged period of killing? Yes, we would have stopped it much sooner.

If we had chosen to enhance the capabilities of UNAMIR in these ways, we could have wrested the initiative from the ex-belligerents in reasonably short order and stymied the aggression for enough time to expose and weaken the "third force." I truly believe the missing piece in the puzzle was the political will from France and the United States to make the Arusha accords work and ultimately move this imploding nation toward democracy and a lasting peace. There is no doubt that those two countries possessed the solution to the Rwandan crisis.

Let there be no doubt: the Rwandan genocide was the ultimate responsibility of those Rwandans who planned, ordered, supervised and eventually conducted it. Their extremism was the seemingly indestructible and ugly harvest of years of power struggles and insecurity that had been deftly played upon by their former colonial rulers. But the deaths of Rwandans can also be laid at the door of the military genius Paul Kagame, who did not speed up his campaign when the scale of the genocide became clear and even talked candidly with me at several points about the price his fellow Tutsis might have to pay for the cause. Next in line when it comes to responsibility are France, which moved in too late and ended up protecting the génocidaires and permanently destabilizing the region, and the U.S. government, which actively worked against an effective UNAMIR and only got involved to aid the same Hutu refugee population and the génocidaires, leaving the genocide survivors to flounder and suffer. The failings of the UN and Belgium were not in the same league.

My own *mea culpa* is this: as the person charged with the military leadership of UNAMIR, I was unable to persuade the international community that this tiny, poor, overpopulated country and its people were worth saving from the horror of genocide—even when the measures needed for success were relatively small. How much of that inability was linked to my inexperience? Why was I chosen to lead UNAMIR? My experience was in training Canadian peacekeepers to go into classic Cold War–style conflicts; I had never been in the field as a peacekeeper myself. I had no political expertise, and no background or training in African affairs or manoeuvring in the weeds of ethnic conflicts in which hate trumps reason. I had no way to gauge the duplicity of the ex-belligerents. The professional development of senior officers in matters of classic peacekeeping, let alone in the thickets of the post-modern version (which I prefer to call conflict resolution), has often been reduced to throwing officers into situations and seeing whether they can cope. While the numbers of UN troop-contributing nations has increased well beyond the more traditional contributors (among which Canada was a major player), there are still no essential prerequisites of formal education and training for the job. As the conflicts grow increasingly ugly and complex and the mandates fuzzy and restrictive, you end up with more force commanders like myself, whose technical and experiential limitations were so clear. There will continue to be a need for UN-led missions and these missions will continue to increase in complexity as well as have more international impact. As a global community, it is crucial that we develop an international pool of multidisciplinary, multi-skilled and humanist senior leaders to fill these force commander billets.

Still, at its heart, the Rwandan story is the story of the failure of humanity to heed a call for help from an endangered people.

The international community, of which the UN is only a symbol, failed to move beyond self-interest for the sake of Rwanda. While most nations agreed that something should be done, they all had an excuse why they should not be the ones to do it. As a result, the UN was denied the political will and material means to prevent the tragedy.

Like many governments and NGOs, the UN more or less muddled through the tumultuous 1990s, a decade marred by the proliferation of armed conflicts that defied the codes of former wars. My own country, Canada, was carried by altruistic impulses into operations in places such as the former Yugoslavia, Somalia, Cambodia and Mozambique. During the Cold War, peacekeeping missions generally monitored the implementation of peace agreements and prevented isolated incidents from leading to a resumption of conflict. In the nineties the focus shifted: the mission aim was to bring about a form of order, whether it be a system of humanitarian relief or an agreement forced on warring factions. UNAMIR started out as a classic Cold War–style peacekeeping mission but then found itself in the middle of a civil war and genocide. In all these situations, a humanitarian catastrophe was either the catalyst for the security problem or the result of it. Displaced and refugee populations were on the move, in numbers rarely ever witnessed, and were prey to extremists, warlords and armed bandits. More often than not, peacekeeping missions had to make ad hoc responses, mounting tardy attempts to assist in the resolution of both the conflicts and the humanitarian crises.

How do we pick and choose where to get involved? Canada and

other peacekeeping nations have become accustomed to acting if, and only if, international public opinion will support them—a dangerous path that leads to a moral relativism in which a country risks losing sight of the difference between good and evil, a concept that some players on the international stage view as outmoded. Some governments regard the use of force itself as the greatest evil. Others define "good" as the pursuit of human rights and will opt to employ force when human rights are violated. As the nineties drew to a close and the new millennium dawned with no sign of an end to these ugly little wars, it was as if each troubling conflict we were faced with had to pass the test of whether we could "care" about it or "identify" with the victims before we'd get involved. Each mission was judged as to whether it was "worth" risking soldiers' lives and a nation's resources. As Michael Ignatieff has warned us, "riskless warfare in pursuit of human rights is a moral contradiction. The concept of human rights assumes that all human life is of equal value. Risk-free warfare presumes that our lives matter more than those we are intervening to save." On the basis of my experience as force commander in Rwanda, *j'accuse*.

We have fallen back on the yardstick of national self-interest to measure which portions of the planet we allow ourselves to be concerned about. In the twenty-first century, we cannot afford to tolerate a single failed state, ruled by ruthless and self-serving dictators, arming and brainwashing a generation of potential warriors to export mayhem and terror around the world. Rwanda was a warning to us all of what lies in store if we continue to ignore human rights, human security and abject poverty. The tens of millions of three-year-olds like the one I met on that Rwandan road deserve and must have nothing less than a chance at life as a human being and not as someone's slave, vassal, chattel, or expendable pawn.

Are there any signs that we are prepared to take the higher road in international human relations? Not many. Look at the conflict that has engulfed the whole Great Lakes region of central Africa since the genocide. In September 1994, when I returned to New York for a debriefing after my mission, I arrived determined to argue one last time for Homeward Bound, my operational plan, which I personally presented to the Secretariat, to the troop-contributing nations and to the media. UNAMIR 2 was designed to support the swift return of the more than 2 million refugees hunkered down in camps within kilometres of the Rwandan border, as well as to move 1.7 million internally displaced persons in the HPZ toward their homes. NGOs, UN agencies and the RPF would be called upon to sort out resources and the fair redistribution of land and homes, while UNAMIR 2 would guarantee the security and coordination of the return journey. With Shaharyar Khan's full support, I lobbied extensively to persuade people of the necessity of the exercise: the refugees could not be allowed to settle into the camps or disaster would follow. We needed to separate the displaced Rwandans from the génocidaires—arresting the perpetrators so they would face justice—and then get the Rwandans back to Rwanda.

We needed to mount this operation or face the consequences, I argued. The two million Rwandan refugees in neighbouring nations, still suffering in horrendous conditions in refugee camps under the thumb of the génocidaires, living on the scraps of international conscience, with no voice and little hope, were the fuel that could ignite the entire Great Lakes region of central Africa into an even larger catastrophe than the Rwandan genocide.

At the meeting of the troop-contributing nations, the French ambassador to the UN rose as soon as I had finished speaking, and pronounced my plan unworkable. He left before hearing my response. His attitude infected the other nations, who as a result suffered severe cold feet on account of the admittedly risky nature of my plan. Ultimately, however, it was the apathy of the United States, whose conscience had apparently been satisfied with the over-aid effort to Goma, that once again stifled any urge to act. From 1994 to 1996, the génocidaires in those camps launched raids in Rwanda, Uganda and Burundi. In 1996, Rwanda's RPF regime invaded Zaire in retaliation and forced most of the refugees to return home. Hundreds of thousands of others perished on the roads and in the jungles of the Kivu region, once again running from the RPF.

The result has been a continuing regional war. From the Rwandan exodus in 1994 until genocide broke out once again in 2003, it has been estimated that four million human beings have died in the Congo and the Great Lakes region and, until very recently, the world did nothing except to send an undermanned and poorly resourced peacekeeping mission. Five times the number murdered in Rwanda in 1994 have died and, once again, only when the television cameras of the world captured the event were nations embarrassed into sending a half-hearted temporary mission to try and stop the killing. For the veterans and survivors of Rwanda, watching the recent events in the Congo has been like watching an instant replay of the horror we lived in 1994—only worse. It is heart-rendingly obvious that a decade after the disaster in Rwanda, we are once again witnessing human destruction on a grand scale, which is inspiring the same Pontius Pilate reaction from the developed world. The only difference this time is that the international media have been far more aggressive than they were in 1994 (whether because of the recent memory of Rwanda's genocide or the need to fill the proliferating twenty-four-hour news channels) and have been able to move public opinion. However, the mission, from its conception, has suffered the same financial, logistical and political deficiencies that UNAMIR faced in Rwanda. And as in Rwanda, once again France is sending in troops, ostensibly to keep the peace, but also insisting that they be kept outside of the UN command structure. They do not want to be curtailed in their initiatives and actions on the ground by the overly restrictive and still ad hoc DPKO military command structure, and I acknowledge that there is some wisdom in that. But the downside is that the new French intervention in central Africa is another example of the First World's growing tendency to work around the UN and take action either unilaterally or in concert with a small coalition to impose its will on others—which does absolutely nothing to reform or strengthen the UN's capacity to resolve conflicts that threaten international peace and security. The authority of the UN to conduct conflict resolution is being eroded, not strengthened.

What is the reason for this *marche seul* by the developed nations? In the last decades of the twentieth century, self-interest, sovereignty and taking care of number one became the primary criteria for any serious provision of support or resources to the globe's trouble spots. If the country in question is of any possible strategic value to the world powers, then it seems that everything from covert operations to the outright use of overwhelming force is fair game. If it is not, indifference is the order of the day.

To imagine that these same world powers have magically leapt ahead in this new age of humanity (as Kofi Annan named it in his seminal speech at the millennium UN general assembly in September 2000) could not be further from the truth. It will take the world's dedicated will and means to move from the twentieth century—the century of genocide—to the century of humanity.

Although often couched in the empathetic phrases of humanitarian aid and of supporting the right of persons to be free from tyranny, ephemeral interventions and relief efforts tend to dry up as soon as CNN puts yet another disaster on prime time to capture the fickle heart of the international community. Though I too can criticize the effectiveness of the UN, the only solution to this unacceptable apathy and selective attention is a revitalized and reformed international institution charged with maintaining the world's peace and security, supported by the international community and guided by the founding principles of its Charter and the Universal Declaration of Human Rights. The UN must undergo a renaissance if it is to be involved in conflict resolution. This is not limited to the Secretariat, its administration and bureaucrats, but must encompass the member nations, who need to rethink their roles and recommit to a renewal of purpose. Otherwise the hope that we will ever truly enter an age of humanity will die as the UN continues to decline into irrelevance.

At the Canadian Forces Peace Support Training Centre, teachers use a slide to explain to Canadian soldiers the nature of our world. If the entire population of the planet is represented by one hundred people, fifty-seven live in Asia, twenty-one in Europe, fourteen in North and South America, and eight in Africa. The numbers of Asians and Africans are increasing every year while the number of Europeans and North Americans is decreasing. Fifty percent of the wealth of the world is in the hands of six people, all of whom are American. Seventy people are unable to read or write. Fifty suffer from malnutrition due to insufficient nutrition. Thirty-five do not have access to safe drinking water. Eighty live in sub-standard housing. Only one has a university or college education. Most of the population of the globe live in substantially different circumstances than those we in the First World take for granted.

But many signs point to the fact that the youth of the Third World will no longer tolerate living in circumstances that give them no hope for the future. From the young boys I met in the demobilization camps in Sierra Leone to the suicide bombers of Palestine and Chechnya, to the young terrorists who fly planes into the World Trade Center and the Pentagon, we can no longer afford to ignore them. We have to take concrete steps to remove the causes of their rage, or we have to be prepared to suffer the consequences.

The global village is deteriorating at a rapid pace, and in the children of the world the result is rage. It is the rage I saw in the eyes of the teenage Interahamwe militiamen in Rwanda, it is the rage I sensed in the hearts of the children of Sierra Leone, it is the rage I felt in crowds of ordinary civilians in Rwanda, and it is the rage that resulted in September 11. Human beings who have no rights, no security, no future, no hope and no means to survive are a desperate group who will do desperate things to take what they believe they need and deserve.

If September 11 taught us that we have to fight and win the "war on terrorism," it should also have taught us that if we do not immediately address the underlying (even if misguided) causes of those young terrorists' rage, we will not win the war. For every al-Qaeda bomber that we kill there will be a thousand more volunteers from all over the earth to take his place. In the next decade, terrorists will acquire weapons of mass destruction. It is only a matter of time until a brilliant young chemist or smuggler obtains a nuclear, biological or chemical weapon and uses it to satisfy his very personal rage against us.

Where does this rage come from? This book has demonstrated some of the causes. A heightened tribalism, the absence of human rights, economic collapses, brutal and corrupt military dictatorships, the AIDS pandemic, the effect of debt on nations, environmental degradation, overpopulation, poverty, hunger: the list goes on and on. Each of these and so many other reasons can lead directly to a people having no hope for the future and being forced in their poverty and despair to resort to violence just to survive. This lack of hope in the future is the root cause of rage. If we cannot provide hope for the untold masses of the world, then the future will be nothing but a repeat of Rwanda, Sierra Leone, the Congo and September 11.

Several times in this book I have asked the question, "Are we all human, or are some more human than others?" Certainly we in the developed world act in a way that suggests we believe that our lives are worth more than the lives of other citizens of the planet. An American officer felt no shame as he informed me that the lives of 800,000 Rwandans were only worth risking the lives of ten American troops; the Belgians, after losing ten soldiers, insisted that the lives of Rwandans were not worth risking another single Belgian soldier. The only conclusion I can reach is that we are in desperate need of a transfusion of humanity. If we believe that all humans are human, then how are we going to prove it? It can only be proven through our actions. Through the dollars we are prepared to expend to improve conditions in the Third World, through the time and energy we devote to solving devastating problems like AIDs, through the lives of our soldiers, which we are prepared to sacrifice for the sake of humanity.

As soldiers we have been used to moving mountains to protect our own sovereignty or risks to our way of life. In the future we must be prepared to move beyond national self-interest to spend our resources and spill our blood for humanity. We have lived through centuries of enlightenment, reason, revolution, industrialization, and globalization. No matter how idealistic the aim sounds, this new century must become the Century of Humanity, when we as human beings rise above race, creed, colour, religion and national self-interest and put the good of humanity above the good of our own tribe. For the sake of the children and of our future. *Peux ce que veux. Allons-y.*

GLOSSARY

5ième Brigade-Group 5th Canadian Mechanized Brigade Group (CMBG), an all-arms francophone formation, based in Valcartier, Quebec

5ième Régiment d'artillerie légère du Canada (5 RALC) The francophone artillery regiment of the Canadian Army, Regular Force, based in Valcartier, Quebec, which General Dallaire joined and later commanded

ACABQ or Fifth Committee The UN General Assembly Committee, which meets in private closed session to establish and approve the budgets of peace-keeping missions

Lieutenant Colonel Joe Adinkra, CO Ghanaian Battalion advance party A small, select group of officers that is deployed prior to a main body to handle operation and administrative matters that will facilitate the deployment of the main body (mission)

Madame Agathe Agathe Uwilingiyimana, prime minister of the interim government

Aide-de-camp An officer assigned as personal assistant to a senior commander

Akagera Park (also known as Kagera Park) The last refuge of grassland wildlife in northeastern Rwanda. Due to its remote location, the only RGF camp in the area at Gabiro was a site suspected as a training centre for the Interahamwe. Also known as A'Kagera Park

Akagera River The river that divides Rwanda from Tanzania and flows into Lake Victoria

General Jean Victor Allard A famous World War II hero and subsequent Canadian CDS

Amahoro Stadium Complex consisting of a stadium, training facilities, parking lot and an athletes' hotel located in the east end of Kigali; was the location of the UNAMIR headquarters. Amahoro means peace in Kinyarwanda

Hedi Annabi Head of Africa Section in the Political Division of the DPKO

Kofi A. Annan Under-Secretary-General for Peacekeeping Operations (March 1993–December 1996). DPKO, Secretary-General of the UN 1 Jan 1997–present. Ghanaian

Brigadier General Henry Anyidoho Ghanaian UNAMIR Deputy Force Commander and COS, 21 Jan 94 until after General Dallaire left Rwanda

APC Armoured personnel carrier

Arusha Peace Agreement Also known as Arusha accords, Arusha negotiations or Arusha. Peace agreement between the RPF and the Government of Rwanda consisting of five protocols (accords) which ended the civil war in Rwanda and started a peace process that would result in the establishment of democracy and human rights in Rwanda, signed on 4 Aug 93

Lieutenant Colonel Mike Austdal Canadian reinforcement Officer worked as Contingent Commander

José Ayala Lasso UN High Commissioner for Human Rights, visited Rwanda in May 94 and described his observations of the situation in Rwanda as genocide

Camp Bagogwe RGF commando training camp in northwest Rwanda.

Colonel Théoneste Bagosora Chef de cabinet of the minister of defence, RGF, known Hutu extremist, currently awaiting trial, International Criminal Tribunal Rwanda

Lieutenant Colonel Walter Ballis Belgian Staff Officer, employed as UNAMIR Deputy Chief Operations Officer

Jean-Bosco Barayagwiza One of the heads of the extremist CDR party

General Maurice Baril Canadian Military Adviser to the Secretary-General of the UN and head of the Military Division of the DPKO

Battalion Ideally, a homogeneous unit of 800 soldiers with a headquarters, an integral service support company and four rifle companies

BBTG Broad-Based Transitional Government; was never installed due to political impasse

Major Brent Beardsley Canadian Military Assistant to General Dallaire

Commandant Mohammed Belgacem Tunisian Company Commander in NMOG, UNAMIR 1 and 2

UNAMIR, Jul 93–1 May 94, medically evacuated to Canada, did not return to mission

Jérôme Bicamumpaka MDR Hutu extremist who was appointed foreign minister of the interim government and tried to spread disinformation and cover up the genocide in Europe and New York

Jean-Damascène Bizimana Rwandan Ambassador to the UN in Sep 93, Member of the Security Council from Jan 94

Augustin Bizimana Minister of defence, extremist MRND, Hutu

Lieutenant Colonel Augustin Bizimungu Promoted Major General at the beginning of the conflict, Chief of Staff RGF, assumed the position in late Apr 94 replacing Marcel Gatsinzi, who had replaced Déogratias Nsabimana, extremist hard-liner, Hutu

Pasteur Bizimungu RPF's senior political adviser, member of the Executive Committee for the RPF and Commissioner for Information and Documentation, Hutu. Became president of Rwanda, Jul 94–Mar 2000

Brigadier (Retired) Paddy Blagdon Head of the UN De-Mining Program

Manfred Bleim Head of the UN Civilian Police Division

Blue Beret Slang term for United Nations Peacekeeper, term taken from the light-blue berets (or blue helmets) worn by peacekeepers

Jacques-Roger Booh-Booh SRSG 22 Nov 93–May 94, former Cameroonian foreign minister and diplomat

Boutros Boutros-Ghali Secretary-General of the UN Jan 1992–Dec 1996

Brahimi Report Internal UN study of UN Peacekeeping, conducted post-Rwanda and that produced comprehensive recommendations to improve the UN capacity for peacekeeping operation

Brigade A formation of several units under a Brigade Headquarters. Numbers can vary from 3000–6000 personnel depending on nation and type of brigade

Martin Bucyana National president of the CDR extremist Hutu party, murdered by moderates near Butare on 22 February in retaliation for the assassination of Félicien Gatabazi on 21 Feb 94

Prudence Bushnell US Deputy Assistant Secretary of State for African Affairs

Major Michel Bussières Canadian officer transferred from Somalia during the genocide and employed as Chief Military Personnel Officer

Butare South-central Prefecture in Rwanda, capital also named Butare, location of UNAMIR Southern Sector HQ

Byumba North-central Prefecture, capital of same name, location of the UNAMIR demilitarized zone Sector HQ. RGF camp located in same area, close to the DMZ. Bizimana's hometown

CAO Chief Administration Officer

Linda Carroll Canadian Chargé d'affaires in Rwanda who led the successful evacuation of over one hundred Canadians

CDR Coalition pour la défense de la république, Hutu extremist party, splinter group of the MRND, led by Jean Shyirambere Barahinyura, Jean-Bosco Barayagwiza and Martin Bucyana. CDR leadership refused to sign the Arusha Peace Agreement and Statement of Ethics and were shut out of the transitional government. Openly and violently anti-Tutsi

Chapter 6 peacekeeping Classic peacekeeping, term used to describe United Nations Peacekeeping conducted under Chapter 6 of the UN Charter

Chapter 7 peacekeeping Peace Enforcement, term used to describe United Nations Peacekeeping conducted under Chapter 7 of the UN Charter

Commander Charles *Nom de guerre* of the RPF Battalion Commanding Officer in Kigali

General Jose Charlier Chief of Staff of the Belgian Army

Chief Administration Officer (CAO) Senior UN civil servant in a UN mission responsible for administration and logistics. First UNAMIR CAO was Hallqvist, followed by de Liso and Golo

Chief of Staff (COS) Senior staff officer in the HQ directly subordinate to the commander, responsible for controlling the staff branches (personnel, operations, logistics, plans, etc.) in the performance of their duties

Willy Claes Belgian foreign minister, visited Rwanda and UNAMIR in February of 1994

Captain Frank Claeys Belgian Para-commando and Special Forces Officer, head of UNAMIR intelligence section

CND Congrès National de Développement or Conseil National pour le Développement. Site of the National Assembly and a resident hotel in Kigali. The RPF leadership and security battalion resided in the hotel side of the complex. UNAMIR occupied the National Assembly portion of the complex and the perimeter for security

Code Cable Secure fax capability between UN HQ in NY and UNAMIR HQ in Kigali

Code of Ethics (Also known as the Statement of Ethics) The Arusha Peace Agreement had called for each political party to sign a Statement of Ethics if they were to be included in the BBTG. Each party had to sign every other party's Code of Ethics form. The CDR refused to sign the Arusha Peace Agreement or the Code of Ethics and therefore the RPF and the moderates refused to have them included in the BBTG. Also known as the Statement of Ethics

Collège militaire royal de Saint-Jean (CMR) Francophone military college in Canada. General Dallaire attended CMR as an Officer Cadet and later served as Commandant

Command and Control Military term defining how authority is exercised by a commander and his staff through a chain of command

Command post Field headquarters of a unit responsible for the control of subordinate units and responsible to a senior headquarters. Used primarily for communications, planning and coordination

Commune Political subdivision of a prefecture, equivalent to a county

Company A sub-unit of a battalion, approximately 125 personnel

Concept of Operations A general description of how a commander intends to accomplish the assigned mission

Contingent Commander Each nation contributing troops to a UN Force appoints a National Contingent Commander who is responsible for national discipline and administration, provides a link from the mission area to his home nation and provides a single point of contact for the Force Commander on matters relating to that nation's contingent. Considered to be a secondary duty and usually the officer is also appointed to a primary command or staff position within the force

General Roméo A. Dallaire Canadian Force Commander of UNAMIR, and Chief Military Observer UNOMUR Oct 93–Aug 94, promoted to the rank of Major General in the field, 1 Jan 94, retired at the rank of Lieutenant General in Ottawa, 22 Apr 00

General John de Chastelain Canadian Chief of Defence Staff

Captain Willem de Kant Dutch Officer, selected by General Dallaire from service in UNOMUR to serve as Aide-de-camp in UNAMIR, Oct 93–Mar 94

Christine De Liso Acting CAO following Hallqvist's departure in Feb 93 replaced by Golo May 94

CIDA Canadian International Development Agency

Defensive stores Items such as barbed wire, sandbags, corrugated iron, lumber, etc., that can be used to protect/defend an area

Defensive position Field defences like trenches and bunkers used to protect and defend a certain location

Leo Delcroix Belgian minister of defence, visited UNAMIR Mar 94

Major Eddy Delporte Belgian Military Police Officer, in Rwanda for the Technical Mission, conducted the analysis of the Gendarmerie, transferred from MINURSO to UNAMIR, stayed until Apr 94

Captain Amadou Deme Senegalese Officer, served in UNAMIR Intelligence Sector, viewed the arms cache in Jan 94, became head of sector following Belgian departure in Apr 94

Demilitarized zone (DMZ) DMZ located in northern Rwanda between RPF and RGF forces. Approximately 120 km long and from 100 metres at its narrowest to up to 20 km at its widest point. The DMZ was the last line of forward troops of each party when the ceasefire went into effect in 1991. Neither party was permitted in the zone, which was under NMOG and later UNAMIR control

Beadengar Dessande Former Ambassador from Chad and political officer on the SRSG staff

Lieutenant Colonel Joe Dewez Belgian Commanding Officer of the second Belgian Para-commando unit from 1 Apr–20 Apr 94, replaced LCol Leroy

Major Diagne Senegalese UNAMIR Staff Officer became FC's note-taker during the conflict

DHA UN Department of Humanitarian Affairs

Dom Bosco School Location of Belgian Camp in Kigali and site where Belgian troops abandoned hundreds of Tutsis who were subsequently massacred. Also known as École technique officielle (ETO)

Mark Doyle BBC reporter and the only reporter to remain in Rwanda throughout the genocide

DPKO UN Department of Peacekeeping Operations

DPA UN Department of Political Affairs

Extremists Believers in Hutu Power, not prepared to bring refugees home, and unwilling to share power in a multi-ethnic, multi-party democracy respecting human rights. Predominantly MRND and CDR, but present in all parties other than the RPF

FC Force Commander

Joe Felli Political Adviser to the OAU's Neutral Military Observer Group and later OAU representative in Rwanda

Field Operations Division (FOD) Part of DPKO that provides administrative and logistics (such as communications, transportation, finance, procurement, construction, information systems, contracting, general services) support to deployed peacekeeping missions

Colonel Herbert Figoli DMZ Sector Commander, Uruguayan, left UNAMIR mid-January

FOD Field Operations Division

Force Commander (FC) Commands all UN military personnel in a peacekeeping force

Bob Fowler Canadian Deputy Minister of Defence

Louise Fréchette Permanent Representative of Canada to the United Nations from 1992 to 1995. Deputy Secretary-General of the UN, 2 Mar 1998–present

Gabiro RGF camp on the eastern side of the DMZ close to Akagera National Park

Philippe Gaillard Chief Delegate of the International Committee of the Red Cross in Rwanda before and throughout the genocide in Rwanda, the only humanitarian agency to remain for the duration of the crisis

Garrison The home camp of an army unit

Dr. Anastase Gasana A Hutu moderate and Minister of Foreign Affairs until 6 April when President Habyarimana kicked him off his airplane just before it was shot down. Spent most of the war in Tanzania and returned to his post after the RPF won the war

Félicien Gatabazi Head of the Social Democratic or PSD party; a well-known Hutu moderate from Butare

Colonel (later Major General) Marcel Gatsinzi Appointed RGF Chief of Staff to succeed Nsabimana on his death 7 Apr 94, replaced less than two weeks later by General Augustin Bizimungu. Gatsinzi was a moderate Hutu Army officer from Butare who later deserted to the RPF

Gendarmes/Gendarmerie Para-military force of 6,000 members, the national police force in Rwanda, controlled by the regime, based in Kigali and Ruhengeri, trained by both Belgian and French advisors, modelled on the French equivalent. Used mainly as a police force, however units were sometimes mobilized to the front to augment the army

Génocidaire French term to describe someone who participates in a genocide

Chinmaya Gharekhan Senior political adviser to Boutros-Ghali, and under-secretary-general of the UN

Gisenyi Northwestern prefecture in Rwanda, capital also named Gisenyi, tourist town on Lake Kivu, heartland of the extremist CDR

Gitarama Approximately 40 km from Kigali, location of the interim government

Allay Golo Chadian CAO, replaced De Liso in May 94

Marrack Goulding Under-Secretary-General for Political Affairs, from Great Britain, replaced James Jonah

Grasshopper Codename for events requiring a very high level of security

Major General Juvénal Habyarimana Rwandan president (dictator), came to power in 1973 *coup d'état*, killed in plane crash night of 6–7 Apr 94, Hutu from Ruhengeri, founder and head of the MRND

HAC Humanitarian Assistance Cell

Per O. Hallqvist Chief Administration Officer until resignation 14 Feb 94

Colonel Mike Hanrahan CO of 1ˢᵗ Canadian Headquarters and Signals Regiment (1 CDHSR)

Peter Hansen UN Under-Secretary-General for Humanitarian Affairs. First senior UN official to visit Rwanda after the start of the genocide

Colonel Azrul Haque UNOMUR second-in-command, the Deputy Chief Military Observer, a Bangladeshi. As Dallaire was the Chief Military Observer of UNOMUR, in addition to being the Force Commander of UNAMIR, and living in Kigali, the DCMO of UNOMUR was, in effect, the Commander of the Sector. Replaced Colonel Ben Matiwaza in Feb 94

Hard-liner Slang for extremist

Head of Mission The individual designated by the SG of the UN to be in overall command of all divisions within the UN mission. Usually the SRSG, however for periods during UNAMIR, the FC was designated Head of Mission as well

Arturo Hein UNREO Coordinator

HPZ Humanitarian Protection Zone

Humanitarian Assistance Cell (HAC) Formed 13 Apr 94 to work in close support of UNREO, aided in security of humanitarian aid and other issues

Humanitarian Protection Zone (HPZ) Area of Rwanda secured by Op Turquoise, also known as Sector 4

Hutu Majority ethnic group in Rwanda, comprising approximately 85 percent of the population

Hutu Power Extremist movement dedicated to the dominance of the Hutu in all aspects of Rwandan affairs, appeared in several political parties

ICRC International Committee of the Red Cross

ICTR International Criminal Tribunal Rwanda

Impuzamugambi Kinyarwanda for "those who have a single aim," CDR youth wing/militia, trained, armed and led by the Presidential Guard and other elements of the RGF closely linked to the Interahamwe, participated in the killings during the genocide

Inkotanyi Kinyarwanda for "those who fight courageously." Units of the RPF

Interahamwe Kinyarwanda for "those who attack together." Militant young men attached to the youth wing of the ruling MRND party, trained and indoctrinated in ethnic hatred against Tutsis. Dressed in cotton combat fatigues in the red, green and black of the then Rwandan flag, carried machetes or carved replicas of Kalashnikovs, often incited violence, largely responsible for the killings during the genocide

Interim government Appointed 7 Apr 93 by Habyarimana, to be in power until the BBTG would take over. During the UNAMIR period led by Madame Agathe until her assassination. On 7 Apr 94, a Hutu extremist–dominated interim government led by Jean Kambanda seized power until defeated and driven out of Rwanda in Jul 94

International Committee of the Red Cross (ICRC)

International Criminal Tribunal Rwanda (ICTR) UN-sponsored judicial body prosecuting war criminals in Arusha, Tanzania

Inyenzi Kinyarwanda for "cockroach," a term used by Hutu extremists to describe Tutsis

Dr. Jacques *Nom de guerre* of an RPF political officer at the CND during the genocide

James O.C. Jonah Under-Secretary-General for Political Affairs, from Sierra Leone, replaced by Marrack Goulding

Jean-Pierre Informant who described the arms cache in Jan 94, was once a Commando and a Presidential Guard, the chief trainer of the Interahamwe

Joint Military Commission A joint body made up of General Dallaire, the COs of the RGF, the COs of the Gendarmerie and the commander of the RPF designed to set the agenda and approve the proposals of a number of sub-committees planning the details of the disengagement, disarmament, demobilization, rehabilitation/release and reintegration processes for the security forces of both sides as called for in the Arusha Peace Agreement

Kabale UNOMUR HQ, located in Ugandan border town of Kabale

Dr. Abdul Hamid Kabia Acting Executive Director UNAMIR. Began mission as Political Officer with UNOMUR, later moved to Kigali; UN diplomat and political expert with considerable field and HQ experience, from Sierra Leone

Kadafi Crossroads Critical intersection of several major roads in and out of Kigali in the northwest corner of the city

Major General Paul Kagame Military Commander of the Rwandese Patriotic Army—the military wing of the RPF—Tutsi, media nickname "the Napoleon of Africa." Inaugurated 5th President of Rwanda 22 Apr 00

Robert Kajuga President of the Interahamwe, responsible for most of the killings during the genocide

Jean Kambanda Hutu extremist in the MDR, became the figurehead interim prime minister of the genocidal government 7 Apr 94, convicted as a génocidaire at ICTR and sentenced to life in prison

Major Frank Kamenzi RPF Liaison Officer to UNAMIR

Mamadou Kane Political Adviser to Dr. Booh-Booh, the SRSG

Kangura Extremist newspaper filled with ethnic and anti-UNAMIR propaganda

Camp Kanombe RGF military camp at east end of Kigali International Airport

Colonel Alexis Kanyarengwe Chairman of the RPF, Hutu

Froduald Karamira Vice-President of the MDR

Commander Karake Karenzi First RPF Liaison Officer to UNAMIR

Judge Joseph Kavaruganda President of the Constitutional Court

Grégoire Kayibanda Leader of Hutu-dominated Rwandan government following uprising and independence of 1961, deposed and killed in coup by Habyarimana in 1973, former president and prime minister of Rwanda

Ambassador Colin Keating New Zealand Ambassador to the UN, President of the Security Council Apr 94

Major Henry Kesteloot Kigali Sector Operations Officer, Belgian

Shaharyar M. Khan Pakistani career diplomat, appointed SRSG by Boutros-Ghali June 94

KIBAT Nickname for the Belgian Battalion located in Kigali

Camp Kigali RGF camp in the centre of Kigali, housed headquarters, reconnaissance battalion, maintenance transport unit and military hospital/convalescent centre

Kigali Hospital Civilian hospital located near Camp Kigali

Kigali Sector HQ in Kigali, commanded by Colonel Marchal, who was also the Belgian Contingent Commander, located at a compound near the Meridien hotel, UNAMIR area of operations within the KWSA, consisted of Belgian Battalion (KIBAT), Bangladeshi Battalion (RUTBAT), MILOBs, and occasionally Tunisian Company

Kigali Weapons Secure Area (KWSA) Agreement made whereby military units in Kigali would be required to store all weapons and ammunition, and weapons or armed troops could only be moved with UNAMIR's permission and escort, signed 23 Dec 93, actual area radius of approximately 20 km from the centre of the city

King Faisal hospital Brand new but unused hospital, used as a field hospital by UNAMIR, and to treat the local population. Taken over by MSF

Kinihira Abandoned tea plantation in the heart of the DMZ; several articles of the Arusha Peace Agreement were signed here, often used as a neutral meeting place

Kinyarwanda The official native language of Rwanda, spoken by Hutus, Tutsis and Twas

Captain Apedo Kodjo Togolese MILOB who witnessed the initial attack on the ten Belgian and five Ghanaian UNAMIR soldiers on 7 April 94

Bernard Kouchner Former French politician and founder of Médecins Sans Frontières, he made two trips to Rwanda during the genocide

KWSA Kigali Weapons Secure Area

Brigadier General Jean-Claude Lafourcade Commander of the French Opération Turquoise

Captain Sarto LeBlanc Canadian reinforcement officer

Major Phil Lancaster Canadian MILOB, replaced Major Brent Beardsley in May 94

Lieutenant Colonel André Leroy Commanding Officer of the first Belgian Para-commando Battalion (KIBAT), Oct 93–Mar 94

Light battalion A dismounted infantry unit of varying size

Light infantry Dismounted infantry

Lieutenant Thierry Lotin Belgian Para-commando platoon commander of mortar section guarding Prime Minister Agathe, killed 7 Apr 94

Amadou Ly UNDP Resident Representative, Senior UN authority in Rwanda prior to UNAMIR, Senegalese

Major Don MacNeil Canadian reinforcement Officer, employed in the Humanitarian Assistance Cell during the genocide and responsible for saving thousands of lives, known by call sign MamaPapa 1

Major Peter Maggen Belgian Senior Duty Officer UNAMIR Force HQ Operations Centre who supervised and trained the Bangladeshi Duty Officers

Bernard Mamiragaba National Committee of the Interahamwe leader

Colonel Luc Marchal Belgian, Kigali Sector Commander and also the Belgian Contingent Commander in UNAMIR

Ambassador Jean-Philippe Marlaud French Ambassador to Rwanda

Major Miguel Martin DPKO UNAMIR desk officer in New York, Argentinian Army Officer on loan to UN, was also concurrently desk officer for several other missions, promoted lieutenant-colonel Jan 94

Ben Matiwaza UNOMUR second-in-command, the Deputy Chief Military

Observer, in effect the commander of the Sector since Dallaire was in Kigali. Sep 93–Feb 94, based in Kabale, a Zimbabwean Zulu

Patrick Mazimhaka 1ˢᵗ Vice-Chairman of the RPF, Minister Designate of Youth and Sports of the BBTG, after RPF victory became a minister in the new government, was often the chief negotiator for the RPF, name often spelled Mazimpaka

Captain Diagne Mbaye Senegalese MILOB who saved the lives of Prime Minister Agathe's children and was later killed by mortar fire in Kigali

Major John McComber Canadian reinforcement officer who worked with FC as chief logistician

MDR Mouvement démocratique républicain (Democratic Republican Movement) now known as Rwanda Democratic Movement, the main opposition party to the Habyarimana regime (MRND), party split contributed to political impasse, many members of the MDR joined the genocide, while others were victims

Médecins Sans Frontières (Doctors Without Borders) Independent humanitarian medical aid agency dedicated to providing medical aid wherever needed

Merama Border crossing between Rwanda and Uganda, close to the Tanzanian border

Militia Political parties in Rwanda all had youth wings that were covers for a party-loyal security force to protect party leaders and meetings

Military Adviser Belgian and French military advisers to the Rwandan forces, advising the inner core of officers in the RGF

MILOB Military Observer, unarmed military officers loaned by their respective nations to the UN, formed in multi-national teams and sent on tasks of monitoring, observing and reporting. Also known as United Nations Military Observers (UNMOs)

MINURSO UN Mission in Western Sahara

Moderates Prepared to bring refugees home, and share power in a multi-ethnic, multi-party government respectful of human rights

Colonel Moen Chief Operations Officer of UNAMIR, Bangladeshi

Moustache Codename of the Security Officer for the UNDP, French citizen

Movement-control platoon Thirty troops trained to receive, load, unload and dispatch personnel and *matériel* from aircraft

MRND Mouvement révolutionnaire national pour le développement, political party formed in 1975 by then President Habyarimana, former ruling party in

Rwanda under Habyarimana, party changed name to Mouvement républicain pour la démocratie et le développement (National Revolutionary Movement for Democracy and Development) in 1993, Hutu extremist party

Justin Mugenzi Parti libéral president, hard-liner, currently under indictment at the ICTR

Mulindi A former tea plantation 60 km north of Kigali and used as the HQ of the RPF in Rwanda

Faustin Munyazesa Minister of Interior, MRND extremist

Vice-Admiral Larry Murray Canadian Deputy Chief of the Defence Staff responsible for all Canadian Forces members serving in operational theatres

Yoweri Museveni President of Uganda, head of the New Resistance Army, sponsor and supporter of the RPF

President Ali Hassan Mwinyi President of Tanzania and facilitator of the Arusha Peace Agreement negotiations

NATO North Atlantic Treaty Organization

NCO Non-Commissioned Officer

Landoald Ndasingwa Tutsi head of the moderate Parti libéral, known as Lando, Minister of Labour and Social Affairs in the interim government and the BBTG. Married to Hélène Pinsky, Canadian, owners of Chez Lando hotel, bar and restaurant, he and family killed 7 Apr 94

Captain Babacar Faye Ndiaye FC's Aide-de-camp, Senegalese

Colonel (later Major General) Augustin Ndindiliyimana Chief of Staff of the Gendarmerie, reported to the minister of defence for operational taskings, support and logistics but to the minister of the interior for day-to-day police work around the country, became Major General at the beginning of Mar 94. Hutu, member of the MRND, confidant and supporter of Habyarimana, currently under indictment at the ICTR

Mathieu Ngirumpatse Hutu extremist and President of the MRND party

Ephrem Nkezabera Interahamwe leader, special councillor

NMOG OAU Neutral Military Observer Group composed of a few dozen military observers and a light company of Tunisian infantry, located mainly in DMZ, absorbed by UNAMIR 1 Nov 93

Non-Commissioned Officer (NCO) Junior leader between soldiers and their officers

NRA (New Resistance Army) Ugandan Army

Colonel (later Major General) Déogratias Nsabimana RGF (Army) Chief of Staff, strong supporter of President Habyarimana, killed along with President in plane crash night of 6–7 Apr 94

André Ntagerura Hutu extremist and acknowledged dean of the MRND

Cyprien Ntaryamira President of Burundi, killed in plane crash along with President Habyarimana the night of 6–7 Apr 94

Colonel Ntwiragaba Head of military intelligence for the RGF

Joseph Nzirorera Secretary-General of the MRND

OAU The Organization of African Unity

Opération Amaryllis The French expatriate evacuation operation conducted in April 94

Operation Clean Corridor Operation to prepare a secure route for an RPF battalion and politicians to travel into Kigali to a secure location in the city. Conducted 28 Dec 93, in accordance with the Arusha Peace Agreement

Operation Lance Canadian Forces operation contribution to UNAMIR 2, 1994–1996

Operation Passage Canadian Forces operation to provide assistance to Rwandan refugees in 1994

Operation Silverback The Belgian expatriate evacuation expanded to include their contingent in UNAMIR conducted in April 94

Opération Turquoise Controversial UN-sanctioned French operation for a Chapter 7 intervention into Rwanda Jun–Aug 94

Operations Officer Staff Officer responsible for planning and controlling military forces conducting tasks assigned by the Commander

Dr. James Orbinski Canadian surgeon who served as a doctor at the King Faisal Hospital in Kigali throughout the genocide and saved the lives of hundreds, perhaps thousands, of people

The Organization of African Unity (OAU) Organization founded in 1963, based in Ethiopia, its primary aim is to promote unity and solidarity among African countries. Other aims and objectives include improving the general living standards in Africa, defending the territorial integrity and independence of African states, and promoting international co-operation. Membership of the OAU includes 53 of the 54 countries of Africa. The only African state that is not a member is the Kingdom of Morocco, which withdrew in 1985 following the admittance of the disputed state of Western Sahara as a member in 1984

Papal Nuncio The Pope's Ambassador to Rwanda, Monsignor Giuseppe Bertello, who also served as the Dean of the Kigali Diplomatic Corps

Para Battalion French parachute battalion stationed in Kigali, left Dec 93 returned Apr 94 to evacuate non-African expatriates

Para-Commando RGF parachute commando regiment

Para-commando battalion Belgian parachute commando battalion

Parti libéral (PL) Liberal Party, moderate political party headed by Lando Ndasingwa and Justin Mugenzi, popular among the business community and some Tutsi groups, split along ethnic lines in Sep 93

Major Marek Pazik Polish Officer, worked with the HAC, callsign MamaPapa after his initials

PDC Parti démocrate Chrétien (Christian Democratic Party), moderate political party led by Jean-Népomucène Nayinzira

PDI Islamic Democratic Party

Macaire Pédanou UN Political Observer in Arusha

Suzanne Pescheira Force Commander's Secretary, Ecuadorian UNESCO employee originally based in Paris, on loan to UNAMIR

Charles Petrie Deputy UN humanitarian coordinator in Rwanda and Burundi

Major Jean-Guy Plante Canadian officer transferred from Somalia to Rwanda during the genocide and employed as media information officer

Hélène Pinsky Canadian, married to Landoald Ndasingwa, killed 7 Apr 94

PL Parti libéral (Liberal Party)

Platoon Sub-unit of a company of up to 35 personnel commanded by a Lieutenant

Colonel Poncet French Army Commander of Opération Amaryllis

Prayers Military meeting where a commander issues orders to subordinates, also known as an orders group or O Group

Prefect of Kigali Tharcisse Renzaho

Prefect Political head of a prefecture, political division of Rwanda, similar to a governor

Prefecture Political divisions of Rwanda based on the Belgian colonial system. In 93–94, Rwanda consisted of ten prefectures led by prefects, and sous-prefects. Rwanda is now divided into eleven prefectures/provinces

Presidential Guard Highly trained, well-equipped, ruthless RGF bodyguard unit, based in the centre of Kigali, with detachments all over the city including near the airport in Kigali, Hutu extremist group intensely loyal to President Habyarimana

PSD Parti social démocrate, united and influential moderate political party, known as "the intellectuals' party." Led by the triumvirate of Fréderic Nzamurambaho, Félicien Gatabazi and Théoneste Gafarange, based largely in Butare, Southern Rwanda, made up of moderate Hutus

Major Luc-André Racine Canadian reinforcement MILOB employed on challenging tasks by General Dallaire due to his excellent language skills and extensive experience. Worked with recce as Sector Commander in HPZ, and as Liaison Officer to Human Rights Mission

Radio Muhaburu Radio station operated by the RPF

Radio Rwanda Government-controlled radio station

Radio Télévision Libre des Mille Collines (RTLM) Kigali independent radio station with strong links to extremist elements in and out of the regime

Ambassador David Rawson US Ambassador to Rwanda, left at the beginning of the war

Lieutenant Commander Robert Read Canadian reinforcement Officer transferred from Somalia to Rwanda during the genocide and employed as Logistics Base Commander

Recce Reconnaissance

RGF Rwandese Government Forces

RGF Headquarters Located in Camp Kigali

RGF Sector HQ in Ruhengeri, south of the DMZ, encompassed government-controlled areas in northern Rwanda consisted of MILOBs only

Isel Rivero UN DPKO Political Desk Officer for Central Africa, Cuban

Iqbal Riza Assistant (Deputy) Secretary-General, DPKO, Pakistani diplomat and long-time UN employee

ROE Rules of Engagement

Colonel Jean-Pierre Roman Belgian Commander of the Belgian Para-commando brigade, visited Rwanda at the same time as Minister Claes

Colonel Cam Ross In spring 1993, led first UN Technical Mission to Rwanda and recommended the deployment of a peacekeeping force. During UNAMIR, was Director of Peacekeeping Operations for the Canadian Forces at NDHQ in Ottawa

General Armand Roy Canadian Army Military Area Commander for Quebec in 1993

Royal Canadian Regiment The senior serving infantry regiment in the Canadian Army

Royal Military College (RMC) Located in Kingston, Ontario, Canada

RPA Rwandese Patriotic Army

RPF Rwandese Patriotic Front

RPF Sector HQ in Mulindi, co-located with the RPF HQ. Its area of operation was the area under RPF control in northern Rwanda. Consisted of MILOBs only

RTLM Radio Télévision Libre des Mille Collines

Ruhengeri Northwestern prefecture, capital of same name, location of the Virunga Mountains, heartland of the extremist Hutu regime, location of the Gendarmerie school, including rapid reaction forces

George Ruggiu Belgian mercenary who ran RTLM, which incited genocide against Tutsis

Enoch Ruhigira Chef de cabinet of the president and former prime minister of Rwanda, confidant of Habyarimana

Rules of Engagement (ROE) Establishes rules for the use of military force in a mission, updated as risk factors change

Colonel Léonidas Rusatira Head of the esm or Military College, senior colonel in the rgf, later promoted to general, Hutu moderate, deserted to the rpf near the end of the war

Tito Rutaremara Proposed RPF national assemblyman, Tutsi extremist

Lieutenant Colonel Ephrem Rwabalinda RGF liaison officer to UNAMIR, killed in early July 1994

Rwandese Government Forces (RGF) Hutu-dominated Rwandan Government Army, Kinyarwanda- and French-speaking

Rwandese Patriotic Army (RPA) The military wing of the RPF

Rwandese Patriotic Front (RPF) Tutsi-dominated military and political movement, disciplined rebel army composed of Rwandan refugees raised in Ugandan refugee camps, supported by the Ugandans, English-speaking, led by Kagame, originally the Rwandese Alliance for National Unity (RANU) started in 1979, changed to RPF in 1987

Major Jean-Yves St-Denis Canadian reinforcement Officer, UNMO

Sainte Famille A large church/school complex in the centre of Kigali that served as a protected site for thousands during the genocide

Dr. Salim Ahmed Salim Secretary General of the Organization of African Unity, Tanzanian

Marcel Savard Ex-Canadian Forces Logistics Officer, leader of the UN Field Operations Division team on the Technical Mission

SC The UN Security Council

Lieutenant General Daniel Schroeder American commander of the U.S. Joint Task Force to Africa

The Secretariat The administrative support organization of the UN

Special Representative of the Secretary-General of the United Nations (SRSG) The political head of mission appointed by the SG, usually appointed Head of Mission. SRSG UNAMIR was Jacques-Roger Booh-Booh from Cameroon from Nov 93–Jun 94 and Shaharyar M. Khan of Pakistan from 1 Jul 94

Section A squad or group of soldiers usually eight to eleven in number and commanded by a junior NCO or Sergeant

Security Council UN decision-making body of ambassadors representing their respective nation-states charged with monitoring and ensuring international peace and security. The council receives reports from the SG and in turn issues the SG with guidance. The Security Council issues the mandates for peacekeeping missions

Seth Sendashonga RPF political leader, fled Rwanda to join the RPF in Uganda, Hutu

SG The UN Secretary-General

Théodore Sindikubwabo Hutu MRND extremist appointed President of the interim government after the assassination of Habyarimana

Sitrep Situation Report, provides details of current situation

Major Manuel Sosa Uruguayan MILOB killed by a rocket

Southern Sector HQ in Butare, area of operations was government-controlled area of southern Rwanda, consisted of MILOBs only

Sous-prefect Assistant political head of a prefecture

SRSG Special Representative of the Secretary-General of the United Nations

Status of Forces Agreement (SOFA) Agreement between the UN Force and a host nation, concerning administrative and legal matters such as immunity from national law, exemption from duties and tariffs, etc.

Status of Mission Agreement (SOMA) Agreement between the UN Mission and a host nation, concerning administrative and legal matters such as immunity from national law, exemption from duties and tariffs, etc.

Johan Swinnen Belgian Ambassador to Rwanda, left in April 94

Technical Mission UN term for a multi-disciplinary reconnaissance or information-gathering team sent to a problem area to observe and report back to the SG who in turn reports to the SC

Theatre command Operational command in the field

Third force Name given by UNAMIR to an extremist group that was out to derail the peace process

Colonel Isoa Tikoka UN Military Observer during Arusha Peace negotiations, and later became UNAMIR Chief Military Observer, known as Tiko, of Fiji

Major General Guy Tousignant Canadian Force Commander of UNAMIR, replaced Major General Dallaire Aug 94

Triumvirate General Dallaire's nickname for Major-General Maurice Baril, Kofi Annan and Iqbal Riza

Master Corporal Philippe Troute FC's personal driver, Walloon Belgian Para-commando

Tutsi Minority ethnic group in Rwanda comprising approximately fourteen percent of the population

Twa Minority ethnic group in Rwanda comprising approximately one percent of the population, mainly pygmies

Faustin Twagiramungu Prime Minister Designate for the BBTG, selected in Arusha, member of the MDR, moderate Hutu during 93–94, varied political background, became prime minister after the RPF victory in July 1994

UN United Nations

UNAMIR United Nations Assistance Mission for Rwanda

UNAMIR 1 Established by Security Council Resolution 872/05 Oct 93, to assist in the implementation of the Arusha Peace Agreement

UNAMIR 2 Established by Security Council Resolution 918/17 May 94, to contribute to the security and protection of displaced persons, refugees and civilians at risk in Rwanda

UNCIVPOL United Nations Civilian Police Division

UNDP United Nations Development Programme

UNHCR United Nations High Commissioner for Refugees

UNICEF United Nations Children's Fund

UNITAF Unified Task Force Somalia, to establish a safe environment for the delivery of humanitarian assistance

UNMO United Nations Military Observer

UNOMUR United Nations Observer Mission Uganda-Rwanda, treated as a Sector within UNAMIR. HQ in Kabale, area of operations was the Ugandan side of the Uganda/Rwanda border opposite the area under RPF control, to monitor the flow of men, arms and supplies from Uganda to the RPF in Rwanda, consisted of MILOBs

UNREO The United Nations Rwanda Emergency Office, established to coordinate all humanitarian aid efforts for Rwanda

UN Protected Sites Protected areas for people at risk (such as the Amahoro Stadium, the Meridien hotel, the King Faisal hospital, the Hôtel des Mille Collines, the Belgian camp at the Dom Bosco school)

General Uytterhoeven Belgian Senior Military Officer, visited Rwanda at the same time as Minister Claes

Agathe Uwilingiyimana Prime minister of the interim government, MDR Party, moderate Hutu, put in power 7 Apr 93, killed 7 Apr 94, known as Madame Agathe

Captain Robert van Putten Dutch Aide-de-camp replaced Captain Willem de Kant, Feb 94

Valcartier Home base of 5ième Brigade-Group, located outside Quebec City, Quebec, Canada

Vital points Installations or locations considered to be mission-essential property that merits security, for example, airports, power stations, etc.

Butch Waldrum Retired Canadian Air Force General, employed in FOD New York, visited UNAMIR 5 Apr 94, caught on the ground during the events of 6–7 Apr 94, evacuated to Nairobi and established the air bridge to support UNAMIR

Weapons-secure area/zone The RGF and the RPF would secure their weapons and move them or armed troops only with UN permission and under UN escort

Colonel Clayton Yaache Ghanaian Demilitarized Zone (DMZ) Sector Commander before 7 April, and later, after withdrawal to Kigali, head of the Humanitarian Assistance Cell in UNAMIR HQ during the genocide

RECOMMENDED READING

Perhaps some of you who have read this book will be encouraged to study the Rwandan genocide in greater detail. The following is a list of books and reports that I recommend for their accuracy, the quality of their research and the way they present the facts. I emphasize that this is a personal reading list, which reflects my opinion and perspective.

The best brief history of Rwanda culminating in the genocide is the work by French social scientist Gérard Prunier, *The Rwanda Crisis: History of a Genocide* (New York, Columbia University Press, 1995). Prunier is a Rwanda scholar who has lived in the area and studied its people and their history in the depth that can only be achieved by a brilliant academic.

The best overall account of the background to the genocide, and the failure to prevent it, is Linda Melvern's *A People Betrayed: The Role of the West in Rwanda's Genocide* (London: Zed Books, 2000). I provided the author with information and consulted on some of the chapters; the investigative work is hers and hers alone. She discovered so much that we did not know, and her book remains one of the best sources available.

Two worthwhile works by American academics are Samantha Power's *A Problem from Hell: America and the Age of Genocide* (New York: Basic Books, 2002) and Michael Barnett's *Eyewitness to a Genocide: The United Nations and Rwanda* (Ithaca: Cornell University Press, 2002). They give the reader an inside look at decision-making in the U.S. government and in the halls of the UN, using Rwanda as the case study. I strongly recommend both works for the reader who wants to better understand why no one came to help in 1994.

The best account of the actual genocide, one which is also very detailed and very painful to read, is a book by the American human rights activist Alison Des Forges, called *Leave None to Tell the Story: Genocide in Rwanda* (New York: Human Rights Watch, 1999). Alison is an expert on the history of human rights in Rwanda and was one of our greatest allies in 1994 in trying to encourage the international community to intervene in Rwanda and to expose the genocide for what it was. She has testified at the International Criminal Tribunal for Rwanda at Arusha and is considered an expert on all aspects of the genocide.

The most disturbing account on the tragedy of genocide, written from a personal perspective, is Philip Gourevitch's *We Wish to Inform You that Tomorrow We Will Be Killed with Our Families: Stories From Rwanda* (New York: Farrar, Straus and Giroux, 1998). Gourevitch was one of the first journalists to enter post-genocide Rwanda and speak directly with survivors. He took that information and produced a work that strikes directly at your soul.

For a picture of post-genocide Rwanda, Shaharyar Khan's *The Shallow Graves of Rwanda* (London: I.B. Tauris Publishers, 2000) is the most complete account of how the international community failed to help the survivors of the genocide. Khan was the UN's Secretary-General's Special Representative in the last days of UNAMIR. We served a little over a month together, and I found him to be a superbly experienced diplomat, an innovator, a talented leader and a wonderful human being.

The official Canadian Forces history of UNAMIR was written by Dr. Jacques Castonguay, a military historian who was principal of the Collège militaire royal de Saint-Jean and was a professor when I attended that institution as a cadet. From the start, I wanted an official history of the mission, the sort the Canadian Army used to produce during military campaigns in the past. Dr. Castonguay travelled to the mission area while the headquarters was still in place and reviewed documents that have since gone missing. His account also reflects Brent Beardsley's and my own thinking about the genocide immediately after it occurred.

Two senior officers have written excellent books on the complex military command and political interface on the ground during the mission. The first was written by my deputy force commander, Ghanaian Brigadier General Henry Anyidoho, and is called *Guns over Kigali* (Accra: Woeli Publishing Services, 1997). It is the story of the mission from the perspective of an experienced African soldier and peacekeeper. Henry served under me and my successor; he had the opportunity to view Rwanda first-hand both during and after the genocide. His insight on the command of African troops is particularly valuable. He, too, returned to a nation where colleagues were jealous and the government apathetic. The Ghanaian troops of UNAMIR never received full recognition from their government, their army or their fellow citizens for the courageous work they performed in Rwanda. The other work I want to mention is *Rwanda: la descente aux enfers: Témoignage d'un peacekeeper Décembre 1993–Avril 1994* (Brussels: Éditions Labor, 2001) by Colonel Luc Marchal, who served as my Kigali sector commander as well as the Belgian contingent commander. He has written a first-class account of leadership in a peacekeeping mission in crisis, where one is torn by loyalty to country and loyalty to the mission and morality. He had the most difficult command in UNAMIR, the Kigali Weapons Secure Area, and his book is an extremely personal reflection on the complexities of this new era of conflict resolution. He performed his duties beyond the call; his actions and his high personal moral standards permitted Belgium to be perceived as behaving with a modicum of dignity as its government abandoned us in the field and then attempted to influence the rest of the world not to help. In response, his home country did nothing less than try to destroy him. There is no better example of the risks of command in operations.

During the genocide, I produced a plan for an emergency international intervention of 5,500 troops to stop the slaughter, a plan that was never adopted. In 1997, this plan was subjected to international military analysis at Georgetown University, where Colonel Scott Feil of the U.S. Army was studying under a fellowship from the Carnegie Commission on Preventing Deadly Conflict. The plan was assessed by high-ranking officers from several nations. Their analysis was published

INDEX